Roland Hardenberg
Children of the Earth Goddess

Religion and Society

Edited by
Gustavo Benavides, Frank J. Korom,
Karen Ruffle and Kocku von Stuckrad

Volume 73

Roland Hardenberg
Children of the Earth Goddess

Society, Marriage, and Sacrifice
in the Highlands of Odisha

DE GRUYTER

ISBN 978-3-11-068497-1
e-ISBN (PDF) 978-3-11-053288-3
e-ISBN (EPUB) 978-3-11-053176-3
ISSN 1437-5370

Library of Congress Cataloging-in-Publication Data
A CIP catalog record for this book has been applied for at the Library of Congress.

Bibliographic information published by the Deutsche Nationalbibliothek
The Deutsche Nationalbibliothek lists this publication in the Deutsche Nationalbibliografie;
detailed bibliographic data are available in the Internet at http://dnb.dnb.de.

© 2019 Walter de Gruyter GmbH, Berlin/Boston
This volume is text- and page-identical with the hardback published in 2018.
Index: Jochen Fassbender
Printing and binding: CPI books GmbH, Leck
♾ Printed on acid-free paper
Printed in Germany

www.degruyter.com

for
my wife Andrea,
my son Janik, and
my daughter Ravina

Preface

It all began in the millennium year 2000, when my mentor Georg Pfeffer and I together toured the highlands of Orissa (since 2011 Odisha). During our visit to the Niamgiri Hills in Rayagada District, I was instantly captivated by the beauty of the landscape and by the proud, brave and independent character of its inhabitants, the Dongria Kond. My first impressions left me with no doubts: this was the place where I wanted to conduct the fieldwork for my next research project. I returned a year later and remained with two brief interruptions until 2003.

Towards the end of my research, I could already see the signs of some oncoming changes. Locals were talking about foreign people with machines that gave them the ability to look into the mountains and see the wealth stored there. In some villages, I suddenly met outright hostility towards me. For example, in April 2003, I was threatened by a group of local youths carrying a gun, who said that I should not come to their village since foreigners were not welcome in the mountains. Only later did I learn that the state government had signed a memorandum of understanding with Vedanta Aluminium Ltd. to set up a refinery, a power plant and a bauxite mine in the tribal areas. The construction of the refinery and the power plant began in nearby Lanjigarh in 2004, and the Niamgiri Hills were selected as a suitable site for bauxite mining.

Soon opposition arose against these mining plans, which were expected to have disastrous effects on the lives of the indigenous population (*adibasi*) and their whole environment. While the refinery began operation in Lanjigarh in 2007, the mining plans for the Niamgiri Hills were soon stopped by the strong protests of the Dongria Kond, the local tribal community that claims indigenous rights to the land and worships the mountains and rivers as their gods. They were supported by various national and international non-governmental organizations (NGOs), as well as by social activists, politicians and celebrities from all over the world.

This was to a large extent the result of the activities of Survival International, a movement for the protection of indigenous people worldwide. Their activists came into close contact with the Dongria Kond, most of whom could not read or write and had no access to any form of public media. Survival International produced short films about the Dongria's way of life and their protests against the bauxite mining. These were distributed widely through Survival International's own internet platform and various social media. As a result, the voices of this small group of tribals, at the time of my research no more than perhaps eight thousand people, were suddenly heard all around the world.

The Dongria Kond were called the "real Avatars," as their life situation was compared to that of the Na'vi in James Cameron's Hollywood blockbuster *Avatar*, which was released in 2009 and received three Oscars. All over the world, various organizations wrote petitions to support the Dongria Kond in their fight against the bauxite mining, a fight which soon began to concern various courts in India. Committees were set up to investigate the situation. While Vedanta Aluminium Ltd. was first granted permission to continue with its plans, the Environment Ministry later stopped its activities in the Niamgiri Hills for the time being. The Vedanta Group appealed, but the appeal was rejected by the Supreme Court of India on 18 April 2013. The judges stated that the Dongria themselves should determine whether bauxite is to be mined in their mountains. On 19 August 2013, residents of twelve villages unanimously rejected plans for the mining project. Since then, the struggle between the company and the tribals goes on, even if the company is not allowed to mine the mountains. However, the refinery continues to operate in Lanjigarh with bauxite from different sources, and according to the latest reports, the state government has recently granted the company permission to increase its production.

For non-Indian scholars, these developments have made it increasingly difficult to conduct research in the area. During my last stay in Odisha in 2015, I was told that the tribal areas through which I travelled fifteen years ago were now officially closed to foreigners. Several reasons are given by the government for imposing these restrictions, but one major cause apart from the protest movement is the activities of a Maoist group, called the Naxalites, who have initiated a guerrilla war against the police, politicians and wealthy local landlords. Already in 2003 I had heard about their activities in certain areas of Odisha, but since then their activities seem to have expanded immensely. The fight between the government and these rebels has become more violent and has destabilized internal security in the region. The Odisha government restricted access to the highlands after two Italian tourists were kidnapped by Maoists in 2012 and only released after the chief minister set free a number of arrested rebels.

Under these conditions, anthropological research by non-Indian scholars has come more or less to a standstill. It is therefore fortunate that different research projects that began prior to these developments have in the meantime produced a number of scholarly works on the highlanders of Odisha. Among the various publications, I would like to stress the valuable works produced by a group of my fellow researchers under the guidance of Georg Pfeffer at the Free University of Berlin. Their research projects began in 1999 and were finished during or after the completion of my own fieldwork. For example, Peter Berger published his comprehensive study of the rituals of the Gadaba tribe of Koraput District first in German in 2007 (*Füttern, Speisen und Verschlingen: Ritual und Gesellschaft im Hochland von Orissa, Indien,* Berlin: LIT Verlag) and later in an English translation in 2015 (*Feeding, Sharing, and Devouring: Ritual and Society in Highland Odisha, India,* Boston: De Gruyter). Lydia Guzy finished her work on the Alekh Dharma in highland and lowland Odisha and published her results in a book that appeared in 2002 (*Baba-s und Alekh-s – Askese und Ekstase einer Religion im Werden: Vergleichende Untersuchungen der asketischen Tradition Mahima Dharma in Orissa/östliches Indien,* Berlin: Weissensee Verlag). Tina Otten, who has conducted intensive fieldwork on healing rituals on the Koraput District plateau, brought out her monograph in 2006 (*Heilung durch Rituale: Vom Umgang mit Krankheit bei den Rona im Hochland Orissas, Indien,* Berlin: LIT Verlag). Uwe Skoda completed his research on a peasant population in the frontier zone between caste and tribal society and made an important contribution to the study of dominant castes and little kingdoms in Odisha with a book that appeared in 2005 (*The Aghria: A Peasant Caste on a Tribal Frontier,* New Delhi: Manohar). Christian Strümpell pursued his research interest in the industries of Odisha and, following the publication of his monograph on a power plant in the Odisha highlands in 2006 (*"Wir arbeiten zusammen, wir essen zusammen": Konvivium und soziale Peripherie in einer indischen Werkssiedlung,* Münster: LIT-Verlag), is continuing his fieldwork on the Rourkela steel plant in Odisha. These authors have produced numerous articles on the highlanders of Odisha and are pursuing further research on different socio-cultural dynamics in this region of India.

My own work on the Dongria Kond of Odisha first resulted in a post-doctoral thesis entitled "Children of the Earth Goddess: Society, Marriage and Sacrifice in the Highlands of Orissa." In 2005, I submitted this thesis to the Faculty of History/Pholosophy at the Westphalian Wilhelms University of Münster, Germany. On the basis of this thesis and an oral examination I was granted the *venia legendi* for "Ethnologie" (Social and Cultural Anthropology) on 6 February 2006. From this time onwards I was planning to publish my thesis, but new research projects soon prevented me from doing so. It was only in 2015, when time and some additional funds were available, that I could again pursue my publication project.

The outcome is a book that in a certain sense has many authors. I could only write this monograph with the help, support and knowledge provided to me by the Dongria Kond. I especially express my thanks to the villagers of Sikokagumma, who built a house for me, accepted me as a member of their community, and shared with me the good and bad moments of their lives. My particular thanks go to Brundabati Kondapani and Sandyarani Kadraka, the two "Multiple Purpose Workers" (MPW) of the local development organization whom I addressed as *didi*, 'elder sister', because they protected me like a younger brother. They taught me the Dongria language and shared with me not only their food, but also their immense knowledge. I feel very sorry that in recent years I have been unable to meet either with them or with the many Dongria Kond who became my friends, brothers and sisters, fathers and mothers, grandfathers and grandmothers. I sincerely hope that they are all well and that we soon have a chance to meet again.

I would also like to express my gratitude to my academic teachers, advisors, colleagues and friends. First of all, Georg Pfeffer deserves my deepest gratitude for supporting me throughout my career for more than two decades. He introduced me to the cultural wealth and natural beauty of the highlands of Odisha and made me see and understand the highlanders' way of life. Another colleague and friend who deserves my deepest appreciation is Peter Berger. When I began my fieldwork in 2001, he accompanied me into the mountains and shared his immense experience and knowledge about tribal life with me. In India I also received continuous support from Deepak Kumar Behera and Prasanna Kumar Nayak. I am very thankful to them for treating me not only as a colleague but as a family member. Back in Germany, many scholars supported me in the process of analysing my data and writing up my thesis. My special thanks go to Chris Gregory, Tina Otten, Josephus Platenkamp, William Sax, Uwe Skoda and Christian Strümpell.

I am not sure whether I would have managed to endure all the hardships of fieldwork in the Niamgiri Hills without my wife Andrea Luithle-Hardenberg. She visited me several times in Sikokagumma, and we even got married in this village, as I describe in this book. She interrupted her own fieldwork among the Jains of Gujarat to spend time with me among people whose cultural practices are the opposite in many ways of the norms and values of the non-violent, vegetarian Jains she was acquainted with. I know how difficult it was for her to adapt to these very different circumstances in the Niamgiri Hills. That she nevertheless stayed and even returned to the highlands gave me the feeling that somebody really cared for me while I was staying in this remote area, and this gave me the strength to continue my research against all odds. During the time I was writing this book, in 2004, my son Janik was born. Three years later, in 2007, when I had shifted my research focus towards Central Asia, my wife gave birth to our daughter Ravina. I dedicate this book to all three of them.

For many years, this thesis circulated only as a PDF file among certain specialists. However, many people requested that I publish my results in a proper book. In 2015, the anonymous reviewers for De Gruyter's book series "Religion and Society" positively evaluated my manuscript and accepted it for publication. Subsequently, a thorough revision was conducted by Jennifer Ottman, who corrected the entire text and immensely improved the manuscript in both style and format. I cannot image a better proofreader, because she identified mistakes and inconsistencies that had escaped me and other readers of the text. Finally, Jochen Fassbender created a very useful index, and the De Gruyter editorial team, especially Eva Frantz and Florian Ruppenstein, very professionally and smoothly coordinated all the necessary changes. My thanks go to all of them. As a result of these collaborative efforts, my research conducted about fifteen years ago will now be available to those interested in the study of the tribal religions of India.

Contents

Figures, Tables, and Photographs —— XIX

Abbreviations —— XXIII

Spelling of Dongria words —— XXV

1	**Introduction —— 1**	
1.1	The people —— 1	
1.2	Theoretical framework —— 6	
1.2.1	Value-ideas —— 8	
1.2.2	Hierarchy —— 9	
1.2.3	Whole, contexts, and levels —— 10	
1.2.4	Universalism, holism, and comparison —— 11	
1.3	Representing fieldwork —— 12	
1.3.1	*Writing Culture* —— 12	
1.3.2	The fieldwork situation —— 16	
1.4	Content and organisation of the work —— 37	
1.4.1	Chapter 2: "Tribal society" in the Niamgiri Hills —— 37	
1.4.2	Chapter 3: Dongria social categories, rules, and practices —— 39	
1.4.3	Chapter 4: Negotiation, violence, and love —— 42	
1.4.4	Chapter 5: The clan sacrifice: Creating Niamgiri society —— 46	
1.4.5	Chapter 6: Conclusion: A system of ideas and values —— 51	
2	**"Tribal society" in the Niamgiri Hills —— 52**	
2.1	Introduction —— 52	
2.2	Theoretical concepts —— 54	
2.2.1	The notion of "tribe" and its critique —— 54	
2.2.2	Tribe and caste in Odisha: The debate —— 60	
2.2.3	"Tribals" and "untouchables": Kond and Dombo —— 63	
2.2.4	Untouchability, the *jajmani* system, and patron-client relations —— 65	
2.3	Value-ideas —— 71	
2.3.1	Kond "inside the village" (*rechagiri*), Dombo "outside the village" (*akagiri*) —— 72	
2.3.2	Kond as "kings" (*raja*), Dombo as "subjects" (*praja*) —— 74	
2.3.3	Kond as "senior" (*kaja*), Dombo as "junior" (*icha*) —— 75	
2.3.4	Kond as "humans" (*kuang*), Dombo as "ghosts" (*marha*) —— 78	
2.3.5	Dombo and Dongria as "one clan" (*ra kuda*) —— 79	

2.3.6 Dombo and Dongria as "friends" (*tone* / *ade*) —— 82
2.4 Social boundaries —— 87
2.4.1 Closed spaces —— 87
2.4.2 Prohibited food —— 89
2.4.3 Forbidden women —— 92
2.5 Forms of interdependence —— 93
2.5.1 Dombo as generalists —— 93
2.5.2 Allocation of land and agricultural cooperation —— 96
2.5.3 Wet rice cultivation and individual property —— 99
2.5.4 Small village traders and influential urban dealers —— 102
2.5.5 Sharing and selling of alcohol —— 107
2.5.6 Dombo as traders and herders of animals —— 109
2.5.7 *Barika*: Village trader, arbitrator, messenger, and politician —— 113
2.5.8 Money and the "other," sharing and the "own" —— 121
2.6 Ritual interaction —— 127
2.6.1 The debate —— 127
2.6.2 Religious status and ritual office —— 128
2.6.3 Dombo as "communicators with the divine" —— 129
2.7 Conclusion: Tribal and caste societies —— 132

3 **Dongria social categories, rules, and practices** —— 140
3.1 Introduction —— 140
3.1.1 Terminology, norms, and practice —— 142
3.1.2 Diachronic alliance with relatives: The "South Indian kinship system" —— 149
3.1.3 Perpetuating alliance through gifts: The "North Indian kinship system" —— 155
3.1.4 Alternation and delayed alliance: The "Central Indian kinship system" —— 160
3.2 Terminology —— 171
3.2.1 The data —— 172
3.2.2 Analysis —— 174
3.2.3 Interpretation —— 189
3.3 Rules —— 191
3.3.1 The concept of "clan" (*kuda*) —— 196
3.3.2 Kond "totemism": Relations between clan and territory —— 199
3.3.3 Affines (*gota*), siblings (*tayi bai*), and friends (*tone*) —— 202
3.3.4 "Dongria clans" and "Desia clans" —— 206
3.3.5 Prohibited degrees for marital relationships —— 209

3.4	Practice —— 215	
3.4.1	The treatment of clan incest —— 216	
3.4.2	Marriage between brother clans? —— 217	
3.4.3	Marriages between clan territories (*muta*) —— 220	
3.4.4	Marriages between villages (*padari*) —— 228	
3.4.5	Marriage with "relatives" —— 236	
3.5	Conclusions —— 244	
3.5.1	Descent, territory, and residence —— 244	
3.5.2	Comparison of terminology, rules, and practice —— 248	
3.5.3	Proximity and incest, distance and fertility —— 249	
3.5.4	Violent habitus, status, and strategies —— 251	
4	**Forms of marriage: negotiation, violence, and love —— 256**	
4.1	Introduction —— 256	
4.1.1	Approaches to bride capture and marriage —— 257	
4.1.2	Kond marriage and the legacy of John F. McLennan —— 258	
4.1.3	Understanding present forms of Kond marriage —— 267	
4.1.4	Anthropological approaches —— 268	
4.2	Categories of Dongria Kond marriage —— 271	
4.3	Collective contracts: Arranged marriages —— 277	
4.3.1	Prestations: An overview —— 283	
4.3.2	*samudi sehena* ("we discuss with in-laws") —— 285	
4.3.3	*karjame* ("serving son-in-law") —— 292	
4.3.4	*mahala takang* ("betrothal fee") —— 297	
4.3.5	*ijo henga hana* ("we go to see the house") —— 311	
4.3.6	*tone paga tinja hana* ("we go to eat the rice of friendship") —— 314	
4.3.7	*hedi tana* ("we bring the girl from far away") —— 315	
4.3.8	*giri takoli* ("to bring the path") and *wenda kodang* ("old legs") —— 340	
4.4	Youthful deviation: Love marriage, bride capture, and collective settlements —— 344	
4.4.1	Youth within the age system —— 345	
4.4.2	Dormitories —— 353	
4.4.3	Bride capture (*ahpa tana* or "let's catch and bring") —— 383	
4.4.4	Conflict settlement —— 389	
4.5	Conclusion: Forms of marriage, reciprocity, and social distance —— 403	

5 The clan sacrifice: Creating Niamgiri society —— 412
- 5.1 Introduction —— 412
- 5.1.1 From human sacrifices (*meria*) to buffalo sacrifices (*kodru parbu*) —— 414
- 5.1.2 Interpretations of Kond human sacrifice (*meria*) —— 418
- 5.2 The buffalo sacrifice (*kodru parbu*): An overview —— 423
- 5.2.1 Place: The sacred layout of a village —— 423
- 5.2.2 Time: Date and intervals —— 436
- 5.2.3 Costs: Financing the sacrifice —— 444
- 5.3 Preparations —— 451
- 5.3.1 *kanga parbu*: The "pigeon-pea festival" —— 451
- 5.3.2 Purchasing the sacrificial animals —— 462
- 5.3.3 Preparing the sacrificial site —— 467
- 5.3.4 Showing round (*trehnari*) and feeding (*tisnari*) the buffalo —— 494
- 5.4 Sacrificial objects —— 499
- 5.4.1 Sale of village territory: Transfer of pots (*daka*), hearth (*halu*), and spoon (*hetu*) —— 503
- 5.4.2 Clearing the village land: The axe (*tangi*) of the first settlers —— 506
- 5.4.3 Clan land and rulership: The umbrella (*satara bonda*) of the king —— 510
- 5.4.4 Clan land and sacrifice: The knife (*suri*) that "eats" the victim —— 516
- 5.5 Sacrificial specialists —— 518
- 5.5.1 Historical and modern accounts —— 518
- 5.5.2 Forms of ritual specialisation among Dongria —— 522
- 5.5.3 Worshippers of the earth goddess: *janinga* —— 530
- 5.6 Performing the sacrifice —— 535
- 5.6.1 Preparations —— 536
- 5.6.2 *sukruwar satara line* ("on Friday the umbrella will stand") —— 542
- 5.6.3 *saniwar desa rundam ane* ("on Saturday non-relatives will assemble") —— 553
- 5.6.4 *adiwar kodru mada ane* ("on Sunday the buffalo will be killed") —— 564
- 5.6.5 Distribution of the meat —— 574
- 5.7 Conclusions —— 579
- 5.7.1 *kodru parbu* and feasts of merit —— 579
- 5.7.2 Creating society: Sacrifice and social structure —— 583
- 5.7.3 Sacrifice and marriage —— 591
- 5.7.4 Ritual and political organisation —— 596
- 5.7.5 Myth and ritual —— 599
- 5.7.6 Fertility: Exchange and violent appropriation —— 605

6	Conclusion: A system of ideas and values —— 609
6.1	Introduction —— 609
6.2	Female values: "life" (*jiu* / *jela*) and "wealth" (*lahi*) —— 609
6.3	Male ways of obtaining "life" and "wealth" —— 614
6.3.1	Violent appropriation: Hunting (*beta*) —— 615
6.3.2	Negotiation and bargaining: Reciprocal exchange (*hinga tana* or "to go, give, and bring") —— 616
6.3.3	Sharing (*bat kina*) —— 617
6.4	Male values: Senior (*kaja*) and junior (*icha*) —— 619
6.5	The whole —— 620

7   Glossary —— 623

Appendix 1:
Family tree of icha jani segment (Gumma) —— 631

Appendix 2:
Marriage relations between Gumma and other villages —— 632

Appendix 3: Numbers and names of villages —— 634

Appendix 4:
Plan of a Dongria house —— 635

Appendix 5:
Plan of a Dongria house (profile) —— 636

Appendix 6:
Myths about Duke and Dumbe —— 637

References —— 640

Index —— 653

Figures, Tables, and Photographs

Figures

Figure 1: Map of Odisha – Location of study area —— 5
Figure 2: Map of Sikokagumma —— 32
Figure 3: Categories implied by reference terminology —— 178
Figure 4: Relations between reference terms for spouse's siblings and siblings' spouses —— 183
Figure 5: Relations between reference terms for spouse's sibling's spouse —— 184
Figure 6: Address terms for cross-cousins —— 185
Figure 7: Levirate and sororate —— 187
Figure 8: Phratry relations —— 192
Figure 9: Phratry (kuda), clan (kuda), and descent group (punja) —— 193
Figure 10: Clan (kuda), sacrificial community (muta), and villages (padari) —— 194
Figure 11: Village (padari), settlement (nayu), and village territories (padari) —— 195
Figure 12: Dominant and dependent clans in a village —— 196
Figure 13: Social categories and marriage relations —— 209
Figure 14: Locality and marriageability —— 210
Figure 15: Dissolved arranged marriage —— 212
Figure 16: Marriage relations over five generations —— 214
Figure 17: Four circles of affinal villages —— 235
Figure 18: Sister exchange between two families —— 238
Figure 19: FZ and BD married to three brothers —— 239
Figure 20: Marriage with two local lines of the same village —— 241
Figure 21: Marriage with two local lines of the same village —— 242
Figure 22: *Samdin* and *sadu* relations between two local lines —— 243
Figure 23: *Sadu* relationships within the Sikoka clan of Gumma —— 244
Figure 24: Occasions, objects, givers, and receivers in Dongria marriage transactions —— 286
Figure 25: Age system in the Dongria community —— 352
Figure 26: Model of negotiations concerning the reimbursement of a "betrothal fee" —— 397
Figure 27: Abductor's gifts to four villages —— 401
Figure 28: Types of reciprocity, forms of marriage, and degrees of distance and hostility —— 411
Figure 29: Sacred sites in a Dongria village —— 425
Figure 30: Diagram of the *jakeri* of Gumma —— 432
Figure 31: T-shaped sacrificial post (*panikimunda*) —— 456
Figure 32: Basic frame of sacrificial hut —— 472
Figure 33: Layout with three types of posts —— 473
Figure 34: Frame of the roof —— 475
Figure 35: Spatial oppositions in the village —— 478
Figure 36: Different types of sacrificial stakes (examples) —— 484
Figure 37: Wall for the husband of the earth goddess (*koteiwali palawara*) —— 488

Figure 38: Marriage relation between gods and humans —— 525
Figure 39: Territorial organisation —— 584
Figure 40: Descent and status categories —— 585
Figure 41: Descent groups and houses (hypothetical example) —— 586
Figure 42: Villages interconnected by the *kodru parbu* —— 589
Figure 43: Relations based on territory —— 590
Figure 44: Relations based on affinity —— 590
Figure 45: Relations based on rivalry —— 590
Figure 45: Female creation —— 614
Figure 46: Relations between goddesses and human beings —— 614
Figure 47: Obtaining "life" through "hunting" —— 616

Tables

Table 1: Dongria Kond terminology —— 172
Table 2: Agnates and affines —— 194
Table 3: Mythological explanation of clan titles —— 200
Table 4: Etymology of clan titles —— 200
Table 5: Different sources for Kond sibling clans (e = elder, y = younger) —— 203
Table 6: Phratries (*tayi bai kuda*) —— 205
Table 7: Local categories —— 208
Table 8: Marriages —— 218
Table 9: Villages of the Sikoka (I) *muta* and local lines —— 222
Table 10: Thirteen *muta* of the Niamgiri Hills —— 224
Table 11: Marriages (Village: Gumma) —— 226
Table 12: Proportion of dominant and affinal clan members in different villages —— 231
Table 13: Distribution of marriage alliances between villages —— 232
Table 14: Status and category of married women —— 275
Table 15: Types of marriages of householders in Gumma —— 276
Table 16: Types of marriages in polygamous households in Gumma —— 277
Table 17: Recipients, names, and amounts of different shares of the "betrothal fee" (Dongria Kond) —— 300
Table 18: Name, meaning, and number of "betrothal fee" items among Jreda Kond (Ramnagar, 2003) —— 302
Table 19: Amounts paid by the *member* of Phakeri to the *member* of Lamba (2002) —— 303
Table 20: Dongria age-and-status categories —— 346
Table 21: Types of dormitories in tribal Middle India —— 357
Table 22: Dongria body ornaments —— 364
Table 23: Mythic correspondences between time and sexual acts —— 368
Table 24: Structures of the creation myth, the *bali yatra,* and social life —— 375
Table 25: Buffaloes presented as gifts by abductor —— 398
Table 26: Gifts and payments by Sikoka Kangu —— 399
Table 27: Differences between forms of marriage —— 407

Table 28:	Buffalo sacrifices (*kodru parbu*) observed by the author (year, name of village, community) —— 417	
Table 29:	Binary pairs structuring the sacred village layout —— 435	
Table 30:	Harvest ritual (*neta dakina*) and buffalo sacrifice (*kodru parbu*) —— 439	
Table 31:	Three-year ritual sequence and agricultural cycle —— 440	
Table 32:	Animals bought for the *kodru parbu* —— 447	
Table 33:	Oppositions on the day of *kudi bhoji* —— 491	
Table 34:	Types of relations —— 498	
Table 35:	Hierarchy of "umbrellas" (*satara bonda*) —— 515	
Table 36:	*jani* and *dehri* according to Macpherson —— 519	
Table 37:	Distinction between *janni* and *kutaka* according to Niggemeyer —— 520	
Table 38:	Ritual specialists among the Dongria Kond according to Jena et al. —— 521	
Table 39:	Ritual specialists among the Dongria Kond according to Hardenberg —— 529	
Table 40:	Worship of weapons and the three main deities —— 559	
Table 41:	Differences between the two types of affines —— 578	
Table 42:	Social and territorial organisation in relation to the *kodru parbu* —— 586	
Table 43:	Forms of marriage and sacrifice compared —— 595	
Table 44:	Levels of royal organisation among the Kond —— 599	
Table 45:	Sacrifice and marriage and the hierarchy of relations —— 608	
Table 46:	Obtaining "life" through reciprocal exchange —— 617	

Photographs

Photo 1:	Niamgiri Hills (2002) —— 2	
Photo 2:	Dongria building the author's house in Gumma —— 29	
Photo 3:	Heap of turmeric rhizomes in a Dongria village —— 105	
Photo 4:	Dombo *barika* and his wife —— 114	
Photo 5:	*Beju* in trance (right) and young *bejuni* —— 129	
Photo 6:	Village of Phakeri and the remains of the earth goddess's house —— 424	
Photo 7:	*Jakeri* inside the house of the earth goddess (Kanharu, 2001) —— 429	
Photo 8:	A swidden in the Niamgiri Hills (near Kadrakabondeli, 2001) —— 442	
Photo 9:	Sacrificial stake placed near stream (Railima, 2001) —— 482	
Photo 10:	*Koteiwali* —— 487	
Photo 11:	Fence at entrance to village (*kodru parbu* in Railima, 2001) —— 490	
Photo 12:	Feeding and anointing the buffaloes —— 496	
Photo 13:	Pots placed near the earth goddess (at night in Mundawali, 2001) —— 504	
Photo 14:	Jani carrying the sacrificial axe (*tangi*) (Mundawali, 2001) —— 507	
Photo 15:	*Bonda* (Tebapada, 2001) —— 511	
Photo 16:	*Satara bonda* with white cloths (Tebapada, 2001) —— 512	
Photo 17:	*Daka jani* and *bahuki* carried into the village on a cot —— 532	
Photo 18:	*Palawara* with banana trees (Kuskedeli, 2001) —— 546	
Photo 19:	Winnowing fan with "weapons" of *lada penu* (Tebapada, 2001) —— 555	
Photo 20:	Dongria shooting a gun during the worship of *lada penu* (Tebapada, 2001) —— 557	
Photo 21:	Dongria with drums during *kodru parbu* (Mundawali, 2001) —— 561	

Photo 22: Buffaloes tethered to a post two days before the sacrifice (Tebapada, 2001) —— **569**

Photo 23: Leg of sacrificial victim placed on the roof of the *jani*'s house (Tebapada, 2001) —— **575**

Parts of this book were previously published in:

1. Hardenberg, Roland 2003. "Friendship and Violence among the Dongria Kond (Orissa/India)." *Baessler Archiv* 51: 45–57.
2. Hardenberg, Roland 2006. "'Hut of the Young Girls': Transition from Childhood to Adolescence in a middle Indian tribal society." In *Childhoods in South Asia*, edited by D. K. Behera, 65–81. Singapore: Pearson Education.
3. Hardenberg, Roland 2009. "The Buffalo Sacrifice of the Kond and the Creation of Society." In *Contemporary Society: Tribal Studies,* vol. 8, *Tribal Society: Category and Ritual Exchange*, edited by G. Pfeffer, 52–66. New Delhi: Concept Publishers.
4. Hardenberg, Roland 2009. "'Village Relations': Exchange and Territory in the Highlands of Orissa." In *Contemporary Society: Tribal Studies,* vol. 8, *Tribal Society: Category and Ritual Exchange*, edited by G. Pfeffer, 135–158. New Delhi: Concept Publishers.
5. Hardenberg, Roland 2017. "'Juniors', 'Exploiters', 'Brokers' and 'Shamans'— a Holistic View on the Dombo Community in the Highlands of Odisha." In *Highland Odisha. Life and Society beyond the Coastal World*, edited by U. Skoda and B. Pati, 135–174. Delhi: Primus Books.

Abbreviations

M	mother
F	father
Z	sister
B	brother
D	daughter
S	son
W	wife
H	husband
P	parent
Sb	sibling
Sp	spouse
C	child
e	elder
y	younger
BG	bride-giver
BT	bride-taker
+2	grandparents' generation
+1 (+)	parents' generation (older than ego's F or M)
+1	parents' generation (no age distinction)
+1 (-)	parents' generation (younger than ego's F or M)
0 (+)	ego's generation (elder than ego)
0	ego's generation (no age distinction)
0 (-)	ego's generation (younger than ego)
−1	children's generation
−2	grandchildren's generation
−3	great-grandchildren's generation
−4	great-great-grandchildren's generation
−5	great-great-great-grandchildren's generation

Spelling of Dongria words

The Dongria language, which is not a written language, has so far not been the object of any linguistic research. It differs from the two Kond languages for which we have professional studies, Kuwi (Israel 1979) and Kui (Winfield 1928, 1929). I myself learned the language in the field with the help of local informants. Since I am not a trained linguist, I did not record the language using linguistic methods. In order to avoid mistakes in a field in which I have no expertise, I do not attempt to apply phonological rules in this study. I write the words the way I, as a German speaker, recorded them. Apart from names of people, social units, or places, I write all Dongria words in lowercase letters and in italics.

1 Introduction

1.1 The people

This study focuses on the inhabitants of the Niamgiri Hills,[1] a mountain range in the Rayagada district of Odisha. The majority of the population in this area consists of approximately eight thousand Dongria Kond residing in just over one hundred villages, spread over an area of about two hundred and fifty square miles. They coexist with a smaller population[2] of people known as Dombo, who often reside in hamlets situated in close proximity to the villages of the Dongria Kond. For administrative purposes, the Dongria Kond are classified as a "scheduled tribe", whereas the Dombo are considered a "scheduled caste". This distinction, however, is dubious, as both communities share ideas and values, are dependent upon one another, and display substantial interaction on a daily basis. They may therefore be considered part of the same society. The major focus of this book is the Dongria Kond's social and cultural representations, which have not previously been described in detail. However, it must be emphasised that the social system that exists in the Niamgiri Hills can be understood only by taking into consideration specific forms of interaction between members of both the Dongria Kond and the Dombo communities.

The name Dongria Kond is used by that people to describe themselves, particularly when dealing with outsiders such as government officials or development workers. The word Dongria derives from the Oriya word *dongor* meaning "mountain" or "hill," specifically one that is tree-covered, and can be translated as "mountain dweller." The etymology of the word Kond remains doubtful but probably derives from the Telugu word for "mountain" (*kondh*) (Nayak 1989,

---

[1] The mountain range occupied by the Dongria derives its name from its highest peak, the sixteen-hundred-meter-high Niamgiri, locally also called Nebaharu. It is considered the seat of their divine king, Niamraja, who is said to have been selected by the sun god, Dharam Devata, to rule over the people (Jena et al. 2002, 159–63). The word *niam* means "moral law" and describes actions considered to be in accordance with the rules and traditions laid down by the gods.

[2] According to a study undertaken in 1975, the 110 villages in the Niamgiri Hills at that time were inhabited by 5,618 Dongria and 1,173 Dombo (Das Patnaik 1984, 23). According to the statistical data published by Nayak in 1989, 7,858 Dongria occupied 116 villages. In 52 of these villages, they lived together with a total of 1,365 Dombo. Kanungo (2004) provides statistical data for the Dongria Kond only. According to his source (DKDA Chatikona and Parsali), 112 villages are today inhabited by 1,813 Dongria Kond families with a total population of 8,042 individuals. The male / female ratio for the Dongria Kond stands at 1000 : 1030.

Photo 1: Niamgiri Hills (2002)

25). Thus, from the perspective of the Oriya, their habitat, the forested hills, characterises these people more than anything else.

The Kond are spread over the whole of the Eastern Ghats, the major mountain range of eastern India, and together form a population of about one million people (Padel 2000, 12). Depending on the region, the Kond are classified into different subcategories. In the mountains of Phulbani district, the so-called Kondmals of Odisha, they are known as Kui Kond, Kuttia Kond, and Malliah Kond. Towards the south, in the former undivided Koraput district,[3] they are referred to as Dongria Kond, Desia Kond, and Kuvi Kond. These local Kond communities differ markedly from one another in culture and are not united in any kind of social or political corporation. There are, however, certain features that are considered typical for the Kond, although they are not necessarily characteristic of all communities throughout Odisha. Such features include i) village layout, which is usually in the form of two rows of houses; ii) the existence of localised, exogamous clans; iii) a distinction between secular (*majhi* or *bismajhi*)

---

[3] Before 1993, the Rayagada district was part of the Koraput district. As part of an administrative reorganisation, the Koraput district was divided into four separate districts: Koraput, Nawrangpur, Malkangiri, and Rayagada.

and sacred (*jani*) leaders; iv) the worship of the earth goddess represented by stones; and v) the performance of human sacrifices in the past and of buffalo sacrifices today.

Linguistically, the Kond are far from homogenous. Linguists distinguish between the Kui language spoken by inhabitants of the Kondmals (see Winfield 1928, 1929) and the Kuvi (or Kuwi) language of the less numerous southern branch of the Kond (see Israel 1979).[4] Both belong to the Dravidian linguistic family, which explains why Trautmann in his seminal work on Dravidian kinship also discusses Kond kinship terminology (Trautmann [1981] 1995, 140–43). Dongria themselves refer to their language as Kuang Kata. The word *kuang* has the same root as Kui and Kuwi, *ku-*, which in Dongria is used to denote male in opposition to female, marked by the prefix *as-*. For example, *kumila* denotes a male child, *asmila* a female child. However, when Dongria wish to distinguish between themselves and individuals belonging to other communities, they refer to themselves as *kuang*. Used in this way, the term *kuang* means "men" and has the connotation of "human being." This corresponds to the observation that tribal communities in India and elsewhere define themselves and their way of life as "human" and attach less value to the society and culture of others (Dumont 1986, 207; Padel 2000, 12).

In the Rayagada district, the Kond classify members of their community (*jati*) into two categories on the basis of their place of residence. The Dongria refer to those Kond living in the valleys and flatlands along the rivers as Desia Kond in Oriya and Pangenga in their own language. Desia means "people of the land (*desa*)," while Pangenga derives from the Dongria word *panga*, which indicates more specifically the flat areas used for cultivation. The "flatlanders" (Pangenga) refer to the members of their community who reside in the steep hills of the Niamgiri range as Dongria or Jarnenga. The latter term derives from an Oriya word, *jharana*, that means "spring" or "mountain stream" and alludes to the fact that the Dongria live near the sources of the numerous small streams that run down from the hills. The Dongria and Desia Kond exhibit differences in culture and language and ridicule one another by pointing out these dif-

---

[4] According to Israel, Kui and Kuwi are different languages and not simply dialects of the same language (Israel 1979, xv). Although I am not a linguist, I remain doubtful about this. In my view, Kui and Kuwi are simply the least related of the Kond dialects. When learning the language of the Dongria, I found that the vocabulary and grammar showed similarities to both "languages" described by Israel and Winfield. In my experience, dialects exhibit differences every twenty kilometres in this mountainous area. The differences between Kui and Kuwi correspond to the relatively great distance between the areas occupied by the Kui and Kuwi speakers studied by these two authors.

ferences in dress code, behaviour, and pronunciation. However, people identify with one of the two Kond categories solely on the basis of one criterion, namely their place of residence: the Dongria live in the mountains, the Desia on the flatlands.

Although their marriage rules differ, the Desia and Dongria nonetheless intermarry with one another and prohibit marriage relations with any other groups. They explain this by claiming membership of the same *jati*, a word commonly translated as "caste." In the valleys inhabited by the Desia Kond, it is indeed possible to speak of the existence of a caste system, as people are divided into ranked endogamous communities. From the perspective of the Desia Kond, society is divided into the "small," unclean castes, such as the Ghasi (brass workers), Leli (sweepers), Komti (Telugu traders), and Dombo (Oriya traders); the lower, but relatively clean castes, such as the Lohar (blacksmiths)[5] and Sundi (alcohol distillers); and the "big," high castes, such as the Paika (soldiers), Gouda (cowherds), Kumbhara (potters), Karana (scribes), and Bamana (Brahmins, priests). The Desia Kond occupy a middle position in this local hierarchy and in some areas may be referred to as a dominant caste because they are in possession of the land and form the majority of the population.

However, despite their inclusion in such a caste network, and despite the strong influence of mainstream Indian culture and politics, the Desia Kond differ from, say, a peasant caste in the coastal plains of Odisha. They are organised in exogamous, territorial clans that form phratries with other clans, including those of the Dongria Kond. People of the same clan may not intermarry but must cooperate in the worship of the earth goddess. Marriage follows the bridewealth pattern, not the Brahmin ideal of the gift of a virgin (*kanyadan*). Each clan is divided into certain status categories, within which, as in the clans in a phratry, senior and junior units are distinguished. The Desia Kond may participate in local Hindu festivals celebrated in nearby towns, but they do not have permanent temples in their own villages. They sacrifice buffaloes and pigs and consume this meat at village feasts. Their villages and houses are built in the same style as those of the Dongria Kond but differ from those of the local potters and Brahmins.

Compared to the Desia Kond, the Dongria Kond are included in such a local caste system to an even lesser extent. They live a relatively isolated life in the Niamgiri Hills together with only one other community, the Dombo or Oriya trad-

---

5 Some of the blacksmiths are classified as Kond. These Lohar Kond intermarry with Desia Kond but are considered to be of lower status. Lohar Kond thus eat in the houses of Desia Kond, but not vice versa.

Figure 1: Map of Odisha – Location of study area (Copyright: 2015@www.mapsofworld.com)

ers, who act as their clients. The Dombo perform the role of middlemen between the Dongria and the people of the lowlands.[6] However, apart from their need for certain items sold in the lowland markets, such as pottery, metal objects, and animals for sacrifice, the Dongria highlanders are relatively self-sufficient. They have their own priests and do not depend on Brahmin priests to perform their rituals or prepare food for their guests. They are skilled fighters, feared for their aggressiveness, and do not depend on members of a warrior caste to protect their land. Almost everything they require they produce themselves, and their yearly income from swidden cultivation is so small that they have no need of accountants to measure the harvest or record revenue payments. Proud landowners, they carry out all agricultural tasks themselves and refrain from employing unskilled labourers to carry out the most strenuous tasks. In ad-

---

6 In recent years, due to the activities of a local government agency, the Dongria have begun to deal directly with the traders of the major market towns.

dition, the Dongria wash their own clothes and bury or burn their own dead, or in other words, do not depend on washermen or "untouchables" to relieve them of their impurities. Essential elements of a caste system are thus absent, which leads to the question of what kind of society actually exists in the Niamgiri hills. The aim of this book is to provide some answers to this question.

1.2 Theoretical framework

This study was inspired by the writings of Louis Dumont and by those anthropologists who have successfully applied and advanced the theoretical concepts he developed. It is generally necessary to draw a distinction between Dumont's theory and the more widely known structuralism of Lévi-Strauss. Dumont's approach to the study of social and cultural phenomena operates with an analytical method commonly known as structuralism, but it also makes use of concepts and modes of comparison not found in the work of Lévi-Strauss.

In the context of South Asian studies, Dumont has exerted an immense influence on anthropologists and Sanskrit scholars who study Indian civilisation through the publication of his opus magnum, *Homo Hierarchicus* ([1966] 1998), his numerous articles in *Contributions to Indian Sociology,* and his very detailed ethnographic study of the Pramalai Kallar of Tamil Nadu, *A South Indian Subcaste* ([1957] 1986). His more general theoretical writings, published in his *Essays on Individualism* (1986), are less known to specialists of Indian civilisation but have influenced a number of scholars studying rituals and exchange systems in other parts of the world.

These scholars have produced a number of studies dealing with various societies, such as the Are Are (de Coppet 1981, 1985, 1995) and Orokaiva (Iteanu 1990a, 1990b, 2004) of Melanesia, the inhabitants of the Kei islands (Barraud 1990a, 1990b; Barraud and Friedberg 1996) and Tobelo (Platenkamp 1988, 1990, 1992, 2001) in Southeast Asia, and the Nyamwezi (Tcherkezoff 1985) and Tuareg (Casajus 1985) in Africa.[7] A group of French anthropologists cooperating in a research team named E.R.A.S.M.E. has been especially responsible for the further development of Dumont's structural analysis of value systems. These anthropologists promoted the comparison of the societies they studied and published papers jointly in collected volumes such as *Différences, Valeurs, Hiérachie: Textes offert á Louis Dumont* (Galey 1984), *Contexts and Levels: Anthropological*

---

[7] For an application of Dumont's notion of hierarchy to the study of Chinese civilisation, see Taylor (1989, 490–511).

Essays on Hierarchy (Barnes, de Coppet, and Parkin 1985), *Of Relations with the Dead* (Barraud et al. 1994), and *Cosmos and Society in Oceania* (de Coppet and Iteanu 1995), as well as in special editions of anthropological journals such as *Ethnos* (Howell 1990) and *Bijdragen tot de Taal-, Land- en Volkenkunde* (Barraud and Platenkamp 1990).

Within the realm of South Asian studies, Dumont's concepts have remained relevant to the study of both caste and tribal society. Dumont's theory of hierarchy as the fundamental principle of caste society has stimulated both ethnographic research and the promotion of sociological theories. In recent years, anthropologists interested in the study of caste who have worked with Dumont's concept of hierarchy have placed particular focus on royal institutions and concepts of divine kingship (Apffel-Marglin 1985; Galey 1989; Hardenberg 1999, 2000), aspects neglected in Dumont's own studies.

In his writings on Indian society, Dumont also disregarded the many different tribal communities and their specific values. The ethnographic description and analysis of these societies became the focus of Georg Pfeffer's work. Over a period of more than two decades, Pfeffer carried out fieldwork in various parts of Odisha, an Indian state with sixty-two different officially recognised tribes, who comprise one fourth of the total population and are protected by special, constitutionally guaranteed reservation rights. Pfeffer convincingly applied Dumont's concepts and developed them further in his studies on marriage and kinship systems (e.g., Pfeffer 1982, 1983, 1999, 2004a), in his analysis of rituals and social structure (e.g., Pfeffer 1991, 2001), and in his comparison of value systems (e.g., Pfeffer 1997b, 2000, 2004b).

Some decades ago, the study of tribal value systems in new ethnographic fields has been made possible through a research programme financed by the German Research Council. Pfeffer designed a research project with a team of social anthropologists from the Free University of Berlin who conducted long-term fieldwork in an industrial setting within the "tribal belt" (Strümpell 2001, 2006, 2008), in a "mixed zone" inhabited by both caste and tribal communities (Skoda 2000, 2001, 2005), among the Rona of the Koraput plateau, who were formerly recognised as tribals before being reclassified as an "Other Backward Class" (Otten 2000a, 2000b, 2006), and among people living in both coastal and tribal Odisha who have adopted the new ascetic faith of Mahima Dharma (Guzy 2000, 2001, 2002).

As a member of the same research team, Peter Berger (2000, 2002, 2004, 2007, 2015) conducted twenty-two months of fieldwork among the Gadaba of southern Odisha. His study of the Gadaba ritual system attains the same depth of analysis and understanding as Vitebsky's (1993) famous work on the dialogues with the dead among the Sora. Berger studies the rituals as a system, i.e., he looks at the relations among those rituals concerned with the construction of the person (Berger 2015, 221–363), the production of crops (Berger 2015, 364–474), and the healing of disease (Berger 2015, 475–519). Applying concepts developed by Dumont, de Coppet, and Barraud, he distinguishes three types of relations expressed in local terms through metaphors of consumption: to feed, to share, and to devour. The first two types of relations, associated with feeding and sharing, are seen as stable, predictable, based on the moral order (*niam*), and linked to a value Gadaba express in the words *bol soman*, "good and even." Berger identifies a third set of relations in contexts of sickness, disease, and black magic, which are seen as opposed to the moral order and linked to concepts of misfortune (*bipod*). The three forms of consumption do not simply occur within a ritual framework, but in Berger's analysis are ritual actions that creatively represent and change social relations. Using a concept developed by Dumont and de Coppet, he describes them as "value ideas" (Berger 2015, 43–44).

In the context of South Asian studies, the exceptionally coherent model presented by Dumont, in particular his concept of the "encompassment of the contrary" (see below), opened the way for new questions and influenced a whole generation of anthropologists who went on to conduct intensive fieldwork in various parts of India. Although the critics of Dumont's work outnumbered those scholars who found his approach helpful in understanding the social and cultural phenomena they studied, it would be fair to claim that the critics who were prepared to study values and ideas radically different from those of modern ideology were far fewer than those who never seriously attempted to apply Dumont's concepts. What are these concepts? In what follows, I briefly summarise Dumont's most important concepts – value-ideas, hierarchy, whole, context, and levels, and universalism and holism – as these provide a framework for my analysis of Niamgiri society.

1.2.1 Value-ideas

The term "value" as used by Dumont must be distinguished from the concept of value or value orientations as developed by Clyde Kluckhohn. Dumont applies the concept of value in his analysis of representations of social facts and not in order to understand the behaviour of individual actors. In what Dumont calls "non-modern"[8] societies (Dumont 1986, 234–68), society is seen as part

---

8 The term "non-modern" is not used by Dumont to characterise members of other societies as backward or as being of lower value. He simply states a difference between our society, which

of the cosmos, i.e., as governed by the same principles as the universe and ordered according to a common set of values. These "values have nothing to do with the preferable or the desirable" (Dumont 1986, 249), because their primary role is not to regulate the actions of "individuals." In non-modern societies, they express the order of relations that permeates the entire cosmos, including society itself. In modern societies, this unity of the cosmos has, in Dumont's view, been replaced by the absolute distinction of values. Values are divided into distinct, strictly separated domains such as science, aesthetics and morals. This separation corresponds to the distinction between what *is* and what *ought* to be (see also de Coppet 1992, 3). In Dumont's view, the transformation from non-modern to modern ideology can be seen as the transformation of a society understood as a community ("Gemeinschaft") governed by the principles of the cosmos into a society understood as a collection of individuals ("Gesellschaft"). As part of this transformation, values relating to the social and cosmological order are replaced by values relating to the individual. In modern ideology, values (what *ought* to be) bear exclusively on individual, "subjective" morality (Dumont 1986, 247). While modern ideology separates values and facts (or science), non-modern ideologies embed values in their worldview. Since values express the order of the whole cosmos in the latter type of ideology, these values are often linked to ideas about the world, and Dumont therefore speaks of "value-ideas" (Dumont 1986, 252).

1.2.2 Hierarchy

The term hierarchy as used by Dumont is unrelated to social stratification, military ranking, or power inequalities, and instead refers to a special configuration of values. Hierarchy does not derive from empirical relations but rather provides the form according to which these relations are ordered in a specific ideology. Hierarchy as defined by Dumont distinguishes between higher and lower values and organises them according to a principle he refers to as the "encompassment of the contrary" (Dumont 1998, 240). By this he means that a higher value is not only opposed to a lower value but also identified with the whole. Dumont adopted this concept from Apthorpe (Dumont 1998, 241–42) and applied it to the study

---

defines itself as modern, and other societies, which differ in values, social morphology and collective representations. Modern society has an ideology that valorises the individual in the sense of an "independent, autonomous moral and thus, essentially non-social being" (Dumont 1986, 279). Non-modern societies have a holistic ideology that "valorises the social whole and neglects or subordinates the human individual" (Dumont 1986, 279).

of collective representations in a given society, the caste system of India. In Dumont's view, this configuration of values corresponds to a particular relation between the castes. On the one hand, the higher and lower values, purity and impurity, are complementary, corresponding to the division of society into complementary but opposed elements, the castes. On the other hand, the higher value of purity encompasses the lower value of impurity, since it stands for the unity of the whole and thus corresponds to the idea that the status principle represented by the highest element, the pure Brahmin caste, is the principle according to which the whole of society is ranked (Dumont 1998). This means that the elements of an ensemble are ordered in two ways: when dealing with the whole ensemble, one element encompasses the other, and when dealing with the parts of the ensemble, the elements oppose each other. According to Dumont, a hierarchical system of value-ideas usually shows the following three features (Dumont 1986, 252–53): first, a ranking of value-ideas; second, a possible reversal of that ranking in concrete contexts; and third, in its application, a hierarchy that leads to a fluid, constantly changing segmentation of collective representations. The concept of reversal is of particular importance to Dumont, for it shows that hierarchy is "bidimensional" (Dumont 1986, 253), i.e., it operates on different levels.

1.2.3 Whole, contexts, and levels

Inspired by Mauss and his concept of the "total social fact,"[9] Dumont aims to study "wholes," i.e., those representations of social unity that show internal consistency. For Dumont, a social whole consists of parts ordered according to the principle of hierarchy. The "parts" or value-ideas relate to social representations that are enacted in concrete contexts. Contexts are therefore structured by value-ideas, and since these value-ideas are ranked, the contexts are also divided into higher and lower contexts. The ranking of value-ideas is not absolute. In non-modern societies, we often encounter situations in which the order is reversed, i.e., in which value-ideas that are lower in one context become higher in another. This opposition or complementariness of value-ideas is a typical feature of the lower dimension of hierarchy, i.e., at the level of the parts. However, according to Dumont, there is a second dimension, i.e., that of the whole, and at this higher level of the overall configuration, one value is identified with the whole. Contexts pertaining to this value are higher in contexts stressing the

---

[9] For a detailed interpretation of this concept, see Gofman (1998).

whole, while in contexts relating to only a part of the whole, the same value may be subordinated to another. We thus have two levels or dimensions, that of the whole and that of the part. The evaluation of a concrete context or situation thus depends on whether it refers to the higher level of the whole or the lower level of the part. To illustrate this point, Dumont discusses the distinction into right and left (Dumont 1986, 248–50), which is used in symbolic classification all over the world (see Needham 1973b). When studying the opposition of right and left in relation to collective representations expressed in concrete contexts, Dumont suggests distinguishing between situations expressing the opposition of parts, i.e., the distinction between right and left, and situations pertaining to the whole, the body, usually represented by one of its parts, the right hand.

While Dumont himself did not study rituals in detail, others applied his concepts to the analysis of complex rituals and exchange systems. Following Dumont, Barraud and Platenkamp, for example, do not separate ritual from other social facts but emphasise the close link between ritual activities and the basic structure and values of a society. They suggest studying the way in which a single ritual relates to other rituals and how these activities structure the society under study (Barraud and Platenkamp 1990, 104). For Platenkamp, rituals reveal "the hierarchical order of relationships which constitutes the social morphology" (Platenkamp 1992, 74).

1.2.4 Universalism, holism, and comparison

Dumont distinguishes between universalism and holism. Holistic ideologies stress the distinctiveness of their own society, which is seen as being of higher value than any other society. The existence of other societies and their ideologies is not denied as such, but less value is attached to them, sometimes to the extent that members of external societies are not even regarded as human beings. In contrast, modern ideology denies the distinctiveness of its own society through its universalistic outlook. It claims to apply this to the whole of humankind and rejects other ideologies and their societies (Dumont 1986, 207). Anthropology deals with both the global and the local. Following Mauss, Dumont defines anthropology as the science that starts from the idea of the unity of humankind. This implies that beyond all differences, "there exist a few categories applicable to all societies, a few social universals, and that is enough for differences to be transcended, and talked about" (Dumont 1986, 206). Differences within the human species are related to the existence of local societies with their own holistic ideologies. In Dumont's view, anthropologists should study such societies as wholes before comparing these wholes. In this way, comparative analysis of several societies can reveal how similar elements are valued differently in relation to these individual wholes.

Anthropologists working with Dumont's concepts have developed this idea further in their study of rituals and exchange systems. Rituals are not studied in isolation but as part of a system that reveals those values structuring structure society as a whole, i.e., its social morphology, collective representations, and actions. Holism implies that ritual elements acquire their meaning from their position in the overall configuration of values. When comparing rituals of different societies, this holism requires the comparison of societal wholes (Barraud and Platenkamp 1990, 104).

1.3 Representing fieldwork

1.3.1 *Writing Culture*

Since the 1980s, when anthropologists turned to literary studies for new theoretical inspirations, it has become fashionable to focus on "representation" rather than on the data themselves. It is assumed that both data collection and interpretation are essentially subjective undertakings: ethnographers, in the individual circumstances of their fieldwork, compile data that have been constructed by individual informants and process them, i.e., transform them into a published text that relies on the ethnographer's sole authority in an effort to impress readers, earn a degree, or obtain other personal benefits. The writer's commanding position is unavoidably carried into the content of the writing. From a post-modern point of view, the anthropologist should as far as possible refrain from making abstractions and rather give the individual self and individual experiences a significant place in the text:

> Post-modern ethnography captures this mood of the post-modern world, for it, too, does not move toward abstraction, away from life, but back to experience. It aims not to foster the growth of knowledge but to restructure experience; not to understand objective reality, for that is already established by common sense, nor to explain how we understand, for that is impossible, but to reassimilate, to reintegrate the self in society and to restructure the conduct of everyday life. (Tyler 1986, 135)

Given this "post-modern" vision of the world, older notions of culture stressing coherence or the systematic nature of symbols and their meaning are naturally regarded with suspicion. The authors of *Writing Culture* (Clifford and Marcus 1986) on the one hand accepted Geertz's idea that an ethnographer is constructing data in conversations with informants; on the other hand, they went beyond him by rejecting his notion of culture and blaming him for not revealing his own subjectivity in his texts. Rabinow states this point clearly:

> At first glance James Clifford's work, like that of others in this volume, seems to follow naturally in the wake of Geertz's interpretative turn. There is, however, a major difference. Geertz (like the other anthropologists) is still directing his efforts to reinvent an anthropological science with the help of textual mediations. The core activity is still social description of the other [...]. The other for Clifford is the anthropological representation of the other. (Rabinow 1986, 242)

The whole idea of anthropology as a science producing cumulative and revisable knowledge about other people's cultures by means of comparison and generalisation of ethnographic data becomes questionable to those convinced that everything is in permanent flux, an object of personal contestation and subjective manipulation.

> If "culture" is not an object to be described, neither is it a unified corpus of symbols and meanings that can be definitively interpreted. Culture is contested, temporal, and emergent. (Clifford 1986, 19)

Inspired by literary criticism, some anthropologists began to see ethnographic texts as the products of authors who use a specific strategy of authority to present readers with a convincing account of their subjective experiences. Attempts to establish a certain order by constructing models or establishing relations among the data were now exposed as a strategy aimed at persuading the reader of an objective truth. Anthropologists inspired by literary critics detect in such texts attempts to camouflage the means by which the authors gathered the knowledge they present with such authority:

> Since Malinowski's time, the "method" of participant-observation has enacted a delicate balance of subjectivity and objectivity. The ethnographer's personal experiences, especially those of participation and empathy, are recognised as central to the research process, but they are firmly restrained by the impersonal standards of observation and "objective" distance. In classical ethnographies the voice of the author was always manifest, but the conventions of textual presentation and reading forbade too close a connection between authorial style and the reality presented. (Clifford 1986, 13)

The editors of *Writing Culture* further uncover a science-oriented, authoritarian, and imperial strategy in the systematic presentation of facts. For example, they oppose those anthropologists who, when systematizing their insights, present their findings in an impersonal, generalised way, although the data were originally collected from individuals in very specific contexts. For some critics, such generalisations not only obscure the subjective nature of our data in the name of a false notion of objective science, but worse, they take away the "voice" of the people involved, their agency and individuality, and treat them as objects rather than as human subjects. Thus, Clifford in his summary of Said's arguments states:

> This Orient, occulted and fragile, is brought lovingly to light, salvaged in the work of the outside scholar. The effect of domination in such spatial/temporal deployments (not limited, of course, to Orientalism proper) is that they confer on the other a discrete identity, while also providing the knowing observer with a standpoint from which to see without being seen, to read without interruption. Once cultures are no longer prefigured visually – as objects, theatres, texts – it becomes possible to think of a cultural poetics that is an interplay of voices, of positioned utterances. (Clifford 1986, 12)

To counteract these developments in anthropology, the self-reflexive fieldwork account emerged as a genre. Classical accounts written by Malinowski, Firth, Leach, and Evans-Pritchard, to mention but a few, also contained personal notes, allowed insights into fieldwork methods, described individual informants and their life histories, and gave "voice" to the people studied by quoting songs, myths, and recorded conversation. However, these personal narratives have been criticised for three reasons: first, in their style they resemble earlier travel writing that mystifies the author and his or her experiences; second, they serve merely to establish that the author has really been "out there"; and third, they are always given a subsidiary role in relation to the main text dealing with the people's culture and society (Pratt 1986, 35). The "experimental ethnography" favoured by Clifford, Marcus, and others goes beyond these classical accounts. For these critics, the author's reflection on fieldwork methods and writing styles, as well as the people's polyphony and contestation, becomes the central issue of ethnographic writing.

As is well known, anthropologists have always more or less revealed their methods, reflected on their writing, and presented us with context and polyphony. The novel aspect of the "literary turn" proposed by Clifford and Marcus is the rather radical position that ethnographic writing should always be reflexive and experimental and constantly reveal the subjective, contextual nature of our fieldwork experiences. In contrast to Evans-Pritchard (1962, 22–23), who sees writing ethnography and building models as two different but equally important steps in our work, Clifford and Marcus want to restrict themselves to the first step only. The real difference between the kind of ethnography produced by Malinowski and Evans-Pritchard, for example, and the experimental ethnography envisaged by Clifford and Marcus is not so much the latter's greater reflexivity as it is the latter's idea (or lack of an idea) of culture. When everything is considered to be in constant flux and subject to individual contestation, when in Clifford's words ethnographies are "true fictions" (Clifford 1986, 6), then any separation between observer and observed, between ethnographic work and ethnographic writing, appears superfluous:

> In fact, it [post-modern ethnography, R.H.] rejects the ideology of "observer-observed," there being nothing observed and no one who is the observer. There is instead the mutual, dialogical production of discourse, of a story of sorts. (Tyler 1986, 126)

If, on the other hand, ethnographic writing refers to something beyond the individual, i.e., to culture in the sense of something produced and transmitted through collective efforts, then experimental ethnography as suggested by Clifford and Marcus is a welcome addition to, but not a substitute for cultural analysis. If this is the case, it raises the question of the extent to which such "experiments" should influence our rhetoric and the content of our writing. Can they be as marginal as in many classical accounts, or do we have to give them a central place in all of our published work?

Answers to these questions depend on the focus and scope of the particular work. Is it an article or a book? Does it aim to present a complex system of ideas or to make a specific event intelligible? Does it deal with the formal aspects of a culture or with specific performances? Is it addressed to students or to colleagues? Is it published in a journal, a magazine or newspaper, etc.? Further, any information concerning the empirical basis of our authorship is helpful, as it allows the reader to judge the value of the data presented: How were the data collected? How long was the ethnographer in the field? How intimate were his or her relations with the people in the field? How competent was he or she in their language? What problems did he or she have to face in the field situation? Answers to these questions help the reader to judge the strengths and weaknesses of the ethnographic work (Evans-Pritchard 1940, 9). However, in my view, authors do not need to recapitulate these particular circumstances in every piece they publish or recount these conditions every time they speak at an ethnographic event.

In a rather old-fashioned way, I decided to answer these questions in this introductory part and refer to it whenever necessary. I will refrain from exposing my fears and frustrations in minute detail and present mainly those problems that clearly derived from a clash of values and thus enhance our understanding of the culture under study. The description of my fieldwork will not provide the reader with an "authentic" picture, since I refer to only a few events and omit others. Even if it were twice as long, it would not, in my view, be more authentic, as it would still present only a very limited picture of my total experiences.

My fieldwork account will focus on three aspects. First, I will show that my research depended on the help of many different people at home as well as in the field. Second, I will describe my achievements and failures in order to allow the reader to judge the value of my data and the limits of my attempts at understanding Dongria Kond society. Finally, I will recount some events involving conflicts and acts of aggression against me or my colleagues in order to introduce the reader to important aspects of this and other tribal societies: the lack of a central authority that can be called upon to establish peace and the absence of contractual reliability when making arrangements with people who change their loyalties contextually.

In the cultural analysis presented in the following five chapters, the Dongria will be given a voice by quoting their myths and songs and by describing in detail actual cases of bride capture and buffalo sacrifices. Yet for me, such "voices" are not in themselves the object of my study, and presenting them is not my only mode of ethnographic writing. In my view, there is something beyond these individual utterances and discursive dialogues, a collective system of ideas and representations, which deserves a different – perhaps old-fashioned – treatment.

1.3.2 The fieldwork situation

The fieldwork project on which this book is based began to take concrete form in 2000, when I accompanied Georg Pfeffer, professor at the Free University of Berlin, one of his students, and a young man from Sambalpur University on a visit to the highlands of Odisha. On our month-long trip, we visited the villages of Olari and Gutob Gadaba in the district of Koraput, Koya in Malkangiri, Dongria Kond in Rayagada, and Kuttia Kond in Phulbani with the explicit aim of finding a research topic and a suitable place for my fieldwork. In more than twenty years of field experience in Odisha, Pfeffer had visited most of the districts we went to and was familiar with many facets of tribal life through his own research and his knowledge of the few existing ethnographies. Yet on this trip we visited many places he himself had never seen, and we came across a number of aspects of tribal life that appeared to both of us worthy of further investigation. In Koraput, for example, we met Gadaba who had only recently left their original villages and migrated into another area where they were busy building new villages, constructing shrines, and establishing social relations with their new neighbours. In Malkangiri, we visited a village with an impressive "graveyard," where a number of stones and wooden posts had been set up in the course of funerals and where the village chief explained to us the links between certain mythological events, these memorial stones and posts, and the different Koya phratries and clans. Among the Kuttia Kond, we witnessed a buffalo sacrifice as part of a naming ceremony for three young boys that involved extensive rituals and invocations of the ancestors.

In all these places, the people were obviously quite unlike the poor, suppressed tribals who figure so prominently in the numerous publications concerned with their "development" and "uplift." They were neither undernourished nor living in a state of poverty. Their houses were not rich and did not contain the same luxuries as those of many wealthier Hindu peasants, but they were not the crumbling, dirty huts of the poor either. These were not resettled, depressed people deprived of their culture but members of vital societies, people who actively shaped their fate in their own, culturally specific ways.

When we arrived in the Niamgiri Hills to visit villages inhabited by Dongria Kond, I knew that I had found the place for my next fieldwork. What attracted me most on this first short trip into the hills was the beauty of the place. In contrast to most areas I had seen in the Koraput and Malkangiri districts, the Niamgiri Hills are still densely covered with forest, and travel through the valleys requires crossing numerous streams of clear water flowing down from the mountains. Compared to the rather dull countryside in coastal Odisha or on the Koraput plateau, the home of these hill dwellers is a spectacular landscape with an immense variety of flora and fauna. My romantic picture was somewhat tarnished later when I learned about deforestation and excessive hunting by townsmen, but I still think that the Niamgiri Hills are one of the most beautiful and best preserved natural landscapes in Odisha.

Right from the beginning, I was less romantic about the people, the Dongria, who never appeared to me as noble savages in a Garden of Eden. On the contrary, after reading the only book then available about the Dongria, Prasanna Kumar Nayak's *Blood, Women, and Territory* (1989), I perhaps fell prey to another distorted image, that of the wild man in the wild jungle. Nobody can read the sixty-six pages filled with Nayak's descriptions of bloody clan feuds without thinking that there are better and safer places to spend time and conduct research in this world than the Niamgiri Hills. Most of the time, I managed to push memories of these brutal conflicts away, but later, when I had personally experienced such events, I had to come to grips with situations in which I felt surrounded by people who might have killed me at any time. Such fears were certainly exaggerated and an expression of the insecurity felt by every person entering a new, unknown field, but they were not products of sheer fantasy either. On the one hand, to this day, the institutions of the Indian state are far from controlling the Dongria people and the Dongria region. The Niamgiri Hills remain remote, and the inhabitants continue to regulate their affairs according to the tribal system, which might, under certain conditions, include the application of brute physical force. Sahlins's concept of *warre* as "an underlying circumstance," a "potential inclination" to secure safety, gain, and status by means of force (Sahlins 1968, 7), appropriately captures this aspect of tribal society. On the other hand, Dongria culture positively values a certain degree of manliness and aggressiveness and of resistance against outsiders. Especially when drunk, male Dongria can quickly become inflamed with rage, lose all inhibitions, and go berserk. Hardly anybody dares and is able to control a Dongria man when he is in such a condition. These are the situations in which people are wounded and even killed in axe battles.

A first impression of this male, drunken aggressiveness was forced upon us in the first days of our stay in the Niamgiri Hills. Following the advice of Prasanna Kumar Nayak, at that time a professor of anthropology at Bhubaneswar University, we entered the hills via the small town of Kalyansingpur. Nayak had recommended a visit to this western part of the Niamgiri Hills for two reasons: first, he regarded the southern part of the region, including the villages of Kambesi and Kurli, where all previous anthropologists had conducted their fieldwork,[10] as not suitable for research, since people there were involved at the time in serious conflicts about land and had on several occasions shown their aversion to the outsiders who from time to time intruded into their villages in tourist groups; second, the government had established a second branch of its local development agency (the DKDA or Dongria Kond Development Agency) in the hills

---

10 The first surveys and ethnographic studies among the Dongria Kond were conducted by Patnaik and Das Patnaik, both members of the Tribal and Harijan Research-cum-Training Institute, who published their results in a book (Patnaik and Das Patnaik 1982) and in various articles that appeared in *Adibasi*, the institute's official journal. Among their research staff was Prasanna Kumar Nayak, who later became director of the institute, which has been renamed the Scheduled Tribes and Scheduled Castes Research-cum-Training Institute. His research work began in 1975 and resulted in a PhD thesis published in 1989 and dealing with Dongria Kond clan feuds. The first really extensive fieldwork, about fifteen months long, was conducted by Dagmar Stachowski in the 1980s. Due to a prolonged illness, she unfortunately could not write up her thesis. Thanks to her supervisor, Georg Pfeffer of the Free University of Berlin, I had access to two of her unpublished manuscripts (Stachowski unpublished a, unpublished b). Upali Aparajita conducted research in five villages, including Kurli and Kambesi, in the late 1980s and published her results in 1994. I found it difficult to establish how long she actually spent in the field, and most questions concerning her field methodology etc. remain unanswered. Finally, a research team consisting of four Indians worked at Kurli in the 1990s under the guidance of Klaus Seeland. Their results were published in the Man and Forest Series (Jena et al. 2002). Again, the length and circumstances of individual fieldwork remain unspecified. It should, however, be stressed that starting with Patnaik and Das Patnaik, all these fieldworkers conducted their research in the same area, probably for the simple reason that the villages of Kurli and Kambesi are accessible by the only proper road in the Niamgiri Hills.

above Kalyansingpur, and many of its most experienced and reliable staff members had been stationed in this new project settlement, called Parsali.[11] Nayak knew these DKDA officials well and provided us with a letter of recommendation, which facilitated our entry into this rather remote area.

The start of our time in the Niamgiri Hills coincided with the main days of the *siva yatra*, an important Hindu festival celebrated annually at a temple located on top of an impressive rock formation near Kalyansingpur. On this occasion, young Dongria men and women come down from the hills into town to attend the festivities. On one of these festival days we, along with the Amina, a land record officer who was an important official of the DKDA, went by jeep from Parsali to Kalyansingpur to buy rice and vegetables. On our way back, we made the mistake of giving a lift to two young Dongria men. The road from Kalyansingpur to Parsali is nine kilometres long, but it takes about an hour to cover the whole distance, because the road is stony and bumpy and crosses several streams. Apart from bullock carts, only motorcycles and all-terrain vehicles can be used in the upper, hilly sections of the road, this being perhaps the main reason why up to now outsiders have not yet managed to remove large amounts of timber from this part of the Niamgiri Hills. On the day we drove up into the hills, a large number of young and mostly drunk men were on their way back to their villages. When they saw their two brothers sitting in our vehicle, they immediately stopped our jeep and demanded to be given a lift up to Parsali. Within minutes, almost twenty men were sitting either inside or on top of the vehicle, obviously enjoying our irritation and helplessness. The Amina sat more or less silently inside the car and made only half-hearted attempts to drive the Dongria out of the vehicle. The less experienced among us – the driver from Koraput district, Georg Pfeffer, and myself – got out of the jeep and began a discussion with the Dongria, trying to convince them to leave the vehicle and walk on foot back to their villages. Many laughed at us and passed comments we could not understand, while others behaved more aggressively, shouted at us, and demanded to be given a lift. We refused, as we were afraid that on this bumpy road the drunk men might fall off the jeep and receive serious injuries.

Faced with our refusal to drive on, the young men continued arguing with us, obviously sensing our fear – as always when walking through the hills, these young men carried axes and knives – and taking advantage of being in the majority. We had two options: either to continue on our way up into the hills together with this crowd of drunk young men, or to go back in the direction

---

11 The first DKDA office was established in 1978 in a village called Chatikona near the town of Bissamcuttack.

of Kalyansingpur and wait somewhere long enough to allow these men to reach their villages on foot. We decided in favour of the second option and, under the Dongria's protests, turned our vehicle. We slowly drove back, stopped about half a kilometre later, parked the jeep in the shadow of a tree, and waited for more than half an hour. When we again continued our drive up into the hills and reached the place where we had first confronted the young men, we found our path obstructed by massive rocks. We had to get out and remove the rocks, not once but several times before we finally reached Parsali. The message was clear: we were outsiders intruding into their country, and we were expected to either submit to their rules or stay away.

For the next few days we stayed in a bungalow belonging to the Special Officer of the DKDA in Parsali.[12] Apart from this bungalow, the small project settlement consists of a small school for young boys and an attached dormitory, four tin-roofed houses used by staff members as residential quarters or storehouses, a deep well, and some gardens. The road from Kalyansingpur ends here, and only small footpaths lead further into the hills, where most Dongria villages are located.[13] On our visits we were guided by a DKDA Multiple Purpose Worker (MPW), a Muslim named Abdul Rauf who could look back on more than twenty years of service in the Niamgiri Hills. The DKDA in Parsali employs about six MPWs,[14] who live in either Kalyansingpur, Parsali, or interior areas of the Niamgiri Hills, each one being responsible for a certain number of villages. They are expected to visit these villages regularly, supply them with the various items provided free of cost by the government (e.g., orange trees, pineapple and banana plants, fertiliser, school uniforms for children, medicine), give polio vaccinations, teach the children reading and writing, introduce new forms of agriculture (e.g., fruit tree plantations, potato cultivation), and resolve conflicts when necessary.

---

12 The name Parsali actually refers to a small Dongria village located about two hundred meters up the hill.
13 In 2002, the Indian government spent a great deal of money building more roads in the Niamgiri Hills, and for some months I was able to ride my motorbike further into the hills, up to the next village, named Sana Denganali. In 2003, the monsoon destroyed almost all of these new roads, and nothing remained but the stones that Dongria had put into place in weeks of hard labour.
14 Their wages are extremely low, about Rs 1,200 a month, and are paid very irregularly. It is therefore not surprising that most MPWs work only as much as necessary, which basically means that they turn up when the Special Officer from Rayagada pays a visit to the area. Since it is a government job, the position offers a certain security, but most MPWs seek other jobs to earn extra money. Of all the MPWs I met, only two women took their work seriously and actually lived in Dongria villages.

In these few days, we visited several villages and were everywhere welcomed with respect, but also reserve. People knew our guide, and they were used to official visitors, usually Indian development officers, doctors, or political representatives, who turn up in long trousers, white shirts, and American baseball caps, put some questions to the villagers, take notes, and leave again. On these first visits we were treated exactly like these people, as I understood much later when I experienced such visits from the perspective of the villagers: we were offered a cot to sit on, and the village chief, the local messenger from the Dombo community, and some elders were assembled and took responsibility for answering our questions. Some children, especially from the Dombo community, gathered around to get a look at the strange-looking foreigners, while most Dongria women remained inside their houses or watched us only from a distance. No water, food, or drinks were offered us, as everybody expected that such "high-status people" (*bada loka*) would not be willing to accept anything from them.

During these first short visits, I was often strongly impressed by the shrines Dongria build for the celebration of their most important festival, the buffalo sacrifice to the earth goddess. Such a shrine usually consists of a house constructed of massive, carved pillars made of teak wood, bamboo walls plastered with mud and painted with colourful triangles, and roofs thatched with the long, shining mountain grass (*wikang*) or, in more recent times, with corrugated metal provided by the government. The shrine usually stands in the centre of the village, and depending on the time that has passed since the residents celebrated their last buffalo sacrifice, the house may be either fully intact and used as an assembly hall by the male villagers or slowly falling apart, still useful only as a shelter for cows and goats when it is raining.

Georg Pfeffer had earlier told me about these sacrifices, which he himself had witnessed together with his student Dagmar Stachowski more than two decades previously. He now suggested to me to make these events the focus of my ethnographic research. It was clearly a relevant topic, given the lack of empirical studies of this phenomenon. Most earlier writings dealt with the Kond's human sacrifices (*meria*), which continued in the form of buffalo sacrifices (*kodru parbu*) after the British in the middle of the nineteenth century prohibited the offering of human victims to the earth goddess. In many areas of Odisha, especially those where Christian missionaries had been converting people for decades, these buffalo sacrifices were discontinued, but here in the Niamgiri Hills they were still celebrated in grand fashion. They were clearly important events for the people. For example, we found that villagers answered most of our questions with reserve and in a matter-of-fact tone, but when our questions addressed these buffalo sacrifices, discussions became more lively, and it was obvious that they considered this event to be one of the most important in their lives.

After leaving the Niamgiri Hills, we continued our trip and went to Phulbani district, where the Kuttia Kond live in another steep mountain area near Belagad. However, I had already made up my mind that the buffalo sacrifices of the Dongria Kond were a suitable topic for further research. At the same time, I must admit that I was also worried. After experiencing the difficult living conditions in the hills, I could foresee the various problems I would have to face in the field: Where would I live, get my food, or take a bath? How could I communicate with the people, and how long would it take me to understand their conversations? Who could accompany me when walking through the hills, and would it be dangerous for me to live there? These and other questions continued to bother me for a long time, and I never found satisfying answers to all of them. When back in Germany, I wrote up a research proposal together with Professor William S. Sax, who had been appointed head of the Department of Ethnology at the South Asia Institute in Heidelberg and was interested in my research topic. We applied for a grant from the German Research Council, which at that time was sponsoring the second phase of an overall six-year research programme focusing on the Indian state of Odisha and bringing together anthropologists, archaeologists, historians, geographers, and Indologists in an interdisciplinary project.

The council decided to sponsor an initial two-year research period, and I was able to start my fieldwork in February 2001.[15] When I arrived in Odisha, I first met with my friend and colleague Peter Berger, who was involved in the same research programme and had meanwhile gathered several months of fieldwork experience in a relatively remote tribal area in Koraput district. He was carrying out research on the rituals and society of the Gadaba tribe, work that has since resulted in an excellent PhD thesis.[16] Peter and his wife Amrei accompanied me to Rayagada, the administrative centre of the district, which became a kind of refuge for me whenever I felt tired and overworked during my fieldwork. This rather shabby, often dirty, and extremely dusty town provides its few visitors a recently built, excellent hotel named Sai International, a number of good restaurants, a market with fresh vegetables and fruits, gas stations, garages, and good shops for purchasing everything from batteries to razor blades. On our arrival in town, Peter helped me to buy all those things that according to his experience were necessary when living in the Odishan highlands without elec-

---

15 The project officially began in May 2001, but the Free University of Berlin, where I was then employed as an assistant professor, allowed me to take leave and start my research project earlier.

16 Peter Berger, "Füttern, Speisen und Verschlingen: Ritual und Gesellschaft im Hochland von Orissa" Berlin: LIT Verlag. This work has also been translated into English (Berger 2015).

tricity and running water: matches, lighters, batteries, lanterns, torch lights, cooking utensils, kerosene stoves, metal boxes, *jori* (cheap plastic bags), blankets, raincoats, *lungi* (a kind of loincloth), *gamcha* (a multipurpose towel), handkerchiefs, sandals, *bidi* (a kind of cigarette), and many more items to add to the mosquito net, air mattress, sleeping bag, cassette recorder, microphone, and other things I had brought along from Germany. Peter further aided me when I purchased a motorbike, a light Suzuki, which proved highly reliable and useful for traveling on the often washed-out roads in the hills.

On one of these first days in Rayagada, we contacted the DKDA Special Officer at the time, Sarat Chandra Dash, whom Georg Pfeffer and I had met the year before on our first visit to the Niamgiri Hills. He promised to accompany us to Parsali to see that everything would be arranged for my stay in the project settlement. My initial plan was to move into one of the MPW residential quarters, which remain vacant for most of the year, as many of these staff members prefer to reside in Kalyansingpur. From Parsali I intended to make excursions into the hills in order to find a suitable village and either move into an empty house or build a new house. In the end, I managed to implement this plan, but it took me much longer than expected.

On the day of our departure from Rayagada, everything went well: Mr. Dash turned up with his jeep, we managed to fit all our equipment plus several bags filled with potatoes, rice, and vegetables into the vehicle, and Peter and I took turns riding the motorbike and sitting inside the car until we reached Parsali in the afternoon. We moved into one of the staff quarters, which became my home for the next two months. The next day, we decided to pay a visit to Phakeri, one of the largest villages in this area with approximately sixty houses, to find out whether they had a vacant house for me or were willing to build me one. Peter's wife stayed back in Parsali, as rumours were spreading that some villagers were suffering from "smallpox," locally referred to as *ma budi* or *aji budi*, but it turned out that they were suffering from the less serious chicken pox, which is called by the same name.[17] When we arrived in Phakeri, hardly any villagers were present, as most people had gone to work in their fields in the surrounding mountains. As I soon found out, this situation was not exceptional. The practice of spending most of the day with the whole family working in the swiddens became a major source of frustration to me, as often nobody was there when I arrived in a village to conduct interviews. On this day, too, only a few people were

---

17 Like everywhere else in the world, smallpox was eradicated in this area many years ago, but some middle-aged and elderly people can still be seen with the typical scars caused by this disease.

present, and one of them, a young man who later became a village leader, complained that many people in Phakeri were suffering from disease and even dying, that the water pump – locally called *boring* – was not working properly and water supply a constant problem for the people, and that the villagers were now thinking of deserting the place and building a new settlement in another part of the hills. His talk was not encouraging, and when he informed us that no vacant house was available in Phakeri, I had already made the decision to find a place in another village. When we got back to Parsali, we discussed the matter with the Special Officer and some other staff members, who suggested several places to me, but the matter remained undecided when Peter and Amrei left the Niamgiri Hills to continue fieldwork among the Gadaba.

I did not remain alone for long, as soon after their departure a student named Promod Ratha arrived in Parsali. At my request, Deepak Kumar Behera, my "elder brother" and professor at Sambalpur University, had asked him to join me for an initial period of one month as a translator and assistant. I had promised to pay him well, but until he actually turned up in Parsali, I was worried he would not come. He proved to be one of the best field assistants I ever had. Although he was brought up in an urban Brahmin family and had never studied anthropology, he quickly adjusted to the different living conditions in the hills, and confronted with what must have appeared to him as rather strange customs and forms of behaviour, he reacted with curiosity rather than with repudiation. Although he too was a stranger in this area, he was of immense help to me. First of all, he improved my Oriya speaking skills. Four years had passed since I had completed my first fieldwork in coastal Odisha, and I had forgotten quite a number of words and expressions. Second, he was a good companion, who escorted me on all my tours and made me feel less insecure and unprotected. Third, everyone liked him, and he had a good way of talking to government officials, to Dongria, and to Dombo too.

Soon after his arrival we found out that several villages were planning to perform the buffalo sacrifice (*kodru parbu* or *meria*) within the next four weeks. Every day we received new information concerning the various preparations for this festival either from DKDA staff members or from one of the many Dongria who came to the project settlement to buy rice or kerosene. It turned out that Parsali was a kind of "news centre" in this rather remote place and a perfect location for getting an overview of the different activities and events in the Niamgiri Hills. One day we rode the motorbike to a village named Railima to observe the construction of the shrine for the earth goddess, and another day we walked on foot to a village called Kuskedeli to see the ritual feeding of the buffalo. In the evening we usually returned to our house in Parsali, where the staff members shared their food with us and where we discussed the events of the day. The

Amina and some of the MPWs narrated their experiences and provided us with stories about certain people we had met, about particular villages where we had been, and about earlier buffalo sacrifices they had either witnessed themselves or heard about. Finally, towards the end of Promod's stay, we managed to observe the buffalo sacrifice in three different villages (Kuskedeli, Tebapoda, and Mundawali), where we stayed overnight in school buildings or in houses of the Dombo community.

On all these occasions, I used a small digital video camera to record the events. Dongria sometimes expressed their disagreement with my video shooting, and women often avoided the focus of my camera by disappearing into a house or hut as soon as I turned up. Some demanded money or alcohol from me in return for the right to film certain rituals, and when I turned down their demands, they actively prevented me from continuing my video shooting by moving into my way or by trying to take away my camera. Although I actually shut off the camera in such situations, I am still at a loss to understand my initial inability to comply with the wishes of my hosts. In retrospect, I think my inappropriate behaviour had two reasons: first, I felt it necessary to record everything in order to have a more or less complete visual documentation of the events to be used for ethnographic analysis and to be presented to the academic audience at home; second, and perhaps more importantly, I felt absolutely overwhelmed by the events and considered video shooting a way of coming to terms with the situation. To participate in these events was out of the question, as I was a complete stranger and did not even know what would happen next. In this situation, I felt secure behind my camera and thought I was at least doing my "job" instead of just simply standing around and observing events.

Later, I began to behave in a different, perhaps equally exaggerated way when with the beginning of my second fieldwork period I completely stopped using either a photo or a video camera. This was partly due to the new circumstances of my fieldwork. By that time I had moved into a village where the uninvited use of a camera would have offended people who were my neighbours and who were becoming my friends and "relatives." After living in this village for some time, I learned that their refusal to be photographed had religious as well as aesthetic reasons. For example, a photograph taken during a major religious event when the gods and ancestors are considered to be present is seen as an attempt to take away, to steal, these spiritual beings. In an everyday situation, Dongria do not like to be photographed when they are engaged in work and wearing their usual, perhaps dirty or torn clothing. Things were different when people had time to dress up for the occasion. For example, after I had started distributing photographs to them, Dongria explicitly invited me to take photographs on festive occasions, when they put on all their jewellery, wear colourful *sari* or *shirt-pant,* and face the camera with pride while standing in a row, shoulder to shoulder.

After a month of very successful cooperation, Promod went back to Sambalpur, and I immediately felt his absence when I witnessed the next buffalo sacrifice in the village of Railima. I suddenly had nobody to talk to, I felt insecure without the help of a translator, and I could work only with difficulty, as nobody kept away at least some of the drunk young men who tried to extract money from me for a drink but were not willing to answer any questions. I was reminded of the Nuer in Evans-Pritchard's famous account of his fieldwork, in which he describes how people constantly evaded his questions until he suffered from "Nuerosis" (Evans-Pritchard 1940, 13). During the three days of this festival, I spent hours sitting on a rock near a stream trying to calm down and find enough strength to continue my observations among people who frightened me. I spent the night under a mosquito net in front of a Dombo's house and felt like a visitor from an alien planet. The next day, that Dombo's wife scolded me for sleeping the whole night while everybody else had so much fun, and I definitely knew by then that something was wrong.

Back in Parsali, I talked to the DKDA staff members about my problems, and one of them promised me to ask a young man living in Kalyansingpur to join me as a field assistant. He seemed to be the ideal assistant in this situation, because he was able to speak some English and claimed to know the Dongria language as well. After one or two meetings, in which I promised him Rs 2,000 per month, he agreed to work for me. He had completed his higher education at a college in Koraput district, but like many other young men with good qualifications could not find a job in this remote area. He lived with his mother and his younger brother in a small house near the river, a rather dirty and shabby place inhabited mostly by people belonging to the lower castes and by Desia Kond from whom he had learned the Kuwi language. He asked me to call him by his surname, Hial, a title used by members of the sweeper caste, who have a very low status in this Hindu community. Although he had grown up and spent most of his life in Kalyansingpur, he, like most residents of the town, had never set foot in the Niamgiri Hills. However, he was acquainted with the Dongria who regularly go to Kalyansingpur to sell their cash crops or to buy new cooking utensils, clothes, or vegetables in the market.

Before Hial joined me in Parsali, some staff members of the DKDA introduced me to a Dombo family living in a Dongria village named Gumma or Sikokagumma, Sikoka being the name of the clan whose members own the land belonging to this village. The Amina and the MPWs argued that I should first establish good rapport with these Dombo if I intended to stay in Gumma, because they have a strong influence on the opinion of their patrons, the Dongria.

Gumma was recommended to me for another reason. Two women employed as MPWs were staying in this village from time to time and could help me find a house. I talked to them a little later, and they indicated their willingness to aid me in my efforts to find a place to live in Gumma. The Dombo family suggested I could move into an empty hut on their lane in the village, but the two women advised me to refrain from doing so for two reasons: first, I would be considered a Dombo, i.e., somebody of low status, and probably would not be admitted into the Dongria's houses; second, they warned me that Dombo dry animal skins and buffalo meat in front of their houses and that this practice causes a terrible smell, especially in the hot season.

While we were discussing these different opportunities, Peter and Amrei suddenly turned up one evening and stayed with me for the next couple of days. On the second day, we went to Gumma, about an hour's walk from Parsali. On our arrival, we were welcomed by the two women working for the DKDA, whom I, like others, had started calling *didi* (elder sister) or *guruma* (female teacher). They sent a young boy to call the *member* or village chief. In other regions of Odisha, the word *member* denotes the elected representative of a "ward," i.e., the lowest level of the local political organisation (*panchayat*). In this area, however, the title *member* is not derived from a position in the local *panchayat* organisation – Gumma and other villages only formed the so-called Parsali *panchayat* in 2002 – but from functions in the administrative system established by the DKDA, which appointed one man in each village as a kind of spokesman and village representative. These were usually influential men who were able to organise collective work due to their charisma as well as their inherited status. The *member* of Gumma appeared after some time, and the authority emanating from him was immediately perceptible. Although he was a bit drunk, was dressed only in a dirty loincloth, and looked relatively weak and old – he must have been around forty-five or fifty years old at the time – in comparison to the young, sturdy men standing around us, he looked like a leader to me. He threw a disapproving glance at us, sat down, and inquired in a very self-confident way why we had come. The *didi* explained my intention to live in Gumma and started to discuss this plan with him. I understood only about half of what was discussed, but Peter, who in the meantime had acquired fluency in this so-called Desia dialect of the Oriya language, briefly translated what the *didi* and the *member* said to each other. After some time, everybody stood up and went to an open space next to the house where the *didi* resided. In their usual energetic way, the two women explained to the *member* where the villagers could build a house for me, how large it should be, and how it should be constructed. Meanwhile, a number of people had gathered to listen to our conversation, among them a Dombo man who was quite drunk and from another village, as I learned only later. He immediately took on the typical role of the Dombo middlemen, commented upon everything, and gathered momentum as soon as we addressed the costs of building a new house. After some bargaining, I agreed to buy a buffalo, a keg of country liquor, and some rice with which to give a feast to the village. The *member* in turn promised that the villagers would soon start constructing my new house.

After Peter and Amrei had left, my new assistant Hial came to Parsali, but it soon turned out that he was not robust and strong enough to live in the hills. After the first day and an admittedly very long walk through the hills after which he returned to Kalyansingpur by foot, he felt so weak that he could hardly walk for days. He was not used to walking on dirt paths at all, and some of his toenails turned black after this first day. Yet he was eager to continue the work, and I was glad to have an assistant. For the next three weeks, he stayed with me in Parsali, where we had begun to cook for ourselves, which, however, meant that some of the DKDA staff members no longer ate with us due to my assistant's low status. In these weeks, we went to Gumma almost every other day to see how the house construction was progressing. On some days, I returned depressed when no work had been done; on others, I felt extremely happy when the villagers indeed brought the necessary materials from the forest or began to set up posts and walls. The *didi* were urging them every other day to continue their work, and I am sure that without them, the villagers would never have completed building the house. Finally, on May 1, 2001, the house was ready, and the *member* and four young Dongria girls turned up in Parsali to escort me – Hial had gone home to Kalyansingpur – to my new home in Gumma.

I stayed in Gumma until mid-July 2001, and in these two and a half months I experienced many ups and downs in my attempts to assimilate to village life. For some weeks I thought I had to get up at four-thirty every morning to join the Dongria men who met on the village plaza to discuss village affairs or just sit and smoke a cigarette or chew tobacco. On such occasions they usually light a fire, because even in summer it is quite chilly early in the morning before sunrise. Hial and I sat next to them and listened to their talk, and from time to time I asked my assistant to translate what they were discussing. I felt like a spy, and in a way I think the Dongria felt the same. To my frustration, Hial could not understand much more than I did, and it turned out that the Desia Kond language he had learned from the Desia is quite different from the dialect spoken by the Dongria. After some time, we gave up these futile undertakings and slept until the sun or a crying baby woke us up.

My next attempt at becoming incorporated into the village community involved rather hard work. Between April and May, Dongria annually thatch the roofs of their houses with mountain grass (*wikang*) they either cut in their swid-

Photo 2: Dongria building the author's house in Gumma

dens or buy from relatives. For this task they form work gangs consisting of four to six men from closely related families who thatch one another's houses in rotation. They begin by taking away the old grass, then remove the old bamboo posts, if necessary, and finally tie bundles of grass to the roof in layers, starting from the bottom. The work starts early in the morning and can be completed by midday if enough people assist the householder. As a reward for their efforts, the helpers receive a meal consisting of boiled rice and cooked pulses and one or two glasses of distilled liquor. I joined one of these work gangs, which included the *member* and some of his "younger brothers" who would later become my closest friends. They gave me some minor tasks like throwing the grass bundles onto the roof where the others were tying the bundles to the bamboo frame. After some time, my participation showed some effect, because the members of the work gang I had joined started calling me "younger" or "elder brother," and since I was sharing their meals, our relations became more intimate.

Hial, however, refused to eat with them, just as the Dongria would not have taken food from him. It became more and more problematic to live with Hial in Gumma, as he found it difficult to go into the mountains and help the Dongria in their agricultural work, to drink alcohol with them, as he was a complete teetotaller, and to listen to the often obscene talk among the young men. One day we accompanied the *member* and a group of ten young girls to a village in Kalahandi district to buy paddy for a big feast, and when we returned in the evening, he immediately fell ill and ran a high temperature. Another day he stumbled in a swidden, hurt his feet, and could not walk for some time. Contrary to our agreement, he had told everybody that I paid him Rs 2,000 per month for his assistance. Dongria, Dombo, and the two women started asking me how I could afford to pay him so much money and what it was that I was paying him for. Two thousand rupees is quite a considerable sum in the eyes of the Dongria, more at least than I had paid the whole village for the construction of my house. I discussed all these problems with Hial and finally told him that I had decided to continue my fieldwork without his assistance. I think we both had mixed feelings about this, as he needed the money but at the same time disliked his stay in this remote place inhabited by people whose manners irritated him deeply.

During these first months in Gumma, the *member* became an important person in my life. From time to time he invited me to his house for "lunch" or "dinner," meals eaten from leaf cups or aluminium plates while sitting on the floor inside the relatively dark house. He started becoming my main informant, and soon I addressed him as "older brother" (*tada*) and his spouse as "older brother's wife" (*awa*). Later, when other people tried to establish fictive kinship relations with me, they first considered their relationship with the *member* and then addressed me accordingly. Everybody told me that the *member* was the most knowledgeable person in the village, and I soon found out that he was indeed well informed, but often reluctant to part with his knowledge. He expected presents, alcohol in particular, to get into the right mood for answering my questions, and sometimes he deliberately lied to me. One reason why he tolerated my stay in the village was that my presence raised his status. For example, he liked to call me to the veranda of his house when other villagers or some visitors had assembled and then used the situation to teach me something, to make me recite the kinship terms I had learned from him, or to ridicule me in the knowledge that I would not dare to oppose him. He could be very pleasant, too, but his moods changed quickly, and I soon became aware that the other villagers suffered from his outbursts of anger in the same way as I did. In the following months, I slowly reduced my contact with him, trying not to offend him, since I knew that without his assistance I could easily be thrown out of the village.

In July, after spending five months in the field, I went to Germany, returning to Gumma in early September of the same year. This second phase of my fieldwork lasted for another eight months, until April 2002. This time I changed my approach and decided not to depend on an assistant anymore. This meant that I had to learn the language. Again, I received the greatest help from the two women of the DKDA, my neighbours, who now spent most of their time in

Gumma after their second house in another Dongria village had burned down. Both had more than twenty years of experience in the Niamgiri Hills. They had begun working for the DKDA as MPWs in the first project settlement set up in Chatikona in 1978. About ten years before I met them, they had been asked to shift to Parsali when the second DKDA office was set up in this western part of the Niamgiri Hills. Both were in their forties at the time of my fieldwork and unmarried. One, Brundabati Kondapani, belonged to a low-ranking caste with origins in Ramnagar (Koraput district), while the other, Sandyarani Kadraka, stemmed from a family of Desia Kond and was born near Bissamcuttack (Rayagada district). Both are fluent in the Dongria language and have completely adjusted to the living conditions in the hills. I often admired them for their strength and for the way they could handle the most difficult situations. They never seemed to be afraid, even though they told me that one of the female staff members had been killed by Dongria some years ago, and they never showed any weakness when quarrelling with the Dongria. They were very popular among the Dongria women, who often came to our veranda to have a chat with them. To be their neighbour was my great good fortune, and I think I would not have managed to live in the area for so many months without their help and their encouragement.

They taught me the language by translating Oriya words into Dongria, by translating whole sentences for me, and by answering my numerous questions concerning grammatical rules. They gave me lessons almost every morning for several weeks, and I then practised with the people who came to our veranda or whom I joined on the village plaza or under palm-wine trees, where from time to time I joined the drinking groups that assemble three times a day at these palm trees to drink their alcoholic sap, which is available in varying amounts almost year-round. When the juice is abundant, Dongria men may spend up to six hours a day walking through the jungle to their various trees, where one of them climbs the tree, brings down the sap in a gourd, and distributes it in equal shares to all present. Men chat and make jokes, and I often learned more about people on these informal occasions than when trying to conduct a formal interview. Apart from two or three young men, hardly anybody had gone to school, and those who had, had not remained for more than a few months. The *didi* had been teaching the small children from Gumma in their house, but all in all, hardly anybody had experienced the discipline imposed on children in a regular school. I consider this one of the reasons why Dongria found it so difficult to sit with me for more than fifteen minutes and answer my questions. After some frustrating attempts, I finally gave up this formal interview technique and instead tried to grasp as much as possible on more informal occasions. I also learned that it was more successful to ask questions concerning

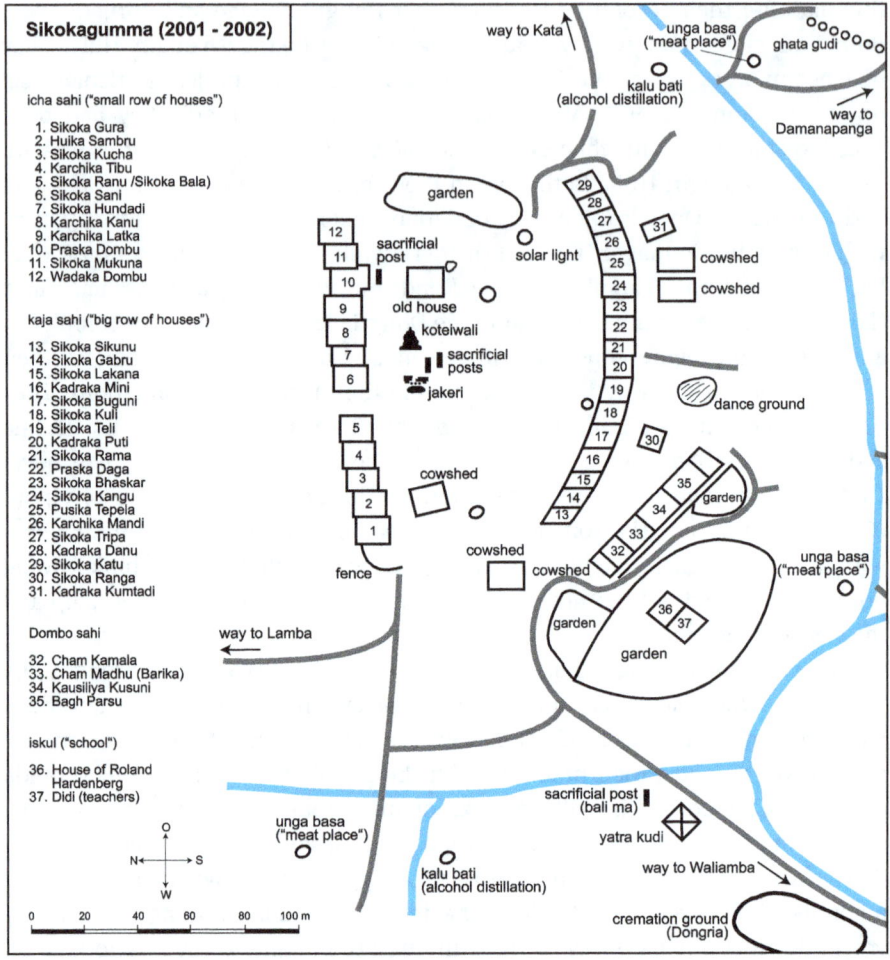

Figure 2: Map of Sikokagumma

some actual, recent events, rituals, or ceremonies than to inquire about past happenings or imagined situations. My attempts to conduct a census completely failed, as people found it extremely boring to recite all the names of the relatives I asked about and pretended to have forgotten these names when I continued to bother them for more than ten minutes with my inquiries. Things were different when I asked about these relatives in a concrete context, like a marriage or death, which made it, however, more difficult to get a complete picture, even though the village consisted of not more than thirty-one houses of Dongria and four houses of Dombo.

This second phase of my fieldwork began with an event that improved my relations with the villagers and my status in the community considerably. Before my departure for Germany I had informed the *didi* and the *member* that I was planning to bring my fiancée, Andrea Luithle, to Gumma. Since we were not yet married at the time, I suggested celebrating the wedding on our arrival in Gumma. When we arrived in the Niamgiri Hills in September, the *didi* had already begun preparations for the wedding: they had purchased rice for a feast, asked the villagers to set up a canopy on poles in front of my house, and sent four young Dongria girls to Parsali to escort us to Gumma. Andrea was given a chicken to carry under her arm to the village, and on our arrival, it was sacrificed in front of my house. The local shaman blessed us and gave her a name, Sonari, by which she was called by the villagers from that day on. I bought a large buffalo, which was slaughtered some days later when all the villagers joined in a large feast I sponsored. We were given a bath in turmeric water and received gifts of money from all our neighbours. Andrea left after two months, but our wedding had a lasting effect on my status in the village. Women now came more freely to my house or talked to me in public, and more and more people started addressing me with kinship terms.

A woman belonging to the Dombo community, Kamala Cham, whom I addressed as "elder sister" (*nana*), proved to be particularly helpful and knowledgeable. She had been married twice, but both her husbands had died, and she now resided in Gumma with her two grown daughters. Her two sources of income were trading in cash crops she either cultivated on her own or received from the Dongria and distilling alcohol, which is officially forbidden and not usually done by women. She constantly suffered from one or another sickness but possessed such strong willpower and charisma that all the villagers, even the *member*, listened to what she had to say. Her house was often a meeting place, since she sold alcohol, and even people from other villages came to her veranda to have a drink. For this reason, she kept informed about the latest events in the region and constantly provided me with news about what was going on in our village or in neighbouring ones. The same can be said about one of her close relatives, Madhu Cham, who worked as the messenger (*barika*) and provider of sacrificial animals for Gumma and two other villages. Since Dongria needed his services in order to celebrate a marriage, a funeral, or any other ceremony involving sacrifices, he was always informed about upcoming ritual events in the area. What is more, he remembered in detail rituals and gift transactions that had occurred years back and was thus an amazing source for a curious anthropologist. For many months, I accompanied him on his trips to other villages when he sold a buffalo, bought a goat, or received his share from a funeral or wedding feast. Our relations cooled when he started drinking strong alcohol and was not sober for days at a stretch. When drunk, he could become very offensive and aggressive, and it was impossible to have a proper conversation with him.

Towards the end of this second research period, two incidents occurred that almost made me break off my fieldwork. The first incident occurred in February 2002 when I was riding my motorbike from Kalyansingpur to Parsali. A Dongria friend from Gumma had asked me for a lift and was sitting behind me on the motorbike when we passed a store where Dombo sell country liquor. My friend saw his mother's brother and asked me to stop for a moment. When we entered the hut, we met a young Dongria man from Phakeri who was quite drunk. He had sold his cash crops in Kalyansingpur, had several hundred rupees with him, and had obviously spent some of this money on alcohol. He asked me to buy him a drink, but I refused, which made him angry, but he managed to control himself. A little later, when we were about to continue our trip into the hills, he asked for a lift, and I again refused, explaining that the condition of the road was too bad for a motorbike with two passengers. This time he really got angry and threatened to beat me up and to set fire to my motorbike. My friend tried to intervene and calm him down, but nothing helped, and I decided to return to Kalyansingpur and talk to the police about the incident. After I had left, some other men from Gumma passed by, and my friend informed them what had happened. They, too, were drunk and probably thought it a good opportunity to teach this man from Phakeri a lesson. They started beating him up and reportedly – I still do not know – stole his money. After consulting the police, I received an escort from two policemen who accompanied me on their motorbike up to Parsali. Shortly before we arrived in the project settlement, we came across the Dongria from Phakeri, who was bleeding slightly and had a stone in his right hand with which to defend himself. The policemen managed to calm him down, I apologised for not giving him a lift, and he agreed to part in peace but at the same time threatened to take revenge on the men from Gumma who had beaten him up.

Two days later, a handwritten letter was delivered to the Dombo messenger (*barika*) of Gumma, inviting him and the villagers to come to Sana Denganali, a village halfway between Gumma and Phakeri, to attend a meeting concerning the incident. The letter had been written by the *barika* of Phakeri, a village with about twice as many residents as Gumma. The people from Phakeri were seriously angry and blocked the way to Kalyansingpur, only allowing the Dombo to use the path. I accompanied some men from Gumma to the meeting, where the *barika* from Phakeri was expecting us and informed us that the man who had been attacked demanded to be given the money stolen from him plus a buffalo as a fine to be paid to his whole village. My companions did not accept this demand and started arguing with the *barika*, reminding him of other incidents that had occurred long back. People started exchanging harsh words and finally told the *barika* they would "fuck his wife" (*ni dakeri kai*), which made him so angry that he left the meeting immediately.

Some days later, the people of Gumma and I were called to attend a second meeting. That day, I was woken up early in the morning and asked to come to the village plaza, where the influential men from Gumma had assembled. They confronted me with the demand that I should pay the fine as I was "responsible for the situation." I argued that I had done nothing wrong, the man from Phakeri had threatened me, and the men from Gumma had beaten him up. The men assembled, on the other hand, kept reiterating that everything had happened because of me, which in a way was true. Later, one of them told me straight out that I should either pay the fine or leave the village. About half of the men from Gumma then started walking to Sana Denganali to meet the people from Phakeri, while the rest first went to another village to have some drinks. When we reached the meeting point, we immediately saw a crowd of at least sixty young men from Phakeri waiting for us on the other side of the river, shouting and threatening us with their axes. At that moment, I saw the two DKDA women from Gumma, who had just returned from a trip to their natal villages. They asked me to cross the river and talk to the people from Phakeri. They received me in a friendly manner and asked me to inform my friends from Gumma that they expected to be given a fine of several hundred rupees. I discussed the issue with the *didi* and two outside Congress Party workers from Kalyansingpur. These politicians had heard about the meeting and had come to try to resolve the problem because they were afraid that a feud between two Dongria villages might pose a threat to their election campaign in the area. They urged me to contribute a substantial amount to the fine and persuaded the villagers from Gumma to pay the rest. After handing over some money, the chiefs of the conflicting parties sat down, a local religious specialist recited verses to establish peace, and alcohol was exchanged. The whole event showed that my integration into the village community was a matter of context: when I was attacked, I belonged to them; when they had to pay a fine, I was an outsider.

The second incident occurred during a buffalo sacrifice about a month later. At that time, Professor Pfeffer paid me a visit, and we decided to go to Hundijali, a village near Kambesi in the western part of the Niamgiri Hills, to observe the ceremony. We hired a car and drove up to Mundawali, a village where I had been the year before and which was only two kilometres away from the location where the sacrifice was supposed to take place. We went straight to the house of a Dombo whom I knew from my previous visit and were invited to stay in his house during the days of the festival. In the afternoon I decided to take Professor

Pfeffer to the earth goddess's shrine, where I had witnessed the buffalo sacrifice the previous year. In contrast to other places, the Mundawali goddess's house is not located inside the village, but a few hundred meters away in the jungle. On our way to the shrine, our host's son accompanied us. After reaching the place, I started describing to Professor Pfeffer where and how the sacrifice had been performed, when suddenly three drunk men from Mundawali arrived and told us that we had committed a serious mistake by coming there. They demanded to be given a hundred rupees, and when we declined, threatened us by holding a knife to Professor Pfeffer's throat. The young Dombo urged us to place the money on the earth goddess's stone and leave as quickly as possible, and we followed his advice, hearing the three men's loud laughter as we returned to the village. Back in the Dombo's house, we told him what had happened and decided to demand the money they had stolen from us. Discussions about the incident continued until late in the night, until finally the three men came to our house and returned the money, not without further threatening us. We stayed two more days, but after being confronted with a demand for Rs 3,000 for being allowed to attend the buffalo sacrifice in Hundijali, we left and returned to Gumma. As we learned later, the incident was most probably related to the visit of another research team that had visited this area some months ago and had paid large sums of money for being allowed to make a cartographic survey of the village. Naturally, it was now expected that every foreigner should pay for collecting information, and those unwilling to do so had to learn who has the power in this area – the Dongria.

I left the Niamgiri Hills in April 2002 and did not return until mid-January 2003, after recovering from malaria. This third research period lasted for three months, until April 2003, and allowed me to answer a number of questions that had come up while I was reviewing my data in Germany. At the beginning of this third phase, when Professor William Sax was visiting me in the field, one of my "younger brothers" from Gumma one day asked me whether I was interested in recording a trance session performed by his mother, a local shaman (*bejuni*), for the gods of his swidden. Previously, I had used my cassette recorder only to tape songs, and this was the first time somebody requested me to record a shamanic possession. It continued for an hour and a half, and people immensely enjoyed listening to it again afterwards. Several days passed before the next trance session took place, and when I asked whether I could record it again, nobody said no. In this way, I recorded several shamanic possessions, as well as one long incantation by a religious specialist (*jani*). These tapes became very popular among the villagers. In the evening, people sometimes came to my house just to listen to these tapes, and the young man who first allowed me to record his mother's trance quickly learned how to use the cassette recorder and demonstrated it to all his visitors.

I spent much of this third research period trying to translate these tape recordings, which was only possible with the help of the *didi* and the local shamans, because the expressions used in them are highly metaphorical and need detailed exegesis to become intelligible. Without the *didi*, their good relations with the shamans of Gumma, and their infinite patience, I would never have gained access to this realm of Dongria knowledge, which proved essential for understanding some of the ritual practices I describe in this book.

1.4 Content and organisation of the work

A major aim of this book is to identify the system of values and ideas that gives order to social relations, collective representations, and actions in the Niamgiri Hills. For this purpose, I will inquire into the forms of interdependence between Dongria and Dombo (chapter 2), study Dongria social categories, rules, and practices (chapter 3), describe and analyse their forms of marriage (chapter 4), and finally attempt to understand their most important ritual event, the buffalo sacrifice to the earth goddess (chapter 5). This main part of the book is divided into four major chapters in which I present and analyse ethnographic data I collected during my fieldwork.

1.4.1 Chapter 2: "Tribal society" in the Niamgiri Hills

The second chapter focuses on social relations between Dongria and Dombo. According to the Indian state's administrative categories, Dongria are a "scheduled tribe", while Dombo are classified as a "scheduled caste". This categorisation implies that members of the two communities belong to two different types of society, tribal society and caste society. From an anthropological point of view, this classification is dubious, since Dongria and Dombo reside in the same villages, interact in daily life, and have many cultural features in common. They form one society, which in my analysis is essentially different from the society existing in the lowlands, where Kond and Dombo are part of a caste organisation. In other words, the two communities, Kond and Dombo, are found in the highlands as well as in the lowlands, but their relations differ in accordance with the society they are part of, a "tribal society" in the hills and a "caste society" in the plains. While anthropologists typically characterise tribal societies as "egalitarian" and distinguish them from "hierarchical" caste society, I will not use this distinction to differentiate these two types of society. In my view, they are both "hierarchical" in the sense given to the word by Louis Dumont. In both tribal and caste society, value-ideas are ranked, characterised by reversals, and segmented in their application.

What differentiates the two types of society is not the presence or absence of hierarchy, but the concrete form hierarchy takes in each case. In caste society, the opposition between the value-ideas of purity and impurity is related to the segmentation of society into a large number of ranked, more or less endogamous units that depend on each other for various purposes. Interdependence between castes is expressed primarily in terms of the removal of impurity by the lower for the higher castes, whose members guarantee the wellbeing of society through their rituals, their duties as rulers, and their agricultural work. In the tribal society existing in the Niamgiri Hills, purity and impurity are not major value-ideas. Instead, the oppositions between senior and junior, kings and subjects, inside and outside, and the living and the dead are correlated with the segmentation of society into higher (Dongria) and lower (Dombo) groups. Interdependence exists between them in relation to the exchange of objects in trade, some of which objects will enter the exchange between humans and gods / ancestors in the context of sacrifice.

To clearly bring out similarities and differences between this "tribal society" of the Niamgiri Hills and the "caste society" of the plains, the second chapter is divided into six major sections. Following an introduction, the second section offers an overview of various theoretical approaches to the study of tribal society and addresses some of the critical arguments made against the notion of "tribe." Since Dombo are often represented as "untouchables" in the literature, I will further introduce some major theories of untouchability. This will help us to understand the major differences between "untouchables" in caste society and the Dombo's position in the society of the Niamgiri Hills. In the third section, I will introduce the reader to some important value-ideas that order relations between Dongria and Dombo. These value ideas stress either the hierarchical segmentation or the unity of both communities. In the fourth section, I will discuss the three realms of social life in which hierarchy manifests itself: space, commensality, and marriage. In the fifth section, I will address the various forms of interdependence between Dongria and Dombo, which in my interpretation are linked to the exchange between humans and gods / ancestors in the context of rituals. To clarify the relations between Dombo and Dongria with regard to rituals, the sixth section will provide data showing that Dombo as individual actors are not excluded from the ritual realm. However, their ritual functions have to be distinguished from their role in the society as a whole, which consists in enabling the Dongria to link the short, individual cycle of exchange to the long, collective cycle of exchange. This collective cycle includes gods and ancestors on whom the wellbeing of all people, Dongria and Dombo, depends.

1.4.2 Chapter 3: Dongria social categories, rules, and practices

After the second chapter's discussion of the "tribal society" of the Niamgiri Hills and its major parts, the third chapter focuses on one of these parts or "sub-wholes", the Dongria community. As in the caste system, some of the principles that structure relations between segments of society also order relations within segments. The principle of seniority, for example, is not only linked to the status distinctions between Dongria and Dombo, but also differentiates senior from junior clans, senior from junior local lines, and senior from junior siblings within the Dongria community. Just as society as a whole is divided into landowning patrons (Dongria) and serving clients (Dombo), each Dongria village is divided into members of the dominant, landowning clan and the tenants who depend on them. Finally, ideas of brotherhood and friendship not only create relations between Dongria and Dombo but also connect the various segments within the Dongria community. The major difference between the higher level of Dongria-Dombo relations and the lower level of relations within the Dongria community is with regard to marriage. While marriage relations between members of the two communities are forbidden, they are allowed, yet highly regulated, within the Dongria community.

In order to understand relations between the segments that make up the Dongria community – defined as a part of the overall "tribal society" – it is necessary to understand the organisation of marriage relations. Such a study of marriageability, however, requires us to distinguish different levels of data, as Needham (1973a) suggested: classification (or terminology), rules, and behaviour. First of all, affinity often works as a principle defining relations between categories in a relationship terminology. Such a terminology is a form of classification and an expression of values and ideas about the order of the world rather than a means to regulate the world. It should, therefore, be distinguished from address terminology, marriage rules, and rules of behaviour that are more closely related to people's practical concerns. Finally, actual behaviour, such as marriages recorded by the anthropologist in the field, forms a third level of analysis. Ideas about marriage and affinity are expressed on all three levels, but they may not be congruent, because each of the three levels, i.e., terminology, rules, and behaviour, exists to some extent independently from the others. For this reason, I follow Needham's advice and study Dongria affinity separately for each level before I compare them in my conclusion.

Marriage and affinity have been major issues in the debates about "kinship systems" in India. Initially, debates focussed on the opposition between North and South Indian kinship systems. Only since the early 1980s have attempts been made to generalise the categories, rules, and practices of the many millions of mostly "tribal" people inhabiting Central India. Despite local variations, relationship terminologies of various ethnic groups in this region show certain features in common. These common features distinguish the Central Indian system from both the prescriptive two-line system in South India and the descriptive system in North India. In more than thirty years of work, Pfeffer compared the data from a great number of Central Indian communities, distinguished them into several "complexes," and summarised their common features.

Dongria Kond relationship terminology, rules, and practices show many features that, according to Pfeffer, are found among many people all over Central India. Other features are typical of what Pfeffer calls the "Kond complex." However, certain aspects stand out as unique and have so far not been reported for any other community in Central India. On the level of classification, Dongria Kond relationship terminology contains a large number of genealogical levels represented by reference terms in descending generations. On the level of rules, the Dongria system is singular in the sense that it prohibits a repetition of marriage between two local lines for three generations. This is also expressed in a positive rule stating that members of the −4 and −5 generation can again marry. This marriage rule corresponds to a peculiarity of the address terminology that has, to my knowledge, not been reported for any other Central Indian ethnic group. In address, not in reference, Dongria classify cross-cousins into either an upper or a lower generation in relation to themselves; in other words, they use the technique of "skewing" known from so-called "Crow-Omaha" terminologies. Finally, on the level of behaviour, Dongria show a marked tendency to spread marriage relations over the whole Niamgiri Hills. While marriage with "strangers" is an ideal implicit in the terminology and the rules, the opposite, marriage with members of "related" local lines, is a feature of the system that can be detected on the level of actual marriage practices. Thus, Dongria sometimes contest the rules by "readjusting" genealogical relations, or they marry with a local line closely related to them but in ways not explicitly prohibited by the rules.

This complicated system deserves a careful presentation of data and a separate analysis of categories, rules, and practices. For this reason, I divide the third chapter into three major sections. After a lengthy introduction to the major debates about "kinship systems" in India, I first deal with the Dongria terminology. I begin this section by presenting the reference terms, which I then analyse by identifying the configuration of terms within each generation. This is supplemented by information about marriage rules, norms of behaviour, and address terms. While reference terms belong to the level of classification, which does not *necessarily* reflect social relations "on the ground" but rather expresses the culturally variable structures of thinking, address terms and rules contain important directives for actual behaviour and must therefore be discussed separately. A careful comparison of these two levels of data reveals that the configuration of reference terms both differs from and shows similarities to the system of relations expressed by marriage rules, norms of behaviour, and address terms. One level of data cannot simply be deduced from the other, and when similarities between the levels occur, they may be seen as correspondences between two dimensions of social life rather than as effects of common causes.

In the next section, I elaborate the rules mentioned before by linking them to the relevant social categories. Two types of rules can be distinguished. First, socio-centric rules regulate marriage relations between the collective categories irrespective of a particular ego. Second, ego-centric rules are applied by each individual to his or her circle of kin in order to either identify or rule out certain relatives as marriage partners. The most important socio-centric rule is that of clan or *kuda* exogamy. Among the ego-centric rules, those prohibiting marriage with the house of the MB/FZH (*mama ijo*) and with the house of a child's in-laws (*samdhin ijo*) serve to define the non-marriageable category, while the rule allowing marriage between cross-relatives in the −4 generation and below classifies certain relatives as marriageable. The latter rule is one of the most fascinating aspects of Dongria culture, because it corresponds to a doubling of the alternation rule and stretches the memory of social relations to its upper limits in a society without extensive pedigrees.

In the third section, I present and analyse my statistical data about actual marriages. Using data I collected in the village where I lived, I give a case study of the marriage relations of one local line, showing that in practice Dongria adjust their genealogical relations in order to comply with the rules. Further, I use my data about the marriages of this particular village to show how Dongria in fact spread their affinal relations geographically across the entire area in which the Dongria live. Finally, I demonstrate that despite this geographical spread of alliance, Dongria do not in fact always marry "strangers." On the contrary, both locally close and distant marriages occur between parties who are related through prior marriages.

In my conclusion, I summarise the importance of territory, descent, and affinity as principles structuring the Dongria system of social relationships and compare the three levels of data discussed in this chapter. This comparison reveals discrepancies between categories, rules, and practices, which in my view are related to Dongria ideas about distance and proximity, their status system, and their constant feuding. "Distant marriages" as implied by the equations of the reference terminology and by the marriage rules create high status and serve to establish alliances between potential enemies. Avoidance of incest is at stake in every Kond marriage but can never be absolute, because all Kond descend from an original sibling pair. However, in the case of "distant" marriages, the parties involved are far apart from each other in terms of incest. "Close marriages" do not increase status but may help to continue well-functioning alliances. However, since the partners are "close," their marriage comes closer to incest than distant marriages. Such unions potentially endanger society, because incest destroys the fertility of both the people and the earth. The opposition between distance and proximity, between high and low status, also characterises the two forms of marriage discussed in the fourth chapter.

1.4.3 Chapter 4: Negotiation, violence, and love

Kond forms of marriage figured prominently in the debates among nineteenth- and early-twentieth-century evolutionists about the origin of human society and culture. They were first described by two Scottish soldiers posted to Odisha in the first half of the nineteenth century to put an end to human sacrifice and female infanticide. These two Scots, John Campbell and Samuel Charters Macpherson, saw a causal connection between the practice of female infanticide among the Kond and their specific marriage customs. According to Campbell, female infanticide is related to the instability of marriage relations among the Kond. To acquire a wife, Kond have to make high betrothal payments, which have to be returned in the event of divorce. Given the notorious "unfaithfulness" of Kond women, this situation arises quite often and causes endless conflicts between the parties. A Kond daughter thus presents an immense burden to her father, and according to Campbell, this is a primary reason why families decide to kill their daughters. Female infanticide produces a scarcity of women, and for this reason Kond men have to seek their wives in "distant places" by way of bride capture. Campbell himself gives a good description of one such case of bride capture he personally observed during his stay in the Kondmals. For Campbell, then, arranged marriages with large prestations lead to female infanticide, which is in turn the cause of bride capture.

Macpherson's argument runs differently. In his opinion, the practice of female infanticide is most prevalent among the followers of the sect of the sun god. According to the myths of this sect, the sun god, after contemplating the evil caused by the creation of the goddess, gave the Kond permission to kill their daughters. Among members of this sect, women are considered notorious adulteresses, and their behaviour is regarded as the main cause of conflicts.

For Macpherson, the religiously enforced practice of female infanticide and women's behaviour react upon each other as alternately cause and effect: on the one hand, female infanticide produces the scarcity of women that raises the marriage payments, and this may lead to conflicts in cases of divorce; on the other hand, women's adulterous behaviour becomes the source of conflicts involving whole clans, and to prevent this, people reduce their number of daughters by practicing female infanticide. In contrast to Campbell, Macpherson did not include bride capture in his reasoning, and the only example he gives of this custom is one of a mock battle in the context of a formal wedding.

This example was later quoted at length by the Scottish evolutionist McLennan, who explained the origin of human society by reference to forms of marriage. In McLennan's view, Kond may justify female infanticide in religious terms, but he sees the "real" origin of this institution in the superiority of men over women in protecting and feeding the members of the group. The practice of killing female babies naturally leads to an imbalance of the sexes, the lack of women in their own group forcing young men to seek wives among people outside their own tribe. According to McLennan, this practice later became protected by the rule of exogamy, which prohibits intra-tribal marriage as incestuous and punishable. The mock conflicts in a Kond wedding, which McLennan considers an example of "ceremonial bride capture," are in his view reminders of an earlier state, when capture was the only way to get a wife. In other words, bride capture in McLennan's view characterises an earlier stage of evolution, marriages with weddings a later stage when exogamy became an established rule. Bride capture developed out of the scarcity of women caused by female infanticide, which in turn has its cause in the greater importance of men for group survival.

Of these three theories, only Campbell's approach has any relevance for understanding present forms of marriage among the Dongria, because he is the only one who sees a connection between bride capture and arranged marriages. Both forms of marriage coexisted in Campbell's time, as they do today, a fact that puts McLennan's evolutionary argument into question. However, to view arranged weddings as the cause and bride capture as the effect, as Campbell argues, does not do justice to the fact that bride capture is also an established institution among the Kond and not simply a reaction to particular circumstances. Moreover, none of these customs seems to be causally connected to the practice of female infanticide, which does not exist among the Dongria, although bride capture is an important form of acquiring a wife among them. For this reason, later theories of bride capture and marriage rejected such causal reasoning and focussed instead on the analogies or ideational connections between forms of marriage and other aspects of culture within a given society.

R. H. Barnes (1999) summarised these approaches and several studies of bride capture from all over the world in an article published in *Man*. He points out that several authors have identified a correlation between types of marriage and concepts of social distance, but he rejects any attempt to construct a coherent, institutional complex linked to a particular stage of evolution. He thus gives priority to the study of concrete cases that demonstrate the variability of forms of marriage and their corresponding values and ideas. I follow this approach in my study of Dongria forms of marriage, which according to my interpretation are intimately linked to local concepts about "life" and culturally prescribed ways of obtaining this "life."

To understand Dongria forms of marriage, it is necessary to take into consideration that according to Dongria myths, the power to create resides in the female goddess. The goddess brought the world into being and continues to create life by giving her "daughter," the crops of the land, to the people and by impregnating women with "souls" (*jela*). The male god does not create, but protects and rules over everything originating from the goddess. In the same way, Dongria men are "owners" but not creators of the products of the land and of their children. To establish this ownership, they must become active, and they have two ways to acquire the "life" quality of women: they can engage in exchange activities or appropriate "life" through violence. On the one hand, arranged marriages are a form of exchange, because the bride-takers first have to give extensive prestations before the bride-givers agree to part with their daughter. Bride capture, on the other hand, is a form of violence and likened to hunting. In some cases, bride capture is only a ceremonial way of legitimising a union between a man and a woman who love each other. In such cases, the capture does not involve any real violence, and only very few prestations will be exchanged between the parties. Although Dongria distinguish linguistically between bride capture and such love marriages, in practice they are often the same.

These forms of marriage coexist in Dongria society, but they are differently valued. Love marriages and bride capture lead to unions of a lower status compared to arranged marriages. They may involve only a few people in cases of love marriage, but also whole villages in cases of real bride capture. When a man captures a woman he has fallen in love with, she usually comes from the dormitory of a neighbouring village and has been known to the young man for a long time. Bride capture usually causes conflicts, and to settle them, the capturers have to pay a fine and make prestations to the young woman's people. In cases of real bride capture, the relations between the parties are thus characterised by "negative reciprocity" (Sahlins) or what I call "violent reciprocity." Higher status pertains to arranged marriages, which in contrast to bride captures are based on the idea that the bride-takers must first provide the bride-givers with gifts of goods and animals and with services. Only when all the required services have been performed and the demands for gifts fulfilled will the bride-givers send their daughter and a great number of prestations to the groom's people. The status of the arranged marriage depends on the number of things given and on the relationship between bride and groom. In an arranged marriage of the highest status, bride and groom are promised to each other as children. Such marriages are always highly collective in nature and join individuals who should not know each other and come from "distant" places. Over many years, prestations flow from the bride-takers to the bride-givers before finally, with the wedding ceremony in sight, gift-giving becomes more symmetrical, and on the day of the wedding, the bride-givers give a large gift to the bride-takers when they send their daughter along with a large number of gifts. The value of the gifts given by both sides marks their respective status, and I therefore define this kind of exchange as "prestige reciprocity" instead of using Sahlins's concept of "generalised reciprocity." Comparing these three forms of marriage, my conclusion, in contrast to Sahlins's model of the segmentary tribe, is that violence does not necessarily characterise the most distant relations. In the Dongria case, the greatest violence occurs between people at a medium distance, whose daughters one captures, while marriages between very distant partners involve violence only in a very formalised way, such as ceremonial mocking, and are instead based on mutual exchange.

In order to illustrate these conclusions, I divide the fourth chapter into four main sections. In the first section, I summarise Campbell's and Macpherson's reports on Kond forms of marriage, discuss how McLennan used this information for his evolutionary speculations, and answer the question of the relevance of these early reports and hypotheses for understanding present forms of Dongria Kond marriage, before addressing some of the more recent approaches to the study of these phenomena. In the second section, I give an overview of the three main forms of marriage among the Kond. Of these three, love marriages are relatively insignificant for understanding Dongria collective social relations, because they are basically individual affairs and require neither collective action nor reciprocal gift-giving. The main ethnographic part of this chapter instead deals with the two forms of marriage that require elaborate collective activities in the context of rituals and conflict settlements. I begin the third section by giving a detailed account of those marriages that are arranged over a long period of time. I describe the many different stages of such a matrimonial "contract" and illustrate them with concrete case studies and rituals I observed in the field. In the fourth section, I contrast these arranged marriages with the unions that develop in the dormitories and are turned into a collectively recognised relationship by means of bride capture. In this section, I will also explain local ideas about conception and sexuality. One way men can have access to the female powers of creation is through bride capture, and I will provide several cases of this practice and the subsequent attempts to resolve the conflicts arising out of them.

The violence, conflict and negotiation described in this chapter characterise not only Dongria forms of marriage but also another important event in Dongria life, the sacrifice to the earth goddess.

1.4.4 Chapter 5: The clan sacrifice: Creating Niamgiri society

In the past, Kond used to perform human sacrifices on a regular basis, until British soldiers suppressed this practice and "persuaded" the Kond to replace the human being by a buffalo. Since then, many Kond continue to give buffaloes to their earth goddess, except for those who were forced to abandon this custom by other outsiders with a religious mission, the Hindu nationalists and the Christian preachers. Among the Dongria, neither Hindu nor Christian missionaries have worked with any measurable success, and the executive powers of the Oriya government do not fully operate in this remote area. This may account for the fact that Dongria celebrate their buffalo sacrifices in grand style, even though such killings are contrary to Hindu ethics and against state law.

At different times in their history, Kond thus faced outsiders who tried to suppress their sacrificial practices. The fact that they continue to perform these ritual events against all odds might be interpreted as an expression of resistance or as a way to construct Kond identity. In my view, something different is at stake. In the second chapter of this book I argue that "tribal society" in this area is made up of two communities, Dongria and Dombo. This, however, is only part of the whole picture. Society in its full extent is made up not only of relations between humans but also, and even more importantly, relations between humans, gods, and ancestors. Relations with gods and ancestors are established in the context of a number of different rituals and festivals, but the grand buffalo sacrifice is the occasion when the most important relation is at stake, that between the mother or earth goddess and her children, the people. In the context of this sacrifice, the results of various short-term exchanges between individual Dongria and Dombo flow into the collective, long-term exchange between gods, ancestors, and humans. A part of the prosperity acquired through agricultural work and market transactions must be returned to the source of this prosperity, the earth. The buffalo sacrifice can therefore be said to create Niamgiri society in the sense that it renews as well as establishes relations between gods and humans, between Dongria and Dombo, and between the various segments of the

Dongria community. These buffalo sacrifices will be studied as total social facts, i.e., in all their fullness and complexity and by taking into account how they relate to the social whole. When we compare these sacrifices to other social facts of Dongria society, they may also be called "total" in another sense given to the word by Marcel Mauss. As Gofman points out, Mauss also conceived of total social facts as specific ontological entities that "penetrate every aspect of the concrete social system; they concentrate it and constitute its focus, they are the constitutive elements, the generators and motors of the system" (Gofman 1998, 67). This, I hope to show, can also be said about these sacrifices with respect to society in the Niamgiri Hills as a whole.

During my fieldwork, I observed a total of eleven such buffalo sacrifices among the Dongria Kond and their neighbours, the Desia Kond, who inhabit the valleys. In all cases, the sacrifices required weeks if not months of preparations, continued for several days, and were an occasion for extensive feasting and merrymaking. Among the Dongria Kond, the buffalo sacrifice is performed in the months of *phalgun* or *caitra*, i.e., between February and April, while their neighbours in the valleys, the Desia Kond, usually conduct it one or two months earlier (in *pausa* or *magh*). The festival is celebrated by each Dongria village at irregular intervals of roughly ten to twenty years. The main reason for this sacrifice, locally called *kodru parbu* or "buffalo festival," is the earth goddess's desire for it.

The main sacrificial events take place at various shrines inside and outside the village that is sponsoring the festival. Of these shrines, those of the earth goddess and her husband inside the village become the focus of the most elaborate ritual activities. The earth goddess is represented by a certain number of round, polished and flat, crude stones collectively referred to as *jakeri*. The *jakeri* is often addressed as "mother" (*aya*) by the Dongria; she represents the earth goddess and at the same time a specific incarnation in a certain territory. A myth collected about a hundred years ago (see Thurston [1909] 1987) supports the idea that each *jakeri* marks the site where a part of the flesh of the mother of all Kond was buried. According to this myth, she asked her eldest son to sacrifice her, cut off her flesh, and bury it in the ground to make the soil firm and fertile. The son did as his mother requested and buried her flesh in different places, which he covered with stones. According to Macpherson, Kond used to bury the flesh of their human victims at their shrine stones as well as in their fields. Today, Dongria continue to offer the buffalo flesh obtained at a sacrifice in another village to their own earth goddess by putting it near her stones before consuming it.

Next to the *jakeri*, usually only a few meters towards the east, is a flat, crude megalith that may be as short as twenty to thirty centimetres or as tall as two meters. It stands upright, has a peak, and thus resembles a mountain. Dongria call this stone *koteiwali* and address the deity represented by it as their "father." He is considered the husband of the *jakeri* and may be said to represent the male principle, the sun, in relation to the female principle, the earth. At the sites of both divine beings inside the village, the sponsors will set up shrines with the help of a large number of other people in the weeks preceding the actual sacrifice.

In the centre of the village, above the stones representing the earth goddess, the sponsors of the sacrifice will build a house with one room. They will be assisted in their work by people from brother villages who belong to the same sacrificial community. It takes about three to four days to complete the house, but the work is spread over a period of several weeks. Dongria men are responsible for cutting trees, shaping logs and planks, setting up beams and posts, and making bamboo mats to be affixed as walls on all four sides of the house. Women will smear the ground with cow dung and plaster the bamboo walls with mud. When the mud has dried, they first apply a layer of white colour on the walls before painting them with triangles and lines of different colours. When ready, the house appears to be an image of the goddess herself: the house's beams represent her breasts, the straw on the roof is likened to her hair, and the paintings on the walls show the same patterns as the shawls worn by young girls and boys on festive occasions.

Towards the east, another shrine is built near the stone representing the earth goddess's husband. Instead of a house, the villagers here construct only a simple wall made of two or three posts and a bamboo mat plastered with mud. However, like the goddess's house, her husband's wall has two openings and is decorated with the same paintings. In between these two shrine locations, the sponsors will set up sacrificial stakes. Depending on the number of victims to be offered to the earth goddess, one or more sacrificial poles will be fixed in the ground just in front of the two openings in her house. The victims will be tethered to these poles the night before the actual killing. In front of the wall representing the earth goddess's husband, another, T-shaped stake will be set up. During the festival, the heads of chickens sacrificed in the name of different deities are placed on top of this T-shaped stake.

About a week before the main three days of the buffalo sacrifice, men from a number of other villages will arrive to protect the sacrificial site. These people are not like the sponsors' "brothers" from the same sacrificial community, as they belong to different clans from that of the sponsors. These helpers are potential affines and are called *mudrenga*, a word probably derived from the Oriya term *mudra* meaning "coin," "seal," or in its verbal use (*mudriba*) "to close." These men are responsible for "closing" the village and the sacrificial site by constructing bamboo fences around the whole village and around the place where the victim will be tethered. In addition, they are responsible for protecting the buffalo until the proper time of sacrifice.

The main events occur on three consecutive days, from Friday to Sunday. On Friday, the first guests arrive, and the sponsors erect one or two long bamboo poles, on top of which they attach a brass pot and a small shade made of bamboo or iron. The brass pot circulates within the sacrificial community formed by villages of the same clan and will be retained by the sponsors until the next village celebrates the buffalo sacrifice. On this Friday, the long bamboo poles are carried to each and every house of the village for worship before they are set in place at the wall representing the earth goddess's husband. There, the local shamans climb up the poles, are possessed by the male deity, and bring him down for further worship. At the end of the ceremony, chickens and a white ram will be sacrificed to the god.

On Saturday, the *desa* or "people of the whole country" assemble in the village. Young men and women from various villages and clans arrive throughout the day to enjoy the festival. At night, they will meet in the girls' dormitories or in the woods for sexual experiences. On this day, most rituals are performed at two sites: first, at stones representing the deity of the local line (*kona penu*) and the god of hunting (*lada penu*) outside the village; second, at the wall of the goddess of wealth and prosperity (*sita penu-lahi penu*) inside the house.

During the night, ritual specialists invoke the earth goddess by sitting in her hut and chanting verses for hours and by offering alcohol, incense, and small pigs to her. When these incantations come to an end on Sunday morning, the festival reaches its climax. The main sacrificial specialist takes a knife and thrusts it through one of the openings in the eastern wall of the hut. When he touches the victim tethered to a post in front of the house, this will be the sign for the young men to kill the buffalo. The protectors of the victim withdraw, and the young men run towards the fence, pull it down, and with their axes hack the victim to death. In most festivals I witnessed, however, the sacrificial specialists could not complete their rituals, because the young men managed to break through the fence and kill the victim in the dead of night. Once the victim has been killed, someone will hurry to cut off its head and take it inside the hut, where it is placed in front of the stones, together with a piece of liver and a coin. One of the ritual specialists will hurry to collect some of the buffalo's blood in a bowl or with his bare hands and carry it to the earth goddess. This is considered to be the major gift, as the blood stands for the victim's life.

On this day, pieces of flesh are distributed to the sacrificers, who leave the village with gestures of triumph. Upon reaching home they bring the buffalo meat to the shrine of their own *jakeri*. In the past this meat used to be buried near the *jakeri* and in the fields; nowadays it is cooked and consumed by the sacrificers. The rest of the dead animal will be divided into different pieces, distributed to some individuals to mark their status, and finally cooked and consumed by all present on the following day.

In my interpretation of this festival, I point out the correspondences between ritual events and status categories, social structure, mythological events, and concepts of fertility. A comparison between the buffalo sacrifice and the forms of marriage reveals that in both cases men acquire access to fertility through either exchange or violent appropriation. The sponsors give a gift, the victim's life, to the earth goddess in exchange for the "wealth," the harvest, they have received from her. The relation between sponsors and the goddess resembles that between bride-takers and bride-givers in an arranged marriage between "distant" parties. On the same occasion, young unmarried men act like bride-capturers when they either steal a whole leg of the buffalo in an attempt to make a claim on the sponsor's land or take home portions of the victim's flesh with gestures of victory. The sponsors are linked to the gods' realm through exchanges that, like the gifts given to affines, are signs of their wealth. In contrast, the young men who perform the role of sacrificers more or less violently obtain fertility in an act of "violent reciprocity," which also characterises bride capture.

In order to provide a comprehensible account of this very complex festival, I divide the fifth chapter into several sections, each of which deals with different aspects of the event. After an introduction describing the historical events that led to the change from human to buffalo sacrifices, the second section provides a general overview of the location of the sacrifice, its timing, and its costs. This is followed in the third section by a detailed description of the preparations for the festival, which include the holding of the pigeon pea festival (*kanga parbu*) a year before the sacrifice, the construction of a hut for the goddess, the building of a wall for her husband, the planting of a sacrificial post, and the fencing of both the whole village and the site of sacrifice. In the fourth section, I describe the different objects worshipped during the festival. Each of these objects is used in the sacrifice and expresses a certain aspect of landownership: the pots are used for cooking and are transferred between the owners at the time of a land sale; the axe is both an instrument of sacrifice and a tool for cutting down trees on the hill slopes used for cultivation; the brass pot or "umbrella" is set up on the first day of the festival and represents the divine ruler who controls the land inhabited by the Dongria; and finally the knife "eats," i.e., kills, the victim and thus helps the sponsors to fulfil their gift obligations to the goddess. All these ritual activities require elaborate organisation and the cooperation of a large number of ritual specialists. These specialists and their titles, status, and functions are described in the fifth section, in which I first summarise earlier accounts of Kond priesthood before providing my own ethnographic data. In the sixth section, I give a detailed description of the actual sacrificial events I observed during my fieldwork. I had to decide whether to present an ideal model of the festival by generalising from the specific cases or to describe each concrete sacrifice I observed separately. I decided against both approaches, because on the one hand, I was afraid that the description might loose its vividness if I only presented the structure of the performance detached from actual events; on the other hand, I had collected so many details during the eleven sacrifices I witnessed that a presentation of all these events would be too lengthy and perhaps confusing to the reader. I therefore decided to select one sacrifice I observed as a kind of ideal model and describe it in all its details. This account is further enriched by data collected on other occasions. In this way I hope to achieve both my aims: to provide a lively but structured and comprehensible description of the Dongria's most important festival.

1.4.5 Chapter 6: Conclusion: A system of ideas and values

In the conclusion of this work, I take up Dumont's concept of value-ideas and apply it to the contexts discussed in this book. I identify two major sets of value-ideas. The first I call female values, i.e., those ordering situations in which "life" and "wealth" are obtained through either exchange or violent appropriation. I contrast these with a second set of male values comprising values and ideas pertaining to the segmentation of society into different status categories. The central status opposition is that between "senior" and "junior." In my final analysis, female values are not merely opposed to male values; they encompass the latter, because they are identical with the whole, represented by the mother goddess. "Mother" earth is the source of life, wealth, and wellbeing, which she can give but also destroy.

Up to now, two monographs (Nayak 1989; Jena et al. 2002) on different aspects of Dongria culture and society have been published by professional anthropologists. However, Dongria social forms and practices, as discussed in this book, have never been described and analysed before. The following monograph offers the first detailed anthropological treatment of social relations between Dongria and Dombo, of Dongria relationship terminology, marriage rules, and practices, of Dongria forms of marriage, and of the Dongria's grand buffalo sacrifices.

2 "Tribal society" in the Niamgiri Hills

2.1 Introduction

Earlier studies of tribal people often bore titles such as *The Oraons* (Roy 1915), *The Karias* (Roy 1937), *The Raj Gonds of Adilabad* (Führer-Haimendorf 1948), and *The Bondo Highlanders* (Elwin 1950), implying that these people belong to independent cultural and social units. However, none of these tribal communities exists in isolation. Apart from a number of other tribal and caste communities, whose names and status differ from region to region, we everywhere come across a community alternatively named Dom, Dombo, Pan, or Pano.[1] In the past, these people worked as weavers and traders. Nowadays they have given up weaving, mostly because the very simple cloth they produce cannot compete with the factory products available from local markets. Presently, their main sources of income are trading cash crops, selling alcohol, and working as agricultural labourers. Most researchers report on them in a negative or even derogatory manner. In the past, they were mostly blamed for providing the Kond with human victims for their sacrifices. For example, in 1864 Major General John Campbell, a British special officer assigned to suppress human sacrifice among the Kond, wrote about the Pano:

> These Panoos are base and sordid miscreants, who, without the excuse of superstition and ignorance, carry on a profitable trade in the blood of their fellow-men. Unfortunate people of the low country are decoyed into the hills by these miscreants, and then sold to the Khonds for Meriah sacrifices. (Campbell 1864, 52–53)

Nowadays anthropologists often regard the Pano or Dombo as migrants who came into this area for business reasons and blame them for "exploiting" the "innocent" tribals with their "cleverness" (e.g., Das Patnaik 1988, 11; Jena et al. 2002, 76). Administrators and development officers also take up public prejudices against the Dombo, regarding them as "thieves." Thus, the authors of the Orissa District Gaz-

---

[1] Berreman reports a caste called Dom in the Himalayas. They are the second largest group and often described as the aborigines and predecessors of the Kasas (Rajput and Brahmin), who represent the majority in this region. They are considered "untouchables" and are divided into several castes (Berreman 1963, 20–21). The Dom castes differ in status according to their traditional occupations (Berreman 1963, 212–15). The situation in Odisha is different, because Pan (or Dombo) are not differentiated into endogamous castes. The only exception is reported by Bailey for the Kondmals, where the Oriya Pan claim to be of higher status than the Kond Pan (Bailey 1960).

etteers take up a local explanation and derive the word Dombo from *dhumba* and translate it as "devil," a word that in their view refers to "the thieving propensities of the tribe" (Senapati and Sahu 1966, 92). According to the same source, most cases of housebreaking and theft in Odisha are committed by Dombo who are "professional criminals" (Senapati and Sahu 1966, 315) and "traditional cattle lifters" (Senapati and Sahu 1966, 454). Campbell's statement that most human victims were stolen from the plains "by professed kidnappers of the Panoo caste" is based on the same biased opinion (Campbell 1864, 52). As Pfeffer rightly remarks with reference to the equally derogatory comments on the Dombo by Verrier Elwin, the representation of this caste "is one of the most obvious cases of academic discrimination in Indian anthropology" (Pfeffer 1997b, 7).

My own approach to the representation of society in the Niamgiri Hills neither neglects the Dombo nor takes a moral stance towards their alleged or actual forms of interaction with the Kond. On the contrary, I analyse how their identity is constructed within the particular form of society that developed in the Niamgiri Hills. In this way, I do not start from the idea of an unchanging "tribal society" but rather take into account the permanent adaptations and innovations these people make in relation to the outside world, including both the kingdoms of the past and the political organisations and local economies of the present.

In this chapter I will further compare my own ethnographic data with studies of "caste society" in India, particularly those relating to untouchability, the *jajmani* system, and patron-client relations. The Dombo inhabit both the Niamgiri Hills and the valleys, where they reside in multi-caste villages. In such villages, Dombo and castes with a similar low status are treated as highly polluted and even "untouchable", because they perform impure functions. As specialists in removing pollution from dominant castes, they are integrated into an organisation that has been termed the *jajmani* system. The position of "untouchables" as ritual specialists and as agricultural labourers for landowners is sometimes expressed in terms of patron-client relations, which are said to be typical of "caste society". It will be asked here whether the Dombo of the Niamgiri Hills are engaged in similar relations, or whether their status and functions are valued differently. Should we interpret their interactions with Dongria within the framework of "caste society" or as part of a different cultural logic of social relations?

In this chapter I address the following main questions:
1. How do Dongria value their relations with Dombo? How greatly do these value-ideas differ from those identified by different authors in the various forms of the Hindu caste system of India?
2. In what terms is the interdependence between Dombo and Dongria expressed? Are the relations similar to the *jajmani* system or patron-client relations?

3. Are the Dombo part of the local religious system? Do their religious functions differ from their impure services in "caste society"?

In this chapter I will address these three questions consecutively. First, I will explain my use of the comparative method and of the concept of "tribal society" by taking into account the arguments made against the notion of the "tribe". Next, I will present a short overview of the existing literature on the relations between Kond and Dombo. In my opinion, the present state of debate does not properly represent the nature of interaction between them. I will then summarise the most important arguments concerning untouchability, the *jajmani* system, and patron-client relations in order to define a model for comparison with my own ethnographic data. The main part of the chapter will address the questions raised above by presenting and analysing ethnographic data, including the following points:
1. The local ideology defines status in relation to the opposition of insiders and outsiders, kings and subjects, "senior" and "junior," and the living and the dead. This ideology differs markedly from Brahmanical concepts concerning purity and impurity.
2. The interdependence of both communities, Dongria and Dombo, is not based on a division of labour for the removal of pollution but rather on two different cycles of exchange, which are connected by the Dombo's economic activities, maintained by the Dongria's agricultural labour, and expressed in terms of relations to the goddess of wealth and rice (*sita penu lahi penu*).
3. In contexts where money, commodities, and gifts are exchanged, Dombo are seen by Dongria as the "other" of lower status, while such status distinctions are neglected in contexts of sharing. Sharing does not involve the constant demands that are so typical of gift-giving and market transactions.

2.2 Theoretical concepts

2.2.1 The notion of "tribe" and its critique

In the introduction to a collection of papers dealing with so-called "tribal societies" in India and elsewhere, Pfeffer (2002a) presents basic concepts of "tribal society" expounded by authors more or less belonging to three schools of anthropological thought, i.e., evolutionism, functionalism, and structuralism. Furthermore, he draws a distinction between substantialist approaches and ones that reject any "efforts to conceive definite boundaries of a human assembly called tribe." His summary identifies the central differences between various concepts of the tribe in the history of our subject. I will, however, present these distinctions in a slightly different way. The various concepts of the "tribe" or of "primitive society" in general can be seen as combinations of three oppositions: substantialism versus structuralism, ethnocentrism versus relativism, and empiricism versus generalisation. I will briefly define these analytical concepts before going on to show how these distinctions help us to evaluate the critique of "tribal studies".

1. A substantialist approach defines the tribe as a unit by asking what elements or features it consists of. A structuralist approach focussing on social relations tries to describe these relations and to identify the logic by which these relations are systematically ordered. When viewing the "tribe" as a unit, boundaries are taken for granted, because the tribe is defined with reference to particular, "typical" criteria. When viewing "tribal society" as made up of certain social relations, these relations are seen as depending on particular contexts, and group boundaries are considered to be constructed in the process of social interaction.
2. In any attempt to define "tribal society" – either as a unit or as a relation – the data are ordered from a particular point of view. Pfeffer states in his introduction that certain approaches use Western values and define a society as "tribal" when it has different, allegedly less developed forms of economy or technology, while others show a concern with "a particular cultural logic" (Pfeffer 2002a, 15).
3. Finally, we may distinguish definitions of "tribal" units or societies as empirical phenomena from anthropological constructs used for analytical purposes. Empirical approaches aim to define a particular tribe or certain tribal relations as experienced in a certain area, while generalisations about the "tribe" as a concept use definitions based on abstractions and models more or less carefully derived from ethnography.

These distinctions help us to deal with the critique of the concept of "tribe" or "primitive society", which often rejects only certain approaches mentioned above. I will demonstrate this by discussing two major critiques, the first by Aidan Southall in his article "The Illusion of Tribe" (Southall 1970) and the second by Adam Kuper in his book *The Invention of Primitive Society* (Kuper 1988).

Southall has three main points of critique. On the one hand, he argues that tribes nowadays – i.e., in the seventies – do not exist anywhere, because there is no place on earth not claimed by a state, and since the lack of a state is considered a defining criterion of a tribe, tribes must be regarded as social forms of the past (Southall 1970, 29). He further criticises social anthropologists working in

Africa for regarding certain categories, like Luyia, Sukuma, or Nyamwezi, as large tribal units, although these have little basis in native societies (Southall 1970, 36). Using historical data, Southall demonstrates that they were colonialist creations later taken up by the local population (Southall 1970, 38), an argument made earlier by Morton Fried, who points out that "tribalism can be viewed as a reaction to the formation of complex political structure rather than a necessary preliminary stage in its evolution" (Fried 1968, 15).[2] Finally, Southall argues against any attempt to search for fixed boundaries for any particular tribe, since the segmentary character of "tribal society" makes such attempts a meaningless exercise. The first point of critique targets any substantialist and abstract approach to defining the "tribe", the second and third any substantialist and empirical approach. In essence, according to Southall, there can be no tribal unit, neither in abstract nor in empirical terms. His argument shows a concern with the nature of social relations in a segmentary system and is certainly based on empirical studies, but he does not offer these as alternatives. Instead, he favours a change of labels, referring to a tribe as an "ethnic group."

Kuper's critique starts where Southall's ends. His main argument is that for the last hundred and thirty years our discipline has fostered a cherished idea of "primitive society" (Kuper 1988, 230 ff). The original model of this kind of society, invented by the early evolutionists, has been changed or, in Kuper's phrasing, "transformed" by each consecutive new approach in anthropology, but the idea of primitive society has persisted. For Kuper, the whole idea is an illusion, and our constructions are merely mirror images of ourselves. The focus of Kuper's critique is not empirical definitions of certain tribes or tribal relations, but attempts to generalise social forms from empirical facts.

I find both Southall's and Kuper's critiques too rigorous. For example, the fact that there is no place on earth not claimed by a state does not exclude the possibility that in some areas the state is more distant than in others, thus allowing tribal organisations as defined by Southall to exist. Beteille makes a similar point in his critique of Sahlins, who divides the category of "tribe" into different forms but makes no corresponding distinctions within the category of "state." In Beteille's view, we can distinguish various forms of the state, as well as different ways these states relate to tribal groups (Beteille 1991, 66). Furthermore, good ethnography is a permanent test of our models, and we often find that authors refine their concepts not because of the latest theoretical fashion but due to new ethnographic findings. The notion that these concepts are embedded in wider theories that are related to certain world views is, however,

---

2 Godelier (1977) argues strongly against this proposition.

an important point, and the best reaction, in my opinion, is to compare these world views, i.e., make the underlying assumptions part of our conscious knowledge of others and ourselves.

Therefore, I suggest considering "tribal society" as an analytical concept that is always being redefined in the process of ethnographic research and anthropological abstraction.[3] As Schnepel states, the "danger is that an analytical distinction which was created for a limited purpose only will be taken for the thing itself" and that such concepts "may be interpreted as monolithic blocks stiffly opposing one another, while the many-sided and existent transitions and permeabilities may be excluded from the field of vision" (Schnepel 2002, 229). Taking these warnings into consideration, studies of "tribal societies" may be of two types, one pertaining to social relations in a particular culture area, the other to the comparison of generalised notions of "tribal society" based on ethnography from different regions of the world. Both approaches depend on each other, since without having a general concept of "tribal society" in mind, it is impossible to identify certain relations as "tribal," and without having ethnographic data, generalisations remain hollow and static.

The general purpose of this effort is not to categorise societies but to achieve a better understanding of them. By using the analytical concept of "tribal society" I do not imply that these people are in any way "primitive" or less "complex". Such judgments are made on a purely technological level, while ignoring the complexities of these people's social forms and cosmology. Whether certain people are considered more advanced than others clearly depends on what is being compared.

In previous decades, anthropologists concerned with the ethnography (e.g., Burghart 1978; Apffel-Marglin 1985; Raheja 1988; Galey 1989; Hardenberg 1999) and history (e.g., Dirks 1987; Tanabe 1996; Bayly 1999) of "caste society" have made us aware of the different forms caste organisations may empirically take and have demonstrated variations in value-ideas linked to them. Taking these insights into consideration, the label "tribal" (like "caste") will similarly be understood here as a very broad category without any definite "essence" or definition. It is assumed that within Odisha we will find variations in tribal organisation and in the value-ideas linked to that organisation. To achieve analytical exactness, we will need to make use of comparison on different levels: on one level, ethnographic facts are compared in order to discern differences between specific local social

---

[3] The terms "tribal society" and "caste society" are always put into inverted commas to stress that they do not relate to any concrete observable units but to abstractions made by anthropologists on the basis of ethnographic and historical data.

forms, the latter being abstractions of the anthropologist; on another level, these social forms embedded in regional contexts are compared in order to construct models that may then enter into a comparative analysis with other models (e.g., "hunter–gatherer societies") on a level far removed from the local context but not necessarily from ethnographic facts. The whole process should continually be re-evaluated on all levels, i.e., in terms of ethnography, the social forms derived from it, and the models built from such abstractions.

Why should these efforts be undertaken? Such an approach improves our ethnography as well as our understanding of the local in relation to the global. General concepts and analytical categories of whatever kind sharpen our awareness for ethnographic data in the field, because certain actions and events only enter our consciousness if they question pre-existing notions. The effort to generalise social forms in their relation to values opens the field for new questions and helps us see existing notions from a different perspective. For example, in this chapter I question the preconceived distinction between the Dongria as a "scheduled tribe" (ST) and the Dombo as "untouchables" or a "scheduled caste" (SC), a distinction based on official categories highly influenced by colonial ethnography. By inquiring into the value-ideas of and forms of interaction between these communities, I am able to identify basic differences between the functions assigned to the Dombo in the Niamgiri Hills, where they are part of a "tribal society", and their position in "caste society".

Seeing social interaction in the Niamgiri Hills as constituting a particular form of "tribal society" further allows us to compare these ethnographic findings with other "tribal studies", as well as with the immense literature on caste in India. We may further relate our findings to debates about how indigenous societies worldwide define themselves in relation to other types of political or economic organisation. As the Indian situation and, even more concretely, the history of Odisha exemplifies, members of "tribal" and "caste society" have coexisted throughout history, neither fully merging with nor completely separating from one another. To my mind, exploring the ways they interrelate is one of the most fascinating undertakings in anthropology and history. Membership in either of these societies is defined in contrast to those people with whom one does not identify. This mutual dependence in terms of cultural and social identity between tribal societies and members of the dominant civilisations was first elaborated by Edmund Leach in his seminal article on the "Frontiers of Burma" (1960–61). He argues that the geological difference between hills and valleys is sociologically linked to two political and social systems that were historically influenced by the two major civilisations bordering this region, India and China. Michael Moerman takes up some of Leach's arguments and generalises them in this statement:

> a Southeast Asian society's membership in the set called "tribal" can be described, defined, and analysed only in terms of that society's contrast to a civilised society which it may fight, serve, mimic, or even become – but which it can never ignore. (Moerman 1968, 153)

Surajit Sinha (1980, 1981) comes to a similar conclusion, but he stresses the isolation of tribes rather than their relationship with Indian states. He points out that tribal societies in this region may be defined in opposition to the core peasant and urban population of Indian civilisation. Following Redfield, he defines "civilisation" as a society having a body of written literature produced by an elite and characterised by the existence of various urban centres where "culture" achieves its highest elaboration. In India, these centres are intimately linked to the immense number of small villages, the inhabitants of which provide the economic basis for this civilisation by their work in the rice fields. Tribal societies, according to Sinha, remain relatively isolated from this network of villages and urban centres:

> In their isolation the tribal societies are sustained by relatively primitive subsistence technology such as shifting cultivation and hunting and gathering and maintain an egalitarian segmentary social system guided entirely by non-literate ethnic tradition. (Sinha 1980, 3)

As far as the future of tribal societies in India is concerned, he discerns two trends. On the one hand, he identifies the various processes of absorption that have existed for millennia and result in a loss of tribal identities. On the other hand, he recognises different forms of resistance, which he divides into six main types: political solidarity, preserving one's own worldview, withdrawing into an ecological niche, adopting aggressive behaviour, economic specialisation, and developing wide-ranging forms of communication (Sinha 1980, 10–11). The Dongria of this study may clearly be termed a "tribal" group in the sense that they have remained relatively isolated from mainstream Hindu civilisation. They have managed to maintain this isolation by withdrawing into a relatively inaccessible habitat and by adapting to this "ecological niche." In my opinion, there are two reasons why they, unlike so many other groups who used to live in similar conditions, have not been absorbed. One is the lack of infrastructure in this area, which prevented British colonialists and Hindu businessmen from exploiting the forest. The other is the hostile stance adopted by Dongria towards outsiders. Both conditions are changing as roads are constructed in this area and as schools are built to teach Dongria children the values of modern Indian society. Compared to other Kond groups I encountered in Odisha, however, I find it impressive that the Dongria have managed to preserve their social and cultural distinctiveness for so long.

This distinctiveness may have been favoured by their isolation, but as argued by Leach and others, it has also been achieved only through the long process by which a group builds up its own identity in relation to others of whom it often has only limited knowledge. These "others" are represented from the group's own point of view and in relation to what it considers its "own" traditions. This became clear to me during my two extended periods of field research, the first among Hindus in the coastal area of Odisha (Hardenberg 1999, 2000), the second among so-called *adivasi* in the highlands of the same state. My first study, on the *jagannatha* cult, examined how a Hindu cult incorporated qualities ascribed to the indigenous people or *adivasi* into its complex ritual organisation for the regeneration of life and the liberation of the soul. The ritual specialists in Puri, who are considered to be descendants of the deity's original tribal worshippers, have more in common with the rest of Puri's town dwellers than with any *adivasi* I met in Odisha. However, in the context of the *jagannatha* cult's elaborate rituals they play the role of tribals. From the perspective of the Hindu worshippers, these people are associated with certain abilities, and the rituals' main aim is to integrate these qualities into the ritual system. In this study of the Dongria Kond, I will explore how these indigenous people integrate their "outside world," i.e., the caste system, into what they consider of value in this world and beyond.

2.2.2 Tribe and caste in Odisha: The debate

Beteille, perhaps inspired by Southall, has convincingly argued that "the concept of tribe based on the experience of Australia or North America – the richest fields of classical anthropology – can do little justice to the realities of the Indian situation" (Southall 1980, 827). He points out that in India, tribe and civilization – meaning Hindu "caste society" – have coexisted for millennia, while in other parts of the world, the contact was rather sudden and often disruptive (Southall 1980, 827). These forms of coexistence between caste and tribe have become the focus of social anthropologists doing fieldwork in Odisha.

Although Bailey titled his paper "Tribe and Caste in India" (Bailey 1961), his idea of a continuum based on politico-economic factors seems to be restricted to the Kondmals of Odisha, where he did fieldwork in the 1950s. The Kond have territorial clans, a fact that supports Bailey's claim of a strong connection between segmentary clan organisation and territory, a connection he holds to be a defining feature of "tribal society" (Bailey 1961, 12). He contrasts segmentary tribal organisation with the organic relations that ideally characterise relations between castes in an Oriya village (Bailey 1961, 12). "Oriya village" again must be understood in the context of the Kondmals, where Bailey studied a multi-caste village called Bisipara and dominated by a warrior caste (Bailey 1957). Such multi-caste villages are not omnipresent in Odisha. For example, coastal villages populated only by Shasan Brahmins are an exception. After claiming that segmentary and organic principles characterise "tribal" and "caste society" respectively (Bailey 1961, 12), he goes on to show that these ideal types are empirically not totally distinct, since the Kond have an organic relationship with a local "untouchable" caste called Pan, and the villages dominated by the warrior caste can be seen as segments similar to the Kond territorial clans (Bailey 1961, 13). Bailey's whole method seems somewhat unconvincing to me, since he generalises from a specific case only to turn the same case against his own abstractions, causing the reader to wonder why he did not consider those exceptions in the first place. If Bailey intended to deal with social types in India, his models of "tribe" and "caste" would have gained further analytical value if constructed on a much broader ethnographic basis.

Following the publication of Bailey's article, Louis Dumont (1962a) briefly commented on it, mainly criticising Bailey's self-imposed restriction to politico-economic aspects (Dumont 1962a, 121). Dumont suggests a multidimensional comparison involving the relative scales of values of the societies concerned (Dumont 1962a, 121). For example, in order to understand the place of the territorial factor in both societies, it has to be related to the values on which social organisation is based in each case. For Dumont, territory is not the defining factor of "caste society", although it may affect the position of a particular caste in a given area (Dumont 1962a, 122). Almost in passing, Dumont points to the important fact that the two extreme ends of Bailey's continuum are of unequal value, a tribe being regarded as a whole society, a caste as part of a whole society (Dumont 1962a, 120). In my opinion, this is one of the major questions any generalisation must attempt to answer: What defines a tribe?
1) A collection of clans belonging to a named category like the Dongria Kond?
2) A collection of sub-tribes seen as part of a larger category like the Kond?
3) A segmentary society consisting of different groups and categories sharing common organisational principles and cultural values?

If we use the third definition, we have to change the other end of Bailey's continuum by replacing caste by "caste society" and comparing it to "tribal society" as a different kind of order based on other principles and values. Almost thirty-five years after Dumont published his critique, Pfeffer (1997b) took up the task of comparing "tribal" and "caste society" as wholes. In contrast to Dumont, who never focused his studies on tribal values, Pfeffer has conducted ethnographic studies of different tribal groups in Central India and presented his data and analysis in many publications since 1982. His latest essays present a kind of summary of his basic comparative findings concerning either tribal relations in Central India (Pfeffer 1997b) or the modifications of tribal principles in different parts of the world (Pfeffer 2000, 2001). In his paper concerned with the former level of analysis, i.e., social relations in a given cultural area, he comes to the conclusion that hierarchy is not absent in the "tribal society" of Central India. For Pfeffer, tribal hierarchy is often expressed in the language of seniority (Pfeffer 1997b, 13–14) or by reference to an opposition between sacred and secular leadership (Pfeffer 1997b, 19–21). He further points out that the *varna* scheme has no importance in tribal Central India, that the *karma* ideology is absent, and that no one is opposed to anyone else as twice-born. On the organisational level, Pfeffer contrasts the bilaterally ascribed caste, divided into unilineal and hierarchical clans (Pfeffer 1997b, 12), with the tribal distinction of exogamous clans into agnates and affines that he calls "clanship I" (Pfeffer 1997b, 13) and the differentiation of patrilineally ascribed status segments not governed by the rule of exogamy that he refers to as "clanship II" (Pfeffer 1997b, 18).

Along with his students, Pfeffer designed a project studying the social relations of different groups and categories commonly called the Desia, the inhabitants of a plateau with an elevation of approximately three thousand feet in the district of Koraput. Taking up a sociological perspective, Pfeffer speaks of a Koraput complex (Pfeffer 1997b, 19), despite the fact that some Desia would be termed "tribals" and others "caste people" by the Indian administration. In opposition to Bailey's view, Pfeffer makes the important point that not only values but also social interaction in Hindu "caste society" differ markedly from those in the "tribal society" of Central India. For Pfeffer, the relationship between a tribal patron and his clients is different from the relationship between a dominant and a dependent caste in a Hindu village (Pfeffer 1997b, 11), whereas for Bailey they are basically the same (Bailey 1961, 13).

Peter Berger discusses this topic in an essay dealing with social relations on the Koraput plateau (Berger 2002). He first studies the traditional work, diet, and social divisions of the people who are not considered scheduled tribes but nevertheless live in the same or neighbouring villages. He finds that their internal divisions usually have a tripartite structure and are patterned hierarchically in terms of the opposition between "senior" and "junior" elements (Berger 2002, 87). The relations between these categories are regulated by prohibitions against intermarriage and interdining, just as in the caste system of the plains (Berger 2002, 71). Next, Berger analyses relations in a particular village where the Gadaba, officially a scheduled tribe, are the major landowners, while members of the non-scheduled-tribe group (non-ST) are their clients. While commensal rules and marriage prohibitions separate the local groups, ritual and agricultural work create a specific bond between the villagers, in which the Gadaba as landowners are higher or "senior" in relation to all others. This is expressed in gift-giving in connection with the harvest (Berger 2002, 72–77), as well as in sacrifices at village rituals (Berger 2002, 77–79). The Gadaba patrons present a gift to their clients (Berger 2002, 73), while the latter reciprocate with a token of "respect" to the village goddess and their patrons (Berger 2002, 75). The division of the sacrificial animal (Berger 2002, 84–85) becomes an expression of the village hierarchy, demonstrating the superiority of the original settlers over the latecomers, the members of the local dominant clan over their affinal clans, and all Gadaba over their clients (Berger 2002, 85–86).

2.2.3 "Tribals" and "untouchables": Kond and Dombo

In contrast to the Gadaba described by Pfeffer and Berger, most Dongria villages are not located close to villages of the non-ST category. We may visualise a hill territory with peaks of almost five thousand feet inhabited by Dongria and valleys where the situation resembles that of the Koraput plateau: a landowning tribal population, the Desia Kond, living next to a wide range of people of the non-ST category.

The steep Niamgiri Hills form a natural barrier, more often crossed by the Dongria visiting the market towns than by the Desia, who despite possible business interests are often unwilling to cope with the difficult travel conditions in the hills. This will certainly change – and in some places already has changed. Once proper roads are built, the natural resources of the area will be easily taken away in trucks.

However, when concentrating on relations in the hills, we should modify the picture I drew above, since the Dongria do not inhabit this area alone but rather live alongside people called Dombo, who officially belong to the category of "Scheduled Castes" (SC). In about half of all villages, there is a majority of Dongria households, usually not more than twenty to thirty, and a few Dombo households, usually only one to ten. According to a study undertaken in 1975, the 110 villages in the Niamgiri Hills were inhabited by 5,618 Dongria and 1,173 Dombo (Das Patnaik 1984, 23).[4] In the 1980s, the number of people and villages increased. According to statistical data published by Nayak in 1989, the number of villages had increased to 116, inhabited by 7,858 Dongria and a

---

4 For a small demographic study comparing Dombo and Dongria in the village of Kambesi see Panda (1969/70).

total of 1,365 Dombo. However, Dongria and Dombo lived together in only 52 of those 116 villages (Nayak 1989, 221–26). Apart from the Dombo, we sometimes come across a few households of blacksmiths (Lohar), sweepers (Leli), and brass workers (Ghasi), some of whom have only recently migrated to this area. While the Dombo are usually present in all larger villages, members of these three groups live in very few villages and often do not exceed one or two households.

The coexistence between Kond and the groups mentioned above is not a new phenomenon, whereas the distinction between "scheduled castes" and "scheduled tribes" is. In his mid-nineteenth century account of the *meria* sacrifice, Macpherson still considers the "Panwa" (Pano), "Dombango" (Dombo), and "Gahinga" (Ghasi) to be "aborigines" like the Kond themselves (Macpherson 1865, 115), while modern sociological writers are divided in their opinion, some stressing the social and cultural unity of Kond and their clients, others describing the latter as representatives of Hindu caste society essentially different from the tribal Kond. The relations between Kond and Dombo have been discussed by Bailey (1960, 1961), Niggemeyer (1964a, 1964b), Pfeffer (1982, 1997b), and more recently by a group of Indian social anthropologists and ethnobotanists under the guidance of Klaus Seeland (Jena et al. 2002), working in a Dongria-inhabited area different from the one in which I did my research.

Niggemeyer points to the fact that Kond and Pano – as the Dombo are called in the Kuttia Kond area – form a community (Niggemeyer 1964b, 407). The Kond are landowners and cultivators, while the scheduled-caste people work as traders and supply the Kond with items ranging from alcohol to sacrificial animals and clothes. The Pano are considered socially inferior by the Kond, but this does not hinder them from entering into ritualised bonds of friendship (Niggemeyer 1964b, 411). From an economic point of view, the Pano may be classified either as poor village servants or as rich bankers to whom the tribals are indebted (Niggemeyer 1964b, 411).

In comparison to Niggemeyer, Bailey presents a slightly different social situation for the Kond of Phulbani. In this area, the Pano are distinguished into Kond Pano and Oriya Pano, the latter regarded as having a higher status than their "tribal" caste fellows (Bailey 1960, 121). Furthermore, Bailey reports that the Pano actually work as agricultural labourers on the fields of their Kond masters (Bailey 1960, 140), who regard them as their subjects (*praja*) (Bailey 1960, 133).

Pfeffer bases his analysis on Niggemeyer's findings and his own fieldwork among the Kuttia Kond. He again stresses the role of the Pano or Dombo as "intermediaries" or "culture brokers" (Pfeffer 1997b, 11, 13), preserving the Kuttia Kond's purity by allowing them to avoid contact with the supposedly polluted outside world. Pfeffer regards the Dombo and Pano as part of the tribal world of ideas, and he criticises the derogatory manner in which government officials, as well as ethnographers such as Elwin, write and talk about them (Pfeffer 1997b, 7). Their standard view is that these clients migrated into the hills much later and became exploiters of the "simple-minded" tribals. In his analysis of Kond and Pano relations Pfeffer comes to the conclusion that tribals may be seen as "communicators with the divine" in contrast to their clients who are "communicators with human beings" (Pfeffer 1997b, 13).

Another book on the Dongria, written by Indian authors in cooperation with Klaus Seeland (Jena et al. 2002), completely ignores Pfeffer's work, but the authors also see economic and political interdependence between the communities: "Due to a little literacy as well as greater exposure to the plains people, the Domb are aware of the rationale of official matters, legal matters and market transactions. They act as middlemen or consultants for the Dongaria (sic). It is through the Domb that the Dongaria (sic) have got some access to the world outside their community" (Jena et al. 2002, 70). They state that Dombo are regarded as "untouchables" by the Dongria, who do not allow them to enter their houses. In contrast to Pfeffer, who sees the function of "communicators with the divine" as restricted to the Dongria, the authors report the Dombo's participation in festivals and Dombo adoption of shamanic practices. The Dombo are considered to be late migrants who first came as traders and later settled among the Dongria, whom they soon started to exploit with their "cleverness" (Jena et al. 2002, 69–70, 76).

To what extent are the Dombo indeed considered "untouchables," and what are the associations of this term? In what ways do Dombo and Dongria depend economically on each other? How far can they be said to be part of the same religious community? In order to answer these questions, I will first summarise the most important arguments concerning the relations of "untouchables" and dominant castes before examining my own ethnographic data.

2.2.4 Untouchability, the *jajmani* system, and patron-client relations

The literature on untouchability is immense and analyses this phenomenon from various angles and theoretical perspectives. At this point I will only address that part of the anthropological literature that deals with the ideology of untouchability, in order to compare its content with the system of ideas and values I studied in the Niamgiri Hills.

All over India, we find people belonging to castes (*jati*) called Harijan, Dalit, Scheduled Castes, "Untouchables" (in English), or Achut (in Hindi), each of which terms has its own meaning and history (see Randeria 1992, 9–21; Charsley 1996). These castes are similar in that their position in the caste organisation is extremely low, which often accounts for their poverty and various forms of discrimination against them. Traditionally, members of these castes were associated with certain occupations, such as weaving, sweeping, music making, scavenging, tanning, or basket making, which they performed in segregated quarters. They were, and are, excluded in various ways from the life of the higher castes, whose houses and temples they were prohibited to enter, whose village tanks and wells they could not use, and from whom they had to keep a fixed spatial distance. These forms of discrimination were explained by reference to the extreme impurity inherent in members of these castes from birth.

The ideology of the caste system has been identified by Dumont as based on the opposition between the pure and the impure. For Dumont, the concern with purity is connected with hierarchy, seclusion (or segmentation), and interdependence in the sense that castes are ordered into higher and lower units, the higher castes try to protect (or seclude) themselves from the lower castes, and the purity of the higher castes depends on the removal of impurity by the lower ones (Dumont [1966] 1998, 59–60). The criteria for what constitutes impurity are numerous and include certain organic aspects of human life, but also forms of diet and etiquette and a range of relative criteria, for instance who exchanges what with whom (Dumont 1998, 55). For Dumont, Brahmans and "untouchables" form the extreme poles of a totality based on the ideas of purity and pollution. In his opinion, the hierarchy of the different castes is based on the same principle (Dumont 1998, 54–55), with the exception that in the middle ranks of the system the opposite of status – power – manifests itself as an organising principle (Dumont 1998, 78–79).

While Dumont was mainly concerned with isolating the ideological principle on which the social system is based, Marriott asked himself how hierarchy was established in practice. As his ethnography shows, the hierarchy among various castes living in a certain locality is expressed in terms of exchanges of ranked substances. As described by Marriott, the status of each caste in the local hierarchy is constituted and defined by the nature of exchanges it is involved in, as well as by the codes of conduct it follows. Thus, in his example, the Brahmins give three types of food, including leftovers and garbage, to all other castes and receive only the highest-ranking type of food from clean castes, while the "untouchable" Sweepers give only to the equally low-ranking Kanjar Hunters, but receive food, including the lowest types, from all (Marriott 1968, 159–60).

According to Marriott, South Asians do not separate the giver from the objects he or she gives. Following Schneider, he speaks about "substance-codes" (Marriott and Inden 1974, 983–85; Marriott 1977, 235), but distinguishes his usage from Schneider's American one, which refers to norms of interaction. In South Asia, as Marriott points out, a substance is understood to include a moral code, and the exchange of substances has an effect on the morality and body of the receiver (Marriott 1977, 235). Castes are related to each other by the exchange of services and substances, which they have to control in order to preserve their specific norms and morality. From a comparative point of view, Marriott distinguishes between this Indian idea of a "dividual" (Marriott 1976, 111; 1977, 232) and the Western notion of the "individual." In relation to the upper castes, the lowest castes have the most impure forms of exchange and interaction and are therefore given the lowest rank in the hierarchy of relative purity and impurity (on pessimal strategies see Marriott 1976, 128).

Authors like Gough (1956), Mencher (1974), and Berreman (1971) ascribe the ideology of purity and pollution to the higher castes and view this ideology as a false consciousness that masks the suppression of the materially poor. These authors detect the development of forms of resistance and of alternative values among the lowest castes. In contrast, Moffatt (1979) holds the view that Tamil "untouchables" believe deeply in the dominant ideology. He agrees with Dumont in seeing "untouchables" as an integral part of "caste society", and like the ethnosociologists, he sees indigenous concepts as cultural principles that, like the grammar of a language, are deeply engrained in thought and action (Moffatt 1979, 29–31). From his fieldwork he concludes that "untouchables and higher-caste actors hold virtually identical constructs" (Moffatt 1979, 291), and "they not only share these orientations, but they appear to believe in them as strongly and unquestioningly as do those higher in the system" (Moffatt 1979, 292).[5] How, then, is untouchability defined in the area of his research? Like Dumont, Moffatt argues that the Harijan's status is derived from ideas involving their collective impurity, in particular the extreme impurity associated with life processes such as birth, menstruation, and death (Moffatt 1979, 87). In agreement with Marriott and other ethnosociologists, he further states that untouchability is expressed through preventing these lower castes from interacting with higher castes, thereby "limiting the flow of bodily substances upwards" (Moffatt 1979, 87). This principle structures the whole system and can be found in the relations between all castes, but its most profound expression, the prohibition on touching somebody and territorial segregation, is found only in relation to the lowest castes (Moffatt 1979, 88).

---

[5] The most impressive evidence for these statements is Moffatt's field data concerning the internal ranking of "untouchables" into five castes that replicate the order of the higher castes (Moffatt 1979, 99–153).

Moffatt intends to describe the overall cultural framework on which the Tamil "untouchables" agree, but he does not exclude the possibility of conflicts and the operation of power within the caste hierarchy. This arena of contestation and discourse becomes the focus in Randeria's work (1992). In contrast to Moffatt, she does not analyse the untouchables' position in relation to the higher castes, but rather concentrates on the lower castes and their lived experiences, their categories, and their forms of interaction (Randeria 1992, 6). Like the ethnosociologists, her focus is on transactions, which she combines with an interest in the way in which "untouchables contest and manipulate categories and classifications, challenge the nature of their stigmatised identities and formulate alternative self-representations" (Randeria 1992, 6). Randeria examines the "untouchable" castes on four different levels (Randeria 1992, 2–3), the second of which is of direct relevance to this work. This second level of analysis in her work deals with what has been called the *jajmani* system, i.e., the relationship between each caste and the dominant landowning caste. Like the topic of untouchability itself, this system has been discussed extensively in the literature on caste, and I will again concentrate on only those aspects that enable us to compare the situation of the Dombo in the Niamgiri Hills to that in "caste society".

The term "*jajmani* system" was coined by the missionary Wiser (1936) for a village economy based on services offered by castes whose members perform their hereditary occupations in exchange for ritual and economic prestations such as food, grain, or money. As Dumont points out, the system is symmetrical overall, i.e., every caste except the lowest is in one context a patron and in another a client, but the principle of the system is fully employed by the dominant caste in its relations with various client castes. The dominant caste uses the wealth and power connected with land to integrate the service castes into a system that allows the latter an indirect access to the products of the land (Dumont 1998, 101–2). While Pocock (1962) wants to restrict the term "*jajmani* relations" to relationships between patrons and their religious specialists, which would exclude relationships with craftsmen and unskilled labourers, Dumont argues for a unitary definition. According to Dumont, the system values the interdependence of the elements in relation to the whole, whether these elements are religious castes, craftsmen, or labourers. Therefore, this system, purely religious in nature, differs from the Western market system (Dumont 1998, 105, 107). Dumont's ideas about the division of the grain heap on the threshing floor have been criticised by Fuller, who employs historical evidence to show that actual revenue systems were often based on monetary assessments and exchanges (Fuller 1989, 42–45).

"Untouchables" may be classified into two of Pocock's categories, since they both perform services related to the removal of impurity and also often constitute the bulk of the agricultural labourers. Moffatt describes in detail the relationship between the Tamil "untouchable" agricultural labourers in his area of research and the dominant caste, the Reddiyars, a relationship that has changed considerably in the last two centuries. In the first part of the twentieth century, the two groups were linked in a *jajmani* relationship. The patrons paid the "untouchables" in kind for a fixed amount of work in their fields, presented them with gifts on ceremonial occasions, and aided them in times of distress (Moffatt 1979, 79). This institution has been officially abolished and replaced by a wage labour system, though some individuals still continue this personal relationship with a patron. A second type of relationship is based on land tenancy, which is of two types, depending on whether the payment is fixed in advance or calculated in proportion to the actual harvest (Moffatt 1979, 78). Third, in pre-British times Harijan had access to some dry fields only in return for their services to the village, but from the middle of the nineteenth century, "untouchables" started to acquire land and become small peasants themselves, thereby gaining some economic influence (Moffatt 1979, 72–73). Apart from work related to agriculture, the five "untouchable" castes in Moffatt's area of research held traditionally impure occupations such as drummer, cattle scavenger, cremation ground attendant, announcer, and watchman. Drummers are impure not only because they touch cowskin with their hands when beating the drum but also because of their association with demons, whom they frighten away with their drums (Moffatt 1979, 113). The same holds true for the other four occupations, which are linked to these bloodthirsty beings in one way or another (Moffatt 1979, 113–17).

In order to demonstrate how Dombo and Dongria are related in different spheres of life, I will describe their ideas and values and forms of interaction in various contexts. My aim is to understand the content of a relationship that has at times been described as one between patrons and clients (Pfeffer 1997b, 13, 19–20). The terms "patron" and "client" are often used in accounts of Mediterranean societies (Gellner and Waterbury 1977). Depending on the ethnographic background and theoretical orientation, the patron-client relationship is defined in various ways. Gellner, for example, introduces a collection of papers on such relations with the following definition of patronage: "Patronage is unsymmetrical, involving inequality of power; it tends to form an extended system; to be long-term, or at least not restricted to a single isolated transaction; to possess a distinctive ethos; and whilst not always illegal or immoral, to stand outside the officially proclaimed formal morality of the society in question" (Gellner 1977, 4). Gellner seems to be interested in cross-culturally establishing a type of relationship that can then be explained by external factors, such as "the incompletely centralised state, the defective market or the defective bureaucracy which would seem to favour it" (Gellner 1977, 4). The articles in this book start from very different ethnographic conditions, some dealing with an actual *padrone*, or patron, like Silverman's discussion of Colleverde (Italy), where "all *mezzardia* contracts were phrased as patronage. The landlord was referred to and addressed as padrone. The personal relationship between the contractors and their own families used the idiom of patronage – symbols of command and deference, protection and loyalty, concern and affection" (Silverman 1977, 12). Others refer to ethnographic instances from Malta, Turkey, Cyprus, Lebanon, Jordan, or Algeria, presenting ethnographic data for what they define as "patron-client-relations," which differ, however, in the status and behaviour of the people involved in such a relationship. Some authors seem to justify this use of the term by assuming, like Gellner, a certain type of relationship characterised by "inequality" and a "disparity in their relative wealth, power, and status" (Scott 1977, 22). Others, like Peters, suggest that the patron-client relationships found in the Mediterranean world are spreading until they "will become universal phenomena, appearing in increasing varieties and entering into increasingly disparate sets of relationships" (Peters 1977, 275).

No one will assume that the relationship between Dongria and Dombo is somehow derived from the Mediterranean world. However, it may be useful to describe their relationship as one between patrons and clients, on the basis of their unequal status and access to land, the Dongria's numerical and political dominance, and the respect shown – mostly in ritual contexts – by Dombo. Further, we can follow Gellner and point to the correlation between the spread of the state, the market economy, and democracy in this remote area and the existence of such relations. In my opinion, we can call the Dongria "patrons" and the Dombo "clients" as long as we do not assume that their relationship is just one variation of a universal type having a particular essence and depending on certain well-defined material, political, or social conditions. We can use these terms for the purpose of translating indigenous concepts into our language, but it still remains necessary to describe the relationship between a "patron" and his "client" in detail. When using the terms "patron" and "client" in this work, my aim is not to put them into a scientific category used for comparative analysis in any essentialist manner but rather to translate a local concept for which the people themselves use the words *raja* and *praja*. Such relations are embedded in and defined by this society with its particular configuration of value-ideas. To my mind, it makes more sense to compare the social wholes they are part of, rather than the parts themselves.

Further, the terms carry meaning only in relation to a concrete society. For example, for Dumont the relation between a member of a dominant caste and his dependents is comparable to that between patrons and clients (Dumont 1998, 98). The word he translates as "client" is *praja*, i.e., the same word Dongria use when referring to Dombo. However, as I will show in this chapter, the relations between dominant caste members (*jajman*) and their clients (*praja*) differ from the relations between tribal landholders (*raja*) and the Dombo (*praja*).

I will now present my field data concerning the status, relations, and forms of interaction between Dombo and Dongria in the Niamgiri Hills of Odisha.

2.3 Value-ideas

During my first fieldwork among the temple priests of Puri, I constantly came across notions of purity and impurity as people discussed such topics as the status of various people, the prohibition against taking food or water from certain castes, the rules pertaining to the performance of rituals, and the different spaces within the temple or the town. People used words such as *asuddha, apariskara, papa, sutak, asaucha, mara,* or *maila* to describe various forms of impurity or "uncleanliness," and depending on the knowledge of the informant, these impure conditions were related to concepts concerning diet, profession, mixing of substances, the handling of bodily effluvia such as menstrual blood, leftovers, faeces, or dead bodies, and transgressions of the moral order.

My argument in this case is that Dongria Kond, too, have notions of high and low status, but that these notions are not related to exactly the same set of ideas expressed by high-caste people in coastal Odisha. What superficially appears to be the same turns out to also be partly different when examined more closely. This will become apparent through a discussion of the value-ideas pertaining to relations between Dombo and Dongria. To make this point clearly, I will first discuss one example that reveals all the difficulties involved in the notion of "impurity" so commonly used in descriptions of "tribal" life in Odisha.[6]

---

[6] In many publications dealing with rituals or social relations among tribal people in India, authors write about "pollution" or "impurity" as if these notions were universal concepts and do not deserve further explanation. I attended a conference at which one of the contributors explained to the audience that the Kond celebrate the *meria* sacrifice when the earth is considered "impure." When asked what people had actually told him in Oriya, he explained that his informants used the expression *khorap* to describe the condition of the earth. The word *khorap* literally means "bad" and surely implies other ideas than those expressed by Hindu informants when talking about the impurity of the earth during the festival of the menses, *raja parba*, studied by Apffel-Marglin (1995).

2.3.1 Kond "inside the village" (*rechagiri*), Dombo "outside the village" (*akagiri*)

Among high-caste Brahmins in Puri, there is a special room reserved for women where they must stay during their menstrual period. A woman is said to temporarily become a kind of "untouchable" (*achutia*) during this time, as contact with her is considered defiling (*apariska*). She does not cook, she eats from separate plates, and she remains secluded in her room for up to seven days. Afterwards, she either washes her clothes herself or gives them to a washerman, whose low social status is explained by reference to his contact with impure (*mara*) menstrual blood (*raja*). As Apffel-Marglin (1995) describes in her study of the "festival of menses," *raja parba*, in coastal Odisha a woman is likened to the earth, and her menstruation is considered equivalent to the hot season of the year. Women must rest just like the earth before the rains, and men must abstain from sexual intercourse with women just as they do not plough the earth during the hottest time of the year. Women are considered "untouchables" during their menses because their touch "weakens" men and causes fever and many different illnesses (Apffel-Marglin 1995, 113).

Among the Dongria, we come across very similar practices, but partly different explanations. During her menstruation, a Dongria woman has to stay in a room towards the back of the house. She may neither cook nor eat from the same plate as her other family members, and at the end of her seclusion, usually after three days, she will take her clothes to the river for washing. Only then is she allowed to mix with the other villagers and to continue her work in the swiddens.[7] The explanations Dongria give for this set of rules differ from those provided by coastal people, because unlike them, Dongria do not have any words that label the woman as "untouchable" and her blood or the time of her menstruation as "impure." To indicate that a woman is menstruating, Dongria will say *akagiri hace,* meaning "she has gone to the backside road." As an explanation for this seclusion, they will refer to the wrath of the gods, in particular of the earth goddess, in the event that a woman should come close to their dwelling during her menstruation. As the earth goddess is present in the centre of the village, the woman must stay away from her by remaining in the back of the house, on the side farthest removed from her shrine-stones. If she does not obey this rule, she commits a *dosa*, a serious mistake or offence, and the goddess will punish her, her family, or even the whole village by withdrawing her protection against diseases and different calamities. A menstruating woman should not

---

7 For rules concerning menstruation among the Kui Kond see Boal (1999, 80–81).

be seen by anybody; she must be like the moon, who disappears from sight during her "menstruation," i.e., during the phase of the new moon, when it is said to have gone "to the backside" (*lenju akagiri hace*). As long as the woman complies with these norms, she acts in accordance with *niam*, the order given by the gods. Whenever women move around, they normally do not enter the village on the main road, but always use the roads behind the two rows of houses to avoid any accusations of arousing the earth goddess's wrath. I witnessed the same practise being followed by Dombo traders travelling to the markets and avoiding trespassing the inner village boundaries.

The area behind the houses is the daily meeting place of the village women, whereas men assemble on the main road (*rechagiri*) between the two rows of houses. The stones representing the earth goddess and her husband are located on this main road, while the area behind the houses is associated with death and ancestors. When somebody dies, the dead body will be carried behind the houses to the cremation ground, and dead persons' souls are said to return to their houses the same way. The houses of the Dombo are normally found behind the village, and even if their houses are located at one end of the village rather than behind a row of houses, the Dombo are always said to live *akagiri*. As the Dongria's pigs live behind the house, and as Dongria throw their garbage into these backyards, the place behind the row of Dongria houses is always a very filthy and muddy place, in particular during the rainy season. Thus, the Dombo live on the Dongria's rubbish heap, and like women during menstruation, their houses are out of sight of the gods and the male villagers.

In relation to the Dongria as a whole, the Dombo thus have the same lower status as menstruating women, and it may even be said that like women, they are "outsiders" to the village community. The earth goddess is considered the "mother" of the Dongria, in particular of the descendants of the village's original founders, who belong to the same clan. While men usually remain in the village of their own earth goddess throughout their lives, their sisters will leave and their wives will enter the village. Just like the Dombo, these women are not directly related to the earth goddess of the village where they reside with their husbands. In times of menstruation, this similarity is stressed, as women, like Dombo, are banned from the sphere of the earth goddess and the men. I therefore agree with Barbara Boal, even if I have reservations concerning her use of the word "polluting":

> I suggest that this concern for the polluting of the *Darni* God is not so much an indication of women's inferiority as of the fact that the *darni* shrine stones are very definitely for that particular village alone, whereas women have come in marriage from elsewhere and their daughters will move away in marriage to join their husband's villages. Thus men

alone are permanent to the situation, and they alone can touch it in safety or eat food offered at it. (Boal 1999, 81)

It may be added that Dombo, like women, are not permanent members of a village, as they normally change villages quite often during their lives. As they are traders, their profession demands a certain mobility, and as they are normally landless, they have no reason to remain in a certain place for generations. In a way, they always remain "outsiders."

2.3.2 Kond as "kings" (*raja*), Dombo as "subjects" (*praja*)

An idiom that is sometimes used by members of both the Dongria and Dombo communities to describe their relationship is that of ruler/patron (*raja*) and subject/client (*praja*). When angry, the Dongria shout that they are not small people (*ichun loku*), but children of the king (*raja mila*). They consider themselves the legitimate owners of the land given to them by the gods. In myths (see below) pertaining to the first phase of creation, their father is the sun god, *dharmuraja* or "king of order"; in those relating to the time after a great flood, their culture hero is *niamraja*, literally meaning "king of rules" or "king of tradition". Their relationship to the king, both the mythological one and the former historical one living in Bissamcuttack or Jeypore,[8] defines their status as subjects (*praja*), a status they are very proud of. In relation to the Dombo, they consider themselves kings or patrons and regard the Dombo as their subjects or clients.

The higher status of the Dongria as "kings" is clearly expressed at the time of *dipawali*, when they are honoured by the Dombo living in their village. On the third day of this festival, the Dombo slaughter a buffalo and sell the meat to the Dongria. However, one portion of the meat, the loin (*bema*), is kept separate and divided into four parts. In the afternoon, the Dombo carry each portion on a stick to a different Dongria house, where they sing a song, present the meat as a gift, and receive some rice and money from the head of the household in return. Some hours later, the Dongria who were given the meat will one after the other pay a visit to the street where the Dombo live. The Dombo will set a cot in front of their houses and ask their Dongria patron to sit down. Then they pour water on their patron's head, hands, and feet and give him alcohol to drink. The patron is

---

[8] When talking about the *raja* Dongria are never quite specific about whether they mean the gods who are represented as kings or the kings living in the palaces in the plains.

only allowed to get up once he has given money to the Dombo.⁹ In Gumma, the meat was given to the village's four leaders, two traditional (*jani* and *bismajhi*) and two modern (senior *member* and junior *member*), who all belonged to the dominant Sikoka clan.¹⁰ The meat is kept on the roof or in front of the house as a sign of their superior status, but in the evening it is taken away by some villagers who cook it on the village plaza and share it with everybody who comes to attend this small feast.

2.3.3 Kond as "senior" (*kaja*), Dombo as "junior" (*icha*)

Another idiom used to define the relations between the two communities is that of seniority. As described by Pfeffer (1982, 29; 1997b, 13 – 14) and Berger (2000, 19; 2002, 87) for other communities in the Odisha highlands, the opposition between "big" or "senior" (*kaja*) and "small" or "junior" (*icha*) is one of the main value-ideas that structures social relations in this region. The implications of this opposition will be clarified by the following more detailed description of relations between Dombo and Dongria.

In the context of village relations, members of the Dombo community often address Dongria as elders. For example, a Dombo sometimes addresses a younger Dongria as "wife's elder brother" despite the fact that his wife is much older than the man he is talking to. When a Dongria affectionately calls an older Dombo "mother's brother," the Dombo will usually not respond using the reciprocal term, i.e., sister's son, but instead will also call him "mother's brother" in return. These forms of address are linked to the idea that the Dongria are "senior," i.e., they were the first people who appeared on earth, and all people are descended from their ancestors. This is clearly expressed in Dongria myths about the origin of humankind. According to these myths, first the Kond and then all other people were created by the goddess *jamarani* inside the earth, where they lived in darkness. The goddess then created the sun god (*dharmuraja*) to rule the people, and when his rays pierced the earth through a small hole, the people saw the light and came out, first the Kond, then the higher castes, and finally the lower ones, like the Dombo. The Kond divided themselves into several groups and established the first villages with sites of worship for the earth god-

---

9 The amount of money expresses the status of the patron. For example, in Gumma the man who at that time was respected as the main leader of the village explained to me that he was expected to give more money than the others.
10 The senior *member* (*kaja member*) is authorised by the development agency (DKDA), the junior *member* (*icha member*) by the education department (DPEP).

dess (*dharni penu*), their mother. Later, the sun god punished human beings by sending a great flood, and all of them were killed except a brother (Duku) and a sister (Dumbe). *Dharmuraja* disfigured the sister's face with smallpox so that her brother could no longer recognise her and agreed to take her as his wife. With the help of the sun god, the soil became firm, and life on earth again became possible. The Kond began to populate the land, which the gods divided among them. They were divided into different castes, all of which are considered descendants of twelve brothers born of Dumbe.

The origin of human beings is represented as an act of creation by the goddess in the earth, the role of the father being limited to "opening" the earth and showing the way out of her. He is a king who punishes, destroys, and restores order, but who is not a creator. After flooding the earth and killing most of his children, the sun god helps to make life on earth possible again by joining brother and sister in marriage and by re-establishing order. Hierarchy is expressed in terms of the order of creation and the order of emergence from the earth. In the context of the original creation, the Kond are the first to be created and the first who come out of the earth, followed by the different castes in order from high status to low status. In the second phase, they become the ancestors of all human beings, who are divided according to territory and service. The Kond are generally known as hunters and agriculturalists, whereas people from other castes perform services such as cooking (Brahman), distilling alcohol (Sundi), making iron tools (Lohar), and sweeping the streets (Dombo).

The Kond have the highest status because they were the first; they are the "seniors," while the other castes appeared later and were ascribed different functions. The unity of society is explained in terms of kinship, because all human beings are basically alike as children of the earth in the first phase and as descendants ("brothers") of the ancestral tribal couple in the second phase. The castes are united as brothers and differentiated by their birth order. This is clearly different from the conception of *varna* based on the distinction of higher and lower parts in the body of the original man (Dumont 1998, 66–72) or the conception of caste as based on the opposition between the pure Brahmin and the impure Shudra represented by the cow (Dumont 1998, 54). Further, the incest of brother and sister is not represented as a sin explaining a fall from status.[11] It should rather be seen as solving the problem of how the different clans existing today could have come into being.

---

11 The incest is of course a sin, as indicated by the smallpox the sister suffers from. The fact that the Kond committed a sin is concealed by making the incest the outcome of the disease and not its cause. The myth also shifts the responsibility for the incest onto the god.

Dongria are, of course, aware that from the perspective of others they are not higher than for instance Brahmins, whose cooked food everybody eats. A Dongria once proudly explained to me their status as people of the king, but also pointed out that because of certain habits like eating meat and drinking alcohol, people from the plains consider them to be of "junior" status. It is with reference to food and the idea of an original sin that Dombo explain their present low status:

> We are not a small caste, we are Brahmins. Once there was a Brahmin who had seven sons. One day one of his cows died, and the father sent his sons off to cremate the cow. They carried the cow to a river, hung up their sacred threads on a tree, and placed the cow on a fire. Then they took a bath in the river, put on their sacred threads, and went away. On the way, the oldest brother told the youngest to return and see whether the cow had been properly burned up. When he arrived at the place of cremation, he smelled the meat, and since the cow had been very fatty, the smell was very good. He took off his sacred thread, placed it on the tree, and began to eat the meat. His middle brother had followed him, and when he saw that his younger brother was eating the meat, he quickly informed his other brothers. They came and scolded the youngest brother, took away his sacred thread, and reported everything to their father. The father repudiated his son. He told him that he was no longer a Brahmin and that no one [from another caste] would ever eat with him again.

Very similar myths are told by "untouchables" all over India (e.g., Kolenda 1981b, 175–76; Moffatt 1979, 120–21; Raheja 1992, 132, app. 213–19). The common theme of all these narrations is the fall of the narrator's caste from high status due to a very grave sin, proven or alleged, in this case eating the meat of a sacred cow. The myth's main plot refers to popular Hindu ideology and not to ideas expressed by the Dongria. Eating beef is not considered a sin according to Kond values. Cows are sacrificed by Dongria Kond on certain ritual occasions, and only medicine men sometimes take a vow to avoid beef, because they are assisted in their work by very powerful gods who would refuse their help. The social reference of this Dombo myth is clearly the caste system with its two extreme poles of the status hierarchy: the pure Brahmin and the impure Shudra. Status is expressed here in the code of eating, a code also often used by Kond to express their social relations. Whenever they discuss the Dombo's status, Kond people will hurry to explain that they do not eat with them, nor with the Ghasi or the Leli, two other castes considered "untouchables" in the caste hierarchy. When asked why, Dongria will say that all these people are *icha* (small or junior), while they are *kaja* (big or senior). My point is that these words indeed imply ideas of high and low status, but not in exactly the same sense used, for example, by the Hindu temple servants I studied in coastal Odisha. I will now explore another way in which Dongria consider Dombo inferior, apart from the idea mentioned above that they were the last to emerge onto the surface of the earth.

2.3.4 Kond as "humans" (*kuang*), Dombo as "ghosts" (*marha*)

Dongria refer to themselves as *kuang*, a word meaning literally "men" and in the extended sense "human being." Dongria call their own language *kuang kata*, and all Kond people are said to be *kuang* in contrast to Oriya people, *kaska loku*, from the plains. They often use the word *kuang* to distinguish themselves from the Dombo, whom they equate with ghosts or with dead people. Dongria and Dombo distinguish two types of death, good and bad.[12] A bad death results in the living person's transformation into a violent soul (*marha*) that wanders around and is capable of inflicting its own death experience on others. When a Dongria dies such a death, for example by falling from a tree, he is considered to lose his caste and become a Dombo. Such a violent soul is not considered a "proper ancestor" (*mahane*) and will not, therefore, be called into the house. In other words, like a Dombo, such a ghost is restricted from entering the house. Because these violent souls do not belong to the Dongria community any more, they receive offerings in a space separate from the place where the proper ancestors are fed. When such a violent soul gets reincarnated in a Dongria child, a ritual must be performed to reintroduce the ghost into the Dongria community.

Dongria say that Dombo worship these ghosts on *dipawali*. On this day, Dombo first offer cooked rice, different curries, and beef to their ancestors inside the house. They then go outside, take some rice in their right hands, throw it onto the roof, and summon different types of ghosts, such as the following (all expressions in local Oriya):

sapa taki dela loku ("people who died from a snake bite")
gacha padhi mari gala loku ("people who died by falling from a tree")
nadi nei gala loku ("people who died by drowning in a river")
baga khaila loku ("people who died by being eaten by a tiger or bear")
ucch ki hela loku ("people who committed suicide by hanging").

Finally, they place the rice plates with curry and meat on the roof while shouting *pau*, which means that the ghosts have "received" their share and should take it

---

[12] For a discussion of the concepts of "good" and "bad" death, see Bloch and Parry (1982).

and go. The offering remains on the roof throughout the night, and the next day, the Dombo children take the food and go to the small stream that marks the border of the village. There they drop some food into the water, cross the stream, and eat the offerings. The Dongria call the ritual *pau kina,* meaning "to make receive," and point to the fact that the Dombo feed the ghosts with cooked food in the same way that they feed their own ancestors. In other words, the Dongria who have lost their right to belong to their community by dying a bad death turn into Dombo, from whom they accept cooked food. Not only that, the Dombo themselves exhibit their close relations with these ghosts when they send their children to eat their leftovers.

Not only these ghosts, but sometimes even the pacified souls who died a good death are compared to Dombo. When no Dombo is around, Dongria jokingly call the Dombo *dhumba,* the Oriya word for ancestor, obviously playing with the phonetic similarities. It is said that the *dhumba,* like the Dombo, belong to a "smaller" community (*jati*). The *dhumba* live on the cremation ground, which like the Dombo's houses is always outside and to the west of the village. This stands in contrast to the Dongria, whose houses are located to the east of the Dombo's houses and the cremation ground, the east being associated with life in many contexts (see section 4.2.1). The idea behind this association of the Dombo with the ancestors seems to be that the dead are inferior to the living just as the Dombo are inferior to the Dongria.

The following is a summary of these value-ideas. Like menstruating Dongria women, Dombo live outside or on the "backside" (*akagiri*) of the village in order to be kept away from the earth goddess. They are the Dongria's "junior" or "smaller" (*icha*) brothers and dependent "clients" (*praja*), who emerged on the surface of the earth last and who perform different services in order to make a living. Finally, Dombo are associated with ancestors and in particular with evil ghosts (*marha*). I will now deal with the concept of brotherhood, which creates unity between the Dongria and Dombo communities.

2.3.5 Dombo and Dongria as "one clan" (*ra kuda*)

The two communities, Dongria and Dombo, are organised in named clans that are spread over a vast territory. The number of clans is not limited, and I have not come across a mythological story that connects all the clans in a definite sequence of events. As I will explain later, Dongria clans have a clear territorial reference even if, due to migrations and land purchases, the members of a clan do not occupy a discrete territory with fixed boundaries. Dombo clans are linked to Dongria clans in a system of analogies. For example, the main Dongria clan in the area where I did research was Sikoka, a name that is probably derived from Hiko,[13] the Kuwi word for little millet (*Panicum miliare* L.). When I first visited a neighbouring village at the time of a buffalo sacrifice and did a household survey, one Dongria informant often mentioned the title Kausilya as a clan name of different householders. When I got back from the village to my quarters at a nearby project station of the government development agency (called DKDA or Dongria Kond Development Agency), a local officer told me I must have been collecting wrong data, because no Dongria bears the title Kausilya. I was confused and went back to the village the next morning and angrily accused the informant of giving me wrong information, but he insisted on the correctness of his answers. He then explained to me that Kausilya is the Oriya translation of Sikoka. Some weeks later I found out that Kausilya is the name of a Dombo clan prominent in this area. It then became clear that the name Kausilya is derived from *kosala*, the Oriya word for little millet. I then started to search for other cases of clan analogy, and it became clear that each Dongria clan has one corresponding Dombo clan. When asking about such correspondences for a variety of clans, I often got quite different information from various informants.[14]

An explanation for the association of Dombo and Dongria clans was once given to me by a Dombo belonging to the Kausilya clan. He insisted that the correspondence was based on marriage between the two communities. According to him, his forefathers were originally Dongria belonging to the Sikoka clan. One of his "grandfathers" then married a Dombo girl, and they all became Dombo and accepted the corresponding Dombo clan title, Kausilya. This may indeed have been the case, because the Dongria husband, as well as the children born to this union, will belong to the Dombo caste and can no longer bear the original Dongria clan name. But the theme of this "personal history" is so similar to the theme of other myths told by Harijan about their fall from high status that there is reason to wonder whether it is not simply a repetition of the idea of the original sin, in this case marriage with a low-caste woman.

---

13 The sounds "h" and "s" seem to be interchangeable, and Kuwi-speaking people living in two adjacent mountain ranges may differ in pronouncing a word either with "h" or with "s."
14 For example, one old Dombo woman mentioned the following clan analogies: Wengesika = Benia; Mandika = Barasagudia; Wadaka = Gurida; Himberika = Manandia; Kurtruka = Dongri; Pusika = Takri, Huika = Mongri. A young Dongria man gave me the following equivalences: Wengesika = Benia, Karchika = Kurkuria, Palaka = Palkia, Jakesika = Batria, Kundika = Mandika. Another Dombo informant mentioned slightly different analogies: Kadraka = Bagha, Palaka = Hial, Wadaka = Kakaria, Jakesika = Kondapani, Mandika (here considered a Dongria clan) = Batara, Pusika = Takri. Further equivalences were collected from different informants throughout the period of research, for example Praska = Chati, Saraka = Kataria, Perisika = Ganta.

If the Dongria are asked about the existence of such clan analogies, they give a range of answers. As already mentioned, some consider this a matter of translation, while others see it as a result of the work of government officials who wrote down clan analogies. Some Dongria distinguish between the fact that both communities have the same clan and the status differences deriving from belonging to "different castes." A Dongria is always aware of his higher status but at the same time considers a Dombo to be either a member of his own clan, whom he addresses like an agnate, or a member of an unrelated clan, whom he addresses like an affine. For example, Dongria often address Dombo of their affiliated clan as "brother" or "father's brother" and are addressed with the reciprocal terms in return. If, however, they are closely related but do not belong to associated clans, they are often heard addressing each other as "sister's son" or "mother's brother" if they belong to different generations or as "wife's brother" and "sister's husband" if they belong to the same generation. The clan system provides a classification of people into either "brothers" (*bai*) or "affines" (*bondu*). In practise, this does not mean that status differences are neglected. For example, a Dombo will often address a younger Dongria as a senior.

I was often astonished that Dongria use the same word for clan and caste, calling both *kuda*,[15] while Oriya clearly differentiate the two (*bongsa* and *jati*). I think that Dongria consider *kuda* as a territorial unit in one context and as a functional unit in another. For example, the following myth I collected states how the land was divided among the people by the gods, thus creating different clans, and how at the same time people were distinguished according to the functions they performed:

> Long ago there was neither sky nor earth. The gods lived above; below them was only mud. During this time there existed besides the gods two Kond, a brother called Duku and a sister named Dumbe. They said to the gods, "We want to live on earth; give us a *dharni* [shrine of the earth goddess], a village, and land where we can live and work." Thereupon the gods sent out two crows. They flew around and viewed everything. When they returned, they informed the gods that there was nothing below, no soil and no plants. Hence the gods started to search for a worm. When they found the worm, they killed it. Because the worm had eaten the soil and produced the water, the earth now started to dry up. Then the gods sowed seeds and plants, and trees began to grow. Duku and Dumbe, who belonged to the Wengesika clan, could now live on earth, but because they were brother and sister, they could not marry each other. Thereupon *aji budi* disfigured the sister's face [by smallpox], and because he could not recognise her any longer, the brother married his sister. From them we all descend. When we became many, *niamraja* started to divide us and ascribed different territories and names to us: Sikoka, Jakesika, Kadraka, and so on. Those

---

15 When talking about castes, Dongria may sometimes use the word *jati*, but when I asked them what the corresponding word in their language was, I always received *kuda* as the answer.

who were experts in cooking became Brahmin, those who produced alcohol became Sundi, those who swept the street became Dombo, and the one who called everybody to a meeting in the morning became the *barika*. But in the beginning all were Kond.

What this myth clearly expresses is that people were divided according to two principles, a territorial and a functional. Therefore, people may belong to the same *kuda* or clan in terms of territory but to different *kuda* or castes in terms of occupation. Each use of the word *kuda* is different. When a Dongria is asked which territorial unit (clan) is higher or lower, the answer is always that they are the same. Neither the Dongria territorial clans nor the Dombo clans living in the territories of their patrons are ranked. This means that territory itself is not a status criterion. Hierarchy in relation to clans is only recognised in the context of clan associations or phratries (see section 3.3.3). For example, if two or more clans are seen as "brother-and-sister" clans (*tayi bai kuda*),[16] they are always ranked according to the principle of seniority. This principle is further linked to hierarchy expressed in terms of the division of labour when distinguishing different communities. The functions performed by the senior people are considered higher than those of the junior people.

In summary, *kuda* in the sense of communities differentiated by birth order and/or occupation has hierarchical implications, while *kuda* in the sense of a territorial clan is not ranked. In the first meaning of *kuda*, Dombo and Dongria are considered two communities of different status. When the word *kuda* is used in the second sense, however, the status differences vanish and are replaced by a distinction between one's own clan and all other clans. This is applied to the whole of humankind, because all people belong through descent to a particular territory that gives them their identity, and since this aspect is non-hierarchical, it ignores other status distinctions and allows for the possibility that a Dongria clan and a certain Dombo clan can be seen as one (*ra kuda*).

2.3.6 Dombo and Dongria as "friends" (*tone / ade*)

The association of clans creates a non-hierarchical relationship between Dongria and Dombo on a group level. Similarly, the institution of friendship establishes

---

16 The two words, *tayi* and *bai*, seem to be of Dravidian origin. Israel translates *tayi* as "brother" and mentions the expression *tayi tangi* meaning "brother and sister" (Israel 1979, 371). The word *bai* is not mentioned in this Kuwi dictionary, but we do find it in Winfield's Kui dictionary, where it is translated as "elder sister, paternal cousin (female)" (Winfield 1929, 10). The expression *tayi bai* thus appears to combine words from both Kuwi and Kui.

long-lasting bonds of an egalitarian character between clans, villages, and families. In this chapter, I will only address the last type of bond, which is forged by individuals but often connects whole families for several generations. This kind of relationship may be established between Dongria on all levels, i.e., between members of two different lineages or clans, but not to my knowledge between two brothers. Empirical instances of such friendship relations can further be found between Dongria and Dombo and between people from the hills (*horu raji*) and from the valleys (*panga raji*). For example, Dongria men and women from Gumma have friendship relations with members of their own community both within and outside the village, with Dombo from their own and from different localities, and with members of different castes, in particular Paika (soldiers) and Gauda (cowherds) residing in villages near Kalyansingpur. A Dongria can have more than one friend, and they can belong to different communities. Male friends address each other as *tone* or *sai*, female friends as *ade* or *ali*. This bond is ritually established in childhood on the parents' initiative, but adults may also decide to become friends at any age. During my fieldwork, a Dongria became my *tone*, and I will describe this relationship as an illustration of the rules and rituals involved in such a friendship.

In the early phase of my fieldwork, one man from the village invited me to join him at a drinking party. He was building a wooden cot with the help of some villagers, and as a gift to his helpers he had bought two bottles of *mohua* liquor. I reciprocated his invitation another day when I was building my own cot. Some time later I brought him a cap that he had asked for from the market town. In the following weeks I ate at his house in the mornings, helped him thatch the roof of his house, and worked with him in the fields. One day, a woman working for the DKDA suggested we should become *tone* by sharing food at the next *kodru parbu*, the buffalo sacrifice to the earth goddess. A year later, at the time of the sacrifice in a neighbouring village, we carried out our plan: I brought a fat broiler from the market, and he contributed rice and *mohua* liquor. I cooked the rice and the chicken in my house, and we invited two others as witnesses. All four of us sat on the flour, and while we ate, one of the witnesses instructed us to exchange food and drink, i.e., drink and eat what the other had already touched. After we finished eating, we were further asked to wash our hands jointly and clean each other's plates. Then one of the witnesses told us that from now on neither of us could any longer refer to the other by any of his names, in particular not the name given him by his parents.

Within Gumma, most Dombo children had ritual friends among the Dongria. The relationships had been established in childhood in ways similar to my own experience. For example, one man who already had four children of his own had started such a bond with two slightly younger Dongria men in his childhood. As just described, they had eaten together from the same plate, something Dongria refrain from in other contexts. This commensality has the effect of creating a new relationship, but the breaking of the commensal rules itself is not continued. Thus, his Dongria friends do not eat in his house, although they engage in mutual visits. At the time of *dipawali*, the two Dongria men will come to his house, drink some liquor, and accept uncooked rice and some lentils as a gift from him. On *dasera*, the Dombo will pay a visit to the house of his ritual friends and eat boiled rice and curry before being sent away with some bananas or other gifts.

A relationship between friends does not end with the death of the individuals but is inherited by at least one of each friend's children. Ideally, the bond should be repeated in each of the next four subsequent generations.[17] I was astonished to find that this is more than an ideal in Gumma. For example, the father of the eldest person (Sikoka Ranu) alive in Gumma had established a *tone* relationship with another man from the same village perhaps a hundred years ago. Sikoka Ranu and the already-deceased father of one of the village leaders had continued this bond. In the next generation, this village leader and Sikoka Ranu's son started a *tone* relationship. When Ranu's son became a father, he made sure that his son performed the ritual with the son of the village leader's brother. After the next generation, i.e., when the SSSS of the two men who initiated the friendship have become *tone*, this bond will come to an end.

As indicated above, a friendship involves certain prohibitions. The strongest are linked to the friend's name and to contacts with one's husband's friend. From the day of the ritual commemoration of the bond, the friend's name may never be uttered again. Most commonly one refers to the friend by his or her youth name,[18] but some people feel that they should not even mention this name and instead refer to the person simply as "my friend." In this case the others either know whom he or she is talking about, or they will suggest different names until the speaker shows agreement. When two men have a friendship, their wives are expected to avoid their husband's *tone*. This goes so far that a woman will run away if her husband's friend comes into sight. Once as I was sitting with a woman on my neighbour's veranda, her husband's *tone* turned up. She saw no other way to escape him than hiding in my neighbour's house, where she had to remain for a long time, since the man she had to avoid was in a talkative mood and did not intend to leave for a while. This avoidance

---

17 This positive rule appears again in its negative form in the context of marriage rules (see later). Here the rule states that the descendants of two lineages that have entered an affinal relation cannot marry for the next three generations.

18 It is possible that the friends may also give each other new names, but I found no instances of this practise.

rule sometimes puts women into a difficult position, especially if their husbands' friends live in the same village, but it is strictly observed by Dombo and Dongria alike. When referring to her husband's friend, a woman has to call him "*tone aba,*" meaning "friend's father," while he in return will refer to her as "*tone aya,*" "friend's mother." These are terms of respect and simultaneously exclude the friend's wife and the husband's friend from the category of people with whom one can have a sexual affair.

Among the Gadaba such friends are called *moitr*. They greet and interact with each other in a particularly polite way and may under no circumstances demand anything from each other (Pfeffer 1991, 2001; Berger 2000, 22). This norm does not apply to friendships in the Niamgiri Hills. One has to joke with friends and should not quarrel, but friends neither greet each other in a certain way nor are expected to be particularly polite. Friends are constantly asked for help and assistance. In Niggemeyer's opinion, Kond and Pano enter a friendship bond when they have established a working business relationship and find their cooperation mutually advantageous: the Pano gains a permanent customer, while the Kond knows that his friend will not pressure him too much when it comes to repaying his debts (Niggemeyer 1964a, 18). A similar interpretation may be applied to the information provided by Das Patnaik that before the land settlement Dombo used to work on fields provided to them by their Dongria friends (Das Patnaik 1984, 30) and that Dongria may quarrel with a Dombo but may still approach him for a loan on the basis of their friendship relation (Das Patnaik 1988, 11).

As with family members or co-villagers, one feels free to ask a friend for help or money. Material and financial interests may indeed be the reasons why someone intends to establish a ritual friendship. For example, during my second visit I brought a half dozen watches for the village leaders in Gumma and two neighbouring villages. A young Dongria man who had not received anything became very envious and tried to convince me to give him one of the watches. He offered me *salap* wine and signalled his readiness to share his knowledge with me in return for one of my gifts. I refused, because I had already promised these watches to others. One evening, he, his wife, and his in-laws unexpectedly appeared at my house, his wife carrying a small chicken under her arm, his mother-in-law holding a basket full of rice. They told me that they had come to give me these gifts and to tie the bond of friendship between me and the young man. Clearly, the watches had become status objects because of my intention to distribute them to the village leaders, and one way to acquire one was to enter into a gift-giving relationship with me.

In the same way, I think it is quite possible that the Dombo try to establish friendship in order to be able to ask for land or to secure a business partner. It may even be argued that the rule to continue a bond for the next four generations is meant to ensure that debts will be cleared in the long run. However, it should be stressed that such economic interests are not the only and not even the most important reasons for establishing friendship. In particular, friendship among young Dongria visiting the youth dormitories is based on common experiences, emotions, and activities. Friendship is linked to joy (*rasa*) expressed in dancing and singing during festivals and in sharing alcohol and getting drunk together. Friends are expected to share in the way that same-sex siblings are and to help one another in times of crisis, but in contrast to relations with same-sex siblings, friends do not interact like "seniors" and "juniors." Existing kinship ties and differences of age or of status due to one's belonging to a "junior" or "senior" community are neglected in several ways. First, by eating from the other's plate, thereby denying – at least temporarily – any differences in terms of community. Second, by using special terms of reference and address on a reciprocal basis, thus avoiding the use of other relationship terms that convey distinctions of age, generation, or affinity. For example, the terms for brother and sister are distinguished according to seniority (eB / yB, eZ / yZ), while friends call one another *tone* or *ade* whatever their actual ages. Third, by ignoring an individual's hierarchical relations with parents, parents' siblings (MB, MZ, FB, FZ), or affines (WP, HP), expressed in the names given by them, and using a name that has been given by "equals" of one's own age group or dormitory instead. These names often have a humorous content and can also be used in the context of making jokes (*sedrombi*), something unimaginable with names given by one's kin relations. For example, during my fieldwork I once used the first name of the village elder, Sikoka Mukuna, in a conversation that he by chance overheard. He scolded me, "How can you use the name of a big man? You should know that this is a mistake! I am your elder brother!" Afterwards, I mostly addressed him by the proper term for eB, *tada*, but from time to time when we were making jokes, I called him by his "youth name" (*dawe daru*), Bhimo, and he responded by mentioning the youth name he had given me, Majhe.

Like marriage, friendship establishes relations beyond the individual by linking whole families over a time span of several generations. In contrast to marriage, which creates a status distinction between the higher bride-giver and the lower bride-taker, friendship begins by annihilating all status distinction in an act of commensality. Affinal relationship terms are also clearly hierarchical, in reference as well as in address, while friendship terms are not. In summary, friendship establishes relations similar to those of brotherhood and affinity but different from them in that the relationship is one of equals.

In my analysis, friendship functions in two ways, both of which are important for an understanding of Dombo-Dongria relations. First, friendship creates a sense of relatedness similar to brotherhood, affinity, and joint territoriality between members of different communities and villages. Once such a relationship has been established, sharing, demanding, and exchanging become legitimate ways of interacting. Thus, when I came to Dongria villages less known to me, I was always astonished by how reserved people were in their demands in contrast to the people whom I regarded as my family members, friends, or co-villagers. From a strategic point of view, it makes sense to expect the Dombo to consciously use this institution to pursue their economic interests. Similarly, some of the Gaudo and Paika who had friendship relations in Gumma often came as hunters, and it is not unreasonable to assume that they established such a bond in order to have a place to stay and companions during their expeditions. Second, friendship superimposes equality on status relations. This is of particular importance within the group of youths, who at night escape their elders' authority to meet with "equals" behind the village or in dormitories, where they dance, sing, joke, and sleep with each other. I therefore conclude that friendship in the Niamgiri can be seen as a relationship that is conceptualised in contrast to relations based on communality, clan or lineage membership, and affinity, because it creates egalitarian bonds characterised by joking. I will now examine how in contrast to these rather egalitarian relationships, hierarchy is expressed in forms of segregation in many contexts of daily life.

2.4 Social boundaries

As in caste society, the value-ideas discussed above are linked to rules that separate the two communities of the Niamgiri Hills, Dongria and Dombo. The forms of segregation related to these norms are essentially the same as those found in caste society. Like castes, Dongria and Dombo are segregated in terms of space, food, and marriage.

2.4.1 Closed spaces

The Dombo's lower status is made apparent in daily life in a set of prohibitions. A first restriction applies to spatial boundaries. Dongria will not enter the inner part of a Dombo's house, because this would make them "small persons." This avoidance becomes a rule when applied to the Dombo. Dombo should not enter the inner part of a Dongria house, because that would make the goddess of wealth and rice, *sita penu-lahi penu*, leave the house. This goddess is worshipped at a wall called *handani kuda*, which in Desia Kond houses is one of the walls where grain is stored, grain being the representation of the goddess. In Dongria houses, the room behind the *handani kuda* is usually empty and used only for ritual purposes, especially for invocations to the ancestors. Grain is stored in the attic, where Dongria also keep sacred pots (*bohandi*) and bamboo baskets (*buldang*) containing paddy (*kulinga*) and husked rice (*manjinga*) and gourds (*kaktedia*) filled with rice and millet (*hiko*), which represent different forms of the goddess. Myths and rituals relate to the coming and going of this goddess: her presence brings wealth, her absence leads to poverty. When Dombo started offering me cooked food, I was warned by one of the local development officers that I should not accept it, because the Dongria would then prohibit me from entering their houses, in particular at the time of rituals when the gods are summoned. If a member of either community enters the house of a member of the other community, he or she will commit a "mistake" (*dosa*) that will disturb relations with the gods. This is expressed in the following short myth told to me by a Dongria:

> In the past, *niamraja* used to walk around a lot. But one day he came into one of our villages where somebody with the name "Dombo" lived. He was a Kond, but his name was "Dombo." When *niamraja* heard others calling this man "Dombo," he thought that these people are not Kond but Dombo, and he went into hiding. Since that time *niamraja* cannot be seen any more.

What this myth expresses is the general idea that the gods fear having contact with Dombo. If a Dongria transgresses the rules restricting contact with the Dombo, he disturbs the proper order of relations and risks the gods' withdrawal and even punishment, in particular of his own house. This spatial separation between Dongria and Dombo also governs the layout of the village as a whole. Although Dombo are not restricted from moving around freely in the village, their houses may never be in the same row as those of the Dongria. Dongria build their rows of houses on both sides of the shrine of the earth goddess (*dharni*) and her husband (*koteiwali*), while Dombo should build their houses west of the village. The west is associated with sunset, considered the death of *dharmuraja*, and with the ancestors, who live in the cremation ground to the west of the village. The Dombo's cremation ground is located in a place separate from that of the Dongria. When asked, Dongria will always say that the Dombo live outside (D: *akagiri*; lit. back side) the village, while they themselves live inside (D: *rechagiri*; lit. front side). The back of the house is the place where women spend most of their time, where rubbish is thrown and pigs are kept, and from which the ancestors enter the house.

The rules against building a house inside the village and entering a Dongria's inner house are obeyed by every Dombo. A Dombo may be allowed to sleep on the inner veranda of a Dongria's house at night, but under no circumstances will he dare to step inside the main house. In the same way, I often saw Dongria sitting on the veranda of a Dombo's house chatting and drinking alcohol, but I never saw a Dongria entering the inner part of the house.

2.4.2 Prohibited food

A second restriction concerns the sharing of food. According to the following myth, which I heard from a *gurumeni*, the gods once wanted to attend a feast in the house of a Dombo family, but the god *bima* prevented this by destroying everything:

> In the old days a group of hunters went out to hunt a mouse deer (*gensi*). They reached a place with a big flat rock. They were tired and sat down, and because they wanted to smoke, they lit a fire. They took a stick and started chafing it between their hands in a hole of the big rock. From the dust of the wooden stick arose the gods, followed by the different castes, like Ghasi, Dombo, Kumti, and Lohar. After *lahi penu* came out of the hole, she went around looking for grain. She went to the house of a Dombo, because once a year the Dombo receive grain from the Kond for herding the cows. When she arrived at the Dombo's house, she asked for grain, but while the Dombo man was willing to give her something, his wife refused. Because her wish had been denied, *lahi penu* told the gods accompanying her to transform their hair into rats. They did as requested, and the rats ran into the Dombo's house, took away all the grain, and carried it to heaven. When the Dombo woman saw that all her grain had disappeared, she thought, "Oh, these people asking for grain were not humans but gods. Had I given one *ada* [approximately one kilogram], they would have returned two *ada*. Had I given two *ada*, they would have returned one *mana* [approximately four kilograms]. Now we have nothing." They recognised their fault and therefore wished to give a feast to the gods. They slaughtered a goat, cooked rice, and distributed everything on leaf plates. Then they called the gods, but the moment the gods arrived, a huge storm broke out, and everything became dusty. *lahi penu* took cover in a piece of bamboo. When the storm died, the gods saw that everything was gone, and disappointed, they went back to heaven. There *lahi penu* realised that they had no food. Therefore she returned to earth. Halfway there she met *bima penu*, her mother's brother. He talked to her and tried to prevent her from going back to earth, but *lahi penu* responded, "I am going back to the humans and will settle down near the *dharni* [earth goddess]. I will request feasts for you and the other gods." Nowadays, for this reason we bring *akat manjing* [sacred rice representing *lahi penu*] to the *dharni*.

This myth deals with several aspects important for the discussion of the Dombo's status. First, the Dombo refused to give grain when asked, and now they are punished for this by having all the grain they possess taken away. When the Dombo woman regrets her behaviour, she expresses a basic Kond paradigm: when asked by a higher person one should give, because one can expect greater gifts in return. This is the basic logic in all Kond rituals, and because the Dombo did not act accordingly, they are of a lower status, deprived of *lahi penu*, who is represented by grain in many rituals. One could say that the original "sin" was the refusal to give what belongs to the goddess, which is certainly different from the "sin" expressed in the myth about the fall from Brahmanical status. Second, when the Dombo want to present the gods with cooked food, the gods are ready to attend the feast, but they are taught a lesson by *bima penu*, who destroys everything. The message is that people of higher status can demand raw rice from Dombo, but not cooked food.[19] Third, when *lahi penu* returns to earth, she settles near the *dharni*, i.e., in a Kond village. From them she can demand grain, because she can be certain that it will be given to her. It is implied that the Kond understand the essential norm of reciprocity: *lahi penu* has given a part of herself, the grain, to the Kond, and when she demands it at the time of sacrifice, they will return it to her and the other gods.

Dombo often claim that the Dongria do not strictly obey the food restrictions. In public, I never saw a Dongria eating in the house of a Dombo, but the latter often assured me that Dongria sometimes come at night and eat their meat. They also claim that in other villages at the time of *dipawali* Dongria and Dombo will sit together nowadays and attend the feast given by the Dombo. When I once declined to eat in the house of a local home guard belonging to the Dombo community by saying that the Dongria of my village would otherwise

---

19 The same idea is expressed in the following part of a myth collected by another research team:

"Having cleared the hill slopes, the men turned to *dharam devata* to inquire about when the slashes should be burned. After some thought, he advised them not to light a fire without the permission of *bima penu*, who, if irked, would become wrathful. He told them to appease *bima penu* on a Sunday and also to worship the hill god (*danda penu-horu penu*) on the same day; the slashes were to be burned on Monday. After this, the men asked *dharam devata* for seed to sow and he gave them some which he had taken from the demon's tongue. Since they did not suffice, they went in search for more seeds, and hoped to acquire them in a distant village from a Domb boy who sold clothes and had large amounts of seed. They offered to pay three times the price, but the boy was only willing to part with the seed on condition that the men ate at his house. The men were in a quandary as they had vowed never to accept food in a Domb's house. Thus, they went to *dharam devata* for a solution. He told them to agree to a meal at his home, provided the seed were delivered beforehand; but, upon getting the seed they were to rush back, thus avoiding the meal. The Domb boy promptly delivered the seed; then he began to prepare the meal, and killed a goat for this purpose. While he was doing so, *dharam devata* create [sic] wind and rain as a ruse, so that the men could flee. Then he asked them whether they had eaten at the Domb boy's house, and hearing that they had not, told them to claim that they had indeed eaten there" (Jena et al. 2002, 152–53).

prohibit me from entering their houses, he assured me that even the chief of the village where I was staying had eaten cooked food in his house.

Dongria's reaction to the suggestion that they may take food from the Dombo depends completely on the context. When, for example, explaining the status differences between communities, they will say that the difference between them and the Dombo is that the latter will accept cooked food from them but not vice versa. To prove this claim of higher status, they will point to the fact that Dongria give *gandi kahpe* to the Dombo. This word refers to cooked food, in particular boiled rice and gruel, that is given to the Dombo as a remuneration for services they provide. Thus the *barika* of the village, as well as the Dombo children who look after the Dongria's livestock, receive *gandi kahpe* twice a day, in the morning and the evening. It is given to them either in leaf plates or in aluminium pots the Dombo themselves bring to the veranda of the Dongria's houses. This offering is one of the most explicit markers of the status difference between members of both communities, not because of any impurity involved, but because of the clients' dependence on their patrons.

When, however, sitting with Dombo around a *salap* tree drinking and chatting, Dongria will publicly deny that these restrictions carry any relevance. The myth quoted above and collected by Jena et al. ends with the god advising the hunters to pretend they accepted the Dombo's food even if they have not. This reflects the general diplomatic attitude of the Dongria, who will not insist on status differences when Dombo are around. For example, when a Dombo from elsewhere once came to visit our village, he told the Dongria with whom he was drinking that nowadays there are only two castes, the caste of men and the caste of women and nothing else. The Dongria happily agreed. This was certainly due to their idea of polite behaviour but equally due to the context of drinking. Drinking wine from a *salap* tree is an occasion when status differences are denied, except for those between men and women, who never attend these drinking sessions. Dongria will not drink from a cup or gourd touched by a Dombo's lips, but since everybody avoids drinking in this way, this status marker plays no role.

When discussing the topic of eating a Dombo's food in an interview situation, Dongria give different responses. One of my best friends, who also had a ritual friendship with a Dombo of his village, told me that he does not care about any restrictions but will eat food from everybody. Others declined to take food from the Dombo in their village, but expressed their readiness to accept food from everybody in the "plains" (*panga raji*). However, when Dongria travel to the smaller towns or to market towns in the valley, they always take cooked food with them, which they eat somewhere on the way, never in the vicinity of any settlement or market.[20]

At village feasts, Dombo and Dongria always eat together, but everybody considers the Dongria to be the sponsors and cooks, even if the Dombo help by cutting the meat. If the location allows it, all the men will sit more or less in a circle, with the fire and the cooking pots in the centre. However, despite the circular form of the seating arrangement, I often had the impression that Dombo and Dongria behave like two groups facing each other, because the Dombo always sit together in one part of the circle. The Dombo will never serve the Dongria; rather, the young Dongria boys will go around and divide the cooked meat and boiled rice or millet among everybody, including the Dombo. The idea, of course, is that the Dongria give "their" cooked food to the Dombo, not the other way around.

2.4.3 Forbidden women

A third restriction applies to marriage relations. Dongria boys and Dombo girls often joke with one another using language with a clearly sexual content. According to one of my informants, at least half the Dongria boys have slept with a Dombo girl, an estimate that I think is exaggerated. However, such casual sexual relations certainly occur, but are not openly talked about. A Dombo girl who has sexual relations with Dongria men is called Minkawani, "wife of the fishes," a derogatory term that implies that she is promiscuous. Such women sometimes dress like Dongria girls and dance and sing with them.[21] However, if a Dongria falls in love with a Dombo woman and takes her permanently as his consort, he commits a great "mistake" (*dosa*) that will lead to his expulsion from society. In the area where I worked, I heard about two cases in which Dongria entered into permanent liaisons with Leli women, who are regarded as even more inferior than the Dombo. In one case, the Dongria committed suicide due to rejection by his family members; in the other, the man had to leave his village and settle some hundred meters away from the main settlement of another village. If a Dongria takes a woman from a "smaller" caste as his wife, the members of his village will call the *bismajhi* or, according to others, the *mondal*. They watch over the observance of social rules. According to Nayak, the *mondal* can

---

20 But when I invited some Dongria friends to eat with me in the local restaurants, they agreed happily as long as I paid the bill.
21 I am not certain whether these Dombo women also sleep in the girls' dormitory, which is not usually entered by Dombo women.

reintegrate a Kond who marries outside the community by touching his tongue with heated gold. The *mondal* keeps the gold for himself, and the Kond thus reintegrated has to give a feast (Nayak 1989, 181). I have also been told that the *mondal* can expel a Kond who takes a Dombo girl as his wife, probably in the event that he is not willing to give up this relationship. He will perform a ritual to reintegrate the outcaste's household into the clan community. The members of the household then have to provide the village community with a feast. The culprit himself will lose his status as a Dongria and will become a member of the "smaller" caste, just like the children born of this union. I have never heard of any case of a Dombo man taking a Dongria woman as his wife,[22] but I recorded cases of marriages with men from higher castes like Gauda and Brahmin among the Kond in the plains. Again, joking with a Dombo man is allowed for a Dongria woman. I watched for several weeks as Dongria girls tried all their charms on a handsome Leli boy, and nobody talked badly about them or prohibited them from visiting his house.

In a previous section, I showed that the value-ideas structuring the relations between Dombo and Dongria are not exactly the same as those found in "caste society". In this section, I have demonstrated that the forms of segregation nevertheless appear to be quite similar to those found in "caste society". I will now address how interdependence between the segments of society is created and maintained. In what terms do Dongria express the forms of interdependence that exist in the Niamgiri Hills? I will attempt to answer this question by providing ethnographic evidence for the forms of interaction between Dombo and Dongria in different spheres of life. In my view, the forms of interdependence found in the Niamgiri Hills differ markedly from the *jajmani* relationships of "caste society".

2.5 Forms of interdependence

2.5.1 Dombo as generalists

A major difference between the position of "untouchables" in "caste society" and relations between Dombo and their patrons in the Niamgiri Hills is found in the evaluation of their socio-economic relations. Dombo are considered generalists who live by working for others, in contrast to the Dongria who depend

---

[22] Nayak only states in brackets that sometimes "Domb also took away Dongria Kond girls" (Nayak 1989, 181).

only on their own land. Dombo perform various functions that in coastal areas are usually ascribed to members of different castes of higher status. In the past, some Dombo used to work as weavers, a craft they have given up for economic reasons.[23] Nowadays – as in the past – they work as agricultural labourers, some even possessing land themselves. They also deal in various products and work as traders in the market.[24] Many Dombo distil alcohol and sell it to their patrons. Children and younger Dombo often look after their own or their patrons' cows and goats. None of these tasks are mutually exclusive, so the children may herd cattle while the wife goes to the market to trade or helps her husband with agricultural activities if he is not busy distilling alcohol. None of these functions is considered particularly impure, and I never heard a Dongria explaining the Dombo's lower status by reference to impurities involved in their work. For a Dongria, his own status derives from the land he cultivates, the hills given to him by *niamraja*, while a Dombo's lower status stems from the fact that he has to perform various functions for others in order to receive rice or money from them. Thus Watts, who visited the Niamgiri Hills in 1968, states:

> In most Dongaria villages there are three Dom families in residence. They are servants of the Dongarias and treated as such. One acts as a liaison between the Dongarias and the outside world; the second family looks after the cattle; the third are the sweepers of the village. (Watts 1970, 44)

The cultivator is in a direct exchange relationship with the gods: they have given him land that he cultivates. The harvest is a representation of the goddess who nourishes him, and it is his duty to perform the rituals in order to return a gift, either individually for his own land or collectively for the village land. While the Dongria depend on the gods, the Dombo depend on the Dongria. A Dombo has no access to the gifts of the gods, i.e., land and the harvest, except through a Dongria who shares with him, sells him his produce, or gives him rice and food in return for his services.[25] As mentioned above, this logic of relations is not expressed in terms of states of purity and impurity, but in terms of land

---

23 Niggemeyer narrates a myth told by the Kuttia Kond that explains how the Pano (Dombo) became weavers (Niggemeyer 1964a, 15).

24 Another myth collected by Niggemeyer narrates how the Kond once asked the god *nirantalikapantali* for help because they did not know how to find the market. The god advised them to send the Pano to the market on their behalf. If they were to bring buffaloes home from the market themselves, the animals would die on the way (Niggemeyer 1964a, 15).

25 As I will describe below, a major change in this arrangement was introduced by the government when they introduced the idea of private land, which allowed the Dombo to become landowners themselves.

and seniority and by reference to the relationship between kings and their subjects. Without the Dombo, however, Dongria cannot transform their individual products into money (or animals) that may then be given as gifts to affines and gods in order to meet their obligations for reciprocity.

In my analysis of these forms of interdependence, I take into account two important contributions to the understanding of economic transactions in non-industrial societies. The first is Bloch and Parry's insights into the incorporation of monetary economies into local transactional systems linked to particular cultural ideas and values (Parry and Bloch 1989). On the one hand, both authors reject different universalistic conceptions of the inherent "powers" of money. Thus, they argue against notions that the existence of monetary exchange necessarily leads to profound social and cultural transformations threatening the existing moral order. They further question the radical distinction between traditional economies and modern social systems operating with money by pointing to the importance of money in many societies considered "traditional." In particular, they express their doubts that commodity exchange is founded on entirely different principles from the exchange of gifts. On the other hand, they see a recurrent pattern in the transactional systems found in the different cultures dealt with in their book. They identify a pattern of two related but separate transactional orders. They call the first one the "short cycle of exchange," since it is linked to individual competition and reproduction, while the other is referred to as the "long-term cycle of exchange," since it is concerned with collective efforts to uphold the social or cosmic order. Both cycles are linked in many ethnographic instances by procedures that convert goods – or money – derived from the short cycle into objects circulating in the long cycle. My argument here is that the interdependence of the Dongria and Dombo communities is based on this transformation or conversion of agricultural goods into money and gifts accomplished by the Dombo. I further support the authors' doubts about the opposition between gift and commodity exchange by suggesting that these two types of exchanges are identical in their moral aspects and in their opposition to the egalitarian mode of sharing. Monetary transactions and gift exchanges take place between "others" and involve demands and bargaining, while sharing depends on and creates a sense of social unity and forbids any haggling. However, within the Dongria community sharing is often restricted to certain contexts within the wider and more important system of exchanges between "others."

The concept of sharing has received particular attention in the literature dealing with hunter and gatherer societies. Of the existing literature on this topic, I was particularly inspired by those authors dealing with the general principles and values of such societies. Thus, Woodburn identifies in societies of the "immediate return type" strong levelling mechanisms that prevent the accumulation of property and the creation of dependence. Equality in such societies is based on "the ability of the individual to attach and to detach themselves at will from groupings and from relationships, to resist the imposition of authority by force, to use resources freely without reference to other people" (Woodburn 1982, 445). In the case of my field study, I also encountered forms of sharing, which were, however, restricted to certain contexts. The equality expressed in such contexts is different from that described by Woodburn, because it consists in the conscious and situational denial of the demand, bargaining, and reciprocity typical of exchange and gift relations with "others" who belong to a higher or lower status category.

To understand why people in certain contexts stress the idea of sharing, I take into consideration Bird-David's work. Comparing the Nayaka to their neighbours, the Bete and Mullu Kurumba, she overcomes Woodburn's concern with subsistence technology, in particular with agricultural techniques characteristic of "delayed return systems". Looking at ideological conceptions in both societies, Bird-David finds differences in their respective ideas about the environment. She then explains the modes of sharing she finds among the Nayaka, which are also typical for Woodburn's "immediate return systems", in relation to their concept of nature as "parent." Here it is suggested that in those contexts in which Dongria and Dombo alike find themselves obliged to share, the "root metaphor" of the earth as mother and of the bringer of all natural objects as "father" finds its application. However, I would argue that the forces of nature in the Dongria case are not as "undemanding" as among the Nayaka but rather demand a gift in return. Sharing thus appears as a feature of relations among "children" as receivers but not of relations between "parents" and their "children." To substantiate these claims about these particular forms of dependence in Kond society, I will now address the Dombo's different socio-economic activities.

2.5.2 Allocation of land and agricultural cooperation

As will be described in more detail later (see section 3.4.3), the Niamgiri Hills are from the Dongria's perspective[26] divided into clan territories called *muta*. Within

---

[26] The land categories introduced by the land survey and settlement operations of 1961 are quite different from Dongria land categories. For a detailed description of the settlement and its effects see Das Patnaik (1984, 28–32).

such a territory, the members of the dominant clan[27] have rights to the land of the mountain ranges or valleys belonging to a particular village. For example, a Sikoka *muta* consists of a certain number of villages mainly inhabited by members of the Sikoka clan, and each of these Sikoka villages has its own territory, called *padari*. In former times, such village land could be sold as a whole to Dongria belonging to different clans or a different *muta*, who thereby acquired collective rights to the land and all its produce. After buying the land, the new owners would start acting as organisers of the *kodru parbu* (buffalo sacrifice; see chapter 5) and purchase the buffalo to be sacrificed to the earth goddess.

The members of the dominant clan in a village divide the land among themselves. The rights to particular stretches of land are passed down by inheritance from a father to his sons. When approached by others, these right-holders will share their land. These others may be Dongria of a different clan or Dombo who settle in the village. For example, there were several Dongria households in Gumma not belonging to the dominant Sikoka clan. Their forefathers had built houses in the village, usually in the context of marrying a daughter of the village and taking up uxorilocal residence after marriage. Further, the village presently has four Dombo households, two of which were actively engaged in shifting cultivation in the recent past. These two households were given land on a mountain slope when the Dongria of the village decided to cultivate a neighbouring valley three years prior to my fieldwork. The Dombo engaged Dongria men to cut down the forest and then began to prepare the ground, sow the seeds, and weed the fields. The other two households did not demand any land, because in one case the household consisted of an old woman incapable of taking care of a swidden, and in the other case the man earned his living as a trader and *barika* for the village. During the last year of my fieldwork, the two other households also gave up their agricultural activities. In one household, a woman with two daughters fell sick, and since she had no husband, she could no longer take care of the fields. Her elder son moved from his wife's village to her village, along with his family, but he showed no interest in helping his mother tend her fields. Her neighbour met a similar fate when her husband left her a year ago and she remained alone with her children, unable to continue her work in the swidden. Both families nowadays depend on income from their trading activities, which I will describe below.

---

27 By dominant clan I mean the clan that is considered to "own" the village land and has the right and duty to buy the buffalo to be sacrificed to the earth goddess. Within the village, members of this clan normally form the majority and make up the village council.

The Dombo help the Dongria in their swidden fields in the context of a particular institution for mutual help called *bati kam* (or sometimes *buti kam*). For very time-consuming work like cutting down the forest or weeding the fields, each household can ask the village community for help. For a whole day, either the boys or the girls or at least one person from each household works in the swidden of a particular family. Assistance from the boys (*dangananga buti*) will be demanded for cutting trees, removing bushes, or setting fire to the dry wood, while women and girls (*daaska buti*) will be employed in weeding. Sometimes all the households may form one collective work group (*kutumba buti*) representing the whole village, for example when preparing the village shaman's swidden. A further type is the collective work of a group formed on the basis of mutual agreement. Such a group (*punda buti*) will consist of a number of households who agree to help somebody with a given task. For other types of *buti* work, the person will not make the arrangement himself but will approach the village chief and ask him to assemble the boys or girls in his swidden on a specific day. On this day, his wife will cook enough food to feed the helpers at midday, and in addition, the family will pay a nominal amount of money, normally twenty rupees for a full day of work. This amount is very small in comparison to the payment for contract work, which is about forty rupees per person per day, an indication that the work is not performed in order to earn money. On the other hand, it is also not a free service. When several households have made use of this institution, and enough money has accumulated, a buffalo will be bought, slaughtered, and shared by the whole village at a feast. The Dombo are included, because they earned a right to a share by participating in the village work. If somebody assembles a particular work group (*punda buti*), he will either pay them the nominal amount of twenty rupees, or if the work extends over a long period of time, he will agree to buy a buffalo and hand it over to this group at the end of their work. A Dombo may also make use of this collective help from his co-villagers. For example, one Dombo from Gumma gave a buffalo to seventeen households for preparing his swidden for cultivation. The possibility of asking for collective help is not restricted to agriculture. The village leader of Gumma once needed rice for his big-men feast, and he asked the girls of the village, including the Dombo, to help him carry the rice he bought in the plains to his house. For this *buti kam* he paid twenty rupees to the girls' fund. When Dongria recently started building new houses with the help of development funds, one of them asked a group of co-villagers to assist him in making the bricks, a task that took several weeks. When the work was finished, he remunerated them with a buffalo.

Sometimes, either the whole village or a few people agree to do a certain task classed as *kuli kam* for the Dombo or the government. This kind of work, which includes thatching a roof, digging up turmeric, and building a road, for example, is paid per person in money, the sum being agreed upon in advance. If many people will be involved in such a task, it may also be agreed to give the "employees" buffaloes as a payment. A Dongria will not perform any work falling into this category of *kuli kam* for any other Dongria, but instead only for outsiders.

A third type of assistance is work-sharing, which is always remunerated in kind, not in money. When, for example, a Dongria is reaping his harvest, others may "join" (*adina*) him and receive a share of the harvest, which is calculated in baskets of grain. I have personally never seen Dombo "joining" Dongria in reaping, but I also did not ask whether there were any rules against it. A similar idea of work-sharing is practised when threshing the harvest, a task that can hardly be done by a single household and requires the help of several people. Dombo often assist Dongria in threshing their harvest and later join the feast given by the swidden's owner in the context of the harvest ritual. In exchange for their help, they have a right to a specific share of the harvest consisting of the grain that sticks to the straw after threshing. Mutual assistance structures the composition of groups that help each other in thatching houses. These small groups are constituted on the basis of kinship, neighbourhood, or friendship. The owner of the house has to provide his helpers with food and alcohol, but no payment is required. These groups, however, exclude the Dombo, because the Dongria do not allow Dombo to climb on the roofs of their houses, since the attic (*papi, atu*) and the central beam (*tudi*) are places where the house gods reside. Dombo can thus be seen employing Dongria to thatch their roofs, but not vice versa.

Dombo are included in almost all institutions of mutual help on the village level. Their status prohibits them from participating in mutual services only in the context of thatching houses, not any other activities. They may be "employers" as well as "employees" in the context of *kuli kam*, and they may both ask for collective help called *buti kam* and provide such help.

2.5.3 Wet rice cultivation and individual property

While few Dombo are engaged in shifting cultivation, many cultivate wet rice and dry fields if these are available in their area. Dry fields and land used for wet rice cultivation have been privatised as part of land settlement operations by the government since 1961 (Das Patnaik 1984, 28–32) and can be owned by individuals. Dombo were excluded from the settlement, i.e., they did not receive any land in their names. The hill slopes, which Dongria refer to as *horu* and which are categorised as "reserved forest" by the government, should technically not be used for agriculture. However, since the forest guards do not visit these areas and no one enforces the law, the locals continue to treat it as their clan land, and nobody has interfered so far.

The general impression of people from the plains coming to visit the Niamgiri Hills is that the Dongria are "lazy folk", because they do not convert flat land into cultivable rice fields.[28] For example, Gumma was once visited by a group of Lanjia Soara from Ganjam district who were engaged by the DKDA to build a school. Lanjia Soara are experts in rice cultivation, and they were obviously shocked by the Dongria's "primitiveness," pointing out all the places with ideal conditions for constructing rice fields. In some of these places, rice fields had in fact been built, but Dongria do not put much effort into rice cultivation, using only very simple methods and spending only as much time as necessary on sowing, weeding, and harvesting. The situation is different in areas where there is less hill land but wide stretches of flat land for dry or wet cultivation, and where there is usually a higher concentration of Dombo than anywhere else in the hills. There is no reason to believe that this is a new development. According to Das Patnaik, the leader of each *muta*, the *mondal*, allowed the Dombo in his clan territory to use the flat land for cultivation. The Dombo contributed to the revenue collected for the king, and trouble only started when, acting according to the land settlement, Dongria claimed "their land" from the Dombo who had been using it on the basis of individual friendship relations (Das Patnaik 1984, 27, 30). In other words, Dongria always farmed in the hills, considered the abode of the gods, while Dombo were given the flat land at the foot of the hills where the cremation ground, the abode of the dead, is found.

In the area of my research, I found the following arrangements between Dombo and Dongria. If wet or dry fields were available, some were cultivated by Dongria on their own or in cooperation with a Dombo. For example, two brothers who were referred to as the Naika[29] of the village own a field in a neighbouring valley used for wet rice cultivation. Two years before the time of my fieldwork, they cultivated these rice fields along with two related Dongria households and divided the harvest with them. A year later, a young Dombo moved into the village with his family, and since he was a hard and experienced worker, he was asked to join the group and later received an equal share of the harvest. The rice fields were officially owned by one Dongria from the dominant clan, but

---

28 According to Das Patnaik, out of twenty plot owners in the Kurli area, only eight have taken up paddy cultivation systematically. The income from paddy cultivation has been decreasing (Das Patnaik 1984, 30).

29 This title was probably given to them in the context of the king's revenue system.

since he did not want to do the work alone, he shared the work and harvest with others, Dongria and Dombo. On the day the rice was brought to the threshing ground, each household that had participated in the work received an equal share of the harvest. A heap of rice was set aside, and each household from the village could come and ask for one basket of grain. This "sharing" cannot be compared to the division of the grain heap in the *jajmani* system, because those who received a basket of grain had not performed any functions for the landowner, and nobody expected any reciprocity.

A second, more common arrangement I came across was based on rent. For example, a person from the village I lived in owned a stretch of rice fields but was not interested in cultivating them at all. Instead, he gave the land on lease to a Dombo from a different village for the small sum of Rs 500 for a period of five years.[30] In this case, the fields were cultivated by the Dombo, and apart from the rent, he did not owe anything to the Dongria. However, one Dombo told me that his family living in the Muniguda area holds land given to them by the Kond for cultivation and that his brothers were expected to offer a goat and rice as a counter-gift to their patrons at the time of the *kodru parbu* (buffalo sacrifice), which is held in order to worship the earth goddess.

The third arrangement was mentioned only by the government officials working in the area. They claimed that vast areas of cultivable land were taken away from the Dongria by the Dombo. According to law, only tribal people can own land in this area, and ownership is proven by certificates (*pota*), one copy of which is kept by the tribal landowner and another by the revenue department. If a Dongria falls into debt or urgently needs cash, he can mortgage his plot or agree to transfer his land certificate to a Dombo, who will then bribe the revenue officers to sanction this transfer by writing the Dombo's name on the certificate. Particularly in the less inaccessible areas around Kalyansingpur, some Dombo are said to have accumulated significant wealth due to this practise.

To summarise: in contrast to the swidden fields in the hill forest, wet rice fields and dry fields are considered individual property and can be rented out or sold. Dongria put all their effort into swidden cultivation on the hill slopes belonging to their village and given to them by their ancestors. They will perform the most time-consuming agricultural labour with their whole family and practically throughout the whole year. Only when time allows do they pay attention to wet rice fields. Since they use very simple methods, the harvest is very small, but

---

30 When a Dongria leases his land to a Dombo, this is called *kada taki praca maneyu* ("for rent he sells it").

even then, the work and the harvest are divided and shared with the village. Dombo, on the other hand, try to rent or buy these fields wherever they are available. They are most numerous where good conditions for this kind of agriculture exist, and in these areas their main work is agriculture. If nothing else is available, they will also join the Dongria in shifting cultivation, but not on a long-term basis. As soon as other opportunities arise, they will neglect the swidden and start another enterprise.

2.5.4 Small village traders and influential urban dealers

In the Niamgiri Hills we encounter two kinds of "market" centres. One is found in the small towns (*gada*) in the valleys, such as Bissamcuttack, Lanjigada, Muniguda, and Kalyansingpur, with tea stalls, small restaurants, shops offering everything from clothing to jewellery, and street vendors selling vegetables and fish. Some of the shops specialise in trading products produced by the Dongria, with whom they maintain long-standing business relations. Economic transactions between the shop owners and the mountain dwellers usually take place in town or somewhere in the foothills. For example, one Telugu trader from Kalyansingpur owns a shop on the main street of Kalyansingpur where he and his family sell rice, millet, lentils, spices, sugar, salt, oil, etc., but he can frequently be seen riding his motorbike into the hills as far as the first Dongria village (Patalamba), which is still accessible by road. At the entrance to the village, he keeps a large scale on which he measures the products brought to him. He either buys these products for money or barters rice for them. The advantage for the Dongria and Dombo selling their products is that they do not have to carry their heavy loads all the way to town. The trader, on the other hand, has the advantage of controlling all the products coming from the hills and only has to arrange for transport.

The second type of market is the weekly market (*hata*) held in various villages in the foothills, such as Majhiguda, Chatikona, and Tirumui, and in some of the towns mentioned above, such as Muniguda and Lanjigada.[31] These markets closely resemble the one in Bastar district (Madhya Pradesh) described by Alfred Gell (1982). As in Bastar, such markets are divided between stallholders and open market traders, the latter sometimes including dealers in livestock such as cattle, buffaloes, goats, and chickens. These markets are con-

---

31 Kalyansingpur and Bissamcuttack do not have their own weekly markets, probably because there are important market places such as Majhiguda and Chatikona nearby.

ducted in a festive, almost ceremonial mood and offer an opportunity for amusement and entertainment. Gell's interpretation that such markets provide a ground plan for group relations, a hierarchy of goods, and a reference for time similarly holds for the markets mentioned above. If, however, we compare the different markets around the Niamgiri Hills, it becomes clear that they differ in size and in the exact types of transactions taking place. For example, the market in Tirumui was only initiated a year before my fieldwork and is rather small in size, consisting of only a dozen shops. The traders are mainly interested in buying certain products from the Dongria, such as lentils, castor beans, and jackfruit seeds, while only a few traders offer items sought by the Dongria, such as vegetables, tobacco, and cheap jewellery. This is in contrast to the large and important market in Majhiguda, attended by people from all over the region and sometimes even visited by foreign tourists.[32] Here, government officials, rich storeowners from the district capital, and sellers from all castes can be found, including the Dombo, who mostly deal in cattle and other livestock. Dongria do not generally attend the markets as sellers. Only on very rare occasions did I see one or two Dongria men sitting on the ground at the market, looking rather insecure and selling what the government calls "minor forest produce." Taking into account Gell's observation that a market is "a compendium of social relations" (Gell 1982, 480) and "serves very much as a ground plan of inter-group relations" (Gell 1982, 483–84) expressed by the seating arrangement of the various sellers, this behaviour can be used as a good illustration of the Dongria's relation to the dominant culture of the plains; the fact that Dongria do not sit in the market can be seen as an indication that they are socially and spatially not a part of this society, but their participation in its economic relations also shows that they are not fully independent of it. The Dongria are not given a fixed place in the market (or society), or from their point of view, they do not want to take up such a position. They come and go as they please and cannot easily be fitted into the scheme of "hierarchical relations" (Gell 1982, 483) exhibited at the market.

Trade in the Dongria's products in the hills ideally involves two different communities. In the villages, the Dombo buy the products of the land from the Dongria and carry these to the nearest town. In town, the village Dombo will sometimes sell the products to another Dombo but more often to a Komti. The Komti (or Kumti) are a Telugu caste renowned for their trading skills. They

---

32 Another market, Chatikona, is also regularly visited on market days (Wednesday) by tourists participating in tribal tours. These tours are mostly organised by travel agencies in Bhubaneswar and can be booked via internet. The tourists come mostly with the intention of taking pictures of the "exotic" Dongria.

are considered to be of lower status than the Dombo, but they do not live in the mountains. Instead, they reside in small cities in the foothills, like Bissamcuttack, Chatikona, and Kalyansingpur, where they have their own shops or act as moneylenders (Sahukar).[33] Niggemeyer narrates a myth that explains the origin of this arrangement and the financial inequality between the Dombo and the Komti:

> A Kuttia, a Pano, an Oriya, and a Komati went to Nirantali-Kapantali and said, "We do not have anything to eat. What shall we do?" Nirantali-Kapantali gave fields to the Kuttia and seeds of all kinds and beans such as castor beans for sowing and planting. She commanded the Oriya to rule and reign over the Kuttia and Pano. The Pano and Komati she asked to come again the next day. On the next day she gave a pot for measuring four *ser* to the Pano and said, "With this pot you will measure the Kuttia's grain and make your profit." To the Komati she gave a bamboo pole for carrying the goods. But the Komati stole the pot for measuring from the Pano. The Pano became angry and complained, but Nirantali-Kapantali said, "What can I do? You take the bamboo pole and do your business. Make your deals with the Kuttia and carry those things you bought from him to the Komati and sell them to him. If he had not stolen the measuring pot, he would have carried these things. Now it is the other way around." (Niggemeyer 1964a, 16; my translation)

In which products do these traders deal? The major cash crop in this area is turmeric (*hinga / merka*), which is nowadays provided on a large scale by the government. Some years ago, the government started a programme through their development agency (DKDA) supplying each household with two hundred kilograms of turmeric rhizomes free of cost.[34] The Dongria plant the turmeric rhizomes in small fields on their hill slopes and dig them up after a period of two years.[35] Turmeric cultivation is not very intensive work except for the fact that the fields must be cleared of all roots, something the Dongria do not do in their regular fields.[36] When a Dongria is in urgent need of cash, he will sell the whole

---

33 This system of transactions between Kond, Dombo, and Komti has been previously described by the Orissa District Gazetteers: "During hard months, the tribal people particularly the Soaras and the Khonds get loans from the Sahukars who are mostly the Kumuti businessmen or the Sundhi (wine sellers) through the Dombs. The money-lenders who are but casual visitors to tribal villages come in direct contact with the Dombs and transact through them" (Senapati and Sahu 1966, 203).
34 The DKDA provides two hundred kilograms for free and buys the harvest back after cultivation at fixed rates. These rates are going down, decreasing during the period of my research from five to four rupees per kilogram.
35 It is generally believed that the yield is seven to one.
36 It is my impression that in the long run, intensive turmeric cultivation will destroy the forest much faster than the local practise of shifting cultivation, because once the roots are taken out,

Photo 3: Heap of turmeric rhizomes in a Dongria village

field to a Dombo for a price lower than what the Dombo will receive when he later sells the crop back to the government. In addition to the amount given for the field, the Dombo will have to pay the Dongria to dig up the turmeric. If a large part of or even the whole village is involved in digging up the turmeric, the Dombo will give them one or two buffaloes as compensation (*kuli kodru* or "labour buffalo"). The Dombo will boil and dry the fresh rhizomes and carry them to town to sell them.

Dombo living in Dongria villages also trade in bananas, oranges, pineapples, and castor beans. Most Dongria keep only those bananas that they can cook for consumption and give the rest to the Dombo, who carry the bunches to the local shop owners. The lowest segment of each bunch is given to the Dombo as their profit (*laba*). The Dongria calculate one rupee for four bananas, while the Dombo receive one rupee for two or three bananas from the shop owners. Normally the Dongria selling his bananas will not accept money but will ask the Dombo for alcohol, which he then shares with everybody present. In this way, the Dombo makes a double profit, and the Dongria raises his status as a generous man.

---

the forest will not recover. In the Kambesi area I already saw wide stretches of land without forest, overgrown by a particular grass.

Oranges and pineapples, which are not eaten by Dongria, were introduced on a large scale by the DKDA, but in contrast to banana plantations, these plantations are less successful and profitable. In some areas, Dongria have given up pineapple cultivation completely, because the plants are eaten by porcupines. If the harvest is successful, the Dongria carry the fruit to town themselves, because they will make a larger profit by selling the fruit on their own than by giving it to the local Dombo. The Dombo from the plains will wait on the road to town in order to buy the pineapples for a slightly lower price, and sometimes Dongria agree because they need cash to buy alcohol in a nearby Dombo house. The same happens with oranges, but because Dongria leave the trees almost unattended, the harvest is usually so small that trading in oranges has almost no economic importance. Castor beans are grown by Dongria in large quantities in their swiddens and are then carried to local markets, where they are either sold (*prana*) or exchanged (*patela kina*) for rice.

While the local Dombo formerly acted as middlemen in this trade, the Dongria nowadays carry their products to the markets and towns themselves, where they sell their products to businessmen, mostly Komti. The same happens with brooms (*bedunika*) made by the Dongria from grass. Both the grass itself, which Dongria collect on their hill slopes, and the ready-made brooms are exchanged with the local Dombo for money or alcohol, but the majority of the brooms will be bought by a trader from the plains, usually a Dombo or a Komti. A village will often collectively sell its brooms to one trader – a Dombo but more often a Komti – from the nearest market town for a fixed price. Other crops, such as pigeon peas, arrowroot, and chillies, are always sold or exchanged for rice by the Dongria directly, without the help of the local Dombo. This means that those making the largest profits from trading with the Dongria are living in the market towns in the plains, mostly the Komti, and not the Dombo living in the Niamgiri Hills. Some Dombo from the plains are also involved in small-scale trade, travelling through the hills carrying dried fish, tomatoes, or sweets. These they exchange for cow peas or dried tamarind.

According to Niggemeyer, the Pano not only sell the Kond's products, but also buy items such as salt, tobacco, pots, baskets, cheap jewellery, cloth, and modern industrial products in the markets and resell them to the Kond in the villages (Niggemeyer 1964a, 16). This is not – perhaps no longer – the case in the Niamgiri Hills, because the Dongria go either to the markets or to the smaller towns and buy these things themselves. Sometimes Ghasi come into the mountains to sell pots or exchange new ones for old, but usually Dongria buy new cooking pots or pots for storing water when they visit the valleys and plains, in particular at the time of major Hindu temple festivals. Niggemeyer reports that the Kuttia at the time of his fieldwork were familiar with coins but not with notes and most often paid the Pano in kind and not in cash (Niggemeyer 1964a, 16–17). Dongria nowadays can recognise all kinds of money including notes and, except for a few old men, are all able to count and calculate with money. This is of course the basic prerequisite for a certain kind of independence from the Dombo in market affairs.

Dombo and in particular the Komti are making a good profit, either by buying things for lower prices than they sell them for or by exchanging products of a low market value, for example rice, onions, or tomatoes, for products of higher value. Dongria accept this for two main reasons. First, they say that Dombo live by eating "profit" (*laba*), while Dongria live from the products of their land. Second, the Dongria accept this arrangement because rice and certain vegetables are not available in abundance in the hills. Generally, Dongria will prefer to barter when they are in need of food, while they will prefer to sell their products when they need money, for three purposes: first, to buy items linked to what Dongria consider enjoyment and pleasure, such as alcohol, meat, tobacco, and cheap jewellery; second, to purchase sacrificial animals for the performance of important rituals; and third, to pay the often very high price for a son's wife.

Dombo will spend much less for the first two purposes, at the same time that they may also accumulate money for marriages, which will go to the husband's side. However, in contrast to Dongria, Dombo will use most of their money for reinvestment in their businesses. Some of them are very successful in their business undertakings, which get their start by trading with the Dongria but can extend to other enterprises, for example buying land or becoming a moneylender (Sahukar). Nowadays, one of the highest achievements a Dombo or Komti can strive for is to transform his money into political influence by getting elected to the local government. As can be expected from the economic chances of a Dombo from the hills compared to Dombo or Komti from the valleys and plains, the really successful traders live in or near the major towns. Apart from shifting, wet rice, or dry field cultivation, the Dombo living in a Dongria village has two further ways to make an income. One is the selling of locally produced alcohol, and the other is trading in animals.

2.5.5 Sharing and selling of alcohol

The main type of alcohol is made from the fruit of the *mohula* tree, which ripens between March and May. The trees grow everywhere in the mountains but usually not in large numbers. Early in the morning, Dombo and Dongria will go to these trees, which are not owned by anybody in particular, to gather the fruit from the ground, take it home, and dry it in baskets on their roofs. Once it is dried, the Dongria will sell it to the local Dombo, who store it in their houses. If they run out of dried fruit, they can buy it in the towns, where it is heavily mixed with chemicals for preservation and sold for comparatively high prices. From time to time, the Dombo will ferment the fruit with water and a local starter (*kara*) and take the mixture to a stream for distillation, which takes about two hours. This work should be done by men, but if no men are available in the household, a woman is allowed to do the task. After distillation, a Dombo will sell the alcohol to the Dongria at his home by the bottle (*kanch*), while the Dombo themselves usually abstain from drinking distilled alcohol. A second type of alcohol made in this way is produced from sugarcane molasses (*gudu*) that the Dombo buy in the market by the kilogram. The amount of alcohol produced varies from village to village. Some of the more populous Dombo villages are renowned as places where alcohol can be bought every day. Dongria will visit these places to buy alcohol for ceremonial occasions or when "thirsty" following a trip to the market or a distant village. Dombo in less accessible villages, like the one I lived in, usually make alcohol only on the eve of a village feast or when they have no other source of income. The amount of money that can be earned from distilling and selling alcohol is hardly enough to feed a family if there are no other sources of income. For example, if the Dombo have to buy dried *mohula* fruit, they will have to pay three to five rupees per kilogram. One pot of fermented fruit contains around ten kilograms, so the Dombo's expenses will be either thirty to fifty rupees or nothing if he collects the fruit himself. Through the process of distillation the Dombo will produce between twenty and twenty-five bottles of alcohol, which he sells for ten rupees per bottle. The profit of one distillation process will therefore be around Rs 200 to 250 minus the cost of buying the fruit. If there is no feast or any other occasion for which alcohol is needed, however, it may take days before the Dombo is able to sell his product. Making alcohol from sugarcane molasses will allow him to make a similar profit. One kilogram costs fifteen rupees in the market. If a Dombo spends Rs 200 on molasses, he can make a profit of around the same amount by distilling alcohol from it. When the mangoes ripen, Dombo also make alcohol by distilling fermented mango juice. This raw material is free, but the amount of alcohol gained from distillation is relatively small. To increase the amount, Dombo mix the alcohol with water. Another reason the alcohol made from mangoes is not a very lucrative source of income is the widespread availability of fruit alcohol at this time of the year, when apart from mangoes, jackfruit also ripen. Almost every Dongria household is then engaged in distilling alcohol from its own fruit, and the need for them to buy it from the Dombo is minimal.

The status difference between both communities is made very explicit with reference to alcohol. A Dongria who distils alcohol will share a part of the product with the people present at the distillation site in the forest, then carry the rest to his house, where he drinks it together with family members or close friends. This is done more or less secretly, because everyone who enters the house at the time of drinking can expect a share. A Dombo, on the other hand, will also share part of the product at the forest distillation site, but will then take it home to sell it to others. Dongria often say that they would never sell fruit alcohol, because otherwise they would be like Dombo. What they mean is that they would never sell it to other Dongria, but they may sell their share to the Dombo if they are in urgent need of money.

The same idea about sharing and selling exists concerning palm wine (*mada kalu*). Palm-wine trees are owned by Dongria and Dombo. While the Dongria inherit these trees from their parents who planted the seeds, the Dombo buy the trees from those Dongria who already possess many.[37] A Dongria owning a tree will always share the alcoholic sap with everybody present. A Dombo owning a tree will also be obliged to share some of it with the people who come and wait under the tree while he or a Dongria authorised by him cuts the inflorescence. But if the flow of sap from the tree is strong, he can retain a portion for himself, which he may sell or share with others in his village. In certain months, when palm sap is available in great amounts, Dombo sometimes make an agreement with one or two Dongria from a particular village. The Dongria will sell a certain amount of sap either every day or on the eve of certain festivals to the Dombo, who will come in the morning with a canister to collect it. The Dombo will then carry the sap to his own village or to a village where a festival is taking place and sell it to the Dongria. I once witnessed a young Dongria from a village selling the sap to an old Dombo woman, who then resold it to other Dongria boys in the presence of the original owner. The Dombo woman earned approximately double the amount she paid to the Dongria boy, but the boy would never have sold the alcohol to the other Dongria himself.

2.5.6 Dombo as traders and herders of animals

A second source of income for the village Dombo is trading in animals and their skins and horns. This is often considered the work of the *barika*, whose functions I will describe later. For various festivals and ceremonies, Dongria need animals

---

37 A tree is sold for about fifty to one hundred rupees.

as sacrificial victims. These are bought by Dombo at local markets (*hat*) in the plains. In such places, people from all castes assemble to trade various things, but the animal market is always dominated by Dombo who come to sell buffaloes, cattle, and goats. A Dombo from a Dongria village will mostly be interested in buying old buffaloes that can no longer be used for ploughing and are, therefore, relatively cheap, in the range of Rs 900 to Rs 1,300. These are sought by Dongria for village feasts and gifts to their affines. He will rarely buy goats and never chickens, because these animals are also available in the hills, where he can often buy them for cheaper prices and with less effort than at the market, which is several hours walking distance from his village.

A Dombo will usually go to a market where he is well known and, therefore, will not be bothered by the police. Once a Dombo from Gumma went to a market different from the one he usually visited for buying animals. There he faced problems with the police because he had no bill of sale (*rasida*). When dealing in cattle and buffaloes, the dealers need to issue bills listing the names of the buyer and seller as well as the price, sex, colour, and appearance of the animal, and the purchaser must carry this bill with him. Normally, neither buyer nor seller can read or write, and since they usually want to save the costs of hiring a professional writer who offers his services at the market, they mostly settle the deal without any paperwork. In this case, the Dombo was not well known in the marketplace, and the police stopped him, asked for his bills, and since he had none, put him in jail on suspicion of theft. It took him several hours and a bribe of Rs 1,000 before he was released.

On the eve of a feast or marriage ceremony, the Dongria will ask a Dombo to buy a buffalo, and he will go to the market to try to find a bargain. A Dombo who regularly trades in animals usually has a fixed number of villages as his clientele, and if other Dombo try to sell animals in his area, a serious quarrel or even a fight between them is assured. At the market, he will usually buy more buffaloes than required if cheap animals are available, because there is a constant need and he can be certain of selling them in the near future. If he buys too many, however, he will have two problems, first that of taking them into the hills and second that of herding and looking after them once they are in the village.

On the day of the feast or before leaving the village to visit his affines, the Dongria will call the Dombo to the village plaza. The Dombo will bring the buffalo with him, and the Dongria will start inspecting it, making comments on how thin and weak it looks. One of the influential Dongria of the village, usually a village elder, will ask the Dombo to name a price, and then the bargaining starts. The Dombo will keep the price for which he bought the animal secret, but Dongria are experienced enough to estimate it correctly. The Dombo will appeal to the Dongria's generosity by saying that he has to feed his children or that he has no rice of his own but has to buy it with money. He will be less demanding if he has two or three buffaloes to sell in other villages, knowing that his efforts will yield enough profit. Because the Dombo can sell the buffalo's hide to Muslim traders ("Pathan") in town, he may reduce the price if the Dongria promise not to mutilate the hide when killing the buffalo. A reduction of about Rs 200 will be calculated for the hide, but often the Dongria boys cannot resist slaughtering the buffalo by hacking it into pieces, a way of killing that is considered particularly joyful. The buffalo's horns will not be included in the price. They belong to the Dombo, who will sell them for five rupees apiece in town. From what I witnessed, the parties will finally agree on an amount that is between Rs 150 and Rs 300 more than the price for which the Dombo bought the animal. A Dongria elder will give ten rupees or a stone to the Dombo as a sign that the deal is settled and nobody else can buy the buffalo.

The money will be collected by the Dombo himself. If the buffalo was bought for a village feast, the Dombo will calculate the number of participating households and divide the amount accordingly. Every morning after sunrise, he will stand on the village plaza and demand the outstanding debts, but it often takes weeks before he has collected the money from everybody. In the event that a single person bought the buffalo as an affinal gift or for a death ceremony, the Dombo will from time to time visit his house and demand the money. Often, he will not be paid all at once but will be given small amounts each time he comes. A Dombo (and *barika*) of the village in which I lived once explained to me that the Dongria owed him an amount of money totalling Rs 32,000. Since he was illiterate, he had to keep all the sums in his mind and be an expert in mental arithmetic. He stressed the reliability of the Dongria, who may pay with a delay but will eventually always clear their debts. He contrasted this with the attitude of people from his own community, who in the event of his death would not pay their debts to his wife, whereas the Dongria would honour their obligations.

The demand for cattle is lower than the demand for buffaloes, because they are not given as gifts to affines[38] and are sacrificed only on rare occasions. Dongria buy cattle for varying reasons. If they buy an animal collectively, they intend to sacrifice it to the goddess protecting the village (*yatra kudi*). If they buy one individually, they may either use it for a sacrifice to a violent ghost (*marha*), keep it as a kind of security they can convert to cash in times of need, or use it for ploughing and threshing. When Dongria use their cattle as a kind of finan-

---

38 Desia Kond give cattle as part of the gifts to the bride's kin.

cial security, it may happen that one animal is sold back and forth between the same two owners. Whenever a Dongria needs cash, he sells the animal to a Dombo, only to buy it back again when he has enough money. In the area of my research, only a few Dongria owned wet rice fields and dry fields, but several families kept cattle for ploughing and threshing on their affines' fields in another village. Such cattle cost between Rs 1,000 and Rs 2,000 and are often bought in pairs. Possessing cattle is a status marker, and a person's wealth is sometimes expressed by reference to the number of cattle he owns. Dombo also keep cattle, sometimes even buffaloes, for ploughing and threshing on fields located in the valleys, either their own fields or those of close consanguinal kin. At the time of ploughing and again at the time of harvest, they take their cattle to the village and keep them there until the work is over. They also sacrifice cattle at the time of their major festival, the *dipawali* ceremony in the month of *karttika*. While Dombo milk their cows for their own consumption, Dongria do not, because they do not drink milk. In comparison to the Kond in the valleys, Dongria appear to be rather inexperienced in keeping cattle, and they do not feel a particular affection for their animals. They are not experienced in breeding, and I had the impression that many cows died due to lack of proper care. Dombo, on the other hand, know how to keep and treat cattle. If an animal is injured or has to be castrated, for example, Dongria will bring it to the local Dombo for treatment.

Apart from buffaloes and cattle, Dombo also deal in goats, which are kept by Dongria for financial security and for ritual purposes, in particular for sacrifices to the house gods. Since the amount of meat is small in relation to the high price of a goat, goats are never slaughtered for village feasts. The demand for goats is therefore limited, and they are sold only if the owner is in need of urgent cash. Cattle as well as goats are looked after by the young boys of the village, Dongria and Dombo alike. Each boy is assigned to care for animals belonging to one or two households, and if he is a Dombo, the household will provide him with cooked food (*gandi kahpe*) twice a day, in the morning and in the evening. Once seeds have been sown in the fields and on the hill slopes, the boys take the animals into the forest and keep them away from the areas of cultivation. When the harvest is over, they stop herding the animals and let them roam freely.

Trading in animals is one of the main sources of income of the *barika*, the most respected Dombo at the village level.

2.5.7 *Barika:* Village trader, arbitrator, messenger, and politician

The term *barika* means "barber" in Oriya, but the person who bears this title is not at all associated with a barber's functions. He always belongs to the Dombo caste and may be responsible for one or more villages. If the village is very big and factions exist among the Dombo, the duties of a *barika* may also be shared by two persons.[39] If the villages are small or the *barika* is very influential, one Dombo may be responsible for three or four villages. For example, in the village I lived in, one Dombo was officially recognised as the *barika* for three villages with a total of seventy-nine (34+26+19) Dongria households and additionally provided sacrificial animals for a fourth village without being acknowledged as its *barika*.

The position of *barika* is not hereditary and must be confirmed once a year. In the month of *phalgun*, at the time of the *ambadadi* festival,[40] a Dombo will be acknowledged as the *barika* of the villages for which he works. He has to give a buffalo to each village, as well as one *mana* (around four kilograms) of rice for cooking the sacrificial food (*bana paga*) offered to the gods. If he neglects this duty, or if the Dongria accept a buffalo from somebody else, he loses his position as *barika*. The Dongria consider this festival and the giving of the buffalo by the *barika* as the beginning of the new year. A second obligation of the *barika* is to give one buffalo to the villages he is responsible for at the time of *dipawali*, when the Dombo worship their ancestors. The buffalo will be slaughtered outside the village where the *barika* resides, and representatives of all the villages he works for will come and take away their respective share. On the day of the *dasera* festival, the *barika* will go to each house in the villages he works for, together with his wife and children carrying large baskets, and ask for his share (*gandi*). He will be given bananas and cooked rice. Every day, he sends his children to the local chief's house to ask for gruel (*dare kahpe*). After harvest, he has the

---

39 As in the village of Phakeri with its sixty households, for example, where two *barika* divide their responsibilities according to the two rows of houses.
40 This festival is also the occasion for cancelling or renewing two other contracts. The first is the contract with a labourer (*halia*) who works for a certain household for a whole year. A Dombo can hire another Dombo, a Dongria somebody from his own community. The labourer receives food and clothing, sleeps on the veranda of his master's house, and does all work assigned to him by his master. The second is the contract with the Dombo who herd cattle for a certain household, which is renewed on the day of this festival.

Photo 4: Dombo *barika* and his wife

right to demand a share of the harvest, usually one basket (*mana*) from each house.⁴¹

A *barika* has the following functions:

---

41 Banerjee reports that in the Kuwi Kond village he studied near Rayagada, the *barika* is given an earthen pot by the village headmen when he first takes up his post. With this pot he goes to every house in the village to ask for gruel, which is given in return for his services. Further, the *barika* has a right to "one full measure of a winnowing fan, of all the articles grown by them, namely, paddy, mandia, *kandala* and *kassala* which is sufficient for him and his family to pull on for a year apart from the paddy fields he had on his own possession" (Banerjee 1969, 104).

1. If a meeting (*bereni kina*) has to be held because of a dispute or an urgent collective task, he wakes up the important Dongria men and asks them to assemble at the village plaza. He leads the discussion and announces the decisions. When it is considered necessary to summon a person not present at the meeting, the *barika* will go to summon him or her.
2. He buys everything needed for the performance of collective festivals, in particular the sacrificial animals, but in some villages also other items like alcohol, pots, or baskets. He decides where to store the items and what to do with them. He collects the money for all expenditures related to festivals.
3. He settles disputes within a village and between members of different villages by holding meetings and paying or accepting fines. The *barika* is sent by the bride's or groom's party to discuss anything concerning marriage payments and gifts and to settle disputes between affines.
4. He is a messenger in the event of death. When somebody dies, the *barika* will go to summon the deceased person's relatives and people from neighbouring villages to attend the funeral ceremonies.
5. He represents the village in all matters relating to the "outside world." If visitors arrive, he will receive them, and if somebody is killed or dies under unnatural circumstances, he has to inform the police.

The *barika*'s first function is founded in mythology. Jena et al. collected a myth about the sun god's birth, which was witnessed only by a young Harijan boy. The gods, who had fallen asleep, were envious and killed the boy. The boy's soul went up to the sun god, who condemned the act of killing and gave the Harijan the following boon:

> "You will always be the first one to see me rising from the east. You will be the one who can watch me performing my ablutions, or bathing, who will be able to see me picking up my sword, raising my umbrella over my head and placing myself on my throne, with my crown on, to rule over the people. Only through you, will others learn about how all this became possible", said the sun god. He then turned him into a cock, this being the first creature to watch the sun rise, as it wakes up before the others. When the sun god takes a bath, water is said to drip on the wings of the bird, causing the cock to crow and thus announce daybreak. The sun god's daily habits and his work are a secret kept by the bird, who, being unable to speak, cannot reveal anything to the people. (Jena et al. 2002, 141)

When I discussed this myth with one Dongria informant, he explained to me that the cock is like the *barika*, because they both wake the villagers up in the morning. The *barika* of the village in which I lived always kept a cock in his house, which around four o'clock in the morning started flapping its wings rapidly before it began to crow. As in the myth, this was explained by my informant by reference to the sun god's bathing water that falls on the bird's wings. When the cock crowed, the *barika* of Gumma used to get up, walk to the village plaza, and sit down with the Dongria. Sometimes he started to summon certain Dongria to attend a meeting or to bring him payment for outstanding debts for sacrificial animals. Like the *ambadadi* festival, in which the *barika*'s gift represents the new year, this myth associates him with time, here with the beginning of the day. The Dongria distinguish thirteen different times of day, but the first one is called *kayu knepa*, "cockcrow."

My informant also commented on the story by saying that the sun god gave another boon to the Harijan. After the gods had killed him, the sun god promised the Harijan that he would never die again except when being sacrificed to the gods. This refers to the fact that Dongria do not kill a cock for the sole purpose of eating but for offering to the gods. A share of the sacrificial animal, usually blood and the cock's head, will be given to the gods first, before the Dongria cook the animal and share the meat among themselves. Outside ritual contexts, cocks are never killed.

A further aspect of the *barika* implied in the myth quoted above is his trustworthiness. The sun god confides in the cock, which cannot speak and will, therefore, keep his secret. Dongria sometimes say that all Dombo are thieves and cannot be trusted. However, I was often impressed by the deep confidence they placed in their own *barika*, to whom they entrusted their money and their personal affairs. If outsiders arrive, the *barika* will always speak in the interest of his own villagers, and if he visits another village to settle a dispute, he will be trusted to strike the best deal on their behalf.

The *barika*'s main duty is to purchase sacrificial animals, just as in the past he used to buy the human victims sacrificed to the earth goddess at the time of *kodru parbu* (buffalo sacrifice). The *barika* of Gumma explained to me that nowadays, when he sells a buffalo to the Dongria for the purpose of performing the *kodru parbu*, he receives one *ada* (one kilogram) of rice and ten rupees from the village as a kind of compensation for the sin he commits by providing the *meria*, the word referring to the sacrificial victim. He himself identifies the sin as the purchase of a young buffalo that will be brutally killed by the crowd (*dunia loku* or "people of the world," i.e., people who come from faraway places) instead of the old and "useless" buffaloes that will be slaughtered at other festivals by one or more people from the village. However, I think this gift may well be a survival from the time when the *barika* bought a human victim and sold him or her to the Dongria.

The trade in sacrificial animals is a very lucrative business for a *barika*, in particular if he is a clever bargainer and supplies several villages. He can achieve considerable influence due to the fact that a vast number of people become indebted to him, and he may even rise to the status of a small village "banker" in the sense that people will come and ask him for money in times of need. My experience in Gumma was that many festivals could only be held because the *barika* did not insist on immediate payment but was able to advance the money on loan.

Das Patnaik reports that, apart from collecting money for festivals, the *barika* was historically responsible for collecting the tax revenue from the villages he worked for: "Since land is owned as per Mutha, land revenue too, was not paid individually, but on the basis of Mutha. Each occupant paid a nominal amount, that is, one anna to the village Barika (messenger) who deposited the amount with the Jani and Bismajhi. The Jani and Bismajhi of each village deposited the amount with the Mandal who subsequently deposited the same in the court of Jeypore Maharaja" (Das Patnaik 1984, 26–27).

The second major function of the *barika* is that of a mediator and arbitrator, in particular in matters concerning marriages. For example, if the people of his village have abducted a woman, her relatives and fellow villagers will come, sometimes bringing their *barika* along, and start demanding either the return of their daughter or considerable sums of money (see section 4.4.4). This usually leads to open quarrels, and the *barika* will be called on to intervene and discuss the matter with the bride's family members and *barika*. If a daughter of the village runs away with somebody other than her fiancé, the fiancé's *barika* will soon visit the woman's village and that of her new husband to demand a fine. In such cases he will often come alone and discuss the matter with the whole village, including the *barika*. When someone is demanding money for giving his daughter to another village, the *barika* of both parties will be present. During such negotiations, one *barika* will put forward his party's demands, while his opponent from the rival party will argue against these demands and will try to reduce them. Normally, such disputes are not settled in a few hours or a single day, because the *barika* will go back and forth, each one reporting back to his party and getting new instructions from them. The *barika* will also be responsible for handing over money to another party, or if he belongs to the receiving party, for counting it. In the same way, he will sometimes be summoned as an arbitrator if a fight erupts. In such cases he will go back and forth between the conflicting parties until a settlement is reached. He will then assemble the conflicting parties in one place and make sure that fines are paid. A ritual will then be performed to guarantee peace for the future.

A "good *barika*" can enforce the will of the individual or village he represents and at the same time reconcile the conflicting parties. In practise, however, *barika* are rarely good peacekeepers, because of their loyalties to one of the parties. For example, one *barika* from the village of Phakeri was renowned for his commitment to the interests of his villagers, but he was equally known for his bad temper, which often prevented the settlement of a conflict. The *barika* of Gumma had both abilities, but during the season when palm wine flowed abundantly, he usually started drinking heavily and ignored his duties. He also faced the problem of being the *barika* of three villages. When quarrels flared up between them, he was caught in a dilemma, because whichever side he took, he neglected his loyalties to the other. In such instances I often saw him avoiding the role of an arbitrator.

This is possible because the Dongria will often involve the police in their quarrels. The police have representatives called *chaukidar* who normally live in remote areas, while the actual police officers live in the towns and only visit the villages in serious cases, such as murder. The *chaukidar* in the area of my research originally came from Andhra Pradesh and was married to a local Dombo woman. Her brother was working as the *chaukidar*'s assistant (called *grama rakhyaka*), a very low position in the police hierarchy, often held by local Dombo. The *grama rakhyaka* accompanies the *chaukidar* when he visits the villages assigned to him, and at the time of *kodru parbu* (buffalo sacrifice) they work as peacekeepers.

The *chaukidar* alone or with the help of his assistants will perform all duties traditionally assigned to the *barika*. According to my observations, Dongria call for these low-ranking police officers when the local *barika*'s efforts do not yield any results. For example, when a village does not give its daughter to the groom's village despite having received all the payments they asked for, the Dongria will first approach the *barika*, and if he fails to resolve the dilemma, they will then approach the *chaukidar*. The *chaukidar* and his assistants sometimes carry truncheons (*lati*) as a symbol of their authority, especially at the time of the *kodru parbu* (buffalo sacrifice), when they try to prevent the young Dongria boys from killing the buffalo ahead of the appropriate time. In contrast to the *barika*, they can read and write, and since the Dongria consider this ability to be a sign of their power, these officers are sought after as mediators in various types of disputes. For example, if a father wants to ensure that his son's father-in-law does not withhold his daughter any longer but sends her to her husband's house, he may approach the *chaukidar*. He will pay him to write a letter in which he threatens the father-in-law if he does not release his daughter. If two people are engaged in a fight and call the *chaukidar* to resolve the conflict, he will come and listen to the complaints from both sides before he asks them to pay a fine. In most cases I witnessed or heard about, both sides were fined; sometimes one side was fined less than the other, but rarely was all the blame put on one side only. The *chaukidar* will then write two letters stating the names of the persons involved, the reason for the fight, and the request for a peaceful settlement. These letters will then be exchanged by those who started the conflict. The *chaukidar* will get a small fee or a chicken from both sides for resolving the dispute.

If no settlement can be reached, or if the quarrel involves physical violence, Dongria will threaten to contact the police in the nearest town to start a "case". In practise, this rarely happens, because everybody knows that a "case" will be a costly affair for all parties involved. The word "case" should not be confused with a "court case", because it involves only police officers, to whom the local people ascribe judicial powers. Like the *chaukidar*, the police officers will fine one or both parties, but usually much more heavily than the village guards do. In the past, feuds between the Dongria were more frequent than they are nowadays, certainly because the police always intervene in cases of serious injury or even murder. When a feud takes place between the Dongria of two different villages, the Dombo of the conflicting parties will not be involved in the fight and can move around freely and follow their trade.

In minor cases of conflict, I often heard the *barika* of Gumma saying that the Dongria should contact neither the *chaukidar* nor the police but rather the "big people" (*kajaru*) of the village. Apart from the *barika*, these are charismatic and often elderly Dongria, who may belong to families bearing the traditional titles of village leaders, such as *naika*, *bismajhi*, and *jani*. These influential people will assemble on the village plaza in the early morning before dawn and call the conflicting parties to a meeting. Once, I myself was involved in such a conflict and could experience how the *barika* settled the dispute. On the day before the meeting, I was told by the village leader's son that a notorious troublemaker had spread rumours about me while he and others were drinking at a *salap* tree. I became angry and confronted the man, who denied the allegations. I then declared my intention to clarify the situation in a meeting, and the next morning before sunrise the *barika* called me to sit with the village council on the plaza. The *barika* inquired about my complaint, I told him what had happened, and he then asked the Dongria who had allegedly spread rumours about me about the matter. When he denied it, the *barika* summoned the Dongria who first made these allegations. The *barika* told him why he had been asked to come and started questioning him about his allegations. Faced with the village council, he denied that he had heard his fellow villager spreading rumours, either because he had indeed lied to me or because he did not dare to confront him openly. The *barika* then came to the conclusion that, in fact, nothing had happened. The mood quickly changed from serious to light-hearted, and after some time everybody left to go drinking by the palm-wine trees.

The *barika* also performs the function of a messenger, particularly at the time of the death of someone in the village. If somebody dies, he has to inform the deceased's fellow villagers and his relatives living in other villages to come to the funeral ceremonies. This is particularly necessary if somebody dies unexpectedly, for example, when a young boy suddenly fell ill and died the same day. In such instances, witchcraft or poisoning is suspected as the cause of death. The relatives must be given an opportunity to inquire into the death before the body is cremated. If somebody dies an unnatural death, like falling from a tree, the *barika* will go to the nearest town and inform the police. The police will come and investigate the possible causes of death, along with the *barika*.

As the last example illustrates, the *barika* represents the village to the outside world. According to Nayak (1989, 178), a *barika* used to accompany a Dongria with the royally granted title *mondal* to give a gift of honour called *bheti* to the kings of Jeypore and Bissamcuttack.[42] The *barika* had a variety of contacts with the people of the plains and with the police officers to whom he reported events that took place in the village. In Nayak's opinion, "the role of the *barik* has been minimised so far as interconnections of regional polity with village polity is concerned" (Nayak 1989, 178). My own experiences lead me to hold the opposite opinion. With the increasing number of people coming into the Dongria hills as representatives of the state or of non-governmental organisations, the *barika*'s functions have become increasingly important. In the village where I lived, hardly a fortnight passed without the visit of an official from either the development agencies (e.g., DKDA), the education projects (e.g., DPEP), various health organisations (e.g., UNDP), or the public works department (e.g., BDO). When traveling in the hills, they are usually accompanied by a young Dombo or by the Dongria *sarpanch*, and when they reach a village, they will be welcomed by the *barika* and some of the local village chiefs. Once the visitors have left, the villagers will discuss what was talked about further, and very often the *barika* will be expected to make recommendations. His opinion is very influential, and Dongria often trust his advice, because they consider him experienced in dealing with people from outside their village. For example, when I was searching for a village to live in, I was told by a very experienced DKDA officer to first persuade the Dombo and the *barika* of my good intentions. His argument was that once I convinced these people, the Dongria would no longer oppose my residence in their village.

As these examples reveal, the *barika* traditionally plays a major political and economic role in society, despite being of lower status. Depending on his personal abilities, he may rise to become a village banker or a judge and extend his influence from one to several villages in the region. He influences decisions at the village level and beyond and mediates between political forces from outside the

---

[42] Nayak does not mention any source for this information.

village and the local village leaders. A *barika* will often pay deference to local Dongria leaders due to his status as a Dombo, but most Dongria consider him to be among the "important people" of the village. A good *barika* will be respected for his wealth, his experience, and his influence outside the village, even if the Dongria will not eat his food or allow him to enter their houses. While the Dombo as a whole can be seen as clients in relation to the landowners, the situation is somewhat reversed when we consider the relationship between the *barika* and the Dongria. The latter are his clients in the sense that they have become dependent on him. He does not appear to be a subject ruled by kings, but rather a leader who rules by making political and legal decisions, organising festivals, and arranging marriages. His functions are related to all important aspects of life in the local society: he helps to keep peace in an environment characterised by personal insecurity and violence (*warre*; see Sahlins 1968), he enables the Dongria to perform sacrifices in order to ensure their own wellbeing and the fertility of their land, and he helps them to establish contacts with a potential bride, to acquire the money necessary for marriage, and – most important – to bring the bride to the groom's village after all payments have been made. Nowadays, his judicial functions are minimised due to the slowly increasing influence of the state, the powers of which, however, are far from being omnipresent.

2.5.8 Money and the "other," sharing and the "own"

Writing about his experiences in the Ghumsur district in the 1840s, Macpherson states:

> The use of money, with the exception of cowries, was until recently, nearly unknown to the Maliah Kond, and the value of all property is estimated by them in "lives," a measure which requires some adjustment every time that it is applied, a bullock, a buffalo, a goat, pig or fowl, a bag of grain, or a set of brass pots being each with any thing else that may be agreed upon a "life." A hundred lives, on an average, may be taken to consist of ten bullocks, ten buffaloes, ten sacks of corn, ten sets of brass pots, twenty sheep, ten pigs and thirty fowls. (Macpherson [1842] 1863, 50)

This statement clearly suggests that, to the Kond, objects of exchange acquired from outside one's own community are representations of a highly valued power that animates all beings. What Macpherson translates as life is what is called *jiu* or *jela* by Dongria, words that have a variety of meanings, including soul, life force, and value (see pp. 375–76, 481 and section 6.2). Money, livestock, grain, and valuable brass pots given at the time of marriage all contain "life" and can be exchanged against the "life" of the bride. Multiple forms of "life" are contained in rice, which represents the goddess *sita penu-lahi penu* or *sita-laksmi*. This goddess is also referred to in ritual invocations as *sita gati lakmi gati* ("Sita's knot, Lakmi's knot"), referring to knotted bundles of rice straw placed under a canopy set up for the worship of the goddess, and as *jale gati muna gati*, meaning "knotted purse, knotted bag." The word *jale* is used for a small bag in which Dongria keep their money. In these invocations Dongria ask the goddess to provide them with a sufficient harvest and with money, both forms of the goddess herself. She is requested to come into their houses and stay there for the wellbeing and prosperity of the inhabitants. The markets where Dongria barter and sell their products are also invoked in rituals to the goddess by saying *saraji raji hata banaji hata andu hari barsa hari*, meaning "all country, country market, exchange market, become more every year," which probably means that the prices for the Dongria's products should increase. What is seen by a Western observer as an economic transaction depending on the laws of the free market is interpreted here as a change of form by the goddess. I would even suggest that for the Dongria, buying and selling is in essence a continuous transformation of "life" or "wealth," of which the highest form is rice, i.e., the goddess herself. The success of any such economic transaction does not depend simply on economic partners or market forces but rather on one's relationship with the goddess, which is maintained through rituals. Whether the harvest will be good, prices will increase, women will bear children, and the land will be fertile all depends on the goddess's goodwill.

For Dongria, money and certain other types of property are forms of the life principle that can be exchanged with "others." The definition of who is regarded as "other" depends on what is being acquired by the transfer of money or other valued forms of property. Depending on what is being sold, money or livestock or other manifestations of the life principle may be given to a different localised clan, to affines, or to the people of another community, such as the Dombo. For example, the clan territory of a particular village can only be sold to people who are "outsiders," i.e., either Dongria belonging to a different clan, or if they are from the same clan, belonging to a different *muta*. From the Dongria perspective, a village's dominant clan is the smallest and most important unit of "landownership." The land must be shared within the village community, but it can be sold to "others." Another occasion when Dongria "buy" something from members of their own community is marriage. In the context of marriage, the bride-taker will give considerable sums of money, as well as livestock and grain, to the bride-giver. A woman, as a manifestation of the life principle, can only be given to another clan, which thereby acquires rights to her and her children.

Ownership of fruit trees exists only in the context of the exchange of such manifestations of "life." Some fruit trees, such as jackfruit and orange trees, are "owned" individually. People know who planted these trees, and sons inherit them from their fathers. The fruit is taken to the market and sold to the Dombo for money. If somebody picks fruit from the tree without permission, it will be considered a serious theft, and the person will be punished. The tree itself can be sold to a Dombo, in which case the original owner loses all rights to it. When somebody asks for fruit, however, the Dongria will always give it, and from what I witnessed, a Dongria never sells jackfruit to another Dongria. Again, jackfruit, like other fruit, will be taken to market, sold to a local Dombo, or given as a gift to ritual friends. Other fruit trees, such as mango and *mohula* trees, belong to everybody in a village and cannot be sold. During the mango season, groups of young boys or young girls will set out early in the morning to collect – or in their language "to hunt" (*beta*) – mangos that are then either consumed, processed, or sold at the market.[43]

The *salap* tree belongs to the former category of trees, as it is "owned" individually. Taking its sap is considered theft. It can be sold to a Dombo, but it must be shared with other Dongria and cannot be sold by one Dongria to another. In this way, the "ownership" of a tree and its produce exists only in relation to the "other," in this case the Dombo who will replace the "life" of the tree with the "wealth" of money or other manifestations of the goddess. A Dongria may sell the produce of his land or his tree to Dombo or others with whom he bargains and exchanges one form of "life" or "wealth" for another. However, when he shares "life" or "wealth" with others, no such demands for counter-prestations will be made. In other words, individual ownership of manifestations of "life" exists in contexts of exchange with "others," while the idea of ownership is denied in contexts of sharing with one's "own" people. Who is considered to be "other" or "own" is thus defined by the form and content of the transaction, not by membership in certain fixed groups.

The fact that transactions involving money, livestock, and other forms of "wealth" are a means to define and to deal with the outside world gives the Dombo a very powerful position, because they are the ones who can transform what all Dongria own, the products of the land, into money, livestock, or brass pots. Without a Dombo, a Dongria normally cannot acquire a wife, at least not in the prestigious way that includes the transfer of considerable sums of money and buffaloes. The same holds true for land transactions, since in former

---

[43] Quarrels arise only when Dombo collect too many mangos for themselves in order to sell them at the market.

times Dongria could only gain access to new land by giving money – or equivalent forms of "life" mentioned by Macpherson – to a different lineage that was willing to sell. Finally, without a Dombo who buys and sells sacrificial animals for money, the Dongria cannot repay their gift obligations to the gods. As will be seen in the chapter on the *kodru parbu* (buffalo sacrifice; see chapter 5), the most important sacrifice is the gift to the earth goddess, for which the Dombo provide the victim, a human being in the past, a buffalo in the present. Without sacrificial animals, a Dongria's land will not be fertile, and without fertile land, he will not be able to get a wife and assure the fertility of his family or purchase new land where his descendants can settle. In other words, while Dombo accept Dongria's higher status on the basis of their superior relation to the land, Dombo are, in fact, more powerful, as they are able to convert crops into different manifestations of "wealth." We can say that the Dombo link what Bloch and Parry (1992) call the "short cycle of exchange" with the "long cycle of exchange," because they allow the transformation of crops produced by individual effort into money used to sustain the community's wellbeing.

This monetary exchange and gift-giving may involve hierarchy in the sense that the "other" defined by the transaction is seen as standing in a higher or lower position in relation to oneself. The Dombo to whom one sells products and from whom one buys them are always in a lower position, and the gods to whom one gives gifts and from whom one receives them are always in a higher. Thus, the transaction itself does not create status differences, because they already exist beforehand, but it does confirm them. In barter and monetary transactions, the positions of Dongria and Dombo are unequal. The former sell the crops they produce themselves on their land, while the latter depend on the monetary transaction itself. This stands in contrast to transactions within the Dongria community, which may at least temporarily establish a status difference that did not previously exist. Thus, giving a daughter is higher than taking a bride for one's son, but the inequality established in the context of the betrothal turns into equality over time due to counter-gifts. Sharing, on the other hand, ignores status distinctions, forbids the bargaining characteristic of market transactions, and prohibits the demands for reciprocity typical of gift exchanges.

Sharing occurs most commonly in three contexts: feasts, land divisions, and drinking sessions. Some village feasts are based on the idea of pooling, meaning that all contribute either labour or money to buy an animal that is then sacrificed or slaughtered. Since all, including the Dombo, contribute equal amounts of money or labour, they receive equal shares when the raw or cooked meat is divided among all present. The situation is different when it comes to feasts in the context of gift exchanges. For example, on the occasion of a death or marriage, animals are given to close kin, who often live in different villages. Those who receive a buffalo will never consume the meat alone but will instead share it with – or rather distribute it among – their co-villagers. The same holds true for fines paid in the form of buffaloes or money for taking someone's bride or killing someone's brother. The fine will be paid to one household but will be shared by all households in the village, including the Dombo. No one will need to demand a share of meat, because arrangements are made so that the meat is divided into equal shares according to the number of households present. Such feasts take place within the morality pertaining to gift exchanges with its demands and haggling, but differ from them in the sense that the morality of sharing among one's "own" people is applied. In such contexts, the village and the gifts given to the village are often called *kutumb*, a word derived from Oriya and meaning "family" or close agnatic kin. In other words, someone shares with his fellow villagers, including the Dombo or a foreign anthropologist, just as he shares with the members of his own household.

A second context in which sharing is the norm is the division of land among co-villagers. All land is considered to have been originally given by the gods to the Kond. The earth goddess, a stone arrangement found in each village, is referred to as "mother" by the Dongria, while the *koteiwali*, a stone representing the culture hero *niamraja*, is considered their father. Within each village, some Dongria belonging to the dominant clan of the territory (*muta*) are regarded as the descendants of the founders who either first occupied the land or bought it from others. These families "own" the village land, which was divided among them at some point in the past. Households without such rights to land, such as the Dombo and Dongria from elsewhere who have settled in the village, have to approach these men of the dominant clan and demand a share of land from them. If available, it will be given without discussion or quarrelling, and nothing will be demanded in return. Like the buffaloes given as part of a gift exchange but shared among the villagers, however, this land sharing is embedded in a cycle of exchange. Since the land was originally a gift from the gods, upon whose goodwill its fertility depends, the villagers must reciprocate for their right to use the land and its produce by giving sacrifices in return.

A third important context is the drinking of *salap* sap, which is likened to mother's milk. The tree as such was given to the Dongria by *niamraja* to nourish them, and each individual tree was planted by parents (father or mother) in order to provide "milk" for their children, although in fact it is mostly the men who drink it. Just as different parts of the village land have "owners" who inherited their rights from their ancestors, each tree is owned by a particular person who received the rights to the tree from his parents. When he harvests the tree's sap, however, he is expected to give an equal share to everybody present. Nobody needs to request a share of the sap; being present suffices. I also never heard any demands for reciprocity from the *salap* tree's owner. Dongria will, however, repay their gift obligations by performing a sacrifice under the tree in order to obtain the goodwill of the gods, who first provided the tree and are responsible for the sap's continuing flow.

Concerning land and the fruits of the land, we find among the Dongria a "root metaphor" similar to the one identified by Bird-David among the Nayaka: "Nayaka look on the forest as they do on a mother or father. For them, it is not something "out there" that responds mechanically or passively; it provides unconditionally to its children" (Bird-David 1990, 190). Bird-David distinguishes between a view of the environment as a parent, which involves the obligation to share, and a view of nature as an ancestor, with whom one maintains a relationship of reciprocity (Bird-David 1990, 191). In my opinion, Dongria and Dombo do not clearly distinguish nature in this way, but rather perceive the gods and ancestors as family members who, like living elders, expect to be honoured and taken care of. They do not give "unconditionally." This kind of expectation for reciprocity was once expressed by an old man from Gumma. While sitting under a *salap* tree, he told a young village boy that he had planted *salap* trees for his children and had climbed up the trees when he was young. He further explained that he now expects the young boy to bring him *salap* sap and to provide him with alcohol even after his death.[44] In daily life, elders are, in fact, often neglected, but when they die and become ancestors, their powers increase, and they become more like gods possessing the power to inflict disease on a person. In other words, "parents" (gods, ancestors, elders) give gifts to their "children" (humans, descendants, juniors), who share these gifts equally among themselves as "children" (co-villagers, family members, brothers) but have to reciprocate the original gifts of their "parents." As clearly expressed in the myth about *lahi penu* quoted above (see section 2.4.2), the gods live from the sacrifices given by humans. Sharing is thus an encompassed feature of a "delayed return system" and not a dominant ideology as in the "immediate return systems" analysed by Woodburn (1982).

What is clear from the ethnographic data presented above is that sharing and the cycles of exchange are separate but not independent. The separation is not created by the objects shared or exchanged, but by the morality of the social relationship through which the transfer of these objects takes place. Thus, *salap* may be shared in one context, but sold or given as a gift in another. Dongria will bargain in the market, and they will demand gifts or argue to reduce the

---

44 When Dongria drink distilled alcohol, they always spill some drops on the ground for the gods and the ancestors first.

demand for gifts, but when it comes to sharing, they will make sure that the shares distributed do not become the objects of such haggling. Among one's "own people," one shares equally what has been given freely by one's "parents," while in relation to "others" one sells, buys, or gives objects and the products of one's own labour. Dombo are considered members of the village, and as such they are included in the process of sharing on the village level and have the right to demand their share.

These relationships between Dombo and Dongria are clearly different from the *jajmani* system. The Dombo are generalists who perform several functions assigned to different castes in the plains. They have various sources of income and may be engaged in shifting and wet rice cultivation on their own fields. They work as agricultural labourers, but since the system of private landownership is not very developed in the hills, the Dongria as landowners do not depend on their labour force. Furthermore, the Dombo are not religious specialists who remove their patrons' pollution and receive prestations in return. However, they may become powerful "communicators with the divine."

2.6 Ritual interaction

2.6.1 The debate

The previous section explains how Dongria and Dombo are related in terms of status and power and how these relations are different from those between landlords and "untouchables" in "caste society". This difference was first noted by Pfeffer, who also stressed the importance of the opposition of "senior" and "junior" as the major value configuration in this region. As described above, however, he reintroduces the idea of impurity by ascribing the Dombo's lower status to their "impure" trading activities involving the crossing of boundaries. Focussing on their economic and political functions as traders and mediators, he further sets up a distinction between the Dombo as "communicators with human beings" and the Dongria as "communicators with the divine" (Pfeffer 1997b, 13). To draw such a radical distinction, however, does not accord with my ethnographic data, which clearly shows the Dombo's involvement in diverse rituals. If we examine the local categories of ritual specialists, it becomes clear that the Dombo are excluded from some forms of communication with the divine, while they are included in others. I will address these categories in more detail in a later chapter (see section 5.5), but in order for my argument to be understood, it is necessary to make some introductory remarks on religious functionaries at this point.

2.6.2 Religious status and ritual office

Dongria do not clearly differentiate between different ritual offices in the way assumed in the literature on them and on other Central Indian communities classified as tribal. In the literature, we often find an enumeration of titles like *jani, pujari, dissari, beju, bejuni,* and *gurumeni* accompanied by a description of their respective functions, such as village priest, cook, medicine man, and male and female shaman. Several comments have to be made on such classifications. First, it should be pointed out that none of these people can be called priests, because they do not depend on their ritual performances for a living, and their work does not consist mainly of conducting rites and ceremonies. All of these people are involved in agricultural work in their swiddens and only put their special powers at the service of the community when needed. Second, none of these positions excludes any of the others. This means that in terms of functions, not of status, someone can simultaneously be a *jani* and a *dissari* or a *pujari* and a *beju*. In reality, most specialists will fall into more than one of these categories, because to perform any of these functions, it is necessary to have a "divine blessing", and somebody having these special powers will often be able to "communicate with the divine" in several ways. Third, when dealing with the titles mentioned above, we should clearly distinguish between the function and the status associated with them. All these titles can be separated into two categories. The first category contains those specialists who perform the functions associated with the status positions of *jani* and *pujari*. Somebody may have the status of a *bismajhi*, but may act as a *jani*. The second category contains titles related only to certain ritual specialisations, not to status positions. It includes titles like *dissari, beju, bejuni,* and *gurumeni*. By status I mean a position that derives from belonging to one of the collective categories of which society is made up. As will be addressed later, every Dongria belongs to one of several status categories, such as *jani, pujari, mondal, bismajhi,* and some others of less importance. These categories are ordered hierarchically in relation to the opposition of "senior" and "junior," and they are probably derived from positions in a royal Hindu cult. In other words, when somebody is said to be a *jani*, this can refer to the fact that he belongs to this status category, or that he knows how to recite the invocations to the gods, or both (for details see section 5.5). However, when somebody is called a *beju* or a *dissari*, the reference is always to his functional specialisation, never to any status category.

This distinction is important for my main argument concerning the inclusion of Dombo in "communication with the divine." The Dombo are excluded from all of the status categories mentioned above. They carry clan names that may be correlated with Dongria clan names, but their lineages are not named or associated

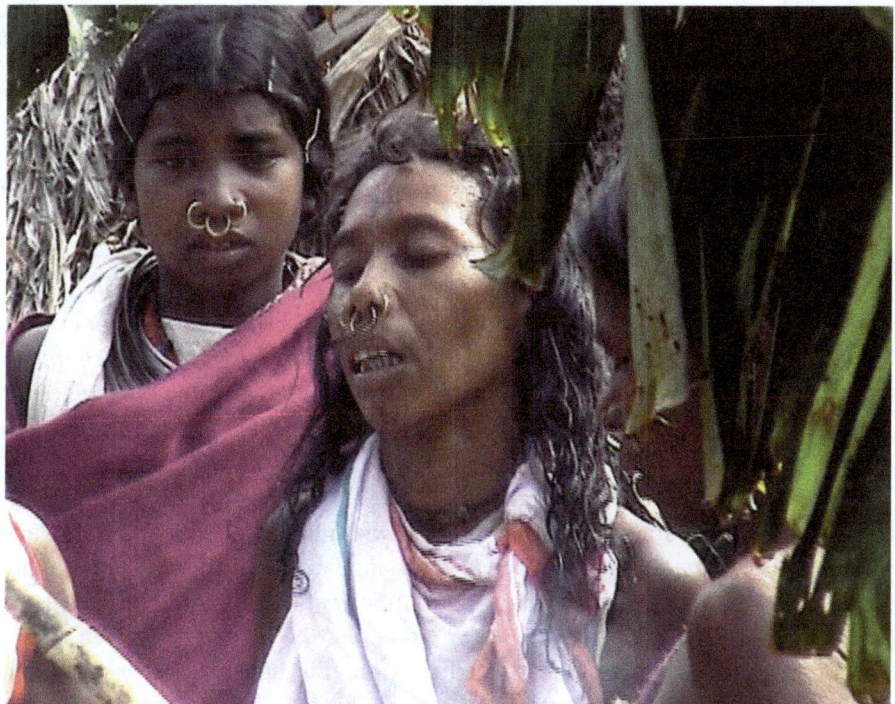

Photo 5: *Beju* in trance (right) and young *bejuni*

with the status categories of their patrons. They are their "subjects" and, therefore, cannot carry the titles of the "kings," the Dongria. But the Dombo may and indeed do perform the functions related to titles in the second category.

2.6.3 Dombo as "communicators with the divine"

At the beginning of my fieldwork in Gumma, I attended a festival for the goddess of smallpox. The festival began with the local female Dongria shaman (*bejuni*) bringing small pots filled with grain from each Dongria house to the centre of the village, where a small canopy was set up. Some Dombo women were also present, but since, to my knowledge, Dombo were excluded from ritual performances, I did not expect them to participate. As my following field notes show, my expectations were proved wrong:

After some time, the [Dongria] *bejuni* woman stood up, the others [Dongria boys] started drumming, and she began to dance. The *member* and one female assistant [*gurumeni*] spoke animatedly to the [main] *bejuni,* and she answered them. The *bejuni* let down her hair. In the meantime, the old Dombo woman from Lamba [an adjacent village] had arrived, the one who is building a house in Gumma. She sat on the ground with unbound hair and swung her head back and forth. Suddenly she fell into trance, tried to get up, but needed the help of two Dombo girls. Like all other *bejuni*, the Dombo *bejuni* started rubbing the rice [in the winnowing fan] with her hand, recited, and danced. There was no difference between her and the other [Dongria] *bejuni.*

This last statement was made too rashly, because in the course of further events, certain differences became apparent. For example, shortly after the dance finished, the Dongria and Dombo called the children to sit down on the village plaza to receive a protective mark (*linga*) on their foreheads. The *bejuni* divided this task between them according to the children's status: the female Dongria shaman touched the Dongria children, the female Dombo shaman the Dombo children. A similar separation became apparent when the two *bejuni* left the village to go to the shrine of the smallpox goddess and had to cross a small stream. Since they were possessed by the goddess, they were not allowed to touch the water with their feet and had to be carried across the water by the men. When the Dombo *bejuni* reached the stream, the Dongria men refused to carry her, and she had to wait until members of her family came to help her.

In the remainder of my time in the village I learned that one of the major duties of a Dongria shaman is to heal by falling into a trance, communicating with the gods, and inquiring into why a particular person has been struck by symptoms of disease.[45] I was again astonished when one day I visited a Dombo's house where such a healing session was taking place, and instead of a Dongria *bejuni*, the old Dombo woman conducted the inquiry in a state of trance. When asked, people confirmed that shamans will only perform the healing ceremony for members of their own community. The conclusion I drew from these instances was that both communities have a similar shamanic tradition, and that they celebrate independently in the context of their household affairs but jointly in the framework of village festivals. I understood the separation as an expression of the hierarchy between the two communities, the Dongria expressing their higher status by not touching the Dombo *bejuni* and the Dombo children. Indeed, in the context of festivals I experienced many other markers of Dombo inferiority. For example, a village festival can take place without the participation

---

45 On "untouchables" acting as shamans see Berreman (1964), Moffatt (1979), and Kolenda (1981a).

of the Dombo *bejuni*, but not without the Dongria religious specialists. Further, in the example above, the Dombo do not bring a pot with rice representing the goddess, this being a privilege of the patrons. When at the time of the *kodru parbu* the buffalo is driven from house to house to be fed, the Dongria are allowed to give him boiled rice, while the Dombo may only offer paddy. In the same way, when the Dongria summon the ancestors at a village festival on the central village plaza, they will only summon their own ancestors and feed them boiled rice. They will then proceed to the row of Dombo houses, so that the Dombo can give alcohol and paddy to their patrons' ancestors. Only at the end of the festival, when they all go outside the village to a shrine (*yatra kudi*) where they will send away the gods and ancestors, will the shamans also make a small offering in a separate place to the ancestors of other communities like Leli, Ghasi, or Dombo.

Another typical sign of the Dombo's inferiority is, however, absent in the context of village festivals. In the plains, Harijan often perform the function of musicians, especially of drummers and flutists. When Dongria celebrate a village festival, the situation is reversed, because the drums are played by the Dongria. These drums are kept by the Dongria in their houses and are worshipped like gods at the time of festivals, receiving chicks and rice as offerings. Without the drums, the gods cannot dance. Only in the context of the *kodru parbu* (buffalo sacrifice) did I witness the participation of Dombo musicians, who played the oboe (*mohuri*). An indication that playing the drums is an inferior activity became apparent only at the time of the big-men festival, the *ghanta parba*. At the end of this festival, the Dongria drummers will be called to the house of the big men and sprinkled with turmeric water by the female shaman. When asked why, they responded that for the time of the festival the Dongria have become Dombo and Ghasi. For this reason they are prohibited from entering the house of the big-men for the time of the festival. The turmeric water was used as a purifying substance, this being one of the few occasions when Dongria showed concern about ritual pollution. The reason, I think, was that the Dongria performed music for somebody else in return for payment in rice and meat. They behaved like Dombo, who work for a patron in order to receive something to live on.

Assuming that Dombo could only participate in festivals in an inferior position, I was astonished to find out at a *kodru parbu* (buffalo sacrifice) that many of the major rituals were performed by a Dombo from the plains, who looked like a *sadhu* with his matted hair and was addressed as *dissari* or *beju* by the Dongria. At first, I thought this might have been an exception, but a year later I attended another buffalo sacrifice in a completely different area and witnessed the worship of one of the highest deities of the Dongria, the god *niamraja*, and again the main shaman was a Dombo, this time from the organisers' village. He performed the ritual alongside three or four female Dongria shamans, but he was clearly the leader of these ritual specialists. The reason why in both cases a Dombo could perform these rituals must be thought about in terms of the position of shamans. A male shaman (*beju*) is always considered more powerful and knowledgeable than a female shaman (*bejuni*). If a Dombo has enough experience and has a reputation as a powerful shaman, he will be selected as the chief ritual specialist, whatever his social status outside the ritual sphere may be. Male shamans, in general, are less easy to fit into existing social categories, because they are highly individualistic and try to cross boundaries, not only in the ritual but also in the social sphere. For example, many male shamans do not marry, are cross-dressers, and act like women, some of them engaging in homosexual relations with men from different communities.

We can, therefore, conclude that Dombo may perform all ritual activities except those associated with Dongria status categories, i.e., *jani* and *pujari*. The functions and titles connected with these status categories are reserved for Dongria only, perhaps because they mark positions in a royal organisation and define the Dongria as the "ruling elite" in contrast to the Dombo, their subjects. The latter are clearly "communicators with the divine" when performing the functions of *dissari*, *beju*, or *bejuni*, and while they are often in an inferior position when compared to Dongria ritual specialists, they may become very powerful and are then asked to conduct the most important rites for their patrons.

2.7 Conclusion: Tribal and caste societies

To what extent are these value-ideas, norms, and forms of interdependence comparable to what we know from "caste society"? Following Dumont's highly influential work on caste, other authors have made the criticism that purity and pollution are not the sole ideological references in Hindu life. Apffel-Marglin's (1985) ethnographic work among the *devadasi* in Odisha provided evidence for the importance of concepts of the auspicious and inauspicious. Likewise, Raheja (1988) demonstrated the existence of ideas about inauspiciousness in the context of gift exchanges in North India and linked these ideas to a principle different from hierarchy, which she calls "centrality." Studies on Indian kingship (Dirks 1987) often contradict Dumont's view that the caste system is essentially based on the idea of purity and the pre-eminence of the Brahmin. For example, Burghart (1978) expresses his dissatisfaction with Dumont's restriction of his analysis to this binary opposition and widens the perspective by including additional ideals in his analysis of society. In his sources about a Hindu-ruled Himalayan kingdom in Nepal, Burghart identifies three principles, each of which is a path to virtue and a source of cosmic harmony: *dharmic* caste code, ascetic renunciation, and royal power (Burkhart 1978, 533). Similarly Veena Das, using Gujarati "community histories", identifies a series of conceptual pairings that derive their meaning from a "latent" third value. For example, in her opinion the relation between Brahmin and king is defined by the "latent" principle of the renouncer (Das 1982, 49). In Dirks's (1987) opinion, caste relations do not mainly emphasise religious values like purity and impurity, but rather action and power deriving from indigenous cultural concepts. The kings and the dominant castes are seen as standing at the apex of the caste organisation and are the reference point of the moral order. Ethnological studies (Apffel-Marglin 1985; Galey 1989; Hardenberg 2000) of royal rituals show that the royal function is itself considered a religious value, as it is linked to ideas about the cosmos, fertility, and regeneration. While no one will claim that purity and impurity and Brahmanic ideology are of only minor importance in India, all of these authors try to present a broader picture of the cultural and social reality they have encountered in the field or in their historical sources. As Bayly (2000, 23) states, all these ideologies and forms of social organisation conceptualised and interpreted by anthropologists and historians may indeed have existed in India, but at different times and in different places. If we agree that hierarchy based on the ideas of purity and impurity is an Indian phenomenon, perhaps more important in centres of Hindu worship than in their periphery and probably of greater relevance just before and after colonialism than in the Middle Ages, then this statement does not exclude the possibility of finding other value-ideas and forms of social organisation as well, depending on the region and its particular socio-cultural history.

The Niamgiri Hills clearly belong to the periphery in terms of remoteness from the centres of power and Hindu worship. Here, Brahmins and Hindu ascetics are absent, and no one follows in their footsteps by taking over their functions. Dongria are not concerned with the results of their actions for a future life (*karma*), with attaining divine bliss (*bhoga*), or with achieving liberation (*moksa*). Forms of asceticism are not highly valued, while enjoying life in the form of eating meat, drinking alcohol, and having sex are. The Dongria language does not have any words for purity and pollution except those derived from Oriya (e.g., *dosa*), and apart from certain ritual contexts and times of menstruation, birth, and death, they are not often concerned with purification. Dongria express their relations with the Dombo in terms of "seniority," a value linked to the origin of humankind, birth order, and brotherhood, of landownership versus dependent work, and of life in opposition to death and the dead.

The degree to which local kings influenced the Dongria's values and social organisation is difficult to answer. Schnepel (1993, 347; 2002, 288–90) collected data concerning the participation of Dongria Kond in the *durga puja* of the petty king of Bissamcuttack that showed that the Kond were organised into groups to which different functions in the festival were assigned. In return for their ceremonial services, the Dongria were granted signs of honour. In this way, the kings included the tribals in their system of royal organisation. Nayak states that "the control exercised by the king and the king's men over many aspects of their socio-cultural, religious and economic life, was remarkable" (Nayak 1989, 182) He further writes that "a number of traditional customs, practices, beliefs, ideas and activities of the Dongria was partly but significantly the contribution of the king of Bissamcuttack and his administration" (Nayak 1989, 182). In his interpretation, the titles used by the Dongria were related to functions in a regional structure of authority for the administration of the hills (see diagram in Nayak 1989, 179). Part of this organisation were the Paika, infantry soldiers who in the past assisted the petty king (*thatraja*) in his battles against the high king (*maharaja*) of Jeypore (Schnepel 1993, 345–46) and who communicated the king's orders to the inhabitants of the hills (Nayak 1989, 182). A Dombo official called *barika*, who was responsible for accompanying selected Dongria to give gifts (*bheti*)[46] to the king, is said to have occupied the lowest rank in this administration (Nayak 1989, 178). Since Nayak does not mention any sources, it is not clear whether his descriptions are based on historical evidence or on information collected in the field from the memory of his informants.[47] He seems to contradict his own assumptions about the importance of the king and his administration when he states a few pages later that from the perspective of the Dongria, "they are not to be ruled but they themselves are the rulers [...] they do not believe in any other kingship" and that the "acknowledgement of their glory and political importance in relation to their land is of primary importance to them over any other affairs related to the zamindar king" (Nayak 1989, 184). In other words, as long as the ritual exchanges honoured the "royal" status of the Dongria, they came to attend, but this did not mean that they submitted to the king's rule and power. Edmund Leach arrived at a very similar conclusion when studying the relations between the "hill people" and the "valley people" in the frontier region of Burma, where the whole ecological and social situation shows close similarities to the situation in Odisha (see Pfeffer 2004b):

---

46 *Bheti* are gifts acknowledging the king's authority; see Hardenberg (2000, 141–48).
47 Schnepel relies on information provided by a local priest and a local historian, as well as on a description of the *durga puja* in Bissamcuttack by Sahu.

In Burma proper the Hill Chieftains whom the first European travellers encountered were often dressed in Chinese, Shan, or Burmese style and took pride in listing honorific titles which had been bestowed on them by their elegant Valley overlords, but at the same time they themselves claimed to be lords in their own right, subject to no outside authority. (Leach 1960–61, 60)

The issue of royally granted titles used by the Dongria will be discussed in more detail later (see section 5.7.4); however, I will at this point express my doubts that these titles were ever linked to clearly described functions in a workable royal administration in the Dongria hills as described by Nayak. In my opinion, they were emblems of honour that became part of the social organisation because Dongria see themselves as "children of the king" (*rajamilang*). I have doubts as to whether Dongria were ever incorporated into the king's system of justice, of ritual worship, and of revenue collection, as Nayak claims. It is also questionable to what extent the Paika, who live in the valleys but not in the hills, ever functioned as intermediaries between the Dongria and the king. There is no doubt that Dongria were part of a "little kingdom" as defined by Cohn (1962), but it has yet to be established through historical sources whether the military and political power, as well as the ritual authority, the petty kings exercised was as strong in the hills as in the valleys, where they had their temples, palaces, and soldiers. The situation may be compared to the Dongria's incorporation into the modern Indian state: the government works in complex ways in the political centres but does not have the infrastructure to operate fully in the hills.

Dongria have probably never inhabited the Niamgiri Hills alone. We do not have any historical proof, but there is no reason to believe that Dombo are only recent immigrants to the area. Brahmins may be absent in this area, but if Dumont is correct in stating that the lower castes are an essential functional part of the caste system, and if we take into account Moffatt's finding that "untouchables" share the caste system's dominant ideology, the Dombo provide the main link between this hill society and the pan-Indian ideology of the plains people. An indication that the Dombo are indeed a major factor in the spread of "Brahmanical" ideas is their concern with impurity. Dombo will strictly avoid any contact with a mother who has given birth. When I once entered the house of a Dongria woman who had given birth and needed medical treatment, none of the Dongria were concerned about my pollution, while a Dombo woman who heard about the incident immediately called me to her veranda and told me to purify myself by taking a bath in the river before entering my house. After birth, Dombo will strictly observe a time of impurity, while Dongria mothers often leave their houses a few days or even hours following birth. Once a

Dombo woman suffered from what may have been a psychotic attack and was unable to talk or to recognise anybody for several days. This was explained by the other Dombo by reference to her visit to the house of a mother who had just given birth and was thus highly polluted. I was also struck by the different attitudes members of both communities exhibit in relation to impurity in the context of death. Dongria will say that there is *dosa* for three days when somebody dies in their village, but except for a quick bath in the river with mango bark powder following the funeral, they will not be concerned with purification. In contrast, once when a child died while I was visiting a village where many Dombo lived, purification became a major issue. For the next two days, the Dombo women hardly got any sleep, because they had to purify everything in their houses. They whitewashed the walls over and over again, took their clothes to the river to wash, and even immersed their cots in the water.

The similarities that can be found between forms of segregation in "caste society" and the rules pertaining to space, food, and marriage in the Niamgiri Hills may be explained by referring to, first, the operation of hierarchy as defined by Dumont, and second, an on-going process of exchange of ideas. Dumont and his colleagues have shown that hierarchy in the sense of "encompassing the contrary" (Dumont 1998, 244) is a concept found in many societies and is linked to a variety of value-ideas. These value-ideas divide societies into higher and lower segments while at the same time creating dependence between them. In this way, the Dongria opposition of "senior" and "junior" is not fundamentally different from the Hindu opposition of the "pure" and the "impure", even if the meanings and social forms associated with it are. For Dongria, the origin of society can be traced back to a brother and a sister, thus affirming the difference between man and woman from the start, and to the brothers born to this woman, who are different because of their birth order. Just as Brahmin and "untouchable" are a pair representing the unity of "caste society", siblings serve as the model of society in tribal Central India.[48]

One of the main features of hierarchy, as described by Dumont, is the tendency of those with higher status to separate themselves from those of lower status. In the same way, Dongria and Dombo observe rules concerning space, food,

---

48 The "tribal model of society" appears to be less "hierarchical" – in the negative sense in which this word is often used in Western societies – because status differences are not linked to any bad deeds (*karma*) in a previous life or to any inferior bodily states but simply to the fact of being "junior." Discriminatory behaviour is easier to justify in a system in which status is linked to pure or impure social institutions and states of mind and body than in one in which it is linked to the order of birth. However, in the Niamgiri Hills as well as in "caste society", value-ideas also express the unity of the unequal segments of which society is made up.

and marriage that clearly serve to create and to maintain a boundary between them. The rules are the same as those in a Hindu village occupied by different castes, but Dongria do not explain them by reference to a Brahmin concept of purity. However, it seems that their value-ideas function in the same way, and therefore, we may assume that "purity" in a wider sense is indeed involved. Purity and pollution can be understood as cultural concepts, which in India have been elaborated in Brahmanical writings, or they can be seen as analytical concepts for understanding very widespread ideas about the maintenance of groups and categories (Douglas 1966). The fact that the regulations themselves are so similar in the context of tribal and caste interaction may be understood in the following way. First, identities are often constructed in relation to space, food, and marriage, not only in Hindu India but elsewhere. Second, Dongria are aware of the existence of different castes in the plains. They are familiar with their status differences, and they know that the Dombo belong to the lowest caste. Since they consider themselves to be of higher status and regard the Dombo as lower, they treat the Dombo in the same way as they are treated by higher castes in the plains and valleys. On the other hand, Dombo accept the higher status of the Dongria and explain their lower status in terms of Dongria ideology by describing themselves as "junior" and in terms of purity by explaining their fall from Brahmanical status as due to the sin of eating beef.

Therefore, apart from the features of hierarchy in general, the similarities can be understood as the result of a continuous exchange of ideas. Local ideologies and the regulations and norms linked to them are never completely separated from the surrounding dominant ideologies, like ideas about purity and pollution or kingship. These ideas are partly integrated, but are simultaneously redefined in relation to the already existing ideology. The ethnographic data above provide many examples of this, like the inclusion of the "impure" Dombo in the category of the "junior" segment of society or the adaptation of the word *dosa*, which in Oriya is used for all situations in which members of a caste organisation are called impure, while Dongria employ it in opposition to *niam*, the proper order of things or "law" given by the gods. Another good example is the idea that Dombo are like ghosts, an association also reported by Moffatt in reference to the "untouchables" in Tamil Nadu. According to Moffatt (1979, 112–16), Harijans are said to have a particular relation with demons (*peey-piasu*) and ghosts (*bhut*). The "untouchable" drummers control these malevolent beings, the cattle scavengers come in touch with the decay caused by these demons, the cremation ground attendants work at the place where ghosts are present, and the watchmen protect the village from these spirits. Dombo do not work for the Dongria in any of these functions, and they are not the only ones who can control the unhappy dead. For example, on several occasions I have seen Dongria shamans summoning, embodying, and sending away these violent spirits. In other words, from their patrons' point of view, the Dombo are not linked to ghosts and ancestors on the basis of any impurity inherent in their work but rather due to their commensality with the dead, their segregation, and perhaps their restlessness.[49]

This last example directs our attention to the forms of interdependence between Dombo and Dongria. If interdependence is an integral feature of hierarchy, and if hierarchy in the Niamgiri Hills is not expressed in the Brahmanical terms of purity and impurity, then how is interdependence between the segments of society created and maintained? In what terms do Dongria express the existing forms of interdependence in the Niamgiri Hills? What I have argued is that it is the transformational function of the Dombo, who link the "short cycle of exchange," i.e., trading in crops, to the "long cycle of exchange," i.e., gifts to affines and gods. Through the Dombo, a Dongria acquires money that he can use for individual pleasures (e.g., alcohol or tobacco) or for restoring or continuing relations important for the wellbeing of his collectivity, whether this be his house, lineage, village, clan, or the "whole world" (see the buffalo sacrifice, chapter 5). The Dombo are seen as one's "own" people in contexts of sharing, when gifts from "parents," the gods, are divided among all humans as their "children." In such contexts, the "juniority" of the Dombo is ignored, while equality is stressed. Money transactions and gift exchange, in contrast, often occur between people of different status and are founded on the idea of reciprocity. The system is based on dividing and merging "wellbeing" in an oscillatory movement: the land is divided among the clans, the villages, and all households, which produce their own crops; these crops are sold to the Dombo, who transform them into money; the money is then used by each household for individual wellbeing and for merging its individual profits with those of other households in the village or the clan in order to conduct rituals aimed at maintaining the relations on which the fertility of the land and the wellbeing of the community depend. The idea of wellbeing is manifested in the form of the goddess *sita penu-lahi penu*, who is represented by rice or crops in general and by money. She receives wealth in rituals and gives wealth in the form of a bumper crop or a good deal at the market. The ethnographic data clearly shows that the market is not outside the religious sphere but embedded in it and that money is not excluded from the moral sphere but an integral part of it. The same holds

---

49 This last point was never explicitly expressed by my informants, but there is an obvious similarity between the Dombo, who travel a lot as traders and often change their places of residence, and Dongria ideas about ghosts, who are restless, unsettled, and roam around in the night.

true for the Dombo themselves, who are engaged in individual market transactions, but whose functions are not independent of but rather directly linked to collective rituals. Considering their key position in this unified moral economy, in which economic transactions are linked to ritually maintained wellbeing, it would be astonishing if the Dombo's functions were restricted to an economic sphere devoid of religious significance. As demonstrated in the last part of this chapter, Dombo, apart from dealing in goods, do indeed "communicate" with the divine as ritual specialists. They are excluded only from those functions that are connected to status positions reserved for Dongria, and in contrast to their role in "caste society", their religious function is not defined by the removal of impurity. By seeing the Dombo as an integral part of a society that is based on different value-ideas and on a moral economy encompassing the market in an exchange relation between humans and gods, we have moved far away from the conventional view that Dongria are "tribals" and Dombo are "untouchables" or a "scheduled caste."

3 Dongria social categories, rules, and practices

3.1 Introduction

In this chapter, the focus of study will shift from the consideration of relations between different communities in the Niamgiri Hills and neighbouring valleys to the study of social relations and categories making up the Dongria Kond community. Membership in this community is first of all defined in terms of three principles: marriage, descent, and territorial affiliation. The following analysis of Dongria Kond terminology, rules, and practices will identify the culturally specific ways in which these three principles combine to structure this particular society. In my view, of these three principles, affinity (or marriage) provides the most encompassing framework, as it establishes relations between social categories otherwise separated in terms of descent and territory.

Marriage and affinity have been major topics of South Asian anthropology since Dumont's first article of 1953. Debates have been concerned with these phenomena in South Indian as opposed to North Indian "caste society". Several renowned scholars (e.g., Dumont 1983; Trautmann 1981; Uberoi 1994) compared marriage norms and practices, as well as terminological patterns, all of which suggested that the repetition of intermarriage from one generation to the next, i.e., "marriage alliance," exists in the south but not in the north of the subcontinent. In contrast, several publications by Pfeffer (e.g., 1982) and Parkin (e.g., 1985) added data on affinal relationships as found in the very heterogeneous ethnographic literature on tribal Central India or resulting from Pfeffer's extended fieldwork. The two authors also developed hypotheses about the Scheduled Tribes speaking languages of the Munda family (Parkin 1992b) and all language families (Pfeffer 1983), since tribal relationship terminologies and marriage rules could be classified neither as "southern" nor as "North Indian," though they bore resemblances to both of these general "types."

Regarding marriage practices, or the implementation of specific and far-reaching affinal norms, only McDougal's dissertation (McDougal 1963, 160 f.), based on long-term field research among the Juang, has supplied reliable data from Central India, though these were not compared or contrasted to the data on terminology and rules. As a result, the anthropological public has been informed about rather complicated sets of marriage regulations and rather intriguing terminological structures in this region without convincing reports on the practical management of the rules or the application of the relationship terminologies. The co-ordination of these three dimensions of affinity, i.e., terminology, norms, and behaviour, is generally of great importance and even more so among the Dongria Kond and other Scheduled Tribes, since these ethnic units lack any other type of formal constitution. In these societies, kinship and affinity offer the parameters for organisational achievements and interpretative efforts otherwise associated with the domains of economy, religion, power and conflict resolution, or any other such field.

My contribution is an attempt to close the lacuna described above. As part of this introduction, I will initially summarise the main debates concerning the existence of different kinship "systems" on the Indian subcontinent. Next, I will offer a rather complicated introduction to Dongria terminology (3.2. Terminology). A discussion of the marriage rules will follow, which is encumbered by references to unfamiliar Dongria categories and ethnographic illustrations and could be difficult going for anyone not familiar with the socio-cultural logic involved (3.3. Rules). An even greater challenge to the patience of my readers will come next, when I reveal how Dongria practical politics offers room for multiple manipulations of the marriage rules, so that an altogether different picture, compared to the formal rules, arises from the given conditions "on the ground" (3.4. Practice). Again, these manipulations will be demonstrated in ethnographic cases that reveal unfamiliar logical ground.

Pan-Indian debates on kinship and affinity are concerned with the issue of marriage alliance, i.e., the repetition of intermarriage from one generation to the next. In contrast, Dongria Kond have strict rules *against* such intergenerational affinal ties. In fact, the meticulous prohibitions do set out typical ideas of alliance, but they articulate them in an *inverse* manner, forbidding the repetition of intermarriage and the symmetric exchange of marital partners between two "sides." In observed practice, however, my ethnography will reveal numerous manipulations to achieve the exact opposite, i.e., repeated marriages between the same "sides" from one generation to the next, as well as mutual "give and take" between the two "sides." No such contradictions have been reported so far in the literature. The explicit rules to avoid "holistic" marriages and the overwhelming practical implementation of what has been prohibited must be regarded as a central feature of Kond sociability, Kond conflict, and Kond values discussed in the conclusion (3.5. Conclusions). Compared with observations in other Indian regions or ethnic units, it is far from clear whether these Dongria contradictions have any parallels elsewhere.

3.1.1 Terminology, norms, and practice

> Any consideration of marriageability in a given society must [...] investigate separately, and compare: the terminological prescriptions (if any); the institutionalised exchange preferences; and the behavioural practices of that society. (Barnard and Good 1984, 102)

This statement is meant as advice to research scholars dealing with phenomena summarised under the broad labels "marriage" or "kinship," but it also contains the conclusion drawn by these authors from a long debate that basically began with Morgan's seminal work on "Systems of Consanguinity and Affinity" (Morgan 1870). The basic question is how the terms denoting relatives – the kinship *categories* – relate to other aspects of social life. Morgan concentrated on the study of kinship terms and related a particular structural feature, the existence or absence of the terminological merging of lineal and collateral relatives, to wider aspects of society, in particular the division of societies into two types, *societas* and *civitas*. Due to the evolutionary straitjacket imposed on Morgan,[1] he abandoned his earlier approach of seeing different kinship systems as expressions of two types of classification, the natural or "descriptive," which supposedly follows relations imposed by nature, and the artificial or "classificatory," which classifies relatives independently from natural relations (Trautmann 1987). Influenced by McIlvaine, a Presbyterian minister, Morgan later began to "naturalise" classificatory relationship terminologies by seeing them as a direct result of certain marriage practices, which he then arranged into an evolutionary sequence.

Rivers adopted Morgan's opposition of two types of terminologies, the "classificatory" and the "descriptive," and added a third one, the "kindred system" (Rivers [1914] 1968, 54–62). He further related the classificatory system to a system of clans arranged in moieties, so-called "dual organisation" (Rivers 1968, 67), and to particular marriage rules. Rivers insisted on the necessity of relating kinship terms to social functions, rights and duties, privileges, and avoidances and demonstrated how classificatory terminologies were derived from the equation of relatives belonging to the same clan and from marriage to a "cross-cousin" (Rivers 1968, 69–70). Like Morgan, Rivers thus treated terminologies as a direct outcome of marriage rules and practices and speculated about possible evolutionary sequences.

---

[1] Morgan's work has been re-examined by Trautmann ([1981] 1995, 1987). On the basis of Morgan's original manuscripts and his correspondence with his editors, Trautmann is able to demonstrate how Morgan had to change his original treatment of kinship terms in order to adapt it to the mainstream evolutionary theory of his time.

Kroeber was one of the first researchers to break away from this intellectual fashion by treating relationship terminologies on their own, independent of social rules, in his short but highly influential article published in 1909. He suggested eight possible ways to order kinship relations, which can be found in different combinations in various actual terminologies. Kroeber's approach was later adapted by other anthropologists interested in setting up typologies of classification. The most famous are the typologies of Lowie (1928) and Kirchhoff (1932), who classified relations in the first ascending generation ("generational," "bifurcate collateral," "lineal," and "bifurcate merging") and of Murdock (1949), who distinguished certain equivalences on different generational levels and named them rather arbitrarily on the basis of their occurrence in the terminology of one particular ethnic group (e. g., Hawaiian type, Eskimo type, Sudanese type, Iroquois type, Crow or Choctaw type, Omaha type).

Kroeber and Rivers set the trends in dealing with kinship terminologies for most authors throughout the whole twentieth century; terminologies were either taken out of their social context and treated like linguistic categories, an approach that led in its extreme form to so-called "componentional" or "transformational analysis" (e.g., Goodenough 1956; Lounsbury 1956; Scheffler and Lounsbury 1971), or they were seen as embedded in social contexts, which led to the question of the extent to which they are indeed related to other social phenomena. Among the authors following the latter approach, a further distinction may be drawn between those who related terminologies mainly to aspects of descent and group affiliation and those who laid stress on systems of opposition and exchange and examined terminologies in association with different rules of marriage. These distinctions led to well-known debates between the proponents of the "descent theory," in particular Radcliffe-Brown, and the advocates of the "alliance theory," like Lévi-Strauss and Louis Dumont.[2] The debate first appeared as a confrontation between the two intellectual traditions of British social anthropology, with its stress on jural and legal aspects of social organisation, and French ethnology, with its interest in mental evolution and total social phenomena based on exchange. A major point of discussion was the definition of "descent" and its role as a principle in organising society. While Radcliffe-Brown suggests that descent defines group membership and thereby serves to structure society into groups controlling different kinds of rights (Radcliffe-Brown 1952, 44–45), Dumont and others choose to follow Rivers, who defines de-

---

[2] The debate has been well summarised by Dumont (1971), Barnard and Good (1985), and Kuper (1988).

scent as a mode of affiliation into exogamous groups (Rivers 1968, 86; Dumont 1971,[3] 34). While "descent" as a principle appeals to those interested in defining *groups* or *corporations*, followers of alliance theory emphasise the aspect of exogamy because it calls for a theory of marriage, i.e., of *relations* between groups.

Soon, these intellectual borders became blurred, in particular in the writings of Edmund Leach (1951, 1954, 1955) and Rodney Needham (1966, 1967, 1971, 1973a), who combined insights into models of social organisation based on exchange with a strong empirical approach and rigorous analytical methods distinguishing different levels of data.

This leads me to the second trend within the tradition of kinship studies that relates relationship terminology to other social phenomena. In his analysis of Omaha relationship terminologies, Radcliffe-Brown (1952, 71–88) argues against Kroeber's treatment of kin terms independently from the social context. According to Radcliffe-Brown, correspondences between kinship nomenclature and social practices are found all over the world. He holds that kinship systems everywhere group people into categories, and the relations between people classified in this way are characterised by certain rights and duties, as well as socially approved attitudes and modes of behaviour (Radcliffe-Brown 1952, 62–63). The categories relate to existing social relations, which are again structured by certain "principles." It is these principles of social organisation that Radcliffe-Brown is interested in analysing, rather than relationship terminologies. Thus, he relates the terminology of the Fox Indians to a system of descent and the "principle" of the unity of the lineage group. His "principles" all start from the idea of the importance of relations established in the elementary family:

> The classificatory system, as thus interpreted, depends upon the recognition of the strong social ties that unite brothers and sisters of the same elementary family, and the utilisation of this tie to build up a complex orderly arrangement of social relations amongst kin. (Radcliffe-Brown 1952, 67)

Such a statement, of course, goes against the fundamental ideas of proponents of the alliance theory, particularly the atom of kinship proposed by Lévi-Strauss (1969) and related ideas about marriage as the fundamental principle on which certain societies are built. This difference led to a famous debate between Radcliffe-Brown and Dumont after the latter had published his analysis of the Dravidian kinship system (reprinted in Dumont 1983, 3–23). The main difference is

---

[3] The page numbers refer to a manuscript containing an English translation by Robert Parkin of the original French text. The manuscript is available at the Institute of Ethnology, Free University of Berlin.

that Radcliffe-Brown starts from the assumption that the system is based on relations of consanguinity, while Dumont begins from the idea that the system derives its logic from relations of affinity. According to Dumont, the system of classification expresses the value of affinity, which, combined with the rule of cross-cousin marriage, leads to alliance as an enduring institution, i.e., the consecutive repetition of marriage relations through the generations (Dumont 1983, 14). In other words, in such systems affinal relations are inherited and are given primary value, just as consanguinity is valued and inherited in Western society (Dumont 1983, 22).

Like Radcliffe-Brown, Dumont thus proposed to understand relationship terminology as an ordered whole and to analyse it in relation to social practices. However, these similarities are superficial. When Dumont speaks about the concept of a whole, he does not mean a functional whole in Radcliffe-Brown's sense, and when he considers practices, he is not interested in attitudes. According to Dumont, a whole is an idea that encompasses social aspects according to a certain principle or opposition. Thus, Dravidian terminology is a whole in the sense that everybody is encompassed in a structure that unites by distinguishing between kin and affine. It may operate in an ego-centred way, but it is oriented towards the whole, i.e., society (Dumont 1983, 17). When analysing Indian relationship terminologies, Dumont relates them to marriage rules, the "caste system", or gift exchanges (Dumont 1983, 36–104), but unlike Radcliffe-Brown, he is not interested in identifying individual kinship relations and the attitudes and codes of conduct linked to them. Further, Dumont is always careful to distinguish between the terminological system, "an abstract frame of reference" (Dumont 1983, 76), and kinship behaviour in his analysis, i.e., he always explicitly marks which level he is talking about.

His distinction of two levels of data, categories and behaviour, was further refined by Needham (1973a) in his highly influential article on prescription, in which he argues that kinship terms are a system of classification.[4] He distinguishes the classification of relatives from the rules expressing preferences in a society and from actual practices. Needham thus advocates a differentiation of three levels of data that have to be examined separately, since it cannot be assumed that they are necessarily congruent.

Needham does not restrict himself to describing and analysing "kinship," understood as an "odd-job word" (Needham 1974, 42), but suggests analysing re-

---

[4] These ideas had already been proposed by Needham in earlier articles, in particular in 1966 and 1967, but in this article he summarises them most clearly.

lationship terminologies in a comparative way. However, he simultaneously expresses two warnings:

> What I am arguing against is, in the first place, the conventional typology which – by the very fact of assigning terminologies to named substantive types – leads us to imagine that the form of a society's relationship terminology tells us more than it ever can. Secondly, I am arguing against the related assumption that societies with similar terminologies [...] are thereby sociologically similar also. (Needham 1974, 59)

On one hand, by insisting on the analysis of principles instead of types he reaffirms the importance of Kroeber's contribution to the study of kinship and overcomes the typologies created by Murdock. On the other hand, by linking the study of principles with the comparison of rules and practices he overcomes Kroeber's strict separation between categories and practice. This leaves us with two compatible approaches: we may compare relationship terminologies abstracted from any particular context as an expression of a certain system of classification, and we may relate a relationship terminology to the rules and practices found in a particular society.

Lévi-Strauss never fully agreed with Needham on the separation of terminology and rules and the related distinction between prescription and preference (Lévi-Strauss 1965, 1969). Instead, he drew a different line by distinguishing between a "mechanical model," in which marriage may be called prescriptive because the elements fit neatly into the envisaged model, and a "statistical model," in which marriages may be said to be preferred only because deviations from the ideal occur due to individual choice, demography, probabilities, etc. (Lévi-Strauss 1965; 1969, xxxv). Thus, marriage rules may be said to be prescriptive on the level of the ideal or mechanical model and preferential on the level of observation or the statistical model. Dumont seems to agree with this proposition, because he believes a rule may serve to integrate ideas in the mind even if it does not have the same force in actually organising social groups.[5] Therefore, in his opinion, the marriage rule he encountered during his fieldwork in South India "turns around an ideal formulation, more or less realized in fact, of the role of the maternal uncle as identical to the father-in-law (of a man), a role concerning prestations and ceremonies which dramatically opposes him to the father [...]. The rule thus works to model actual reality in conformity with a formula of order, of honour and may we say of beauty which is present in mind" (Dumont

---

5 In his stocktaking in 1981 Dumont uses the word "mandatory" instead of "prescription" for the terminological level and "preference" for the level of the rule applied to particular groups (Dumont 1983, 171).

1971, 114–15). We might further note that restricting the term "prescriptive" to the categorical level of terminology unnecessarily limits the range of data forming the ideal model. Dumont mentions ceremonies and gift exchanges as examples, and we might also add the rules implied in mythological charters about the constitution of society or of proper marriages.[6]

However, for analytical reasons I suggest differentiating between three levels of data and reserving different technical terms for phenomena of an ideal and classificatory type. Thus the discrepancy between the prescriptive marriage of cross-cousins on the terminological level and the preferred marriage of the Pramalai Kallar for the matrilateral cross-cousin can only be recognised when, following Needham, we distinguish between these two levels. How we interpret this matter and how the rules relate to a "formula of order" is an altogether different question. Second, it is advisable to use the term "prescriptive" only for a certain type of terminology as defined by Needham[7] in order to be able to make comparative statements. Only if certain terminologies can be termed "prescriptive" because they are based on particular principles of classification can they be distinguished from terminologies that lack such features. Other terms can be found to describe the imperatives attached to rules expressed in mythological charters or collective rituals.

The leading proponents of these debates have never wandered far from the intellectual interests exhibited by Lewis Henry Morgan more than a hundred years ago in his study of relationship terminologies, although each of them has given priority to certain aspects of Morgan's work. Morgan collected terminologies all over the world and developed a comparative approach that was never abandoned, although many authors restricted themselves to certain cultural, linguistic, or geographical areas rather than studying terminologies worldwide. Further, apart from approaches stressing the linguistic aspects of terminologies, most authors have, like Morgan, tried to link them to other social and cultural phenomena, whether modes of agricultural production or bureaucracy, forms of social organisation, or marriage rules and practices. It might have been expected that Morgan's evolutionism would be abandoned in the study of relationship terminologies, but this would be correct only with respect to his later attempts to correlate kinship and forms of marriage or kinship and technology (see Morgan's *Ancient Society*). With regard to his original interest in the evolution of types of terminology, attempts to speculate about how and why cer-

---

6 For Trautmann's position on the matter see Trautmann (1981, 217). It seems he was unaware of Needham's proposal, since Needham's works do not appear in his bibliography.

7 "Prescriptive terminologies can readily be identified, by the invariant relation that articulates relations between lines" (Needham 1974, 56).

tain forms evolved can be observed in the Oxford tradition in particular (Allen, 1975, 1976, 1986; Pfeffer 1983, 1993; Parkin 1992a, 1992b). Typologies as Morgan first used them have never been completely abandoned, although they have come under attack, in particular by Needham, who prefers the study of principles instead of types (Needham 1974, 5), and by Barnard and Good, who question the usefulness of "pseudo-ethnographic labels" in the study of general principles (Barnard and Good 1984, 59). Finally, Morgan's insight into different ways of ordering the world of social relations and – even more important – into the nature of classification has been in the background of many debates, in particular about the difference between descriptive and holistic terminologies and about the question of whether or not people universally define kinship with regard to genealogy (see Scheffler vs Dumont). In this chapter I will argue that terminologies are a part of classification and that they may differ according to whether or not they involve the systematic order of a whole (in the Maussian sense) and whether or not they define "kin" in genealogical terms or otherwise. For this reason, I will from now on use the expression "relationship terminologies" (Barnard and Good 1984, 37) instead of kinship terminologies, in order to express the possibility that the "relations" expressed in these terms are not necessarily ordered by kinship understood as a genealogical link.

All these debates have had an impact on the study of relationship terminologies in India. Starting with Morgan, the so-called "Dravidian kinship system" became a standard case for a certain type of relationship terminology in many authors, although it did not enter Murdock's ethnic typology.[8] Later, first Irawati Karve ([1953] 1965) and then Louis Dumont (1962b, 1966, 1975) compared terminologies, rules and practices in the whole of India, and Dumont and Vatuk (1969, 1975) in particular concentrated on similarities between North and South India. The central region, although also dealt with by Karve, became a topic of research and analysis first by Pfeffer (1982, 1983) and to a certain extent by Trautmann ([1981] 1995) and later by Parkin (1992a, 1992b). The following chapter will present a short summary of these debates, which directly affect our analysis of a Central Indian "tribal society" whose members speak an Indo-European and a Dravidian language, and some of whom adhere to the rules of "cross-cousin marriage" while others adhere to rules also observed by many people in North India.

I will use various terms, such as "Dravidian terminology," "North Indian terminology," "Munda terminology," or "kinship system," because these were the terms that the authors I cite used in discussing the various issues. However, at

---

8 The "Iroquois type" resembles certain "Dravidian" equivalences most closely.

the same time, I have reservations about these analytical expressions. My strongest reservations concern the use of labels derived from linguistics for phenomena grounded in culture and society. Barnard and Good (1984, 49) make this point in arguing against the very widespread use of the term "Dravidian system," and Pfeffer (1993, 49) convincingly brings into question the construction of a "Munda" (Parkin 1992b) social organisation as if there were a necessary link between a language family and a certain type of social formation. This is particularly questionable in an area like Central India, where people speak languages belonging to three different language families but share very similar value-ideas and forms of social organisation (Pfeffer 1997b, 6–7). Again, the expression "kinship system" should be used with reservation, because it conveys the idea that there is a strong congruence between all levels of data, something that in general cannot be expected (see Good 1981) and in any case must be proven empirically. In general, I think it is better to distinguish between "kinship regions," with two reservations: First, none of these regions should be seen as discrete areas, neither in linguistic nor in kinship terms. For example, Barnard and Good point to the fact that "some Dravidian-speakers, such as the Nayar (Gough 1952) and groups practising eZDy marriage (Good 1980), do not have "Dravidian" terminologies according to any of the formal definitions, whereas some non-Dravidian speakers in the same region, such as the Kandyan Sinhalese, do" (Barnard and Good 1984, 59).[9] Second, the goal is not to define a type, but to describe and analyse the ideas and principles underlying the categories, norms, and practices of the people we encounter in our fieldwork.

3.1.2 Diachronic alliance with relatives: The "South Indian kinship system"

Indian relationship terminologies stood in the centre of long and very difficult debates continuing from the 1950s to the 1980s, but afterwards the new protagonists of the discipline lost interest in them, and nowadays most readers, even among anthropologists, find it hard to understand these highly complex issues. The following is not intended to give a thorough summary of these debates but rather to point out the basic issues discussed during this period of time.[10]

---

9 See also Majumdar (1960) on "Dravidian" equivalences in a Himalayan region.
10 The different "kinship systems" are well summarised by Karve (1965) for India and by Pfeffer (1985) for South India in general. Skoda (2000) gives a short but very good introduction to the three "types" of Indian terminologies. For the presentation of North Indian terminology he relies heavily on the summary by Trautmann (1995, 91–103). While Skoda concentrates on the characteristics of each terminology, I will put a greater emphasis on the development of the arguments.

The most important figure in these debates was Louis Dumont, who aimed at understanding fundamental sociological categories by way of comparison – comparison between our genealogical understanding of kinship and other people's universe of kinship and between South and North Indian concepts of ordering social relations. His starting point was the Pramalai Kallar and other castes he studied during an intensive two-year period of fieldwork. While his doctoral thesis was mostly neglected, even after its publication in English in 1986, Dumont "shocked" the discipline with a purely structuralist interpretation of what he – following the practice established by Morgan – called the Dravidian kinship terminology. This terminology had exercised the minds of leading anthropologists for many decades: Morgan (1870) derived his second stage or *punaluan* family from the terms sent to him by a missionary working in Tamil Nadu (Arcot Mission), Rivers (1968) dealt with it as an example of a previous dual organisation in which cross-cousin marriage and a distinction between cross- and parallel cousins "survived" as a practice, Lowie (1928) used it as an example of the type of equation called bifurcate merging, and Radcliffe-Brown (1952) "explained" it by reference to his allegedly universal principle of the "solidarity of the sibling group."

It was the last of these who reacted with a deep sense of irritation to the new interpretation proposed by Dumont in the early 1950s. For Radcliffe-Brown, the most disturbing element of Dumont's article was his claim that in the terminology under study the mother's brother was not considered to be a cognate, i.e., a "brother of the mother," but an affine, i.e., the representative of a whole category of people who are classified as standing in an affinal relationship to ego's father. The whole proposal was such a radical break with conventional definitions of and approaches to "kinship" that Radcliffe-Brown admitted that he did not understand it and asked Dumont "to be enlightened as to its meaning" (quoted in Dumont 1983, 18). What Dumont, in fact, attempted to achieve in this article was indeed impressive in light of the few (fourteen) pages he devoted to the matter. What are these major shifts in the study of "Dravidian terminology"?

First, unlike Radcliffe-Brown, Dumont did not bother to write about behavioural aspects of the "mother's brother," how he acts, what people think about him, or how he is treated by others. Instead, he concentrated on the terminology as distinct from kinship behaviour. Second, neither specific terms nor the four principles of the terminology were of importance to him, and consequently, he presents them at the beginning of his article as a kind of standard knowledge[11]

---

[11] Classification according to generations, distinction of sex, distinction of two kinds of relatives within certain generations, distinction of age.

and then proceeds with what is of real interest to him. In his response to Radcliffe-Brown, he explains his own approach in the following way: "we take the terminological system as a whole and try to determine from its structure what the content of each of its categories is" (Dumont 1983, 21). This leads to the most revolutionary aspect of this article, because by giving priority to the local system of defining "kinship" relations, he sets up a distinction between "us" and "them," i.e., our understanding of the categories of kinship and the definitions implied by the Dravidian system of classification.

These findings are at the core of the article and may be summarised as follows: like our own terminology, the Dravidian system operates with the distinction between affines and kin, but it defines them in a different way. The distinction is based on a relationship created by marriage that divides the whole social universe into terminological affines, i.e., a relationship of alliance, and terminological kin, i.e., a relationship from which alliance is excluded. This kind of classification differs from ours in several ways. First, it orders the whole according to a simple opposition and can thus be termed a "system." Second, the terms stand for whole classes of relatives and not for certain persons linked to ego genealogically. Third, marriageability become the major principle for defining categories of relationships. Finally, fourth, the terminology implies alliance across generations,[12] and the perfect way to achieve this in practice is the so-called "cross-cousin" marriage. What Dumont claims here and in later articles is nothing less than a fundamental shift from "our own way of thinking, unconsciously superimposed on the native thinking," to an understanding of local categories implied in the terminology. His major argument is that Western anthropologists start from the notion that consanguineal relations come prior to affinal relations and that in their perspective affinal relations are ephemeral, while "blood-relations" are inherited across generations. In contrast, the Dravidian terminology in his analysis values affinity, i.e., the transmission of marriage relations across generations, which leads to alliances or inherited marriage relations on the practical level.

A final novelty of this early article was the way Dumont presented the terminology in a diagram. In accordance with his aim to capture the terminology's systematic character,[13] he did not bother using particular terms, their linguistic

---

[12] The MB is not only an affine of F but as a SpP also in an affinal relationship to ego. The MB's children are ego's potential marriage partners, and the osSbC are the potential marriage partners of ego's children.
[13] In a later article on North Indian terminology, Dumont (1966, 96) describes his method in the following way: "The attempt is as usual to extract from the configuration of the system of kinship terms the definition of the fundamental categories of kinship. The concrete linguistic form

forms, or their etymology, but instead used different capital letters for the various words that in different Dravidian languages denote certain relationships. He then ordered these letters not in a typical genealogical diagram but rather in boxes ordered by the principles of the terminology itself: sex, generation, cross/parallel, and relative age. This kind of diagram has been accepted by many anthropologists (e.g., Good 1981; Trautmann 1981; Pfeffer 1982; Parkin 1992a, 1992b) dealing with "lineal terminologies," defined by Needham as a "classification in which the typical feature, in the medial three genealogical levels at least, is the distinction of statuses according to whether relationship is defined through persons of the same sex or not." As Pfeffer (2004a) points out, in agreement with Needham's works, the expression "lineal" should not be assumed to be related to descent, because the diagram does not take into account group affiliation but rather only the logical order of categories.

Subsequently, in an article first published in 1957 (see Dumont 1983, chapter 2), Dumont elaborated his argument, in particular researching kinship behaviour, which in his analysis confirms the overall importance of alliance in South India despite, for example, the contradiction between the symmetric terminology and certain asymmetric prestations or the asymmetric preference of the Pramalai Kallar groups for the maternal cross-cousin (from the male perspective). One new point of interest compared to the earlier and much shorter article was Dumont's analysis of the relation between kinship and caste, which led him to propose that "there is no absolute difference between what happens inside and outside a caste group" (Dumont 1983, 37). Later, after having examined kinship data from North India in more detail, he refined this statement from a comparative point of view by suggesting that in South India the hierarchical principle of caste did not enter into the basic kinship categories, defined by the distinctive opposition between kin and affines (Dumont 1983, 166).

These far-reaching claims led to new research and various responses by authors belonging to different schools of thought. Those who were in favour of the descent theory of kinship, for example Kathleen Gough, argued that the terminology cannot be understood independently from the particular organisation of South Indians in descent groups. Others, in particular Scheffler, favoured an approach developed by the proponents of "componential" analysis and explained the categories by reference to the principle of extension, i.e., the broadening of the meaning of a kinship term from "primary relatives" to "secondary relatives," thereby bringing into question the whole structuralist approach to

---

of the terms, their etymological meanings, etc., will be disregarded in an effort to draw boundaries between what is fundamentally different from the point of view of kinship."

the terminology as a system. Finally, members of the so-called ethnosociological school followed David Schneider's (1968, 1972) suggestion that "kinship" is basically a cultural construct and McKim Marriott's (1990) application of some of Schneider's ideas derived from the study of American kinship to India. This approach produced a number of important contributions to the study of kinship in North (Fruzetti, Östor, and Barnett 1976) and South India (David 1973; Barnett 1976) concerning the question of how kinship categories are defined in cultural terms, in particular in relation to concepts about bodily substances and certain codes of conduct. In his "Stocktaking 1981" (Dumont 1983), Dumont discusses some of these research results and their contribution to the understanding of South Indian kinship. Therefore, I will not go into further detail but instead concentrate on two other important developments.

In the same year in which Dumont summarised the state of research on South India, Thomas Trautmann published his seminal monograph on Dravidian kinship. Combining methods and sources from philology, history, and anthropology, Trautmann presents the most comprehensive treatment of so-called Dravidian kinship terminologies available at this time. He deals with terminologies from South India and Sri Lanka, as well as many variants from the so-called "ethnographic frontiers of Dravidian kinship" that are of particular importance to this chapter. Through this comparative study Trautmann (1995, 229–37) aims to reconstruct a proto-Dravidian relationship terminology. Although he explicitly differentiates between his own "historical" method of defining the system and "a formal abstraction that generalises the common features of the particular Dravidian systems," i.e., Dumont's approach, the result (Trautmann 1995, 232) is remarkably, though not entirely unexpectedly, quite similar, except perhaps for the stronger stress put on the principle of relative age. Trautmann examines the nature of cross-cousin marriage in the past by studying Sanskrit sacred law, literature in Sanskrit, Pali, and Prakrit, and inscriptions and chronicles about dynastic marriages.

Of all the authors who address Dravidian kinship, Trautmann is perhaps the one who examines the concept of "crossness" (Trautmann 1995, 41) most elaborately. For him, cross-cousin marriage is "at the heart of the characteristically Dravidian discriminations made within ego's generation" (Trautmann 1995, 47), i.e., the distinction between parallel and cross-cousins. In an almost algebraic approach to kinship, Trautmann finds different rules for determining "crossness" or its opposite and presents complex tables of equations for different kintypes. Apart from the difficulties of understanding this kind of presentation, another point of critique may be raised, one first articulated by Dumont decades before Trautmann's publication. In his 1953 article he expresses almost in passing his dissatisfaction with the expression "cross-cousin marriage," because it uses the imagery of "kin" or genealogy to convey the idea of alliance (Dumont 1983, 14). In another statement published in the same volume, he makes his point more explicit in a critique of Carter:

> For our forerunners, it [i.e., cross-cousin marriage, R.H.] was a label designating a particular form of marriage between close relatives. Then, on closer inspection, it turned out that there was a transition from the immediate *genealogical* cross-cousin to more remote relatives falling into the same *category*. [...] What Carter is doing is to separate the two and to maintain the existence of "intermarrying classes" while denying that marriage with the immediate genealogical cross-cousin plays any significant role. [...] It is of course true that to translate the *category* as "cross-cousin" is misleading. Roughly speaking, I proposed to translate it as "affines". (Dumont 1983, 163; emphasis original)

In other words, when Trautmann stresses "crossness" as a principle of the terminology, he in fact defines an affinal category with reference to a genealogical link that is only important (or not) at the level of marriage practices. This leads to the conclusion that it is advisable to name the categories according to the principle – "alliance" – and not "crossness," while the study of marriage practices should consider "crossness" as part of the selection of marriage partners. Good does not agree with Dumont on this point and comments, "In my view, it is precisely the neutral character of the terms "parallel" and "cross" which makes their use desirable" (Good 1981, 115).

Good conducted anthropological fieldwork in Tamil Nadu and applied Needham's distinction of three different levels to his data. I will also use this approach in this chapter and will, therefore, concentrate on this aspect of Good's work and neglect his second major contribution, the study of "elder sister's daughter marriage" in South India.[14] In an article published in 1981, Good first attempts to analyse the terminology of his informants and basically follows Dumont's identification of four different principles and his portrayal of the terminology in a linear diagram. Further, he identifies the terms for the terminologically prescribed spouse of a male or female ego (*kolundiyal* and *attan*): "That is a man has to marry a junior cross-relative of his own terminological level and a woman a senior cross-relative of her own level" (Good 1981, 115). He continues on in a separate chapter to discuss the "rules and preferences" of the group under study. In this part of his paper he considers negative rules related to exogamous groups and groups defined by family deities, as well as positive rules or

---

[14] See Good (1980) on how caste groups among whom marriage with the eZD is prevalent employ a system of categories not structured by the ideal "Dravidian" type. See also the critical comments by Trautmann (1995, "Preface to the Indian Edition," xiv) on Good's claim that eZD marriage constitutes the normal pattern in South India.

"preferences" for a certain kind of marriage on the basis of "genealogy," in this case with the patrilateral cross-cousin (male perspective). Other rules or attitudes concerning village exogamy, direct sister exchange, and status differences between spouses are also addressed. In another chapter he presents the statistical data he collected in two different places concerning actual marriages. The data show only slight differences between the numbers of FZD and MBD unions and a very high proportion of marriages with actual cross-cousins, in particular when taking into account the number of cross-cousins in a given sample.[15] In his conclusion, Good compares the three levels and finds that the overall symmetric pattern of the terminology is *not consistent* with the preference for one type of cross-cousin, yet there is *no contradiction* because the rule makes only further discriminations but otherwise "operate[s] within the framework of categorical boundaries" (Good 1981, 124). When taking into account actual marriage practices, Good concludes that they correspond more closely to the symmetry implied by the categories than to the asymmetry contained in the rules. This need not be the case in all sub-castes, and as Good is eager to point out, the statistical behaviour cannot be inferred from the rules. There is always a certain autonomy of each level that prevents us from making any predictions. Inconsistency, rather than contradiction, between categories and rules is probably a very essential feature of most systems, because otherwise rules in general would be superfluous (Good 1981, 127). The distinction of three levels of data thus not only imposes itself as a proper way to present ethnographic data but also encapsulates a theory of change!

As described in this chapter, Dumont's 1953 article influenced further research and a joint effort by many scholars to concentrate their attention on a topic imposed on them by the intricacy of the data. He achieved exactly the same result a decade later when he shifted his attention to the study of North Indian kinship.

3.1.3 Perpetuating alliance through gifts: The "North Indian kinship system"

In the 1950s and 1960s Dumont was mainly concerned with understanding the principle of hierarchy, an endeavour that culminated in his major work, *Homo Hierarchicus*, first published in 1966. His comparison of North and South Indian kinship should be seen within this framework, as well as his overall question

---

15 On this important point for the analysis of statistical data about cross-cousin marriage see in particular Trautmann (1995, 221).

about the role of hierarchy in India and the question "Is India one?" (Dumont and Pocock 1957). As mentioned above, in his study on South Indian kinship he had already pointed out that hierarchy is not absent, because it does not stop at the boundaries of caste but pervades kinship. In his further study of Nayar kinship (Dumont 1964) he refines this notion by showing that endogamy is encompassed by the hierarchical principle (Dumont 1964, 91), but he also contrasts the isogamic pattern of the south with the hypergamic pattern of the north (Dumont 1964, 92). The question then is whether the North Indian terminology can be said to encapsulate the alliance pattern (or "kinship") in the form of a distinctive opposition, as in the south, or whether it is instead pervaded by the hierarchical principle (or "caste") of the encompassment of the contrary.

Before we enter into this debate, let us first consider quite generally what the main features of North Indian, i.e., first of all Hindi, terminology are in comparison to South Indian, more exactly Tamil, terminology. In this discussion I will closely follow Trautmann's (1995, 92–103) excellent summary. In general, the number of terms on each generational level is much higher in Hindi than in Tamil. Thus, Hindi has eight terms for the +2 generation compared to two in Tamil, fifteen for +1 compared to eight, fourteen in ego's generation compared to eight, and so on (Trautmann 1995, 102). The large number of terms in the +2 generation is due to the fact that not only are maternal and paternal relatives named differently, but in contrast to Tamil, one's spouse's grandparents are also denoted by separate terms (e.g., HFF, WFFF is *dadsara*). In the first ascending generation, Hindi has three separate terms for F, FeB, and FyB, while Tamil contains only one word (*appa*), to which prefixes denoting relative age (*periya* for elder, *cinna* for younger) are added (Trautmann 1995, 40). Again, while Hindi restricts the relative age distinction in the +1 level to the paternal side (maternal side only M = *ma*; MZ = *mausi*), Tamil applies it to both sides and in contrast to Hindi, also to members of ego's own generation (e.g., eB = *annan*, yB = *tampi*). Another major difference exists in the distinction Hindi makes between one's parents' opposite-sex siblings and one's spouse's parents (e.g., MB ≠ SpF). Hindi does not classify parent's siblings and parent's sibling's spouse in the same way as Tamil does (MB = FZH, FZ = MBW, FB = MZH, MZ = FBW) but has separate terms for each of these relations (MB ≠ FZH, FZ ≠ MBW, FB ≠ MZH, MZ ≠ FBW), and it also does not make the typical Tamil distinction between cross and parallel linked to the sex of the speaker in the −1 generation (BSws = ZSms, ZSw = BSms = S, ZDws = BDms = D, ZDms = BDws) but individualises these relations (ZS ≠ BS ≠ S and D ≠ BD ≠ ZD). This leads Trautmann (1995, 96) to the general conclusion that "Hindi terminology is, speaking broadly, much more analytic, the Tamil comparatively synthesizing." The only example Trautmann himself provides that contradicts this statement is the previously mentioned recognition of relative age in Tamil terminology, which is missing in Hindi except in the relation between HB and BW.[16] Another sharp difference between both terminologies becomes apparent when we consider categories for "consanguines" and "affines"[17] in ego's generation. Since this problem is at the heart of the debate, we will return to it after presenting Dumont's initial attempts to analyse the North Indian terminology.

Dumont's first major attempt to answer the question of the relation between South and North Indian kinship was in an article published in *Contributions to Indian Sociology* in 1966.[18] It was based on fieldwork he had conducted in eastern Uttar Pradesh, and the starting point was the differences between North and South Indian kinship mentioned earlier by Karve (1965). Dumont, while agreeing in general that the two systems differ from each other, questions the magnitude of these differences by asking whether the importance of affinity he identified in South India is absent in North Indian kinship. While fully aware that his endeavours were premature, he nevertheless analyses ceremonial prestations, North Indian terminologies, and marriage rules and comes to the conclusion that it is possible to identify a common pattern in North and South India, consisting in the "*consequent elaboration and ordering* or *patterning, of affinal relationships*" (1966, 113; emphasis original).

This conclusion was based on the following observations. First, an analysis of ceremonial prestations brings to the fore that *irrespective of generation* bride-givers and bride-takers of an agnatic group are linked by the exchange of certain categories of gifts. In other words, in North India the continuity of affinal relations is expressed on the *practical level* of prestations. This result was basically confirmed by Vatuk (1975) in a later article dealing with similar prestations in the context of funerals. Her data show the existence of a status difference between bride-givers and bride-takers that is upheld through the generations by a unidirectional flow of gifts to a category of bride-takers called *dhyana*.

Next, Dumont turns to the terminological level. From the start, he acknowledges that the terminology does not separate a category of "bride-givers" and that affinity is not transmitted from one generation to another (Dumont 1966, 93). He describes the problems he encountered when trying to follow the method

---

16 Trautmann (1995, 98) links the terminological separation of HeB and HyB to the institution of levirate (a woman can marry her HyB when her husband dies but not her HeB).

17 Both these terms have to be understood as open categories that change their exact meaning according to the society under study.

18 Already in 1962, Dumont (1962b) had published an article in French dealing with North Indian terminology, in which he gave the details of the terminology he discussed in his 1966 article.

he had applied to the South Indian material, because the North Indian terms cannot be represented in a simple system of oppositions. They do not have a "structure," or in Needham's terms, it is not a "lineal terminology." Instead, Dumont prefers to call it a "configuration" or "texture" that orders fundamental relationships by starting from an ego and can, therefore, be termed (in conscious opposition to Morgan) "descriptive" in contrast to the "classificatory" (or structural) system of the South, which orders the whole social "universe" (Dumont 1966, 96). This point, as well as Dumont's analysis of the categories *bhai* and *mama*, was later sharply criticised by Vatuk (1969) on the basis of her own very detailed ethnographic study. Her contribution and critique will be discussed below.

At this point I only want to draw attention to the last part of Dumont's analysis. Here he examines the marriage rules and practices of the Sarjupari Brahmins and makes the very important observation that the character of these rules is not completely different from that of those in the South. The main purpose of these rules is *not to prohibit* marriage alliance but *to limit* it, which otherwise means that a repetition of marriage alliance is generally *permissible* (Dumont 1966, 105). The same holds true for other rules prominent in the whole of North India, like the *sapindya* rule or the four-*gotra* rule. The former prohibits a large number of relatives as marriage partners on the basis of shared substance, but it does not prohibit certain marriages practised by the Brahmins under study, like MZHBD or FZHBD. Again, the four-*gotra* rule prohibits marriage with the same clan as one's grandparents (FF, FM, MM, MF), but it does not prohibit marriage with the clans of one generation beyond (e.g., FFF's clan). As he points out, this corresponds to rules linked to a three-generation gap. Vatuk confirmed this general argument with reference to her own data, although she expresses doubts about Dumont's data concerning the way in which the Sarjupari Brahmins elude the *sapindya* rule. Her general impression is that the people she studied do not marry close affinal kin but tend to repeat the direction of previous marriages in an indirect way (Vatuk 1969, 111). It was Pfeffer (1985, 178) who first described this phenomenon as "Zerstreuung" or dispersal, later called "dispersed alliance" by Parkin (1992a, 255), thereby adapting an expression commonly found in discussions of so-called Crow-Omaha systems (e.g., McKinley 1971).

According to Dumont, these are not really "kinship rules," because they are linked to status in the sense that their function is to uphold a difference of rank and privileges between bride-givers and bride-takers. When his view is expressed in this way, it is possible to agree with Dumont on this particular point, but it should be kept in mind that when he speaks of status, he means caste (Dumont 1966, 106), or the opposition of the pure and the impure. It may be appropriate to link such rules to status in the "caste system" of North India, but what intrigues me is that I found very similar rules in a local context where caste – as an organisation and as a "state of mind" – is relatively weak. This will be discussed in more detail in my analysis of "exogamy" among the Dongria Kond, but at this point it should be noted that rules may be related to status and hierarchy, but the definition of status and the social organisation linked to it may vary within India.

Let us now turn to the analysis of North Indian kinship. According to Dumont, this kinship is not a "system," it is descriptive rather than classificatory, and it does not show any clear patterns of affinity. Vatuk brings all of these statements into question after analysing her very elaborate data on the terminology of a local Hindi dialect spoken by urban people (Meerut) in western Uttar Pradesh. In her opinion, this terminology is classificatory, because people try to fit everybody into their social universe by finding an appropriate relationship term and because the terms denote whole classes of kin or kin categories. She is certainly correct on this point, but we can nevertheless see a difference between a structure that orders the social whole into such "classes" and a terminology that creates these classes in relation to an ego, i.e., the individual. Her second point of critique is more convincing, because she can demonstrate that marriage orders North Indian categories in a particular way.

Vatuk can convincingly show that the Hindi terminology in ego's generation contains three classes of relatives: a class of siblings and "quasi-consanguines," a class of bride-givers, and a class of bride-takers. Vatuk chooses the term "quasi-consanguine" in order to come to terms with the fact that the category *bhai/bahen* includes an important category of affines, for example BWZH/BWZHB/BWZHZ.[19] These terms indicate that "persons married to same sex "siblings" are "siblings" of one another" (Vatuk 1969, 101), an idea that corresponds to rules prohibiting the reversal of the marriage direction. In relation to bride-givers or bride-takers, ego and these quasi-consanguines have the same status, i.e., they both either give or receive.[20] This leads Vatuk to the most important pattern of the terms in ego's generation, the distinction between a class of bride-givers (including bride-giver's bride-giver etc.) and a class of bride-takers (including bride-taker's bride-taker etc.). For a male all bride-givers are either *sala* or *bhabi*, whereas for a female they are only *bhabi*, and all bride-takers are *jija* for a male but either *jija* or *nanad* for a female. This leads to the conclusion that there is an asymmetric pattern of marriage relations built into the terminology, in contrast to the symmetric alliance of the Dravidian terminology. Again, this corresponds to Vatuk's finding that there is a unidirectional flow of presta-

---

19 It should be noted, however, that WZH and HBW are called *bhai/bahen* only in address, not in reference.
20 See Jamous (1992), who refers to this phenomenon as "meta-siblingship."

tions from the lower bride-givers to the superior bride-takers. However, in contrast to South India, this clear pattern of affinity is not found beyond ego's generation, or in other words, the clear distinction between bride-givers and bride-takers can be identified in neither the +1 nor the −1 generation.

We will now turn to consideration of debates concerning the principles of kinship found in a region lying between North and South India, the area where the "tribal society" I studied is located.

3.1.4 Alternation and delayed alliance: The "Central Indian kinship system"

Compared to the other two major "regions," Central India became the focus of intensive comparative kinship studies very recently, the major attempts having begun in the early 1980s. Before this time the literature offered bits and pieces of information collected by various authors of Indian origin or from abroad, describing more or less unsystematically and without any knowledge of either descent or alliance theory diverse nomenclatures, marriage rules, and practices. An exception to this "piecemeal ethnography" is represented by the excellent doctoral thesis by McDougal (1963a), who conducted fifteen months of fieldwork among the Juang of Keonjhar district. While his articles (McDougal 1963b, 1964) were easily accessible to the public and quoted by various authors, his doctoral thesis remained unknown for a long time, as it was only published on microfiche. McDougal himself showed no inclination either to put his findings into a theoretical framework or to compare them with data from other tribes in the region.

While anthropologists before the Second World War concentrated their studies in India on "tribal societies", the post-war period saw a rapid decline in interest in tribal studies. Instead, the impressive Hindu civilisation, well documented in thousand-year-old sources and easily observable in accessible villages and vivid temple towns, became the focus for generations of anthropologists. Even kinship studies, normally considered the reserve of studies on "primitive" societies, were carried out with an intensity previously unknown, and the complexity of the interpretations was supported not only by extensive field studies by dozens of anthropologists from all over the world but also by reference to ancient sources made accessible by generations of Indologists (e. g., Tambiah 1973b; Trautmann 1995).

Compared to these ideal conditions, the situation for studying kinship in Central India appeared daunting, and it is to Georg Pfeffer's credit that under these conditions he single-handedly began the project of comparing and analysing the collective representations and social practices of several million people with diverse "tribal" names and languages populating a vast region. Such a situation demands an approach combining ethnographic work, the study of the existing literature, and comparative analysis. After initial fieldwork among the Shasan (Vedic) Brahmins of Odisha (1976), Pfeffer shifted his attention to the highlands, where he initially spent five months in 1980/81 traveling through several districts. This was followed by further research almost every other year with stays of between two to six months among people living in an area ranging from the extreme south of Odisha up into northern Odisha and Bihar. By now, this long-term research activity has led to the publication of many books and articles dealing with all aspects of social life, from the intricacies of kinship and marriage to complex feasts of merit. Pfeffer's own ethnographic efforts in the study of kinship and ritual have been supplemented by long-term fieldwork conducted by his students in Koraput district among the Gadaba (Berger 2000, 2002, 2007, 2015), among the Rona community (Otten 2000a, 2000b, 2006), and in a small industrial town (Strümpell 2006), as well as in Sambulpur district among the Aghria (Skoda 2000, 2005). A further project compared the religious movement called Mahima Dharma in Dhenkanal and Koraput (Guzy 2002).

Using Boas's (1914) insight into the absence of any deterministic relationship between language and culture, Pfeffer from the start approached these seemingly diverse people as inhabitants of a major *culture area* that could be distinguished into different types or "complexes." The differences and similarities between these types are seen by Pfeffer as "family resemblances" (Wittgenstein) and not as deviations from a particular "original" form. All in all, Pfeffer distinguishes four major "complexes" in the region, differing in socio-cultural rather than in linguistic terms. Within these complexes, he identifies two concepts of patrilineal affiliation, one linked to exogamous categories ("Clanship I"), the other to categories distinguishing sacred from secular status ("Clanship II"). From south to north, the complexes identified by Pfeffer (1997b) are:

1. the **Gond complex**, comprising several million people united by a system of phratries identified by numbers and/or totemic species (Clanship I); the clans are divided into a priestly segment, a secular or guardian segment, and a segment of "commoners" (Clanship II);
2. the **Koraput complex**, defined by a total of eight totemic clans shared by all tribes, although some make use of only a limited selection of these totems; in Pfeffer's analysis the totems are part of a symbolic classification indicating zones of altitude (Clanship I); all clans are divided into status segments referred to as *kuda* and distinguishing sacred (*kirsani, sisa,* and *pujari*) from secular (*badanaika, munduli,* and *chalan*) leadership (Clanship II);
3. the **Kond complex**, consisting of about a million people, the majority of whom inhabit the valleys and hills south of the Mahanadi River; they are re-

ported to be organised in territorial clans called *kuda* (not to be confused with the status category *kuda* in the Koraput complex) forming phratries or brotherhoods (Clanship I); each clan is again divided into segments called *punja* by some; these segments are distinguished on the basis of the binary opposition between secular (*bismajhi, mondal*) and religious (*jani, pujari*) specialists (Clanship II);

4. the **Chota Nagpur complex**, in which some groups (Kharia, Santal, Bhumji) have a limited number of clans, while others (Ho, Munda, Kisan, Oraon) recognise multiple distinctions (Clanship I); the famous institution of the *khunt* divides these clans and villages into senior and junior segments, a distinction that is related to the status of sacred or secular leadership or to the opposition between original settlers and latecomers (Clanship II).

Within these four complexes, Pfeffer identifies a wide range of terminologies belonging linguistically to three major language families (Indo-European, Dravidian, and Munda), a number of different rules, mostly of the negative type, and variations in marriage practices. Despite all this variation, nevertheless, he comes to the conclusion that the whole region is characterised by "a uniform set of relational directives" (Pfeffer 1982, 39) and that "social behaviour, rules and categories express a uniform human conception of the societal whole" (Pfeffer 1982, 39). What are these "directives," and how are they expressed on all three levels of data?

Pfeffer's major findings are, first, that all people in this culture area, independent of the language they speak, value symmetry as a principle of social relations. Second, people everywhere follow the imperative to continue affinal alliances, but normally this directive is linked to a "principle of distance." Pfeffer places the latter observation into the pan-Indian context. He arrives at the conclusion that the main difference among North, South, and Central India has to be seen in the relative elaboration or simplification of these two principles, none of which "may demand a logical priority" (Pfeffer 1983, 119). Pfeffer interprets the principles organising social relations in India within the framework of the evolution of social forms. The Central Indian pattern is seen as a synthesis of both principles and may be regarded as the starting point. The South Indian pattern emerges when the principle of distance is neglected and the principle of prescriptive symmetric alliance is made the focal point of the system, while the North Indian pattern results from the opposite development, i.e., the elaboration of the principle of distance combined with a neglect of the principle of the symmetric pattern under the influence of the "caste system".

What are the facts that support these far-reaching abstractions? Pfeffer analysed around fifty different terminologies and came to the conclusion that all of them are clearly symmetrical. Further, none of them exhibits the descriptive features of the North Indian terminologies, but instead they resemble the classificatory terminology of the south. However, Central Indian terminologies differ from the clear two-line pattern of the Dravidian terminology. Thus, in the three medial generations, most Central Indian terminologies distinguish further types of affines from one another, whereas the South Indian terminologies often combine them. For example, in the +1 generation, MB is equated with FZH and FZ with MBW, but both are distinguished from the affines of ego, i.e., SpF and SpM.[21] In the 0 generation, most terminologies lack the equation of SbSp and SpSb and, even more important, do not clearly distinguish between Sb, PssSbC, and PosSbC. The −1 generation lacks the identification of osSbC and CSp. Further, Pfeffer identifies certain terms that do not fall into any of the mentioned categories of affines, and their specifications reveal that they have taken or given brides to the same group as ego. Pfeffer follows Vatuk (1969) in referring to these relatives as "quasi-consanguines" (Pfeffer 1982, 65).

In the following years, Pfeffer developed the idea of a four-line structure for Central Indian terminologies. In his earlier writings (Pfeffer 1982, 1983), he concentrated on a particular kind of equation relatively unknown in South Indian terminologies, the identification of alternate generations, which appears in two forms: in the simple form of an identification between two generations separated by the existence of a single intermediate generation (e.g., +1 and −1 or +2 and 0) or in a more complex form in which the distance between the generations is doubled and two generations separated by three intermediary generations (e.g., +2 and −2, +1 and −3) are equated. When compared to the clear two-line system of South India, these two types of identification between alternate generations are seen by Pfeffer as expressing the idea of a society that is divided into four or even eight intermarrying sections. Thus, terminologies like that of the Juang operate with a simple identification, and in each generation, ego's line is allied to at least two other segments. Taking into account the alternation after two generations, this implies that two generations are linked with two other segments, thus dividing society into four segments. In cases where the alternation occurs only after a gap of three generations, the structure of the system is, logically, doubled, producing eight intermarrying segments. Pfeffer points out that the latter is practically inconceivable, particularly in large societies, but the terminolo-

---

[21] HW and WF, as well as HM and WM, are referred to by only one term, thus clearly expressing the symmetrical nature of the terminology. In an asymmetrical terminology, HF is referred to by a different term from WF, and HM is distinguished from WM.

gies, nevertheless, show clear signs of its existence (e.g., Ho terminology, Pfeffer 1982, 85; 1983, 114).

In later years, Pfeffer developed this idea by ordering Central Indian kinship terms in a four-line scheme adapted from the two-line scheme used by Dumont for the Dravidian terminologies (Pfeffer 1999, 2004a). The first line is that of kin, the second that of affines of the first order (M, MB, MZ, Sp, SbSp, CSp). These are terminologically different from another, third line of affines of the second order, such as SpP, SpSb, CSpP, and osSbC. The fourth line consists of terms that do not fall into any of the first three orders but are clearly related to them. These include the quasi-consanguines, i.e., the givers and takers of ego's own affines (of the second order). In other words, in relation to ego's line of kin, the other three lines stand in different relations. Affines of the first order are directly linked to ego's line of kin as either bride-takers or bride-givers. Affines of the second order may provide brides to ego's kin or take them from them, but they themselves maintain alliances with a marriage class different from ego's. This implies a fourth line, which indeed exists and may be termed quasi-consanguines because they are the exchange partners of affines of the second order.

Can the two principles identified by Pfeffer be found on the levels of rules and practice? What are the rules substantiating the claim that people not only distinguish different types of affines but also positively value the repetition of past alliances? The material concerning the Juang became the test model for these hypotheses, partly because no other society was better documented at that time. Juang terminology has several terms that clearly express the principle of equating alternate generations (e.g., *aji* = FFZ, eZ, MBD), and it provides clear categories for spouses. Thus, the perfect affine for a man is his *saliray*, which among other meanings denotes an eBWyZ and an eZHyZ, thereby implying classificatory sister exchange, as McDougal (1963a, 165) himself remarks. On the village level, the Juang distinguish between two generation sets joining members of alternate generations. Marriages take place between members of the same generation set belonging to affinal villages (*bondhu*), which are distinguished from consanguineal villages (*kutumb*). In practice, Juang tend to avoid groups from which members of previous generations have selected their spouses, meaning, in other words, that cross-cousins are not preferred spouses. Instead, there is a strong tendency towards direct exchange between groups of classificatory siblings. Considering all this information, Pfeffer finds a strong indication that the marriage alliances created in one generation ideally cannot be renewed in the next generation but rather in the alternate generation, or in other words, that a village's two generation sets have separate affinal links with distinct groups in other villages. Seen from a global perspective, therefore, four sections can be identified, even if the Juang themselves do not group themselves explicitly in this way. Pfeffer (1982, 53) concludes, "They therefore maintain a structure which Dumont defined as characteristic of the Aranda system."

The model of an eight-section system is more difficult to derive from the existing data, and as Pfeffer himself writes, is quite impossible to uphold in practice (Pfeffer 1982, 88; 1983, 112). Nevertheless, he finds certain indications that this kind of order may be behind certain terminological equations and rules. An indication of an eight-section system exists in the equation of generations separated by three intermediate generations as found among the Ho (e.g., *gungu* = FeB, MeZ, SSS). This may be interpreted to mean that members of ego's and of the following three generations must ally themselves with different groups, and only the fourth generation may be seen as entertaining the same relations again. In a closed system, this suggests the existence of eight intermarrying sections, each being allied with four others in four consecutive generations. Such a conclusion may be further supported by marriage rules prohibiting the repetition of a marriage alliance for the next three consecutive generations. Such negative rules are documented for the Munda, Oroan, Santal, and Kond. However, Pfeffer could find only one example in the literature (Yamada 1970, 385, cited in Pfeffer 1982, 58)[22] of a positive rule supporting his interpretation that such systems prescribe the repetition of an alliance after an interval of three generations. Another indication is provided by Pfeffer from his own fieldwork when he states that the Ho informed him that all those eating from the same pot may not marry and that this includes all people with whom they have been allied for the last three generations. The Dongria Kond play an important role in Pfeffer's argument for the possible existence of an eight-line scheme, because among them Pfeffer traced the existence of a terminology that uses the same terms for consanguines and affines down to the −5 generation (Pfeffer 1982, 84; 1983, 112–13; 1985, 186). This finding and the rule that prohibits Dongria from repeating a marriage with the same local group for the next three generations, first reported by Pfeffer (1982, 57), will be discussed in the section on exogamy.

The three structures presented by Pfeffer – two-line, four-line, and eight-line – are very plausible, and for the first two we indeed find strong evidence on all levels of data. The third model, however, the eight-line system, appears to be relatively weakly developed and is very difficult to derive from the existing data.

---

22 Pfeffer (1982, 58) cites him as Ryuji, which in the Japanese system is his given name. Parkin (1992b, 162–63) cites him correctly but without referring to Pfeffer, who first acknowledged the importance of Yamada's findings for the study of kinship in Central India. In general, I find it incomprehensible why Parkin often does not recognise the similarities between Pfeffer's work and his own conclusions. A misplaced striving for originality and a general reluctance to acknowledge others' achievements may account for such behaviour.

There are rather few indications of a systematic articulation of the "alternation of alternation" on the terminological level, a fact Pfeffer himself acknowledges by writing that he is putting together "Gelenkstücke" ("disarticulated components"; 1985, 185). On the level of rules, the situation is better, because we find many instances of an interval of three generations and indications that following this interval a line of kin turns – and even should turn (see Yamada) – back into a line of affines. Starting from the assumption of a closed system, such rules combined with the alternation of alternation logically suggest an eight-line system, but in my opinion, the people concerned have not developed this idea to a great extent in their classification, neither in their terminology nor on the "global level" (see Dumont 1971) of social segments. However, whether or not more traces of such an eight-line classification can be found, Pfeffer must be credited with isolating the principles that govern these terminologies, rules, and actual marriage behaviour, i.e., the principle of symmetric alliance combined with the principle of "extended distance." In my view, the latter principle became in certain areas the central value opposed to the continuous repetition of alliance, where it destroyed closed systems rather than creating them. Distance must be understood in the genealogical as well as the territorial sense. The Kond, for example, usually bring their marriage partners from far away (Pfeffer 1982, 49–51), which leads to a situation where ideally "foreigners" marry each other. In my opinion, the rules of distance and the practice of marrying "foreigners" contradict any attempts at the systematisation of regular alliance.

Parkin's work differs from Pfeffer's in three major points. First, he selects tribes speaking a Munda language to study. The area thus covered in his study is, in fact, almost identical to the region dealt with by Pfeffer, because Munda-speaking tribes are spread from the south of Odisha (e.g., Gadaba, Sora) up into the north (e.g., Munda, Ho, Santal). Second, he is critical of the existence of a four-line terminology and instead presents his data in a three-line scheme. Third, he proposes a different evolutionary scheme, one that begins with a hypothetical stage comparable to Allen's (1986) tetradic society.

As the two other "kinship systems" are often equated with language families, a procedure I criticised above, it may be for this reason that Parkin selected tribes speaking languages belonging to the Munda family as the focus of his study. He himself states that his work should be seen in relation to Trautmann's research on "Dravidian kinship," which lacks any thorough account of "Munda kinship" (Parkin 1992b, ix). Envisaging criticism of this identification of sociocultural and linguistic forms, he states in the preface to his major monograph that he does not "argue in favour of any sort of linguistic determinism in cultural matters" (Parkin 1992b, ix), but throughout this and other publications he speaks about the "Munda organisation" or the "Munda system." In linguistic terms, the

Munda language family is divided into three zones – North, Central, and Koraput Munda – and Parkin uses this classification when discussing kinship in tribes whose primary language belongs to this language family. Probably because none of his publications are based on primary research and personal acquaintance with the region, he creates a completely artificial unit of study, which may be justifiable in linguistic but not in socio-cultural terms. He justifies this by arguing that the people belonging to "'tribes' and 'low castes'" have a degree of "separate identity through language" (Parkin 1992b, ix). Identity among tribal groups in Central India has hardly been studied, but from my experience in the field I can certainly state that language, at least in the sense of the purely theoretical concept of a language family, is not a marker of identity among the people I have gotten to know. It escapes Parkin's attention that every twenty kilometres or so, people speak a different dialect and have to shift to Oriya (or more precisely its local forms) as a lingua franca to converse with each other. Again, to distinguish between "tribes and low castes" united by language does not agree with my analysis of the situation presented in chapter 1.

Within this artificial unit Parkin identifies a three-line terminology that merges cross- and parallel cousins with siblings and has a separate terminology for those affines who are not merged with consanguines (e.g., SpP or CSp; see the diagram in Parkin 1992b, 138).[23] In ego's generation, Parkin cannot identify "lines," but only a distinction between terms combining cognatic and affinal specifications and those covering only the latter (Parkin 1992b, 187). Thus, what Pfeffer terms "quasi-consanguines" (e.g., SpSbSp, SpSbSpSb, SbSpSbSp) and what Parkin seems to regard as the combination of "affinal and cognatic specifications" appear in his diagram in the same category as B and Z,[24] while the "purely" affinal terms are represented in a separate category normally reserved for the cross category in the Dravidian scheme. While Parkin identifies the cross/parallel distinction in the +1 and –1 generation, he interprets the relative lack of this distinction in ego's generation by reference to a different system of alliance (Parkin 1985, 716). The "Munda system" differs in two aspects from the "Dravidian system." On the one hand, "Munda" are said – with exceptions – to prohibit cross-cousin marriage. Therefore, alliances are not directly repeated from one generation to the next. On the other hand, marriage may be renewed after a delay of one or three generations, an aspect that is seen as related to

---

[23] This diagram has been adopted by Skoda (2000, 286) for presenting the terminology of the Aghria, despite his critique (Skoda 2000, 283) that this diagram opposes the affines and the MB, thus depriving the latter of his affinal status.
[24] The same procedure can be found in Trautmann (1995) for other Central Indian tribal people, for example for the Kond (Trautmann 1995, 141).

the equation of alternate generations. After taking note of McDougal's monograph and being informed about the positive marriage rule among the Munda (Yamada 1970), Parkin in his later publications (Parkin 1992a, 1992b) elaborates this "Munda" alliance system by adopting McDougal's ideas about "classificatory sister exchange."

Two aspects are characteristic of this kind of marriage alliance among the Juang. First, a younger sibling may only marry the younger sibling of his or her own classificatory elder sibling's spouse, a rule which serves to mark the status distinction between juniors and seniors. Second, the preferred spouse of a Juang is his *saliray*, which among other meanings denotes eBWyZ and eZHyZ. In McDougal's (1963a, 166) words, "exchange may take two forms: (1) a brother and sister A marry a sister and brother B; (2) two brothers of A marry two sisters of B; two sisters of A marry two brothers of B." In the metalanguage of anthropological scholarship, McDougal's two forms are called symmetric and asymmetric exchange, depending on whether the women marry into the same (asymmetrical) or opposite (symmetrical) lines (Parkin 1992b, 179–81). The question is to what extent such marriage relations are renewed in successive generations. According to McDougal, a Juang will have to know the marriages of a previous generation, because he cannot marry into the same group again. Once this negative rule has been applied and ego has made sure that "no marriage ties to a particular group were established by members of the *kutumali* ["family," R.H.] in the previous generation, Ego will trace an affinal relation through any classificatory sibling" (McDougal 1963a, 168). The explicit marriage rule mentioned by McDougal states that a man should not take a bride from his opposite generation set (+1 and +3), while he should take a bride from his own generation set (0 and +2) (McDougal 1963, 155–56). Therefore, it is not conceivable why Parkin states that "the alliances of his generation are peculiar to it and are not those of any previous generation before the fourth, in most cases" (Parkin 1992b, 183). The model McDougal (1963a, 169) uses for illustrating this system is based on four intermarrying units (*kutumali* or "families") that marry with the same two local groups in continuous alternation very similar to the model of the Aranda system. McDougal does not report a three-generation delay. He does, however, say that contrary to his model, there is practically "no marked empirical tendency for the members of *kutumali* units to obtain spouses from the same local descent group in alternate generations" (McDougal 1963a, 169). The reason is that the main exchange units are villages, and on this level of social organisation there are "relatively permanent marriage alliances, which each village maintains with few others, exchanging brides with them in every generation" (McDougal 1963a, 175) All this casts serious doubt on Parkin's (1992a, 256) statement that Juang observe a rule of a delay of three generations, a rule not reported by any ethnographer (Pfeffer 1993, 49). Parkin is, however, certainly right to follow McDougal in his emphasis on classificatory sister exchange, because when combined with a rule of marriage within one's own generation set, it leads to a model of four intermarrying sections and to an empirical situation of a small number of villages joined by marriage.

Starting from the – most probably wrong – idea that Juang observe a three-generation delay typical of the North Indian system while preserving features of prescriptive symmetry in the +1 and −1 generations, Parkin (1992a, 257) regards this Juang system as "clearly transitional, a symmetric prescriptive system in process of decay." In his analysis of the terms of ego's generation, he thus arrives at a conclusion diametrically opposed to Pfeffer: while Parkin regards the separate affinal terms in that generation as indicators of decay, McDougal and Pfeffer interpret them as signs of a system of diachronic alliance among a small number of groups and categories. Considering the relatively clear alternation of terms, the terms for kin in opposition to three types of affinal terms, the marriage rules in combination with the existence of generation sets, and the practical alliances between a small number of villages, the reader indeed wonders how such a well-integrated and functioning system can be considered to be in a state of decay and transition.

All this casts doubt on the place of the Juang in Parkin's evolutionary scheme, although it does not in itself make the overall scheme questionable. According to Parkin, we can envision an evolution of kinship systems starting from a hypothetical society similar to Allen's tetradic society and evolving into the Dravidian system, followed by a Juang-type system, which then further disintegrates into the "Malto" and "Malpahariya" system (see critique in Pfeffer 1993, 49) and the Jat system, until in the last stage, found in North India, the idea of renewal is completely absent from the terminology. We are, thus, faced with two "grand narratives": while Pfeffer sees two opposing developments – simplification and elaboration – linked to overall changes in values and in social, economic, and political organisation (Pfeffer 1982, 1983, 1993), Parkin (1992a) envisions a unidirectional decline of the principle of prescriptive symmetric alliance. It will never be possible to prove either of these sequences. In my view, their main function for anthropological understanding seems to lie in the fact that they force us to compare systems in different regions that, historically and logically, must be related to one another. Such comparison increases our understanding of each single model, even if we never arrive at hard and fast conclusions about evolution.

My own efforts are not directed at establishing such overall evolutionary sequences. Nevertheless, the models employed by these authors serve as useful orientation when discussing Dongria Kond terminology, rules, and behaviour.

My data will throw new light on many aspects discussed above. Until now, Kond society has played only a very minor role in the on-going debates. Trautmann analyses the Kond terminology collected and published by Ray (1950) as part of his chapter on the "ethnographic frontiers of Dravidian kinship." He arranges the material in the standard "Dravidian" manner, i.e., in a two-line system (Trautmann 1995, 141). Trautmann does not analyse the terminology on its own, because he compares everything to a kind of "standard" (Tamil) Dravidian model. What fits this model is "normal for Dravidian terminologies," "characteristically Dravidian," or "based on the Dravidian logic of cross-cousin marriage." Everything else is "most striking," but then "there is no reason that we must not regard it as non-Dravidian" (Trautmann 1995, 142). Trautmann (1995, 142–43) identifies only two "anomalies," one being the existence of separate terms for MZC and FBC that can be explained by reference to neither the Dravidian nor the Indo-Aryan and may be attributed to the existence of patrilineal descent groups. The main problem is that for Trautmann the terminology can only belong to either the Dravidian or the North Indian system, and if analysis reveals "anomalies," these are interpreted by him as local features requiring a sociological explanation (Trautmann 1995, 143). In this way, Central Indian societies are not given independent status but seen as societies that developed certain peculiar institutions reflected in anomalies within an otherwise Dravidian system.

In Parkin's work, the existing literature on the Kond is *a priori* excluded from analysis because they speak a Dravidian language. In Pfeffer's work, the Kond figure prominently as a whole "complex," and data concerning their marriage system is discussed by Pfeffer in different publications. He collected most of the relevant data during fieldwork among the Kuttia and Dongria Kond. However, he neither analyses a Kond terminology in detail nor compares Kond marriage rules and practice in detail. As he himself states, knowledge about the marriage practices of these people is difficult to obtain, because "small villages, the obligation to marry far away, and the frequent prohibition against marrying people related in one of the previous generations seem to be responsible for the rather thin data on marriages in the north" (Pfeffer 1982, 51). In the framework of Pfeffer's overall argument concerning the relation between alliance and distance, the Dongria Kond occupy a central place, because their terminology is mentioned several times as an indication of the distance implied by an eight-line scheme. Considering the difficulties of obtaining data and the importance of Kond kinship for understanding kinship systems in India, the following presentation and analysis of new fieldwork data is a necessary step for a better understanding of the whole region. For each level of data – terminology, norms, and practice – I will address whether my material collected among the Dongria Kond exhibits symmetrical or asymmetrical features, whether it shows a tendency towards direct repetition or employs the principle of distance, and whether the system is defined in positive terms or only in negative ones. By finally comparing these three levels, we achieve a clearer understanding of a social system based to a very large extent on marriage.

3.2 Terminology[25]

The following analysis identifies the most important categories implied by the Dongria Kond relationship terminology. Generation, sex, affinity, and relative age are the principles structuring this particular terminology. In comparison to other Central Indian terminologies, the Dongria terminology includes a large number of genealogical levels represented by terms in descending generations. Since ascending generations above the +2 level are not marked by any additional terms, the terminology includes a certain asymmetry between ascending and descending generations. Sex distinctions are absolute, never relative. They may, however, be indifferent, as in the −3 and lower generations, for example, where a single term is used to denote relatives of both sexes. The number of terms (forty, or forty-five when counting all alternative terms) is relatively large when compared to South Indian terminologies (e.g., twenty-six Nanjilnattu Vellalar terms in Trautmann 1995, 34–35) but not as large as in some Hindi terminologies (e.g., fifty-eight, or including all alternatives, sixty-seven terms mentioned by Vatuk 1969, 98–100) or those collected by Skoda (2000, 2005) among peasants in North Odisha. The distinction between senior and junior relatives carries great importance, but in the reference terminology the age marker occurs only in ego's and in the first ascending generation, while it is neglected in all others. Age distinctions are usually absolute; only siblings of ego's spouse are referred to according to whether they are older or younger than the latter. Self-reciprocity is restricted to a few terms and occurs only between speakers of the same sex (*sadu-sadu, mehna tayi-mehna tayi, mehna tangi-mehna tangi, samndi-samndi, samndini-samndini*).

---

25 I thank Georg Pfeffer and Chris Gregory for comments on an earlier version of my analysis of Dongria Kond terminology. Georg Pfeffer inspired me to look at the role affinity plays in structuring this terminology, while Chris Gregory made me aware of the importance of the address terminology and the behavioural rules for understanding the underlying principles of the overall kinship system.

3.2.1 The data

The following table contains the Dongria Kond relationship terminology I collected during my fieldwork. My data correspond in many respects to the list of terms provided by Nayak (1989, 41–42) but add certain terms and denotata. Further, I write some of the terms differently. These changes are indicated in footnotes. The denotata are given in the right column. Terms for relations belonging to distant genealogical levels like +2 and above or −2 and below have a wide variety of meanings, of which only the most important are mentioned. The two terms for the +2 generation are used for all persons belonging to this generation and above.

Table 1: Dongria Kond terminology

+2	
tadi	FF, MF, etc. [all old men]
aji	MM, FM, etc. [all old women]
+ 1 (+)	
kaja aba	FeB, MeZH
kaja aya	MeZ, FeBW
+ 1	
mama	MB, FZH
ama	FZ, MBW
pateleyu[26]	WF, HF
para (pada)	WM, HM
aba	F
aya	M
+ 1 (-)	
ichun aba, pabu [koka]	FyB, MyZH [MyZH]
Ichun aya [koki] [mila aya]	MyZ, FyBW [MyZ] [FyBW]
0 (+)	
tada	eB, FBS(e), MZS(e)
awa	eBW
nana	eZ, FBD(e), MZD(e)
mechu (or *bato*)	eZH
hasu	WeZ, HeZ
husreyu	WeB, HeZH, HeB

---

[26] Nayak: *patieyu*.

jawadi	HeBW, WeBW
0	
sadu	WZH
samndi	SWF, DHF
samndini	SWM, DHM
mehna tayi	FZS, MBS
mehna tangi	FZD, MBD
dakera	H
dakeri	W
0 (-)	
buda	yB, FBS(y), MZS(y)
kduwa	yBW, SW, WyBW, HyBW
boi	yZ, FBD(y), MZD(y)
mrandeyu[27]	WyB, HyB
jame[28]	yZH, DH, HyZH
nanjo	WyZ, HyZ
- 1	
mireyu	S, BS (ms), ZS (ws)
maga	D, BD (ms), ZD (ws)
banaja	ZS (ms), BS (ws)
banaji	ZD (ms), BD (ws)
- 2	
nati	SS, DS, ZSS, BSS etc.
nateni	SD, DD, ZSD, BSS etc.
- 3	
puti	SSS, SDS, DSS, DDS, SSD, SDD, DSD, DDD, ZSSS, BSSS, ZSSD, BSSD etc.
- 4	
nali	SSSS, SSSD etc.
- 5	
sunga	SSSSS, SSSSD, etc.

---

[27] Nayak: *mrandeya*
[28] Nayak: *janwa*

3.2.2 Analysis

In the following analysis, I will discuss the different generational levels separately, starting with the +2 generation. Within each generational level, I will first address the reference terminology and the social categories implied by the specific configuration of terms. In the second step, I will identify the social categories implied by the address terminology and norms of behaviour. In my interpretation at the end of this section, I will view the terminology as a whole and compare the different levels of data.

+2 generation
reference terms
There is only one term for each sex designating all people belonging to the +2 or any higher generation. The terms do not distinguish between agnates and cognates or consanguines and affines and hence include kintypes not mentioned in the table, such as spouse's grandparents. The reciprocal terms are *nati* and *nateni*, designating all members of the –2 generation. An ego will refer to relatives of descending generations below the –2 generation by using the terms *puti* (–3 generation), *nali* (–4 generation),[29] and *sunga* (–5). Dongria do not have any separate reference terms for members of the +3 and higher ascending generations.

address terms and behaviour
The terms *tadi* and *aji* are used in address for any older person. Older men are also sometimes addressed with the respectful term *musela*. The strong asymmetry between ascending and descending generations probably derives from the fact that the terms used for members of descending generations are important in the context of marriage arrangements. The rule is that a marriage between two local lines can only be repeated after a lapse of three generations, i.e., in the –4 generation (*nali*) (see p. 189). A person has to remember his or her grandparents' marriages in order to apply this rule to the marriage of his or her grandchildren. A repetition of ego's grandparents' marriage relation would be forbidden for ego's children, but not for his grandchildren.

Strong mutual affection and mild forms of joking often mark relations between grandchildren and grandparents. A grandchild has a joking relationship with both maternal and paternal grandparents. Grandparents often take care of their grandchildren while the parents work in the fields, and when a member

---

29 In Tamil, *nale* means "four."

of the +2 generation dies, the person's soul (*jela*) is often believed to be reborn in a member of the −2 generation.

+1 generation
reference terms
The +1 generation is split into three age levels distinguishing father (*aba*) and mother (*aya*) from their siblings according to relative age. The kintypes are referred to by two words, *aba* and *aya*, with an additional distinction of relative age expressed by the prefixes *kaja* and *ichun*. The word *ichun* means younger (or smaller) and has as its opposite the word *kaja* (elder or larger) on the senior level. The terms imply sister exchange in the sense that (*kaja* / *ichun*) *aba* and (*kaja* / *ichun*) *aya* must be married to each other if they belong to the same intra-generational level. On the younger level, additional basic terms exist, such as *pabu* and *koka* on the male and *koki* on the female side. The word *pabu* is often used in address and less often as a term of reference and has exactly the same meaning as *ichun aba*. The pair *koka* / *koki* is derived from Oriya and in my experience is mostly used by Dongria when speaking Oriya to somebody.[30] Therefore, both terms can be neglected in our analysis, but it should be mentioned that Oriya has different *basic terms* for parents' younger and elder siblings, while the Dongria terminology contains only two basic terms, *aya* and *aba*, further differentiated by *age markers* only.

The distinction of relative age is lacking in relation to a parent's opposite-sex siblings, a feature reported for other Central Indian terminologies as well (Pfeffer 1982). Thus, no distinction is made between FyZ and FeZ or between MyB or MeB. The equations (FZH-MB and FZ-MBW) of *mama* and *ama* are clearly prescriptive in the sense that a *mama*'s wife is an *ama* and an *ama*'s husband is a *mama*. What has been said so far corresponds completely to a classical two-line South Indian terminology. The main difference is that the terms *mama* and *ama* do not include the spouse's parents, who are referred to by two different terms. These terms, *pateleyu* and *para*, are clearly symmetrical in the sense that each term is used for bride-givers and bride-takers depending on the speaker. Thus, a *pateleyu* for a female speaker is a bride-taker (HF), while he is a bride-giver (WF) for a male speaker. The spouses' parents are collectively called *para-*

---

30 In the Dongria terminology, as well as in the Kond terminology recorded by Ray and analysed by Trautmann (1995, 140–43), Indo-European terms (*koka, koki*) are adopted for parents' same-sex siblings but not for parents' opposite-sex siblings. Further, the Indo-European terms are used only for parents' *younger* same sex siblings (FyB, MyZ), *not* for their elder same-sex siblings.

liska (plural of WM, HM) or *patka loku*, *−ka* being a plural marker while *pat−* is a shorter version of the term for wife's or husband's father (*pateleyu*).[31]

From this configuration of reference terms in the +1 generation we can derive three important categories of relatives. The first category consists of *aya* and *aba* and their same-sex siblings. The two sides are joined by marriage. This category is divided according to age levels due to the distinction between senior and junior siblings. The second category contains the opposite-sex siblings of both "mothers" and "fathers." Age markers do not distinguish them. However, like the same-sex siblings of *aya* and *aba*, the opposite-sex siblings are classified as being married to each other.

What unites the first and the second category is the idea that one group of siblings marries another group of siblings in a symmetrical fashion, i.e., each sibling group gives and takes women from the other. From ego's point of view, they are in one way of the same category but in another are divided into two categories. They belong to one category because they are all siblings of *aya* and *aba* and are members of one of the two groups of intermarrying siblings. This unity is expressed more clearly in the address terminology, which uses the basic terms *aya* and *aba* plus age markers for both the same-sex and the opposite-sex siblings of the speaker's parents (see below). However, in the reference terminology opposite-sex siblings of *aya* and *aba* are distinguished from same-sex siblings by different basic terms and by the lack of age markers. The presence of age markers expresses difference *within* a category including ego; the absence of age markers conveys the idea of the otherness of the whole category in relation to ego.

The second main group in this generation is ego's in-laws. Ego's relation to them is defined in terms not of his or her "mother's" and "father's" marriages but of his or her own marriage. This means that ego's marriage must create a relationship with a category of people who do not belong to the "cross" category as in the classical Tamil system. The configuration of terms thus implies that ego's marriage cannot be a repetition of the marriage relations between the groups of siblings in the +1 generation. As will be discussed below, this corresponds to the

---

31 There are two possible etymologies for these words. The word *pateleyu* may be derived from the word for "exchange," *patela*, which is again an adaptation of the Oriya word *badala*, while the suffix *−eyu* indicates a male in the third-person singular. On the other hand, the root *pat* and the expression *patka* may also derive from the word *panda* (or *pandina*), "to send." According to Winfield (1929, 90–91), *patka* is the plural action form of *panda*, which he translates as "to send, depute, commission." In this sense, the expression *patka loku* could be translated as "the people who give us many things."

rule that one cannot marry the children of one's *mama*, which in practice leads to a spread of marriage alliances.³²

The particular constellation of reference terms identified for the +1 generation occurs again in ego's generation. Terms in ego's generation will be discussed in more detail below, but in order to bring out the symmetry of the configuration of categories in both generations it is necessary to introduce some of these terms at this point. Ego refers to all children of *aya* and *aba,* including those of their same-sex siblings, as *boi* (yZ) / *nana* (eZ) or *buda* (yB) / *tada* (eB) depending on alter's relative age and sex. Different reference terms are applied to the children of their opposite-sex siblings, who are called *mehna tangi* (PosD; "cross-sisters") or *mehna tayi* (PosS; "cross-brothers") depending on alter's sex but not on relative age. They are again distinguished from ego's spouses, who are referred to as either "husband" (*dakera*) or "wife" (*dakeri*). In other words, just as all siblings of *aya* and *aba* are united into one category and yet distinguished into two subcategories, their children are in one sense all "brothers" and "sisters" of ego, yet distinguished into two subcategories by the use of separate reference terms and the application of the relative-age marker. In relation to ego and his "parallel" siblings, this *mehna* or "cross" category is defined as "other." However, this "otherness" does not serve to define marriageability in this generation, because ego's spouse does not belong to the cross category. Similarly, the spouses of ego's siblings are not identical to his or her cross-siblings, nor to the siblings of ego's spouse, but fall into different categories (see fig. 3).

address terms and behaviour
Address terms used by ego for members of the +1 generation define the latter as parents, since all are called either *aya* or *aba*. A distinction, however, remains between father, mother, and their siblings on the one hand, and the in-laws on the other. The former category of relatives is distinguished according to relative age, while the latter is not. The mother's younger brother will be addressed as *pabu* or *ichun aba* (yF), the mother's elder brother as *kaja aba* (FeB). Similarly, the father's younger sister will be addressed as *ichun aya* (MyZ), the father's elder sister as *kaya aya* (MeZ). The husbands of FyZ and MyZ will be addressed as *ichun aba*, the husbands of FeZ and MeZ as *kaja aba*. The address terminology

---

32 In this respect, the Dongria Kond terminology does not differ from many other Central Indian terminologies. In an article, Pfeffer (2004a) summarised the major differences between the classical two-line system found in South India and most Central Indian terminologies. In contrast to the former, the latter distinguish, first, sibling's spouse and spouse's sibling (Pfeffer 2004a, 393); second, parents' siblings and parents-in-law (Pfeffer 2004a, 394); and third, opposite-sex sibling's child and child's spouse (Pfeffer 2004a, 395).

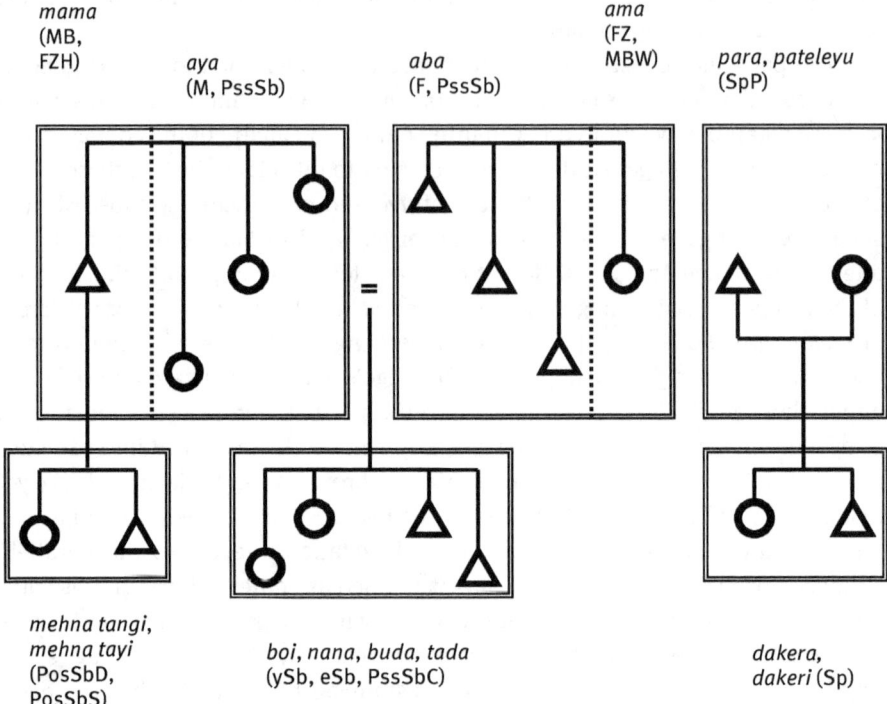

Figure 3: Categories implied by reference terminology

thus reveals more clearly than the reference terminology the unity of the two categories of intermarrying siblings.

As a whole, these "parents" are differentiated from the in-laws, who are addressed as *aya* and *aba* without distinguishing relative age. Thus, address and reference terminology both use the presence or absence of relative age to distinguish between "us" (age marker) and "them" (no age marker). However, they apply the age marker for different purposes. In reference terminology, relative age is used to define father, mother, and their same-sex siblings as "us" in opposition to "them," the parents' opposite-sex siblings. Address terminology uses the relative age marker to define all siblings of mother and father as "us" in opposition to them, the in-laws.

In terms of behaviour, we can state certain differences in the relationships between ego and his or her parents, cross-relatives, and in-laws.

behaviour: ego – parents
Ego is expected to show respect to his or her parallel parents and assist them in all kinds of work. Parallel parents assert their authority over their children on many occasions and can punish them for misbehaviour. While daughters are usually very obedient towards their "fathers" and quarrel with their "mothers" from time to time, sons tend to be very dutiful, protective, and affectionate with their "mothers" but sometimes refuse to obey their "fathers," particularly as they grow older. The relative age distinction is quite important, and children are expected to show more respect to their father's elder brothers than to their father's younger brothers.[33] A father's younger brothers are addressed as *pabu*, the father as *aba*, and the father's elder brothers as *kaja aba*; a mother's younger sisters are addressed as *ichun aya*, the mother as *aya*, and the mother's elder sisters as *kaya aya*. In return, the "parallel parents" mostly use the name given to "their" child after birth.

behaviour: ego – cross-parents
On the behavioural level, the MB is clearly distinguished from the FZH. While reference and address terms for both kintypes are the same, their physical representatives play quite different roles in relation to their sister's or wife's brother's children. The FZH does not have any particular function; he has no intimate relations with his wife's brother's children and hardly ever sees them if they do not reside in the same village. In contrast, the MB performs various functions for his sister's children. Dongria say that a mother's brother (*mama*) is like a god and one should not quarrel with him. The mother's brother is expected to be generous and to give to his sisters' children if they are in urgent need of something. Young men are often seen going to their mothers' brothers to demand something from them, particularly when they need money for performing a certain ritual, and their demands are rarely turned down. At the time of marriage, the mother's brother and his wife are expected to bid farewell to the bride in a ceremonial way and contribute an important share to her wedding gift (see section 4.3). A mother's brother can give a name to his sister's children, and at the funeral of a sister's child, the descendants of the mother's brother will get the neck (*herki*) of the buffalo slaughtered on this occasion.[34] A special ritual has to be performed after

---

33 A Dongria of the village I lived in called me *pabu*, father's younger brother. In return, he requested me to call him *pabu* too. This self-reciprocal use of the term *pabu* seems to imply mutual respect without a great social distance.

34 All those who have given a name (*daru*) to the person get a particular part of the buffalo. Name-givers are usually the parents, the mother's brother, the sisters, the in-laws, and the friends. When these are no longer alive, their direct descendants receive the share. The mother's

the birth of the eighth child of a man's sister. It is believed that without this ritual, in which the *mama* smears the blood of a sacrificial animal on the child's forehead before he names it and shoots an arrow into a corner of the mother's house, the mother's brother would die.

These examples reveal that rituals serve to distinguish between mother's brothers and father's sister's husbands and that sister's children have expectations different from those of wife's brother's children. A mother's brother clearly has a higher status than a father's sister. When dealing with address terminology and behaviour in ego's generation, we will find a very similar distinction. A person generally has a higher status when compared to his patrilateral cross-cousins and a lower one in relation to his matrilateral cross-cousins.

behaviour: ego – in-laws
The third category comprises ego's in-laws. There is a kind of one-sided avoidance relationship between ego and ego's opposite-sex in-laws, i.e., between DH (*jame*) and WM (*para*) and between SW (*kduwa*) and HF (*pateleyu*). A child's spouse is expected to address his or her spouse's opposite-sex parent in a formal way and behave towards him or her with reserve. While doing census work I discovered that a man cannot mention his wife's mother's name and a woman cannot mention her husband's father's name. On the other hand, mother-in-law and father-in-law can joke with a child's opposite-sex spouse in a mild way. WM and DH, as well as HF and SW, are allowed to look at each other and remain in the same room or place.[35] Ego will address his or her in-laws as "father" (*aba*) and "mother" (*aya*), while they use in return a special name given to the SW/DH at the time of marriage. This name is used by the parents-in-law as well as by one's spouse's siblings and often has a humorous meaning. The relationship between ego and in-laws of the same sex is very similar to that between M and D or F and S. A woman often treats her son's wife almost like her own daughter, and I have witnessed situations of conflict in which a woman sided with her daughter-in-law against her son. When a young man performs some years of service in his in-laws' village (see section 4.3.3), he may develop a very close personal relationship with his father-in-law. He may become like a "son" to the father-in-law, particularly when the man has no sons of his own or when his sons live in another village.

---

brother's people (*mama*) get the neck (*herki*), the parents or brothers get a collection of different pieces of flesh called *kundera*, the sisters (*tangi*) receive the buttock (*tikuni*), the in-laws (*patka*) a leg (*pade*), and the friends (*tone*) a piece of loin (*bema*).
35 A real "avoidance" exists to my knowledge only between a man and the wife of his ritual friend (see section 2.3.6).

In summary, it can be said that the address terms stress more clearly than the reference terms the identity between same- and opposite-sex siblings of ego's parents. In address, age markers are used for both same- and opposite-sex siblings of ego's mother and father. The whole +1 generation is thus divided into two categories: first, ego's parents, consisting of two groups of intermarrying siblings (M, MeZ, MyZ, MyB, MeB married to F, FeB, FyB, FeZ, FyZ); second, ego's in-laws (WF, HF, WM, HM). In terms of behaviour, relations between ego and members of the three categories differentiated by reference terms are clearly different. However, while reference terms classify mother's brother and father's sister in one category, in practice the two play different roles in ego's social and ritual life.

0 generation
According to my analysis of reference terms in ego's generation, Dongria Kond terminology classifies seven different categories of relatives in relation to ego: 1) siblings; 2) cross-cousins; 3) spouses; 4) siblings' spouses; 5) spouse's siblings; 6) spouse's siblings' spouses; 7) children's spouses' parents. In the following analysis, ego's spouses will be omitted, as the terms and their relevance for the kinship system have already been discussed above. Further, I will not analyse siblings' spouses and spouse's siblings separately but discuss them in a single subsection.

reference terms: siblings
Siblings are the children of ego's father and mother and the children of ego's parents' same-sex siblings (MeZ-FeB, M-F, MyZ-FyB). They are referred to as either younger or elder sister / brother (*boi* / *nana* and *buda* / *tada*) according to their place in the birth order in relation to ego. Thus, a FeBS will be called elder brother if he was born earlier than ego, and younger brother if he was born later. In other words, the age distinction between parents and parents' siblings is not transmitted into the children's generation.

reference terms: cross-cousins
Cross-cousins are the children of "father's" and "mother's" opposite-sex siblings (MBC, FZC) and are referred to as *mehna tangi* ("cross-sisters") and *mehna tayi* ("cross-brothers"). Dongria thus use Indo-European reference terms for siblings and parallel cousins and Dravidian reference terms for cross-cousins.

reference terms: siblings' spouses and spouse's siblings
The terminology distinguishes four types of siblings' spouses and four types of spouse's siblings. Siblings' spouses are distinguished according to two princi-

ples. First, whether the relation exists through a sister or a brother and, as a consequence, whether alter is male or female (ZH, BW); second, whether the sibling is elder or younger than ego (eSbSp, ySbSp). Each of these four types of siblings' spouses is referred to by a separate term: eZH = *mechu / bato*; yZH = *jame*; eBW = *awa*; yBW = *kduwa*). Spouse's siblings are distinguished according to the sex of alter (SpZ; SpB) and the relative age of alter in relation to ego's spouse (SpeSb, SpySb). Each of these four types of spouse's siblings is referred to by a separate term: SpeZ = *hasu*; SpyZ = *nanjo*; SpeB = *husreyu*; SpyB = *mrandeyu*).

Relations between siblings' spouses and spouse's siblings are thus expressed by eight reference terms, each of which has two reciprocal terms. Due to the distinction of relative age and sex of alter, the two terms for younger siblings' spouses (*kduwa* and *jame*) are linked to the two terms for a spouse's elder siblings (*hasu* and *husreyu*), and the two terms for elder siblings' spouses are linked to the two terms for a spouse's younger siblings. In other words, the reference terms distinguish the relationship between spouse's younger siblings and elder siblings' spouses from the relationship between spouse's elder siblings and younger siblings' spouses. This corresponds with the distinction of these relationships in the rules pertaining to sororate and levirate (see fig. 4).

reference terms: spouse's siblings' spouses
There are only two distinct terms denoting spouse's siblings' spouses: *sadu* and *jawadi*. *Sadu* is one of the few self-reciprocal terms and is used by two men who are married to two sisters. In other words, the age difference between the sisters is neglected. The other term, *jawadi*, is not self-reciprocal. It is used by both male and female speakers for spouse's elder brother's wife. The reciprocals for *jawadi* are *kduwa* and *jame*. When two women marry two brothers, the one who married the elder brother will be the *jawadi* of the woman who married the younger brother, her *kduwa*. When a woman will be referred to as *jawadi* by a man, the reciprocal term for this man is *jame*. This means that *jawadi* has the same reciprocals as *hasu* (reciprocals: *kduwa* and *jame*). A *jawadi*, thus, falls into the same category as wife's elder sibling (*hasu*). In a *jawadi* – *jame* relationship, the woman (*jawadi*) is married to the elder sibling, the man (*jame*) to the younger sibling. The opposite case is expressed by the reciprocal terms *kduwa* and *husreyu*: the woman (*kduwa*) is married to the younger sibling, the man (*husreyu*) to the elder sibling. The same reciprocals, *kduwa* and *husreyu*, are also used between spouse's elder sibling and younger sibling's spouse.

reference terms: children's spouses' parents
A final pair of terms belonging to this third unit is *samndi* and *samndini*, i.e., the parents of ego's children's spouses. Both terms are of Indo-European origin and

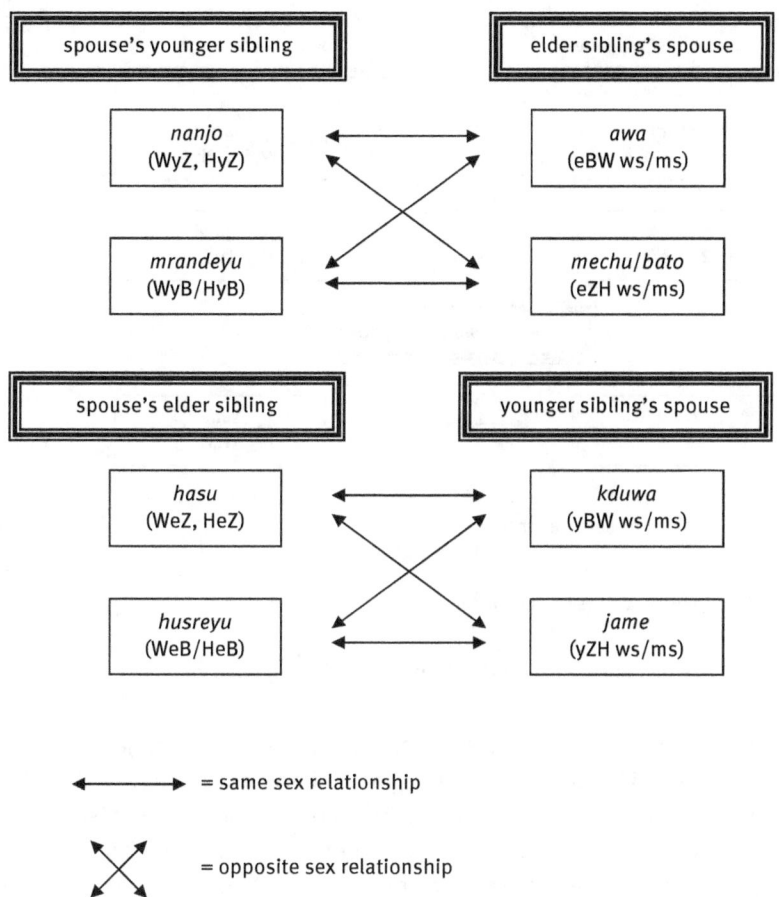

Figure 4: Relations between reference terms for spouse's siblings and siblings' spouses

can be translated as those "bound together" (*sambandhan*) by marriage. In a typical South Indian terminology, the prescriptive formula would include them in a category along with PosSbC/SposSb/osSb/osSbSp, but here they are clearly distinguished. Thus, as in the first ascending generation, the marriage relations established in ego's generation are not implicitly transmitted to the next generation. In the overall configuration, the terms *samndi-samndini* in ego's generation are structurally similar to the terms *patelyu-para* in the *+1 generation*.

The most obvious difference between a typical south Indian terminology and this Dongria terminology with regard to the arrangement of terms in ego's generation lies in the fact that the latter does not prescribe a direct exchange of sisters. On the contrary, it rules out this possibility, because siblings' spouses and

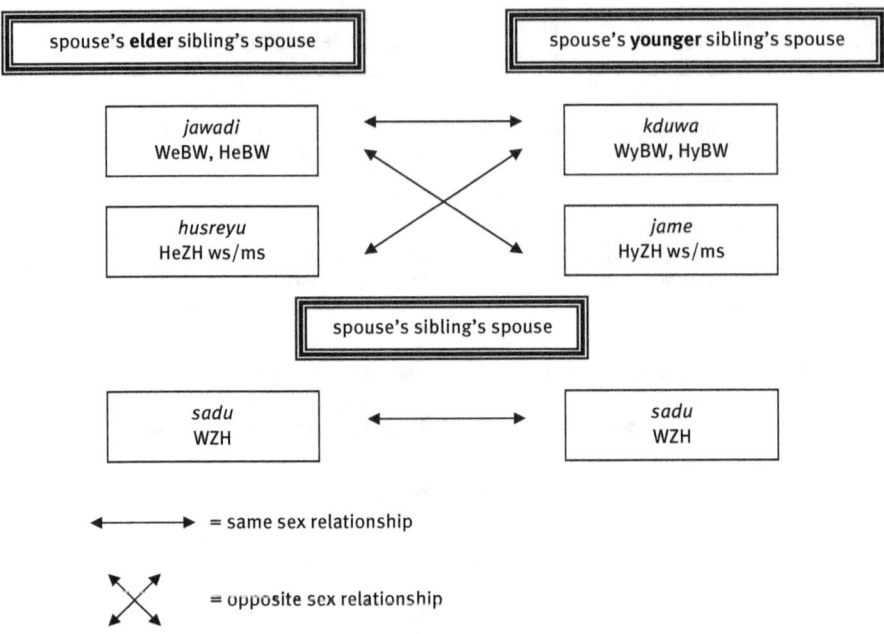

Figure 5: Relations between reference terms for spouse's sibling's spouse

spouse's siblings are never equated, the latter having their own affines. Further, Dongria terminology distinguishes between parallel and cross relatives, but the latter are not identified with ego's spouses. This corresponds to the distinction between SpP and PosSb identified in the +1 generation and to our observation that the marriage relations established in this generation are not transferred to the next.

address terms and behaviour: siblings
Younger siblings address their older siblings by using the reference term, i.e., either *nana* (eZ) or *tada* (eB). In contrast, older siblings call their younger siblings by name. Brothers often quarrel with each other, and serious fighting may even erupt between them. In such cases, other relatives or villagers will immediately try to bring an end to the quarrel.

address terms and behaviour: cross-cousins
In contrast to reference terms (*mehna tangi, mehna tayi*), address terms distinguish cross-cousins according to relative age and by their line of descent. A MBS will address an elder FZS as *kaja banaja* (ZSe) or *tada* (eB), a younger one as *ichun banaja* (ZSy). This means that, in relation to the FZS, the MBS

uses the same term of address as his father, *banaja*, and additionally applies the age marker to mark the birth order between him and his cross-cousin. The FZSy, in return, will address his MBSe as either *mama* (MB) or *aba* (F), i.e., he will use the same term for the MB and the MBS. If the MBS is younger, the elder FZS will address him as *buda* (yB). The MBS will call the FZSS *nati* or "grandson," i.e., classify him as belonging to a lower generation than his own children. In the next generation, the MBSS will again address his FZSS as *kaja / ichun banaja* and his FZSSS as *nati*.

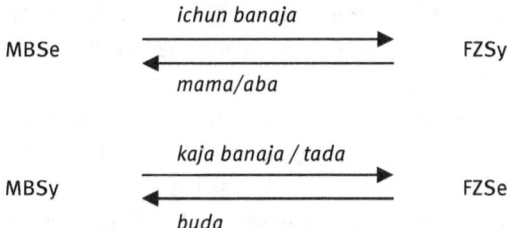

Figure 6: Address terms for cross-cousins

The address terms thus express a status difference: the MBS defines the FZS as junior, i.e., belonging to a generation below him. The FZS in return will put the MBS in the category of his MB when older, in the category of a younger brother when younger. On the local level, this status distinction corresponds to the difference between original settlers and immigrants. In a village, ancestors of the dominant clan established the settlement, and their descendants are responsible for the major rituals, particularly the buffalo sacrifice to the earth goddess (see chapter 5). Others are classified as "sister's sons", the descendants of men who left their original villages and took up residence in those of their wives. They inhabit land owned and ritually made fertile by their mothers' brothers and the latter's children. In practice, cross-cousins often ask each other for help and assistance. They cooperate in many contexts, such as thatching houses and performing rituals. During the buffalo sacrifice to the earth goddess, the "sister's sons" can act as protectors (*mudrenga*) of the buffalo and often help build the new shrine for the deity (see p. 486).

address terms and behaviour: siblings' spouses and spouse's siblings
In address and behaviour, the two sets of relations, i.e., between SpySb and eSbSp and between SpeSb and ySbSp, differ markedly. The relation between a SpySb and a eSbSp is one of joking. A man addresses his eBW as *awa*, and she will address him either as *buda* (yB) or with a "calling name" (*arpa daru*)

given to him by his elder siblings or friends. In the village in which I lived, the wife of my "elder brother" was the Dongria woman I had closest contact with. I often ate in their house, even if my "elder brother" was absent, and she regularly teased me for various reasons. Similarly, a woman will have a joking relationship with her eZH, her *mechu*, whom she calls *bato*. Among men, the relationship between eZH and WyB is also marked by mutual joking. For example, when Dongria men thatched my house, two of them were related as eZH and WyB, and they threw thatching grass at each other and each tried to ridicule the other in various ways. I have no data concerning the relationship between a *nanjo* and an *awa*, but I assume that it also falls into the category of joking relationships. The joking clearly corresponds to marriageability, because a younger sibling can marry an elder sibling's spouse in the event that the elder sibling dies.

In contrast, if a younger sibling dies, an elder sibling cannot marry his or her spouse. The relationship between SpeSb and ySbSp is characterised by mild forms of avoidance. The younger sibling's spouse will address his or her spouse's elder sibling like a parent-in-law. Thus, a woman addresses her HeSb like her HF, *aba*, and a man addresses his WeSb like his WM, *aya*. In return, these relatives will use a "calling name" or address the younger sibling's spouse like a younger sister or younger brother. For example, when my wife came to visit me, my "elder brother" taught her to address him in a respectful way by saying *oh, aba*,[36] while he in response addressed her as *oh, Sonari*, i.e., by using the "calling name" given to her by the village shaman, my "mother," on the day of her arrival. While my wife was expected to address him in a formal way, my "elder brother" often teased her in a mild way. In other words, he behaved like a father-in-law in relation to his daughter-in-law. It corresponds to this observation that the reference terms used by spouse's elder sibling for younger sibling's spouse also denote SW (*kduwa*) and DH (*jame*).

In summary, we can state that the relationship between spouse's younger sibling and elder sibling's spouse is marked by mutual joking and includes the possibility of marriage in the context of sororate and levirate. In contrast, younger siblings' spouses are expected to avoid their spouse's elder siblings and treat them like a father-in-law or mother-in-law. This excludes any marriage between them in the event that the spouse dies, but the mild joking engaged in by the spouse's elder sibling hints at possible sexual relations.

---

36 Whenever addressing somebody, one should first say *oh* and also respond in the same way. For example, when friends meet each other on the path, they mutually address each other as *oh, sai*.

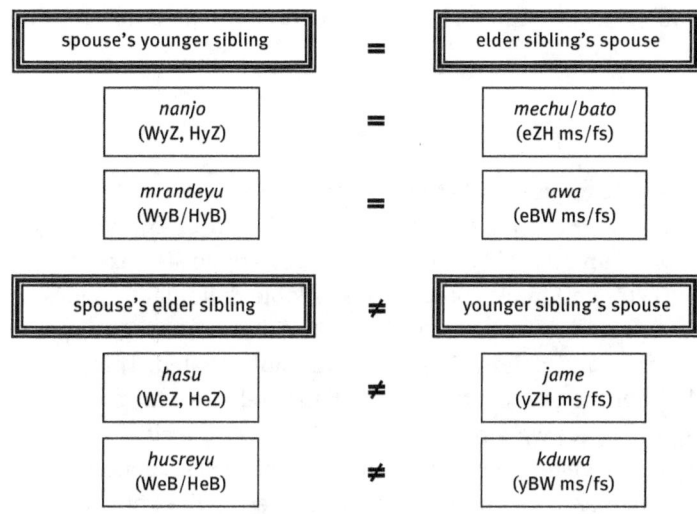

Figure 7: Levirate and sororate

address terms and behaviour: spouse's sibling's spouse
The relations between spouses' siblings' spouses of opposite sex closely resemble the relations between spouse's elder sibling and younger sibling's spouses. When of opposite sex, ego will address spouse's elder sibling's spouse like a parent-in-law, i.e., as either *aya* (WeBW) or *aba* (HeZH ws), and will be called by a "calling name" in return. I do not know how HeWB (*jawadi*) and HyBW (*kduwa*) address each other, but I assume that their relationship is modelled after the relationship between *hasu* and *kduwa*. Joking and mutual affection characterise the relationship between two men who are married to two sisters and call each other *sadu*. In contrast to the relationship between *mrandeyu* and *bato*, the *sadu* relationship does not recognise the principle of seniority. A *sadu* is classified as a brother, but the relationship is more like that between ritual friends. The *sadu* and *tone* (ritual friend) relationships are very highly valued in this society.

address terms and behaviour: children's spouses' parents
Both in reference and address, the terms used for children's spouses' parents are self-reciprocal for speakers of the same sex, i.e., men call each other *samndi*, women *samndini*. The relationship is essentially symmetrical and characterised by mutual affection. Thus, I once witnessed a man bringing a sacrificial buffalo to his *samndi's* house. On his arrival, they both hugged each other, laughed, and expressed their joy at seeing each other. As described in more detail in the con-

text of marriage relations (see chapter 4), relations between *samndi* may also be very strained.

-1 generation
reference terms
Only six different reference terms denote the relations between ego and members of the −1 generation. *Maga* and *mireyu* denote the children of ego and ego's same-sex siblings, *banaji* and *banaja* the children of ego's opposite-sex siblings, and *kduwa* and *jame* ego's children's spouses. It is notable that relative age is no longer relevant from here on. In contrast to South Indian terminologies, opposite-sex siblings' children and children's spouses are not equated. This can be interpreted in the light of the non-continuity of alliance relations from one generation to the next, an aspect we already identified in the opposition between PosSb and SpP in the +1 generation. The terms for children's spouses (*jame* and *kduwa*) are the same as those used for direct affines of the younger level of ego's generation. I came across this kind of classification in all Kond and Dombo terminologies I collected in Rayagada district, but it is absent in the list provided by Ray (1950). In view of the importance attached to the distinction of generations and of age levels within generations, this feature is striking. It may be interpreted as a way to stress the non-marriageability of the younger siblings' spouses, who are classified along with the strongly avoided category of children's spouses. The two terms for cross-relatives (*banaja* and *banaji*) in the −1 generation show a structural similarity to the two terms for cross-cousins (*mehna tayi* and *mehna tangi*) in ego's generation. In South Indian terminologies these cross categories represent the affines in ego's and ego's children's generation, while they lack this meaning in the Kond and most other Central Indian terminologies.

Address terms and norms of behaviour will not be discussed, as they are the same as those between members of the +1 and 0 generations.

-2 and lower generations
Like the +2 generation, the −2 generation contains only two reference terms, *nati* and *nateni*, denoting agnatic and cognatic as well as affinal and consanguineal kintypes. The terms are the same as in Oriya. Starting from the −3 generation, we come across only one term for both male and female relatives. The designation of relatives in the −4 and even −5 generation is remarkable and was first reported by Pfeffer (1982, 1985). As will be seen in the next chapter, the −4 generation plays an important role in the context of marriage rules.

Dongria address terminology uses the technique of "skewing" characteristic of so-called Omaha classifications, which are often linked to a prohibition on repeating marriages from one generation to the next. Among the Dongria, this "skewing" creates a distinction between two local lines mutually related as bride-takers and bride-givers and appears to be linked to a particular marriage rule. As mentioned above, when a man gives his sister in marriage to another man, the descendants of the two men are prohibited from renewing the marriage relationship in the following three generations. During these three generations, address terms continue to mark the initial relationship between bride-givers and bride-takers. As mentioned above, a MBS will call his FZSy *banaja* and his FZSS *nati* or "grandson." He thus continues to use the terms used by his father, the initial bride-giver, for the descending generations of his father's bride-takers. In relation to the MBS's children, the FZS's children will be classed one generation below. This "skewing" of generations may explain why Dongria express the marriage rule described above by saying *nali sunga hedi ane*, which means "our descendants in the −4 and −5 generation can marry." This rule may derive its meaning from the practice of marking the status difference between the MB's people and the FZ's people by using address terms belonging to adjacent generations for relatives of the same generation.

3.2.3 Interpretation

At first glance, the Dongria kinship system seems to follow a simple principle: marriage draws people from outside of ego's kin universe into its cycle of kin and marks them as non-marriageable for subsequent generations. The reference terminology does not provide ego with a category of spouses as in the so-called Dravidian kinship system. Children of ego's affines are categorically excluded as marriage partners in subsequent generations, i.e., each generation has to find its own marriage partners outside the circle of relatives defined by the terminology. However, when taking into account other levels of data, a different picture emerges. On the one hand, spouses must belong to different clans, and the children of both parents' same-sex and opposite-sex siblings are excluded from the pool of ego's potential marriage partners. For this reason, Dongria must seek their spouses outside the circle of relatives by descent or prior marriages. On the other hand, two types of relatives within ego's kinship universe are marked as marriageable. This cannot be derived from the reference terminology and only emerges from the consideration of address terms, behaviour, and rules.

The two categories of marriageable relatives are, first, spouse's younger siblings / elder sibling's spouse, and second, the relatives called *nali* and *sunga*. The former can marry each other in the context of sororatic and leviratic unions, and their potential marriageability is marked by mutual joking. Such unions follow the logic that a younger sibling can substitute for an older sibling as a spouse but not vice versa. The second category of marriageable relatives is mentioned in the rule pertaining to the repetition of marriage relations. A prior marriage between two local lines does not permanently prevent the descendants of these local lines from marrying again. Dongria say *nali sunga hedi ane,* which literally means that members of the −4 generation can marry members of the −5 generation. However, this would be an incorrect translation, because it does not take into account the classification of relatives according to Dongria address terminology. In address terminology, the bride-givers call the bride-takers of the same generation by a term denoting a person of a lower generation. To say that a *nali* marries a *nali* would imply the possibility that two descendants of the same line could marry each other. In order to point out that a descendant of the bride-givers can again marry a descendant of the bride-takers, Dongria use the asymmetrical address terms, *nali-sunga,* instead of the symmetrical reference terms (*nali*). By using reciprocals (in address) of adjacent generations for cross-cousins, i.e., members of the same generation, it is possible to distinguish between the line of former bride-takers and the line of former bride-givers and express the prohibition of marriage between them.

In the *reference terminology* the cross/parallel distinction is of importance even if it is not linked to the immediate repetition of marriage as in the Dravidian system. The descendants of opposite-sex siblings are distinguished from the descendants of parallel siblings. This distinction of two lines corresponds to the rule that after a lapse of three generations, they again become potential marriage partners. Marriage thus turns "them" into "us," but only for a limited time before they again become "them." Reference terminology provides the following distinctions between "us" and "them": 1) children of a male ego are distinguished from his sister's children; 2) ego's father's children, i.e., ego's brothers, are distinguished from ego's father's sister's children. Dongria *address terminology* further employs the technique of "skewing" and thereby separates the two lines of bride-givers and bride-takers. A father's sister's descendants who belong to the same generation as ego are classified as belonging to the next lower generation. In this way, the affinal relationship remains marked, but the concrete individuals classified as "mother's brother" and "sister's children" are defined as non-marriageable. However, the prohibition on repeating a marriage does not last forever. The rule that allows marriage between *nali* and *sunga* points to the fact that Dongria positively value the repetition of marriage before the earlier affinal relations are completely forgotten. After a lapse of three generations, the descendants of bride-takers and bride-givers continue to be classified as members of adjacent generations, but now they are called *nali* and *sunga*. When the relationship between *nali* and *sunga* replaces the relationship between *mama* and *bhanaja* (or *bhanaji*), a renewal of the former marriage relation becomes possible. The terminology may not prescribe the union, but within the framework of rules, such a *nali-sunga* union may be interpreted as a preferred one. It is, to my knowledge, the first instance of a rule being expressed by a terminological constellation referring to the −4 and −5 genealogical levels. In conclusion, we can say that except for sororatic and leviratic unions, Dongria highly value marriage with relative strangers. They are strangers in the sense that they are not part of the kinship universe defined by the reference terminology or in the sense that time has again turned former relatives into relative strangers. The rules are, therefore, mostly negative, i.e., they function to prohibit marriage within certain descent categories and with past marriage partners. Only the rule pertaining to the repetition of marriage defines certain relatives as marriageable and creates an identity between the +2 generation and the −2 generation. These rules and their effects will be discussed in detail in the following section.

3.3 Rules

In this section I will discuss the rules of marriage in relation to Dongria social and territorial organisation. I will start with the most inclusive categories before addressing those groups that actually intermarry, i.e., "local descent groups" (*punja*) and "houses" (*ijo*). To facilitate a better understanding of what follows, I will first briefly describe the most important elements of Dongria Kond social and territorial organisation.

Dongria Kond as a whole consider themselves to be people of the "steep country" (*horu raji*) in opposition to the Desia Kond of the "flat country" (*panga raja*). Within these steep Niamgiri mountains, Dongria are divided into different clans, some of which can be called dominant because their members claim to be owners of the hill land used for shifting cultivation. According to a Dongria myth (Nayak 1989, 39–40), there were originally six such dominant clans. Today, the whole territory of the Niamgiri Hills is divided among nine clans (Jakesika, Kadraka, Kruska, Nandruka, Niska, Pusika, Sikoka, Wadaka, Wengesika). Except for the Nandruka,[37] each of these clans is linked to a varying number of "brother-and-sister clans" (*tayi bai kuda*)[38] to form a phratry. These brother-and-sister clans are associated with certain territories in the valleys or

---

37 Only Nayak (1989, 54) mentions that the Nandruka are linked to the Tidumaska as clan brothers.
38 For an explanation of the expression *tayi bai*, see footnote in section 2.3.5.

the "flat country" of the Desia Kond, where they own villages. A phratry is thus based on sibling relations between a single dominant Dongria clan and members of Desia Kond clans. While the majority of these associated clan members still live in the Desia country, some have at some point in time moved into the Niamgiri Hills. For this reason, we find in the hills not only members of the nine "Dongria" clans but also members of about sixty other clans (see details below) who, by taking up residence in the mountains, became "Dongria."[39] However, in contrast to the people of the nine dominant clans, the immigrants do not own any hill territories. Among the nine dominant clans, the Kruska are to a certain extent an exception, as they seem to be latecomers to the Niamgiri mountains. The majority of the villages owned by this clan are located in the Desia Kond country, while only a few Kruska villages can be found in Dongria country. In the latter villages, the Kruska are considered to be "Dongria Kond." Another indication that they do not have the full status of a Dongria clan can be derived from the fact that their phratry is dominated by another Dongria clan, the Niska, who, according to all sources, are considered to be their seniors.

HORU RAJI ("steep country")   PANGA RAJI ("flat country")

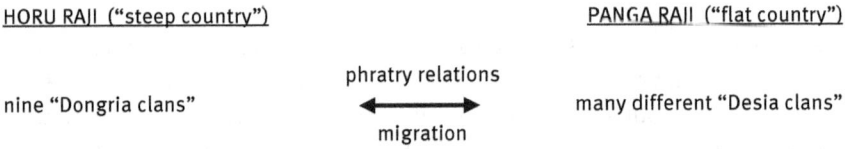

nine "Dongria clans"   many different "Desia clans"

Figure 8: Phratry relations

In a phratry, Dongria and Desia Kond territorial clans are united as "siblings" (*tayi bai loku*) who cannot intermarry. The same holds true for the elements of each phratry, the clans. Both phratry and clan are called *kuda* in the Dongria language, and only the context of the term *kuda* makes it possible to determine whether a Dongria means the people bearing the same clan title or all his brothers of the same phratry. A *kuda* is divided into an unspecified number of descent groups called *punja*. Within a *punja*, people should be able to state the genealogical relations between them, but since descent lines are not remembered for a long time in this society, there is much space for contesting old or constructing new genealogical relations. Each descent group has a title derived from one of the status categories similarly referred to as *punja*. The major status

---

39 The migration occurred in the opposite direction, too. Thus, Dongria set up residence in a Desia Kond village and thereby became Desia people while still retaining their clan title, which identifies them as people from the Niamgiri Hills.

categories are *jani*, *pujari*, *mondal*, *bismajhi*, *saanta*, and *naika* (or *kirsani*), and each of these categories is again divided into a senior (*kaja*) and a junior (*icha*) category. Not every clan has members belonging to all of these status categories. Descent groups of the *mondal* status category in particular are relatively rare in the Niamgiri Hills and found in a few clans only.

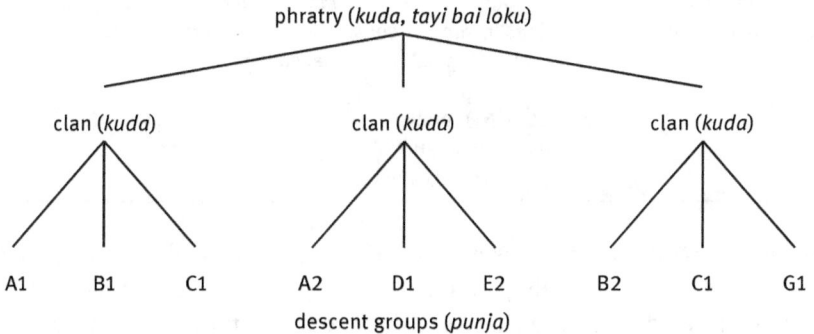

A, B, C, D, E, F, G = titles of status categories (e.g., *jani*, *pujari*, *mondal*, etc.)
A1, A2 = senior and junior segment of the same status category (e.g., senior *jani*, junior *jani*)

Figure 9: Phratry (*kuda*), clan (*kuda*), and descent group (*punja*)

In contrast to one's brothers, i.e., members of the same clan and phratry, members of all other clans are considered to be "affines," locally referred to as guests or *gota*. With these people, marriage is possible in principle but restricted under certain conditions. One restriction applies to villages owned by other clans with which one's own village has long-lasting friendship relations (*tonenga*). Other restrictions apply to descent groups or "houses" with which one's family members established affinal relations in previous generations. In particular, these are members of the descent groups of the "mother's brother" and "father's sister's husband" (both *mama ijo*) and the people to whom one has already given a son or daughter in marriage (*samdin ijo*). Thus, on the collective level, marriage opposes one's "own people" or *ma kuda* (own clan or phratry) to one's "guests" or *gota* (other clan and phratry), and the latter are distinguished into people with whom intermarriage has taken place in the present or in previous generations and all others. The question of how long a previous intermarriage prevents two descent groups from renewing the marriage relation will be discussed in detail below.

Table 2: Agnates and affines

	AGNATES (non-marriageable)	OTHERS		
CLANS	ma kuda loku ("our clan/phratry")	gota ("guests")		
DESCENT GROUPS	ma punja (our descent group)	ma gota ("our affines"), samdin gota (in-laws), gota pahana (see Nayak 1989, 150–51); previous marriage relation (non-marriageable)	ma tonenga ("our friends") (non-marriageable)	gota (marriageable)

The nine dominant "Dongria" clans mentioned above possess all the hills in the Niamgiri mountains, because they perform the sacrifices for the shrines of the earth goddess located in their territory. For these religious functions, villages belonging to the same clan form a sacrificial community called *muta*. Villages of the same *muta* exchange certain sacred objects used at the time of the buffalo sacrifice to the earth goddess. Large clans like the Sikoka have up to three such *muta* in the hills, while most others have only one. Altogether I identified thirteen such *muta* in the Niamgiri mountains. They do not have "discrete" areas in the sense that all villages belonging to the same *muta* are located in the same neighbourhood. Although villages of the same *muta* are often located within a certain area, it is not uncommon to find villages owned by other clans in the same area.

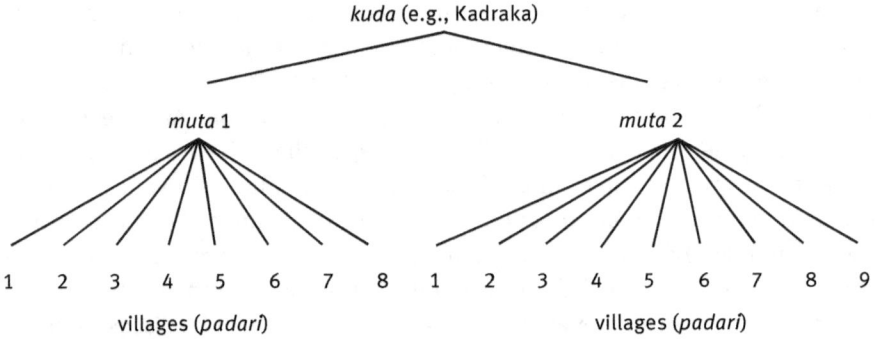

Figure 10: Clan (*kuda*), sacrificial community (*muta*), and villages (*padari*)

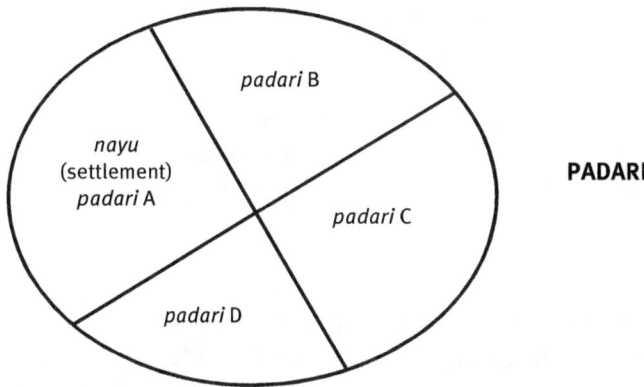

Figure 11: Village (*padari*), settlement (*nayu*), and village territories (*padari*)

In contrast to the *muta*, the village (*padari*) has clear boundaries. Piles of stone (*handiwali*) mark the borders between the hills belonging to adjacent settlements. A village consists of a settlement (*nayu*) built around a stone arrangement (*jakeri*) representing the earth goddess (*dharni*). In addition to the *jakeri* inside the settlement, each village may possess one or more territories, which, like the village as a whole, are also called *padari* and have their own stone arrangements (*jakeri*). These additional *jakeri* are of two types: they mark either a territory used for shifting cultivation or a site where there used to be a settlement in the past or where a new settlement can be built if villagers decide to give up the old one. The Dongria term for "village" (*padari*) thus has two meanings: in its widest sense it means a certain number of territories including the one where the settlement presently stands, and in a limited sense it refers to a single territory-cum-*jakeri* unit only. Thus, *padari* is the whole – the total village land including the present settlement[40] – as well as a part – a portion of the village land (*padari*) with a *jakeri* claimed by some clan members residing in the settlement. As a part, *padari* is opposed to *nayu*, the settlement, which is defined by common residence but not necessarily by common descent. These distinctions are clearly expressed in the way these words are used. For example, people referred to the settlement where I lived as Sikokagumma, meaning the "the settlement owned by the Sikoka clan," and to its territory as Gummapadar or "land of

---

40 Nayak (1989, 183) understands this word in a very similar way: "*Padari* here refers conjointly to the land mass of the clan members as well as to the settlement site being presided over by the earth goddess established by that clan."

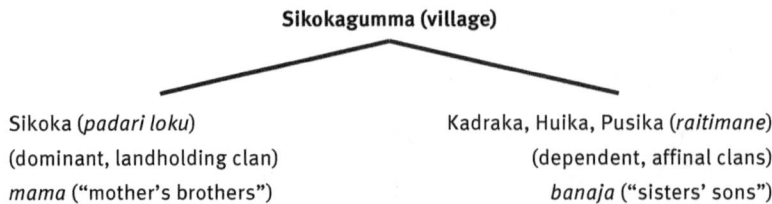

Sikoka (*padari loku*) Kadraka, Huika, Pusika (*raitimane*)
(dominant, landholding clan) (dependent, affinal clans)
mama ("mother's brothers") *banaja* ("sisters' sons")

Figure 12: Dominant and dependent clans in a village

the settlement."[41] Any resident of Gumma belonging to another clan could call the place his or her *nayu* (settlement), but not his or her *padari* (clan land).[42]

In each village, members of only one clan claim to be the descendants of the people who established this stone arrangement or bought this land from another clan. They may be called the members of the dominant clan, as they are usually in the majority and have the sole right to cultivate the surrounding land. If people of other clans are present in the village, they have no rights in the land, but the members of the dominant clan are expected to share their land with them. The relations between the dominant clan and the dependent clan members are expressed in the idiom of kinship, as the former are called "mother's brothers" (*mama*) and the latter "sister's sons" (*banaja*).

Following this brief overview, I will examine in more detail the relation between the social and territorial organisation and the rules of marriage.

3.3.1 The concept of "clan" (*kuda*)

In contrast to the meaning given to the concept of clan by most anthropologists, I will not use the word "clan" in the sense of a unilineal descent group (UDG) when dealing with what Dongria call *kuda*. As Pfeffer (2000a, 2000b) has repeatedly pointed out, the clan system of Central Indian tribes is not identical to the clan organisation described by Evans-Pritchard or Fortes in classical Africanist ethnographies. One of the main differences is stated by Pfeffer as follows:

> Middle Indian segmentary opposition at one level cannot be raised to that of a more inclusive structural frame, because segments are not classified according to the relative genera-

---

41 The word *gumma* is widely used in South Odisha for "settlement" or "place."
42 Thus Nayak (1989, 183) writes, "People use the term *padari* or *padar* with prefix of the founding clan in general and in particular with a prefix of the name of the village. But the term for village is *nayu*."

tional proximity or distance of a particular descent line. No such descent lines exist. Pedigrees are absent. (2000a, 339)[43]

In other words, neither the units – the "clans" – nor the way these units are arranged in a system – the "clan organisation" – are similar. The absence of pedigrees and extensive descent lines means that tracing descent as such is of little value or importance to Central Indian tribespeople. In the Dongria case, such a statement holds true for both levels of segmentation, the *kuda* (clan; in the extended sense also phratry) and the *punja* (local line). When a Dongria meets a fellow clansman, he will call him by the appropriate agnatic kin term, such as elder brother (*tada*) or younger brother (*buda*), father (*aba*) or son (*mila*), grandfather (*tadi*) or grandson (*nati*), depending on age or on existing genealogical relations. But these two men will not engage in a discussion about how their families are related within their *kuda*, because descent lines are not remembered. Within each clan (*kuda*), several local lines (*punja*) are distinguished, but the generational depth of these lines is very shallow. Genealogical links are only stated with some accuracy for the two ascending generations; beyond this point, people begin forgetting first their ancestors' names and then the concrete genealogical links between houses. However, what people do remember is, first, the status category (*punja*) to which each local line (also called *punja*) belongs, and second, the place of origin and the history of migrations of members of their own local line (see p. 587).

A *kuda* cannot be called a descent category in the sense that group membership is defined in relation to a particular ancestor. A Dongria will not argue that he belongs to group X because his ancestor is a man named Y. The *kuda* title may be said to be inherited from one's *pater* or "sociological father'. The latter is the man who has married one's mother. For example, before I arrived in Gumma, a woman became pregnant after sleeping with different men in youth dormitories. Under other circumstances the baby would have been neglected and left to die, but following threats from the local police, the mother did not dare to abandon the child. After more than a year, a man from a neighbouring village whose first wife had recently passed away came to present gifts (*mahala*) to the village in order to take the woman and her baby to his own settlement. Once the woman was properly married in this way, the baby boy acquired the clan title of his mother's husband, whereas before he was considered to be without a

---

[43] Pfeffer uses the expression "Middle India" instead of "Central India", but we refer to the same region.

clan.⁴⁴ In general, it is very rare that nobody will accept the paternity of a newborn child.

Most girls sleep with different boys throughout the time of their on-going marriage negotiations and also in the first year or two after the wedding, in particular when visiting their natal villages. Only when the first child has been born is a woman expected to stop visiting dormitories. In any case, a woman's child will receive the clan title of his or her mother's husband and not of his or her biological father, who may not be known anyway, and Dongria do not exhibit much interest in gossiping about a child's possible *genitor*. Once the mother is married, the children will carry her husband's *kuda* title. If the couple divorces, the children will normally remain with their mother's former husband and will in any event continue to belong to his clan. If the husband dies and the widow marries again, the members of her former husband's local line take care of and raise her children.

In accordance with this rule, people address all their father's brothers as "father" (*aba*). When conducting census work, I was often irritated when informants gave me the name of their father's elder brother as their father's name. When inquiring into the matter, I had difficulties explaining my intention to get the name of the "real" father. In Oriya, one asks for the "real" father by using the adverb *nijara* ("self"), while the only way to express a genealogical relation in the Dongria language is to ask about the "stomach" or "womb" (*pota*). Thus, when I asked a Dongria for the name of his or her *nijara bapa* ("real father"), I could never be sure if I was receiving the "correct" answer in the genealogical sense of the term, because for them all father's brothers are *nijara bapa* in Oriya or *ma aba* ("our father") in Dongria. The best way to get a correct answer was to check in each individual case whether the name given referred to the father (*aba*), the junior father (*ichun aba*), or the senior father (*kaja aba*).

While a man will always bear the clan title of his father, a woman may change her *kuda title* with every marriage, because she takes her husband's *kuda* or clan name. However, whether the woman is married or divorced, she will always *belong* to her father's clan. For example, if her first husband dies, she may marry a man from her deceased husband's clan, but not from her father's clan. For purposes of marriage, she always retains the *kuda* membership inherited from her "sociological father". After her own marriage, she additionally becomes incorporated into the clan of her husband, as indicated by the change in her *kuda* title. In my interpretation she does *not* change her *kuda* affiliation by her own marriage but is only

---

44 When the chief of Gumma explained this situation to me, I could tell from his face the disgust he felt about the idea that the child was without a clan.

named according to the union with her husband. This interpretation is supported by the fact that after her marriage the woman's first name will be composed of her husband's first name and a suffix (-*wani*) meaning "wife," like Majhiwani, "the wife of Majhi." Further marriages by a woman will not change her children's clan affiliation, but if she marries again after being widowed or divorced and gives birth to more children, they will inherit her new husband's clan title. The children of her former husband can marry into the *kuda* of her new husband except when her new husband belongs to the category of her former husband's "elder brothers" (*tada*). This means that marriage, not only descent, creates a legitimate relationship in which the children born to this union are affiliated to the mother's husband's *kuda*.

3.3.2 Kond "totemism": Relations between clan and territory

The higher category uniting all these local lines, the *kuda* or "clan," serves two main purposes: it expresses the relationship between its members and a particular territory (or earth goddess), and it regulates marriage. Each *kuda* is identified by a distinct name. The total number of such names is not limited, and each region where Kond reside seems to have its own range of *kuda* titles. For example, anthropologists who have conducted fieldwork in the Niamgiri Hills together mention more than sixty different clan titles (see table below). Away from the Niamgiris, in other areas where Kond reside, completely different *kuda* titles are found (e. g., Niggemeyer 1964a). According to my estimation, it is no exaggeration to state that the total number of Kond *kuda* names comprises several hundred titles. Some of these *kuda* are dominant, meaning that their members claim rights in the land while others reside and work on their land as affinal guests or poor immigrants.[45] It is difficult to unravel the meaning of the various *kuda* titles, and I suppose most regions have their own myths and stories explaining the titles and putting the local clans in some kind of order by arranging them in a sequence of appearance (Niggemeyer 1964a, 45, 221–22; Jena et al. 2002, 45, 142). Among the Dongria Kond, Nayak collected a myth explaining the *kuda* titles by reference to a feast at which everyone got completely drunk (Nayak 1989, 39–40). Following this feast, they received clan titles depending on the way they drank or the location they were found drunk.

---

45 Even though Evans-Pritchard (1940, 7) speaks of a "dominant clan" within a tribe as having slightly higher status than "Nuer of other clans and Dinka who have been incorporated into the tribe," the Dongria "dominant clan" should not be equated with the same concept in Evans-Pritchard's work (see also Evans-Pritchard 1940, 212).

Table 3: Mythological explanation of clan titles

Kuda title	Characteristics and location of the people
1. Jakesika	people drank from a gourd (*jake?*)
2. Kulisika	people were lying drunk in a rice (*kuli*) field
3. Kadraka	people were lying drunk at the side of a spring (*kadra*)
4. Wadeka	people were lying drunk under a *wada* tree
5. Pusika	people were lying drunk in their own excreta (*pusi*)
6. Melaka	people were lying drunk in a group of peacocks (*mela*)

During my research I often asked people about the meaning of their clan titles. In most cases the whole question was received with a kind of incomprehension not dissimilar to the reaction most Germans show when asked what their family name means.[46] The myth collected by Nayak is the most comprehensive attempt at explaining at least a few of the many clan names found in this area. Most Kond I met bothered to explain neither their own clan title nor those of others. One way to make sense of the clan titles is to explore their etymology. Considering the roots[47] of the different clan titles, some of them may be translated in the following way:

Table 4: Etymology of clan titles

Kuda title	Etymology (O = Oriya, D = Dongria)
Hemberika	*hemberi* (D) = those people from beyond / far away
Hergika	*hergi* (D) = name of a tree (teak)
Kadraka	*kadra gambi* (D) = a red insect that often appears in masses on the ground during the rainy season; *kadra* = spring (according to Nayak)
Kanjaka	*kanja* (D) = a rhesus monkey
Kodruka	*kodru* (D) = buffalo
Kulisika	*kuli* (D) = paddy
Kunaka	*kuna* (D) = a root called *konda* in Oriya
Mandika	*mandia* (O) = finger millet
Manjika	*manji* (O) = seeds
Melaka	*mela* (D) = peacock
Miniaka	*mina* (D) = fish
Nandruka	*nandru* (D) = name of a black edible fruit called *jamokuli* in Oriya
Padgaka	*padga* (D) = stick
Palaka	*pala* (O / D) = sprouts, especially rice sprouts

---

46 Banerjee (1969, 40) writes, "The meaning of clan names is also not known to the local Kandha while only a few could signify their relation with some geographical area."
47 The suffixes *–ka* or *-iska* in each *kuda* title seem to denote a plurality of people.

Table 4: Etymology of clan titles *(Continued)*

Kuda title	Etymology (O = Oriya, D = Dongria)
Pdikaka	*pdeka/pdika* (D) = seeds
Pusika	*puse* (O / D) = in Dongria and Oriya the word refers to a small cat; or *pusi* (O) = in colloquial Oriya the word refers to male semen; often used as a derogative term
Sikoka	*hiko* (D) = little millet; in Oriya *kosala*
Wadaka	*wada* (D) = denotes a tree; the leaves of this tree are used in many rituals
Wengesika	*benga* (O) = in Oriya the word refers to a frog; or *wena* (D) = Dongria term for listening and for demanding something (*wenga* = to go and demand)

It must be remembered that these etymologies are based on my own ideas, because people themselves rarely explain their *kuda* names in this way. For example, I asked several times whether the title Wadaka was derived from the word for the tree named *wada,* but no one was willing to see it this way. The only indication is again the myth collected by Nayak. I also have not heard any stories linking these words to events in the past, as reported by Niggemeyer for a few clan names of the Kuttia Kond.

Taking into account that many names seem to denote either animals, plants, or stages of agricultural growth, an underlying system of classification according to classes found in nature may be supposed. This appears to be the case among the Desia of Koraput district. According to Pfeffer (1982, 56), the following eight clan categories are found in Koraput: fish, cobra, cow, bear, leopard/tiger, monkey, vulture, and sun.[48] Only two[49] of these totemic categories used by the Desia people of Koraput are applied to Dongria Kond clans. One is the Naga or "serpent" category, which is identified with a group of brother clans consisting of Niska, Praska, Piska, Pdikaka, and Pdiska. The other is the tiger clan, Bagha Bongsa, used by the Kadraka people to identify themselves. Some of the other "totems" appear in the list above (for instance, fish and monkey), but there is a general difference between the system of the Koraput complex, which encompasses all clans in a limited number of categories, and the Kond pattern, which is

---

[48] Similarly, units of the larger Gond tribe seem to be segmented everywhere into a senior phratry opposed to four junior ones, within which an earth-bound totem (cobra or porcupine) is opposed to a sky-bound one (bird) and a land-bound totem (tiger) to a water-bound one (tortoise) (Pfeffer 1983, 92–95).

[49] Ethnographers of Koraput (Berger, Otten, Pfeffer) inform me that cobra and tiger are by far the most important totems in that region. See Pfeffer (1982, 56): "All inquiries (and the little literature we have) point to the fact that cobras and tigers make up the overwhelming majority of each of these tribes."

open and allows for immense variation. Furthermore, most clan titles are directly linked to objects or activities associated with the earth. The only bird identified in the list of clans above is the peacock, which spends most of its time on or close to the ground. There is no clan bearing the title of the sun or the moon or of any bird like the vulture.

In my analysis, Kond clan titles are intimately linked to the environment and the activities of a community of cultivators spread over a vast territory. Each title links the members of every *kuda* not only to a particular area but also often to a certain object in the environment or a function in dealing with this environment. In other words, the *kuda* titles express the relation of each element, the segments of Kond society, to the whole, their "mother," the earth. The system is open and at the same time provides a kind of framework. It is open in the sense that the number of clans is not limited; it is closed in the sense that the earth, or more precisely the territories inhabited by Kond, holds them together. They are united and at the same time classified in relation to the earth. This interpretation is consistent with what I consider to be the main message of the myth collected by Nayak. According to this myth, each clan is identified by its location, which is in turn linked to an object belonging to the natural world. As Kond, they are all children of the earth, but as a *kuda,* they are mutually as distinct as each territory and the plants, animals, and agricultural techniques associated with it.

When I once visited the Jreda Kond near Ramnagar, I was astonished to hear that these people do not cultivate little millet. Like the Dongria, they perform shifting cultivation on hill slopes, and the environmental conditions appeared ideal for cultivating this grain. When asked about the cultivation of little millet, the Jreda Kond immediately pointed to the distant hills in the Rayagada district where the Dongria and Desia Kond live. There, the Jreda Kond explained to me, the people who cultivate little millet would reside. Afterwards I always wondered whether this view was just a coincidence, an aspect of the system of clan titles, or even part of a pan-Kond system of classification making the major clan in the Niamgiris derive its name from the millet that identified the whole area in the eyes of non-Dongria Kond.

3.3.3 Affines (*gota*), siblings (*tayi bai*), and friends (*tone*)

This leads me to the second aspect of the *kuda* system, its regulatory functions for marriage alliances. In the eyes of a member of a particular *kuda*, all other *kuda* are divided into those with which marriage is possible and those with which it is prohibited. In many areas of tribal Central India, clans in the marriageable category are referred to as *bondhu*, but among the Dongria this expression is not used in their indigenous language. In the Dongria language the *samdin gota* are opposed as affines to the category of *tayi bai kuda* or "brother-and-sister clans" (see also Nayak 1989, 53). The word *gota* in its widest sense means "guest" and refers to anybody who must be treated with hospitality. The word *gota* also denotes all affines in general. For example, when a bride pays a visit to different villages before her actual wedding, she is said to go and see her *bai, ade,* and *gota,* i.e., her brothers, friends, and affines. In the context of wedding ceremonies, the expression *samdin gota* denotes all people who have come either as bride-takers or as bride-givers. The term *samdin* denotes "child's spouse's parents" (CSpP), but in the context of a wedding the word acquires a wider meaning and refers to all people accompanying the CSpP to attend the marriage feasts. Thus, the word *gota*, like the term *bondhu*, has the general meaning of "affines," while the term *samdin gota* refers to a bride-giver or bride-taker – but not a whole clan – with which a certain local line has established marriage relations.

Table 5: Different sources for Kond sibling clans (e = elder, y = younger)

Brother-and-sister clans (*tayi bai kuda*)			
source: Hardenberg	source: Pfeffer (unpublished)	source: Nayak (1989, 54)	source: Jena et al. (2002, 46)
1. Pusika (or Puika) (e) / Huika (y)	1. Pusika (e) / Huika (y) / Tuika (y)	1. Pusika / Tuika / Huika / Praska / Persika	1. Pusika / Hikaka / Tuika
2. Sikoka (or Hikoka) (e) / Himberika (y)	2. Sikoka (e) / Hikoka (y) / Hemerika (y)	2. Sikoka / Hikoka	2. Sikoka / Hikaka
3. Kutruka (e) / Nundruka (y) / Kadraka (y)	3. Kadraka (e) / Kudruka (y) / Saraka (y) / Karaka (y)	3. Kadraka / Kodruka / Kutruka / Karaka	3. Kadraka / Kutruka
4. Kulesika (e) / Jakesika (y)	4. Jakesika (e) / Kulesika (y) / Himerika (y)	4. Jakesika / Himadka / Himerika	4. Jakesika / Krungelika / Kulisika / Wangesika
5. Wadaka (e) / Nadaka (y)	5. Wadaka (e) / Naraka (y) / Angelika (y) / Wanjalika (y)	5. Wataka / Nadaka	5. Wadaka / Saraka / Nadaka
6. Wengesika (e) / Mandika (y) / Kundika (y)	6. Kundika (e) / Mandika (y) / Manjika (y) / Kumburika (y)	6. Wengesika / Karchika / Wangeleka / Krungeleka	6. Wangesika / Jakesika / Krungelika / Kulisika

7. Niska (e) / Kruska (y) / Piska (y) / Praska (y) / Prikaka (y)	7. Niska (e) / Praska (y) / Piska (y) / Wengesika (y) / Kruska (y) / Nisaka (y)	7. Niska / Kruska	7. Niska / Praska / Piska / Prikaka / Pdiska / Kruska / Krukaka
8. Karchika (e) / Srukaka (y)	8. Karchika (e) / Pirlaka (y)		
9. Miniaka (e) / Tihaka (y)			8. Miniaka / Melaka / Palaka
10. Saraka (e) / Kunaka (y) / Tadika (y) / Karaka (y)			
11. Ataka (e) / Palaka (y)	9. Palaka (e) / Ataka (y)		8. Palaka / Ataka
12. Jalika (e) / Padgaka (y)			
13. Kalika / Kalika [stressed differently; seniority unknown]			
14. Melaka / Tilaka [seniority unknown]	10. Melaka (e) / Kolaka (y) / Urlaka (y)		9. Melaka / Kalaka / Kilaka
15. Urlaka / Hergika [seniority unknown]			
		9. Nundruka / Tidumaska	
		10. Kundika / Kadmakaka / Padkaka	
		11. Mandika / Kulsika	
			10. Nandruka / no fraternal clan
			11. Kumbrika / Kundika / Mandika
			12. Gredaka / Hedaka
	11. Kajamunga (e) / Lipaka (y) / Kondamagar (y)		
37 clans / 15 phratries	37 clans / 11 phratries	32 clans / 11 phratries	36 clans / 12 phratries

Nayak (1989, 54) translates the expression *samdin gota* as "affinal clans" and provides us with a list of such "affinal clans" for each major *kuda* category in the Niamgiri Hills. I, personally, have never heard of any fixed affinal relations between certain clans.

The expression used for a clan with which marriage relations are not possible is *tayi bai kuda*, literally meaning "brother-and-sister clan." Often, several such sibling clans form a phratry within which they are ordered according to their relative seniority. The sibling relations are not remembered in any form of genealogy or mythical charter, and different informants will provide different accounts of what clans are linked in a phratry. The table above includes the phratries I recorded during my fieldwork as well as those collected by others during previous research. Despite obvious differences in the composition of the various phratries, the four columns show similarities in other aspects. Although the total number of clans mentioned by the authors amounts to sixty-one different names,[50] the number in each column only ranges between thirty-two and thirty-seven clans. Again, despite the huge number of clans, all are arranged into a limited number of phratries, ranging from eleven to fifteen. Among these, some clan groups show a certain degree of agreement across all four columns. Taking into account all clans that are mentioned in combination in at least two sources, seven or eight phratries can be identified.[51]

Table 6: Phratries (*tayi bai kuda*)

Dongria Clans	Desia Clans
1. Pusika:	Huika, Tuika
2. Sikoka:	Hikoka, Himberika (Hemerika)
3. Kadraka:	Kutruka (Kudruka), Karaka
4. Jakesika:	Kulesika (Kulesika), Himerika
5. Wadaka (or Wataka):	Nadaka (Naraka)
6. Wengesika (or Wangesika):	Mandika, Kundika, Krungelika (Krungeleka)
7. Niska:	Kruska, Piska, Prikaka

---

50 Clan names that differ only slightly, like Wangesika and Wengesika, are counted as single clans.

51 Nayak (1989, 54) mentions Tidumaska as a brother clan of the Nundruka. My informant considered the Nundruka be part of the Kutruka-Kadraka phratry, which is quite unlikely overall, because the Kutruka are not a "Dongria clan." Further, this informant considered the Kutruka to be senior to both Nundruka and Kadraka, which goes against the pattern that the hill people are senior to the valley people. According to the myths collected by Jena et al. (2002, 142), the Nundruka were the first to emerge onto the surface of the earth. I have been told by my informants that the Wengesika were the first to come out of the ground.

Table 6: Phratries *(tayi bai kuda)* *(Continued)*

Dongria Clans	Desia Clans
8. Nandruka:	unclear

A final non-marriageable category are the people referred to as "friends" (*tonenga*). As described in the previous chapter, friendship may be established between individuals and whole groups but not to my knowledge between entire clans. In the context of the *meria* sacrifice, certain villages belonging to a particular clan will be treated as "friends," but other villages of the same clan can be excluded from this arrangement. These bonds may also be loosened, and then intermarriage becomes possible again. This happened, for example, in the village where I lived, whose members used to have close friendship relations with certain villages of the Wadaka clan. When these friendship bonds were no longer renewed in the context of the *meria* festival, families from Gumma began to establish marriage relations with some houses from these Wadaka villages.

3.3.4 "Dongria clans" and "Desia clans"

The consistency of the data concerning the first seven phratries is unsurprising if we take into account the fact that all the authors collected their data among the Dongria, not the Desia Kond. Each of the first seven phratries starts with a Dongria clan that claims a territory within the Niamgiri Hills. Each of these seven "Dongria clans" (Pusika, Sikoka, Kadraka, Jakesika, Wadaka, Wengesika, Niska) has its own *muta* organisation consisting of villages in the Niamgiri Hills. One further clan with a *muta* in this area is the Nandruka clan, which is not, however, clearly associated with any particular brother clan, except in Nayak's account. Two additional groups of brother clans are mentioned with a certain consistency in all sources. These clans (Palaka / Ataka and Melaka / Kolaka) do not belong to any *muta* organisation in the Niamgiris but are territorial clans of the Desia Kond. The same holds true for all the other clans linked as brothers to these seven "Dongria clans." In other words, in all cases except two,[52] the Dongria territorial clan is considered to be the "elder" brother of the

---

[52] I was told by my informant that the Jakesika are the younger brothers of the Kulesika. The latter clan has no *muta* in the Niamgiri Hills, while the Jakesika do. The same informant considered the Kutruka senior to both Nundruka and Kadraka. Pfeffer's informants considered the Ja-

"younger" clans among the Desia Kond. It should be clearly noted that members of these "younger" clans consider themselves to be Dongria when living in villages in the Niamgiri Hills, but their villages of origin are located somewhere in the valleys. Of the sixty-one clans, only the seven mentioned above plus the Nandruka clan have a *muta* organisation in the Niamgiri Hills and can be considered "Dongria clans." A partial exception is the Kruska clan *muta*. The majority of villages forming this *muta* belong to the Desia country, except for two villages (Kurusmui and Kumbeli)[53] located in the hills.[54]

All the other clans mentioned in the four columns have no territorial rights in the Niamgiri Hills. These clans will be termed "Desia clans," and members of these clans living in the hills (e. g., a Kunaka in a Niska village) will be referred to as "non-local affines" in contrast to "local affines," members of the "Dongria clans" residing in villages outside their own clan territory (for example, a Pusika in a Sikoka village). Taking into account the idea of brotherhood between clans, it is further advisable to distinguish between the dominant "Dongria clans" and their related "non-local brother clans" of the valleys. I term the latter "non-local" brother clans because they do not have territorial rights in the Niamgiri Hills like their Dongria brothers. The sibling clan associations in the valleys are not as clearly described in any of these sources as the *tayi bai* linkages between the Dongria and the Desia clans. The reason, in my opinion, is that Dongria are less concerned with these relations, because the latter do not directly affect their own marriage regulations. For a Dongria, it is necessary to know with which Desia clan he cannot marry, while he is less concerned with the marriage prohibitions of those clans that may intermarry with all Dongria but not with certain other Desia clans.

The analytical terms just introduced partly correspond to indigenous categories. The distinction between "Dongria clans" and "Desia clans" is in accordance with the Dongria distinction between the "hill territory" (*horu raji*, lit. steep country) and the "valley territory" (*panga raji*, lit. "flat country") and between the "hill people" (*jarnenga*, lit. people of the springs) and the "people of the valleys" (*pangenga*, lit. flatlanders).

---

kesika superior to the Kulesika and, in agreement with all other sources, did not include the Nundruka in the same phratry as Kadraka and Kutruka.
53 According to my information, the village of Kumbeli has been abandoned.
54 In the same way, one of the Sikoka *muta* (Sikoka III; see below) includes villages of the Dongria Kond in the hills as well as villages of the Desia Kond in the valleys.

Table 7: Local categories

	Hills	Valleys
Geographical category	*horu raji* ("steep country")	*panga raji* ("flat country")
Social category	*jarnenga* ("people of the springs")	*pangenga* ("flatlanders")

When talking about clans and discussing whether the members of these clans are Dongria or Desia, people can often be heard referring to either the hill territories or the valleys. For example, when a Dongria is asked whether Karchika is a Desia or a Dongria clan, he will certainly respond by saying that the villages of the Karchika clan can be found in the *panga raji* and that these people are Desia, even if quite a few Karchika live in his own village and talk and dress like any other Dongria. In other words, clans and individuals are defined in territorial terms, the clan by its territory of origin, the individual by his or her place of residence.[55]

The distinction between local affines / brothers and non-local affines / brothers does not have a clear counterpart in the Dongria language. All Dongria distinguish between local lines having territorial rights in the land of their village (*padari loku*, lit. people of the communal land), such as the Sikoka families living in a Sikoka village, and their "tenants" belonging to affinal clans. The latter are referred to as *raitimane*.[56] A *raiti* belongs to a clan that is different from the dominant clan of his village, whose members share their land with him. The *raiti* are classified as "sister's sons" (*banaja*) by the members of the dominant local clan, their "mother's brothers" (*mama*). In this sense, the *raiti* are "poor relatives" rather than "tenants," because they do not have to pay rent for the right to use village resources.

There is, however, no word to distinguish a *raiti* of a "Dongria clan" from a *raiti* whose ancestors migrated from the valleys into the Niamgiri Hills. Both have exactly the same rights and status in relation to members of the dominant clan. In analytical terms, the distinction between local and non-local affines / brothers appears useful because of the restrictions on marriage imposed by the system of brother clans. All local affines are possible marriage partners for all members of the "Dongria clans," while among the non-local affines, i.e., members of "Desia clans," members of "brother clans" are not possible marriage partners, due to the assumed fraternal relationship in a common phratry.

---

55 When, for example, Desia people move into the hills, they are said to "become Dongria."
56 *-mane* is the plural marker. In the singular the appropriate term is *raiti*.

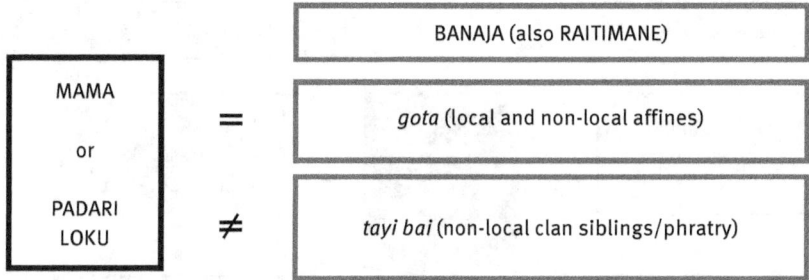

Figure 13: Social categories and marriage relations

As in the case of the association between Dongria and Dombo clans, the idea of brotherhood is part of a system of social classification. While the former clan analogy creates a link between sections of two communities, the latter links the hill Kond to the valley Kond in a system opposing marriageable (*gota*) and non-marriageable sibling clans (*tayi bai*). The origin of these associations is in both cases unknown. Thus, the Sikoka do not know why they cannot marry the Hikoka or the Himberika except for the fact that they were originally "elder" (hill people) and "younger" (people of the valleys) brothers. Like the Dombo-Dongria clan analogy, the names of many brother clans show phonological resemblances, for instance Kadraka, Kutruka (Kudruka), and Karaka, or Wadaka (Wataka) and Nadaka (Naraka). In the case of the association between Hikoka and Sikoka, I have shown that these two names are indeed related by meaning and that their difference is based on a phonological shift (h / s). However, I do not know whether the other instances quoted above reflect a common linguistic origin or simply the idea that what sounds similar must be of the same type, i.e., of the same "brotherhood."

3.3.5 Prohibited degrees for marital relationships

The previously discussed rule of clan (*kuda*) exogamy opposes different marriageable and non-marriageable categories. The rules analysed in this part of the chapter specify which local lines within the marriageable category are prohibited, just as they define the generational depth of such prohibitions.

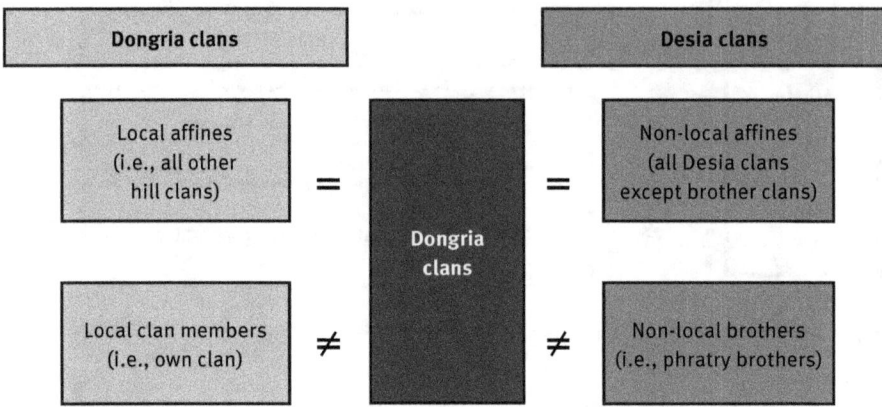

Figure 14: Locality and marriageability

The house of the mother's brother (*mama ijo*)

One rule to which Dongria pay particular attention in discussions about potential marriage alliances is expressed in their own language as *mama ijo ta:ari*. The word *mama* refers to the MB as well as to the FZH, *ijo* literally means "house," and the verb *ta:ari* can be translated as "one should not bring." In other words, Dongria are forbidden to bring a daughter from the house with which the father has established marriage relations as either bride-giver or bride-taker. Dongria stress their obedience to this rule because it goes against the practice of the Desia Kond, whom they regard as their "own people" (*ma jati*) and with whom they intermarry, just as it deviates from the practice of the Dombo, their "subjects." Desia Kond (Banerjee 1969, 43) and Dombo allow and even prefer marriage between real and classificatory cross-cousins.

In my opinion, the Dongria rule prohibiting marriage between cross-cousins is only part of a more complex rule that regulates the repetition of intermarriage. I will elaborate on this hypothesis step by step. First of all, it must be made clear that the prohibition of marrying into one's *mama ijo* applies not to categories but to remembered and recognised relations established by birth and/or marriage. It took me a long time to understand this rule, because in the beginning of my research I assumed that the relationship term *mama* applied to all members of the same clan as a genealogical MB and FZH. However, when discussing possible marriage alliances, it became clear that a man can marry a woman of the same clan as his *mama*. Next, I assumed that the expression *mama ijo* referred to the status category of the *mama*. For example, if a *mama* belongs to the category of "senior *jani*," I assumed that a Dongria could not marry a woman of the same category, but again people denied that the rule is applied in this case. The question of who the people excluded as marriage partners because they belong to the category *mama ijo* are then remained.

In fact, the expression *mama ijo* includes the real MB and FZH and their children, i.e., the people usually referred to as "cross-cousins" in anthropological jargon. It also includes those relatives the metalanguage calls "classificatory cross-cousins." Accordingly, not just all brothers of ego's genealogical mother but also those of his genealogical father's brothers' wives' (i.e., FBWB), as well as the children of these men, belong to the *mama ijo*. In the same way, if a genealogical FZ marries a man having several genealogical brothers, the children of the latter will also fall into this non-marriageable category. This means that the scope of ego's cross-cousins is defined by the marriages of all members of the first ascending generation of his local line and not by his individual father's marriage only. The rule prohibiting marrying into one's *mama ijo* therefore forbids affinal relations with any of one's parents' siblings as well as with any of one's real or classificatory cross-cousins.

A new marriage alliance by any member of a given local line will have an effect on the possible marriages of all its other members. This can best be illustrated by the following example. A man of the Huika clan named Sambru came to Gumma and married a Sikoka woman. Together they had one son named Ghasi, for whom they arranged a marriage with a Kadraka girl from a neighbouring village. The Sikoka woman had many miscarriages and died in the course of the last one. Later, Huika Sambru married again, this time with a Sikoka woman from a different village. During a drinking session under a *salap* tree, when Ghasi's arranged marriage was being discussed, one man pointed out that under the new conditions this arranged marriage must be dissolved because Ghasi and his bride were brother and sister to each other. On inquiry, it was pointed out that Huika Sambru's new wife was the sister of a woman married to the brother of Ghasi's bride's father.

It did not matter that Ghasi's genealogical mother (1.) had no relationship to the Kadraka family. What mattered to the Dongria discussing this issue was his father's second *marriage*. By the logic of this marriage, Ghasi would have married his social mother's sister's husband's brother's daughter, his parallel cousin. The same could apply to a cross-cousin, if a man's second wife was the sister of his son's or daughter's potential father-in-law, for example.

The important conclusions from this example are the following: any marriage by any member of a local line turns the local line of "exchange partners" (*samdin*) into *mama ijo*, thereby withdrawing them from the pool of potential marriage partners. This is best illustrated by considering the vertical dimension of marriage prohibitions.

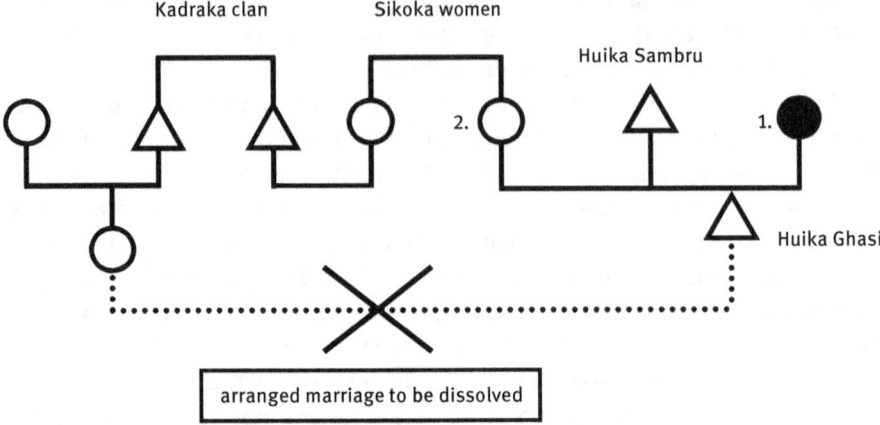

Figure 15: Dissolved arranged marriage

The house of the in-laws (*samdin ijo*)

In ego's generation, the ideal states that a man or a woman should *not* marry a sibling of his or her sibling's spouse (SbSpSb).[57] This rule is expressed by saying *samdin ijo are ta:ari*, meaning that one should not *again* bring a spouse from the house of one's child's spouse's parents.[58] This expression makes sense when considering that ideally parents arrange the marriage of their children. When they have more than one child, the marriage of each one creates a relationship to a group of in-laws from whom, as a consequence, they cannot select another spouse. It is expected that siblings marry according to their birth order, seniors first, juniors next. Thus, an elder sibling's marriage limits the range of possible spouses for all younger siblings. What the rule basically prohibits is the immediate repetition of an intermarriage between two local lines. Not only direct exchange is forbidden by this rule, but also any replication of an alliance established by any other member of ego's local line in ego's generation.

In ego's parents' generation, the mentioned rule prohibiting a marriage with the house of one's *mama* basically means that the alliances established by one's

---

[57] I found two informants who stated that such a marriage was possible. My interpretation is that they were applying the rules practised by the Desia Kond, since both belonged to local lines whose forefathers had migrated into the Niamgiri Hills from the valleys.

[58] Nayak (1989, 151) also states that an ego's brother or sister cannot subsequently marry into the family or lineage of ego's wife and that neither ego nor his brother or sister can marry any member of any other sibling's spouse's family or lineage.

parents and one's parents' siblings cannot be renewed. From this perspective, the rule preventing ego from marrying a SbSpSb is basically the same as the *mama ijo* rule, because in principle, both forbid a younger member of a local line from marrying into the same local line as an elder member. This raises the question of duration. For how many generations should such a prohibition on repeating a "senior intermarriage" be observed?

Generational depth
If a Dongria is asked whether someone can marry a woman from the same local line as a grandfather (e.g., FMBDD), the answer will unequivocally be "no." The same negative answer will be given concerning a repetition of marriage in the +3 generation, although the whole question is more or less hypothetical, since hardly anybody remembers the name or even the local line of his or her FFM, for example.

The depth of the time dimension involved in remembering marriage alliances becomes clearer when the question is about forbidden alliances in descending generations. The alliance with a local line created by the marriage of an ego cannot be repeated by his C (*mireyu* or *maga*), CC (*nati*), or CCC (*puti*). Most of my informants agreed on this point; only two were of the opinion that a new marriage can already be established after the *nati* generation. All others stated that starting with the −4 generation the rule no longer prohibits a renewal of the alliance entered into by ego. In the Dongria language, this is usually expressed by saying *nali sunga hedi ane,* meaning that a renewal of ego's marriage is possible for one's CCCC (*nali* or −4 generation) and CCCCC (*sunga* or −5 generation).[59] These terms and the rule that allows a renewal with the *nali* generation were first recorded by Pfeffer (1982, 84).[60] How can such a rule, extending over three generations and allowing a renewal of marriages only in the fourth generation, work in a society where people do not have extensive pedigrees and usually remember only the marriages of the second ascending generation?

Parkin (1992b, 182) states that a person would have to trace the genealogy of someone like his or her FFFFZSSSS, and therefore, he accuses anybody who discusses the possibility of repeating a cross-cousin marriage in the fourth generation of not doing justice to the "indigenous conception." I believe the problem

---

59 The words *nali* and *sunga* are often used in combination.
60 Pfeffer (1982, 58–59) also surveyed the literature and collected data on the same rule demanding an interval of three generations for any alliance among Munda, Oraon, and Santal. From Nayak's (1989, 151) chart on the forbidden degrees of marriage among the Dongria, only a rule prohibiting the repetition of intermarriage for two generations can be derived.

arises from the fact that he himself is not very familiar with the indigenous conception and is, therefore, inclined to understand the rules from ego's perspective, i.e., from the perspective of the person who is going to marry. Dongria often express the ideal that elders arrange the marriage of their descendants. If, for example, the members of the father's generation arrange the marriage of a son of their local line, they will have to consider two rules to prevent any illegitimate union. First, they should not select a girl from a local line to which any of them refers as *samdin gota,* because that would mean a repetition of a previous marriage. For the same reason, second, they will ensure that the girl does not come from a local line that is related to the boy, his father, and his father's father as *mama ijo*. Although the latter relatives (PPSp) are removed three generations from the boy, they are only two generations removed from his father and one from his grandfathers, so it can be expected that the elders, when discussing the legitimacy of the match, remember the prohibited local lines. To apply the rule in a positive way, i.e., in order to search for a spouse who falls into the categories of *nali* or *sunga*, a grandparent only has to remember his or her grandparents' marriages to identify a line into which his or her grandchild can marry.

If we take into consideration the whole field of relatives affected by these rules, i.e., not only prohibited degrees but also those once again acceptable as marriage partners, another structure emerges. According to the rules, the marriage alliance created by one's FF has an impact on the his descendants' choice of spouses for the next three generations. Starting with the *nali* generation, they can again marry into the same local line. Seen from a sociocentric point of view, every local line is thus divided into a core of five generations, of which the +2 and the −2 generation are identified with one another in the sense that they can marry with the same local line, while the Central three must establish different alliances. Repetition of intermarriage is possible after an interval of three generations. The rules allow a marriage alliance identifying members of ego's upper with ego's lower alternating generations (+2 and −2) but *not* with ego's own generation, as would be the case in ordinary systems of alternating generations. In fact, the latter's interval is doubled in this system.

Local Line A		Local Line B
A+2	=	B+2
A+1	≠	B+1
A 0	≠	B 0
A-1	≠	B-1
A-2	=	B-2

Figure 16: Marriage relations over five generations

3.4 Practice

The following sections of this chapter provide evidence for two tendencies in actual Dongria marriage practices. First, I will demonstrate that all marriages indeed take place between clans and that any union going against the rule of clan exogamy leads to social expulsion. My data further show that exogamy in the territorial sense does, in fact, exist, as almost all marriages take place between clan territories (*muta*) and villages (*padari*). Even if marriages occur within any of these territorial organisations, they are conceived of as unions between members originally coming from different village territories (*padari*). My statistics provide evidence showing that each Dongria village is linked to a high number of other villages and that marriages are highly dispersed in the spatial sense.

Second, my data concerning the actual alliances of particular segments and households of a local line often contradict the principle of distance identified in my analysis of the kinship terminology, the rules of exogamy, and the ideal of not repeating marriages with the same local line. I will provide evidence that sometimes Dongria do indeed marry "relatives," either those of their own prior affines or those of another local line of their own village. They contract marriages with people who are exempt from the negative rules mentioned above but, nevertheless, are closely related to their prior affines. Further, they often dispute existing genealogical links between the lineages of their past and present marriage partners and in this way even manage to directly exchange women.

Taking into account these two tendencies, the question of the extent to which they are compatible arises. How can any dispersal of alliances arise out of marriage practices between relatively closely related affines? The answer seems to lie in the segmentation of each village into relatively independent local lines and in the fact that for these households, marriage entails very practical concerns. As Bourdieu (1977, 36) states, affinal relationships "are the product of strategies (conscious or unconscious) oriented towards the satisfaction of material and symbolic interest and organised by reference to a determinate set of economic and social conditions." Although the marriage arrangements and ceremonies (see chapter 4) leave the impression that villages intermarry, local lines or even houses are, in fact, the units linked by intermarriage. Local lines of the same village make their decisions in matters of marriage relatively independently from each other, even if the arrangement as a whole often involves the active participation of all village members. These local lines or houses are torn between two practical concerns: (1) their status aspirations, which cause them to seek a bride among relative strangers, from whom a woman can be acquired only after making huge payments that increase one's symbolic status; and (2) their intention to continue well-functioning alliances with prior affines with whom new marriages can be contracted without any great expenditure but also without much gain in terms of status and social relations. These contradictory aspirations are encapsulated in the rule that proscribes direct repetition and reciprocity but allows for both in the long run. Actual marriage choices can, thus, be fit into a continuum between two extremes: (1) new alliances with strangers involving expensive weddings, which are celebrated only by those who can afford it and appear to take place relatively rarely; and (2) the renewal of alliances with prior affines, which occurs more often than might be expected given the rules of marriage mentioned by my informants. The variation allowed by the rules, the spectrum of practical concerns, and the segmentation of each village into household units that are relatively independent in terms of their choice of alliance partner together cause the observed territorial and social dispersal of alliances, even if some marriages actually take place between previously allied people.

3.4.1 The treatment of clan incest

In the case of the Kond, the analytical expression "exogamy" means that people belonging to the same clan or to brother clans cannot intermarry and must find their marriage partners outside their own clan category. To what extent is this rule observed in actual practice? In 274 marriages recorded by myself and Pfeffer (for the village of Kambesi), I found no case of a union between a man and a woman with the same *kuda* title. Not only is any form of union between members of the same clan or phratry prohibited, but also any kind of sexual relations. Any breach of this rule has severe consequences, as it is considered a serious mistake (*kaja dosa*), and either the couple will have to undergo a ritual of purification followed by a communal meal, as well as abstinence from any further such relations, or the culprits will be expelled from the Dongria community.

Not long before I arrived in Gumma to conduct my fieldwork, a boy and a girl were accused of having slept together in a dormitory in another village. They denied the accusation, but others insisted on having seen them embracing. The leaders of the village threatened the boy's mother, the local shaman, with the prospect of expelling her son and forcing her whole lineage to leave the village. The mother became afraid and begged them to find a compromise. Thereupon the village leaders decided to call the two *mondal* of the Sikoka to a meeting. In the subsequent proceedings, they decided to drop the charges in the event that no further evidence of a continuing relationship between the two could be produced. Members of the accused's family had to tie a turban around the *mondal*'s head as a sign that they accepted his authority. Furthermore, the shaman's family was forced to sponsor a village feast that included a buffalo, rice, and alcohol. In this way, the accused and his lineage were rehabilitated.

A second case of accusations concerning incestuous inter-clan relations occurred during a marriage ceremony towards the end of my stay. A young woman of the Sikoka clan was sleeping in the back room of the house while her husband had gone out to dance with the girls who had come from other villages for the marriage. Similarly, the village was crowded with young men from various villages looking for girls to dance, sing, and sleep with. Since the village had no girls' dormitory, the boys were meeting the girls in the woods, on the dance floors, or in the houses. One young man from the Sikoka clan entered the room where the Sikoka girl was sleeping. What followed was the subject of quite different descriptions by several witnesses on the one hand and the accused on the other. According to the version of two young men from the village, they opened the door of the back room and saw the Sikoka girl and boy making love on the floor. The accused boy, however, denied this version, stating that he had just entered the room to talk to the young woman when the two men appeared and immediately started beating him. In any case, in the course of this confrontation the girl's husband was informed and, after rushing to the scene, became involved in a serious fight that included the accused, some of his fellow villagers, the husband, and the husband's friends. Finally, the accused was able to escape without being killed, and all the boys and girls from his village left. The next morning, the men returned, and a meeting was held, which soon developed into another physical combat. Since I left a few days later, I do not know how the conflict was finally resolved. In the past, a feud between the villages would have been the outcome of this event, but nowadays Dongria more often resort to the police for conflict resolution. What these examples show is the intense rejection of any sexual relations between clan members even in cases in which there is only suspicion rather than clear evidence.

3.4.2 Marriage between brother clans?

Of all the marriages I recorded, only those between "Dongria clans" and "Desia clans" are significant for answering the question of whether or not Dongria observe fraternal clan exogamy, because this rule does not apply to marriages between the nine (including Kruska) "Dongria clans" of the Niamgiri Hills.[61] Of the

---

61 As explained above, a Dongria can belong to a "Dongria clan" (clan territory in the hills) or

218 — 3 Dongria social categories, rules, and practices

274 marriages in my sample, 203 occurred between "Dongria clans" claiming territorial rights in the Niamgiri Hills. Of the remaining seventy-one marriages, I found only three instances of marriages between members of "Desia clans,"[62] while the other sixty-eight marriages took place between "Dongria clans" and "Desia clans." In none of these cases did men marry women of the same phratry as defined by any of the four authors mentioned in the table above. The seventy-one marriages either between "Dongria clans" and "Desia clans" or between "Desia clans" and "Desia clans" are listed in the following table.

Table 8: Marriages

Kambesi			
Bride-Takers		**Bride-Givers**	
"Dongria Clan"	*"Desia Clan"*	*"Dongria Clan"*	*"Desia Clan"*
Wadaka			Ataka (1), Palaka (1), Kundika (2), Piska (6), Praska (1), Kanjaka (1)
Kadraka			Palaka (1), Kundika (2), Hikoka (2), Praska (1)
Sikoka			Kundika (1)
	Melaka	Wadaka (1)	
	Praska	Sikoka (1), Jakesika (2), Wadaka (2)	
	Karchika		Kundika (1)
	Kundika	Wadaka (2), Sikoka (1), Pusika (1)	Karchika (1)
Gumma			
BT		**BG**	
"Dongria Clan"	*"Desia Clan"*	*"Dongria Clan"*	*"Desia Clan"*

---

to a "Desia clan" (clan territory in the valleys). All "Dongria clans" can intermarry, but "Dongria clans" cannot intermarry with all "Desia clans" because of phratry relations between them.
62 In Dongormati, a man of the Mandika clan married a woman of the Saraka clan. In Kambesi, one Kundika man has given his sister to a man of the Karchika clan, while another Kundika man married a woman of the Karchika clan.

Table 8: Marriages *(Continued)*

			Kambesi
Sikoka			Krungelika (1), Piska (5), Kudruka (1), Kulesika (2), Saraka (2), Praska (2), Karchika (1)
	Piska	Sikoka (2)	
	Karchika	Sikoka (5)	
Kadraka			Krungelika (1), Praska (1)
	Praska	Wadaka (1), Sikoka (3), Pusika (1)	
		Dongormati	
BT		BG	
"Dongria Clan"	*"Desia Clan"*	*"Dongria Clan"*	*"Desia Clan"*
Sikoka			Kutruka (1), Kulesika (2), Praska (1)
	Wandeleka	Sikoka (1)	
	Mandika		Saraka (1)
	Karchika	Wadaka (1)	
		Lamba	
BT		BG	
"Dongria Clan"	*"Desia Clan"*	*"Dongria Clan"*	*"Desia Clan"*
	Kulesika	Sikoka (2), Kadraka (1), Wadaka (1)	
Sikoka			Wandeleka[63] (1), Kutruka (1), Pdikaka (1)

---

[63] The Wandeleka clan, like the Kruska, does not clearly belong to either the "Desia" or the "Dongria" category. The village of Wandeleka Kambesi, for example, is inhabited by people considered to be Dongria, but other villages of this clan are inhabited by Desia Kond.

3.4.3 Marriages between clan territories (*muta*)

As the Kond model of society is based on a system of intermarrying kinship units, we may ask to what extent Dongria observe the rule of clan exogamy in a strictly territorial sense. To answer this question, we first have to take note of the fact that in contrast to the ideal model, clan territories never coincide with discrete areas having clearly fixed boundaries. Although most villages belonging to the same clan are indeed located in close proximity to each other, interspersed villages belonging to other clans are often found. Villages can be bought and sold, they change their location, and certain local lines die out, with others taking over their land. This leads to a situation approximating the ideal but never fully corresponding to it. People speak about their clan territory not in the sense of a bounded area but rather in terms of a set of villages called *muta*. As an example of how the territorial constitution of such a *muta* may change, I will at this point describe the developments within a Sikoka *muta*, before I compare marriage statistics with the norm of clan exogamy in its territorial aspect.

Case study: "History" of the Sikoka *muta*
The village of Gumma belongs to a Sikoka *muta* consisting of a total of twelve villages. Two of these villages are presently deserted, Waliamba and Kadengeyu. Both were still inhabited about forty years ago, when the people of Gumma left their village after many deaths due to attacks by tigers. One group of villagers settled in Kadengeyu, another in Waliamba. About twenty years later, these families slowly returned to Gumma and started building new houses. While the valley of Kadengeyu turned into a dense jungle, the valley of Waliamba has been used for shifting cultivation over the last three years, and some families from Gumma are now planning to build houses at the site where their parents and grandparents had once settled. None of these three villages formerly belonged to the Sikoka clan. Both Kadengeyu and Waliamba were owned by the Jakesika clan, just like neighbouring Bada Denganali, whose land has also been taken over by Sikoka. In this area, only one small Jakesika hamlet named Kuskedeli remains. Only during the *meria* festival do Jakesika from villages located in the valleys of Kalahandi come to Kuskedeli to have the symbol of their clan erected at the location of the buffalo sacrifice to the earth goddess (see below). These are not the only cases of Jakesika being ousted by Sikoka in these *muta*. Three more villages located in Mundawali district met the same fate: Penewali, Atejarana, and Goilunga formerly belonged to the Jakesika clan. Gumma itself was bought from members of the Timaka clan who left several generations earlier.

Two more villages of this *muta* formerly belonged to other clans. The small village of Kata, lying on the other side of the mountains from Gumma in the Muniguda district, was owned by Kadraka but bought by Sikoka. Similarly, the Sikoka acquired rights of landownership from the Wengesika clan for a village named Bada Dengoni. Nowadays, of the twelve villages constituting this Sikoka *muta*, only four villages are said to have belonged originally to the Sikoka clan, and all of them lie in close proximity to each other north of the crest of the Niamgiri Hills. The origins of the Sikoka local lines owning these twelve villages lie either in the four villages just mentioned or in villages in the valleys. In the latter case, these Sikoka came from seven villages (Hatimuniguda, Debguda, Ambguda, Kargodi, Piepadru, Dandra, and Penjo) located around the small town of Muniguda. Some Sikoka from these villages left and moved into the mountains. Except for one village (Penjo), which has been sold to the Niska clan, all other villages remain in the hands of the Sikoka.

In some cases, a village's land was bought by a single local line; in others, members of several local lines shared the costs. For example, in Gumma the ancestors of three Sikoka men belonging to different lines are said to have bought the land originally from the Timaka clan. After some time, one local line again sold part of the land to another one, only to buy it back at a later date. This selling and buying of land rights occurred several times, until finally all Sikoka of the village acquired the rights jointly.

Such land transactions seem to have been quite common in the past and were called *padari mekela kina,* meaning literally "to sell and buy village land back and forth." The relations between those who sold and those who bought land resembled, in some ways, the relations between bride-givers and bride-takers. In most cases, villages and valleys were sold by one clan to another, just as a woman is given to another clan in exchange for money. Nowadays, the mountains and valleys can no longer be sold or bought by Dongria, but in the past, this used to be common practice. The amounts of money were very small by today's standards, but Dongria do take into account that the value of money changes. Thus, in most cases of land sales in the past, people paid one, three, five, or seven rupees. When discussing these transactions, Dongria always point out that one rupee of the past is worth several thousand rupees of the present. From the discussion on the amounts paid for the villages that nowadays belong to the Sikoka *muta* described above, I often learnt that only a part of the agreed sum had been paid, for example, only half of the seven rupees for Atejarana, and that the amount remaining, three and a half rupees, is the equivalent of several thousand rupees today. In almost all cases of land sales, only part of the price fixed had been paid. Demands concerning these outstanding debts are a common cause for conflicts arising at the time of the buffalo sacrifice *(kodru parbu)*. This process of demanding land for money on the one side and of demanding more money on the other side resembles the long process of demanding, bargaining, and haggling between affines in an arranged marriage.

Although local lines often buy land jointly, members of each local line identify themselves with one or more villages of the *muta*. People also talk about villages as if they belong to a particular line, e. g., by saying that a certain village is a *bismajhi padari*, meaning that the village's land belongs to members of the status group of *bismajhi*. For example, in Gumma the Sikoka are divided into six different local lines classified into four status categories. These four categories are the "senior" (*kaja*) and the "junior (*icha*) *bismajhi*" and the "senior" (*kaja*) and the "junior (*icha*) *jani*." Each status category may be comprised of different local lines. Thus in Gumma three Sikoka local lines[64] are grouped into the category of "junior *jani*." Further, one local line is classified as "senior *jani*," one as "senior *bismajhi*," and one as "junior *bismajhi*." Some of these local lines are further identified with a particular royally granted title. For example, the line of the "junior *bismajhi*" of the village is sometimes referred to as *saanta* (deriving from the honorific *samanta*), and one line of the "junior *jani*" is called *naika*. Each of these local lines is identified with one or more of the twelve villages, because their family members reside there or because their ancestors are said to have bought the village. The twelve villages of this Sikoka *muta* are said to belong to seven different local lines, six of which are represented in Gumma. The seventh local line has a particular name (*ganaca jani*) and is linked to one of the seven original Sikoka villages, Hatimuniguda:

Table 9: Villages of the Sikoka (I) *muta* and local lines

SIKOKA (I) *MUTA*	
LOCAL LINES	VILLAGES
senior *bismajhi*	Gumma, Kata, Bada Dengoni
junior *bismajhi* ("*saanta*")	Gahi Monda
senior *jani*	Goilunga
junior *jani* (1.)	Penewali, Bada Monda, Sana Dengoni, Atejarana
junior *jani* (2.) ("*naika*")	Waliamba
junior *jani* (3.)	Kadengeyu
ganaca jani	Duherigadi

---

[64] Two of these three local lines sometimes claim to belong together, but in terms of their original villages and in terms of their house gods they are clearly different.

Not all village land has been transferred from one clan to another in exchange for monetary payments. Whole villages are said to have been given as gifts to affines. For example, the village of Bada Denganali, which does not form part of the Sikoka *muta* mentioned above, is considered to belong to a local line of "senior *bismajhi*" in Gumma. One of their forefathers is said to have come to Bada Denganali during his youth to work for his father-in-law. As will be described later (see section 4.3.3), young men often spend a year or two in their father-in-law's village in order to perform bride service, thus reducing the amount of money their families are expected to give to their affines. At that time, the land belonged to the Jakesika. After some years of service, the Sikoka showed no intention of leaving. Instead, he demanded a house and land by asking the Jakesika *na juta embo tuchi*, meaning "where shall I throw my leftovers?" Some time later, the Jakesika left the village for unknown reasons, while the Sikoka remained, and since that time his line claims rights of ownership in the village. While in this case the claims are accepted, others are the cause of constant quarrels. For example, from time to time the Sikoka of Dongormati, who belong to another Sikoka *muta*, demand money from the people of Gumma for the right to cultivate the village land of Waliamba. An informant from Gumma told me the following story in order to explain the grounds on which the Sikoka of Dongormati claim the land of Waliamba:

> Once a boy from Dongormati came to Waliamba and climbed up a *charkoli* tree (*sreka mara*). He was sitting in the tree eating its fruit when the grandmother of Sikoka Bhaskar [member of the local line of Gumma claiming rights in the land] passed by and saw him. She was on her way to collect greens (*kucha beta*). She called the young man and took him home. He continued to stay with her, and she brought him up like her own son. For this reason, the people of Dongormati nowadays say that the land of Waliamba belongs to them.

Sometimes village land may be transferred from one clan to another as a compensation for theft. For example, many years ago a forefather of one of the "junior *jani*" of Gumma is said to have stolen dried meat from a bamboo pole (*kada*) belonging to the Pusika of the neighbouring village of Lamba, causing a conflict between the two villages that was only settled when the people of Gumma gave away a whole part of their village land, called Gamberi Bondeli, to the Pusika.

Preference: Marrying outside the clan territory (*muta*)
These examples clearly illustrate the flexibility in the constitution of "clan territories" and account for the fact that any particular locality consists of villages belonging to different clans and *muta*. As indicated above, *kuda* and *muta* do

not necessarily coincide, i.e., people bearing the same clan title do not necessarily live in villages of the same *muta*. A *muta* is, first of all, a social as well as sacrificial unit. Nowadays, Dongria talk about their *muta* mostly in contexts of outstanding debts for land transfers, of incest cases punishable by the *mondal*, and most importantly, of the buffalo sacrifice (*kodru parbu*). As will be described later, the unity of the *muta* is articulated in terms of sacred objects exhibited at the time of the buffalo sacrifice. Thus, the Sikoka have three different *muta* in the Niamgiri Hills, and the difference between them is expressed by reference to the different knives and brass symbols each *muta* possesses. Taking into consideration this local definition of a *muta* as a unit of villages that share the same knife (*suri*) and brass symbol (*bonda*) used at the time of the buffalo sacrifice, the villages of the Niamgiri Hills are ordered into the following thirteen *muta*:

Table 10: Thirteen *muta* of the Niamgiri Hills

Jakesika *muta* (7 villages)
Kurli, Mundawali, Hundijali, Tuaguda, Hutesi, Ranibanda, Gondeli
Kadraka *muta* I (12 villages)
Panchkodi, Katigucha, Bondeli, Damanapanga, Tebapoda, Padarmali, Tamkaseli, Taripayu, Giriguda, Badaduari, Puibata, Kodrukheri
Kadraka *muta* II (9 villages)
Kadrakagumma, Kajuri, Arsakani, Patalamba, Jangajodi, Radang, Batigari, Sagdi, Lahunikunti
Kruska *muta* (8 villages)
Kurusmui, Kumbeli (abandoned), Tadamui, Palkamana, Padudiguda, Tendatikera, Kambarabata, Tidimaska
Nandruka *muta* (3 villages)
Kueni Duherigadi, Srambi, Merkabondeli
Niska *muta* (6 villages)
Niskabondeli, Kirida, Kadigumma, Tanda, Kacurala, Hingabadi
Pusika *muta* I ("Huika") (5 villages)
Batigumma, Jangjodi, Talapali, Uparapali, Railima
Pusika *muta* II (7 villages)
Lamba, Gundapayu, Salpajala, Tuduli, Sutangoni, Badabada, Gurta
Sikoka *muta* I (12 villages)

Gumma, Kata, Waliamba, Kadengeyu, Bada Dengoni, Goilunga, Atejarana, Penewali, Bada Monda, Gahi Monda, Sana Dengoni, Duherigadi

Sikoka *muta* II (10 villages)

Phakeri, Patalamba, Tuta, Parsali, Bongapadi, Sana Denganali, Niskhal, Nirgundi, Ambadani, Kucheli

Sikoka *muta* III (17 villages)

Lekhpadar, Dongormati, Sarlenja, Puyubhata, Bhaliapadara, Naringtola, Kauraguda, Baruguda, Hatawali, Pukura, Mandepeta, Tamkisili, Dakansua, Dakabondeli, Tolua, Patalomba, Patangpadari

Wadaka *muta* (5 villages)

Kambesi, Gartali, Kurli, Talagumma, Uparagumma

Wengesika *muta* (3 villages)

Dhanapadar, Chatikona, Bemberi

Dongria do not express any prohibition against marrying within one's own *muta*. On one occasion, I witnessed an arranged marriage between a Sikoka of Kata village and a Jakesika of Sana Dengoni, both villages belonging to the same *muta*. The marriage was celebrated in a pompous style, and nobody seemed to consider this alliance a mistake, never mind incestuous. It may be asked, however, how often such marriages within the same *muta* in fact occur. The following data show that *muta* exogamy may not be a rule but is at least a statistical preference.

I arranged my data concerning marriages in Gumma by distinguishing between marriages of families belonging to the local dominant clan and those of affinal status. In the former category, thirty-six men married forty-nine women from fifteen different clans. These women came from twenty-three different villages, the majority of which were located in the Niamgiri range. Two of these marriages will not be addressed here, because they are exceptional in the sense that Sikoka from Gumma married girls from their own village. In other words, they married the child of an affine who had once come to Gumma to reside with his wife at the time of his marriage. Of all the other marriages, not one occurred between a man from Gumma and a woman residing in any of the eleven other villages belonging to the Sikoka *muta*. When considering the women given by Gumma to other villages, a similar picture emerges. The village gave twenty-two women to seven clans residing in sixteen different villages, only one of which (Penewali) belongs to the same *muta* as Gumma. However, it should be remembered that Penewali was bought some time ago by the Sikoka from the Jakesika.

Furthermore, taking into account all three Sikoka *muta*, the outcome offers almost the same result. Of all brides taken by men of the dominant clan from Gumma, only three came from a village that belongs to a Sikoka clan territory. One of these three cases is an exception in that the girl's original village (Kudruka) is located elsewhere. At the time of the marriage she had moved to her husband's village, but after some time she ran away to her sister's husband's village, Sana Denganali. This leaves us with two cases, both concerning marriages with Saraka women from the village of Phakeri, belonging to a Sikoka *muta*. Of the daughters and sisters of Gumma given in marriage to other villages, none moved to a place within a Sikoka territory except the one who married a Jakesika man from Penewali, mentioned above. If we take into consideration the few marriages of men from Gumma not belonging to the dominant Sikoka clan, a different trend becomes apparent. The nineteen men from Gumma married eighteen women belonging to the Sikoka clan, six of whom came from the same village. Of the remaining twelve other women, only two were taken from a non-Sikoka village, one from a Sikoka village of the same *muta* as Gumma, and nine from Sikoka villages of another *muta*. Only five marriages were entered into with women not belonging to the Sikoka clan or a Sikoka village. Of the nine women belonging to an affinal clan, a total of six married a man of the Sikoka clan, and of these six husbands, three were residing in villages of the same *muta* as Gumma.

Table 11: Marriages (Village: Gumma)

Dominant Clan		Affinal Clans	
Bride-Giving Villages	*Bride-Taking Villages*	*Bride-Giving Villages*	*Bride-Taking Villages*
Kadraka: 8 (2x Chatikona, 3x Buduni, 2x Pusikagumma, 1x Kuskedeli)	Kadraka: 8 (4x Damanapanga, 1x Sagdi, 1x Kadrakagumma, 1x Lahanikuti, 1x Radang)	Kadraka: 2 (1x Buduni, 1x Chatikona)	Kadraka: 2 (1x Tebapoda, 1x Sagdi)
		Sikoka: 18 (6x Gumma, 1x Sutangoni, 2x Sana Denganali, 1x Lekhpadar, 1x Lamba, 1x Sarlenja, 1x Phuldumberi, 1x Berenipinda, 1x Sarlenja, 2x Bada Denganali, 1x Kota)	Sikoka: 6 (2x Kata, 1x Sana Denganali, 1x Dongormati, 1x Nirgundi, 1x Dongoni)

Table 11: Marriages (Village: Gumma) *(Continued)*

Dominant Clan		Affinal Clans	
Bride-Giving Villages	*Bride-Taking Villages*	*Bride-Giving Villages*	*Bride-Taking Villages*
Pusika/Huika: 5 (1x Sutangoni, 1x Mayawali, 3x Jangjodi)	Pusika/Huika: 5 (1x Lamba, 1x Salpajala, 1x Railima, 1x Gundawayu, 1x Mayawali)	Pusika: 1 (1x Gundapayu)	
Piska: 5 (1x Gumma, 4x Musudi)	Piska: 2 (1x Damanapanga, 1x Sagdi)		
Wadaka: 2 (1x Khojuri, 1x Gandeli)	Wadaka: 1 (1x Garta)	Wadaka: 1 (1x Kambesi)	Wadaka: 1 (1x Lamba)
Wengesika: 6 (3x Chatikona, 3x Dhanapadar)	Wengesika: 3 (1x Niskabondeli, 1x Dhanapadar, 1x Musudi)		
Krungelika: 1 (1x Kemdipadar)		Krungelika: 1 (1x Kemdipadar)	
Jakesika: 3 (1x Jalkirda, 1x Nacheniguda, 1x unknown)	Jakesika: 2 (1x Nacheniguda, 1x Penewali)		
Niska: 3 (2x Niskabondeli, 1x Kendugaradi)	Niska: 1 (1x Jalkirdang)		
Kundika: 2 (2x Kambesi)			
Nandruka: 2 (2x Merkabondeli)			
Kudruka: 1 (1x Sana Denganali)			
Kruska: 6 (1x Kurusmui, 4x Kumbuli, 1x Mayawali)			
Kulesika: 2 (1x Railima, 1x Lamba)			
Saraka: 2			

Table 11: Marriages (Village: Gumma) *(Continued)*

Dominant Clan		Affinal Clans	
Bride-Giving Villages	*Bride-Taking Villages*	*Bride-Giving Villages*	*Bride-Taking Villages*
(2x Phakeri)			
Praska 1 (1 x Gumma)			
49 women 15 clans 23 villages (not including Gumma)	22 women 7 clans 16 villages	23 women 5 clans 16 villages	9 women 3 clans 8 villages

From this marriage data, the following marriage preferences can be assumed. First, members of the dominant clan tend to take wives from and give sisters and daughters to villages not belonging to the same *muta* as their own village. Second, a large majority of members of affinal clans take their wives from and give their sisters and daughters to the clan in whose territory they reside. They marry not only within the *muta* but preferably even within the village. This leads me to reconsider the notion of "village exogamy" among the Kond.

3.4.4 Marriages between villages (*padari*)

Most authors writing about Kond villages start from the idea that the villages were originally inhabited by one clan and only later by members of other clans who had migrated (e.g., Niggemeyer 1964a, 46; Jena et al. 2002, 48–49). In this assumed original condition there used to be perfect village exogamy, since all villagers shared the same clan title, and only when affinal clans later started residing in the village did marriages within its boundaries sporadically occur. Such a historical explanation is sheer speculation and cannot be based on any evidence. Dongria themselves speak about their villages as belonging to one clan only when referring to the village land, while in other contexts they present the village as consisting of different clans and local lines with specific rights and duties.

Settlement (*nayu*) and village territory (*padari*)

When Dongria talk about their villages, they often say *ma* ("our") *nayu, ma* ("our") *padari*. The word *nayu* can be translated as "settlement" in the sense of rows of houses, while *padari* is derived from the Oriya word *padara* meaning "village land," including the hill slopes, the forests, and the site where the houses are built. The *padari* has fixed boundaries marked in all directions by stone heaps (*handiwali*), which are worshipped in the course of festivals or in times of crisis such as the occurrence of a violent death. Within each *padari* are the sacred stones referred to as *jakeri*. They represent the earth goddess (*dharni*) and are said to have been established either by the gods or by the first people who came to the place. Each *jakeri* is owned by one or more local lines. In many villages, members of more than one local line of the same dominant clan are present, and together they may own more than one *jakeri* in a village. For example, the village of Lamba consists of three *padari* marked by three stone assemblages, one in the centre of the present settlement and two others located in the surrounding forest.

Some *jakeri* mark the places where a settlement (*nayu*) presently stands or where not too long ago a settlement used to be. In the latter case, such places are called *bondeli*. Other *jakeri* can be found in places where settlements have been built neither at present nor in the past. These *jakeri* usually mark a certain hill slope or hill territory claimed by a particular line (or lines) whose descendants reside in the settlement to which this *padari* belongs. It seems these *jakeri* can become the site for a settlement only after conducting certain rituals. From my inquiries about the buffalo sacrifices (see chapter 4) I developed the idea that these sacrifices are performed at the place of a *jakeri* when the stone representation marks a settlement in either the past, the present, or the future. Thus, when a settlement has been abandoned, people may use the land marked by one of their *jakeri* to build a new settlement, but in this case they have to perform a buffalo sacrifice at this site. Unless people plan to build a new settlement, the other type of *jakeri* found in the hills, in places that were not settlement sites in the past, will not become the site for a buffalo sacrifice (*kodru parbu*). However, a buffalo will be sacrificed for such a *jakeri* in the present main settlement.[65]

When villagers abandon a place, they have two options. Either they move into an existing village, or they build a new village. For example, the villagers

---

[65] For example, the village of Lekhpadar has four *jakeri* in four *padari*. In one such *padari*, the present settlement has been built, while the other three do not seem to be sites of former villages but only hill territories used for cultivation. Buffaloes were sacrificed in the present settlement for all four *padari*. This is different from cases where the buffalo sacrifice is performed for a *jakeri* of a former village site. For example, the village of Railima also organised the sacrifice for four *padari*, but each of these *padari* either presently or in the past contained a settlement. For this reason, I assume, the four buffaloes were sacrificed in four different places.

of Puyubhata abandoned their settlement completely and moved to the village of Patangpadari, the home of their clan and *muta* brothers. In the same way, the people of the village of Cipca abandoned their village and moved to two villages belonging to their clan and *muta* brothers, Phakeri and Parsali. In 2003, they started to build new houses in Cipca and return to their former village site. The people of Gumma, on the other hand, collectively left their settlement many years ago and built new settlements in the territories of Kadengeyu and Waliamba, which were not occupied by anybody else at that time. Changes in and of the residential unit (*nayu*) do not affect the village (*padari*) as a whole. People may die, houses collapse, or the entire village become deserted; none of this changes the fact that the village belongs to a particular clan, whose members must from time to time perform the buffalo sacrifice to the earth goddess of their village clan territory. When a village is sold to another clan, the rights to cultivate and to sacrifice have to be transferred as well. The *padari* differs from the *nayu* in the sense that the former is always associated with one clan only. Accordingly, many villages are named after the clan having the dominant rights in their land, such as Sikokagumma, Kadrakagumma, Pusikagumma, etc. Furthermore, when discussing the question of landownership, most Dongria I talked to could immediately assign a particular clan to each village I asked about. At the same time, all were aware of the fact that members of different clans actually lived in these settlements and jointly cultivated their land. The ideal of "one clan, one territory" contained in the definition of *padari* is thus imposed on the settlement (*nayu*) and creates the image of a rather uniform unit, although in reality the latter changes its composition constantly.

A member of an affinal line belongs to the village community but never to the collectivity defined by the land. For example, when arranging a marriage, all members of a village act as a group. They jointly capture a girl or bring her to the village, and they discuss fines together or fight together in cases of conflict. All are considered to belong to one "family" (*kutumb*), and the residents of a village as a whole are responsible for all of its members, regardless of agnation or affinity. However, as an affine, a man has no right to buy the buffalo that is to be sacrificed to the earth goddess, and he cannot cultivate the soil unless members of the dominant clan share their land with him. As an individual, he may join the village collectivity, but he can never change his territorial identity, which is defined by the village of his ancestors and expressed in his clan title. This distinction leads me to the conclusion that for a Dongria, all marriages are arranged outside the "village" (*padari*), but they may join two individuals residing in the same settlement (*nayu*). In the Dongria case, we may speak of village exogamy in the sense that the system of territorial clans combined with the rule to marry outside one's *kuda* implies that all marriages take place between people who belong to separate territorial-cum-kinship units.

Preference: Spatial dispersal of marriage alliances
Village exogamy in the sense of a rule that prohibits individuals from marrying neighbours does not exist in this society. I asked several informants whether they considered it to be a "mistake" (*dosa*) to marry within the village, and nobody answered in the affirmative. Cases of intra-village marriage are, therefore, no exception to the rule of village exogamy but rather confirm the fact that individual decisions do not matter as long as the proper relations between affinal categories are maintained. However, the majority of marriages take place outside the village. This in itself is unsurprising, considering that in most villages members of affinal clans are in the minority. Take, for example, the percentage of houses belonging to the dominant and to the affinal clans in different villages (data on Kambesi collected by Pfeffer).

Table 12: Proportion of dominant and affinal clan members in different villages

Village	Houses Dominant Clan	Houses Affinal Clans	Percentage Dominant Clan
Tebapoda	9	2	81.8%
Mundawali	21	9	70.0%
Kambesi	28	13	68.3%
Gumma	19 (Sikoka)	11	63.3%
Dongormati	16 (Sikoka)	10	61.5%
Lamba	7 (Huika)	12	36.8%

With regard to marriage alliances between villages, two further aspects deserve attention. First, the number of villages with which marriage alliances exist, and second, the distance between the villages linked by marriage. Concerning the first point, it can be stated with some certainty that Dongria do not marry within a close circle of villages. For example, in Lamba the nineteen householders have taken four women from the neighbouring village of Lekhpadar, but all other wives were brought from sixteen different villages. A similar situation exists in Dongormati. Taking bride-givers and bride-takers (residing uxorilocally) into account, the twenty-six marriages recorded link Dongormati with a total of twenty different villages.[66] In Gumma, the seventy-two women who were brought in by

---

[66] Five marriages occurred with women from Lamba. The corresponding husbands' villages are not taken into consideration.

marriage from the outside come from thirty-three villages, while the thirty-one sisters and daughters who were given away married men from twenty-two different villages. These 103 marriages[67] together establish alliances with a total of forty-four villages, only ten of which are both bride-giving and bride-taking ones. For Kambesi, Pfeffer collected data about the villages from which brides were taken in the past. The sixty-three marriages for which he noted the women's place of origin connect the men of Kambesi with thirty-six different villages. Taking into account the tendency for a decrease in the percentage of new alliances with any increase in recorded marriages, we find that on average the percentage of marriages that create new alliances may approach 40 to 60 per cent in a village consisting of thirty to forty households.

This means that in practice Dongria do *not* tend to repeat marriages with a small number of villages but rather spread out their alliances. The question is whether this statement is valid in spatial terms, too. Do Dongria prefer to marry women from nearby or from distant villages? When asked about their opinions, Dongria responded that marriages with people from the same place or from neighbouring villages are not advisable, because such an arrangement would result in constant quarrels. Affines residing in distant villages were definitely to be preferred, since their regular involvement in day-to-day matters could be ruled out in this manner.

Table 13: Distribution of marriage alliances between villages

Village	Number of Marriages	Number of Villages (Bg / Bt)	New Alliances per Marriage
Lamba	19	16	0.842
Dongormati	26	20	0.769
Kambesi	63	36	0.571
Gumma	103	44	0.427

It is difficult to state in statistical terms whether Dongria prefer to marry women from close or rather from distant villages, as basically all places inhabited by Dongria can be reached within a day's walk, and really distant villages do not exist. Marriages with people living in villages outside the mountain range are rare, at least in the villages I am familiar with.[68] Dongria are used to walking long distances through the mountains but usually only within a fairly limited

---

67 These include intra-village marriages as well as those with uxorilocal postmarital residence.
68 I cannot rule out the possibility that Dongria living in villages closer to the valleys contract marriages with Desia Kond more regularly.

area and often not beyond the towns in the foothills that mark the entrance into the valleys. From Gumma, for example, Dongria can reach villages they consider to be far away (*dipa ane*), like Railima or Musudi, within a five- or six-hour walk. In my estimation, it does not take more than eight or nine hours to walk from Musudi (Kalyansingpur Gram Panchayat) in the southern part of the mountain range to Phuldumberi (Lanjigada Gram Panchayat) in the north-western part of the Dongria-inhabited area.

When describing the approximate distance between villages, I have to rely on my own experience, since I lack a detailed map giving exact distances between Dongria villages. The map presented below is taken from P. K. Nayak's (1989, 32) study and gives a good overview of the approximate location of most Dongria villages. I had to change many numbers indicating the location of villages that were not correctly placed. Further, I included four circles centred on the site of my fieldwork (no. 95: Sikokagumma) to indicate distances to its affinal villages. I frequently walked with my Dongria friends through their mountains and, thus, have a fairly good idea of approximately how long it takes to reach certain villages. The circles thus represent a time dimension rather than absolute distances in kilometres. The circles are drawn on the basis of my estimation of how long it takes to reach certain villages from Sikokagumma. The first circle includes those villages that can be reached within about a half-hour walk. The second circle encompasses all villages within a two-hour walk. The third circle comprises those affinal villages within approximately a four-hour walk. Beyond this we find a number of affinal villages that can only be reached with more than four hours of walking. The following list identifies Sikokagumma's affinal villages[69] according to their approximate distance and the number of marriages (givers and takers).[70] The number in brackets[71] is the village's reference number on the modified map below.[72]

First circle (red): Villages within ½ hour
Sikokagumma: 8 [95]; Lamba: 4 [96]; Sana Denganali: 4 [86]; Bada Denganali: 2 [85]; Mayawali: 3 [87]; Kuskedeli: 1 [112]; Sarlenja: 2 [102]. *Total: 7 villages and 24 marriages*

---

[69] One village, named Kendugaradi, could not be located and is not included in the following figures.
[70] For a comprehensive list of all 103 marriages with a total of forty-four villages, including Kendugaradi, see appendix 2.
[71] The sign ** means that the village is found neither on Nayak's map nor in his table no. 1 (Nayak 1989, 221–26), which lists all the villages mapped.
[72] I have considerably modified the original map (Nayak 1989, 32). All numbers in Arial font are added according to other maps and my own knowledge of the area. For a list with the names of all villages corresponding to the numbers on the map see appendix 3.

Second circle (blue): Villages within 2 hours
Dongormati: 1 [97]; Kumbeli: 4 [70]; Lekhpadar: 1 [98]; Nacheniguda: 2 [**]; Phakeri: 2 [84]; Dhanpadar: 4 [69]; Chatikona: 6 [68]; Kurusmui: 1 [66]; Damanapanga: 5 [60]; Kata: 3 [51]; Buduni: 4 [104]; Nirgundi: 1 [105]; Sutangoni: 2 [49]. *Total: 13 villages and 36 marriages*

Third circle (green): Villages within 4 hours
Kambesi I: 3 [6]; Gundawayu: 2 [46]; Garta: 1 [48]; Salapjhola: 1 [47]; Dongoni: 1 [57]; Tebapoda: 1 [62]; Phuldumberi: 1 [115]; Kemdipadar: 2 [**]; Berenipinda: 1 [**]. *Total: 9 villages and 13 marriages*

Fourth circle (brown): Villages more than 4 hours away
Khajuri: 1 [16]; Kadrakagumma: 2 [8]; Pusikagumma: 2 [11]; Jangjodi: 3 [12]; Radang: 1 [13]; Gondeli: 1 [18]; Sagdi: 3 [19]; Lahunikunti: 1 [20]; Penewali: 1 [43]; Merkabondeli: 2 [52]; Musudi: 5 [80]; Railima: 2 [81]; Niskabondeli: 3 [22]; Jalkirdang: 2 [23]. *Total: 14 villages and 29 marriages*

These figures clearly show the tendency to spread affinal relations over the entire area, from nearby to relatively distant villages within the whole territory belonging to the eight or nine (see above) clans and their *muta* organisations. If we take into account the modern Gram Panchayat organisation,[73] we will similarly find that the people from Sikokagumma maintain affinal links with villages from all major Gram Panchayats.[74]

Sexual relations within the village

So far, what has been said about village exogamy has referred to marriage relations. We may ask whether the territorial aspect also has any impact on the regulation of sexual relations among the Dongria. Nayak states that boys must not sleep in the dormitories of their own village. In my opinion, however, such a definite rule does not exist. Of the two types of dormitory relations, only one complies with the statement made by Nayak. The first type of relation exists between the girls and boys of two villages who from time to time pay collective visits to each other. For example, once or twice a year the girls of Kambesi come to visit the boys of Gumma and vice versa. When, escorted by an older woman, the girls come to dance, sing, and sleep with the boys of Gumma, the latter receive them in the back portion of their houses and participate as expected. Gumma does not have a dormitory, but I have been assured that where such a place exists, the vis-

---

[73] A list of all villages according to Gram Panchayat membership is provided by Nayak (1989, 221–26).
[74] Kurli Gram Panchayat: 11 affinal villages; Patroguda Gram Panchayat: 7 affinal villages; Muniguda Gram Panchayat: 2 affinal villages; Sunkhandi Gram Panchayat: 7 affinal villages; Singari Gram Panchayat: 9 affinal villages; and Lanjigarh Gram Panchayat: 3 affinal villages. Sikokagumma itself belongs to the Singari Gram Panchayat.

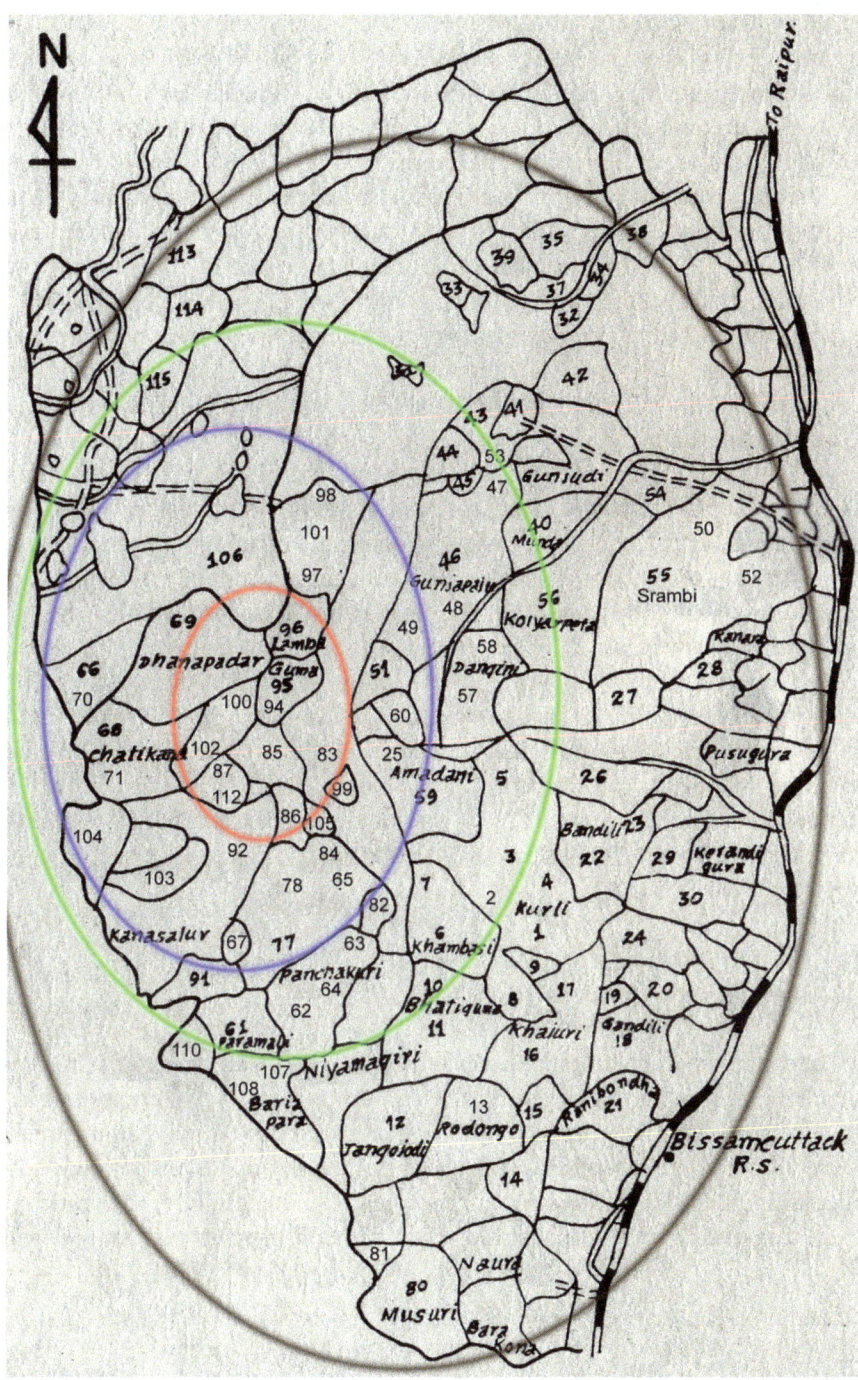

Figure 17: Four circles of affinal villages

iting girls will stay there, and the boys of the village can come at night in order to sleep with them. The same holds true for major festivals or marriages when all available space, including the forest surrounding the village, is used as dancing and sleeping grounds. Therefore, we cannot speak of a general rule that prohibits a boy from sleeping with a visiting girl in his own village. Such collective occasions may be distinguished from individual visits normally undertaken by boys to a girls' dormitory.[75] The boys leave their village at night, often in the company of a senior married man visiting his affines, and stay in a dormitory where they have developed friendships with some girls. All this happens without much public singing and dancing, in an almost routine manner. The boys do not enter the village but proceed directly to the dormitory, which is usually located behind the two rows of houses that make up the village. They will leave the village again in the same inconspicuous way early on the following morning to return home. A man will refrain from visiting the dormitory of his own village, where most of the girls present will fall into the categories of younger or elder "sisters," while his chances to meet a girl with whom sexual relations are permitted are much better in the dormitory of a village belonging to a different territorial clan. Even there, he may meet a girl of the same clan, but older girls will be present to ensure adherence to the clan rules. If, however, girls of an affinal clan come to visit a man's village and stay in its dormitory, no rule prevents him from visiting this place and from engaging in sexual relations with the visitors. The tendency of boys to visit dormitories outside their respective village may, therefore, be seen in the light of the incest rule in combination with the localisation of particular clans in different villages. There is no rule that prohibits a boy from engaging in sexual relations with girls in his own village as long as they are not considered to be his "sisters."

3.4.5 Marriage with "relatives"

To what extent are the prohibitions concerning repeated marriages between local lines mentioned above observed in practice? To illustrate the complexities involved in answering this question, I will first present a case study that illustrates how familiar it is necessary to be with the genealogical and affinal relations of a particular local line in order to find out what is often kept hidden, i.e., the repetition of marriage between local lines. After presenting this case study I will

---

[75] As described in the next chapter, Dongria girls sometimes visit the dormitories of neighbouring villages.

make generalisations from my data and show some methods employed by Dongria to marry people who are not prohibited by the rules and yet are closely related to them in the genealogical or spatial sense.

Case study: Direct reciprocity between local lines
To provide an example of the repetition of marriage between local lines and of the strategies for evading or stretching the rules that accompany such marriages, I will analyse the affinal relations of one local line in Gumma belonging to the status category of *icha jani* and consisting of six households. These can be divided into two segments of three households. In each segment, genealogical relations between the households are known, while people cannot say exactly how the two segments are related except in the sense that the great-grandfathers were brothers, either real or classificatory, a difference that is often not remembered. Despite this lack of genealogical knowledge, all households still consider each other as belonging to one *punja*, an idea expressed at certain collective rituals or in contexts defined as *dosa* (mistake or disorder) that affect members of all six households. Here, I will concentrate on one segment of the local line (see pedigree in appendix 1).

The marriage relations of this local line aroused my interest when one day during my stay, a group of four young Dongria from the village of Railima came to Gumma in the company of their *barika* to bring a fine (*tapu*) for a woman named Sikoka Sukuli. The topic of fines will be discussed in the next chapter. At this point it suffices to say that when a girl has been demanded by one local line but runs away with a man from another, the latter has to pay a substantial amount of money to the girl's village as well as to the village of her former fiancé. In this case, Sukuli had been demanded by Wengesika Kandra from Dhanapadar for his son Drinju. On the village plaza, the visitors and the villagers from Gumma sat down to bargain on the amount to be paid as a fine. Finally, the bride-takers handed over Rs 6,000 and promised to come back the next week to pay the rest of the agreed Rs 15,000. When the visitors had left, a quarrel broke out between Sukuli's FeBS, Sikoka Buguni, and the wife of another FeBS, Sikoka Gabru. The latter originally came from Dhanapadar and argued that Sukuli should be given to her "brothers" instead of being married to the Pusika of Railima, who had captured Sukuli one day when she was staying at her MB's house in Jangjodi (close to Railima). The argument was pursued vehemently by both sides, Buguni standing outside the house, Gabru's wife inside the house, hiding behind the door. For the moment, the dispute could not be settled, but some days later, the objecting side agreed to accept the fine paid by the Pusika and give Sukuli in marriage to them. Following the quarrel, I started inquiring into the marriage relations between this local line and the Wengesika from Dhanapadar and found out, to my astonishment, that marriages between the same local lines, though contrary to the rules elaborated above, had in fact occurred previously.

Gabru's wife and the wife of the *naika* of Gumma are two sisters from the Wengesika clan of Dhanapadar. Their father is Wengesika Daru, who is married to two wives, one Kadraka and one Wralika woman. While Gabru's and the *naika*'s wives are daughters of the Kadraka woman, a man named Wengesika Jogi is the son of the Wralika woman. Some years ago, Jogi married Sikoka Sipu, who is the daughter of Gabru's FeB. In other words, Wengesika Daru from Dhanapadar *gave* one daughter to Sikoka Gabru's local line *and received* one from it. This is a clear example of a symmetric exchange of daughters and would be prohibited by the *samdin gota* rule.

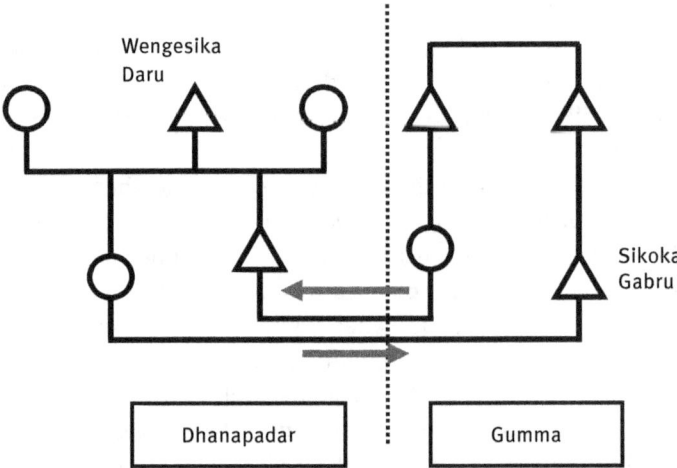

Figure 18: Sister exchange between two families

This was not the only empirical marriage between these two local lines in that generation. Wengesika Daru has a classificatory brother named Wengesika Guse in Chatikona. Despite living in two different villages, they are considered to belong to the same local line, although the exact genealogical relationship is difficult to trace. Guse has two daughters from two different wives. The elder daughter, Wengesika Bami, was promised to Sikoka Gabru's elder brother, one Sikoka Bitu, while the younger daughter, Wengesika Dombadi, was given in marriage to Sikoka Lakana, Gabru's paternal cousin. This implied that two classificatory brothers were about to marry two half-sisters. However, before this could happen, Wengesika Bami ran away with another man, and her fiancé married a woman from the sweeper caste. The situation is further complicated by the fact that according to information given to me by Wengesika Dombadi, Sikoka Gabru's wife is her classificatory FZ, implying that the repetition of marriages occurred not only in the same but also in adjacent generations, with three brothers tied by marriage agreement to a FZ and her two BD, thus violating the prohibition on diachronic as well as synchronic repetition of intermarriage.

If we ignore Wengesika Bami (who ran away with another man), the Wengesika line has given two women to the Sikoka line but received only one woman in return. This, I believe, explains why Gabru's wife argued so vehemently with her husband's younger brother to make him give his sister Sukuli in marriage to her Wengesika line, a step that would have balanced the giving and taking of brides.

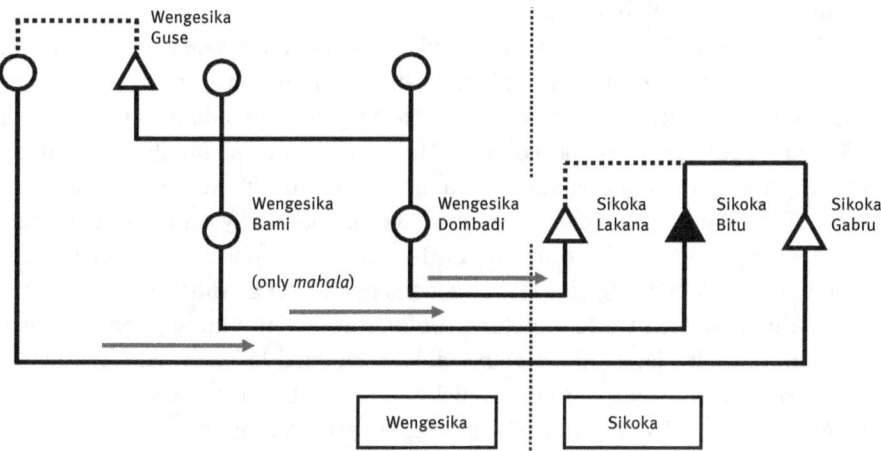

Figure 19: FZ and BD married to three brothers

On all these issues, the Sikoka line was divided into two factions. Lakana and his real brother, Buguni, argued against the marriage for monetary reasons, as some assumed, because the Wengesika from Dhanapadar are relatively poor compared to the Pusika from Railima. Thus, Drinju's father had not given anything but had just come one day and demanded the girl, while the people from Railima had paid an amount of Rs 6,000. According to Lakana, the marriage between Wengesika Drinju and his sister was furthermore unacceptable because Drinju and Jogi were classificatory brothers. Since the latter had married Lakana's sister Sipu, the marriage would not have complied with the rule prohibiting alliances between siblings belonging to two local lines, i.e., men who have become siblings due to the fact that they have both married "sisters". When I confronted him with the fact that he himself had married the sister of his classificatory brother's wife, he answered that his family had given *mahala* for his wife three years earlier than the other (i.e., Bitu's) family, so that he had not broken the rule.

This argument puts all the blame on Bitu's family, which had indeed shown disrespect for rules several times in the past. Thus Bitu himself took a woman from the Reli caste as his wife, just like his younger brother Sorti, who was expelled from the village after falling in love with another sweeper girl. As explained above, their third brother's marriage likewise amounted to a violation of the rules in the sense that it involved a direct sister exchange. In the context of Sukuli's marriage, Gabru and his wife argued in favour of giving her as a bride to Drinju, claiming that Drinju did not belong to the same local line as Jogi. Jogi's forefathers had lived in a different village, named Jalkirida, and had only rather recently moved to Dhanapadar.

The question of whether certain families belong to the same local line or not is often difficult to answer. In particular when there is some uncertainty, for example when detailed genealogical links are forgotten, people may change their affiliation depending on the context. There were several families in Gumma whose affiliation to a particular local line was not absolutely certain. For example, the local line of the *member*, Sikoka Mukuna, originally comes from a village called Monda and is said to belong to the same local line as the *naika* family, although the latter's original village is considered to be Waliamba. In times of cooperation, such as while thatching roofs, in forms of address, and in discussions about their history, the *member* always claimed to be of the same line as the *naika*, a claim that was disputed by others. When the *member* performed his house ritual (*ghanta parba*), he erected a sacrificial hut at a shrine different from that of the *naika*, and he worshipped a house god different from that of the *naika*. In this context, everybody agreed that they indeed constituted two different local lines, and the *member* himself had to admit that his line was "a little different" from theirs.

This clearly demonstrates that once concrete links are forgotten, affiliation to a local line becomes an object of contestation, people sometimes arguing in favour of and sometimes against being a member of a certain local line depending on their interests. As the rules prohibiting marriages apply to local lines, they can be bypassed by contesting group membership. This clearly happened in the case described above, because Sukuli's marriage was acceptable to those who considered Drinju's and Jogi's families to belong to two different local lines, while it was rejected by others who considered them members of the same line.

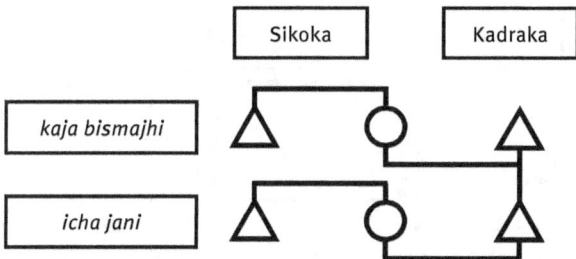

Figure 20: Marriage with two local lines of the same village

Switching between local lines (*punja*)
Taking into account the rules of *kuda* exogamy and the prohibition applying to four generations of people belonging to the *mama ijo* or *samdin ijo*, it would be expected that Dongria would find their marriage partners among people to whom they are only very distantly related. Operating on this assumption, I was astonished that in fact in the village where I lived, almost all houses were interrelated by marriage. A major reason for such an affinal web is that affines, after moving into their respective wives' villages, try to continue or extend their ties with the dominant clan. There are several possible ways to achieve this end. One is to marry one's children to a different local line of the dominant clan from that of one's wife. Thus, a Kadraka had married a woman from the *kaja bismajhi* local line and found a wife for his son among an *icha jani* line of the same village (fig. 20).

Another way to marry as close as possible is to give one's sister to a household whose members live in the same village and belong to the same clan as the people from whom one has taken one's wife but who consider themselves to be of a distinct local line. For example, a Huika was married to a Sikoka of the *kaja bismajhi* line, while at the same time his half-sister (same mother, different father) was given to a man of the *icha jani* local line (fig. 21).

Another aspect that can be derived from the study of the affinal relations of particular local lines is the tendency to marry siblings into the same village. The rules *prohibit* such a repetition of intermarriage between local lines, but they do *not* prohibit such links between villages. An example of a continuing alliance on the local level is the marriage of three sisters from the Kruska clan of the village of Kumbuli into three different local lines of Sikoka from Gumma. First, two men of almost equal age married two sisters, and then much later, a younger male Sikoka took the third, younger sister as his wife. Such cases are not uncommon. In Gumma I recorded five marriages of two or more sisters with Sikoka men from

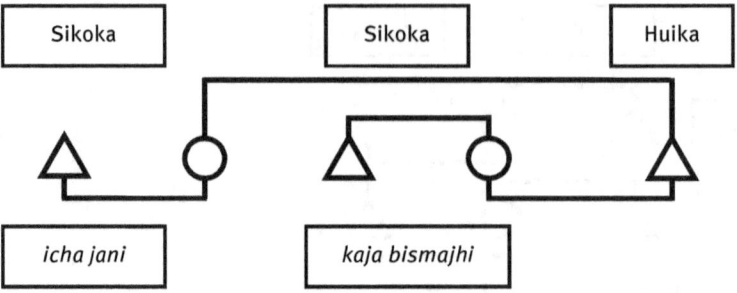

Figure 21: Marriage with two local lines of the same village

different local lines. I once witnessed first-hand how the Sikoka of Dongormati tried to arrange the marriage of two of their village men to two sisters from the village of Wandeleka Kambesi. In other words, what is prohibited for a local line can be practised on the village level.

One way to strengthen an already existing tie within a particular village is to establish a *sadu* relationship with one's affines. A *sadu* relationship exists between two men who have married two sisters, either real or classificatory (i.e., parallel cousins). In contrast to forms of address and reference between brothers, the term *sadu* is used reciprocally and thus excludes hierarchy based on seniority. If more than one "route" to choose an address term is available, the expression *sadu* is preferred between members of the same clan. For example, a young Karchika addressed two Kadraka brothers as *mama* (MB) before his marriage.[76] Then he married a sister of the younger brother's wife. Afterwards, he addressed the younger brother affectionately as *sadu*, while he continued to address the elder brother as *mama*.

A *sadu* relationship, though conceived of as fraternal, is characterised by joking and mutual help. It frequently occurs on the village level between members of the dominant and the affinal clan. For example, a Sikoka of Gumma had given his sister in marriage to a Kadraka from a different village who, following the wedding ceremony, began to live uxorilocally. In the next generation, the sons of both men married two sisters of the Krungelika clan from a different village and thereby *changed* the *samdin*, or affinal, relationship established by their fathers into a *sadu*, or quasi-agnatic, relationship.

---

[76] His mother called the two Kadraka "younger brothers" because they were the children of her classificatory FZ, or in other words, they were younger cross-cousins to her.

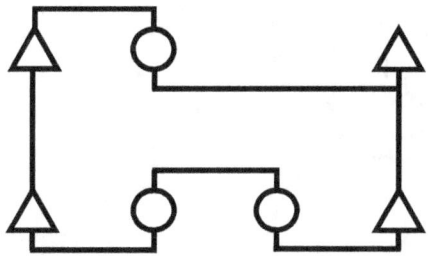

Figure 22: *Samdin* and *sadu* relations between two local lines

A similar marriage was arranged by Huika, mentioned above, for his son: while he himself had married a woman of the *kaja bismajhi*, he planned to arrange a marriage for his son with a girl who was the sister of the girl demanded by his *kaja jani* neighbour for his son. In both cases a *samdin* relationship was replaced by a *sadu* relationship in the subsequent generation, with either the same or a different local line of the dominant clan, thus transforming relations of affinity into relations conceived of as agnatic.

The marriage of two local lines in a village with two or more real or classificatory sisters is a regular link not only between clans but also between local lines of the same clan. In Gumma, local lines of the dominant clan were often linked by such affinal ties in different generations. As an illustration, I will refer to the local line of *icha jani*. Two generations ago, they were linked to the *kaja bismajhi* of the same village by a marriage of two sisters from the Piska clan. One generation ago, the same local line established links with the *kaja jani* and another line of *sana jani* from Gumma by marrying one of three sisters of the Kruska clan. Finally, in this generation, one member of their local line married a sister of the wife of the local line of *naika*:

Symmetric reciprocity: Marriage by capture
In the context of marriage by capture I recorded two cases in which the ideal of symmetric reciprocity, disallowed by the rules, was explicitly expressed by my informants. One case involved two young men from Gumma, Sikoka Teli and Sikoka Dikca. Teli had fallen in love with a girl from the neighbouring village of Lamba, whom he visited regularly in her dormitory. However, she was engaged to a man from Lekhpadar, and Teli could not afford the inevitable fines if she were captured. Dikca, on the other hand, was officially engaged to another girl from Lamba, who was desired by a man from Lekhpadar. When I discussed this issue with a man from Gumma, he told me that the villagers of Lekhpadar were trying to strike a deal with Lamba and Gumma in order to exchange the

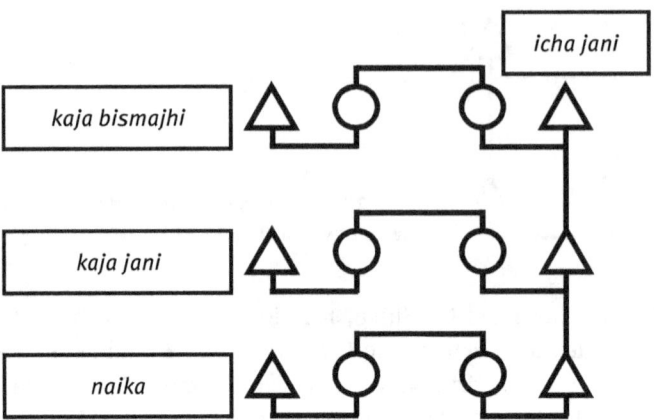

Figure 23: *Sadu* relationships within the Sikoka clan of Gumma

brides; if Gumma was willing to give them Dikca's bride, they were prepared to let Teli marry the bride demanded by them.

Another instance demonstrating the ideal of reciprocity between villages in the context of bride capture had occurred in the recent past. The *naika* of Gumma had an unmarried sister. Some time ago, Kadraka Katu from the village Buduni had come along with his friends to capture her. When they had successfully taken her to Buduni, the villagers from Gumma sat together and decided that since Buduni had taken a woman from them, they would go and capture a sister from Kadraka Katu for Mishra, the son of the *member* from Gumma. They put their plan into action and captured her, but after some time they had to release her, because she was still a very young girl. The *naika*'s sister also returned and is still unmarried. This capture of Katu's sister was called *patela kina* ("to make an exchange"). Balancing the number of brides seems to be particularly important in cases of marriage capture. As will be seen in the discussion of fines in the next chapter, the amount of money is partly determined by the fines paid between the villages in the past.

3.5 Conclusions

3.5.1 Descent, territory, and residence

Following the consideration of rules and practices, the relationship between the two principles that define marriage on the local level, i.e., descent and territory, has to be re-examined. To begin with, the nature of the territorial factor must be elaborated. On the one hand, territory is endowed with an ideological aspect, since according to mythology, the gods divided humans into descent groups and gave them distinct titles and land. This intimate link between descent and territory is reproduced on different segmentary levels of society. Thus, each *muta* consists of a certain number of villages (i.e., comprising territory) belonging to a particular clan (i.e., defined by rules of descent), and each village (*padari*) is in turn associated with a clearly marked patch of land (territory) and a dominant clan (descent). In the context of marriage, the rule of exogamy refers to this categorical level, i.e., all marriages must occur outside of the descent category, which is again irrevocably linked to a certain village and *muta* no matter where the individual actually lives. In other words, everybody inherits not only a title but also a territorial affiliation. As long as *kuda* exogamy is observed, all marriages will – *on the categorical level* – correspond to the ideal of bride-exchanging territorial clans.

On the other hand, territory as an empirical factor never fully coincides with the territorial categories of the descent system. Again, this holds true for each level of the segmentary "tribal structure". Dongria may speak about each particular clan as located in a specific area, but there are no boundaries defining any empirical place as owned by a certain *kuda*. The same holds true for the *muta*, which may change its composition due to the migration of the population of whole villages or because of the sale of village territories. In contrast to the *muta*, the village territory has clear boundaries, but it is hardly possible to find a place where the categorical equation of "one place, one clan" is actually implemented. Instead, settlements (*nayu*) often consist of people belonging to a number of different clans. The relation between *nayu* and *padari* is a good example of what French sociologists call an "encompassment of the contrary," which includes a reversal when moving from the level of a whole to the level of its parts. On the one hand, the word *padari* is used for the highly valued whole of the land and people, the "village." On the other hand, *padari* is also an element of the whole *and* opposed to *nayu*. *Nayu* refers to the residential unit of presently living individuals who cooperate (or quarrel) in contexts of marriage, sacrifice, feuds, etc. As an element, *padari* is opposed to this aspect of the village, as it is associated with soil, land and cultivation. Since *padari* or "territory" is also linked to a particular earth goddess and claimed by clans represented by dominant local lines claiming membership in status categories, it has a transcendental and collective character. The settlement (*nayu*) constantly changes, while the village land (*padari*), through its association with the earth goddess and with a particular clan, gives permanence to the "village" (*padari*) as a whole. It may also be said that collective permanence defined in terms of descent and the cult unit here encompasses its opposite, the constantly changing settlement, its individual residents and their cultivation of different plots of land.

The discrepancy between the categorical and the factual level mentioned above is in itself unsurprising. The question is how the system is able to cope with it. On the one hand, territory is an attribute of clans, but residence does not determine an individual's membership in a certain exogamous category. On the other hand, everybody belongs on the basis of residence to a particular village, which in turn is incorporated into a *muta* organisation. When examining concrete marriage practices like betrothal, wedding, and divorce (see next chapter), we become aware that among the Dongria each individual acts as a member of a village no matter what his or her *kuda* affiliation is. In other words, on this level of concrete marriage practices, residence becomes an additional factor of group affiliation. While on the categorical level territorial clans segmented into *muta* and villages exchange brides, in actual practice residential units give and take women in the process of creating alliances.

The difference may best be illustrated in cases where both principles, descent and territory, contradict each other. We may imagine a situation in which two villages belonging to the same *kuda* x enter into a marriage alliance that involves individuals of *kuda* x and *kuda* y. I indeed observed such a marriage, one of the most prestigious type, and nobody disputed the correctness of the relation. This marriage was in accordance with the rule of *kuda* exogamy, because the bride belonged to the Jakesika and the groom to the Sikoka clan. However, since both resided in villages of the same dominant clan, the alliance neglected the territorial aspect of the ideal model. The implication is that in the event that the two principles come into conflict, the collective aspect, i.e., the *kuda* category, is given primary value, while the individually changeable relationship, i.e., the residential affiliation, is neglected. The higher value is attached to a system of clan categories, including their associated territories, while the lower value refers to an empirical assemblage of people who have chosen to reside in a particular place. The higher value of territory linked to descent is protected by the rule of exogamy and by a terminology that defines any bride as a "woman from far away" (*hedi*) who has to be "brought" (*tana*) or "captured" (*ahpa beta*). The lower value of territory in the sense of residential affiliation is expressed in a statistical tendency to marry outside the village and outside the *muta*.[77]

---

[77] Christian Strümpell pointed out to me this difference between the higher value expressed categorically and the lower value articulated by statistical behaviour.

3.5 Conclusions

The hierarchical relation between "transcendent village" (*padari* as a whole) and "empirical village" (*nayu* or settlement as an element of the whole) contains a reversal when moving from one level to the other. On the categorical level, territory as an aspect of descent overrides all residential affiliations. What matters when considering whether or not a marriage complies with the norms of society are the descent categories of bride and groom, not their residence. On the level of practice, i.e., in the context of actually establishing an alliance, the situation is reversed, because all members of a village join as bride-givers in opposition to the village of bride-takers regardless of their *de facto kuda* affiliation. Joint residence becomes the primary factor in group affiliation and in taking up a position in conflicts that may occur between bride-givers and bride-takers. For example, if a Jakesika woman from a Sikoka village marries a Sikoka boy from a Sikoka village, the Sikoka of both villages will *not* unite on the basis of the same descent category but will oppose each other in cases of conflict on the basis of belonging to different residential groups (*nayu*).

Prohibitions beyond the rule of clan exogamy do not apply to villages, neither in the sense of "transcendent" nor of "empirical villages," but do apply to "houses" (*ijo*) and "local lines" (*punja*). As mentioned above, these marriage rules are expressed in the idiom of the house, such as the "house of the MB/FZH" (*mama ijo*) or the "house of the exchange partner" (*samdin ijo*). A house always belongs to a local descent group (*punja*), whose members affirm their relationship when worshipping a stone outside the settlement. A *punja* often shares a common history of migrations from an original place. After a few generations or when they settle in separate villages, genealogical relations tend to be forgotten, and local lines separate. Migrating families try to claim membership in an important local line of their new village, or they become the founders of a new line.

This means that residence can be a factor for changing one's affiliation to a particular descent group (*punja*), but only to another descent group of one's own clan category (*kuda*). It may also be said that in the system of opposed clans, territory-cum-descent always overrides residence, while within the clan, residence may override affiliations created by descent. This can be understood within the context of marriage rules. Rules of exogamy apply to the clan category (*kuda*), while rules prohibiting the repetition of marriage are observed by local lines (*punja* or *ijo*). The first rule allows no exceptions, as clan incest is considered the gravest mistake a person can make and is punished by expulsion from the community. Repetition of marriage with certain local lines is not met with the same sanctions, and it occurs from time to time but can be hidden by claiming an affiliation with another local line or by contesting the descent relations between local lines.

3.5.2 Comparison of terminology, rules, and practice

When comparing all three levels of analysis presented in this study, i.e., terminology, rules, and practice, an astonishing consistency comes to the fore: each of these levels highlights the contradiction between proximity and distance. Proximity takes the form of the prescription of direct exchange expressed in Dongria terminology, of the constant exchange of brides implied by the rule of clan exogamy, and of marriages between close relatives of prior affines in practice. Distance is expressed by the negative prescriptions in a terminology that rules out any transmission of affinity across generations, by rules that prohibit any repetition of intermarriage for three generations, and in practice by marriages contracted with distant parties.

In Dongria terminology, I identified the positive valuation of symmetrical reciprocity in the +1 generation, where the terms for parents and their siblings contain a clear prescription: father's siblings are married to mother's siblings in a clearly symmetrical fashion. On the other hand, the terminological distinction between parent's siblings and spouse's parents in this generation already points to the opposite, the discontinuity of symmetrical exchange from one generation to the next. Descendants of affines are no longer marked as such but turn into "siblings," "children," "grandchildren," etc. Terms for descendants are used down to the −5 generation, a fact that, in my view, carries the following message: for many generations, former affines become like one's own descendants and are therefore unmarriageable. Through time, distinctions between descendants of different lines become less and less marked, until finally even sex distinctions are omitted.

We would expect that such a terminology would go along with a rule that prohibits the repetition of marriage until any relations between the lines cease, i.e., after the −5 generation. In reality, this is not the case, since Dongria allow a repetition of intermarriage as soon as the −4 generation. As mentioned above, even this rule was contested by some informants, who were of the opinion that a marriage can already be repeated in the −3 generation. Such rules can be changed in both directions, i.e., either to reduce the interval between marriages of successive generations or to extend it. Pfeffer, for example, was informed by Kond living in the northern Sambalpur district that they used to prohibit a repetition of intermarriage for seven generations (personal communication). There are no positive rules of marriage prescribing a direct symmetric exchange between houses and local lines. Yet the rule of exogamy applies to localised, territorial clans and implies the idea that these clans exchange brides on a regular, direct, and reciprocal basis. Delayed exchange is only introduced by the rules that forbid further marriages with the *mama ijo* and the *samdin ijo* or with any prior affinal line down to the −4 generation. This, in my view, leads to the phenomenon of dispersed alliances observed in practice.

On the level of practice I found two trends. First, the members of each village maintain a relatively wide range of marriage relations over the whole area inhabited by Dongria Kond. The importance of the territorial factor for defining clan affiliation leads to a tendency to marry outside one's village and *muta*. Marriages with "strangers" are highly valued, and the highest status is allotted to marriages arranged by people from relatively distant places whose children have not had any prior sexual relations. This certainly corresponds well to rules that prohibit the direct repetition of intermarriage. My analysis of concrete marriage relations in a particular village revealed another tendency, i.e., establishing marriage relations between people who are "close" in terms of space and/or kinship relations. Thus, affines residing uxorilocally attempt to establish further marriages with relatives of their local wife-givers. They may also try to marry a sister of the wife of a member of the local dominant clan in their host village and thereby turn the former affine into a *sadu*, i.e., into a very highly valued, quasi-agnatic relative. In contrast to the ideal of arranged marriages between relative "strangers," my data on bride capture (see also next chapter) lead me to assume that this form of contracting affinal relations positively values direct exchange.

3.5.3 Proximity and incest, distance and fertility

On all three levels, then, we find contradictory trends: relations between affines are characterised by either proximity or distance, direct reciprocity or delayed exchange. I interpret these contradictions to be an expression of Dongria values. Considerations of incest have a major impact on matrimonial alliances. According to the myth about the two human beings who survived the great flood (see Elwin 1949, 41–42, 288; Nayak 1989, 38–39), a brother and sister married after going to distant places or after being disfigured by smallpox, both events preventing them from recognising each other. Following this original incest, the Kond – in some myths all people – were further subdivided by assigning different territories to them. However, since all Kond are descendants of this original couple, they are never *absolutely* but always only *relatively* different. Relative difference is expressed in terms of clan and territorial affiliation. Dongria men and women are closely related, since they all descend from the original brother-sister pair, but the relation between them – like that of the original couple – should ideally be as remote as possible in terms of space and familiarity. In this way, arranged marriages between relative strangers approximate the ideal of non-incestuous relations. Why, after all, is incest feared so much? Barbara Boal offers an answer to this question:

> The strongest of all Kondh examples of the upholding of the social structure by pollution beliefs is in regard to incest, for the whole social system rests on the right patterns of marriage and the integrity of the exogamous patrilineal clan or lineage group. Liaisons within the forbidden relationships call out the strongest of all emotional reactions from all Kondhs. Thus not surprisingly they are said to pollute the land and endanger not only the couple but the entire society of Kondhs and all others living within their clan boundaries, for they evoke the fiercest disapproval of the Earth Goddess. [...] Rains will fail, crops will shrivel, children already born will fall ill and die and new infants will not be born, they say, if she is roused to action through the polluting of land. (Boal 1997, 173; see also 46)

From this statement I infer the following message: on the *relative* scale of incest and territorial proximity, "close" marriages destroy fertility[78] and reproduction, while "distant" marriages enhance wellbeing, create an abundant harvest, and produce many children. A matrimonial alliance turns formerly "distant" families into "close" relatives, and the rules of marriage serve to ensure that these "close" relatives do not renew their relationship. Instead, people should ideally turn to other "distant" families for further marriages. Meanwhile, the "close" families again become more distant with every further generation. In ego's generation, children of prior affines are called "brothers" (*tayi*) and "sisters" (*tangi*),[79] although they are terminologically different from brothers and sisters (including parallel cousins), the latter being referred to by different terms containing age markers (elder brother / sister and younger brother / sister). In the −1 generation, the seniority principle is no longer used as a marker to distinguish one's own children (including children of same-sex siblings) from children of opposite-sex siblings, yet the latter are terminologically differentiated from affines, i.e., spouses of one's children. In the −2 generation, the distinction between agnatic and affinal categories becomes obsolete. In the −3 generation, the sex marker begins to be omitted. Starting from ego's generation, certain markers of kinship relations are consecutively omitted: age, cross/parallel, and sex. Relatives in suc-

---

78 In a different book, Boal (1999, 115) states, "This [i.e., *geka* or "incest," R.H.] is the most serious of all forms of pollution both to that kin group and to the whole community, for it 'Pollutes the Earth' (Earth Goddess). If not fully expiated, it will bring total disaster upon all forms of fertility."

79 As mentioned before, the word *tangi* as used by the Dongria means not only "younger sister" as in other Dravidian languages but "sister" in general. When Dongria speak about "brother and sister," they use either the expression *tayi tangi* or, more often, *tayi bai*, the word *bai* also meaning "sister," more specifically "elder sister" in Dravidian languages such as Kui (see Winfield 1929, 10).

cessive generations thus continuously lose certain characteristics – we may also say that they become de-individualised – until they merge into the large pool of marriageable "distant" people. Distance between parties in a marriage is highly valued, because the relation created in this way is opposed to incest and the dangers incest contains for the fertility of the earth.

Allow me to speculate at this point. A major difference between Dongria and Desia Kond, who have almost identical terminologies (see section 3.2.3), is that the former prohibit marriages with cross-cousins while the latter explicitly allow such marital unions (for different degrees of violence see section 3.5.4). One way to understand this difference is by linking it to different patterns of agriculture. Desia Kond are primarily wet-rice cultivators who cultivate their fields from year to year and observe only short fallow periods or rotations. Dongria, on the other hand, are almost exclusively shifting cultivators who cut the forest and use the land for a few years only. While the first year usually provides an abundant crop, the harvest decreases with every subsequent year, and especially the highly valued forms of rice and millet can only be cultivated on a newly made swidden. When they abandon a swidden, they will observe a long fallow period before returning to the same site, which meanwhile becomes forest again. I never asked whether Dongria themselves recognise this connection, but it appears striking that their marriage rules and their agricultural practice seem to follow the same idea: fertility is greatest when moving to new places – houses or forests – and when returning to them after long intervals. The opposite, i.e., incest and working in the same fields for years, leads to the destruction of fertility in all of its forms. Another major difference between Desia and Dongria Kond is their social environment and habitus: while the former nowadays live under relatively settled and peaceful conditions, Dongria still engage from time to time in feuds and are, in general, more disposed to use violence and aggression than the Desia Kond. Taking into account the prominent place of violence in Dongria society helps us to understand the following phenomena: first, the coexistence of two opposing marriage strategies in the Niamgiri Hills; and second, the difference between Dongria and Desia Kond marriage rules.

3.5.4 Violent habitus, status, and strategies

In classical accounts of "kinship" relations, especially those written from a functional or structure-functional approach, rules were the main focus of analysis. Actual marriage behaviour was only recorded to state either the relative compliance with the rules or the divergences between norms and practice. According to Bourdieu (1979), such studies approach their subject with a false understanding of practice. Practice, in his opinion, has to be understood as part of a complex historical process of human interaction in which objective structures shape people's dispositions (or habitus), which in turn have an impact on the objective structures that produced them (Bourdieu 1979, 82–83). Bourdieu's approach has the advantage of integrating processes of thought and action into the study of objective structures and enables us to understand the principle of their continuity and regularity. It is meant to eliminate some of the most important fallacies of the structural method, in particular its lack of concern with historical processes, "real life," and people's factual interests and decisions.

Problems start when trying to apply these theoretical statements to the analysis of data collected in long and intensive fieldwork. What are the given structures, what are Dongria dispositions, what are their concrete practices, and how do all these aspects react upon each other? In my attempt in what follows to show how these aspects are interrelated in my data, I restrict myself to a certain aspect of Dongria sociability: How are the official representations of kinship expressed by the rules, and how do the actually contracted marriages recorded in my statistics relate to the practical concerns of the Dongria and to their given social environment? In contrast to Bourdieu, I do not speak of "objective structures" in the sense of power relations, since "power" itself is not objective but culturally constructed and valued differently from society to society.

My data clearly show that seen from the perspective of the territorial unit, the village, marriages are indeed dispersed in the sense that alliances exist with a high number of other villages and that these affinal villages are spread over the whole of the Dongria-inhabited area. This dispersal is linked to two territorial aspects of the clan organisation: (1) the village land (*padari*) dominated by one clan and (2) the union of several villages belonging to the same clan, the *muta*. Any marriage choice is shaped by this socio-territorial organisation, which creates a simple opposition: Dongria live among their kin but must seek their affines, more or less, in territorially distant places.

On the other hand, many Dongria do not live among their kin, as they for various reasons decide to move to their bride's village. Further, villages where affines live are often not far away from one's own village. My data also provide evidence that many marriages do not actually occur between socially distant families, even if they may reside in spatially distant places. The rules are meant to control direct reciprocity as it exists in other societies where sister exchange or the exchange of bilateral cross-cousins is allowed. In any concrete case, the Dongria rules, however, leave enough space for marriage with people who are not "strangers." Dongria may seek new alliance partners or continue with their old ones if they successfully defend them as being in accordance with the rules. The data presented above show that some Dongria do indeed marry "close" people – in the territorial and social senses – either by entering into marriage unions with prior affines that are not forbidden by the rules or by contesting genealogical relations between their prior and their new affines.

Within this given social environment, what are the dispositions that produce practices ranging from alliances with relative strangers to marriages with prior affines with whom one is well acquainted? Keys to understanding this particular aspect of Dongria sociability are violence and status aspirations. For example, Dongria and Desia Kond clearly differ in their aggressiveness and readiness to fight. The former always carry knives and axes with them when leaving their village, and they do not hesitate to use them in cases of conflict. In his book, Nayak gives ample evidence of the brutality with which feuds are pursued between Dongria belonging to different clans and villages. Dongria hit their enemies with clubs, throw stones at them, cut them with knives, or even "hack them into pieces" with axes (Nayak 1989). Even nowadays, Dongria must hand over their weapons to the police when attending major Hindu festivals in towns located in the foothills, and although all my Hindu informants agreed that Dongria violence has decreased due to the monitoring of villages by state officials, it is still very much an aspect of daily life. Interpersonal violence is certainly not absent among the Desia Kond, but according to my observation the Desia are not involved in collective fights like those that Nayak reports for the Dongria and that I have personally witnessed during my fieldwork in the Niamgiri Hills. The general atmosphere in a Desia village is more peaceful than in a Dongria village, and I never worried about my personal wellbeing when staying among them. Desia villages are found in close proximity to villages inhabited by members of different caste communities, and state institutions such as the police, forest department, schools, post offices, etc. exercise direct control over the Desia Kond. In contrast to the Dongria Kond, Desia thus find themselves in a situation in which state officials and local authorities rather than allies from the same community regulate conflicts.

How are these dispositions linked to social and territorial structures? Dongria socio-territorial organisation divides them into kin, with whom one shares feasts and engages in competitions concerning status, and affines, with whom one marries and fights. Kin members normally live in a nearby neighbourhood, and relations with them are usually characterised by solidarity and sharing, but also by status distinctions and by rivalry, especially between elder and younger real or classificatory brothers. Status may be gained and increased by give-away feasts like the main house ritual (*ghanta parba*) and by costly forms of marriage, such as arranged marriages or bride captures involving costly peace settlements (see next chapter). Affines, on the other hand, live in more or less distant places and can always be a source of aggression and conflict. One has to seek one's wives among these potential enemies, and by entering into marriage alliances one can turn them into a kind of relative with kin obligations. Given the general lack of social peace in these mountains, where each territorial unit exhibits a strong solidarity against other units of the same kind, the dispersal of alliances by all members of a village is thus of clear advantage to all. However, the system only works when the alliances have some continuity, or in other words, when they are not only relations of a passing and instable nature. A solution to the problem of potentially instable alliances would be the direct repetition of marriages between local lines. However, such a practice has two disadvantages. From the collective point of view of the village community, this practice limits the overall dispersal of alliances, reduces the number of links with other villages, and, thus, functions to decrease stability in the region. From the perspective of each household, a marriage with a former affine may have the advantage of being relatively cheap and of ensuring the continuation of a well-established relationship. However, it would also go against the status aspirations of one's house and lineage, since high status is only derived from marriages with relative strangers.

Each household is thus torn between finding new alliance partners and upholding alliances with prior affines, between costly marriages contributing to the increase of the household's status and cheap marriages intensifying its existing relations. My assumption is that the choice between distant and close marriages depends on the number of children a family has, its existing wealth, and its status in its village. When they belong to the dominant clan in a village, they will try to arrange at least a few of their children's marriages with outside people to raise their status vis-à-vis the other local dominant families. On the other hand, Dongria living as *raiti* on the land of people belonging to another clan have a particular interest in strengthening their ties with this dominant clan. They achieve this through repeated intermarriages with the members of the dominant clan. The latter may agree to such unions for two reasons: first, they cannot afford to arrange an outside marriage for all their children, and second, the *raiti* are important retainers and trusted people.

We may summarise the above considerations in the following way: The region of the Dongria Kond is divided into a large number of territorial kinship units. Within each territory, members are divided by their status aspirations but joined by relatively friendly kin relations and a sense of solidarity. This solidarity is opposed to the solidarity existing within the other units, which are potential enemies but also a source of status. Furthermore, these units depend on each other for intermarriage and for status aspirations. Men are expected to exhibit a disposition towards violence to defend their own territory and group. Each man has to acquire a wife from a potentially aggressive group, either through violent acts like bride capture or through negotiations, which may involve high payments when the bride-givers are strangers or smaller gifts when they are already allies. Higher status is ascribed to expensive marriages, since wealth is only a marker of status when given away; bride capture can turn into a similar giveaway practice when the group decides to enter into negotiations instead of fighting out the conflict with the people from whom the bride has been stolen (see next chapter). The continuation of marriages with prior affines does not increase status but helps to intensify relations within existing alliances. Each household or segment of a local line competes for status and, thus, has to decide for itself what kind of marriage presents a better choice, given its financial possibilities and present status. Within each village we find a continuum between high-status marriages with foreigners and low-status marriages with "relatives." I discern two overall effects of this situation: the high-status marriages contribute to the dispersal of the alliances of the most important territorial unit, the village, while the ordinary marriages strengthen ties with already allied villages and with related lines and houses within the village. The following chapter describes in detail the main forms of marriage among the Dongria Kond and provides evidence that marriages include various degrees of violence and dispersal of wealth depending on the social distance between the parties involved.

4 Forms of marriage: negotiation, violence, and love

> Anthropology has taught us that everywhere marriage goes much beyond linking two people together and controlling sexuality. Marriage organizes relations between two families, two groups, and even sometimes, two moieties. It is an institution and an exchange, for Lévi-Strauss (1969), the most fundamental of them all. It is a way of accommodating society in time, of linking the past to the future, historically, biologically, and politically, a way to metaphorize similarity and otherness; to come to terms with the fact that everything contains its contrary, though not to the same degree; to establish ontology and to put it into question; and to limit the illusion of any sort of teleology. (Iteanu 2004, 217–18)

4.1 Introduction

The two previous chapters addressed the formal characteristics of social relationships between different communities in the Niamgiri Hills (chapter 2) and within the Dongria Kond community (chapter 3). It was argued that relations between Dongria and Dombo are based on interdependence in the context of cycles of "short-" and "long-term exchange," while relations within the Dongria community are expressed in terms of affinity, descent, and territory. Of these three principles, marriage (or affinity) was seen as the major factor in establishing social relations between categories of people otherwise distinguished by territory and descent. In this chapter, the focus of analysis will shift from the formal aspects of marriage relations to the ways in which such relationships are actually created. The forms of marriage that exist among the Dongria Kond will be seen as expressions of conflicting interests and strategies: on the one hand, village elders and parents consider marriages to be a way of establishing a "contract" between two social units such as villages, local lines, or houses; on the other hand, members of the younger generation often select their marriage partners on the basis of attraction and mutual affection. The interplay of these two interests occurs within a cultural framework in which "marriage", in contrast to "love" relations, can be forged in two ways: by arrangement or by capture. Each of these forms of marriage realises different values existing in this society and corresponds to different accepted modes of behaviour: they are based on either negotiation or violence, spatial and social distance or proximity, exchange or appropriation.

Following an introduction to previous studies of bride capture and marriage, the main part of this chapter will provide data illustrating the particular forms of marriage among the Dongria and their embeddedness in Dongria social values. Following a general overview of the major forms of Dongria marriage (section

https://doi.org/10.1515/9783110532883-004

4.2, "Categories of Dongria Kond marriage"), the main part begins with a detailed account of the values, norms, and practices involved in arranged marriages (section 4.3, "Collective alliances: Arranged marriage"). The negotiations may extend over a time span of as many as twenty years, from the childhood of the prospective bride and groom to their adulthood and actual wedding ceremony. Emphasis is put on the way relations between the affinal parties change from overt hostility to amicable cooperation and on the gradual shift from asymmetric to symmetric gift exchange. The next part of the chapter (section 4.4, "Youth resistance: Love marriages, bride capture, and collective settlements") focuses on other forms of marriage that are the result of young people's love affairs and regularly disturb collectively arranged marriages. While the latter are mostly the business of adults, particularly men, bride capture involves the interests and emotions of young people, both boys and girls, to a much greater degree. Since their love affairs often begin in the context of the girls' dormitory, this institution and its relation to concepts of gender and ideas about creation will receive particular attention. The last part of this section provides evidence on how conflicts arising out of the practice of bride capture are settled through the collective efforts of all parties involved. In my conclusion, I address the following questions arising out of theoretical debates: (1) Are Dongria forms of marriage and their rule of exogamy linked to their feuds? (2) Do Dongria forms of marriage correspond with their ideas about social distance? (3) Is it reasonable to distinguish arranged marriages from bride capture? (4) Does gift exchange occur only in arranged marriages? (5) What types of reciprocity correspond to the different forms of marriage?

4.1.1 Approaches to bride capture and marriage

The topic of bride capture and marriage has been addressed in an article by Barnes (1999), who discusses its relevance for anthropological theory and for understanding social relations in a number of different societies. References to Central India are absent in his contribution, although many classical monographs report the presence of bride capture among various tribal groups; indeed the first theoretical study of bride capture, by McLennan [1865] (1970), repeatedly refers to Kond marriage practices. McLennan based his theories on information collected by fellow Scots who worked as agents for the suppression of human sacrifice and female infanticide among the Kond. While these "fieldworkers" interpreted their observations in view of their very practical concerns, McLennan used them to construct a major theory of the evolution of human society. Modern approaches to bride capture have been developed in relation to other societies, such as those studied by Hugh-Jones (1979), Arhem (1981), Jackson (1984), and Barnes (1999). This raises the question of whether these new approaches have anything to contribute to our understanding of Kond institutions.

4.1.2 Kond marriage and the legacy of John F. McLennan

Many famous nineteenth- and early-twentieth-century anthropologists explained human evolution by focusing on one particular institution. For example, Henry Sumner Maine looked at the evolution of law, Lewis Henry Morgan at kinship terminology and corresponding social forms, Marcel Mauss and Emile Durkheim at classifications, Edward B. Tylor at magic and religion, James G. Frazer at beliefs and rituals illuminating ancient Greek traditions, and John F. McLennan at marriage and bride capture. Their search for origins, together with their belief in the progress of humankind, made them look for reports about so-called primitive peoples to prove a gradual evolution from the dark ages of the past to the enlightened civilisation of their own white European society and culture. What exactly these writers regarded to be the central issue of human evolution partly depended on their access to these reports and on the social institutions described in them.

Good and reliable reports were not easily available, but with the colonisation of various parts of the world, more and more knowledge poured in, mostly produced by sailors, administrators, and missionaries. In the writings of the British evolutionists, it is mainly examples from various parts of India that serve as illustrations for their different evolutionary speculations. These examples were partly provided by administrators facing the task of having to eradicate certain social practices they felt to be the "white man's burden," such as the burning of widows (*sati*), high dowry demands (*kulinism*), the practice of human sacrifice (*meria*), and female infanticide. Due to a certain series of historical events described by Boal (1997) and Padel (2000), the Kond people living in the wild jungles of what is now Odisha began to figure prominently in the reports produced by the British colonialists. Around 1830, some officers were suddenly faced with a group of people who seemed to practice two of these "evils," the killing of human beings during the sacrifice to their earth goddess and the killing of female infants at the command of their sun god. To eradicate these practices, an agency was set up, and two Scottish officers, Major General John Campbell (1801–78) and Major Samuel Charters Macpherson (1806–60), began to devote their lives to the high aims of this agency. They produced a series of reports, partly out of jealousy and pride, as each claimed all the merit of "civilising" these people for himself and tried to diminish the achievements of the other (see Boal 1997, 107–8; Padel 2000, 91–95).

As Padel suggests, this conflict may have its roots in old rivalries between their two Scottish families (Padel 2000, 96). Scots figured prominently in the British army, which provided jobs to them after their families had lost their homes following the English conquest of the Scottish Highlands. The Kond "highlands" then came to be administered primarily by these Scottish officers, including Dyce, Cadenhead, and MacViccar (Padel 2000, 96–97). Given this Scottish dominance in the mountains of Odisha, it appears logical that another Scott, John F. McLennan (1827–81), when writing about the evolution of humankind, used the reports of his fellow countrymen to illustrate his hypotheses.[1] In 1865 he published his most important monograph,[2] *Primitive Marriage: An Inquiry into the Origin of the Form of Capture in Marriage Ceremonies*, which is the first serious attempt to explain forms of marriage in terms of other social institutions such as female infanticide, blood feud, tribal exogamy, and patrilineal descent rules. Apart from Australian aborigines, Kalmyk, and Kyrgyz, the Kond are his primary example for illustrating primitive forms of marriage. It may even be assumed that the place given to female infanticide as the primary cause for exogamy and thus for bride capture directly derives from reports about the Kond. In his book, McLennan refers to two works by Macpherson on the Kond, one[3] a general report about their society, the other[4] a detailed description of their religious beliefs and ritual practices. Apart from these two sources, McLennan also cites a later report by Campbell,[5] which must have reached him only shortly before the publication of his own book. In the dispute between Macpherson and Campbell, McLennan clearly takes the side of the former, whom he regards as "a more intelligent witness" and whose view he considers to be "more consistent with other known facts than that of General Campbell" (McLennan 1970, 41).

---

[1] Another of the famous evolutionists who made use of these reports in his writings is James George Frazer, who in his Golden Bough compares the *meria* sacrifice to fertility rites in ancient Europe (Frazer [1922] 1968, 632–50).
[2] John F. McLennan, *Primitive Marriage. An Inquiry into the Origin of the Form of Capture in Marriage Ceremonies* (Edinburgh: Adam and Charles Black, 1865).
[3] Samuel Charters Macpherson, *Report upon the Khonds of the Districts of Ganjam and Cuttack* (Calcutta, 1842).
[4] Samuel Charters Macpherson, "An Account of the Religion of the Khonds in Orissa," *Journal of the Royal Asiatic Society of Great Britain and Ireland* 13 (1852): 216–74.
[5] John Campbell, *A Personal Narrative of Thirteen Years Service amongst the Wild Tribes of Khondistan for the Suppression of Human Sacrifice* (London: Hurst and Blackett Publishers, 1864).

I found one reference[6] by Macpherson to McLennan's book on *Primitive Marriage*, which at first made me assume that McLennan's writings had an impact on how Macpherson presented his Kond data. The reference to McLennan can be found in a book[7] edited by Macpherson's brother and published in 1865 following the author's death. It contains a collection of various diary notes and reports written by Macpherson, among them the *Report upon the Khonds of the Districts of Ganjam and Cuttack* of 1842. While the original report contains, of course, no reference to McLennan's work, which appeared only thirteen years later, the version edited by his brother has a reference to McLennan's *Primitive Marriage*. Macpherson here compares the forcible abduction of a bride among the Kond with similar practices among Hindus, people of ancient Europe, and tribes of the Caucasus. It may be assumed that Macpherson's brother, when later editing the text, included the reference to McLennan's book.

The passage written by Macpherson about Kond bride capture is actually quoted by McLennan in his *Primitive Marriage* in order to exemplify mock capture. In other words, Macpherson did provide MacLennan with ethnographic data concerning bride capture and with the idea of a comparison between Kond forms of forcible abduction and those found in ancient texts and among tribes of the Caucasus. McLennan's second chapter begins with a treatment of various sources, gives evidence of ceremonial bride capture among the ancient Greeks and Romans (McLennan 1970, 11–13), and then continues with examples of Kond bride abduction provided by Macpherson and Campbell (McLennan 1970, 14–15). He gives further examples from the Kalmyk, Kyrgyz, and people of the Caucasus (McLennan 1970, 17), who are mentioned several times in this book (McLennan 1970, 31, 43, 61, 83). From this we may derive a general idea of the influence of Macpherson's ideas on McLennan's comparative approach to bride capture.[8] However, I think the influence went far beyond these methodological questions to the heart of McLennan's argument concerning exogamy, which in his view was caused by a shortage of women due to female infanticide.

---

6 See Macpherson (1865, 70).

7 Samuel Charters Macpherson, *Memorials of Service in India: From the Correspondence of the Late Major Samuel Charters Macpherson, C.B., Political Agent at Gwalior during the Mutiny, Formerly Employed in the Suppression of Human Sacrifice in Orissa, Edited by His Brother* (London: John Murray, 1865).

8 In 1863, McLennan wrote an anonymous article entitled "Hill Tribes in India," which, however, contains no references to Central India but deals with various tribes in Northeast India. Bride capture does not have a prominent place in this article, which is rather a summary of various customs existing in the region. See John F. McLennan (anonymous), "Hill Tribes in India," *North British Review* 38 (1863): 392–422.

To illustrate this point, I will give a short summary of Macpherson's findings concerning Kond marriage, which also provide a good introduction to the main part of this chapter, since some of the rules and institutions described by Macpherson are relevant for the Kond even today.

In his first report, Macpherson ([1842] 1863) presents us with a relatively detailed description of marriage among the Kond. Women enjoy considerable social influence and are treated with respect. At the same time, men are said to mistrust their wives in cases of war with their neighbours. The reason given is that Kond marry "betwixt members of different Tribes" (1863, 54), with whom they are constantly at war. In Macpherson's view, the Kond represent a stage of human development in which intertribal relations are governed by treaties, but in which nevertheless war is the rule and peace the exception (Macpherson 1863, 42). Due to the rule of intertribal marriage, a group's wives come from the "tribe" of enemies, whom they often visit to condole their relatives following killings in wartime (Macpherson 1863, 54). By "tribe" the author – according to the general usage of his day – means an exogamous clan, and like McLennan, he does not clearly distinguish between the exogamous and endogamous units of tribal organisation.

In order to obtain a wife, the father of the groom has to pay "20 to 30 lives" to the bride's father (Macpherson 1863, 54), a gift consisting of bullocks, buffaloes, goats, pigs or fowl, and valuable metallic items such as brass pots (Macpherson 1863, 50). These have to be repaid in the event that the wife deserts her husband within six months of their marriage. Interestingly, no mention is made of the possibility that strained marriage relations or the repayment of betrothal money may in fact be the cause of wars between "tribes." Marriage relations are also not enumerated among the main causes for feuds among the Kond, the primary factors being land disputes, desires for revenge, and the "passions or caprices of the Chiefs" (Macpherson 1863, 43). However, Macpherson does find an element of violence in the Kond wedding ceremony, which includes a mock conflict following a dance between the affines, in the course of which the groom's uncle runs away with the bride. As stated above, Macpherson compares this ceremonial capture to the forcible abduction of women in other parts of the world.

Macpherson further informs the reader that a Kond father chooses his daughter-in-law by taking into account her physical fitness, since she has to work for him as long as her husband is still a boy and does not have a house of his own (Macpherson 1863, 55). According to Macpherson, a Kond wife is usually four to six years older than her husband, who at the time of marriage is hardly ten to twelve years old (Macpherson 1863, 54). After their wedding, the wife stays in her father-in-law's home, "occupying the same couch" (Macpherson

1863, 55), a statement which suggests the existence of formalised sexual relations between father-in-law and daughter-in-law. A man may have a second wife or a "concubine," whose status and rights of inheritance are the same as those of the other wives and their children (Macpherson 1863, 55).

In his book on *Primitive Marriage*, McLennan uses these data to illustrate a number of arguments. The mock battle among the Kond serves to illustrate the difference between "capture de facto," or violent abduction, and "capture as form," i.e., the ceremonial abduction of a bride within the context of a formal marriage arrangement. McLennan regards capture among the Kond as an example of the latter form, a statement which he finds confirmed not only by Macpherson's observations but also by an elaborate description of an abduction provided by Campbell (McLennan 1970, 14–15). Capture as form is considered by McLennan to be a symbol of a previous stage of evolution, when real abduction used to be the standard way of acquiring a wife. Starting from this assumption, he asks himself what the origin of such a custom might have been. He finds the answer in a rule prohibiting marriage within the tribe. Again, the Kond serve as example, and he quotes both authorities, Campbell and Macpherson, who offer him different explanations for this rule.

In Campbell's view, exogamy among the Kond is linked to the "endless difficulties and quarrels" arising out of female unfaithfulness. At marriage, a Kond father receives a substantial gift for his daughter, but later, when she deserts her husband and runs away with another man, the former son-in-law can demand the return of his original payment. In such a case, the actual financial burden has to be carried by the new husband of the girl, since "the paramour then becomes responsible to the father for the equivalent he has been made to restore" (Campbell 1864, 141).[9] As these cases occur quite frequently, most men have to repay substantial gifts when getting married. In order to escape this financial burden, Kond men marry "women from distant places, for whom they give a much smaller sum than for those of their own tribes" (Campbell 1864, 141–42). Apart from these financial reasons, Campbell further mentions certain values responsible for a marriage between members of different, spatially distant tribes. On the one hand, Kond are said to find it "degrading" to give their daughter to someone from their own tribe; on the other hand, the men consider it to be "manly" to acquire a woman from a distant country, obviously because such an enterprise is fraught with various dangers.

---

9 At the end of this chapter I present my ethnographic data concerning the repayment of the "betrothal fee", which basically confirm the information provided on this point by Campbell.

McLennan dismisses these observations in favour of Macpherson's explanation of exogamy, citing the latter's report on the religion of the Kond, which states that marriage within the same "tribe" (i.e., clan) is considered "incestuous and punishable by death" (Macpherson 1852, 271). This rule ensures that Kond marry outside their own group, which as a whole faces the problem that it must obtain women from other, usually hostile clans. To illustrate this hostility between intermarrying clans, McLennan again cites Macpherson's previously quoted statement that Kond marry "betwixt" tribes who "annually engage in fierce conflicts." The conclusion drawn by McLennan from the concurrence of exogamy and intertribal hostility is that "it was *inevitable* that wives should systematically be procured by capture" (McLennan 1970, 57; my emphasis). He thus suggests a close interconnection between exogamy, mock or real bride capture, and inter-group violence. However, McLennan's search for origins does not stop at this point, since he is inquiring into the "real" origin of exogamy.

His suggestion that exogamy originally derives from the practice of female infanticide leads us straight back to the ethnographic findings of Macpherson. Astonishingly, there is no reference to either Macpherson or Campbell in this section on female infanticide, only a footnote in chapter eight stating that among the Kond female infanticide is a religious institution. The absence of any reference to Macpherson's or Campbell's account of female infanticide among the Kond is particularly intriguing because McLennan obviously lacked any other detailed report about this practice. The facts presented by him are very meagre considering the importance McLennan attaches to this phenomenon for his theory of exogamy. In McLennan's view, female infanticide creates a lack of women in any given population and thus gives rise to the capture of women from outside one's own group, i.e., exogamy, and to polyandry (McLennan 1970, 58). The practice disappeared with the introduction of matrilineal kinship but occurred again in an advanced state of evolution in connection with agnation and blood feuds. The argument runs in the following way. In a previous stage of human evolution, children belonged to their mothers, who lived in the group of their husbands. Any killing of either mother or child would have been avenged by the mother's group, and to avoid blood feuds, female infanticide was stopped. When kinship through males ("agnation") was introduced, the conditions for children changed, since they now belonged to the group of their fathers. Killing them no longer included the risk of arousing the rage of their mother's group members, and therefore, we often find the practice linked to systems of patrilineal group membership:

> Accordingly the most impressive systems of infanticide – chiefly systems of female infanticide – now existing, occur among exogamous races which have male kinship. (McLennan 1970, 105)

The question remains as to why female infanticide is practised at all. In McLennan's view, primitive people considered the male contribution to the survival of the community higher than the contribution of women. For this reason, they preferred to rear boys rather than girls, a practice which resulted in an imbalance of the sexes. McLennan is aware that people like the Kond justify the practice of female infanticide in terms of their religion (McLennan 1970, 68), but he sees the real origin of this custom in the "struggle for food and security" (McLennan 1970, 68). Although he mentions no source for the religious justification of female infanticide among the Kond, he certainly had in mind Macpherson's writings. In his "Account of the Religion of the Khonds in Orissa," Macpherson (1852) develops a kind of religious explanation of the relation between female infanticide and marriage customs. Like McLennan, he regards the religious doctrines of the Kond as a "sanction" of the practice, whose real origin is different. However, Macpherson's sociological explanation directly contradicts that of the famous evolutionist, and this may be the reason why the latter does not cite him when writing about female infanticide. Macpherson clearly states that Kond women are highly valued and that their "opinions have great weight in all public and private affairs; and their direct agency[10] is often considered essential in the former" (Macpherson 1852, 271). He identifies the real reason for female infanticide in high betrothal payments – and not in the struggle for food and security.

According to Macpherson, there were certain districts in the Kond area where female children were put to death soon after birth, so that some "villages containing a hundred houses may be seen without a female child" (Macpherson 1852, 270). Whereas the sacrifice of human beings occurred particularly in areas where people worshipped the earth goddess *tari*, female infanticide was prevalent in areas inhabited by members of the "sect" of *boora*, the sun god.[11] As mentioned above, Macpherson had stressed the great influence and status of Kond women in his report, which appeared ten years earlier, but now he claims that it is highest among the followers of the sun god. They are represented as notorious adulterers, who have the right to leave their husbands and contract new marriages. This behaviour creates all kinds of disturbances, since a deserted

---

10 Postmodern and feminist theorists, who regard the idea of female agency in the sense of women's power to affect public matters a highly modern concept overcoming the out-dated theories of old-fashioned anthropologists, will find this quote from 1852 surprisingly trendy.
11 According to Macpherson, the Kond are divided in two "antagonistic sects," the followers of *tari* and the followers of *boora*. The antagonism derives from a mythological conflict between god and goddess. Each of these sects is said to have its own cult practices, the *meria* being the major rite for the followers of *tari* and female infanticide being a typical practice of the sect of the sun god (Macpherson 1852, 231–59).

husband has the right to reclaim from his former wife's father the total sum he paid for her. The father in his turn approaches the new husband of his daughter and demands a corresponding payment to be made by him. As whole groups are liable for the debts and faults of their individual members, the quarrels arising from divorce and remarriage lead to conflicts between groups. Macpherson suggests that female infanticide was introduced by the Kond to prevent such conflicts, the ultimate cause of which is identified as the capricious behaviour of women.[12] He quotes a Kond as saying that apart from rich men, who seek alliances and can afford to pay restitution, all others consider married daughters as a "curse" and that in order to guarantee peace, female babies have to be put to death (Macpherson 1852, 272). This attitude is sanctioned by the sect's main god, *boora penu*, who, after quarrelling with goddess *tari* and contemplating the evil influences of women on creation, gave consent to bringing up only as many female children as necessary (Macpherson 1852, 272).

Let us now compare the opinions on Kond marriage practices of these three Scottish authors. For McLennan, Kond justify female infanticide in religious terms, although the real origin of this institution rests in the superiority of men over women in terms of protecting and feeding the members of the group. The practice of killing female babies naturally leads to an imbalance of the sexes, the lack of women in one's own group forcing young men to seek their wives among people outside their own tribe. This exogamy became protected by a rule that prohibits intratribal marriage as incestuous and punishable. Since Kond, like all "primitive" men, were in a constant state of war and feuds, the intertribal dependency caused by the imbalance of the sexes led them to acquire their wives by capture. The mock conflicts in a Kond wedding are reminders of this earlier state, when capture was the only way to get a wife.

These speculations have, of course, serious drawbacks, primarily because they deny the essential social role of women and fail to explain why Kond and other people actually fight wars. Macpherson and Campbell, whose aim was not to provide an universal scheme of social evolution but to understand Kond social institutions in order to develop effective measures against such practices as female infanticide and human sacrifice, viewed Kond marriages differently. Both of them stress the important position occupied by women in Kond society and the problems arising out of the instability of marriage relations given the local system of betrothal payments. According to Campbell, these mon-

---

[12] Macpherson does not consider the ambivalence of his statements concerning the role of women in Kond society, who on the one hand are considered to be the primary cause of conflicts and on the other hand are intermediaries in cases of war and necessary to restore peace (Macpherson 1852, 271).

etary regulations create a financial burden for the men, who react by seeking "cheaper" women from distant places. Such women have to be captured, an activity that is not only less costly but also regarded as particularly "manly." In contrast to Campbell, Macpherson did not include bride capture in his reasoning, and the only example he gives of this custom is a mock battle in the context of a formal wedding. For Macpherson, betrothal payments in combination with female infidelity lie at the root of the problem, and he elevates this as the primary cause of intertribal conflicts. His writings suggest two Kond reactions to this situation, i.e., either engaging women as peacemakers, since they are attached to both parties, or the killing of female babies. Following this mode of thinking, we may ask why Kond demand such high betrothal payments in the first place, and indeed Macpherson addresses this question in a paper entitled "Measures for the Abolition of Infanticide 1842–1844,"[13] in which he suggests that female infanticide, high marriage payments, intertribal conflicts, and the instability of marriage ties mutually reinforce each other. Given that he wrote in the middle of the nineteenth century, and taking into account that his reasoning resembles structural-functional explanations dating from the twentieth century, his argument deserves to be quoted in full:

> Infanticide produces a scarcity of women, which raises marriage-payments so high, that tribes are easily induced to contest their adjustment when dissolutions of the tie occur; while these dissolutions are plainly promoted by that scarcity, which prevents every man from having a wife. On the cessation of infanticide women would become abundant, and the marriage-payment would become small. (Macpherson 1865, 222)

This argument shares with McLennan's reasoning the idea that the imbalance of the sexes is caused by female infanticide. However, Macpherson differs from McLennan in the sense that he regards the rise of marriage payments, and not bride capture, to be the primary effect of female infanticide. In contrast to McLennan, he also sees marriage arrangements as the main cause of social conflicts. Regarding the scarcity of women as the main problem, Macpherson came up with the ingenious political measure of giving the girls he had saved from being sacrificed to the earth goddess to men who had failed to secure brides due to the practice of female infanticide.

---

13 See chapter 15 in the book edited by Macpherson's brother.

4.1.3 Understanding present forms of Kond marriage

Do these works have any importance for our understanding of Kond marriage practices today? We may approach this question from two sides, one ethnographic and the other theoretical. First, the data provided in this chapter provide clear evidence that many of the details described by Macpherson and Campbell were obviously not invented and continue to be relevant today. I will give ample evidence that Dongria demand high "betrothal fees", that they have various forms of bride capture, that the highest status is assigned to arranged marriages with women from afar, that the dissolution of these arranged marriages leads to social conflicts, and that bride payments have to be returned in complex peace settlements. However, what puzzles me is the matter of female infanticide, which figures so prominently in these colonial texts. Several informants told me that Dongria Kond indeed put small babies to death. The main reasons appear to be the unmarried status of the mother or her death at a time when the baby still needs to be breastfed. Such babies are neglected, suffocated, or burned along with their mother on the funeral pyre.[14] The death of small babies does not require elaborate rituals among the Dongria, as the infants do not as yet have a name or a social status. However, I never heard that only female babies were put to death or that infanticide was committed in any systematic way and for reasons other than those mentioned above.[15] We may assume that traditions have changed and that the colonial power was as successful in the suppression of female infanticide as in the policy of terminating human sacrifices. Another plausible explanation can be derived from Macpherson's statement that female infanticide was practiced by a limited section of the Kond population only. He himself only became aware of the custom on his second trip, when he visited certain areas inhabited by the followers of the "sect of Boora" (MacPherson 1852, 221) in Ghumsur district. According to Macpherson, these people must be distinguished from the followers of goddess *tari*, who demand a human sacrifice. In spite of my doubts regarding the historical existence of such clearly demarcated sects and cults, it is evident that Dongria and many other Kond perform the *meria* sac-

---

14 When the mother dies during delivery, she turns into a special type of ghost called *kacmahane*. Whether dead or alive, her baby is burned along with her. Such a case occurred in a Dongria village during my stay.
15 In a book about Kuvi Kond written by Rev. F. V. P. Schulze (1912), the author mentions the "murder of babies" of either sex if their horoscope reveals that they may become a threat to the wellbeing of the family (Schulze 1912, 37). However, Dongria do not consult an astrologer to cast the horoscope of a new-born child.

rifice (with buffaloes) today, whereas nobody is known to practice female infanticide as described by these three Scots.

Whatever may have been the case, the stated contrast between Kond who practice female infanticide and those who do not undermines the explanatory value of this practice in the context of marriage and exogamy. If female infanticide has always been a *locally limited* phenomenon, how can it serve as an explanation for other social practices that are characteristic of *all* Kond? In other words, why should all those Kond who do not kill their female infants nevertheless demand "betrothal fees", practise exogamy, and capture their wives? This leads me to the second point, the question of how to approach these phenomena theoretically.

4.1.4 Anthropological approaches

R. H. Barnes (1999) raises the question of modern ethnography's position on hypotheses about marriage and bride capture of the kind put forward by McLennan some 140 years ago. McLennan was a classical evolutionist who sought to understand social evolution by comparing sources of the past with information collected among so-called "primitives" of the present. Social practices of the latter were considered to present earlier stages of evolution when compared to the institutions of the "civilised" white European. Nowadays, neither the search for evolutionary stages nor the ethnocentrism and superiority complex characteristic of many nineteenth-century evolutionists are regarded as appropriate for current anthropologists. Rivière, who re-edited McLennan's classic monograph *Primitive Marriage: An Inquiry into the Origin of the Form of Capture in Marriage Ceremonies* and praises McLennan for his sociological method,[16] nevertheless comes to the conclusion that his arguments are "wrong" (Rivière 1970, xxii) and appear "ridiculous" to the modern reader (Rivière 1970, xl). What, then, are the ideas and hypotheses Barnes finds worthy of reconsideration?

In general, Barnes tends to favour the "old" works because McLennan "gave us a theory and a set of institutions about which to argue" (Barnes 1999, 68). In the process of deconstructing the notion of unitary institutions such as totemism or, as in this case, marriage and bride capture, we are said to enrich our knowledge of the variety of forms these institutions may take (Barnes 1999, 69). Furthermore, Barnes points out that some of McLennan's hypotheses fall outside

---

[16] "Furthermore, his method was truly sociological, since he was trying to explain social institutions in terms of one another, to demonstrate their interdependence" (Rivière 1970, xliv).

the standard evolutionary reasoning, as some of his constructs are based on the method of logical transformations of the kind suggested by Lévi-Strauss. As examples he refers to McLennan's idea of a non-historical, purely formal scale into which "tribal systems" can be fitted depending on their similarities with either of two extremes, "pure exogamy on the one hand and endogamy – transmuted into caste of the Mantchu and Hindu types – on the other" (McLennan 1970, 60), as well as to McLennan's writings about the effects of tribal exogamy combined with matrilineal descent.[17]

Among the many observations made by McLennan concerning bride capture, two aspects fascinate Barnes most: the idea of linguistic exogamy and the relation between "ceremonial" and "real" capture. According to McLennan, marriage capture between separate tribes may lead to a situation in which men and women speak separate languages, a situation that according to McLennan used to exist among the Caribs. While Barnes doubts that the Caribs provide an appropriate example for McLennan's concept of linguistic exogamy, he finds ample evidence of this particular kind of exogamy in Vaupés and Northeast Arnhem Land, as well as a single example in New Guinea.

In cases where linguistic exogamy exists, it often goes along with bride capture of the ceremonial type. The distinction between "ceremonial" and "real" capture has been the object of many discussions, and Barnes (1999, 67–68) carefully summarises the main "explanations" put forward by various authors. McLennan himself offers an evolutionist explanation and regards ceremonial forms of bride capture as a symbol of a previous stage of society, when more hostility prevailed between the tribes. He also provides us with another, almost structuralist interpretation when he states a correlation between types of marriage and the degree of social distance (Barnes 1999, 65). Some of the studies Barnes cites suggest a similar continuum between arranged marriages among allied, friendly groups on one end and bride capture between socially distant, often hostile groups on the other. Thus, he refers to Hugh-Jones's (1979) work on the Barasana, for whom force is unacceptable between close neighbours, whereas capture is an appropriate means to acquire a woman from distant com-

---

[17] Rivière also suggests a link between McLennan and Lévi-Strauss: "Thus for example one can trace Lévi-Strauss's distinction between harmonic and disharmonic regimes back through Durkheim to McLennan's realization that if kinship is traced through women and is symbolized by totemic allegiance then marriage by capture will introduce into the horde women whose offspring will be available for marriage; it will result in what McLennan calls a heterogeneous society" (Rivière 1970, xli-xlii).

munities.[18] The ceremonial character of bride capture is interpreted in different ways. While Arhem (1981) considers it to be a reaffirmation of the value of male aggressiveness among the Makuna he studied, Jackson (1984) regards it as an expression of the ambivalence involved in a marriage between people who in social terms are neither very close nor very distant.

In Barnes' view, modern anthropologists – like the nineteenth-century evolutionists – see a correlation between types of marriage and social distance, but they do not similarly take up McLennan's evolutionary speculations. Barnes himself does not offer a general theory, being rightly critical of constructing bride capture as a unitary institution with a singular explanation. Concerning the distinction between "ceremonial" and "real" capture, he correctly casts doubt on the absolute separation of these two types, as in given instances captures may occur either peacefully or violently. However, considering any universal definition and explanation of marriage and bride capture to be highly questionable does not necessarily mean that we have to give up searching for certain meaningful associations between social institutions in particular cases. When McLennan claims to have found "amongst various races of mankind a *system* of capturing women for wives" (McLennan 1970, 39; emphasis original), one part of this statement can be accepted and the other not. On the one hand, McLennan correctly saw that many of the institutions he found in his various sources were interrelated in a systematic fashion, and his aim was to establish not only the evolutionary but also the functional correspondences between these institutions. McLennan's hypotheses concerning the interrelation between bride capture and other social institutions may have been radically criticised (Rivière 1970, xxxvii-xl), but the systematic character of the link between bride capture and other social institutions has been confirmed in the works of the modern authors quoted by Barnes. On the other hand, these latter studies throw doubts on McLennan's claim that there is "a" system, a single coherent institutional complex pertaining to a particular evolutionary stage. Any detailed ethnography provides us with enough evidence to affirm that values, marriage institutions, and their relations with other social phenomena can differ markedly from one society to another.

---

18 In Barnes's own ethnographic region, the Lamaholot-speaking area, the data concerning bride capture are rather scarce, but taking into account reports about this institution in the past, he comes to the conclusion that in this area bride capture occurs among people who are rather well acquainted with one another and does not stand in contrast to the rules of formal marriage (Barnes 1999, 68).

4.2 Categories of Dongria Kond marriage

The Dongria language offers several expressions to describe the processes by which a marriage relation can be established. The English question "Are you married?" is equivalent to the sentence *ninu hedi tatigi?*, which literally means "Did you bring that woman there?" The Kuwi language spoken by the Kond of south Odisha contains four spatial markers (*i-, e-, u-, he-*) that help to define the degree of remoteness of a being or a thing in relation to the speaker (Israel 1979, 82–83). A woman is referred to as *idi* if she is positioned in close proximity to the speaker and as *edi* if she is farther away, as *udi* if she is distant from him and as *hedi* if she resides in a place far away.[19] Dongria is a dialect quite similar to the Kuwi described by Israel (1979), and the demonstrative pronouns are formed in almost the same way. A Dongria refers to a woman at increasing degrees of remoteness as *idi, edi, dedi,* or *sedi,* the last being equivalent to the word *hedi* used by Kond in the valleys and plains. According to Israel, in the Kuwi spoken by the Kond of Koraput district, *hedi* means "she/it, that woman/thing (far)" (Israel 1979, 424), '*he-*' being a sound marking the highest degree of remoteness. The consonants 'h' and 's' sometimes replace each other in different dialects[20] without an obvious change in meaning. For example, the Sikoka clan of the Dongria is called Hikoka by the Desia Kond, *hiko* being the word for "little millet" used by Desia and Dongria Kond alike. While Desia Kond explain their clan name with reference to "little millet," Dongria of the Sikoka clan do not, because due to the change in the first consonant, the former connection to the original noun (*hiko*) has become lost. I think the same happened with *hedi* and *sedi*. While to a Desia Kond the word *hedi* refers to a bride and a woman from beyond, Dongria distinguish between *hedi* and *sedi*. While *sedi* is used to refer to any woman residing in a different village or in a place beyond the mountains of one's own village, *hedi* is restricted to contexts of affinity. It is often used in the compound form of *hedi maga, maga* meaning "daughter" but also "girl," as in the expression *pusi maga* ("girl of the Pusika clan").[21] When asked to translate *hedi* into Oriya, Dongria may mention the word *kanya*, a word used by Oriya

---

[19] Kui, spoken by the Kond in North Odisha, is considered to be different from the Kuwi language spoken by the Kond in South Odisha. However, the Kui language has similar markers of closeness and remoteness: *i-, e-, a-, o-* (Winfield 1928, 43).

[20] Village names, for example, are often pronounced in both ways. Thus, the Dongria village Sutangoni is referred to by many people as Hutangoni. My adopted clan name, Himberika, was pronounced Simberika by the Dongria Kond from Kalahandi.

[21] People of the Pusika clan nowadays often adopt the clan title Huika, the name of a brother clan from the valleys, because *pusi* in Oriya denotes male and female sexual fluids.

speakers to denote a bride. Taking into account the similarity between *hedi* and *sedi*, we may translate *hedi maga* as "girl who stands in an affinal relationship to the speaker and comes from a remote place."²² This means that the Dongria word for "bride" already implies a certain territorial distance between her and her in-laws, which, as I will argue later, corresponds to a social distance between the parties.

A *hedi maga* is always a woman who has been demanded (*wenga wateru*, "they have come to demand her") by the groom's kinsmen in a particular way described later. This engagement often takes place when both are still children. Starting from this event, which is marked by tying a ring made of a creeper around the girl's finger, they are considered "husband" (*dakera*) and "wife" (*dakeri*), and their parents call each other *samdhin* ("bound together"). From this time onwards, the bride-takers are expected to give a series of gifts (*mahala*) to the bride-givers, not only to the family and their immediate kin but to the whole village. If, after exchanging the necessary gifts, both sides fully consent, the affines agree upon a timetable for the wedding ceremony. Until that time, the boy and the girl should avoid each other and behave like brother and sister, i.e., the boy may not dance and joke with her, and he should sleep neither with her nor with any of her friends (*ade*). When the day for the wedding has been fixed, the groom's friends, kinsmen, and fellow villagers can "bring the bride" (*hedi tanari*). The verb stem '*ta-*' means "to bring" in the sense of going somewhere, acquiring something, and bringing it back. In the context of marriage, it implies the readiness of the bride's parents to let her daughter go, something which is often achieved only through years of service by the groom in the bride's village and/or through very large sums of money paid by the groom's parents. Because the full ceremony of such a marriage by consent is mostly carried out by rich and important men of the village, I refer to it as "big-man marriage".

Not everybody's marriage is arranged in this way in childhood, and even if it is, this does not prevent the boys and girls from visiting the dormitories once they have reached maturity. In these "youth hostels," many young people begin love affairs, and some may decide to turn this casual affair into a permanent relationship. This can not be achieved in the way described above, however, which is reserved for arranged marriages. Instead, the boy, his friends, and his fellow villagers have to "capture" the girl in order to solemnise the relationship. The expressions used to describe this action are *ahpa tana*, *ahpa rena*, and *ahpa*

---

22 According to Winfield (1929, 107), the Kui word *seri* means "girl to be betrothed, bride," while the expression *seri tapa*, which according to Friend-Pereira (1902, 23) is the local word for marriage, can be translated as "to bring the bride" (Winfield 1929, 108). In contrast to the Kuvi word *hedi*, the Kui word for bride, *seri*, is pronounced with a retroflex.

beta hana. The word *ahpa* is made up of the verb stem '*ah-*' meaning "to catch," "to fetch" and a suffix '*-pa*' used to denote an active action like "to go and catch." The verb implies the idea of catching something with one's hand, for example in the expression *nanu minka ahpi mai*, "I am catching fish (with my hands)." *Ahpa* is combined with other verbs such as *tana*, "we bring," or *rena*, "we pull." The difference between the two latter expressions is related to the range of possible reactions by the bride, because she may either be informed, agree to be captured, and show no resistance, or be taken by surprise and forcefully resist all attempts to take her away. In the latter case, the men "pull" her in the literal sense of the word along the way from the girl's to the boy's village. The third expression, *ahpa beta hana*, can be translated as "we go and catch in a hunt." *Beta* is derived from the Oriya word for "hunt," *bentha*, which is used to describe the process of gathering something, for example fruit, or chasing an animal. In the context of marriage, the word *beta* means either "chasing" girls in the youth dormitories or "capturing" them.

These two forms of acquiring a wife do not exclude one another, because very often capturing a girl is part of the on-going negotiations between sets of parents who have arranged their children's marriage. If a bride (*hedi maga*) is captured in this way, the women of her village come and demand her return, while the groom's people use the opportunity to bargain with their affines about the outstanding payments. If they do not let her go, the girl may take the next opportunity to run home. Afterwards, the negotiations and gift exchanges are resumed by both parties and may finally end in an agreement for a grand wedding ceremony. Such a wedding between a man and a woman from different villages, united in an atmosphere of mutual consent, is considered to be of high status. A woman married in this way is referred to as *mahala dakeri*. The word *mahala* (in Oriya often *mala*) refers to the whole process of demanding a bride, including all services and gifts given to the girl's side. *Dakeri* is an expression to denote somebody's "wife."

If a man succeeds in capturing a girl his family members had asked for long ago, and she agrees to live with him, he may still have to face high demands from his in-laws. In most cases, the bride-takers sooner or later comply with some of these demands under pressure from her kinsmen and their own fellow villagers. The latter show their solidarity but at the same time press for a compromise, since they are interested in keeping good relations with the bride-giving village in view of future marriages. Since the girl has agreed to live in her husband's family's house, however, they do not have to bring her in a grand way with the full ritual procedures. Such a wedding does not fall into the category of *hedi tana* or arranged wedding, because it lacks the consent between two villages to which Dongria attach high status. Although such a union is established by "hunt" (*ahpa tana*) and therefore less prestigious, the girl is nevertheless referred to as a *mahala dakeri* because of the gifts and payments made by the groom.

A woman acquired in this way has a higher status than a woman for whom the husband has neither worked in his parents-in-law's village nor provided gifts to the girl's village and kinsmen. If a man has more than one wife, the woman referred to as *mahala dakeri* is always called his "senior wife" (*kaja dakeri*), even if she joined the household last. In contrast, a woman who has been acquired as part of a love affair is always considered his junior wife (*icha dakeri*). Depending on how the relationship was established, she is referred to as either *dapada:a*, *datari*, *snapa dakeri*, or *loku dakeri*. The first two words are derived from the verb stem '*da-*', to sleep with, and have the same meaning. Once a couple begin a love affair, others may say that the girl is the boy's *datari* and that the young man is her *datayu*. Both expressions refer to the person with whom one has sex. If the boy decides to capture the girl, and she lives with him, she is referred to by others as his *dapada:a* or "the woman he slept with." The expression *snapa dakeri* refers to the way the boy brings such a girl to his village. *Snapa* has been translated to me in Oriya as *dhari kari aniba*, which basically has the same meaning as *ahpa tana*, "to catch and bring." A second way of acquiring a beloved is captured in the expression *dugi haceru*, meaning "they have gone into hiding." This refers to cases in which a boy and a girl are in love with each other, but their parents do not agree to their marriage. Often they can live neither in his nor in her village and consequently decide to "elope" by night, hiding in a distant village where they have kinsmen or even in the woods. This often happens when the girl is promised to somebody else and does not agree with the decision of her parents.

This leads to the last of the mentioned terms for a woman who is not acquired by mutual agreement, *loku dakeri*. This expression can be translated as "other people's wife" and refers to a woman who has been promised to somebody else and for whom *mahala* has been given, but who wants to live with another man whom she met in a dormitory. This category also includes women who are already living in their husband's village or who have lived there but returned to their natal home after some kind of disagreement. They may also be widows with or without children, in which case their new husband has to make additional prestations to their deceased former husband's village. One of these women may either be captured – usually with her full consent – or go into hiding with her lover, but because she is already engaged or even married, her fiancé's or husband's kinsmen demand fines (*tapu*) from her new husband. She is called *loku mahala kiti dakeri*, meaning "a woman for whom other people have given gifts," and her lover's kinsmen have to begin a complicated settlement involving three parties, the villages (1) of the bride, (2) of her former fiancé or husband, and (3) of her new groom. This may involve considerable sums of money, which are equal to or even higher than the amounts paid in a *mahala* marriage.

If we compare these forms of acquiring a woman without betrothal, the relationship with a *loku dakeri* carries the highest status, because it is often turned into a regular betrothal by gifts to the girl's parents. However, it cannot be celebrated in the same way as a "big-man marriage", and it always carries the dishonour of taking somebody's else woman, which is likened to eating his leftovers. The lowest form of a permanent relation is established by taking a girl without paying any substantial gifts, either for an engagement (*mahala*) or as a fine (*tapu*). In such cases, people say a woman "has gone for nothing" (*bahen hace* or *cuca hace*). This may happen, for example, when a girl for whom nobody has given any gifts becomes pregnant, and the parents are glad if somebody takes her into his house as his wife.

In my analysis, only the expression *hedi tana* refers to marriage as a "contract". The relationship to a woman who had been engaged earlier may come close to this ideal, because the fines paid establish relations between villages that are taken into account in future marriages. But the union is not as pure as the *hedi* type, because the girl is considered to be a "leftover" (*gandi*), and the relationship began out of love and mutual affection. It is, thus, halfway between the pure alliance and the simple love affair between two individuals without any major gift exchanges between affines. Overall, the *hedi* form of marriage is considered to be of highest status because it is ideally a pure "contract", i.e., irrespective of love, sexuality, and aggression. The longer such a marriage has been planned, the more gifts have been given, and the better the understanding between the exchange partners is, the higher the status of such a "contract".

Table 14: Status and category of married women

Status	Category	Gifts	Action
1) high status	*mahala dakeri, hedi maga* ("arranged wife," "girl from far away")	money, gifts, and services (*mahala*)	*hedi tana* ("bringing a woman from far away"): full wedding ceremony
2) middle status	*snapa dakeri, loku dakeri* ("captured wife," "other people's wife")	fines (*tapu*)	*ahpa tana, ahpa rena, ahpa beta hana* ("to catch / hunt and bring / pull"): capturing the woman
3) low status	*datari, dapada:a* ("woman one sleeps with")	no gifts (*cuca / bahen*)	*hana* ("to go"): woman moves into man's house, no rituals

Statistically, the arranged marriage appears to be an important type of marriage. I found it difficult to get exact data on the different types of marriage, particularly those outside my own village. Among my neighbours in Gumma, nineteen of thirty householders had been involved in an arranged marriage (*mahala dakeri*), although it was often not arranged in their childhood and not always accompanied by a wedding of the most elaborate and expensive kind. It is very difficult to get accurate information on this, because people provide very different accounts and often seem either to exaggerate amounts or simply to reiterate standard payments. However, a marriage only falls into the category of *mahala* when money or one or more years of "in-law-service" (see below, section 4.3.1) have been delivered, and this was the case in all nineteen of these marriages by householders in Gumma. Eleven out of thirty householders were not married to a *mahala dakeri* but to a woman of one of the other categories. Four men had brought their lover (*datari*) from the dormitory. Three men had captured a girl (*loku dakeri*) who had been promised to another man. They had paid fines to the girl's village as well as that of her former husband. Three men had taken their deceased brothers' wives (*awa dakeri*); the woman had been formally acquired as a *mahala dakeri* from a different village in two cases, and I have no data about the original type of marriage in the third case. The last man in this sample had originally been part of an arranged marriage, but when his wife ran away with another man, he was given her sister instead. Adding these last three cases to the type of arranged marriage, all in all twenty-two out of thirty unions were established in this way.

Table 15: Types of marriages of householders in Gumma

mahala dakeri	datari	loku dakeri	awa dakeri	other	total
19	4	3	3 (2 *mahala dakeri*)	1 (originally *mahala dakeri*)	30

The situation is more complex if we take into account the fact that a Dongria can keep more than one woman in his house. In the past, some Dongria of Gumma are reported to have had three or four wives, whereas nowadays such large households are unusual. In Gumma, only five householders were married to two women. All of them were married to their *mahala dakeri* and had taken one more wife. In two of these cases, the woman was the deceased elder brother's wife (*awa dakeri*), while two had brought their *datari* to their house. The fifth man had captured a young woman whom he had made pregnant and for whom he had to pay a substantial fine. His first wife (*mahala dakeri*) – upon being unable to bear him a child – had run home to her parents' village. Two young men of the village had first captured their beloveds from the dormitory and later, upon having sufficient funds, brought the women their respective parents had arranged for them in their childhood. One man had not yet managed to induce his *mahala dakeri* to come to his village, though he lived with his lover and his first son in a new house. He is included in the first column (*mahala dakeri + datari*) of the table below.

Table 16: Types of marriages in polygamous households in Gumma

mahala dakeri + datari	mahala + awa dakeri	mahala dakeri + loku dakeri	total
3	2	1	5

In McDougal's more extensive survey of marriage types among the Juang, the author arrives at the conclusion that the majority of primary marriages fall into the category of marriage by capture (55%), while only 27% are formally arranged and 12% informally arranged, plus 4% child marriages (McDougal 1963a, 240).

In the following sections of this chapter, I describe in more detail and compare the three main forms of establishing a marriage relation among the Dongria. After summarizing previous studies of the Kond marriage system, I first describe the formal procedures and interests involved in an arranged marriage. Next, I analyse the different types of abduction and the motives involved in bride capture. Finally, I show how Dongria collectively find a solution to the conflicts arising from the intrusion of individual passions into the contracts between local groups.

4.3 Collective contracts: Arranged marriages

Arranging a marriage among the Dongria is a long process full of difficulties, uncertainties, hurdles, and trials for both sides involved in forging the matrimonial "contract". Not surprisingly, the process as such is not highly formalised but tends to take a different shape in each individual case. However, despite these variations, it follows a certain logic. When talking hypothetically about events leading to a marriage "contract", people do have an ideal sequence in mind. The summary below tries to capture this model on the basis of what Dongria have told me and what they have actually done, either according to their memories or during the time of my fieldwork. As such, the model conveys a message, the encapsulated social values of which I attempt to identify. However, if we use our ethnographic experience only to construct such an ideal model, we deprive ourselves of a highly valuable source for understanding the whole range of ideas and values involved in people's practical management of social relations. Not only the model but also the practice is culturally specific and cannot be reduced to a universal set of individual "interests" (see Bourdieu 1977). When talking about deviations from the model, I am not much concerned with variations in the sequence of events or with differences in the amount of the "betrothal fee" due to disparities in wealth. I intend rather to focus on the contradictions built into the ideal model that lead to certain culturally specific reactions and rearrangements of the matrimonial process. To mention but the most important cultural factors responsible for the uncertain outcome of forging a marriage "contract", we may remember that:

- the families arranging the marriage and having to develop a relation of mutual trust in due course are relative strangers to each other; they have to turn open hostility by the bride-giving side into mutual affection and reciprocity; for a very long time, the bride-takers have to bear humiliation by their future in-laws and constantly provide the latter with gifts and services on top of that, before finally receiving the desired bride in return;
- in the event of feuds, the family's responsibilities towards the new affinal partner will always be curtailed by loyalties to their own village or clan community; therefore, despite the best intentions of the concerned families, hostilities emerging between different collectives on a higher level often endanger the matrimonial arrangements; at the same time, the marriage itself may become the cause of a conflict quickly leading to animosity between groups on a higher level of social organisation;
- bride-givers can make excessive demands while, at the same time, withholding their daughter as long as they wish, whereas bride-takers have a very powerful cultural tool, abduction, to force their prospective affines to hand over their daughter; as any successful marriage depends on the cooperation of both parties, in the end neither detaining the bride nor abducting her achieves the desired result;
- the individuals joined in marriage should be kept apart as long as possible; they are objects of an exchange irrespective of their personal desires and interests; at the same time, society provides the dormitory, institutionalising and promoting social relations between young people of both sexes;
- in an arranged marriage, the elders of the family or the village council make the final decisions without the consent of the individuals thus joined in marriage; on the other hand, boys are expected to be good "hunters," and every man should have captured a woman for himself at least once.

These are the most important cultural ideas and built-in contradictions responsible for the uncertain outcome of the matrimonial process. It is important to note that these are not circumstantial variations based on demographic, economic, or local factors but contradictions built into society. As will become apparent in several case studies, Dongria have highly sophisticated cultural mechanisms for coping with these contradictions and the conflicts arising out of them. The most elaborate and fascinating form is the system of fines designed to resolve disputes due to the contradiction between "contract" and "abduction", between collective structure and individual passion. Before dealing with these issues, I will offer an account of what Dongria consider to be the ideal process of forging a matrimonial "contract" between strangers, the most highly valued form of marriage.

From childhood until the day the bride finally moves into her husband's village approximately twenty years may pass. Ideally, during this time, the following events occur:

1. *samudi sehena* ("we discuss with exchange partners")
   - during a boy's childhood, his parents – in consultation with their fellow villagers – decide to approach another family in a distant village to demand a girl as bride;
   - first, a delegation of women from the boy's village visits the girl's house;
   - later, a delegation of men from the boy's village visits the girl's house;
   - several more meetings between both parties take place in the girl's village in an atmosphere developing from hostility (*hijeda*) towards mutual acceptance (*rasa*);
   - a delegation of men from the boy's village brings gifts (buffalo, alcohol, paddy) to the girl's parents; these may be refused once or several times until finally being accepted, at which point the boy's father is permitted to tie a ring around the girl's finger; boy and girl are now considered to be husband (*dakera*) and wife (*dakeri*);

2. *karjame* (serving son-in-law)[23]

---

[23] This word is probably derived from Oriya *ghara juain*, meaning a son-in-law (*juain*) living in the house (*ghara*) of his father-in-law. However, among Oriya Hindus a *ghara juain* is somebody who permanently lives in his father-in-law's house *after* marriage, often because he comes from a poor family. His existence as a *ghara juain* in some ways contradicts the hypergamous status order of the Hindu marriage system. Other people often look down on him, comparing him to a "dog" (*kukura*) in his affines' family. Among the Dongria, a son-in-law's service is part of the "betrothal fee" to the higher-status bride-givers *before* marriage. It may indeed turn into a permanent arrangement if the son-in-law decides to set up house in his father-in-law's village after

- in the following years, the boy's relatives visit the girl's parents on different occasions, such as house rituals, village festivals, birth, sickness, or death, and present gifts to them;
- at the age of about seventeen or eighteen, the boy is brought in a procession to his in-laws, in the company of his friends;
- upon his arrival, he has to undergo several trials and bear humiliation by the bride-giving people;
- with interruptions, the boy remains in the girl's village for the next two to three years in order to work in his father-in-law's fields;
- during the first year, bride and bridegroom avoid each other, gradually loosening the ban thereafter;

3. *mahala takang* ("betrothal fee")
   - when the girl is about twenty years old, the boy's family sends a delegation to her parents to negotiate the "betrothal-fee"; taking into account the number of years served by the boy, her people demand a certain amount of money;
   - the boy's delegation comes for a second time to hand over some of the money demanded by the girl's side; normally, the bride-takers give at least that share of the "betrothal fee" that belongs to the bride's fellow villagers, who spend the money on a collective feast;
   - these meetings are repeated several times; each time the bride-takers hand over part of the "betrothal fee" while simultaneously negotiating about the outstanding sum;
   - when the full "betrothal fee" has been paid, both sides agree to perform the wedding ceremony in the hot season of the following year;

4. *ijo henga hana* ("we go to see the house" [of the groom])
   - during the hot season (March-May) the boy's family sends a delegation to the girl's house to invite them and some young men of their village to attend a feast in the boy's village; a day is fixed for the feast;
   - the boy's family buys a buffalo and rice; the delegation, consisting of young men and some older men and women of the girl's village, arrives on a Thursday evening in one of the subsequent weeks; the young men are entertained by the dormitory girls;

---

marriage, but in this case, he is not treated with the same mixture of contempt and ridicule as the *ghara juain*.

- next morning the men slaughter a buffalo, half of which they cook immediately, while the other half is given to their guests at the time of departure; the girls and women cook rice;
- the men of both villages entertain each other with alcohol before the guests are called into the groom's father's house, where they receive as much meat and rice as they can eat;
- in the evening, the groom's villagers bid farewell to the bride's people;

5. *tone paga tinja hana* ("we go to eat the rice of friendship")
    - for the next two weeks, the bride is invited by her "relatives and friends" (*gota are geti*) to eat rice and bid farewell;
    - on the first day, she is bathed in turmeric water by her female friends (*ade*) in her own village before she visits her mother's brother' house; together with her friends she is served rice (*tone paga*) and anointed with oil and turmeric by the mother's brother's wife;
    - the same procedure is repeated in all the houses she visits for the next two weeks; she receives gifts including several *sari* and jewellery;

6. *hedi tana* ("we bring the girl from far away")
    - a delegation from the boy's village visits the girl's parents to fix a day for bringing the bride officially in procession to the groom's village;
    - this "wedding ceremony" lasts for three days and always takes place from Friday to Sunday;
    - *sukruwara* (Friday): ritual preparations begin in both villages; towards evening the bride-taking side's fellow villagers as well as young people from all over the region arrive in the girl's village; the bride is bathed, decorated, and led to each house in her village to hold a final farewell ceremony; throughout the whole night the young people sing, dance, and sleep with each other;
    - *saniwara* (Saturday): following a feast for the guests in the morning, the ritual elders begin to perform a ceremony at a river, while the young people resume singing and dancing; after midday the ceremony at the river comes to an end with a sacrifice of a hen and a pig as the bride and her best friend stand in the water weeping and lamenting; the bride-givers feast on the pig, and a second meal is served to the guests in the evening; the young people entertain themselves in the same way as the

night before; a basket of rice representing the bride's life (*jiu manjing*) is carried by the bride-takers to their village[24];
- *adiwara* (Sunday): early in the morning, the girl's fellow villagers take the bride in procession to the groom's village; her friends carry boxes with cloth, big brass pots, and other household items, all of which pre-stations are collectively referred to as "rice-water" (*lahi jau*); at a river near the boy's village, the bride's and groom's delegations meet; the shamans perform a sacrifice at a small canopy, join the husband's and wife's hands, and together circumambulate the temporary shrine; afterwards, all proceed towards the groom's village, and different rituals are performed before the bride crosses the boundary of the clan territory, of the village, and of the house; the guests receive two meals, one in the morning, one in the evening, and several games and playful trials are performed to find out the newlywed couple's destiny; the bride-givers hand over a buffalo and take a buffalo given by their affines when they go home in the evening;

7. *giri takoli* ("to bring the path") and *wenda kodang* ("the old feet")
    - on Monday, the groom's parents ask their shaman to bring the goddess *lahi penu* back into the house in a ritual called *giri takoli* or "to bring the path"; she is considered to have left the house during the marriage festivities because of the waste of money and food on this occasion; the bride's people conduct the same ritual on the day the bride returns home to visit her parents;
    - normally on the subsequent Wednesday, the wife, accompanied by her husband, returns for the first time to her native village; they are served food and sent home with a pig or a small goat and some rice; this is the first of a series of gifts that from now on continue to be given every time the wife pays a visit to her own kin; when she returns to her new home, the gifts are handed over to the villagers, who slaughter and cook the pig or goat.

---

24 Peter Berger (2015, 469–72) has studied in detail the affinal connotations of rice among the Gadaba of southern Koraput/Odisha.

4.3.1 Prestations: An overview

Before presenting the different phases of the marriage process in more detail, I will briefly discuss the issue of prestations exchanged between the parties involved in an arranged marriage. Literature on the topic of marriage abounds with technical terms such as "brideprice", "bridewealth", "brideservice", and "dowry", the appropriate use and definition of which has been extensively discussed.[25] These terms are useful in comparative studies such as those by Goody (1973), who examined bridewealth and dowry in Africa and Eurasia, and Tambiah (1973a, 1989), who analysed marriage payments and gifts in South Asia and later compared the position of women in South Asia to that of women in sub-Saharan Africa. Such comparisons can help us understand each particular society better, particularly if the comparison concentrates on the whole system of payments, gifts, services, and rights involved in the forging of marriage relations. On the other hand, I am very sceptical about the use of these anthropological concepts as labels for whole societies, saying that group X has a "brideprice system" and group Y a "dowry system," for example, because normally the system of marriage prestations is more complex. It is necessary to carefully evaluate the degree of symmetry or asymmetry in the giving and receiving of prestations and services in order to make a statement about the dominant mode of exchange in the marriage system of a particular society.

In the case of a single ethnographic study such as this one, I think it advisable to avoid these *termini technici* and instead use approximate translations of local expressions in order to convey the local people's point of view. Among the Dongria, I recorded various types of exchanges within the context of arranged marriages, some of which have been mentioned in the list of ideal typical events above. Instead of "brideprice" or "bridewealth" I will use the term "betrothal fee" for the main monetary transaction given by the groom's people to the bride's side. This is a quite literal translation of the Dongria term *mahala takang*, but it must be kept in mind that *mahala* or "betrothal" is a long process among the Dongria and not a single event as in many other societies. The groom's years of work in the bride-givers' fields can be termed "bride service", but the local term *karjame* does not include any reference to the bride, but rather stresses the relation between the bride's father and his "son-in-law" (*jame*) who is doing "work" (*karma*) for him. For this reason I will only talk about "in-law service" and not "bride-service".

---

[25] For summaries of these debates, see Comaroff 1980, Barnard and Good 1984, and Tambiah 1989.

On the day of the wedding, the bride's people send their daughter to her husband's village along with many valuable gifts, and these prestations may be called "dowry". The word used by Dongria is *lahi jau*, which literally means "cooked rice and vegetable broth" and implies that the bride comes to cook and feed her in-laws. The food itself is a representation of the goddess of wealth, just as the bride can be seen as the most valuable gift in the whole marriage process. Instead of "dowry", it would thus be most appropriate to call this gift "bridewealth", but since this word has a completely opposite meaning in the literature, I will instead use the expression "wedding gift".

If we want to judge the symmetry or asymmetry involved in marriage transactions, the relative value of each single transaction must be kept in mind. The table below schematically represents the different transactions, which will be described in this chapter. The thickness of the arrows in the table indicates the relative value of the things exchanged. Of the ten types of transactions noted here, six are made by the groom's to the bride's side, one the other way round, and three are mutual exchanges. The character of the transactions changes over the years: at first, all prestations are from the bride-takers, thus asymmetrical in nature; with the wedding in sight, the exchange becomes symmetrical; and finally on the main wedding day, a purely asymmetrical transaction from the bride-givers to the bride-takers occurs. It seems that the groom's people give more than they receive; however, when we compare the "betrothal fee" and the "wedding gift" ("bridewealth" and "dowry"), we will see that their relative value also depends on the mode of transaction. The "betrothal fee" is an object of negotiations in which the bride's people demand and the groom's people attempt to arrive at an agreement that is not too costly and yet allows them to make a public display of their status. From the bride-takers' perspective, the "fee" and the groom's work for his father-in-law serve three functions: first, the services and payments are meant to convince the bride's people of the bride-takers' seriousness and eagerness to marry their daughter; second, once the money has been handed over, the groom's people can be quite sure that the bride-givers will not arrange a marriage with a third group, although they have no guarantee that the girl will not be captured by somebody else; third, the amount of money given is a sign of the bride-takers' status. In this sense, the groom's people do not "buy" the bride by these payments but rather try to solicit a major return gift, the bride. The bride-givers, on the other hand, demand these payments but do not "sell" their daughter. The money is divided among many relatives, and each of them is expected to give a gift to the bride that is sent along with her to the groom's people. "Betrothal fee" and "wedding gift" are intimately linked, with a kind of balance between the sum received as a share of the "betrothal fee" and the value of the "wedding gift" given.

In turn, the total value of everything sent along with the bride to her new husband expresses the status of the bride-givers. Yet there is a difference between the "betrothal fee" and the "wedding gift", because the latter is not the object of any direct demands. Although everybody expects the bride's people to give according to the payments received, the only direct pressures on the gift-givers are status considerations and the social sanctions connected with acts of reciprocity. At least officially, the "wedding gift" is a "free prestation" and symbolises the fertility of the local line. The highest gift of all is the bride herself, since she will bring fertility to the groom's people, whose children she will bear and in whose fields she will work. Taking into account the whole system, we are forced to conclude that the higher status of the bride-givers rests on the fact that they give something more valuable than they receive. This asymmetry of status exists right from the beginning, when the groom's people are humiliated on the occasion of demanding somebody's daughter as a bride.

4.3.2 *samudi sehena* ("we discuss with in-laws")

When men are sitting under a *salap* tree waiting for its owner to make an incision and bring down the alcoholic sap, discussions often turn to marriage politics. One man may ask the others about a prospective bride for his son. Then someone may suggest the daughter of a man who is the neighbour of his own son's father-in-law. Yet another may recommend the daughter of his wife's elder brother. Very often, an existing link is sought, usually through a previous marriage of somebody not too closely related, such as a neighbour or a friend. Once a suggestion is made, others check whether the girl stands in any relationship to the boy that would prevent a marriage and discuss the financial background of the girl's family. In most cases I know of, relatively poor Dongria did not approach a very well-off family or vice versa but chose an exchange partner of almost equal standing. The elaborate form of marriage described below is normally preferred by those who own more land, raise more profitable crops, bring in larger harvests, and have more valuable assets than the average tribesman, and these relatively rich people normally approach a family with an equally strong economic background.

The quality and amount of land owned by a family is the strongest indicator of its economic status. As described in the previous chapter (section 3.4.3.1), a village's land has normally been bought at some point in the past by members of one or more local lines, who divided the different hill slopes among themselves. The boundaries are clearly demarcated, and in each generation the original portion of land owned by the local lines has to be segmented or pooled, de-

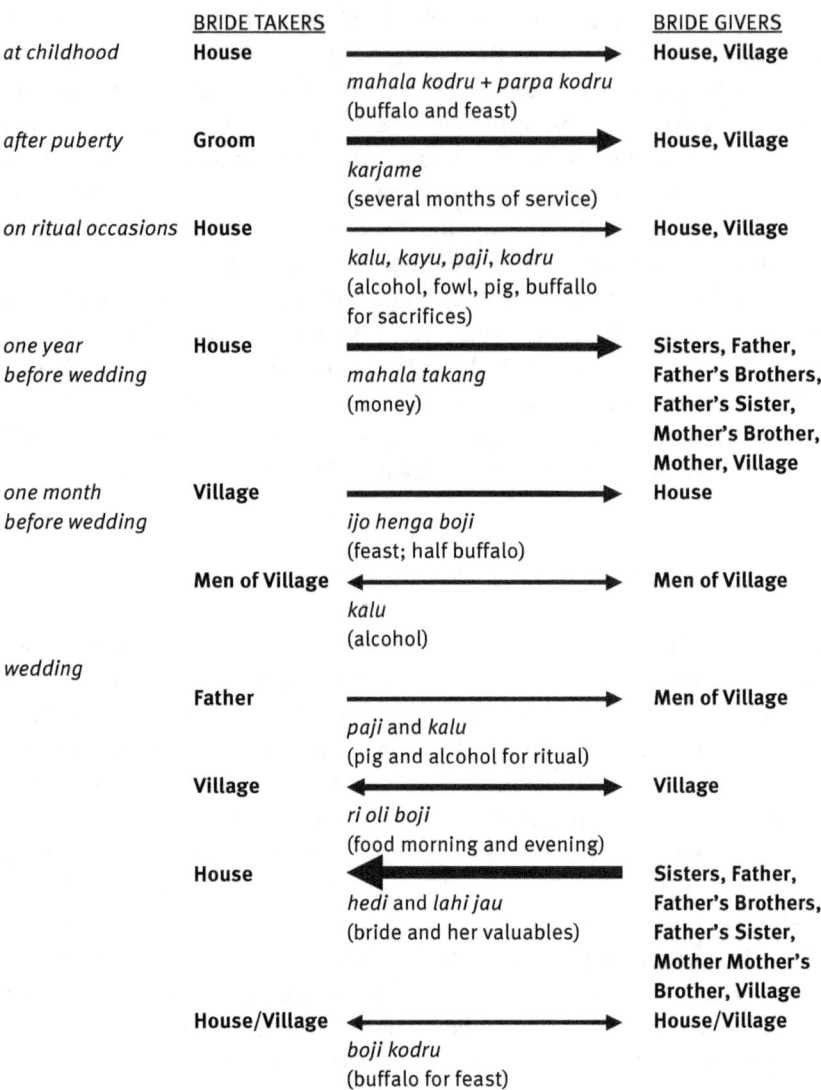

Figure 24: Occasions, objects, givers, and receivers in Dongria marriage transactions

pending on the number of sons. Further segments may be reserved for relatives, such as son-in-laws or sisters' sons, with whom one has a responsibility to share. Therefore, every villager has a hill slope to cultivate, but they differ from each other in several ways. First, some own several hill slopes, while others own nothing but depend on the generosity of others. Second, depending on the number of wives and sons, some Dongria families are able to cultivate two or three hill slopes at a time, while other, much smaller families must be content with managing a single field. Third, the quality of the land differs, some portions being forested, steep, and rocky, others having gentle slopes, good soil, and sunshine throughout the day. As might be expected, poor relatives are often given the first type of land, while the original owners reserve the better parts for themselves. Fourth, fields differ immensely in their value. Poor families with low-quality land usually cultivate only very basic crops, such as millet, pulses, and castor beans, while the rich Dongria, who own the most fertile parts of the hills, have orange groves, turmeric fields, and banana plantations to add to their income. Finally, a few families are in the possession of so-called *pota* or "certificates" guaranteeing their ownership of either wet-rice land or dry fields. These fields can be cultivated by their owners, leased to somebody else, or even mortgaged. These are some of the most important factors creating economic differences among the Dongria.

Arranged marriages of the type described below occur between so-called *kaja loku* or "big men" with high economic and socio-political status. As mentioned above, markers of high economic status are the amount, type, and quality of land and crops and the number of cows and goats owned by the family. These "big men" often, but not always, are descendants of the village's original landowners and carry titles such as *jani* or *bismajhi*. Nowadays, the most important political functions are performed by the *member* of the village, who is usually a charismatic person with a strong economic background. The title *member* derives from the political office of "ward member" or elected representative of a cluster of houses, the lowest level of political administration. Among the Dongria, the title may be used by any person who has been appointed for some purpose by a government institution. For example, there were three *member*[26] in the village in which I stayed. One was appointed by the Dongria Kond Development Agency (DKDA), the second by the District Primary Education Programme (DPEP), and the third by the electoral commission. Among these three, only the *member* appointed by the DKDA was a rich man who had arranged a marriage for his son during childhood, while the others were less well-off, and nobody expected them to marry their children in the most elaborate and expensive way. During the time of my stay, two families from Gumma managed to marry their daughters as *hedi* with the full ceremony, and both belonged to the families of original landhold-

---

26 When written in italics, the word *member* denotes a status position in the Dongria social system and should not be confused with the English word "member." The Dongria word *member* will be used without the plural -*s*.

ers. All this suggests that the high-status form of marriage facilitates "contracts" between "noble" families whose householders have the status of "big men" because they belong to the clan and local line of the original inhabitants. These families are generally richer than others and are ascribed a higher status expressed by their titles and offices. This "nobility" among the Dongria can often be recognised on entry into Kond villages or houses. The original landowners often keep a "big stone" (*kaja wali*) in front of their houses, on which they sit in the morning or evening hours relaxing or discussing village matters. Another, even more important status marker for a "big man" is a wooden post erected either at the entrance door or in the inner part of the house. These posts are put up during the performance of the *ghanta parba*, a very expensive ritual for the particular deity of the house. A rich and influential man sacrifices a great number of goats and chickens and performs the ritual as often as possible. His ability to do so can be judged by the number and condition of the sacrificial posts inside and outside his home.

When a suitable bride-giving family has been selected, the boy's parents decide to send a delegation to them. Such a delegation is normally "disguised" as a dancing party, which consists of a few unmarried girls accompanied by the prospective groom's mother or some other older women of his village. When arriving in the girl's village in the evening, they head towards the house of a relative or somebody they know from previous visits. If unfamiliar with the place, they ask the acquaintance to show the way to the girl's house. Approaching it from the rear, they squat on the back veranda and take up a posture typical of bride-demanding people: they rest their heads on their right hands and keep their right elbows on their right knees.[27] This signifies inferiority and refusal to be treated as guests. Their proposal is only considered legitimate if they do not eat any food in the girl's house. Once I overheard a discussion about a man who had come to our village to ask for a bride for his son. As a relative of the bride's mother, he was served rice and meat, but he rejected the food, saying that he had come to demand the girl. From his perspective, this refusal provided sufficient ground for him to claim later that he had officially asked for the girl, while some of her relatives disputed his rights, as he had never turned up again nor given anything to the bride's people. What this example shows is that both

---

27 Once I took up this posture unintentionally when sitting with some Dongria men under a *salap* tree. Immediately, some of them scolded me, saying I was committing a "mistake" (*dosa*), since only *gota loku*, who come to demand a bride, squat on the ground in this way. To understand why they criticised me it must be remembered that this posture signifies inferiority and a refusal to be treated as a guest. It was, therefore, quite inappropriate in the context of drinking, when equality is the norm and everybody is expected to receive a share.

sides play a role: the bride-demanding people agree to be humiliated, and the bride-giving people are prepared to debase the others in all conceivable ways. The refusal to give any food to guests is one of the worst forms of social misconduct among the Dongria, but in this case it is only the first in a series of humiliations the boy's relatives and the groom himself have to suffer.

The older women in the boy's delegation announce the purpose of their visit by saying *mudi harca manambu* ("we want to bind a ring"). The girl's family members listen and then either ignore them after saying *minge mange gota hile* ("there will be no relationship between us") or talk to them in an insulting manner. Abusive language is highly developed among the Dongria, and the visitors have to bear all kinds of derogatory remarks. If they are unknown to the girl's family, they send some relatives to inquire about them among their neighbours. While the older women keep sitting behind their potential affines' house throughout the night, the girls are normally invited by the young men of the village to join them in the dormitory or in the back room of a house, where they chat and perhaps even sing and dance. Next morning, the boy's delegation returns home. The girl's parents and their fellow villagers take the next opportunity to discuss the proposal and to inquire about the boy and his family. Usually, some weeks or even months pass before the boy's parents send another delegation, this time consisting of some older men, who are sometimes accompanied by their *barika*. Like the women, they arrive in the girl's village in the evening, but unlike the first delegation, they do not go to the back but to the front of the house. They repeat their intention to take the daughter of the house as a bride for their son, and like the first delegation, they have to bear the inhospitable and even hostile behaviour of their potential affines. For example, the woman of the house may start cleaning the veranda on which the visitors are sitting. She begins sweeping the floor as if the visitors were absent. In no time they are covered with dust and symbolically brushed out of the house unless they move away voluntarily.

The accusations made against the outsiders may now be more serious than during the first visit. I have witnessed meetings where the visitors had to defend themselves throughout the night against charges concerning past events. For example, once a delegation of the Praska clan from Damanapanga came to Gumma to demand a girl of the Sikoka clan. The boy's father had a brother whose daughter had been promised to another man from the Sikoka clan of Gumma. When this brother died, the girl ran away to another village and lived with a more distant relative. She refused to marry the man from Gumma, and at the same time, her relatives were unwilling to return the "betrothal fee" already paid for her by the Sikoka. The delegation from Damanapanga returned again and again, discussing this matter each time, until the Sikoka of Gumma finally accepted the gifts offered by the bride-seeking people.

There are many other reasons why a delegation may be abused by the villagers. One common reason is that a relative or fellow villager of the demanding party has married another woman from the bride's village but not treated her properly or even divorced her. The bride's villagers may also be enraged about outstanding payments for the betrothal of one of their daughters, or they may bring up former disputes about land. In any case, the boy's delegation defends itself, but under no circumstances should the bride-seeking people become offensive or aggressive. Knowing how easily Dongria become wild when they suffer minor offences, I was always amazed by how the delegates managed to maintain the patience expected from them. I do not know whether, contrary to everybody's expectations, such meetings sometimes turn into fights between the parties, but in the event that this happens, I assume that it means the end of the marriage arrangements. The negotiations may also come to an end if the visitors and the girl's parents, during their discussions, find out that their children are related in a way that does not permit a marriage between them. As mentioned in the third chapter (section 3.3.5.3), Dongria rules prohibit a repetition of marriage between two "houses" (*ijo*) or local lines (*punja*) for at least three consecutive generations. The parents may not be aware of a link between their families, but these meetings are always attended by the village elders, who may remember a former marriage that turns the proposed bond into an illegitimate union.

After a night of discussions, the delegation returns home early next morning, normally without having received a positive response to their marriage proposal. After a few weeks or months they try again, and, depending on how far the relations between the two villages have been strained by previous disputes, such meetings may be repeated several times. After two or three of these initial discussions, the boy's delegation brings gifts to the girl's house, such as a buffalo, a jug of distilled liquor, and a basket full of rice. Normally, this first offer is rejected, and it is only if the boy's party turns up again, this time with more gifts, that they may be finally accepted as *samdin loku* or "exchange partners" bound by marriage. In the case mentioned above, this process took several years, until in the end the people of Gumma accepted two buffaloes, two jugs of alcohol, and two *puti*[28] of paddy from the Praska family of Damanapanga. The first buf-

---

28 A *puti* of rice ideally consists of twenty *mana* or approximately eighty kilograms of paddy, but in actual practice only six to seven *mana*, one *mana* being about four kilograms, are given. This is just enough to cook rice for one feast for the whole village.

falo is referred to as *mahala kodru*. While *kodru* simply means buffalo, the word *mahala* may be translated as "betrothal."[29] A woman for whom a buffalo has been given as part of her engagement is called *mahala dakeri* or "promised wife," and everybody is aware that abducting her results in a fine (*tapu*). The second buffalo given by the boy's party is called *giri parpa kodru* or "the buffalo to clear the way." The verb *parpa* denotes the action of cutting down bushes to create a footpath through the jungle. Two female workers of the DKDA explained to me that in the context of marriage arrangements Dongria refer to this buffalo as *giri parpa kodru* because the gift creates a friendly relationship between the two villages. The obstacles, i.e., the former quarrels and disputes, are being removed, and thereby the "path" is cleared for both sides to visit each other. If we take into account the three-generation rule, the expression *giri parpa kodru* can further be seen as an indication that marriage relations existed previously. In this sense, the buffalo "re-opens" the path that became overgrown in the long interval since the last marriage connected both houses.

After the gifts are handed over to the bride-givers, the boy's father or an older relative is allowed to tie a ring made from the vine of a creeper plant (*paeri mudi*) around one of the girl's fingers. Soon after, the boy's delegation returns home, while the bride-givers drop their other occupations and begin preparing a feast for the whole village. A message is sent to close relatives of the bride's parents living in other villages to come and attend the feast. The buffaloes are led to an open space outside the village where they can be conveniently slaughtered, cut into pieces, and cooked. Each village has one or more such "meat places" (*unga basa*), mostly near a small stream and in the shade of a large mango tree. Only men assemble there, while women remain in the village, waiting for their fathers or husbands to bring home their share at the end of the feast. A portion of the buffalo meat is boiled, and the rest is cut into equal shares (*kundera*), the number of which corresponds to the number of households in the village. Additionally, a certain number of shares are set aside for the relatives of the girl's parents. Among these, the girl's FF, FFB, FB, FZH, ZH, and MB have a right to receive a share of the buffalo meat. If they are not present, their portion of raw meat must be sent to their houses along with a portion of the cooked food. The people who eat the buffalo meat, i.e., these particular relatives and the villagers, are the same who later receive a share of the "betrothal fee" and are expected to contribute to the girl's "wedding gift".

---

29 Arlo Griffiths suggested to me that the word may be derived from *vadhuvaa* and has undergone the following linguistic development: *vadhuvaa* >> *vaduva* >> *vaadava* >> *maadava* >> *maadala* >> *maahala*.

After cutting the meat into pieces and distributing it in equal shares displayed on large banana or palm leaves, the men sit down, drink alcohol, and eat some of the cooked food, which basically consists of rice, boiled meat, and broth. Each householder makes a certain number of leaf plates and leaf cups, matching the number of family members not attending the feast, and some young men distribute the cooked food. When all have finished eating, everybody puts the raw meat, as well as the leaf plates and cups filled with cooked food, into a basket and goes home, where their wives and daughters are waiting for their shares.

4.3.3 *karjame* ("serving son-in-law")

In the years that follow, the boy's parents provide the girl's family with a series of gifts whenever a ritual or ceremony takes place in the girl's house or village. For example, if the girl's father performs a *ghanta parba*, the boy's father may contribute a goat or at least some hens, as well as rice and alcohol, to the festive occasion. If somebody dies in the girl's family, the bride-takers similarly provide gifts, such as a buffalo or a pig to be sacrificed in the name of the deceased. During a buffalo sacrifice (*kodru parbu*) in the bride's village, the boy's father may give a hen, rice, and perhaps some money or alcohol to his in-laws. All these gifts are considered to be part of the *mahala*, and if the girl later runs away with another man, the boy's parents will demand that these things be returned.

When the boy grows up, his parents discuss whether they should send their son to perform a long and difficult period of service for his father-in-law. I do not know whether this service was a regular feature of all marriages in the past, but nowadays those who can afford it prefer to pay a higher "betrothal fee" and keep their sons at home. Taking into account statements made by my informants as well as my own estimates, a year's service is roughly equal to a payment of Rs 5,000. The boy's parents thus have to decide whether they can afford to pay a "betrothal fee" of Rs 20,000 to Rs 30,000, keep their son at home, and let him work on his father's fields, or send him to his father-in-law for two to three years to save Rs 10,000 to Rs 15,000. Among less well-off families, "in-law service" is very common and may be performed at any time before or after the marriage. For example, the parents of a man who at the time of my fieldwork was about twenty-five years old had arranged a marriage for him during his childhood. Apart from a buffalo and some alcohol, hardly anything had been given to the girl's side, as the bride-takers were not very rich. When the young man began visiting dormitories, he fell in love with a girl and brought her into his parent's house as his wife. She gave birth to two children, but when the young man grew older, he decided to bring his first wife home as well. He was deeply in love with her, but she was not willing to leave her mother, since her father had died some years previously. The young man was now torn between his responsibilities to his first wife living in Gumma, where he cultivated a hill slope with her, and his second wife living in a village two to three hours walking distance from Gumma. He solved the problem by working some days of the week in his own fields and the rest of the week in his mother-in-law's fields. He did not follow a very regular schedule but considered the condition of the fields in both villages and the urgency of the work. After some years passed in this way, his second wife finally decided to move to Gumma. No official wedding took place, and the wife often decided to return home to help her mother or because she had a fight with her husband or with her co-wife. In order to keep his second wife, the young man was forced to continue his services to his mother-in-law. In this way, nothing really changed, and he remained obliged to his in-laws even after the girl had moved into his house.

In a similar case, a boy was officially engaged to a girl in another village, but when he grew up he fell in love with another woman and made her his wife. After she gave birth to a son and a daughter, her husband suddenly decided to bring the woman to whom he had been engaged into his house as a second wife. As his father had died and he himself could not afford to pay the full "betrothal fee", he paid some money and agreed to work for a period of time for his father-in-law. He was a good friend of mine and used to come to my house regularly but suddenly stayed away for weeks, working in his father-in-law's village, while his first wife and his two children remained alone in his house in Gumma. Thus, despite being an adult man in his thirties and despite being a father with his own home and two children, he offered "in-law service" in a distant village, slept on his father-in-law's veranda, cultivated his fields, and supplied him with wood like an unmarried boy. What both these examples illustrate is that bride-givers insist on either "in-law service" or a "betrothal fee" and that poor bride-takers always opt to work for at least some length of time in their in-laws' fields to reduce their financial demands. If already married, they are torn between their family responsibilities and the expectations of the new wife's parents.

Considerations concerning the amount of the "betrothal fee" are not the only reason why Dongria decide to perform "in-law service". Working for a father-in-law is considered to be the best guarantee that the girl's parents do not give their daughter in marriage to another family. During his stay in the girl's village, the boy normally builds up a relation of trust with his father-in-law, and at the end of the service, the girl and her parents often have affectionate feelings for the boy. Following "in-law service", the chances that the girl will run away with somebody else are low, and nobody expects the parents to look for another groom if their son-in-law has served in their house to their satisfaction. In other words, money can "buy" a bride, but service makes sure she actually becomes one's wife.

In most cases I know of, "in-law service" was offered when the boy had grown up and reached the age of seventeen or eighteen. In the village in which I lived, one man began working as a *karjame* in 2001 when I started my fieldwork, and he was only accepted as the girl's husband (*dakera*) as my fieldwork was ending in 2003. The following description of the period of "in-law service" is based on my acquaintance with this case, on interviews, and on descriptions by Nayak (1989, 141–43).

The beginning of the period of "in-law service" for the boy can be compared to the bride's situation shortly after her wedding. Like her, he has to leave his native village to live among complete strangers. Like the bride on her wedding day, he is invited by his friends and relatives to eat food (*tone paga*) and drink alcohol before he is taken in a procession to his in-laws' village. The following days and weeks are particularly difficult for him, as he has to endure humiliation by his affines. According to Nayak (1989, 142), "his entry into the girl's house and the subsequent approval of him as groom by the latter are all beset with trials, hurdles, humiliations, and mental and physical torture." I doubt that any form of "torture" actually occurs, but the boy will definitely be given a hard time. Like the delegation sent by his parents, which was either ignored or abused when coming to demand the bride, his own intentions are now put to a test. Nayak reports different kinds of humiliation that the boy and one or two friends who remain with him have to suffer. For example, on the day of his arrival the boy is not given a place to sleep. The girls of the village sprinkle water over him to make him feel cold when he has to sleep outside. Next day, he and his friends go to fetch firewood, and on their return the girls forcibly untie the firewood bundles to make the transport more difficult. When going to work in his father-in-law's fields, the boy is not given any tools, so that he has to use his hands to carry out his agricultural tasks. I have not personally witnessed such trials, but my impression is that all this takes place in a humorous and lighthearted atmosphere rather than with serious intentions to make the boy suffer. Nayak's descriptions evoke memories of joking between young married men and pubescent boys that may appear cruel to an outsider: the boys are pushed around, abused in humorous language, given ridiculous names, robbed of their shawls and *lungi*, equated with girls, and mocked with obscene gestures. The boys bear this grudgingly and sometimes become angry, which, however, only arouses more laughter and mockery among the married men.

The *karjame* I got to know in Gumma managed to be accepted relatively quickly, as he was rather tall, strong, and hardworking, but he nevertheless had to endure jokes made by others from time to time. In the three years I had contact with him, his behaviour changed considerably. In the first year, he did not drink much and never quarrelled with anybody, but when after two years of service the girl was accepted as his wife, he began to join his father-in-law and other villagers in excessive drinking and lost his restraint in interaction with others. From time to time he got involved in fights with other villagers, and everybody became aware of his rather short-tempered nature.

At the beginning of his service, the *karjame* is expected to behave deferentially and politely towards others. He works every day in his father-in-law's hill slopes and brings home firewood in the evening. Bride and groom are expected to avoid each other. First of all, this means that they should neither talk to each other nor be seen together in public. When working in the fields, they must keep a distance between them and work in different areas of the hill slope. Once I was walking with the *karjame* through the forest when by chance we bumped into a group of women coming from the opposite direction. As the young bride was among them, the *karjame* jumped into the woods in search of cover. His bride hurried along the path and covered her face with a shawl. Although both acted in the right way, everybody was aware of the humour of the situation and laughed accordingly. At night the boy sleeps alone on the veranda in front of his father-in-law's house, while his wife sleeps either inside the house or with some other girls in the room at the back of the house. As dancing and certain songs are loaded with sexual connotations, bride and groom are strictly forbidden to join the same dancing group.

At the beginning of my fieldwork, I was once invited to the dancing ground located behind a village to see the dances of the young people of Gumma. It was evening and already dark outside, and I was talking to some young men, including the *karjame* of the village. Suddenly he ran away and went into hiding behind the fence of a nearby garden, where he sat down secretly observing the dance. Smiling and laughing, the others explained to me that he took cover because his bride had turned up on the dancing ground. A year later, when the avoidance rules had been loosened, the couple still could not attend the same marriage party. That year, two extensive marriage feasts occurred on the same day in two different villages, so the boy and his friends went to one, while the girl and her friends visited the other. In this way, they both respected the avoidance rules and simultaneously seized the opportunity to sing, dance, and perhaps sleep with somebody.

During the period of "in-law service", the girl should not meet other men in the dormitory, nor should the boy sleep with other girls in his father-in-law's village. However, from time to time the son-in-law returns to his native village to help his parents during harvest or for some other urgent work. During this time, he may either pay a visit to a dormitory in a different village or join dancing parties with a group of girls who have come as guests to his parents' village. His wife does the same and more or less secretly sings, dances, and sleeps with those men who visit her village late at night.

Another reason why a *karjame* may return home are village festivals, in particular *dasera* in autumn and *siva ratri* in spring. On these occasions, the *karjame* leaves his father-in-law's village. At the same time, his father-in-law's sons who are providing "in-law service" in other villages return home. In Gumma, the *karjame* rendered his "in-law service" in the house of a man whose own son had left the village to become a *karjame* in Kambesi. On certain festive occasions, he always went home to his parents' village, named Lamba, while his wife's brother came from Kambesi to visit his family in Gumma. When the festival was over, both again left their native places and resumed their work as *karjame*. From the perspective of a father who has a daughter and a son of almost the same age, such an arrangement appears to be very convenient. On the one hand, he loses the support of a son when sending him away to work in another man's fields, but at the same time he tries to find a young man who will do the same in his own hill slopes in order to marry his daughter. I do not have any statistical data to judge how many families employ this strategy, but it can be assumed that parents are more willing to let their sons go when they get a substitute, and it is my impression that this strategy is followed fairly often.

After one or two years, the "in-law service" ends. According to Nayak, the boy now urges the people of his father-in-law's village to attend a feast sponsored by his father in his original village. When the in-laws agree and join the feast, this is interpreted as indicating their willingness to begin the wedding preparations. If they do not agree, the boy has to continue his "in-law service" (Nayak 1989, 143). In my experience, the situation is more complicated, as "in-law service" is normally only the first step in the negotiations about the "betrothal fee". After the boy completes his "in-law service", both sides will meet and discuss the amount of the "betrothal fee", and only once this matter has been settled do the parties involved seriously begin thinking about the wedding. Only if the boy's father is not willing to pay up does service becomes the only way for him to acquire a wife. For example, I know of one young man from Gumma who had been serving his father-in-law for four years, but his in-laws were still not willing to give away their daughter. He was so desperate that he and his parents approached the shaman and asked her to perform a ritual at a river in order to influence their affines to part with their daughter. In such a situation, abduction of the girl is another option to actively change the state of affairs.

The groom's role and status during his "in-law service" shows similarities with that of the bride after her wedding. Just as the bride on her wedding day moves into her new husband's village, the groom at the time of his "in-law service" goes in a procession to live in his future wife's village. Like the bride after her wedding, the boy is a complete stranger in the village of his in-laws and must endure being the least respected member of the household. Not dissimilar to what Dongria expect from a newlywed wife, he must work hard and behave with integrity and discretion. Like a young woman, he can go and visit his native village from time to time, but he should not remain absent for long. Just as people's expectations towards the young woman change the longer she stays in her new village, the boy serving in his in-law's house will after some months be allowed to mix more freely with others, including his future wife. Both boys during their time of "in-law service" and girls after their wedding are slowly accepted as members of their new villages, although nobody forgets their loyalties to their native place. Comparing the movements of boys during "in-law service" and of girls during the last phase of their wedding, we can identify two similar exchange systems. A father who has sent his son away for "in-law service" eagerly accepts a son-in-law in his house to provide the same work. In the same way, a father who has given his daughter away in marriage to another village welcomes an early marriage by his son in order to have a young daughter-in-law in his house. In other words, the system of "in-law service" may be seen as an exchange of men, just as marriage is an exchange of women.

4.3.4 *mahala takang* ("betrothal fee")

As mentioned above, families who are not rich enough to pay the full "betrothal fee" often send their sons away to provide "in-law service". This does not normally exempt them from giving at least a few thousand rupees to the bride's father, but when both sides agree not to celebrate the wedding in a grand fashion, it may happen that two or three years of service are considered sufficient to acquire a wife. This was the case with the *karjame* of Gumma to whom I referred above. After two years of service, a simple ritual at the border between two villages was performed, and the girl was henceforth considered to be his wife. His family was not expected to pay any "betrothal fee", and no one was talking about bringing the girl in a procession to his village. The couple instead remained in Gumma, as the mother could not let her daughter go, and her father had enough land to provide his son-in-law with some good fields in the future.

A family of high status is, however, not content with such a solution and insists on a "betrothal fee" as well as on sending their daughter away in a grand procession. In such cases, several years may pass between the completion of "in-law service" and the actual wedding. During these years, bride-givers and bride-takers enter into negotiations about the payment of the "betrothal fee". A rich family of high status is expected to exact a considerable amount and attempts to postpone the wedding as long as possible. The bride-takers, on the other hand, are torn between the need to prove they can measure up to the demands of their future in-laws and the desire to give less than demanded. In contrast to the bride-givers, they are interested in arranging the wedding as soon as possible. These contradictory interests and expectations set the stage for disputes and conflicts arising out of negotiations for the "betrothal fee". During the time of my fieldwork, I witnessed negotiations characterised by amicable relations between the parties. Such peaceful meetings are considered to be a sign of the high status of the families involved. But I also experienced negotiations that turned into arguments and even fights between bride-givers and bride-takers, and examples of both types are given in the following paragraphs.

When the girl is old enough to be married, the boy's parents fix a day for negotiating the "betrothal fee". In the evening of the day before this meeting, a delegation of bride-takers consisting of some unmarried men, a Dombo *barika*, and some senior agnates of the groom arrives in the girl's village. The young visitors go straight to the dormitories, while their elders sleep in a relative's house. Next morning, before sunrise, everybody assembles on the village plaza, around the one or more fireplaces located there. Then the villagers invite their guests to accompany them to the *salap* trees. There, chatting and joking continues until everybody returns to the village and the serious part of the enterprise begins. The negotiations take place inside the bride's father's house. Since the bride-takers' Dombo *barika* is not allowed to enter the inner room of the house, he sits on the veranda close to the threshold, listening and shouting his comments to the Dongria sitting inside. The women belonging to the bride's village remain in the back room and pass their comments on to the negotiating men from time to time. The bride-takers are represented by the girl's father or his elder brothers, by the village elders, and by men of high status such as the *jani*, *bismajhi*, or *member*. The boy himself and his father are usually absent. Once I even attended a meeting in which the groom's party was represented by men from a village different from his own.

Representatives of both parties sit down on the floor near the *handani kuda*, the wall at which the goddess of wealth and grain, *sita penu-lahi penu*, is regularly worshipped. Among the Desia Kond, who are wet-rice cultivators, this wall is part of a small room in which they store their harvest, the representation of the goddess. A ritual elder of the bride-givers, usually the *jani* or *pujari* of the village, places a winnowing fan filled with rice in front of this wall. He asks for some ember from the hearth and adds resin of the *sal* tree to it in order to produce incense. Next, someone provides a handful of castor beans used for counting. An older representative of the bride-givers begins demanding the "betrothal fee". He mentions a certain amount of money and calls out the kinship term of the prospective recipient. Then, for every one thousand rupees demanded by the bride-givers, somebody places a castor bean in front of the winnowing fan.

The first amount is always demanded on behalf of the village and is referred to as *kutumba takang* or "money for the community." The word *kutumba* means "family" but is often used for the whole village community, which is also referred to as *bara bhai* or "twelve brothers." The amount is relatively standardised and usually does not exceed Rs 2,000 to Rs 3,000, this being enough to buy one or two buffaloes and some rice for a feast. When talking about this share, Dongria often refer to it as *bhojinga*, which literally means "feasts." The groom is not allowed to attend this feast or eat any of the buffalo meat served on this occasion.

When two or three castor beans representing *bhojinga* have been placed on the ground, the bride-givers next demand a share for *amaska*. This word is the plural form of *ama*, an address and reference term for FZ and MBW. In this case, however, the money does not go to the MBW but only to the sisters of the bride's father. The amount demanded on their behalf depends on their number, their relation to the father, and their overall influence on matters concerning the bride's house. In most cases, the total amount does not exceed Rs 2,000 to Rs 3,000. The castor beans representing this share are kept separate from the share of the village community. It is referred to as *ama ada*, meaning "father's sisters' goat." It was explained to me that in the past a goat was given to the *ama* as part of the "betrothal fee".

The next share is demanded on behalf of *taliska* or "her mothers." The plural form signifies that not only the biological mother but all of the bride's father's wives have a right to this share, which is also known as *phingagandanga*. This word can be translated as "clothes [polluted by] excrement." When explaining this expression, Dongria laughingly reminded me of the fact that babies often spit, vomit, urinate, or defecate on their mothers' clothes. In the past, a new dress was given to the bride's "mothers" as a substitute for the dresses ruined by the girl during her early childhood. Nowadays, the "mothers" can expect about Rs 1,000 as their share of the total "betrothal fee".

Next, the bride's older agnates demand money on behalf of her sisters, referred to as *tangiska*. Normally, sisters are called either *nanasika* if older or *boisika* if younger, but in this context they are collectively referred to as "sisters" by using the Dravidian word *tangi*, which in contrast to *nanasika* and *boisika* does not differentiate female siblings according to their relative age.[30] Each sister can

---

30 In Tamil and other Dravidian languages, *tangi* means "younger sister." In the Dongria lan-

expect around Rs 1,500, and their share is called *teduanga*, meaning "bracelet." In the past, these thick bracelets made of brass were given to the bride's sisters as part of the "betrothal fee" and worn by women around their upper arms.

Next, the bride givers demand a share for the mother's brothers (*mamaska*) of the bride. Depending on the status and influence of the mother's brothers, they may be given a substantial share of the total amount. In the cases I recorded, the *mama* received between Rs 2,000 and Rs 5,000. For reasons unknown to me, this share is referred to as *mama pating*, the word *pating* meaning "crossbeams," i.e., wooden beams used to construct the ceiling in a Dongria house.

Finally, the largest share of the total "betrothal fee" is demanded in the name of the people of the house (*ijo*), including the bride's brothers, her father, and her father's brothers. This share is called *mahala* (in Oriya *mala-jula*), and although it is counted as one share, it is later divided among the agnates, the father keeping the largest portion. The exact amount depends on the number of agnates, and in one case I witnessed, the total *mahala* added up to Rs 8,000.

Following the announcement of this last share of the "betrothal fee", the different subtotals are repeated by again counting aloud the castor beans spread out on the ground. After that, the heap of castor beans signifying the village community's share of the village community is put aside, while all the other heaps representing the different relatives' shares are joined in one heap. This heap is again counted, the total amount is proclaimed aloud, and the castor beans are tied in a piece of cloth, which is then placed on the winnowing fan. Just as money is said to be a representation of the goddess of wealth, *sita penu-lahi penu*, the winnowing fan filled with rice and the knot made in the piece of cloth containing the castor beans symbolise this deity.

Table 17: Recipients, names, and amounts of different shares of the "betrothal fee" (Dongria Kond)

Recipient	Category of Payment	Amount (approximate)
village community (*kutumba*)	*kutumba takang* or *bojhinga*	Rs 2,000 – 3,000
father's sisters (*amaska*)	*ama ada*	Rs 2,000 (each)

---

guage, *tangi* refers to all sisters (and female cousins) irrespective of their age. This corresponds to Israel's translation of the Kuwi word *tangi* as "sister; direct cousin sister" (Israel 1979, 371). In contrast, the Kui language distinguishes between elder sister (*bai*) and younger sister (*angi* or *tangi*). As far as I know, Dongria use the word *bai* only as part of the expression *tayi bai* meaning "brother and sister" of the same clan or phratry.

Table 17: Recipients, names, and amounts of different shares of the "betrothal fee" (Dongria Kond) *(Continued)*

Recipient	Category of Payment	Amount (approximate)
mothers (*taliska*)	*phingagandanga*	Rs 1,000 (each)
sisters (*tangiska*)	*teduanga*	Rs 1,500 (each)
mother's brothers (*mamaska*)	*mama pating*	Rs 2,000 (each)
house (father, father's brothers, brothers) (*ijo*)	*mahala* (or *mala*)	Rs 5,000–8,000

The bride-givers declare that if their guests are willing to give this amount of money right now, they are free to take the girl to their village the same day. Everybody knows, of course, that the bride-givers have neither brought so much money nor would be prepared to pay so much. Instead, they begin arguing about the different shares and the total amount and insist that the demands are too high. In one case I witnessed in Lamba, the visitors from Phakeri argued that they should be allowed to take the girl home immediately, provided the money for the village community was handed over. This, of course, was a blunt lie provoking laughter by the people of Lamba. Everybody knew that the father-in-law would under no circumstances allow the guests to take his daughter, even if they handed over a substantial amount of money. In a rather joking manner, the villagers of Phakeri then "threatened" the bride-givers that they would file a "case" against them, i.e., go to the police, make a complaint, and return with some officers in order to take the bride forcibly. If successful, such a manoeuvre would require a substantial bribe to the policemen. As will be described later, "cases" of this sort are indeed filed at times, but normally during the later stage of negotiations, when the boy's parents have paid the full "betrothal fee" and are prevented from taking their daughter-in-law home. When the people from Phakeri mentioned a "case," the bride-givers did not take it seriously but jokingly "threatened" them in return by saying that their police, meaning the officials from Lanjigada district, were more powerful than the policemen of Kalyansingpur, who are responsible for the affairs of Phakeri.

In this way, the negotiations continue until finally the bride-takers hand over the *kutumba takang* by placing the money, normally in hundred-rupee banknotes, on the winnowing fan. The bride's people count the money by making separate piles of one thousand rupees each. Each pile is referred to as *ra mana*, *ra* meaning "one" and *mana* being the local unit of counting rice, one *mana* being equivalent to one particular type of vessel containing approximately four kilograms of grain. This may be seen as an indication that in the past rice or other crops were given as part of the "betrothal fee".

Among the Jreda Kond of Ramnagar, whom I visited in 2003, no money is given as a "betrothal fee", but rather different animals and certain objects. The amount is more standardised and is referred to as *bara konda* or "twelve pieces" because it consists of twelve items divided into six categories. As among the Dongria Kond, these gifts are later redistributed among the relatives. The MB, for example, will claim a cow, the bride's father the axe, and the bride's mother the clothes. This type of "betrothal fee", which consists of livestock and other objects, seems to have been the standard payment at a time when Kond were less familiar with money. According to Macpherson (1863, 50), the Malliah Kond at the time of his work, i.e., in the mid-nineteenth century, estimated the value of property in "lives" of different animals and brass pots. A victim for a *meria* sacrifice was worth fifty to one hundred "lives" (Macpherson 1863, 64), and the parents of a bride could demand up to twenty to thirty "lives" for their daughter (Macpherson 1863, 54). What appears striking is the fact that the Jreda Kond, most of whom have converted to Christianity and adapted to mainstream culture in terms of dress, education, and technology, continue to exclude money from the realm of marriage exchanges, while the Dongria Kond, who in many ways resist attempts to change their way of life, calculate the "betrothal fee" in monetary terms only. This clearly shows that the use of such labels as "traditional" and "modern," or "backwards" and "advanced," to classify whole ethnic groups is wrong not only because of the ethnocentric character of such categories, but also because these ethnic groups do not react to outside influences and imposed changes in a uniform manner. They may be resistant in some spheres of life, while being open to alterations and innovations in others.

Table 18: Name, meaning, and number of "betrothal fee" items among Jreda Kond (Ramnagar, 2003)

Category of Payment	Meaning
ra heru kuruku	one "plough" (two buffaloes)
sengi kodinga	five cows
rinda odanga	two goats
rinda talinga	two food plates
randa beda	one item of clothing
ra tangi	one axe

Among the Dongria, after the visitors hand over the share belonging to the village, they are now served food. In contrast to previous occasions of abuse and humiliation, they are now treated as guests. While in the past the girl's parents refused to treat the boy's delegation as guests, they now want to please their visitors. When leaving, bride-takers should part with a feeling of *rasa*, a word used to signify peace and happiness. To establish *rasa*, the guests are served food and, if available, alcohol at the time of their departure. The dormitory girls make sure that the boys with whom they have spent the night get some cooked food.

Going forward, it may take years until the "betrothal fee" is settled to the satisfaction of both sides. During this time, relations between the villages may become very strained, though ideally the bride-takers return once or twice to hand over the outstanding amounts. I once witnessed such a peaceful settlement between two families whose household heads were political leaders in their respective villages. On their first visit, the bride takers paid Rs 8,500, covering all shares except those for the mother's brothers and for the house. The outstanding payments, adding up to Rs 13,000, were made on a second visit in the following year. On the day of the first meeting, several people told me that they observe the following rule: *ra barca hinambu, ra barca tanambu*, meaning "one year we give ['betrothal fee'], one year we take [the bride]." Indeed, in the year following the second meeting, during which the total outstanding amount had been paid, the wedding took place in a grand fashion.

Table 19: Amounts paid by the *member* of Phakeri to the *member* of Lamba (2002)

Recipient	Category of Payment	Amount
village community (*kutumba*)	*kutumba takang* or *bojhinga*	Rs 2,000
father's sisters (*amaska*)	*ama ada*	Rs 3,000
mothers (*taliska*)	*phingagandanga*	Rs 1,000
sisters (*tangiska*)	*teduanga*	Rs 2,500
mother's brothers (*mamaska*)	*mama pating*	Rs 5,000
house (father, father's brothers, brothers) (*ijo*)	*mahala* (or *mala*)	Rs 8,000
	Total	Rs 21,500

In many other cases, however, the negotiations proceed less smoothly, the basic reasons for disputes being two. On the one hand, some bride-givers keep changing their demands, trying to extract as much as possible from their future in-laws, while others are not willing to give their daughters in marriage even though the bride-takers have fulfilled all their demands. On the other hand, the boy's parents may refuse to pay the full "betrothal fee" and simultaneously exert pressure on the bride-givers, for example by abducting the girl or by filing a "case" with the police. To illustrate both difficulties, I will describe two different cases.

One day the *barika* of Gumma asked me to accompany him to a village named Wadelenka Kambesi located in the foothills of Nebaharu, a high mountain in the neighbouring Kalahandi district, to demand a girl for a young man from the village of Dongormati. In the past, the three villages of Gumma, Dongormati, and Lamba were considered to form a single "village," and the villagers used to act collectively on various occasions, such as marriage arrangements and death rituals. Due to a quarrel over land and a serious fight during one of the last buffalo sacrifices (*kodru parbu*), the unity between the three villages broke. Nowadays, the villagers of Gumma refuse to cooperate with those of the other two, while the people from Lamba and Dongormati, despite belonging to different clans, continue to act as one corporate body. The Dombo *barika* of Gumma, however, still renders his services to all three villages. In this case, I joined him and some men from Lamba on their way to Dongormati, where we were expected by the male agnates of the groom. The groom himself could not join us, as he had fallen ill, but some of his brothers and uncles were ready to bring the girl. Forming a group of fifteen to twenty people, we walked for two to three hours through the mountains and across an impressive plateau (*gati*) until we reached Kambesi by midday. While walking I was informed that four buffaloes, four goats, four jugs of alcohol, and three *puti* of rice had already been given to the girl's parents. Only a week ago, the bride-takers, along with the *barika* and a police official called *chaukidar,* had paid a visit to Kambesi. On this occasion, they had been abused and threatened by young men hitting their axes on the ground in order to frighten them. Following difficult discussions, the bride's people had finally agreed to release the girl if the boy's parents would send their relatives a week later to hand over the "betrothal fee". Our delegation was thus supposed to deliver the money to the bride's parents and take home their daughter. Such an arrangement is called *katada*, meaning "appointment," and it differs from an abduction because the bride-takers are officially invited. When asked about their intentions, the groom's people answered *mambu katata dina maga takoli hanambu*, "we go on the appointed day to bring the girl."

On our arrival, hardly anybody was present to receive, us since the villagers were either working on their hill slopes or drinking wine under the *salap* tree with their friends. After some time, the young men of Kambesi turned up, many of them quite drunk and in an aggressive mood. Our delegation was immediately accused of having stolen wine from a *salap* tree on the way to the village. While most visitors sat more or less silently on the verandas of different houses, the drunken young men of Kambesi shouted at the few guests who dared to oppose them. On such occasions, Dongria men display their culturally specific gestures of aggression: they whistle loudly with one finger between their lips, shout and howl, lift up and rotate their axes in front of them, jump into the air, stamp with their feet, twirl their moustaches, beat their chests with their fists, expose their penises, or throw pubic hair into their enemies' faces while saying *na pida tinmu* ("eat my penis"). The gestures actually performed signify the degree of anger, sexual symbols certainly being the most offensive. On this occasion the latter were not exhibited by the young men, but everybody told me to sit down and wait quietly.

After some time, the more sober men got the upper hand and invited the visitors into the girl's house. Before entering the inner part of the house, the bride-takers had to deposit their axes on the veranda. Then everybody sat down, and instead of a winnowing fan, a brass plate, some rice, and castor beans were placed on the ground. The discussions were led by the girl's mother's brother, a man of the Desia Kond community whom everybody considered to be very clever and able to strike a good deal for the bride's people. Whenever Desia Kond are involved in such negotiations, people expect the Dongria to be fooled, as they are allegedly less cunning. First, a man from Dongormati placed Rs 1,001 on the rice in the brass plate, and then the girl's mother's brother began demanding. Immediately, the negotiations got stuck, since the bride-takers were not willing to pay the high amounts stipulated by the girl's side. Finally, the Desia Kond told his visitors to take the money and leave. They did as suggested and assembled at a little distance outside the village, where they conferred with the *barika*. The girl's party demanded Rs 4,000, of which Rs 2,000 were to be given to the village and Rs 2,000 to the mother's brother. Following their consultations, the bride-takers again entered the village, where they found the mother's brother standing in front of his house and approached him to submit the following offer: the groom's party was willing to give Rs 2,000, Rs 1,000 immediately and Rs 1,000 in a week. Meanwhile, the mother's brother had changed his mind and demanded Rs 5,000, of which Rs 3,000 would go into his own pocket. For a second time, the groom's party assembled outside the village, and the *barika* advised them to accept the demands by suggesting an instalment of Rs 4,000 immediately and Rs 1,000 a week later when taking the bride.

When they communicated this decision to the mother's brother, he consented. Meanwhile, however, the other villagers seemed to disagree, perhaps because their Desia Kond relative planned to take the lion's share. Whatever may have been the reason, the *member* of Kambesi refused to accept the money offered by the *barika*, behaviour that enraged the bride-takers. They left the village in a bad temper, not without threatening the men from Kambesi by saying *mambu minge kodru parbu henambu*, meaning "we'll see you at the buffalo sacrifice." This was intended as a warning, since the next buffalo sacrifice was to be performed a few months later by fellow clan members of the groom's delegation in Lekhpadar, a good occasion to take revenge for the day's humiliation. The people of Kambesi, on the other hand, sent some young men armed with axes to follow us, most probably to prevent us from destroying their palm-wine trees or repeating our alleged theft of the valuable sap. Some Dongormati men hit the trees or the ground before the trees with their axes, and angry comments passed between the groom's delegation in front and the villagers following behind. The latter halted only after we had left their territory. In the following months, whenever I met a member of our delegation, I was informed about the latest events concerning this marriage arrangement. Only later was I told about the real crux of the matter: Dongormati had demanded two "sisters" from Kambesi, and both sides continuously played one case off against the other.

As a second illustration of how negotiations over the "betrothal fee" can turn bride-givers and bride-takers into temporary enemies, I will describe the events surrounding the marriage of a young man from Gumma named Sikoka Dikca. His father, Sikoka Kuca, represents the local "nobility," since he belongs to a line of *kaja bismajhi* ("senior *bismajhi*"), whose members are considered to be descendants of the original village founders. Many villagers of Gumma remembered the time when Sikoka Kuca and his brother, Sikoka Ranu, the oldest men of the village, were very rich, possessing a great number of cows and goats. For several reasons, primarily a fire that destroyed a substantial part of their wealth, their economic status had fallen, although they were far from being considered a poor family. Kuca's eldest daughter and son were already married, but two younger sons, including Dikca, remained to be married, and this certainly put a financial burden on the whole family. Kuca had arranged his son's marriage during his childhood with a daughter of a wealthy man of the Kulesika clan living in Lamba. According to Kuca's statement, he had given his son's father-in-law the standard *mahala* consisting of two buffaloes, rice, and alcohol. Furthermore, his son had served "three years" at Lamba as *karjame*, the length of his "in-law service" being perhaps a bit exaggerated. In Sikoka Kuca's opinion, gifts and service together justified his son's demands to receive the girl, while the girl's parents were not willing to agree to an early marriage, as they expected more money as "betrothal fee" for their daughter.

One morning in June 2001, a few people informed me that a group of men from Gumma had left early to abduct Sikoka Dikca's fiancée. As I had not yet seen an abduction, I immediately followed them, meeting Dikca halfway, where he was accompanied by some other villagers who were trying to force the girl along the path. She resisted as best as she could, beating her abductors with her fists, scratching them with her fingernails, and abusing them verbally. Whenever she got the chance, she tried to run away, but the young men always caught her and pulled her along the path. When the girl refused to walk any further, she was literally dragged and carried away by one or two of her abductors, many of whom showed signs of their victim's forceful resistance. When they finally arrived at Gumma, they took her to Sikoka Dikca's elder brother's house. Before she entered, the oldest man of the village was called to perform a small ritual forming part of any marriage ceremony: the elder takes some long leaves of a plant that grows near the river and a pot of water mixed with mashed turmeric tubers, sprinkles the bride, and pours the water on the roof, from where it drips from the eaves onto the bride as she enters the house. In this way, she is purified. By entering the house she officially becomes the boy's wife. For this reason, this ritual can be performed only once, even if the girl is forcibly abducted several times. In the case of Dikca's fiancée, the girl tried to stop this ritual by kicking the pot of turmeric water. In fact, she succeeded in spilling the water all over the ground, so that a second pot had to be brought. The old man then uttered some ritual verses and sprinkled a few drops of water on her head, but before he could pour the water onto the roof, the girl managed to run into the house. Without stopping, she went straight into the back room, where she sat down in a corner, burying her face in her hands.

The young men were obviously very pleased with their successful abduction and immediately sent the boy's elder brother to the next Dombo village to buy alcohol, as everybody involved in the event was entitled to a bottle of country liquor. A little later, a group of women from Lamba turned up in the village demanding that their daughter be released. As is customary in such cases, the girl's village did not send any men, a rule which is most probably meant to prevent serious fights between the parties. On this occasion, the strategy did not fully work, as the discussions quickly grew excited. The women demanded Rs 30,000 as "betrothal fee" for the girl, assuring the transfer of the girl on receipt. Of course, no one seriously expected such a huge amount of money to be paid on the spot, the sole purpose of the claim being to fix the maximum price for the girl. The abductors, being temporarily in the stronger position, refused to pay anything and claimed that their former prestations to the bride's people gave them the right to retain the girl in their village. Then the members of the girl's party began abusing the boy's family members, particularly his mother and his elder brother, who, having consumed some drinks in the Dombo village, was not in the mood to tolerate this without resistance. Men and women were standing at close quarters, shouting and threatening each other with raised arms. Suddenly, one woman picked up a stick with which to beat the boy's elder brother. At this point the village elders, in particular the *member* of

Gumma, interfered and tried to calm the agitated parties down. Leaf plates with rice and cooked lentils were brought and given to the women from Lamba. Initially they accepted the food, but when unable to achieve the release of their village daughter, they angrily returned it without having eaten anything. This contemporary scene was not so different from what Campbell reported about a hundred and fifty years ago in the Kondmals:

> On one occasion, whilst taking an evening ride, I heard loud cries proceeding from a village close at hand. Fearing some serious quarrel, I rode to the spot, and there I saw a man bearing away upon his back something enveloped in an ample covering of scarlet cloth; he was surrounded by twenty or thirty young fellows, and by them protected from the desperate attacks made on him by a party of young women. On seeking an explanation of this novel scene, I was told that the man had just been married, and his precious burthen was his blooming bride, whom he was conveying to his own village. Her youthful friends, as it appears is the custom, were seeking to regain possession of her, and hurled stones and bamboos at the head of the devoted bridegroom, until he reached the confines of his own village. (Campbell 1864, 44)

Some time after the girl's party had left, a group of men and women from Lamba turned up carrying rice, which they had bought in Patalamba, a Dongria village used by businessmen of the plains for trading with the hill people. On their way back they had heard about the abduction. While the men of Lamba continued their return journey, the women stayed behind and tried to set their daughter free. Again, arguments were exchanged between the parties. At a moment when nobody was paying attention to her, the girl took advantage of the situation and escaped into the woods in the direction of her village. Her fiancé and one of his friends followed suit and caught her after some time. Instead of returning to the village and risking being overpowered by the people of Lamba, they kept her hidden in the forest until the whole group of angry women had left. They then returned with their "prey" to Gumma, and around midday everybody who had attended the successful abduction in the morning was invited to the elder brother's house for a drink of liquor.

Later, when discussing the events with the *barika* of Gumma, he explained to me that Sikoka Kuca had to pay a certain "betrothal fee", or else the marriage would not take place, as the fierce reaction of the girl's fellow villagers had clearly shown. Considering the number of buffaloes and the quantity of rice and alcohol already given by the boy's parents, the *barika* expected Kuca to pay another Rs 10,000 to Rs 12,000, instead of the Rs 30,000 demanded by the bride-givers. He further argued that Kuca would be able to pay this amount, although his family was no longer as rich as in the past, because Sikoka Kuca had earned Rs 8,000 in the previous year by selling turmeric tubers. As described in the second chapter (section 2.5.4), turmeric has become a major source of income for the Dongria since the government has begun to provide each house with two hundred kilograms of turmeric tubers free of cost. As the government also repurchases the crop at standard rates, cash is now rather easily available. According to the *barika*, many Dongria families store substantial amounts of money in bamboo in their houses for purposes such as marriage ceremonies or death rituals.

On the morning following this drama, I was woken up by loud and angry voices coming from the village plaza. When I appeared outside of my house, some villagers informed me that a large number of women from Lamba had come to Gumma in the morning to recover their daughter. They had gone straight to the back of the groom's elder brother's house and forcibly taken the girl. While some had helped the girl to return to Lamba, the others had remained and were now arguing with the boy's parents about the "betrothal fee". Both parties were very angry, as various individuals had received hits and blows during the scuffle in the morning, and the discussions continued for quite some time before the Lamba women went home.

More than a year and a half later, in January 2003, Dikca and his friends again went to Lamba to abduct the girl and successfully returned the same night. This time, the girl had obviously been informed about her groom's plans and agreed to run away with him. When the women of her village turned up in Lamba the next morning, both had gone into hiding (*duga tuhteru*), a clear signal to both parties that the couple was interested in marriage and their parents should arrive at an agreement. However, the dispute continued in the same terms, the bride-givers demanding Rs 30,000 and the bride-takers refusing to pay that much. The Dombo of Gumma suggested that Sikoka Kuca should pay at least Rs 5,000 as *malanga* or the share for the house and another Rs 2,000 to the girl's mother's brother. Including the Rs 2,000 for the village community and some minor shares for other relatives, the total "betrothal fee" would add up to a sum of Rs 10,000 to Rs 12,000, as suggested by the *barika*.

A few days later the couple reappeared, and later when Dikca returned his wife to her natal village, he took a buffalo with him for his in-laws. This gift was meant to improve relations between the affines and was shared in a feast by the whole village. A second buffalo was bought by the boy's father as a gift to his own villagers, who had joined his son in capturing the girl. Such a gift is referred to as *ahpa kodru* or "abduction buffalo," *ahpa* being a word mostly used in the context of hunting, where it refers to "catching" the prey. The whole village is invited to participate in this feast, including the groom and his family.

As the abduction of the girl had not yet achieved the desired result, the boy's father came up with a new plan to force the girl's parents into agreement. One day in February 2003, he went to Mayawali, a small village where the local police watchman lives. This official was convinced by the boy's father to write a formal letter to the people of Lamba stating that the boy's father had demanded a girl for his son long ago, that his son had served three years as *karjame* in his father-in-law's house, and that the following gifts had been given to the Kulesika of Lamba: three buffaloes, three pigs, three chickens, three *puti* of rice, two jugs of distilled liquor, and Rs 2,000 for the village community (*kutumba takang*). In spite of these gifts and services, the in-laws had not been willing to give their daughter in marriage, having instead started a quarrel three or four times and driven Kuca's son out of Lamba at night. In this letter, the boy's father threatened his affines that he would send the *bada loka* or "big people," meaning the watchman and police officers, to Lamba to take the girl if her father would not agree to hand her over to her husband. This letter was then carried by the *barika* of Gumma on behalf of Sikoka Kuca to the girl's people, the Kulesika of Lamba. When I discussed the contents of the letter with the *barika*, he commented that the sole purpose of the letter was to threaten the people of Lamba and to reduce the amount of the "betrothal fee" from Rs 30,000 to around Rs 6,000. I do not know how the girl's father reacted, but as of the day of my departure in April the same year, the matter had not been resolved.

These two extended case studies clearly illustrate how the matter of the "betrothal fee" exerts an immense strain on affinal relations. The whole issue of settling the "betrothal fee" resembles a deal in which both sides employ all sorts of strategies to get the most out of the bargain in terms of status and wealth. The girl's parents will not let their daughter go as long as their in-laws have not fulfilled their demands. They wait for a long time, always hoping to get more than the boy's parents are apparently willing to give. Even if they have received the total "betrothal fee", they may not agree to initiate the final marriage celebrations. Instead, the girl's parents often try to keep her in their house as long as possible, and while one reason is that she is a highly valuable worker, we should also not forget the emotional attachment, particularly that between daughter and mother. As mentioned above, the *karjame* of Gumma was not allowed to take his wife to his own natal village because his mother-in-law was so attached to her daughter that she became desperate and sick whenever her daughter was absent for a day or two.

The boy's parents may follow different strategies. If they are relatively rich and can afford to pay a high "betrothal fee", they will not bargain but hand over the money as soon as possible, thereby managing to finish the marriage arrangements quickly and to increase their status. However, if they are less well-off and cannot afford to fulfil all the bride-givers' demands, they will hand over a portion of the "betrothal fee" stipulated by their affines and wait to see whether the latter are satisfied with less than originally asked for. If the bride-givers insist on full payment, the bride-takers may react by capturing the girl or by threatening the affines in one way or another. In this manner, they may succeed in getting the girl at an earlier date and saving money, at the expense of losing status and of putting a strain upon affinal relations.

After the "betrothal fee" is paid, people have to decide how the girl is to be taken to the groom's village. She may go without any ceremony, or she may be captured, but the highest status goes to a marriage in which the bride is brought in a procession, *hedi tana* (lit. "to bring the girl from far away"), to her new home. This requires a number of preparations, the first being a feast provided by the groom's father to the bride's people.

4.3.5 *ijo henga hana* ("we go to see the house")

When all disputes concerning marriage payments have been settled and both parties seriously intend to finalise the marriage within the year, they begin their preparations at least one or two months before the appointed day. The procession normally takes place in the hottest season of the year, in the months from March to May. As a first step, the boy's parents send the Dombo *barika* and some relatives to the girl's house to invite the father to his son-in-law's village for a feast. This event is referred to as *ijo henga hana* or "we go to see the house [of the groom]." For the first time in the many years since the marriage negotiations began, the bride's people go to the groom's village, marking a first shift in the relationship between the two parties. All former meetings were held in order to settle the demands made by the bride-givers of the bride-takers. The latter were expected to conform to the requirements of courtship by visiting the girl's village, enduring humiliation by her fellow villagers, and transferring a substantial part of their wealth to them. Throughout this time, they are in an inferior position, as they, at least ideally, have to give everything without expecting anything in return. When the boy's parents have fulfilled all the expectations required by courtship, the situation changes, because now the time has come for the girl's parents to meet their obligations. Their role changes from that of gift recipient to that of gift giver, and as part of this change they for the first time go as guests to the boy's village. Paying close attention to the forms of gift exchange between bride-givers and bride-takers, we can notice a gradual shift from asymmetrical to symmetrical relations.

The feast at the groom's house always takes place on a Friday. A day before, the delegation sent by the girl's parents, usually consisting of some older agnates and a few young men, arrives in the boy's village at night. During the previous months and years, the groom's fellow villagers have had many opportunities to sleep in the dormitories of the bride's village whenever they came to negotiate the "betrothal fee". On this occasion, however, the bride's village brothers in return get a chance to stay in the dormitory of the groom's village. They sing and dance throughout the night before they enter the dormitory, or if they are not invited to the dormitory, rest on their hosts' veranda. Next morning, the hosts get up first and begin preparations for the feast. I witnessed such a gathering in a rather remote village named Kata in May 2001 and offer the following account.

When I arrived in Kata on a Friday morning along with the *barika* of Gumma, a few young men were collecting firewood, while most of the guests from Sana Dengoni were still sleeping after a long night of dancing. A few days before, the *barika* had provided the groom's father with a buffalo worth Rs 1,250, and on this day he had come to attend the feast and take the buffalo hide home.[31] The feast was organised by a Sikoka who, according to his own statement, had paid Rs 15,000 as "betrothal fee" to his son's father-in-law. The in-laws belonged to the Jakesika clan and resided in Sana Dengoni, a village belonging to the same clan and *muta* as Kata. In other words, the villages of bride-givers and bride-takers could not be distinguished by their clan identity, yet the members of both villages were linked as affines in the context of this marriage. As dormitory relations[32] are forbidden between members of the same clan, the bride's delegation mostly consisted of young men of the Pusika clan. The Sikoka of this area maintain good relations with two villages (Sutangoni and Badabada) belonging to the Pusika clan, whom they regularly marry and with whom they regularly exchange ritual services, particularly at the time of the buffalo sacrifice (*kodru parbu*), when one group protects the other's buffalo. These Pusika men had come to sing and dance with the Sikoka girls of Kata, and they later took home a substantial share of the buffalo. Although the marriage thus linked a Sikoka to a Jakesika family, the celebration appeared to be an affair between the Pusika and the Sikoka, the two dominant clans and traditional marriage partners in this area. While the Pusika, who mostly came from Sutangoni, represented the "affines" or *gota loku*, about ten young Sikoka from a neighbouring village named Bada Dengoni turned up as "siblings" or *tayi bai*, whose duty consisted in helping the groom's party to prepare the feast.

---

31 Often Dombo try to strike a deal with the Dongria, selling the buffalo at a cheaper rate when the Dongria agree to hand over a complete hide at the end of the feast. However, to the Dombo's dismay, young Dongria often do not like to renounce the joy of killing the buffalo in a wild mob by hacking the animal into pieces, thereby destroying the hide and rendering it worthless.
32 For more details about dormitory relations, see section 4.4.2.

While the Pusika youths slowly got up, the Sikoka of Kata, along with their brothers from Bada Dengoni, led the buffalo to a place near a small stream outside the village and killed the animal on the spot by an axe blow to the back of the neck. The buffalo was then divided into two halves, one half being put aside and later given to the "affines" to take home, the other half being immediately cut into pieces. As is customary on such occasions, a portion of the meat was cooked, while another portion was divided into equal shares of raw meat. However, while on other festive occasion the village always keeps one portion for each house, in the context of this feast nothing was to be retained by the organisers except for "the head and the bones" (*kapada are pdeka*). The different portions of raw meat were later to be given to the villages of "affines" and "agnates," one share for each house. A share (*baga*) always consists of a large leaf plate referred to as *tala* and a smaller leaf cup called *sipidi*, both containing different types of meat. In this case, seventy-three equal shares of raw meat were portioned out and later given to the seventy-three households of three villages, Sana Dengoni and Sutangoni[33] as "affines" of Kata and Bada Dengoni as "agnates." While the men were busy cooking the meat, the women stayed in a different place and prepared the rice. This division of labour is observed on all festive occasions; only at rather informal feasts without guests do the men sometimes cook the rice themselves.

Next, two leaf plates were filled with cooked meat and tied into a bundle (*puda*). Both were carried to the street in front of the groom's house where everybody assembled, the "agnates" sitting in one place, the "affines" in another. The leader of the bride-givers' delegation was a Sikoka and ritual elder from Sana Dengoni who on this occasion represented the "affines" along with one of the girl's brothers. What followed was a direct reciprocal exchange between the parties joined in this marriage arrangement. First, an older member of the "agnatic group" brought a pot filled with distilled liquor and served it to the "affines," before the "affines" did the same for their hosts. Then the two bundles with meat were opened, with each party eating its portion. All this took place in a joking mood, with the anthropologist as the preferred object of mockery.

Following this light snack called *kalu jau* or "alcohol tiffin," consumed in public, the guests were invited to different houses of the groom's village and served a full meal (*paga*) consisting of rice and meat. When leaving, the "affines" took "one half" (*ra pakede*) of the buffalo, and both groups were additionally

---

[33] I assume that the relations between the two villages are similar to those described above for Dongormati and Lamba. In both cases, a Pusika village is joined to a Sikoka village, and the two assist each other with marriage arrangements and on the occasion of the buffalo sacrifice.

given one share of cooked meat for each house of their village. Before the bride-givers' departure, bride-givers and bride-takers discussed when they intended to organise the bride's procession to the groom's village. In this case, the boy's father suggested celebrating this final stage of the marriage the following week, but the girl's delegates disagreed, as the girl was expected to bid farewell to all her friends and relatives before her marriage. For this reason, they asked to postpone the procession for two weeks to give the bride enough time to visit her many relatives living in different villages.

4.3.6 *tone paga tinja hana* ("we go to eat the rice of friendship")

Soon after the bride's relatives pay a visit to her groom's house, she visits her mother's brother to say good bye. On this day, she is bathed in turmeric water by her dormitory friends (*ade*) behind her father's house. She then enters her parent's house and, along with her friends, is served food while her mother applies oil to her hair. Everybody is in a sad mood, the bride and her friends loudly lamenting her forthcoming departure. Afterward, a group consisting of the bride, her friends, and perhaps some elderly women leaves her father's house and goes to her mother's brother's village "to eat the meal of friendship" (*tone paga tinja hana*). Normally, they arrive in the evening and spend the night singing and dancing with the boys before retreating into the dormitory. If the bride intends to sleep with one of the boys in the same place, no one objects. Either the same evening or the next morning, the bride is again bathed with turmeric water by her friends behind the house before they all enter her mother's brother's house to eat the "meal of friendship" (*tone paga*). She is again anointed with oil, and she and her friends lament her fate like women bewailing a death. She may be given some presents, such as a *sari* or some bracelets, but all in all she receives rather few gifts on this occasion. Only later, at the time of the marriage procession, are the mother's brother and the other relatives who received a share of the "betrothal fee" expected to make a substantial contribution to the girl's "wedding gift".

This procedure is repeated in many households in the weeks before the marriage procession. However, instead of a full bath, the friends only rub a little turmeric provided by the relatives on the bride's face, and instead of eating a full meal in each house, the bride and her friends only take a handful of rice and place it next to the plate.[34] People say that the bride is going to visit her *gota*

---

[34] This is the usual procedure followed by Dongria when they want to show that they accept

are geti, the word *gota* here meaning "relatives" in general, while *geti* can be translated as "friends." All in all, she may visit ten to twelve villages, the most important of which are those where her female kin are residing after their marriages. These are the villages of
- her married elder sisters (*nanasika*)
- her father's sisters (*amaska*)
- her mother's sisters (*taliska*)
- her mother's mother (*aji*), if alive

Apart from them, the bride also visits those male agnates who reside in different villages, for example, those who are serving as *karjame* or who have decided to live uxorilocally after their marriage, or if her own father chose to live in his father-in-law's village, those relatives who live in the original villages of her local line.

People told me that the groom similarly bids farewell to his friends and relatives, but in a less elaborate manner. I have not personally seen such an occasion, but I have been informed that the groom and his friends are also invited to eat *tone paga* and to drink alcohol, mostly in the houses of his own village and in a small number of other villages. These visits of bride and groom, of course, also serve to inform the friends and relatives about the date set for the marriage and to invite them to attend the ceremony.

4.3.7 *hedi tana* ("we bring the girl from far away")

The procession is the major event of the marriage festivities and extends over three days, from Friday to Sunday. I personally witnessed the entire event twice and additionally collected information about a number of weddings that occurred in the past. In ritual terms, the main days are Friday and Saturday, when the specialists perform ceremonies inside and outside the village, but from the perspective of the young people, who assemble in large numbers, all three days are equally important as a time of joking, singing, dancing, and lovemaking. First the bride's village and later the groom's village are taken over by the boys and girls and literally converted into a *Kingdom of the Young* (Elwin 1968).[35] In order to present this complex event in a comprehensible way, the three days can be divided into the following ideal-typical sequence of events:

---

the hospitality but do not intend to eat the offered food. When the rice is placed next to the plate and not into the mouth, the food is not considered to be leftovers and can be eaten by everybody.
35 The title of Elwin's own abridgement of his *The Muria and their Ghotul* (1947).

***sukruwara* (Friday):**
- morning:
    - worship of *yatra kudi* (in bride's village)
    - worship of ancestors and house deities (separately in bride's and groom's houses)
- midday:
    - feast (*bana paga*; separately in bride's and groom's villages)
- evening:
    - bride and her friends go from house to house to bid farewell
    - groom's delegation and youth from different villages arrive in the bride's village
- night:
    - singing and dancing by young people; sleeping in the girls' dormitories

***saniwara* (Saturday):**
- morning:
    - feast (rice and lentils) in the bride's village
    - youth resume singing and dancing
    - ritual elders begin a ceremony (*bada*) at the river
    - shamans offer a sacrifice to evil ghosts
- afternoon:
    - bride and friends go in procession to the river
    - ritual elders sacrifice a hen and a pig in the river
- evening:
    - feast (rice and lentils) in the bride's village
    - bride's male relatives cook sacrificial pig
    - bride is bathed in turmeric water; adorning the bride
- night:
    - groom's people take *jiu manjing* ("rice-soul/life") to their village
    - bride and her friends go from house to house to bid farewell
    - singing and dancing by young people; sleeping in the girls' dormitories

***adiwara* (Sunday):**
- early morning:
    - villagers assemble, "wedding gift" is brought to the village plaza
- morning:
    - bride is taken in procession to the groom's village
- late morning:
    - procession reaches the river near the groom's village
    - shamans perform a sacrifice at a canopy near the river

- bride and groom walk around the canopy with their friends
- procession enters the groom's village
- sacrifice to the *koteiwali*
- bride enters the groom's father's house
– midday:
  - feast (rice and lentils; no meat) in the groom's village
  - ritual elders perform worship of new pots at the house shrine
  - groom's sister cooks and distributes *mat manjing* ("rice bundle")
– afternoon:
  - singing and dancing by young people
– evening:
  - feast (rice and lentils; no meat) in the groom's village
  - some people of the bride's party go home
  - singing and dancing by young people; sleeping in the girls' dormitories

These are, in short, the major events, which I will now elaborate and illustrate with concrete observations made during my participation in two such wedding ceremonies. The first marriage took place from 17 to 19 June 2001 in Sana Dengoni (bride's village) and Kata (groom's village), and the second was celebrated from 25 to 27 April 2003 in Gumma (bride's village) and Damanapanga (groom's village).

sukruwara (Friday)

On Friday morning, the bride's villagers prepare for the arrival of many guests by performing a short ceremony at the shrine of the *yatra kudi* or "house of procession [or festival]." This shrine is always located outside the village, usually by the side of the path that leads to the western entrance. The shrine consists of four wooden posts (*munda*) and a few crossbeams (*pate*) forming the roof. In ritual invocations, this place is referred to as *rengena munda rengena pate*, the word *rengena* denoting a withered old teak tree (*hergi mara*). Such a tree can be felled without committing a ritual mistake because the tree is considered to be dead, i.e., without a "soul" or "life" (*jela*).[36] In the centre of the shrine are two ridges made of earth, covered with white dust and forming an X. When invoking the goddess of this place, the shamans call her *chuli bate rupuli bate*, meaning "chalk way, silver way," as an allusion to the two white ridges in the centre.

---

[36] For detailed discussion of the words *jiu* and *jela*, see pp. 375–76, 481 and section 6.2.

On several ritual occasions, the villagers and their shamans celebrate the end of a procession at this place. Most festivals consist of two phases: in the beginning, deities and ancestors are called into the village, and at the end, they are accompanied out of the village as far as the *yatra kudi* in a farewell procession, literally to "throw them out" (*tuchpoli*). The *yatra kudi* thus marks the village border, which the gods and ancestors are requested to cross because their presence in the village may cause not only happiness and wellbeing but also harm and affliction. The realm of the dead and of ghosts, the cremation ground, is always located beyond the shrine, i.e., to the west of the *yatra kudi*. The goddess of this shrine is often associated with *aji budi* or the "old woman,"[37] the name of a highly dangerous goddess responsible for smallpox and other dangerous diseases, which she can cause and cure at the same time. She is further referred to as *thakurani* or "ruling goddess" of the village, as she is responsible for the villagers' wellbeing. As her shrine is located at the western border of the village, the west being the realm of very ambivalent, often potentially evil forces, it is her responsibility to guard the path leading into the village. If the villagers worship her properly, she prevents those coming with evil intentions from entering the Dongria's inhabited space.

For this reason, the shamans of the bride's village first of all perform a sacrifice to this goddess on Friday morning, a day on which they expect many visitors to enter their village. The shamans carry incense, a chick, and raw and cooked rice provided by the bride's house (*hedi ijo*) to the *yatra kudi*. The *bejuni* makes a small heap of paddy in front of the shrine before she takes the chick and holds it above the heap, from time to time coaxing it to peck at some grains. All the while she talks to the goddess, informing her about the events to come and begging her to protect the village from evil forces and to provide wellbeing and wealth instead. Then she twists off the chick's head, places it on the ground near the paddy heap, and simultaneously smears the blood trickling from its neck on the wooden posts and beams of the shrine. Next, she puts two leaf cups near the *yatra kudi*, one filled with paddy, the other with cooked rice. This offering is given to the ancestors and is referred to as *lita manjing* (oblation of raw rice) and *lita paga* (oblation of cooked rice), the word *lita*, like the Hindi word *pinda* (Parry 1985, 618), having the meaning of "body" as well as of "food" provided to the souls of the dead. The ancestors are invited to come from the cremation ground to the *yatra kudi* and partake of the offering of rice and liquor, which the *bejuni* pours on the ground. They are asked not to bring any diseases to the

---

[37] *Aji* is a Dongria term of address and reference for a grandmother, but like the Oriya word *budi*, it also means "old woman" in general.

villagers or their guests and not to disturb the festivities. The same is requested from the "undead" (*marha*) (see section 2.3.4), who are particularly feared because they can transfer their own terrible death experiences to living people. They are not called to the shrine. Rather, the *bejuni* first takes some raw rice into her fist and pleads with the "undead" to stay away and to refrain from causing any harm to the villagers; then she throws the grains towards the west. She then does the same with cooked rice. With this action, this short ritual has come to an end, and the shamans and their assistants, the *gurumeni*, sit down and share the two leaf plates of rice prepared by the bride's parents.

The next events to take place in both villages are ritual invocations and sacrifices, the major recipients of which are the family's ancestors and the house goddess. The groom's and the bride's parents perform this ceremony separately in their respective houses. They invite two specialists, the local *jani* to recite the ritual invocations to the ancestors and the village shaman (*bejuni*) to make offerings to the house goddess and other deities. Although both specialists come together in the same house, they work in different places. In the eastern part of the central room, each Dongria house has a hearth (*holu*) and a wall (*handani kuda*) dividing the ritual space into two parts (see appendixes 4 and 5: Dongria house).[38] The small room east of the wall is occupied by the *jani* and his two assistants (*bahuki*), while the *bejuni* and her helpers sit west of the wall. The small room where the *jani* performs his invocations is called *kandadae* and is used for reciting sacred verses to gods and ancestors during marriage and death ceremonies. During this work, the *jani* never falls into trance, but rather sits cross-legged in this small room, striking small bells against his knee while rhythmically reciting verses to the ancestors, which are repeated in the same singing tone by his assistants. This kind of performance is called *dakina*, a word often used by Dongria to translate the Oriya (and Hindi) word *puja*, but denoting in a more limited sense only this special type of recitation by the *jani*. Common people do not understand the meaning of these recitations, which are said to make the gods and

---

38 The exact position of hearth and wall depends on the location of the house in relation to the stones representing the earth goddess in the centre of the village. The wall for worshipping the house goddess and ancestors is always located close to the door that opens to the veranda and to the shrine of the earth goddess on the village plaza, which is the men's meeting place. The hearth is closer to the back door, leading to the space normally occupied by women and to the realm behind or outside the village. Each house is thus divided into two halves: the "male" half where gods and ancestors are worshipped, and the "female" half with the hearth and the room for birth and menses. House goddess, family ancestors, and male family members represent the permanent aspects of the local community, and it may be argued that the hearth, with its closeness to the room for birth and menses, is associated with the villagers' dependence on women coming from outside, who nourish them and give birth to their children.

ancestors "understand" (*puna*) why a certain ritual is performed and for what purpose. These "explanations" (*wechna* or "we explain") are given in a highly metaphorical language and with frequent reference to mythological events.[39]

By contrast to the *jani*, the *bejuni* falls into a trance (*banga ane*) during her ritual invocations, which are called *male wenbina*, the latter word deriving from a Dongria verb, *wena*, which simultaneously means "listening" and "demanding." This corresponds well to the pattern of the ritual, which consists of two actions, listening to the wishes of the gods and expressing one's own demands to them. The shaman's ritual is essentially a dialogue between humans and gods, the shaman being both, since the gods use her body as a seat and speak through her mouth. She and her assistants (*gurumeni*) sit in front of the sacred wall or *handani kuda* in a space referred to as *madre ijo* or "inner house." Above them is the roof, where the family keeps its sacred grains in a gourd (*kaktedia*) representing the goddess of the house, *sita penu-lahi penu*. From there she descends to be worshipped by the *bejuni*. The rituals of the *jani* and the *bejuni* are clearly ranked in relation to each other, with the *dakina* of the *jani* considered the major work (*kaja kama*). It is always performed by male specialists, usually older men, although I also witnessed a death ritual in which the main *jani* was no older than perhaps twenty-five. Similarly, his two assistants (*bahuki*), who can become the main *jani* in the future, are always men.

At first sight, these two ritual performances do not appear to be so different, as both *jani* and *bejuni* sit on the ground, hold a chicken in front of them, and from time to time coax it to peck at some grains. However, the *jani* recites verses and narrates mythological events repeated by his assistants in a monotonous way, his words being mostly addressed to the house's ancestors, represented by three heaps of rice. Occasionally, he interrupts his recitations and offers alcohol provided by the householder to the gods and ancestors before he and his *bahuki* drink the rest themselves. The whole performance takes about two hours, by which time the *jani* and his assistants are relatively drunk. The end of the ritual is marked by the offering of a chicken and a pig inside the *kandadae* after the ritual specialists have left. The actual sacrifice is performed by a young man of the

---

39 Towards the end of my stay, I was allowed to tape-record such recitations spoken on a completely different occasion, the worship of the mango tree. It is a future project to translate these recordings with the help of the specialists, as they are almost unintelligible to ordinary people. When the *dakina* is performed inside a house or on other major occasions like the buffalo sacrifice, the specialists prohibit any recording, as they are afraid that this may drive the gods and ancestors away or result in a kind of theft of these beings by the anthropologist.

house or a neighbour. Then the *jani* again enters the *kandadae* and offers the blood and head of the victims to the gods and ancestors.

In contrast to the *jani*, the *bejuni* actually becomes possessed by the gods and speaks with their voice. Her assistants, the *gurumeni*, do not fall into trance but function as interpreters, because they understand what the gods, i.e., the shamans, are saying and are able to respond in the metaphorical language they use.[40] The trance session always follows the same pattern. At first the *bejuni* stands in front of the wall holding some paddy in her fist, and explaining the reason for the session, she invites the gods to come to the house. She then throws the paddy against the wall, sits down, and begins to fall into a slow rhythm of utterances interrupted by humming sounds. After about half an hour, her voice suddenly changes to a higher tone, and she increases the speed of her utterances until she gives a shrug, the clear indication that a deity has possessed her. The trance may last for an hour or an hour and a half, during which many gods announce their arrival through the shaman. Each time a deity arrives, the *gurumeni* communicates with the deity, demands his or her help, and offers gifts bought by the house owner, normally paddy and one or two chickens, in return. The shaman responds on behalf of the gods in the same metaphorical way, while holding the chicken in both hands. Before the god departs, she coaxes the chicken to peck at some rice as an offering to the god. Then she tears out a feather, which she puts either into her hair knot or next to the paddy heap in front of her. These actions clearly show that the bird has a double function: it represents the god, who partakes in the rice offering through the chicken, and it serves as an offering to the god, who is given a feather as a symbol of his share of the sacrificial animal. The chickens are only killed at the end of the session, after all the deities have been invited. When the house deities or some other important gods and goddesses arrive, the *gurumeni* calls the inhabitants, especially the children, to make a separate offering. The *bejuni* holds the chicken in the direction of the family member and pours some rice into his or her right hand. The bird pecks some grains out of the person's hand, this being a sign that the deity has accepted the offering.

When all the gods have been invited, the trance session is interrupted, and the *bejuni* and *gurumeni* leave the ritual space. They wait until the woman of the house has prepared some rice called *bana paga* ("rice of the forest") in a new earthen pot on her hearth. At the same time, some men cut the meat of the sac-

---

40 I have recorded such "dialogues with gods" and have translated a whole trance session held during a major harvest ritual with the help of the shamans from Gumma. I plan to publish this translation and my interpretation in the future.

rificial animals (pig and chickens) into pieces and cook it in separate pots. When everything is prepared, the *bejuni* first makes numerous small heaps of boiled and raw rice mixed with small pieces of cooked liver on a leaf plate in front of the *handani kuda*. These are the shares of the different gods invited to the feast. Next, she takes the pot with *bana paga* and spreads a good portion of it onto another, larger leaf plate in front of her. She then sits down and offers the food to the gods by calling their different names and by reminding them again of the purpose of this ceremony. At the end of her recitation, she first calls the male members of the house, who come to her one after the other and stretch out their open right hands. She places a piece of cooked liver mixed with a fistful of *bana paga* from the large leaf plate in their hands, a procedure referred to as *hupinari*. This expression is probably derived from the verb *hupi-*, which means "to spit." Next, the female members and the children of the house are served *bana paga* in the same way, before everybody else gets a share.

There are certain similarities between this distribution of *bana paga* and the allocation of *bhoga* or *prasada* in Hindu temples (e. g., Fuller 1992, 74 ff.). In both cases, the food is first offered to the deities, before the people are allowed to eat. The special way the *bejuni* gives *bana paga* to the members of the house and others may thus be interpreted as the gods feeding the people through the shaman. The shaman is their bodily representation, who "spits out" (*hupina*) portions of what they have eaten. Just as parents feed their children, gods feed the members of the house in this case. Like Fuller, who stresses that the gift of *prasada* is not a transaction because "the deity is served a meal, which the worshipper later consumes" (1992, 78), we may point out that in this feast gods and people do not exchange food; rather, the gods eat the food cooked by the family members and share it with them again by "spitting out" portions of it.

With these offerings and sacrifices, both families try to ensure the help of the gods and ancestors for the following festivities and for the future of the newly married couple. After receiving food and alcohol, they are expected to be satisfied and not interested in doing harm to the people of the house. The small ceremony at the *yatra kudi* and the more elaborate performance in the house thus have the same purpose but different addressees: the first ritual is addressed to the main village goddess and the community's ancestors, while the second ritual seeks the assistance of the house goddess and the family's ancestors in particular.

In the afternoon, before the guests arrive, the bride again goes from house to house with her friends to eat rice and to be anointed with oil and turmeric. When dealing with the events of the buffalo sacrifice (*kodru parbu*) in the next chapter (see section 5.3.4), we will see that the buffalo is treated in exactly the same way as the bride. While the bride laments her fate and says goodbye to her friends, neighbours, and relatives, the groom's fellow villagers get ready to travel to the bride's village. In all villages, the young people dress up for the big event after taking baths and washing their hair with the seeds of the *siali* creeper.

On Friday evening, the groom's people begin heading towards the bride's village, the groom himself usually remaining at home. If they pass through a village of their lineage brothers on the way, they carry some rice and pork prepared in the morning to give to their relatives. The groom's "sisters," i.e., the girls of his village, take a basket full of paddy, some turmeric tubers, a pot of alcohol, and an iron-tipped arrow. All these things will later be given to the bride's people and used on the next day for the main ritual in a river. The groom's people are accompanied by a large number of boys and girls, many of them coming from neighbouring villages that belong to the same clan as the bride-takers.

For example, on the first day of the marriage between a boy from Kata and a girl from Sana Dengoni, I climbed up the steep mountain to the plateau where Kata is located. I was in the company of a group of girls from Gumma, who were carrying all their clothes and jewellery in bundles as it was raining heavily. After arriving in Kata, which belongs to the same clan as Gumma, they straight-away entered the houses, were served with food by their relatives, and dressed up for the event. Meanwhile, several girls turned up in the village, assembled, and then, along with the groom's father and "sisters," went in procession towards the bride's village. On the way, they stopped at a place considered to be the boundary (*handi*) of their own territory. A *bejuni* came, took a small chick, and coaxed it to peck at some rice grains before someone twisted the animal's head off to offer blood to the god of the border. Upon our arrival in the village, the girls went behind the houses to talk to their friends, while the few boys assembled on the village plaza. The young men usually leave their villages much later, shortly before it gets dark, because, I assume, they want to have a drink at their own *salap* tree before they join the festivities. In this case, however, I met many young Dongria sitting in front of the Dombo houses of a neighbouring village, Bada Dengoni, waiting to be served distilled liquor sold for five to ten rupees a *kanch*.[41]

After sunset, small groups of boys and girls enter the village and literally turn it into a huge party ground. The bride stays inside her parents' house, and the groom is absent, but everybody else is busy singing and dancing. Behind and in front of both rows of houses, wherever a suitable place can be found, small groups of boys and girls form. Four or five boys and a similar number of girls form two half-circles facing each other. The girls hold each other by put-

---

41 A *kanch* contains approximately 650 ml.

ting their arms around those standing to the right and to the left, the first one in the half-circle usually being the lead singer. She sets the rhythm with an instrument consisting of small bells (*janjing*), which she keeps in her free hand. When the girls sing, both groups move slowly, step by step, in a clockwise direction. When the boys sing, they all dance counterclockwise. If the girls are leading the dance, they bend down; if the boys are controlling the movement, they do the same, while one or two of them play the flat drum (*dhapu*).

In the past, only boys and girls belonging to different clans could join in a dance, partly because the songs are dialogues with sexual content and are therefore considered inappropriate between brothers and sisters. Nowadays, it is no longer considered a serious mistake if a girl and a boy of the same clan join in a dance, on condition that a special form of address is used by the singers. When affines dance with each other, the girls begin their song by saying *jemu jemu jodi lo*, "let's start, let's start, let's mix," the word *jodi* having a clear sexual connotation, and the boys respond *jemu jemu sarilo*, "let's start, let's start, wives." In a dance participated in by members of the same clan, the girls begin by singing *jemu jemu tadale budale*, "let's start, let's start, elder brother, younger brother," and the boys reply by saying *jemu jemu nanale boile*, "let's start, let's start, elder sister, younger sister." After many hours of dancing and singing, couples go either into the dormitories, into the back rooms of some houses, or into the woods. Older people and unsuccessful boys and girls stretch out on the floor in one of the tidy front rooms of their hosts. One has to watch one's belongings, as people feel at liberty to do things prohibited under normal circumstances.

saniwara (Saturday)
Before sunrise, villagers and guests get up, and the girls immediately begin cooking rice and vegetable broth in their dormitory to be served to all visitors. Meanwhile, the men of the village visit the *salap* trees along with their male guests. As there is never enough *salap* sap for everybody to get drunk, some will have stored country liquor bought from the Dombo the day before. I remember getting up in a Dongria house in Sana Dengoni where I had spent the night along with the groom's father and some of his brothers, and as the first action of the morning they drank a bottle of alcohol they had secretly kept in a corner of the veranda. Throughout the day, the men drink and spend all their money buying alcohol from the Dombo, who turn up late in the morning with large aluminium vessels containing alcohol made from *mohula* flowers (*irpi kalu* or *puyu kalu*), mangoes (*amba kalu*), or sugarcane (*gudu kalu*). Girls also drink, but they usually wait to be invited rather than buy alcohol themselves, and in contrast to men, they never

get seriously drunk. If a girl is very fond of a certain boy, she may also agree to buy him a drink, but more often it is the other way round. Sometimes, older women can be seen getting heavily intoxicated before falling asleep on somebody's veranda, but I have never seen younger women doing the same. For younger boys, a marriage or a buffalo sacrifice is often an occasion to get heavily drunk for the first time and make a fool of themselves. Those who join the dancing groups remain relatively sober and adopt a kind of serious attitude, while the rest often drink as much as they can afford, turning to scrounging once their purses are empty.

On Saturday, more groups of young people turn up, and the village gets crowded. Those who do not dance sit in a corner, and people coming from the same village often stay together in one place. As it is the hottest time of the year, the dancing groups mostly assemble under large trees in the vicinity of the mountain streams near the village. The young people are sometimes joined by the old men of the village, while the middle-aged married men and women do not participate in the dancing and merrymaking. The father of the groom from Kata once explained to me that a married man stops dancing and sleeping with dormitory girls when his beard grows, something that normally happens between thirty and forty. In Sana Dengoni, I saw some old men who were extremely drunk joining the circle of dancers carrying a food plate (*tali*) or a miniature drum normally used by children. To everybody's amusement, they began singing and drumming with these "instruments," imitating and mocking the boys, who in their turn pushed them around and made fun of them. Such joking behaviour between members of alternate generations (e. g., between -1 and +1) is a common feature in many Central Indian societies, particularly among the Juang (McDougal 1963a, 144–46; 1964), where cooperation between boys and elders is highly institutionalised, for example in the context of the men's house (*majang*) (McDougal 1963a, 177–80). Among the Dongria, boys and elders do not form a generation set as among the Juang, but they enjoy a joking relationship, the young men mocking the old people for their childish behaviour, their drunkenness, and their general lack of care for hair or dress, and the old people in return laughing at the boys' seriousness as they try to impress the girls with their drumming, singing, and dancing.

The same elders are responsible for conducting the most important ritual of the marriage ceremony, the invocation of the goddess of wealth, *sita penu-lahi penu*, in a mountain stream (*jodi*) east of the village. This ritual is called *bada* and is performed in the context of all major religious functions concerning the house, like the big-man festival (*ghanta parba*) and the death rites (*dosa karma*) for a family member. It falls into the category of *dakina* rituals, as it is only performed by male *jani* priests, who do not fall into trance but recite incantations to make the goddess "understand" what is going to happen and what they expect from her. The main aim of the ritual is to convince the goddess of wealth to take away all bad influences from the bride and to take care that the girl has a good life in her new home, that she and her children get enough to eat and are treated well. Dongria also say that the purpose of this ceremony is to "meet" (*hena*) the goddess *sita penu-lahi penu*, whom they call *laksmi* in Oriya. The *bada* is always linked to another ritual called *giri takoli* or "bringing the path," the idea being that after worshipping *sita penu-lahi penu* in the river, the goddess is brought from the "path" (*giri*) into the house. The groom's family celebrates the *giri takoli* on Monday following the wedding procession, whereas the bride's people perform it two days later, when their daughter, accompanied by her new husband, returns for a short visit to her natal village. The location of the *bada* ceremony, the river, is linked to the purificatory functions of the rite. For example, after a death of a family member, the householder takes the water (*bada eyu*) from the place of the *bada* ceremony to his house and sprinkles (*raskina*) the walls with it. The same happens during the *bada* of a marriage ceremony, with the difference that not the house but the bride is sprinkled with water.

The position of the sun marks the beginning and end of the ceremony. The three *jani* should begin their recitations in the morning, when the sun is behind them, and finish the sacrifice in the afternoon, when they look into the sun. They sit on stones in the river at a place where it flows from east to west. This is the direction the sun god, *dharmuraja*, travels in his chariot throughout the day before he "dies" in the west at the time of sunset.[42] In the river, at a place with dense forest, three flat stones (*patang*) are carefully washed with water and then used to erect a small altar. The main *jani* sits down on another stone in front of this altar, takes some turmeric powder, and draws a rectangle divided into three parts. On this diagram he puts three leaves of the *wada* tree, five stalks of *bedunika* grass, and on top of that a lump of earth consisting of three types of soil (*wirga*) and representing *sita penu-lahi penu*: soil from the river (*jodi wirga*), soil from the hole of a crab (*janapipi wirga*), and soil from a termite hill (*puci wirga*). Depending on the traditions followed by the *jani*, this lump may be formed into a ball or into a figure. The *jani* of Lamba, for example, always gave it the shape of a small animal resembling a turtle by modelling a body with a head and an open mouth, four legs, and a tail. However, Dongria them-

---

42 Once I was sitting with a Dongria friend in the mountains in the evening, under a *salap* tree, and pointed out to him the beautiful red sun, which was disappearing behind a hill. He immediately scolded me, saying that I should not look in this direction, as the god is dying and it brings bad luck to anyone who sees it.

selves do not compare this object to a particular animal but interpret it as a *linga* or "symbol" of the goddess. This representation of *sita penu-lahi penu* is decorated with grains of rice and a one-rupee coin. The *jani* lights a small lamp and some incense on another stone before he puts the arrow brought by the bride-takers into the water with the point down. A white thread is then made to hang down from the other end of the arrow to the image of the goddess. Dongria explain that the goddess climbs down this thread to be worshipped by the *jani*. The same type of thread is used on a variety of occasions when the goddess is invited, such as house ceremonies and mountain rituals.[43]

Next, the main *jani* and his two assistants (*bahuki*) go to the western side of the stone altar, stand in front of the goddess, hold rice in their right fists, and begin invoking her while facing east, the direction from which she is expected to arrive. They explain to her the purpose of the ritual and invite her to come to the altar. When she is considered to be present, the three specialists throw the rice in her direction and again move to the other side of the altar, where they sit down on three stones and face west, with the main *jani* sitting in the middle. First, they offer some liquor to the goddess before drinking a leaf cup of alcohol themselves. The liquor, as well as the animals to be sacrificed at the end of the worship, have to be provided by the groom's father. The three specialists now begin their incantations, the main *jani* always uttering one sentence, which is then repeated by his two assistants. All three sit on a stone and keep their feet in the water while rhythmically striking small bells (*muyanga*) against their knees. From time to time they interrupt the ceremony to drink more alcohol and to chat and joke with those people who have come to observe the ritual. These are mainly members of the bride's and groom's family, as well as shamans and other more religiously minded villagers.

I observed the *bada* ceremony on several occasions, and it always took place in a more or less peaceful and harmonious atmosphere, except for the second day of the wedding ceremony performed by the villages of Kata and Sana Dengoni. One reason was that the main *jani*, who lived in the bride's village, had started drinking early in the morning, and as he continued to "offer" liquor to the goddess, he became extremely drunk. Most people standing around and watching the event argued about replacing him with another *jani* from the groom's village, who was already present and in a bad mood because he had not been appointed as the main *jani*. When this second *jani* tried to take over the main position in the ceremony, the other one resisted him initially but

---

43 In the context of other rituals, long bamboo or wooden poles serve the same function, as they allow the gods living "above" (*lekha:a*) to come down to the people living "below" (*talani*).

after some time was so intoxicated that he slipped from his stone and fell into the water. This was the moment for the second *jani* to assume control and to continue the recitations in a proper way. The *jani* from the bride's village left angry, and it was only after some of his villagers persuaded him to return that he came back to the river and after some time was allowed to resume the worship, not, of course, without resistance from the groom's *jani*.

While the two main actors took these events very seriously, most onlookers laughed at these two drunken old men and their fights. Only some were worried that the worship was not performed in a proper way and would therefore not yield the expected results. To the *jani*, of course, it was a matter of status to be selected as the main priest, and I have seen similar fights for precedence on the occasion of buffalo sacrifices. I suspect that in this case the direct competition between the two *jani* was a further reason for the conflict. In most cases, the bride's *jani* is from a different clan from the groom's *jani*, and there will be no direct competition between them, as their responsibilities are clearly defined. On this occasion, however, both ritual specialists came from villages belonging to the same clan and even from the same *muta* and were therefore competing directly for the position of the main *jani* in this area.

In the afternoon, the *jani* puts some rice on top of the arrow and coaxes a chicken to peck at these grains as an offering to the goddess. Meanwhile, the bride comes in procession from the village, accompanied by many girls and boys as well as a few older women, all singing *wamule adele*, "come, oh friend." The bride walks while embracing her best friend (*ade*), both being covered by a shawl. When arriving at the river, the two girls jointly step into the water west of the stone and face the main *jani* standing upstream on the other side of the altar. The specialist takes two long leaves, of the type also used at the time the girl first enters the groom's house, and sprinkles both with water while reciting verses for the bride's purification. The main aim of this ritual is to take away *dosa* or "mistakes" and bad behaviour from her and to free her from bad influences, such as those produced by witchcraft (*pangana*). Among the Kui Kond studied by Barbara Boal, it is the duty of the mother's brother to remove spells that might be attached to the bride. Kui Kond do not seem to perform the *bada* ceremony like the Dongria, but when the bride visits her mother's brother's house, he sprinkles her with water while chanting the following verses:

> All those malicious men, spiteful men, men of hatred, men of anger
> Men of sorcery, men of witchcraft,
> Let them not touch my child! Let them not sport with her!
> Let men of hatred, malicious men, be totally destroyed!
> May the young men come to the front of the village and its back for my child!

May she have many children! May she acquire a good home and family.
May everything go well for her. (Boal 1999, 46–47).

As part of these blessings of the bride, the goddess's support of the goddess is ensured by offering sacrifices while the girl and her friend are still standing in the water. First, the *jani* pulls out the arrow, uses its point to cut off the chicken's head, and drops the body into the river. Second, somebody else takes the pig provided by the groom, holds it so that its head is in the water and its body on the riverbank, cuts off its head with a knife, and throws the body into the stream. The blood flows downstream and passes the bride and her friend standing in the water.

At first, I interpreted this event as a sacrifice to the river goddess, *gungi*, but everybody assured me that it is offered in the name of *sita penu-lahi penu*. This, however, left me with the question of why the ritual has to be performed in the water when *sita penu-lahi penu* can also be worshipped on the path or inside the house. Only later, when I began to understand the concept of ancestors and spirits, did I start to comprehend that this ritual is meant to send away those evil forces who surround the bride and may cause harm to her. As mentioned above, the water flows towards the west, the place where the ancestors (*mahane*) and the "undead" (*marha*) live and the direction towards which potentially harmful gods are sent away. All sorts of suffering are created by certain gods, ancestors, and evil spirits who sit on a person and eat her or his "life" (*jela*), contained in the blood. In my interpretation of the event described above, these forces are sent back to their place by giving them a substitute, the blood of a pig, which is carried by the water to the west. As it passes the bride, it attracts the spirits sitting on her body, and the spirits leave her in order to get a share of the blood flowing in the water.

At the place of worship, the villagers remove the stones and throw away the leaves and the lump of earth representing the earth goddess. The pig is taken away by men from the bride's village, who cut it into pieces, cook it along with some rice and turmeric, and share it among themselves. The use of turmeric when cooking pork indicates that it is considered to be impure. When Dongria catch a pig and bind it to a stick for transportation, they usually wash their hands with turmeric paste and water. The pig's jaw or sometimes the whole head, as well as the stomach and intestines, is thrown outside the village behind the two rows of houses.

After returning to the village, some girls begin cooking rice and vegetable broth (*jau*) for the feast in the evening, to which all the guests are invited. Inside the bride's house, the girl's father of the girl measures out one *mana* (about four kilograms) of rice and ties it up in a piece of cloth. This bundle is handed over to the groom's fellow villagers, who immediately leave the village and take it home. This rice is referred to as *jiu manjing* or "rice-soul" and is identified with the "life" of the bride. The bride herself and some of her best friends go straight back to her parents' house, where the young women begin grinding turmeric tubers and bring water from the river. Behind her house, the bride is given a bath, and turmeric paste is smeared all over her body. Next, she is dressed up by her friends, who wrap a new *sari* around her body and adorn her with all kinds of jewellery. I could not personally attend this occasion, but when my wife from Germany visited me during my fieldwork in Gumma, a kind of small marriage ceremony was arranged for the two of us. She was taken behind my hut, bathed with turmeric and water, and dressed in a new white *sari* with a coloured border. On this occasion, a few girls from Gumma played the role of her dormitory friends and joined the bath. As she later told me, a few old women also undressed and took a bath in turmeric water, this perhaps being another indication that members of alternate generations do cooperate in ritual contexts.

In Sana Dengoni, a transgender shaman assumed the responsibility of preparing the bride for the following day. Born as a man, she at some time in her life had begun dressing as a woman and adopted a high voice and female gestures. I knew her well, as she performed the function of the local shaman in a village close to the place where I lived. Imitating the use of female terms by others, I considered her my elder sister and addressed her accordingly as *nana* (eZ). Everybody referred to her as *beju* or "male shaman" only when she worked as a ritual specialist, perhaps because a *beju* always has higher status than his female counterpart, the *bejuni*. In the area where I lived, I knew of at least three *beju* who were transgender, one of them regularly sleeping in the girls' dormitory of her village. In contrast to a female shaman, a transgender *beju* does not marry.[44] On marriage occasions, they stress their social affiliation to the group of unmarried girls by singing and dancing with them. In this case, the *beju* not only took care to bathe and adorn the girl but also accompanied her all the way to her husband's village. She taught the girls songs and dances and was accepted as the leader of their group. During the procession the next day, she never left the bride's side, and when necessary, she carried her in her arms through the river, as the bride is not supposed to touch water on her way. On this Saturday evening, the *beju* accompanied the bride and her girlfriends from house to house, where she is given a plate of rice by her relatives

---

44 This does not mean that all *beju* are unmarried. For example, the *beju* of Lamba is married and has a daughter, and unlike these transgender *beju*, he exhibited no interest in being considered a woman.

and neighbours for the last time. The women of the village wait in the front room of their respective houses and lament the girl's departure by singing *adele badale, gayalo badalo* again and again, the words *ade* and *gaya* meaning "girlfriend," while *bada* is probably derived from the Oriya word for "groom."[45] Inside the house, the householder's wife cries while giving a plate of rice to the bride and her two friends, who wail loudly.

While it is expected of the bride and the other female villagers that they bemoan the girl's departure, the visitors can continue singing and dancing. Towards evening, the boys approach the girls sitting on the verandas of different houses and begin joking with them. If a boy is interested in a particular girl, he asks her whether she can "mix" (*adine*) with him, meaning whether they stand in a relationship allowing them to sleep in the same place. Everybody present discusses their relationship by inquiring into their clan names, their village connections, and possible kinship links between their families. This takes place in a very casual and joking atmosphere, and if they come to the conclusion that a sexual relationship is forbidden between the two, she answers, *adi:e*, "there will be no mixing." If sexual relations are not prohibited, the boy may try to grab the girl's shawl and run away. Taking away the girl's shawl is a clear indication that he wants to sleep with her, and if the girl shows no resistance, she silently agrees to meet him that night, either in the dormitory or some other place. However, if she is not interested in him or if she wants to tease him, she asks her friends to help her chase the boy in order to recover the shawl.

When the young people search for a partner to spend the night with, fights often break out between the boys. As everybody is quite drunk, people lose their restraint, and old disputes may become the cause of quarrels between them. It may further be the case that a boy becomes jealous because somebody else has forcibly taken the shawl of a girl he is in love with. To prevent the outbreak of serious combats, Dongria often arrange for some Dombo to be present who act as peacemakers. The Dombo go around, talk to the enraged boys, calm them down, and take away their axes, as they may quickly turn to physical fighting. The girls perform the same function, trying to separate the fighters or snatch their weapons away from them. The whole atmosphere is characterised by a mix of joking, merrymaking, and sexuality on the one hand, and aggression, threats, and fighting on the other. This is another way in which a marriage cere-

---

45 According to Nayak (1989, 145), the women sing *ademee badale, danse demalo gaya mu badalo,* which he translates as "dear friend, you are leaving us for your unworthy husband's house." The expression *danse demalo* is unknown to me, and I do not see a word or phrase that can be translated as husband's house, as neither the Dongria nor the Oriya word for house, *ijo* or *ghara,* appears in this sentence.

mony closely resembles a buffalo sacrifice, as we will see in chapter five (see pp. 591–95).

adiwara (Sunday)

Early next morning before sunrise, everybody assembles on the village plaza. The bride's friends bring various items given to the girl as a "wedding gift" by her relatives. A standard "wedding gift" includes a number of brass vessels (*dokanga*), small brass containers (*mutang*), food plates (*talenga*), bowls (*kadambanga*), and aluminium boxes (*arkusi*) containing clothing (*gandanga*). The brass vessels are bought in special shops in town for about Rs 500 each. The number of *dokanga* actually given depends on how rich the bride's family is and how much of the "betrothal fee" the bride's relatives have received. In the two marriage processions I personally attended, five and six of such water vessels were given, but I also heard about marriages where between eight and fourteen brass pots were handed over. After attending the marriage ceremony in Kata, some women in Gumma immediately asked me how many vessels the bride's people had taken in their procession to the groom's village, the number being a clear indication of the wealth and status of the bride-givers. As for the boxes, their number usually does not exceed one or two, and as they are closed, nobody can see what exactly is inside. The number of plates, bowls, and smaller brass pots varied between four and six of each in the cases I observed.

In my experience, gift expectations among the Dongria Kond are not highly standardised. Among the Jreda Kond, by contrast, informants were quite certain about the gifts expected from the relatives who got a share of the "betrothal fee". Those who receive a buffalo are expected to reciprocate with ten *mana* of husked rice, two *sari*, one brass pot, one brass mug, and one brass plate. The relatives who take a cow must give the bride five *mana* of husked rice, one *sari*, one brass mug, and one brass plate. Finally, those who accept a goat have to provide a feast to the bride's people. On the day of the procession, the bride is given her "wedding gift", consisting of the mentioned items and many prestations made by various relatives, neighbours, and clan members who come and bring some rice, a *sari*, or a pot. According to Jreda Kond informants, the total "wedding gift" collected consists of about twenty to thirty *puti* of rice, two hundred *saris*, and several brass vessels, mugs, plates, and bowls.

Among the Dongria, the relatives who claimed a share of the total "betrothal fee" are similarly expected to make certain counter-prestations. The parents of the bride usually contribute gold jewellery, a box of clothes, and a few metal items, such as vessels, pots, and plates. Similarly, the father's sisters and bride's sisters make a gift consisting of jewellery or cookware. Each member of the bride's father's local line is expected to give at least one of the expensive brass vessels and may additionally present some plates, mugs, or bowls. The important and wealthy householders of the bride's village add some brass plates and bowls to the "wedding gift" or present money for buying jewellery. Further items may be given by villagers who received a gift from the bride's parents at the time of their own daughter's marriage. Apart from the parents, the mother's brother gives the most substantial gift, but I received different information concerning the relation between his share of the "betrothal fee" and his contribution to the "wedding gift". While the *barika* of Gumma insisted that the mother's brother is expected to make a gift worth double the share he received as "betrothal fee", two experienced development workers rejected this idea and argued that no fixed rules exist concerning the mother's brother's contribution. In their experience, he should not give much less than he received, or else people may talk badly about him. This information was confirmed by a Dombo woman of Gumma who explained to me that Dombo and Dongria have quite different expectations of the mother's brother: among the Dombo, the niece presents a nominal amount, such as five rupees, to her uncle before the marriage and then expects to be given gold jewellery, clothing, and brass vessels by him; among the Dongria, on the other hand, a mother's brother is given a much higher amount of money and is then expected to make an equivalent counter-gift at his niece's marriage. The main gifts expected from a mother's brother are gold ornaments, clothing, and brass items.

This general outline can best be illustrated by data from a marriage that took place in Gumma during the time of my fieldwork. The girl, Sikoka Bambu, belonged to one of the high-status families that trace their origins back to the village founders. She had been demanded by a Kadraka family from Damanapanga, who paid Rs 16,000 as "betrothal fee" to the girl's parents. Out of this total sum, Rs 3,000 were given to the bride's mother's brother, Rs 2,000 to her father's sister, and Rs 2,000 to the village as a whole, and the remaining Rs 9,000 were divided among the members of her father's local line, consisting of eight householders. Within this group, her father took the largest share, while the others got equal amounts. On the day of her marriage, her parents provided her with a box of clothing, a brass vessel, a brass bowl, and a few smaller metal items. Altogether, six of these large brass vessels, along with six brass plates and one bowl, were carried to her groom's village on the day of her procession. Four members of her father's local line had given one brass vessel each, one was provided by her father's sister, and one was given by a fellow villager who was reciprocating a gift he had received from the bride's father at his own daughter's marriage. The bride also received jewellery from the two village leaders, the *member* and the *naika*, and from her mother's brother, although I cannot say exactly how much.

In a second case, I have more, but somewhat inconsistent information concerning the mother's brother's contribution. The bride, named Kurmi, belonged to a Sikoka household of Gumma. The groom's parents, from Sagdi, had paid Rs 16,000 as a "betrothal fee", of which Rs 4,000 were paid to the mother's brother. On the day of the marriage, he reciprocated with a gift to his niece of gold jewellery worth Rs 1,500, according to information given by the *barika*. I remember the mother's brother disputing this amount, claiming to have given more than he had received. The father of the bride, on the other hand, told me that the mother's brother presented jewellery worth Rs 1,000 only.

This illustrates the difficulties in getting correct information about the exact amounts exchanged. The only way to get reliable data is to be present when the "wedding gift" or the "betrothal fee" is handed over, but even then it is impossible to be certain whether the different shares assigned to various relatives are actually distributed or how the share for the "house" is in fact divided among the members of the local line. When it comes to the total amount of the "betrothal fee", the bride-givers usually provide better information than the bride-takers, who exaggerate the amount they paid because it is a clear sign of their wealth and status. The same holds for the different shares of the total "betrothal fee", as the recipients understate the money they received and exaggerate the amount they presented as part of the "wedding gift". The best information is usually provided by the *barika*. He normally has a good overview of the different transactions, because he lends the money or purchases the animals sold by the relatives to fulfil their gift-giving obligations.

In the Dongria language, the prestations constituting the "wedding gift" are collectively referred to as *lahi jau*, *lahi* meaning "rice" and *jau* denoting the cooked pulses or vegetable broth served along with it. These gifts stress the wife's role as the provider of food for her new family. In fact, some of the gift items are clearly linked to cooking, such as the huge brass vessels used for carrying water and the plates and bowls for serving rice and soup to guests. As mentioned above, the goddess of the house is named *sita penu-lahi penu*, as she makes the rice grow and provides food to her "children," the family members. Like the goddess, who is considered a bringer of wealth, similar to *laksmi* in the Hindu context, the bride brings gold jewellery, clothing, and brass items with her to add to the house's wealth. If she dies, her relatives can demand to be shown the jewellery, but they cannot claim it back.

On Sunday morning, the villagers take the bride in procession to her groom's village. The boys belonging to the group of bride-takers go ahead, either the night before or early in the morning. According to Nayak (1989, 145), the boys have to pay some money when they pass through villages belonging to other *muta*. Personally, I have neither seen nor heard about this, and it is not exactly clear what Nayak means by "other *muta*," whether the clan territory of the bride, of the groom, or indeed of people belonging to neither the bride's nor the groom's clan. As they are referred to as *gotanga* (Nayak 1989, 145), which in this case probably means "affines," I assume that the boys may have to pay some money if they pass through a village belonging to the clan of the bride. The bride follows with her girlfriends, some of them assisting her to walk, the others carrying the items making up her "wedding gift". The bride walks under a white piece of cloth and laments loudly, while her friends repeat the song about the bride going to her husband. When they pass through a village where her relatives live, she enters their houses and symbolically accepts the "rice of friendship." Relatives and friends may be very emotional. For example, I remember a Dombo woman who embraced a Dongria bride from a neighbouring village for a long time, both crying and weeping. Just like the groom's people on their way to the girl's village, the bride's people perform a small sacrifice of a hen at the border when leaving their clan territory. According to Nayak (1989, 145), this "is performed because there is a strong belief among them that as she leaves her village, she leaves all her deities behind and has to offer her last homage or obeisance to them."

Such rituals can also be interpreted as markers of the spatial identity of the communities involved in the marriage transaction. Furthermore, they provide a visual representation of the social transition achieved during marriage. In my view, the sacrifice at the border of the village territory (*padari*) is only the first of a series of sacrifices marking the boundaries crossed by groom and bride when leaving behind their previous social existence. On Sunday, rituals accompany the crossing of spatial as well social boundaries. They are performed when the bride leaves her village territory (*padari*) and enters that of her groom, when she enters her husband's village (*nayu*), and when she steps inside the house (*ijo*) of the groom's parents for the first time. In other words, rituals mark the various phases of her movement from her father's village to the territory, village, and house of her new husband. The most elaborate ceremony takes place when the procession approaches the village of the bride-takers. They cross a river where they are received by the bride-takers including the groom, his parents, and his friends. Near the river bank, the shaman and her helper construct a small canopy (*chamda*) with twigs and leaves. At the centre of the area under the canopy they set up a stone decorated with red colour, on top of which they place an earthen pot filled with turmeric water and covered with a leaf. According to some informants, this represents the river goddess, *gungi penu*, who is invoked in the water that is later sprinkled on the newlywed couple. The ritual specialists draw a circle with a cross on the ground to mark the sacred space, within which they place a winnowing fan with rice, a white piece of cloth, and some incense. Additionally, they bring a bowl with flowers and three rings for the deities of the river and put them under the canopy.

The bride-takers provide a chicken and a dove for the next ritual performed by the shaman, who sits in front of the winnowing fan and invokes the deities. Once the gods and goddesses take possession of her body, she either rubs the rice inside the winnowing fan or makes the chicken or dove peck at some rice. While she is in trance, the bride and groom separately approach the temporary shrine, each walking under a white cloth, accompanied by their friends. The women of the groom's village sing *wamuna adele*, "come, oh friend." When a deity comes to the sacred space, the *bejuni* announces the name, and her assistants begin asking the deity for blessings and favours. Depending on the deity,[46] the shaman takes either the chicken or the dove, pours some rice into the groom's right hand, and coaxes the bird to peck at a few of these grains. She repeats the same offering with the help of the bride before the deity is sent away and another god or goddess takes possession of her body. Finally, the *bejuni* gets up, takes the pot filled with turmeric water and the white cloth placed inside the winnowing fan, and walks towards the couple. The cloth is unfolded and spread over the heads of the shaman, the groom, the groom's friend (*tone*), the bride, and the bride's friend (*ade*). The shaman goes in front, holding the little finger of the groom's right hand with her little finger of the same hand; the groom does the same with the bride walking behind him. In this way, they circumambulate the canopy clockwise five times, before the *bejuni* uncovers the earthen pot and pours the water over the heads of both bride and groom. The ceremony ends with the sacrificial killing of the two birds, whose blood is offered to the gods invited to this place near the river bank.

With this ceremony, bride and groom are joined as a couple on the territory belonging to the bride-takers. They have been blessed by the divinities ruling over this area, and they are now invited to come into the groom's village. While the groom himself quickly disappears into a house with his friends to drink alcohol, the bride with all her relatives and friends slowly approaches the entrance of the village near the *yatra kudi*. Before she goes any further, the shaman coaxes a chicken to peck at some paddy from the ground on the path before somebody else sacrifices the animal on the same spot. Nayak

---

46 The colour and type of the sacrificial animal depends on the ritual being performed and who is going to be worshipped. During house rituals, one dark and one white chicken are usually used. On more important occasions, like village festivals, a dove, a cock, or a goat is necessary. At the most important festival, the *kodru parbu* to the earth goddess, a buffalo is required. Several observations lead me to the conclusion that white animals are preferred for male deities and dark ones for female deities, although informants were rather vague about this correlation.

(1989, 146) provides the following explanation for this offering: "They believe that the evil spirit, if any, associated with the girl is thereby driven away, because she comes to their village crossing so many rivers, forests and mountains." As mentioned above, the *yatra kudi* is considered to be the home of the goddess who protects the village from evil outside influences, and her shrine marks an important boundary, which the bride now crosses to become a member of a new village community.

A delegation representing the groom comes to the entrance of the village and offers alcohol to the people accompanying the bride. The bride can now officially cross the next spatial boundary during her social transition from dormitory girl (*dasi*) to married wife (*dakeri*) – the village border – and enter the village plaza. She is immediately taken to the memorial stone representing the *koteiwali*, the male founding deity of the village and husband of the earth goddess. To honour this god, who is considered the father of the Dongria and who represents the authority of the male members of this village, the *jani* of the village performs a *dakina* ceremony. As described above, the main intention of these recitations is to explain to the gods the purpose of the ritual and to ask blessings from them. The *jani* stands in front of the *koteiwali* facing east, holding a chicken in his left hand and some rice in his right fist, and chanting verses. After some time, he first coaxes the chicken to peck at some rice from the stone and then pours paddy into the bride's open palm so that the sacrificial animal can eat some grains, as an offering by the new member of the village, the bride, to its founding deity, the *koteiwali*. The animal's head is twisted off, and some of its blood is smeared on the stone.

From this place, the procession moves towards the house of the groom's parents, as the groom himself normally does not yet have a house of his own. Under the eaves, in front of the door, the *jani* of the village places a pot with turmeric water, as well as a wooden pedestal with a thick rope on top of it. The lower border of the roof that overhangs the wall is called *osona* and marks the boundary between the village and the house. The bride is next sprinkled with water by the *jani*, as described above in the context of a girl being captured. Then her real or classificatory younger sister is asked to come to the place with the pedestal. Throughout the procession, this girl has been carrying a bundle with rice (*mata manjing*) in a pouch in front of her stomach and a chicken (*kayu*) under her arm, and she now hands both of these over to the *jani*, who asks her to move her right foot forward. A real or classificatory younger brother of the groom is next called to join her, and he places his right foot on her right foot. The *jani* takes the chicken, smashes its head first on the feet of both young people and then on the ground. This is the moment the bride can enter the house, but not without the *jani* pouring the rest of the turmeric water on the roof so that it drips onto her head when she passes under the eaves. She is followed by her girlfriends, who take her "wedding gift" inside the house, where the different items are placed next to the sacred wall (*handani kuda*).

Later, a *jani* and his two assistants perform a *dakina* ritual at this place, where the goddess of the house, *sita penu-lahi penu,* is said to reside. She is represented by a gourd (*kaktedia*) filled with grain hanging under the roof and sometimes by a winnowing fan (*heci*) fixed to the wall. Two men hold a white piece of cloth stretched out horizontally in front of the wall, while the three *jani* first stand and later sit in front of it, chanting verses in the same way as they did in the river ceremony (*bada*). From time to time they throw rice grains into the cloth, until it contains one or two handfuls. At the end of the recitation, the cloth is tied into a knot and kept in the attic (*puda gahja itineru* or "they store the cloth tied into a knot"). This is a clear indication that with the bride, the goddess of wealth and of rice, *sita penu-lahi penu*, has entered the house. The bride sitting in a corner and the "wedding gift", *lahi jau*, placed near the wall of the goddess are visible manifestations of this newly achieved wealth. In their recitation, the *jani* ask the goddess to bless both the bride and the items in the "wedding gift" as these are used for cooking by the new daughter-in-law.

The bride's younger "sister" takes a metal cup used for measuring (*lacina*) one *ada*, approximately one kilogram of rice, and fills it with the rice (*mata manjing*) she carried in a pouch in front of her body or in a bundle on top of her head from the bride's to the groom's village. If she brought enough rice to fill up the whole cup, the couple is considered to have a bright future, while the qualities of the bride are put into question if she has not brought sufficient rice. Next, the younger "sister" is expected to cook the rice, but in most cases she just hands it over to the women of the house, who cook it along with the chicken she brought. When this food is ready, the younger "sister" takes rice and meat to the open area in front of the house and calls the young men of the village by saying *awa tati kayu lahi tinga wandu*, meaning "come and eat the rice and chicken brought by your elder brother's wife." On this occasion and at the time when the chicken was smashed to death on the ground, the bride's younger "sisters" and the groom's younger "brothers" joke with each other. The younger "sister" clearly behaves as a representative of the bride: she carries the chicken and cooks the first food in her new house on her behalf. In future, the bride will have a joking relationship with her husband's younger brothers on her own, but on this day she mostly remains inside the house and does not talk much. Nayak further reports a mock fight between the bride's girlfriends, who try to take her back to her village, and the groom's young male friends, who prevent them from doing so. This kind of joking between the younger and unmarried people from both villages may further be interpreted as an indication that future love or even marriage relations between them are positively valued. As stated above, the marriage rules prohibit a direct repetition of marriage between close relatives, but there is no restriction concerning relations between the young people of both villages.

The whole day is spent eating food prepared by the young people. Like the bride-givers, the bride-takers must serve two meals consisting of rice and pulses to their guests, one in the morning and one in the evening. I have been told that this arrangement has been agreed upon rather recently. Previously, the bride's people slaughtered one buffalo on Saturday when everybody came to sing and dance in their village. The animal was cut into two halves, one half being cooked immediately and served to the guests, while the other half was sent to the groom's village. When the bride's procession arrived in the groom's village on Sunday morning, his people in turn slaughtered a buffalo, prepared food from one half of the animal to feed the guests, and gave the other half to the bride's people at the time of their departure. The animal's head was set aside and given to the bride's father when he returned home. This was called *gandi hupinari*, *gandi* meaning "human being" or "body," while *hupinari* denotes the process of giving but is derived from the verb for "spitting," as explained above (see p. 322). According to my informants, this head was given to the bride's parents as a substitute for their daughter, because they were suffering from the loss of their child. This gift can further be interpreted to mark the status distinctions between bride-givers and bride-takers, because the bride's people, like the gods, receive the animal's head. For example, during the buffalo sacrifice (*kodru parbu*), the earth goddess receives the buffalo's head, while the people who have come to attend the festival get a share of the buffalo meat, either cooked or raw. On both occasions, those who take fertility, i.e., the participants in the buffalo sacrifice or the groom's fellow villagers, give the head of the buffalo to those who provide them with fertility, the goddess or the bride's parents. Nowadays, the slaughtering of buffaloes during the three days of marriage is no longer carried out. Instead, the two parties exchange buffaloes in a reciprocal manner on Sunday, the last day of the wedding. The bride's parents bring a buffalo when going in procession to the groom's village in the morning, and they take a buffalo when returning home in the evening. These buffaloes are slaughtered a few days later, most often on Wednesday, and the meat is cooked and distributed to the villagers. This regulation has been introduced in order to provide enough meat for the whole village, because in former times so many guests had to be served that there was hardly enough meat left to feed the villagers.[47]

---

[47] It seems that at the time when Nayak collected his information, the former custom was still

4.3.8 giri takoli ("to bring the path") and wenda kodang ("old legs")

On Monday, the shaman of the groom's village is asked to perform the *giri takoli* ceremony for the house of the groom's parents. The expression *giri takoli* means "to bring the path" and refers to the ritual of bringing the goddess of wealth, *sita penu-lahi penu*, from the path outside the village. She is considered to have left the house in the course of the marriage festivities because the groom's parents have spent so much money on the ceremony and because their guests have thrown away plates with rice following the feast, cooked rice (*lahi*) literally being a representation of the goddess. This "waste" of wealth means that the goddess has left the house and must now be brought back by the shaman. This ritual is always performed after different family rituals, the most important being marriage (*hedi tana*), death (*dosa karma*), the big-man festival (*ghanta parba*) and the harvest of little millet (*hiko*). Following the death of a family member, the *giri takoli* is performed on the western path leading into the village, the path along which the dead person has been carried to the cremation ground. On all other occasions, the goddess is brought from the eastern path back to the village. In the harvest ritual, the house's new wealth, millet, is brought into the house after the family has eaten up its stocks of grain – a symbol of the goddess – since the last harvest. The "waste" of wealth is particularly stressed on the occasion of the big-man festival, when the household spends a great deal of money on sacrificial animals and serves food to the whole village and many guests. After this feast, everybody is requested to deposit the empty leaf cups, which may still contain a few grains of cooked rice, which symbolise the goddess, into a hole dug next to the entrance of the house in order to keep *lahi penu* near the residence.

Jena et al. collected the following story, which explains how the goddess leaves a house due to the housewife's greediness and how she is convinced to return and stay with the Kond. This story deserves to be quoted at length, since many of the ritual elements described below, like the use of bamboo branches and the manner in which the *bejuni* carries a pot representing the goddess, also occur in these mythological events:

> Once, when a yam plant was found on a hill, one of the men tried to remove it by means of a ten-foot long digging rod. Since the tuber was so large and almost reached *narka* (hell), he

---

followed, because he writes, "The boy's party always hurry up the bride's party, but the latter takes its own time so that it will be delayed by the time they reach the boy's village and the boy's party will be embrassed [sic] in entertaining them with good feast, for which the boy's party cook half of a buffalo and the other half is reserved for them raw" (Nayak 1989, 145).

could not remove it fully. *Dharam Devata* told the man that he would only be successful if he would take the goddess Lakshmi (*sita penu*) to the site. The man did so, and the goddess revealed to him that she intended to visit *narka* on the following Thursday. There she came to a house which was owned by an old man and his wife. As she walked on to the nearby river, the old man recognised *sita penu* and followed her. He asked her if he could escort her back to his house, but the goddess was reluctant to do so without receiving an offering from the man. He proposed a sacrifice of several kinds of animals, but she was not satisfied. Then he assured her of the "*soda singi satar lenja*" (sixteen horns, seventeen tails) offering. Although she was unfamiliar with this, she consented, and went to the old man's house. The man was a Kondh and his house was clean and tidy, a lamp lighted the house. *Sita penu* felt very comfortable in the house. The man then went to his swiddens to cultivate various crops, but his wife, being eager to know when the crops would ripen, questioned *sita penu* on this matter. The goddess was annoyed by the question. While she was pleased with the old man who was taking pains to serve the deity (in the form of crops in the swiddens), she was disgusted with his wife who was only thinking of the grand meals she would have when the crops matured. The women's greediness made *sita penu* leave *narka* for her heavenly abode, and, as a result, all the fields became overgrown with weeds. When the old man returned home he was surprised to learn that *sita penu* had gone. He asked his wife whether she had noticed the direction in which the goddess went, but the woman could not tell.

The old man went to search for *sita penu* and found footprints on either bank of the river. He crossed the stream, and asked a mango tree if it had seen *sita penu* passing by. The mango tree replied that it had seen her going that way with a pale face, and that it had tried to keep her from leaving the place. Since the goddess always used mango-bark water to bathe, the tree hoped that *sita penu* would heed its request. The man continued with his search, and met an *irpi mara* [...] and a *paeri laha* [...], which also recounted similar experiences. He also met a bamboo bush which told him that the deity did not heed its request to stay there either. But since the bamboo did not want to lose *sita penu* at any cost, he persuaded her to leave a part of herself there, with the following words: "We are cut to make storage baskets in which you (in the form of grain) are kept; and we would never give cause for you to leave us". Then one of the bamboo baskets succeeded in hiding a single grain of rice in its mesh, and a part of *sita penu* was thus left there.

The old man searched for *sita penu* in vain, and he finally returned home in despair, telling his wife about the sad turn of events. Since he could not forget *sita penu*; he wept for as long as a fortnight. In the heavens, *sita penu's* father felt pity with the man, so he suggested that she went back to *narka*. She, however, was reluctant to do so, owing to the deceptive Kondh woman. Her father assured her that such incidents would not take place again, and argued that, since Niyamraja had left for *narka* with several varieties of seed, she was sure to be protected by him. *Sita penu* agreed to go there provided that she was carried on a person's shoulder half the way, thus being escorted to the Kondh house where rites would be conducted in her honour. The Kondh noticed *sita penu* coming, and their first thought was to wash their houses. Then they trimmed the lamps inside the houses, and lit one at *dharani penu's* altar. After this they went out to escort *sita penu*, carrying her back to their houses on their shoulders while beating drums. This is how *sita penu* came to the Kondh houses, and the act of escorting her for half the distance is called *giri takina* (way bringing). (Jena et al. 2002, 153–55)

Each *giri takoli* follows basically the same pattern. In the morning, the gourd (*kaktedia*) containing the house's sacred grains is brought down from its place under the roof and placed on a winnowing fan on top of a heap of paddy. The shaman and at least one of her assistants come and carry these items to the path beyond the village, to the west in case of a death, to the east on all other occasions. They place the winnowing fan on the ground, sit down in front of it, and begin to invoke the goddess. After some time the goddess arrives, indicated by the shaman falling into trance, and she is requested to come back to the house. As in all these trance sessions, a chicken is used to make offerings to the goddess. While possessed by the goddess, the shaman gets up and puts a folded piece of cloth on her head. She may either carry the gourd representing *lahi penu* on her head or give it to a male member of the house, as I saw on one occasion. Together they walk back to the house, where they are expected by the householder's wife, who holds a pot filled with turmeric water in her hands. She washes the feet of the shaman possessed by *lahi penu*, takes the piece of cloth from her, and pours the rest of the water onto the roof, from which it drips onto the shaman's head. In this way, like the bride on the day of her marriage, the goddess in the body of the shaman enters the house.

Inside the house, the gourd is placed next to the sacred wall, on top of a heap of rice. Somebody brings a small ball of earth and a branch of a bamboo tree, which provides the material for making the baskets in which the goddess in the form of rice is stored, as mentioned in the story quoted above. Bamboo also serves as the goddess's hiding place goddess when her uncle, *bima penu*, comes with a storm, as explained in another story quoted in chapter two (section 2.4.2). A white thread is made to hang down from the wall onto the bamboo branch. The whole arrangement is a representation of the path the goddess takes when moving from the world of the deities down to earth and later back into the upper regions. The wall in the house connects these two worlds existing inside the house, the attic where *lahi penu* resides, represented by the grain stored in large baskets and the gourd filled with sacred grain, and the rooms where Dongria eat, work, and sleep. On the occasion of *giri takoli*, the goddess is next worshipped in the place close to the sacred wall by performing a *male wenbina* ritual, described above. Much emphasis is put on offerings made by the members of the family, particularly by the children, to the gods and goddesses invited on this occasion. Again and again, they are called to offer some rice to the sacrificial animals in their open palms. The chickens are killed at the end of the ritual, cooked, and shared with relatives and neighbours. By sponsoring this ritual, the family makes sure that *lahi penu* returns to their house, where the goddess should stay and protect them.

The bride's family performs the same ceremony on the day the girl, together with her husband and two classificatory brothers and sisters, returns to her natal village for the first time after the wedding, normally on the following Wednesday. This visit is referred to by Dongria as *wenda kodang* or "old feet," because both bride and groom are considered to be tired, having been on the move since the wedding festivities started. They are served food by the bride's parents and are given presents, such as rice, alcohol, and a small pig, at the time of their departure. This is the first of a series of such visits made by the girl to her natal village throughout her life. Whenever there is a major festive occasion or when her parents demand her or her husband's help during the harvest season, she goes back and stays for some days. Normally, the husband, along with an unmarried boy, accompanies her to her village. The husband stays for one night, which the unmarried boy spends in the dormitory of his "elder brother's" affines. When the group arrives, the villagers greet their affines by saying *ubari wate*, "has honour come?"[48] If the husband's help is not required, he and his junior companion return home the next day and come back exactly seven days later to pick up the wife. Again, they may spend one night in the village before all three leave for the husband's village. On their arrival, the husband will be asked by his fellow villagers *ni parasika ana hup:odi panditu*, "what gifts have your in-laws sent?" The word *hupodi* denotes the gifts made by the bride-givers to the bride-takers, which normally consist of at least one small pig worth about Rs 100. This is carried alive by the groom and the boy on a stick over their shoulders and given to the other male villagers on their arrival. Everybody present assembles on the village plaza to cook the pork. Somebody provides an old pot or a pot used only for cooking pork, as pork should not be mixed with other types of meat such as chicken or buffalo. It is always prepared with turmeric paste and often cooked together with rice. When ready, the contents of the pot are poured onto a large winnowing fan, and some boys search the rice for pieces of pork, which they set aside. Then the number of people present is counted, and the rice and meat are distributed in equal shares. When a pig is given by an affine, it is always killed and consumed by the villagers, but when pigs are presented by agnates, these are usually kept and reared. In the former case, male piglets are presented by the affines, while a young sow is an appropriate gift to an agnate.

On the day bride and groom return from their visit to the girl's village, the couple spends their first night together. Ideally, from the time of their betrothal in childhood until this day, they have never slept with each other, although they have most probably gained sexual experience with others when visiting the

---

[48] In Oriya, the word *ubari* is rendered as *majyada*, which means "respect" or "honour."

youth dormitories. A young Dongria assured me that normally during the three days of marriage festivities, both bride and groom can indulge in sexual license, as long as they stay away from each other. Like the other young people, they spend the nights in the youth dormitories or in the back rooms of houses and "sleep" (*dana*) with one or another of the many visitors. As mentioned above, the highest form of marriage consists of a contract arranged by the parents and the village elders without the involvement of the individuals thus joined. After all formal arrangements have been completed and all gifts exchanged between the parties, the couple is finally allowed to experience the more personal and physical aspects of their union. The young villagers lead husband and wife into the inner room of the house, where they can have sexual intercourse. Their friends tell them *kata gada andu de,* "talk, conversation, do it," which is probably an indirect way of prompting them to have sex. Then the girls close the room's back door, the boys close the front door, and the couple remains alone inside. This official arrangement of sexual intercourse stands in sharp contrast to the ways young people normally find their partners for a night in the dormitory, described above. It concludes the long progress of forming a relationship between two young people who are relative strangers to each other.

4.4 Youthful deviation: Love marriage, bride capture, and collective settlements

As described above, society exerts its influence on marriage contracts from the beginning of negotiations until the completion of the marriage ceremonies. However, the concerned individuals often do not accept these collective attempts to forge their marital relations, particularly when they fall in love with somebody other than the partner chosen by their parents. An act of bride capture organised by a young man with the help of his fellow villagers often disrupts the process of on-going marriage negotiations between two other villages, leading to violence and/or negotiations. For a man, a bride capture or a love affair need not stand in contradiction to an arranged marriage, since he can live with more than one woman. A woman, however, is often torn between the expectations of her parents concerning a particular marriage arrangement and her own passions for a boy. By running away with him, by allowing him to capture her, or by refusing to live with her arranged partner, she can actively resist the collective attempts to shape her social existence. When a man captures a girl and she agrees to stay with him despite being promised to somebody else, this is considered a legitimate union. However, this relationship does not stand outside the sphere of collective influence, because the new situation created by the bride capture excites a reaction by several social groups. Youth resistance upsets the relations between bride-givers and bride-takers and induces a settlement process involving at least three parties: the fellow villagers of the woman, of her first husband, and of her second husband. Attempts to reconcile the different parties follow a certain pattern, but like the marriage arrangement itself, these negotiations may be very tense and finally lead to a rupture of social relations or, worse, a feud. The pattern of finding a solution to the conflicts created by the breakup of marriage arrangements will be discussed and illustrated with a number of case studies in this chapter.

The following detailed description of marriages differing from arranged ones is divided into four parts. In the first section, I will describe the age system of the Dongria in order to characterise relations between unmarried young people and other age categories, i.e., small children, married middle-aged people, and old men and women. The second part deals with the centre of life for these unmarried young people, the girls' dormitory. Major issues such as the place of the dormitory within the village organisation, sexual relations, concepts of love, body ornaments, and ideas about procreation will be discussed. I hope to demonstrate that the girls largely control sexual intercourse and that women – like the earth – are the source of procreation and fertility, which men have to acquire through their actions, either in the form of rituals (i.e., arranged marriages) or through violence (i.e., bride capture). The third part provides ethnographic evidence for bride capture. In the last part, I will focus upon conflicts arising out of cases of bride capture, which are then settled through negotiations involving prestations and fines. This will lead me to the conclusion that a correspondence exists between forms of marriage, types of reciprocity, social distance, and territorial segregation.

4.4.1 Youth within the age system

Age distinctions are of major importance among Dongria, although age is not counted in years. I speak of an "age-and-status system," because the categories are not defined by what we call biological age. The system rather derives its logic from a combination of relative age and status, the latter being acquired as part of certain social changes in life, such as entrance into the dormitory or marriage. People remember neither days nor years of birth, keeping only a detailed account of the sequence of births, as far as their own village is concerned. For example, when asked about a girl's age, Dongria respond by listing the names of other boys and girls of the same village who are either slightly younger or slightly older. Age in the sense of position in the sequence of births is linked to concepts of status, as described in the previous chapters.

Table 20: Dongria age-and-status categories

Dongria terms	Age-and-status category (approximate age in years)
kragi	female infants (0–1 years)
kraga	male infants (0–1 years)
asmilang	young girls (1–13 years)
kumilang	young boys (1–14 years)
daasika	unmarried young women (13–22 years)
daweng	unmarried young men (14–22 years)
asika	married adult women
kuang	married adult men; also used for Kond in general in the sense of "human being"
duti	old women (> 60 years)
duta	old men (> 60 years)

Writing about the age categories of the Juang, who live about three hundred kilometres away in north-eastern Odisha, McDougal (1963a, 180) identifies an age system associated with the men's house and consisting of "three formal named groups of either sex, to which distinctive, mutually exclusive sets of rights and obligations are allocated." Among the Dongria, youth activities centre around the female dormitory, and different age-and-status distinctions are linked to various activities and obligations. In certain contexts, groups are formed on the basis of age-and-status, for example when working in the fields, capturing a girl, dancing, and making important decisions. Beyond these contexts, such groups have no formal existence, and we will search in vain for an age system understood as a structure made up of *groups* that are formed around the dormitory institution. We may, however, identify an age-and-status system among the Dongria if we ignore the notion of "groups" and look for a structure of *relations* between the different age-and-status categories.

New-born babies are called *kraga* if male or *kragi* if female until the time they begin crawling or walking around. A wider term for children, which can be used for babies as well as for those older than a year, is *mila* (plural *milang*). In order to stress the sex of the child, a gender prefix has to be added to the word *mila*, either *as-* for girls or *ku-* for boys. Children have hardly any duties except for pasturing and watching the cows, buffaloes, and goats of the village. This task has to be performed from May to December, when the swidden must be protected from the villagers' livestock. Young boys from the age of about eight to ten take them into the woods daily and receive as remuneration a meal of rice or gruel in the evening. When many Dombo families are around, their children are assigned this duty; if not, some Dongria boys are given the responsibility for certain animals. Young girls often help their mothers in the fields in lighter work, but they are more often left to play with each other either in the hut in the swidden or inside the house, where they are watched by grandparents. When visiting a Dongria village at the time of major agricultural work, it is common to meet only old men and women sitting in the village plaza watching their grandchildren at play, while all others are out in their swidden. On these days, a village resembles a huge kindergarten.

When a child reaches puberty, which to my knowledge is not accompanied by any major ritual for either boys or girls, life changes considerably. While small children run around naked most of the time and later wear a small napkin as a loincloth, they now have to cover certain parts of their body more carefully. Girls imitate their mothers by wearing a long white cloth tied around the neck and covering their breasts, while boys, like their fathers, dress in shirt and *lungi*. From now on, girls will not continue to sleep in the inner room of the house like their parents. Once she enters the female dormitories, a girl will be referred to as *dasi* (plural *daaska*) and addressed by the others as *ade* ("friend"). Similarly, boys have to leave the parental room in the evening and find another place to sleep. Accompanied by an elder "brother," a youth visits a dormitory for the first time and henceforth will be called *dawe* (plural *daweng*) by girls and *dangananga* (lit. "sitting in the lap") by boys. During the day, the young people help their parents in their swidden, while at night they visit each other for singing and dancing. From time to time boys or girls join in a labour group to perform tasks for a member of the village community (see section 2.5.2). On festive days, the boys collect the firewood, play the drums, and help to distribute the food, while the girls cook rice or millet in their dormitory.

Following marriage, young people gradually gain independence, taking up more responsibilities for the village community. Men build their own houses, begin cultivating their own fields, contribute their shares to the celebration of village festivals, and join the decision-making groups, while women become more independent upon getting pregnant, rearing their own children, and joining their husbands in the household's swidden. On the birth of the first child, both men and women normally stop visiting the youth dormitories and take off the ornaments typically worn by young people. This change may take some time, and women continue to wear different kinds of jewellery for a long time, while men discard nose rings and necklaces more quickly. Adult men and women are referred to as *kuang* or *aska* respectively, but in order to stress their married status they are more often called *dakera* ("husband") and *dakeri* ("wife"). All important political and religious positions in this society are held by men and women belonging to this age-and-status category. A young married man can become a village *member*, but more authority rests on slightly older and more experienced men. The same holds for religious offices such as those of the *jani* or *bejuni*. The older the officeholders are, the more important are the ritual duties assigned to them. For example, if a senior and more experienced *jani* is present during a ritual invocation, he usually takes up the central position, and the others act as his assistants. However, when an old person is considered to be less knowledgeable than a younger man with special skills, precedence will always be given to the latter. The same holds for shamans. A young woman usually does not play the central role on festive occasions, but leaves it to the older and more experienced *bejuni* to call the gods and make offerings. However, age alone is not a sufficient criterion for a specialist, and many an old shaman must accept the superior abilities of a middle-aged *bejuni* in communicating with gods.

When getting older, men as well as women take rather less care of their appearance. Men stop combing their hair regularly, grow beards, and wear old and often torn clothing. Similarly, old women often look dishevelled and wear no jewellery, and their clothes are more often grey and dirty rather than white. In my experience, they are not systematically classified together with the young residents of the dormitories in a group opposed to the married men and women, as described for the Juang by McDougal, nor do old men have named ritual offices that include certain responsibilities in matters concerning the dormitory. The reason for the lack of male influence on dormitory affairs may be found in the peculiar features of this institution among the Dongria. While the Juang dormitory is managed by the boys in cooperation with the male ritual elders, the Dongria dormitory is organised by the girls with the help of one or more old women. The dormitory belongs to the girls of the village, who are often assisted by an old and usually widowed woman. In fact, many dormitories are houses owned by these widows, who watch over the young people's activities and help them cook.

Old people are called *duta* (old man) and *duti* (old woman). Although we might expect them to be honoured, given the value of seniority in this society, I more often saw them being ridiculed by the younger people. Young men in particular like to make fun of their grandfathers and tease them because of their dress, their smell, or their inability to perform certain tasks. In more serious cases, they may even be neglected, as I experienced in the village where I lived. There, the oldest man was widowed and lived with his son, who forced him to do hard labour and rarely provided him enough food, clothing, or money. However, he was often asked to perform certain rituals, because he knew the incantations of a *jani*. When I inquired about local history, people always referred me to him. Where the invocation of ancestors was concerned, I could be sure that the villagers summoned this old man because he was acquainted with so many deceased people, i.e., he knew not only their names but also the circumstances of their respective deaths. In other words, his age and knowledge gave him a high status in ritual contexts.

In general, it seems that a Dongria man of higher status cannot demand elaborate forms of respect from those of lower status. Others do not treat him with deference, nor do they work for him or present him gifts to gain his favour. The same holds for an old woman, as nobody offers her help when she carries a heavy load or provides her with food and other items to make her life more acceptable. During my previous research in the temple town of Puri, I had experienced various forms of respect shown to old people among high-caste Hindus, and I therefore felt the contrast to the Dongria very strongly. Nobody folds their hands or bows down to touch their feet when meeting elders.

Old people are on the threshold of becoming dead people (*mahane*), and this transition may come quickly through death or slowly through prolonged illness. In the latter case, Dongria may argue that a pregnant woman's foetus is taking away the "life" (*jela*) of the old person, who is viewed as dying at the same time that the foetus is growing in the maternal womb. A ritual performed by the shaman can prevent this "theft" of soul substance. In such a case, the shaman forms a ball made of earth representing the foetus's soul. This ball is then cut into two halves, one containing the old person's soul and the other an empty container for the foetus's soul. The shaman calls the names of several ancestors who have not been reincarnated in another person and asks them to give their soul to the foetus. In this way, the old person can retrieve his or her soul and recover from the illness without depriving the foetus of the essence of life. Very old people and ancestors have a close affinity to members of the youngest age-and-status category, *kraga* and *kragi*, whose life depends on them. Every baby has a deceased person's soul, and a shaman can identify the ancestor reincarnated in the new-born by asking the gods in trance (*male wenbina*). The ancestor, who need not share the baby's sex, usually belongs to the village community but must not be a close lineal ascendant. This ancestor protects the infant, but when enraged may also cause fever and other illnesses in the child. Parents therefore make sure that the baby always gets his or her share of alcohol in order to please this tutelary ancestor, and they may even address the baby by the latter's name. To sum up: the Dongria language offers a set of categories to distinguish people according to their age-and-status. Each category is associated with particular behavioural roles. The transition from one age-and-status category to the other is a gradual process not normally marked by elaborate rituals.

Relations between members of different age-and-status categories vary. While the parental generation tries to impose their commands and authority on their children, the young people openly resist them and do not hesitate to use violent measures. Particularly between sons and fathers and between younger unmarried and older married brothers, relations may be extremely strained and turn into open fights. Several times I witnessed little boys shouting at their fathers and beating them with their small fists, while their fathers tried to calm them down without inflicting any punishment. Once I saw a boy of about eighteen throwing a stone at his father and beating him with the blunt side of his axe because his father had quarrelled with his mother. The father shouted back but did not dare to go against his highly agitated and aggressive son. Family relations were upset for a few days, but then the son returned home and normal life continued, except for the fact that the father, apart from the physical suffering, had also lost his status as the village leader. Following this incident, he hardly left the village, felt depressed, and walked around like an old man, using a stick to support himself. As long as I lived in the village, he never regained his former strength and role as the charismatic leader of the village.

Similarly, love affairs, elopements, and pre-arranged bride captures without the knowledge of the parents may be seen as expressions of this conflict between the young people and the middle-aged married men of the village. By contrast, relations between the youth and grandparental generation are more relaxed and characterised by joking rather than by command and resistance. Old people show a very caring and fostering attitude towards very small children, often more than their parents. Relations between middle-aged and elderly people are not always amicable. Old people are sought out as advisers because of their knowledge of traditions and family histories, but they are not treated with overt deference or explicit respect. While old women are allowed to stay home and take care of the children, old men are forced to work as long as possible and remain independent of their children's help. They cannot demand their children's help and must be content with what is given to them. One day during my fieldwork, the younger brother of the village's oldest man injured himself severely with his knife. His arm was bleeding, and when he came to my house the next morning, he had lost a lot of blood and felt very weak. I decided to go and bring a doctor from a town in the foothills and asked his sons to carry their father on a cot to the closest village reachable by road. However, the elder married son and his friends refused to help the father, and he had to walk slowly with the assistance of his wife and his younger unmarried son.

Dongria often stress similarities and differences between these age-and-status categories. Although far removed from each other in terms of seniority, members of the oldest and the youngest categories are closely linked by the concept of reincarnation and by roles and behaviour. Comparing the appearance of old people and small children, we are indeed struck by certain similarities: both neglect their hair, often wear dirty and torn clothing, and wear only a few body ornaments. Most of the time they stay indoors, either inside the house or in a hut in the swidden. Old people and very small children should not move around a lot, particularly not outside their village territory. On working days, villages become the realm of the very old and very young members of the community, while all others are engaged in agricultural activities in the swidden. A difference exists, of course, in their position in the process of life and death: the old people's souls are vanishing, while the children's souls are growing.

Members of the old and young age-and-status categories may be seen to unite in opposition to the category of middle-aged married people, with whom they both have relatively strained relations. By contrast to these married people, they cannot or should not procreate, and neither weak old men nor inexperienced youths control the village's political affairs. On the other hand, young and old differ in terms of sexuality, which is an important aspect of dormitory relations. Old people often become the object of jokes that target their sexual behaviour. Widowers, for example, are teased about their alleged love affairs and their vanishing sexual powers, and an old man who, like a child, loses control over his bodily functions when drunk is ridiculed.

Members of the young unmarried and middle-aged married categories can be seen to unite in opposition to children and the aged. Both are sexually active, perform difficult agricultural work, and defend the village in feuds and quarrels. The main difference between unmarried and married men and women in the Dongria community revolves around legitimate procreation, as only the latter are entitled to have children. They further differ in terms of their roles, status, and expected behaviour. The two rows of houses forming the village circumscribe the realm within which the married men and women regulate the secular and sacred affairs of the community. Their houses and the village plaza are the places where gods are worshipped, guests are welcomed, and political decisions are made. All important offices are held by members of this age-and-status category, and the general well-being of the whole community depends on them. By contrast, the dormitory and dancing places of the young often lie outside or behind the village and are the realm of those who do not carry the burden of sustaining a family or the community. Neither political issues nor religious matters have an impact on the life in the dormitory: The house of the young should be dominated by fun, joy, and love.

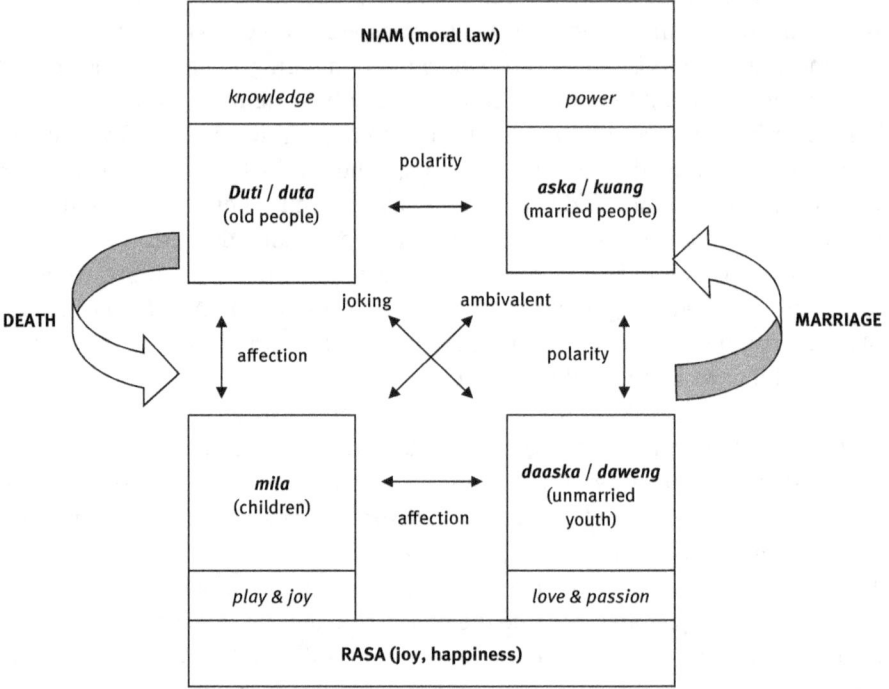

Figure 25: Age system in the Dongria community

In my interpretation (see fig. 25), Dongria age-and-status categories are ordered by two major events in a person's life, the transition from life and death and the transition from unmarried to married status. Old men and children represent the two poles of the first process, which unites and separates them at the same time. Young and middle-aged people similarly represent the two poles in the process of becoming a full member of the village community. Another opposition that structures this age-and-status system is that between the junior categories, whose role expectations are related to ideas about "happiness" (*rasa*), connected with playing, joking, dancing, singing, and learning gender roles, and the senior categories, whose members perform important secular and sacred functions related to the moral law of society (*niam*), such as forming alliances, regulating conflicts, worshipping the gods, and rearing children.

4.4.2 Dormitories

Dormitories of unmarried youths are absolutely unknown in and contrary to the values of Indian "caste society", but in tribal Central India they have been the object of very intensive study, in particular by Sarat Chandra Roy among the Oraon, Charles McDougal among the Juang, Verrier Elwin among the Muria and Bondo, and Simeran Gell among the Muria Gond.[49] These dormitories differ in various ways in their organisation from those existing among the Dongria Kond,[50] but they constitute a centre for the activities of the young unmarried people in all these communities.[51]

The *majang* among the Juang is basically a bachelor's dormitory and a men's clubhouse, usually a large building near the centre of the village (McDougal 1963a, 177). As in the case of the *morung* among the Naga (e.g., Fürer-Haimendorf 1938; Mills 1937), women are not allowed to enter the *majang*, which usually contains a single room, where the most important ritual instruments, the tambourine and the cylindrical drums, are kept. The *majang* is more than just a place where the unmarried boys and widowers sleep; it is the centre of Juang social, religious, and economic life and the symbol of its unity. Every morning and evening the men of the village meet here around the fireplace to discuss judicial and political affairs. Collective activities requiring coordination among many villagers are planned in the *majang*, which is also the place for economic redistribution. Community grain is stored in the *majang*, which on certain occasions serves as a ritual centre. The *majang* is closely linked to the division of Juang society into age groups, and it gives formal emphasis to the dichotomy of the sexes. Unmarried boys and girls do not meet in the *majang*, but they pay each other visits for dancing, singing, and massages (McDougal 1963a, 224 ff).

Verrier Elwin provides us with a very elaborate account of the dormitory institution called *ghotul* among the Muria Gond, which he divides into two types. In the "classical" dormitory (*jodidar*), boys (*chelik*) and girls (*motiari*) belonging to different clans form couples who are expected to stay together throughout the premarital period. They undergo a formal kind of "marriage" and henceforth are expected to be faithful to each other. In the other type of dormitory, which ac-

---

[49] For an overview of youth dormitories in the whole of India see Fürer-Haimendorf 1950.
[50] Fürer-Haimendorf (1950, 129) sees the following major difference: "The youth-dormitories of the Konds, Gadabas and Bondos are of a different order. They are primarily for the use of the unmarried, and nowhere do they serve the purpose of a village-hall. Among these tribes it is the sacred stone circles or built-up stone platforms which are used for public gatherings."
[51] Females are not allowed to enter the *majang* of the Juang, but mutually marriageable girls and boys dance together on the plaza in front of this men's house (McDougal 1963a, 224–29).

cording to Elwin may be a later development, any lasting attachment between a particular boy and girl is explicitly prohibited (Elwin [1947] 1991, 333). Membership in a *ghotul* is highly organised. Following a period of testing, boys and girls are initiated, are given names according to their rank, which changes with their age (Elwin 1991, 354–58), and accept certain social duties. Dormitory boys help to perform rituals at certain festivals, dormitory girls play an important role during wedding ceremonies, and both dance before the clan god and at the great feasts. At the time of funeral rituals, the young people sing songs, particularly in the context of bringing back the deceased's soul (Elwin 1991. 152ff). A *ghotul* has a male and a female leader (*sidar* and *belosa*), who are responsible for upholding discipline in the dormitory. Inside the *ghotul*, boys and girls, apart from singing, dancing, playing games, and telling stories (Elwin 1991, 371ff), also acquire their first sexual experiences (Elwin 1991, 419ff). Members of different *ghotul* may visit each other, but while a boy can easily enter a *ghotul* of a different village, girls are expected to be more hesitant and often wait until they are invited by the girls of another *ghotul* (Elwin 1991, 366–67). Membership in the *ghotul* ceases with marriage, after which neither women nor men are allowed to enter it again.

The *ghotul* became the focus of another extensive study by Simeran Gell, who – unjustly in my view – accused Elwin of presenting a picture of the *ghotul* that "is far too romantic and does nothing to set the *ghotul* in its social context, treating it more-or-less as a dreamland of adolescent sexual bliss" (Gell 1992, 21). Closer reading of Elwin's account reveals that the whole first part of his book[52] is meant to put the *ghotul* "in its place" by providing an account of Muria agriculture, clan organisation, stages of life ("Childhood," "Youth," "Age"), religion, and myths about the origin of the dormitory institution. It is unfair to blame him for misrepresenting the sexual relations within the *ghotul*, since his evidence is overwhelmingly rich in detail and does contain passages in which Elwin provides us with a very balanced view of sexual relations between the young people. We should keep in mind that Elwin himself observed variations among the many *ghotul* he actually visited during his research. It may well be the case that Gell in the group of villages ("Murias of Manjapur") she studied came across just one of the several types of dormitories existing in this area. Furthermore, as she admits herself, her position as a female researcher and her "own moral scruples regarding the intrinsic delicacy of the topic of sex" influenced the data she collected. For example, she describes how difficult it was for her to get the word for

---

[52] This "introduction" of 268 pages is longer than Gell's whole book.

"penis," while in my case this was one of the first words I learned among the Dongria!

According to Gell (1992, 167), the *ghotul* is the centre of the village, even if in many cases it does not actually stand in the physical centre of the village but is situated at the periphery. In any case, it is a kind of "theatre" for collective actions, since villagers are summoned to the *ghotul* to discuss sacred and secular affairs, and visitors, such as high officials, are paid homage at the dormitory: "The values that it strives to instill in its members are those of loyalty to the village and the importance of harmony in intra-village relations" (Gell 1992, 167). Usually, each village has its own *ghotul*, which draws its members from the unmarried girls and boys of the village. According to Gell, boys and girls themselves decide when they want to join the *ghotul*, but at some time everybody will enter it, not only because it is "a social club which caters to the social dispositions of the young and unmarried" (Gell 1992, 170), but also because nobody will attend the marriage of a person who has not joined a *ghotul* previously (Gell 1992, 171).

For a girl, initiation basically consists in publicly announcing her intention to visit a particular *ghotul* regularly, where she is paired off with a boy of her liking, normally after her wish to "sleep" with somebody has been refused once or twice. Such an officially announced partnership is referred to as *jor* and usually brings together a boy and a girl from the same moiety, while those of the opposite, potentially marriageable moiety are not preferred (Gell 1992, 179). Within the *ghotul*, Gell identifies age clusters and certain offices but no elaborate system of titles and duties linked to executive authority as described by Elwin, whom she accuses of mistaking nicknames for social positions (Gell 1992, 189–90). In contrast to Elwin, she understands the *jor* basically as a sleeping arrangement that does not normally involve any sexual acts. She admits that pregnancies among dormitory girls occur, but the relative infrequency of this phenomenon is said to prove her point that the *ghotul* is not a place of sexual liberty. She observes a dichotomy between marriages arranged by the parents and elopements and *ghotul* pregnancies "which are seen as crisis, similar to sorcery accusations" (Gell 1992, 242). Nevertheless, functioning arranged marriages seem to be the exception, since only 20 per cent of the 112 marriages she recorded were with the original *mahala* partner (Gell 1992, 142). In her conclusion, she sees arranged marriages and *ghotul* marriages as primary and secondary marriages similar in structure to those existing among the neighbouring Hindus.

Another variant of dormitories exists in a number of societies that have both male and female dormitories. According to Roy, the Oraon used to have a bachelor house (*jonkh erpa*) (Roy 1915, 211) and a female dormitory (*pel erpa*) (Roy 1915, 260), but the latter was not "a public building, and its location is not supposed to be known to any one except its inmates and to those of the Bachelors' Dormitory" (Roy 1915, 261). Similarly, Roy reports the existence of bachelors' houses called either *giti o* or *gita chari* among the non-Christian Dudh and Dhelki Kharia, where they also serve as guesthouses. At night, the bachelors sleep together in this dormitory, while all the young women sleep together in the house of a lone widow (Roy 1937, 77–78). Roy holds the view that among the Bhuiyas and the Munda-speaking tribes in general the existence of two dormitories, one for boys and one for girls, is the norm:

> Most Munda-speaking tribes have a Bachelors' Dormitory where all the unmarried young men of a village sleep at night. In most of these tribes, the maidens of a village also sleep together in a separate hut, though in most such tribes the maidens have no separate dormitory building specifically constructed for them, and they sleep together in some vacant hut belonging to a fellow villager or in the hut of a lone widow. The Pauri Bhuiyas in the Bonai State maintain a regular dormitory specially constructed for the use of the maidens, generally by the side of the Bachelors' Dormitory. (Roy 1935, 189)

The Bondo seem to fall into this category, too, since they have both a male and a female dormitory, yet they differ from the mentioned tribes because among them people attach more importance to the girls' than to the boys' dormitory. Thus, Elwin in his monograph on the Bondo of Koraput states, "Generally it is the boys' house which is important, the girls' house being definitely subsidiary. But among the Bondos it is the girls house – the *selani dingo* – which matters; the boys' house, the *ingersin*, is simply a basecamp for adventure, from which they go out in search of love and happiness" (Elwin 1950, 72). In this sense the Bondo resemble the Dongria Kond, because among them the girls of a village come together in a dormitory, while the boys, in contrast to other tribal communities in Central India, have no or only a small, insignificant place[53] of their own and always remain only visitors in a place that belongs to the girls. In general, the Dongria dormitory resembles the girls' house among the Bondo[54] more than the highly sophisticated *ghotul* institution of the Muria Gond.

---

[53] According to Jena et al., Dongria do have places for boys, called *dhangdabasa*, where they meet in the evening. I personally have not seen such boys' dormitories, and they seem to be clearly less significant than the girls' dormitories. Thus, Jena et al. (2002, 108) acknowledge that the girls' dormitory "plays an even more active role in Dongria Kondh life.".

[54] "For the Bondo dormitory is nothing more than a sort of matrimonial agency. There are no signs that it was ever a central institution, inspired with magic power, where tribal affairs were conducted. It is not a village guest house; it does not exist to promote the arts of recreation; its organization is sketchy" (Elwin 1950, 72).

4.4 Youthful deviation: Love marriage, bride capture, and collective settlements — 357

Table 21: Types of dormitories in tribal Central India

Mixed dormitories	Public male dormitories	Public female and subsidiary male dormitories	Public male and subsidiary female dormitories
e.g., Muria Gond	e.g., Hill Maria, Juang	e.g., Dongria Kond, Bondo	e.g., Oraon, Kharia

The girls' dormitory (*daaska hada*) among the Dongria

In contrast to a proper house where a family lives and which is called *ijo* or *ilu*, a dormitory is referred to as *daaska hada* or "girls' stable." It usually consists of one room only, except perhaps in those places where the female youth of a village have taken over a deserted house. Some dormitories have cooking areas used at the time of marriages and village festivals when the girls prepare food for their visitors. During the day, the dormitory remains mostly empty, except when the girls have to husk rice or millet. For this work, most of these huts have one or two pits (*häni*) in the ground, into which the girls rhythmically pound (*uhpoli*) the wooden pestle to mash the grains. Only in the evening do activities in the dormitory increase, when the girls meet to comb their hair, put on ornaments, and talk about the events of the day.

Most villages have at least one dormitory, larger ones more than one. In the village where I lived, the dormitory had been demolished because one of the DKDA Special Officers was convinced that it contributed to the moral degeneration of Dongria girls. When this policy changed with the arrival of another Special Officer, the people of Gumma did not rebuild the dormitory, as only a few older girls were living in the village. At the time of my arrival, these girls used to meet their young visitors in an empty house, which was later claimed by a newly married man as his residence. However, he allowed his widowed father's brother's wife, her daughter, and another girl to sleep in the back room of his house, where they felt safe. Whenever boys came to spend the night in Gumma, the girls met them in either this room, the back room of their parents' house, or a widow's house. In other villages I saw similar arrangements; in particular, houses where widows live are favourite places for boys and girls to meet at night.

Proper dormitories are usually erected behind the two rows of houses making up the village. This is the same place where Dongria put up their simple cow barns, which resemble the dormitories except for the fact that they are usually built on small pillars above the ground. Most larger villages have two dormitories, one behind each row of houses, and some have more. The village of Dongormati, for example, has two additional sets of residences in a separate place, apart from the typical two rows of houses, and thus four dormitories altogether. This suggests that each row or set of houses has its own dormitory. In actual fact, however, Dongria girls do not necessarily visit the dormitory belonging to their neighbourhood but select their sleeping place according to their friendship relations. Girls, like boys, have their close friends, whom they refer to as *ade* and whom they meet at night in a dormitory.

As mentioned above, the space behind the two rows of houses belongs to women, married and unmarried. Here they meet to discuss the events of the day or to have a chat with their neighbours. An open level space is used by the girls as a dancing ground. Here they assemble in the evening and practise their songs and dances under the watchful and critical eyes of their mothers. Anthropologists with tape recorders are most welcome guests on such occasions if they allow the girls to listen to their songs once the performance is over. When boys of their own village turn up, the activity may turn into a game in which a blindfolded person has to recognise others by touching their feet and exchanging a standard dialogue with them. The months of February and March, when the evenings start getting warmer, are normally the time when girls begin to practise their songs and dances.[55] Soon, they are given an opportunity to demonstrate their mastery on several festive occasions occurring in the following months: *siva yatra*, *bali yatra*, *kodru parbu*, and marriage ceremonies.

The dormitory system is clearly linked to Dongria rules prohibiting sexual relations within the same clan. When boys and girls reach physical maturity, they are spatially segregated from their parents, who sleep in the inner room of the house near the hearth. Boys normally spend the night in the front room (*duki*), where their parents keep chickens and sometimes even goats. Their sisters sleep at the other end of the house, in the back room (*dapa*), which normally contains a small pigsty. An only daughter often joins her girlfriends and shares a room or a dormitory with them in order to have company during the night, as she may fear being captured by boys from a different village. In this way, parents are segregated from their children and male from female youth. Inside a village, boys and girls regard each other as brothers and sisters, since they – ideally – belong to the same clan and are therefore prohibited from engaging in sexual relations. For this reason, boys have to search for a girl in a village primarily in-

---

55 The year is divided into two periods: the time of happiness, *rasa wela*, from spring to the end of the hot season, and the time of sorrow, *duk wela*, beginning with the rainy season, when diseases and epidemics start spreading, and ending with the difficult harvest in winter.

habited by members of a clan different from their own. Usually, they leave their village in the evening in small groups, after taking a bath, combing their hair, and putting on new clothes. They plan to reach the dormitory with the onset of night. The dormitories that are regularly visited by these young men normally lie at a distance of not more than one or two hours walk, while more distant places are only visited on the occasion of official dancing arrangements. When walking through the jungle, the boys carry large battery-operated torches[56] available in the market to find their way through the jungle and to identify the most attractive girls on major festive occasions like marriages. Sometimes girls choose to visit the dormitory of a neighbouring village. Like the boys, they leave their own village in a group in the evening and return to their parents' houses early the next morning. These casual visits are often made by girls who do not have a dormitory of their own because their village is too small. They are accepted as regular guests in a larger village, where they may sleep with the boys who similarly come as guests from yet other places. According to the information given to me by the two female development officers of the DKDA, Dongria do not prohibit boys from sleeping in the dormitory of their own village if girls from a neighbouring village have come as guests. Similarly, when the young guests and their hosts sleep in the back room of a house, no objection is raised if classificatory brothers and sisters sleep with their visitors in the same room, as long as the hosts keep apart from one another.

Sexual relations (*dapoli* or "to sleep") and love (*mriha* or "to desire")
With the beginning of the time of happiness, the dormitory becomes an increasingly lively place, not only at the time of festivals. As the workload for the boys and girls decreases by the end of the harvest, they have more time to stay awake at night and make up for the sleep lost during the day. In these months, boys and girls can be seen from time to time sleeping on a veranda during the day following a night of singing and dancing.

---

56 During my stay, large silver torches containing two or (even better) three batteries fell out of fashion and were replaced by even larger torches with strong rechargeable batteries. This change was facilitated by the introduction of solar cells provided by the DKDA with the intention of operating a street lamp in the centre of each village. Dongria boys quickly learned how to recharge their torch batteries with the help of these solar cells, with the result that most villages continue to remain in darkness throughout the night, since all the energy goes into the torches. Hunters coming from the valleys into the Dongria hills were also pleased with this innovation, since they could recharge the torches they wear on their foreheads while searching the forests for prey at night.

There are basically two types of visits to a girl's dormitory. When a boy fancies a particular girl in a neighbouring village, he goes to meet her regularly, often accompanied by a good friend. Before leaving their village, they eat in their parents' houses, just as they will be back next morning early enough to have breakfast with their family members. On arrival in the girl's village, they proceed straight to the dormitory without meeting anybody else, and the girls let them in without hesitation. On such regular visits, which are referred to as *daaska beta* or "hunting girls," the boys and girls do not sing and dance, but simply sit in the dormitory and talk for hours until they lie down on the ground in pairs.

Nobody expects the girls to cook anything for the visitors, and the latter leave so early the next morning that hardly anybody in the village really knows who spent the night in the dormitory. Things are different on formal visits, when whole groups of girls and boys meet to entertain each other. Such official visits are called *gota halboli* or "to visit one's affines." A group of girls is normally accompanied by an elderly woman from their village who heads straight to a house where she has relatives upon reaching the host village. The reasons for such visits vary: they may be part of formal marriage negotiations, the group may be on the way to town to attend a Hindu festival, they may wish to bring back a girl who ran away, or they may have been invited by their hosts for a dancing party. The visitors are served food in their relatives' houses before the young people meet on the dancing ground. There they sing, drum, and dance for many hours before finally retiring to the dormitory or into the back rooms of some houses. In the morning, the young hosts prepare food for their visitors, who either leave that day or stay for another night. When leaving, the guests encourage their hosts to pay them a return visit in the future. In addition, long-lasting relations between the young men and women of two villages of different clans are sometimes established at the time of the buffalo sacrifice *(kodru parbu)*. Following this occasion, the girls of the sponsors first send a goat to the boys of a certain affinal village, who react by making a similar counter-prestation some weeks later. In the future, these groups pay mutual dancing visits to each other. In this kind of collective friendship relation, the girls are referred to as *dasi gota*, which may be translated as "marriageable girl who comes as a guest."

I never spent a whole night in a youth dormitory, but I visited these places several times and sat with the young people for some time talking and joking. The following description is based on observations made on these occasions, particularly at the time of buffalo sacrifices and marriage ceremonies, and on informally conducted interviews with Dongria, mostly men, and with two female government workers who regularly sleep in the dormitories when on tour through Dongria villages.

A dormitory always has a leader, usually an elderly unmarried woman or a widow, referred to as *kajari*, "the elder one" or "the big one." It is her responsibility to teach songs to the girls and to watch over the observance of incest rules. When a couple are related in a way forbidden according to the rules pertaining to the clan or to close relatives (see section 3.4.5), she interferes and makes sure they do not spend the night together. The young people sit on the ground and talk with each other, often in a joking mood. After some time, those couples who have been acquainted with each other for a long time go into a corner and lie down on the ground, while the others continue their discussions, sometimes throughout the night. When a boy wants to get closer to a particular girl he is fond of, he asks her if she wants to sleep with him. The term for sleeping is *dapoli* and covers everything from lying next to each other to having sexual intercourse. Many people told me that in most cases girls do not have sexual intercourse with their visitors unless they are regarded as lovers. In the latter case, the boy eventually captures the girl or pays an official "betrothal fee", which is considerably lower than in an arranged marriage.

If they are relative strangers to each other, the girl only allows the boy to sleep on the ground next to her. Someone who enters a dormitory in the middle of the night will see a number of couples side by side, each covered by a white or red shawl, while some people sit in a corner and chat with each other. After several visits by the same boy, the girl may allow her visitor to become more intimate. One evening, some boys from the village where I lived entered my hut after returning from their daily visit to the palm-wine tree, and being in a jolly mood, they wanted to teach me how to behave in a dormitory when meeting a girl. First, they told me, the man has to ask the girl *rahe dana?*, meaning "shall we sleep together?" If she agrees, both will lie down in a free place on the floor of the dormitory. They face each other, and the boy says *banga hiamu,* "give me tobacco," an expression with clear sexual connotations. For example, I once saw a boy furious because somebody else had asked his beloved for tobacco, which he seemed to interpret as an attempt by his rival to flirt with his girl. Sometimes, boys joked with me by telling me I should demand tobacco from a particular girl, and once a friend of mine came to my rescue by informing me that I should never ask a girl for tobacco if I consider her my "sister".[57] When

---

[57] I was accepted as a member of the Himberika clan, considered a brother clan of the Sikoka. Any woman belonging to the Sikoka clan and of roughly my age was therefore related to me as a "sister".

boys demand tobacco from each other, the one who offers it often jokingly says, "Here, eat my penis" (*ida, na pida tinmu*). After exchanging tobacco, the girl rests her head in her hand, keeping her arm in an angle on the ground. The boy comes closer, puts his head into the crook of her arm, and embraces her. Next he invites her to embrace him by saying *ninu pambamu* ("you embrace"). The next step of intimacy is reached when he asks her *kada ladi kiamu*, "open your legs," so that he can place his lower leg between hers and his upper leg on top of her. Finally, if the girl permits, he can penetrate her by saying *kodanga nanu hoti*, meaning "I enter your legs."

One day a young man of the Leli caste (a scheduled caste) was present when discussions turned to the topic of sexual intercourse. Since his childhood, he had spent many years in Dongria villages together with his aunt, who served as a MPW for the DKDA. He was very familiar with Kond dormitories and told me about his experiences with Dongria sexual behaviour in the presence of two Dongria men from Gumma. These men confirmed his statements but were obviously not used to talking about these matters in the same open way as the Leli. According to him, a Dongria girl often only allows a visitor to put his penis between her legs or onto her thighs, where she rubs the organ. He does not penetrate her; rather, they only caress each other in order to reach climax.[58]

The number of rings and necklaces a boy or a girl wears is a clear indication of his or her popularity. When somebody is particularly fond of a certain person, he or she presents the beloved with a blue or red necklace made of small plastic beads or with one of the cheap brass rings available in the markets. I have seen attractive boys and girls who were literally covered with these ornaments, wearing one or two rings on each finger and many plastic beads around their necks and wrists. Some young men put these brass rings around the handles of their axes, which they show to others on festive occasions by holding the axe up in the air while rotating it in their hands. The blade of the axe or knife sometimes has the girl's or boy's name engraved on it, something done by the lover to impress the object's owner.

Dongria lovers behave in ways inconceivable to most Hindus. Westerners, on the other hand, are reminded of the youths in their own countries when watching a Dongria girl teasing and joking with her lover. Girls appeared to me as active in flirting as boys. Rather than playing the role of the "shy" girl to be conquered, they themselves approach a boy they are particularly fond of. On major festive occasions, like the *kodru parbu*, the *bali yatra*, or marriage ceremonies,

---

58 Elwin (1991, 435–37, 468–69) managed to get more detailed information on these practices among the Muria Gond.

young Dongria couples can be observed embracing each other in public in a manner that would arouse outrage among Hindus. However, apart from embraces, other forms of intimacy will not be seen in public. When darkness sets in, lovers retreat to a corner of a house, the dormitory, or the forest, where they are allowed to touch each other. I have never seen Dongria kissing, nor imitating or discussing it, and I therefore think that it is not part of what they consider to be sexual behaviour.[59]

The expression used by Dongria for the love between a dormitory girl and her lover is *mriha*. This word implies sexual desire and passionate feelings for a member of the opposite sex and must for this reason be distinguished from the term *kdenu*, which means "love" in the sense of deep affection felt for a close relative or friend with whom sexual relations are forbidden. The same holds for a third term, *akana*, which expresses a certain sympathy for a person. For example, when I stayed away from Gumma for a couple of days, people often told me on the day of my return *ninge akana mai*, meaning "I worried about you" or "I have been thinking of you.".

Body ornaments

In contrast to older married people, young Dongria, both male and female, show an immense interest in making themselves beautiful by putting on ornaments and wearing colourful clothing.[60] As in Western societies, old fashions die out and new fashions are created with rapid speed. In this section, I present the typical body ornaments of male and female Dongria, those remembered by the elders and those actually worn by members of the younger generation.

---

59 According to Elwin (1991, 432), kissing is known to the tribal people of Central India and goes in and out of fashion: "But even then the kiss does not appear to be on the lips, nor does the tongue play any part; for the Muria the kiss is a highly concentrated massage with the lips upon the skin."
60 Niggemeyer (1964, 65–73) offers some very good drawings of ornaments used by the Kuttia Kond he studied starting in 1955–56. Elwin (1951, 9) presents us with a drawing of a hairpin worn by Dongria Kond. He comments, "Hair pins are not very common. The Konds formerly made them of sambhar bone; they still sometimes make hair-pins of porcupine quills; in Fig. 1 I show an attractive modern substitute from the Niamgiri area" (Elwin 1951, 11).

Table 22: Dongria body ornaments

Body part	Women's ornaments	Men's ornaments
upper body	*ganda* (white cloth as breast cover and colourful shawls)	*angi* (colourful shirt or shawl on festive occasions; otherwise no covering) *kdali* or *simini* (working axe or sacrificial axe)
lower body	*mat ganda* (long white cloth around waist) *atadaru* (snakelike silver chain around waist)	*drilli* (short white cloth around waist) *curi* (knife wrapped in cloth) *katri* (dagger)
hair	*cipenanga* (silver-coloured clips) *jetpurika* (brass-coloured clips) *pungu* (flowers) *kasa* (hair knot behind the left or right ear on young women, at the back of the head on married women)	*cipenanga* (silver-coloured clips) *jetpurika* (brass-coloured clips) *melu kelka* (peacock feathers) *joda* (hair knot at the back of the head) *kaka* or *cireni* (horn comb or plastic comb)
ears	*rupa kutenga* (silver pin in upper part) *rupa murmanga* (silver earrings) *nangulika* (spiral ring in earlobes)	*rupa kutenga* (long silver pin used in the past) *rupa murmanga* (silver earrings)
nose	*suna murmanga* (three gold rings)	*suna murmanga* (two gold rings)
neck	*kakudika* (silver circlet) *mekadika* (chain with plastic beads)	*kakudika* (silver circlet) *mekadika* (chain with plastic beads)
upper arm	*teduanga* (bracelet made of brass)	*mekadika* (chain with plastic beads)
lower arm / wrist	*pajanga* (bracelet made of brass)	*ganta* (watch)
fingers	*murmanga* (usually cheap brass rings)	*murmanga* (usually cheap brass rings)

4.4 Youthful deviation: Love marriage, bride capture, and collective settlements — 365

Table 22: Dongria body ornaments *(Continued)*

Body part	Women's ornaments	Men's ornaments
toes	*amta murma* (ring on big toe) *kada murma* (ring on toe next to big toe) *cingedi capanga* (ring on other toes)	

When attending a marriage ceremony or a buffalo sacrifice, girls normally wear a *sari* that, unlike their ordinary clothing, is not completely white[61] but contains some red or green patterns. They bind the *sari* in the same way as the plain white one; only once, on the occasion of a Hindu festival in Kalyansingpur, did I see a few Dongria girls wearing blouses and binding a *sari* in the way plains people do. When walking through the mountains to the bride's village, they carry a few folded shawls (*ganda*) on their heads, which they later wrap around their bodies or use as blankets while sleeping. While most shawls used by the girls are simple products bought in the market, others show the colourful embroidery done by Dongria women in their leisure time. Around their necks the girls wear two types of necklaces, traditional silver circlets (*kakudika*) and modern necklaces made of red or blue plastic beads (*mekadika*). They part their hair in the middle, and on both sides of the parting they affix a great number of silver- or brass-coloured clips (*cipenanga* and *jetpurika*), which, like the plastic necklaces, can be bought from traders in the weekly market. Their long hair is put up in a knot (*kasa*), which is fastened behind either the right or the left ear[62] and sometimes decorated with a flower, plastic ones being increasingly popular among the girls. The arms and wrists are decorated with bangles and bracelets of different types. Previously, it was a fashion for young women to wear heavy bracelets (*teduanga*) around the upper arm and a second type (*pajanga*) around the lower arm. Nowadays, they are more often seen wearing the typical glass or plastic bangles used by Hindu women in the plains. Many

---

61 Like the Dongria women I know, the women photographed by Watts (1970, Plate IX–XVI) in 1968 covered their breasts with a white piece of cloth and wore a white skirt around their waists.
62 An unmarried girl (*dasi*) normally wears her hair knot (*kasi*) on the right side of her head, while a married woman (*asi*) wears hers at the back of her neck. A woman does not let down her hair in public when other men are around. Appropriate places for her to comb her hair are the back room of her house (*dapa*) and the bathing place near the river where only women are allowed to go.

young women wear three different types of ornaments in their ears. In the upper part of their ears they wear a silver pin (*kutenga*) that looks like the point of a lance. Below that they wear a large number of silver earrings (*murmanga*), from the upper part of the ear to the tip. In their earlobes they wear a spiral (*nangulika*) two or three centimetres long and made of brass. From childhood on girls wear three gold nose rings (*murmanga*), one in each nostril and one in the nasal septum, which they hardly ever take off. For festive occasions, most girls bind at least one long and heavy silver chain (*atadaru*) around their waists. Their hands and feet are adorned with different types of rings, the most popular at present being a brass ring in the shape of a four-leaved clover, which is available for a few rupees in the market. Only a few young women continue to wear different types of rings[63] on their toes as their mothers used to do. The girls wear silver anklets, usually the same chain type worn by Hindu women, but some still have the compact and heavy anklets that were fashionable among Dongria in the past.

The young men do not dress up entirely differently from the girls. Like them, they part the hair in the middle, affix a large number of hair clips (*cipenanga* and *jetpurika*) on both sides of the parting, and put up their long hair in a knot, which they wear at the back of their necks. They wear combs in their hair, either ones made of buffalo horn that they produce themselves (*kaka*) or more colourful plastic combs (*cireni*). In the past, the men used to cut their bangs short and wear their hair knots behind their right ear (see plates XIV–XV in Watts 1970), but this style is now out of fashion and only followed by very old men. The latest trend among the young men, which came into fashion while I was doing fieldwork in Gumma, is to cut their hair short in the style of the Hindu boys in the towns. In the past, when attending a festival, Dongria used to bind a turban around their heads and a white cloth (*drili*) sixteen *hata*[64] long around their waists. The men carried bound into their waist cloths long knives (*curi*) of the type worshipped on the occasion of the buffalo sacrifice. In some areas near Muniguda it was fashionable to wear black shirts available in the local market. Nowadays, Dongria boys, probably in imitation of Hindus, dress in a colourful loincloth (*lungi*) combined with an equally colourful shirt (*angi*) they buy in shops or demand from the anthropologist living in their village. On a festive occasion, they resemble the girls not only because of their hairstyles but also because they wrap the same colourful shawls around their bodies. Like the girls,

---

63 The ring on the big toe is called *amta murma*, the ring on the next toe *kada murma*. The rings on the three other toes are referred to as *cingedi capanga* and look like small shields.
64 One *hata* ("hand" or "arm") is the distance between the elbow and the wrist.

the boys wear necklaces of both types, *kagudika* and *mekadika*, but the silver rings are now more and more out of fashion. Some young men wear bracelets made of brass or silver, but usually only one or two on each arm. It is considered trendy to wear a colourful wristwatch available in the market, even if few people can actually read the time. From childhood on, boys wear two gold nose rings, one in the left nostril and one in the nasal septum, which they usually take off permanently after marriage. Nose rings for men are gradually falling out of fashion, just like earrings. The old men still remember the time when male Dongria wore pins (*kutenga*) in the upper part of the ear, which were much longer than those worn by women nowadays. Some middle-aged men still have holes in both their ears, a sign that they used to wear as many earrings (*murmanga*) as the girls, but nowadays only a few men wear even one earring in their earlobes.

It seems that all the body ornaments that Hindu people today consider to be typically female, such as long hair, nose rings, and earrings, are now gradually being rejected by Dongria men. On the other hand, as Hindu men often wear *puja* rings on their fingers, Dongria perhaps do not feel odd when accepting the rings given to them by the girls. These rings, as well as the cheap necklaces, are appropriate gifts to a girl or boy one is fond of and with whom one has spent a night on an occasion like a marriage ceremony.

Sex and "eating"

A Dongria man from Gumma once told me the following mythological story:[65]

> In the old days there were no plants, no animals, no human beings, only the moon, the stars, the sun, and his seven children. Because of the many suns nothing could grow; it was much too hot. For this reason, the moon thought that she would outwit the sun, her friend. She ate the leaves of a *bja* tree, and her mouth turned red. When the sun saw this and asked what the moon had eaten, she replied that she had eaten her children, the stars. In fact, she was hiding her children in a basket. "Why did you eat all your children?" the sun asked, and the moon responded, "Because I was hungry." Then the moon said to the sun, "You should also eat your children; then you won't be hungry." Following this advice, the sun ate one of his children every day: Somawara, Mangalawara, Buduwara, Lakmiwara, Sukruwara, Saniwara, Adiwara. But when he had eaten all his children, the moon opened the basket and released all her children. The sun became angry due to

---

[65] A similar myth told by Bondo is discussed by Pfeffer in the context of the so-called "hair debate" (Pfeffer 1997a). Very similar myths have been collected among various tribes, but mostly among Kond (see Elwin 1954, 39–40, 47–48, 54–55, 57, 62–63). Particularly strong similarities are evident with stories from the Kuttia Kond of Surangbaro (Elwin 1954, 47–48) and Sutaghati (Elwin 1954, 54–55).

this deceit, and the moon accepted a contract with him: in the morning the sun will eat the moon, while in the evening the moon will eat the sun.

This story can be interpreted in terms of concepts of time, as it relates to the movements of the heavenly bodies and the system of seven days. However, when my informant and I were discussing the story one evening at his house, he explained it in a different way. His interpretation started from the notion of mutual "eating," the exact term used in the story being *guhna*. This verb literally means "swallowing" and has the double connotation of "consuming" and "having sexual intercourse." The idea that a woman's vagina "eats" a man's penis is so widespread among the ethnic groups of Central India that Elwin (1991, 423–26) even speaks of "Vagina Dentata legends." The common idea in all these stories is that the vagina formerly was like a mouth with teeth and could bite a man's penis off. Elwin collected various of these stories, which explain how the vagina lost her teeth and sexual intercourse became possible, among the Gond. In the Dongria language, a man refers to the sexual act by saying *edi guhte, edi kakite*, literally meaning "she swallowed, she disgorged." In a further analogy, my informant equated this act of "eating" with the dormitory relations between young people. In the evening, when the moon eats the sun, the girls allow the unmarried boys from neighbouring villages to enter their dormitories, where they sleep with each other. Next morning, when the sun eats the moon, the girls ask the boys to leave the dormitory.

Table 23: Mythic correspondences between time and sexual acts

evening	morning
moon swallows the sun	sun swallows the moon
woman allows man to penetrate her	woman ends sexual intercourse
boys gain entry into dormitory	boys leave dormitory

Girls' control of sexual intercourse
A striking feature of this interpretation is the stress placed on the girl's power to control sexual intercourse. This corresponds to Elwin's findings among the Muria Gond, among whom the dormitory girls decide whether they want to sleep with someone and with whom:

> There is a good deal of evidence to suggest that just as it is the motiari [dormitory girls, R.H.] who rule the sexual side and make the sleeping arrangements in the modern type of ghotul [dormitory, R.H.], so in both types it is the motiari who take the lead in actual congress. (Elwin, 1991, 436)

Elwin is at pains to explain the low pregnancy rate among the Muria Gond but does not take into consideration that this female dominance in sexual matters may indeed be one of the decisive factors in this phenomenon. Being acquainted with the "Virgin Birth Debate" (Leach 1969), I several times asked young Dongria men whether they thought that a man was necessary to make a girl pregnant. They all assured me that without sexual intercourse a woman cannot become pregnant, but they also insisted that it depends on the will of the girl whether she actually becomes pregnant or not. At first, I assumed my informants to hold some ideas about the power of mind over matters of the body similar to the psychosomatic explanations popular in Western societies, but later I understood that they meant something else. One day I walked with a Dongria man from the market in Kalyansingpur back to our village. On the way our discussions turned to dormitory relations, and I asked him whether Dongria boys and girls actually have sexual intercourse when meeting in the dormitory. According to his experience, he told me, a girl normally does not allow a boy to penetrate her. When spending the night with a visitor, she may allow him to touch her and may caress him in return, but she rarely agrees to sexual intercourse. When both like each other, the boy will visit her regularly. If she still resists him, he may jokingly say *bidema dina nanu bahen watee, ninju nanu ninge posigi*, meaning "I have come so many days in vain; may I today sleep with [lit. penetrate] you?"

This information was later confirmed by others who told me how difficult it was to persuade a woman, as many girls resisted all attempts to have actual sexual intercourse. It thus appears that the girls do control sexual encounters, just as they control who can enter the dormitory. When they meet in the evening, they lock the dormitory door, and when visitors come, they knock on the door with their axe handles, making jokes such as *minkawani duheri demu* ("wife of fishes, open the door")! Only if the girls know the visitors do they open the door and allow them to enter. It seems as if Dongria boys do respect the girl's control in sexual matters, as I have never heard of any bad behaviour against dormitory girls, not to speak of rape. This is confirmed by Elwin, who writes:

> The incidence of crime is very low. An experienced police officer, who had served in the ghotul [dormitory, R.H.] area for twelve years, told me that in all this time there has been no case of murder, riot, assault, hurt, or rape in connexion with the ghotul. (Elwin 1991, 657)

My discussions with Dongria left me with the impression that actual sexual intercourse does occur but is not as frequent as other forms of sex not involving penetration. As described above, girls sometimes allow the man to put his penis between their legs or on their thigh but prohibit him from entering their vagina.[66] Women are considered to become pregnant when they want to, which means when they allow men to penetrate them. One informant further regarded the frequency of sexual intercourse with the same man as a decisive factor in enabling a woman to become pregnant. He had slept with a particular girl only a few times, and when the girl became pregnant, he considered somebody else to be responsible, because this other man had had sexual intercourse with this woman many times. Elwin reports that the Muria Gond (and Gadaba) hold a similar view:

> The Muria believe strongly that conception cannot follow an act of casual intercourse. A woman must remain with the same partner for at least a month and during this time congress must be frequent. (Elwin 1991, 464)

If not considered to be somebody's beloved, most girls change their partners frequently. Once a girl came to me and asked me to write down the names of her lovers in Oriya on a sheet of paper. She mentioned a total of ten different boys, who all lived in one village. This confirmed my general impression that women seek rather short-term relationships with various men instead of having long and intensive love affairs, which might lead to pregnancies. Apparently, girls try to avoid pregnancies by changing their dormitory partners before they enter into more intimate relations. In some parts of his voluminous book on the dormitory system of the Muria, Elwin, too, admits that these people do expect a certain restraint in sexual matters:

> A pregnancy is regarded as a gross piece of carelessness. There is a general belief that no one need conceive unless they want to, that a definite psychological factor is involved. If a boy and girl do not give themselves to one another with too oblivious a passion, if they hold back a little, if they are careful not to love too constantly and too long, conception need never follow. We have seen that too much love is not approved in the ghotul; conception is the punishment of an overpassionate attachment. (Elwin 1991, 465)

---

66 The word used for penetration, apart from *posi-*, which is derived from Oriya, is *kanbi-*, from the root verb *kan-* meaning "to copulate" and the affix *–b–*, indicating an action done repeatedly. In his grammar of the Kuvi language, Israel (1979, 147–51) mentions *–k–* and *–p–* as allomorphs for plural action.

In contrast to the obsession with semen, particularly the loss of semen, in Hindu society and mythology (e.g., O'Flaherty 1973, 1976; Alter 1997), Dongria do not talk much about this male fluid. Semen is not an object referred to in jokes, and I do not know of any mythological story told among the Dongria in which the loss of semen appears as a central motif. It seems to have escaped Elwin that in the hundreds of myths collected by him, semen or the loss of semen is unheard of. In his collection of tribal myths of Odisha, the word "semen" is not even mentioned in the very elaborate motif index, and among the stories falling into his category "Conception and Birth" I found only one story in which a Muni (Hindu ascetic) urinates and thereby drops his seed, which impregnates a she-antelope. (Elwin 1954, 37)

Fürer-Haimendorf managed to get a detailed account about indigenous ideas of conception among the Gond in Andhra Pradesh. In a statement he quotes at length, his informant identifies the following causes for conception: intercourse, which opens the woman's womb; the mixing of male and female "seed" or fluids; the intervention of the god *shambu,* who forms a ball out of these fluids; and the insertion of life or soul (*jiv*) after six months (Fürer-Haimendorf 1979, 286). Gell reports that for the Muria Gond, male and female substances have no place at all in their ideas about conception. The child is thought to be already there, inside the woman, so that from the time of reaching puberty all women are in a state of permanent pregnancy (Gell 1992, 221). A woman is said to become pregnant – we might say visibly – only after marriage (Gell 1992, 220), although no explanation exists as to why this change occurs. In general, according to Gell, Muria Gond do not consider "copulation" to be a crucial factor, while they are said to attach great importance to the woman's sentiments, her happiness and her willingness to conceive a child (Gell 1992, 222).

As among the Muria, male and female substances similarly do not figure prominently in Dongria ideas about conception. The word for semen in the Dongria language is *witanga*, which in my interpretation derives from the verb *wit-*, "to shake," and the noun *anga,* "body." Once a Dongria also told me that the word for semen is *pusi*, i.e., the same word used for vaginal fluids. This suggests that the Dongria, just like the Gond studied by Fürer-Haimendorf, consider male and female fluids basically the same. I have not heard of any equation between semen and seeds (*pdeka*) in the Dongria language, unlike in Oriya, in which it is possible to talk of a man's "seed" (*bihon* or *manji*). In the discussions I had with Dongria about the mode of conception, the mixing of the fluids was mentioned, but particular emphasis was always placed on the matter of penetration (*posina, kanbina*), i.e., male activity. All this leads me to the conclusion that for Dongria "insemination" is a necessary but not sufficient act, while the woman's will, the degree of intimacy between her and her lover, and the frequency of their sexual intercourse, i.e., the degree of male activity, are considered to be primary factors in making a woman pregnant.

Women's control of creation

Following Leach (1969), we may consider Dongria ideas about conception to be part of a dogma different from Dongria's actual knowledge about physical paternity. According to this dogma, male gods do not play any role in procreation. In the mythological stories collected by Jena et al. (2002) among the Dongria, the first divine beings were female deities, the goddess *jamarani* and the goddess *sita penu* (Jena et al. 2002, 136).[67] In the beginning, everything was created by *jamarani* inside the earth, where humans lived as if in a womb, in complete darkness. For this reason the human beings complained and told her:

> ...if you do not give us a king we will not be able to live in this darkness for long, and peace and harmony will not last. Since it was you who created us, it is you who are obliged to save our lives. We cannot move in darkness, and we need a king who will bring us light. (Jena et al. 2002, 138)

With the help of the goddess's female assistants (*jateni*) and a female swan, which lays an egg after eating "coarse sand and rock particles" (Jena et al. 2002, 139), the sun god *dharma devata* bursts out of this egg (Jena et al. 2002, 140). With his help the human beings are rescued from their plight, as the light of the sun god shows them the way out of darkness:

> ...after a long search they spotted a ray of light entering through a small crack. They followed it to its source and thus arrived at *sapangada-(sativada) batangada (batativala)*. (Jena et al. 2002, 142)[68]

---

[67] An old Dongria man once explained to me the origin of the main gods in the Dongria pantheon. According to his statement, all life stems from a female deity called *ui ma*, whose name probably derives from the local word for termite, *ulama*. She created *jamaraja* and *jaura* ("*jamarani*") out of the soil. *Jaura* in turn created one of the main gods, *gajahadi*, who similarly has no father. When *gajahadi* established heaven, *jauragada* or "the place of *jaura*," by putting up an iron pillar on which the sky rests, all the other gods were created. In other words, Gajahadi as a man builds the house, but only the goddess as a woman can create the beings inhabiting this house.

[68] In 2001, along with Professor Georg Pfeffer from the Free University of Berlin, I visited the place that the Kuttia Kond regard as Sapangada, the place where the first humans came out of the earth. It is a rocky place in the forest with a small dark hole overgrown by creepers. An old Kuttia Kond who did not dare to approach the site, as it was worshipped by a rival

Darkness is here linked to being inside the woman, in this case the earth, while light is associated with the male god and the release out of the inner female sphere into the outer male sphere. In the female sphere, creation is possible, while male order and dominance are absent. In the male sphere, in contrast, the sun's light becomes a representation of the powers of the male king, who brings order to the world but cannot create anything on his own. Like the boys who leave the dormitories with the first glimpse of light in the morning, the first human beings could leave their dark habitat inside the earth when they saw a "ray of light." In the same way, married men leave their houses to meet on the village plaza when the cock crows, a sign that the sun god is taking his bath (see section 2.5.8). Just as the sun god establishes order when his light pierces through the darkness, men solve their conflicts when they assemble in the morning, at the time when they see the first light of the sun on the horizon.

The *bali yatra* (Hardenberg 2014) celebrated in some Dongria villages around the full moon in March-April clearly refers to this mythological opposition between the dark but fertile female sphere and the light-filled domain of the male god who destroys and restores order. The main deities worshipped on this occasion are the male god of fire, *bera*, and the female deity of fertility and the soil, *sita penu* or *bali ma* ("mother of sand"). At the beginning of the weeklong festival, the shaman, along with some villagers, goes at night to a river where the group collects soil from different places, which they bring back and store in baskets in a closed hut. In this soil they sow different grains, after which they cover the whole arrangement. Outside this hut, the god of fire is worshipped by sick people twice a day with gifts presented to the possessed shaman, who then offers his body to the god for dancing. While dancing, the god holds swords; while resting, he is represented by a knife stuck into the ground in front of the goddess's hut. On the last day, a swing with a seat made out of wood covered with long thorns is erected opposite the goddess's hut. The shaman, on behalf of *bera penu*, sits swinging while advising patients. A fire pit is dug and filled with burning charcoal. The shaman runs over the hot ashes as a sign of his control of the powerful and potentially destructive heat. At that moment, the sprouts are taken out of the dark hut and brought into the open space. Like the first human beings in the myth, the sprouts were created in complete darkness and sprouted from the soil without sunlight, inside the hut. They are then taken out of the hut and brought to the place where the god of fire, who

---

clan, informed us that a human sacrifice had been performed at the spot a couple of weeks before.

is associated with the sun god and controls destructive forces, is restoring human beings' health.

Depending on context, there are various manifestations of this inner female sphere characterised by darkness, such as the womb, the house, the dormitory, and the earth, and all stand in contrast to the male sphere dominated by the sun god's light. Just as the sun god moves across the sky in his chariot every day, the male sphere is dominated by movement. However, women are the ones who control male movement in their own female "realm," their house, dormitory, and body. They "swallow" (*guhne*) men in the night by letting them enter their house, dormitory, or body, and they "spit them out" (*kakne*) in the morning, when sexual activity ends and the boys leave for their own villages and the men for their fields. Among Dongria, both houses and dormitories are made of wood and clay with only small openings that allow hardly any light to enter the rooms. The interior remains dark most of the time, the only light being provided by the fire in the hearth or by an oil lamp. Being in a house feels like being in a cave or inside the earth. This similarity between the dwelling place of unmarried girls and a cave or a hole in the earth can be seen in descriptions of the youth dormitory among the Bondo. For example, Fürer-Haimendorf states:

> Originally, there were two types of girls' dormitories; ordinary small houses attached to dwelling houses, and underground shelters, dug some ten feet deep into the ground and roofed over with branches, bamboo and pounded earth. (Fürer-Haimendorf 1950, 130)

During the day, men and women rarely stay inside the house or village but move around and work, while at night, everybody stays inside the house or the dormitory. The opposition between mobility and immobility corresponds to the opposition between sun and earth, day and night, working (agricultural reproduction) and sleeping (sexual reproduction).

The sun god in the myth collected by Jena et al. is *not* represented as the primary agent of creation, since his role is limited to showing the way out of the womb, out of darkness. When his light penetrates the earth through the hole made by a small insect (Jena et al. 2002, 135), the human beings already exist. According to this myth, the sun god's role in procreation is limited to "opening" the earth, in order to allow the human beings to come out. The myth therefore contains the following message: men and women are necessary for creation, men's primary role being to "open" the earth so that her creation can be released.[69] The whole process from creation to birth is more or less controlled

---

[69] These ideas about pregnancy may not be so different from Malinowski's famous Trobriand

by women. In the myth, *jamarani* herself creates the human beings and enables them to be "born" by ensuring the birth of the male god, the sun, and allowing him to pierce her with his rays.

Table 24: Structures of the creation myth, the *bali yatra,* and social life

jamarani	*dharam devata*
bali ma (sita penu)	*bera penu*
female	male
earth	sun / fire
soil	knife / thorns
creation	rule
darkness	light
immobility	mobility
being inside the earth ("womb")	moving outside
inside the dormitory	leaving the dormitory
sexual intercourse	political meetings

Where the conception of a child is concerned, Dongria similarly ascribe the most important creative functions to female deities. Thus Jena et al. state:

> When a woman conceives a child, this is understood to be the work of *jaura penu,* as she is believed to be responsible for creating life on earth. [...] It follows that, after death, the soul moves to *svarga* and, at the time of rebirth, it reaches *jauragada,* where *jaura penu* transforms the soul into the seed of life. (Jena et al. 2002, 182)

My own research confirms this view. Dongria explain the conception of a child as the result of the creative functions of the goddess *jamarani* or *jaura penu,* who transfers the soul (*jela* or *jiu*) into the female womb where it slowly forms a body. It is significant that in the Dombo version of this belief, collected by me from an old Dombo woman in Gumma, *jaura*'s husband, the god of death

---

case (Malinowski 1929, 154). Malinowski's "fatherless children in a matrilineal society" (Malinowski 1929, 166) have made a deep impact on generations of anthropologists. The present data, however, seem to indicate that descent rules are hardly functional prerequisites for the idea that "the vagina must be opened" (Malinowski 1929, 154), though insemination by the male is a non-issue.

named *jamaraja*, plays a significant role, as he is said to form the body (*linga*) of the new-born, while the goddess's function consists in writing the child's fate into the foetus. I am not aware of similar ideas concerning the role of male gods in procreation among the Dongria.

Further information from Dongria is needed on this matter, but according to my present knowledge, I understand their concept of creation as follows. All life depends on the existence of souls (*jela* or *jiu*), which are transferred by the goddess of life, *jaura penu*, into various beings, whether human beings, animals, or plants.[70] Just as *jaura penu* created the first beings inside the earth, she puts life inside a woman, into her "belly" (*pota*). When the woman wants to conceive a child, she allows a man to penetrate her, like the sun god penetrated the earth, in order to open her "belly."

What has been missing so far in this discussion of ideas concerning conception is the socio-territorial factor. There is a definite difference between married women, who have sexual intercourse with their husbands in the husband's house and village, and unmarried dormitory girls, who stay in their own village and have sexual affairs with boys who come to the girl's village and house. Marriage reverses the situation for dormitory girls and their lovers. In the context of married couples, everybody expects the woman to become pregnant; in the context of dormitories, sexual relations should not be linked to reproduction. The same attitude is expressed by Muria Gond, according to Elwin:

> there is no doubt that the *chelik* and *motiari* are expected to avoid conception somehow. (Elwin 1991, 465).

This supports the statement, mentioned above, that girls do not often agree to be penetrated, and if they do, they mostly want to become the boy's wife. Taken as an ideal, this means that a man should activate a woman's generative powers in his own house and territory, just as he should ideally cultivate the fields of his own clan land. The division into several clan territories was established by Niamraja according to the myths, but the earth herself and her children were created by the goddess. In a society in which creative powers are ascribed to women, whether a wife or the earth, and in which the earth's products and a woman's children belong to men, there must be ways for men to claim what they them-

---

[70] Niggemeyer collected information among the Kuttia Kond concerning their ideas about conception. According to his informants, the female goddess named *linga pinnu-jaora pinnu* creates the bodies of all human beings with two "machines," one for men one for women, and adds life or "breath" (*jela*) to them. After death, *jela* goes back to *linga pinnu-jaora pinnu*, who keeps it in a dark room (Niggemeyer 1964a, 142–43).

selves cannot generate. Marriage, "betrothal fee", and bride capture are certainly one way, just as another would be patrilineal definitions of clan membership and territorial ownership based on descent. Seen in this manner, the dormitory indeed represents a kind of temporary counter-model to the world of adult married people: the dormitory belongs to the girls, they remain in their own clan territory, they choose their partners according to their own liking, and they have sex ideally without procreation. As a female development officer put it in a typical mixture of Oriya and English, *tara bada power*, "their power is great!"

We may here mark a difference between married and unmarried women. While the dormitory girls control sexual encounters that should not lead to pregnancy, married women are expected to become pregnant after having sex with their husbands. As married women, they have partially lost their dominance and control, since they are no longer in their own villages surrounded by their kin and family members but live in the villages of their husbands. With marriage, the husband acquires a right to the children born to his wife,[71] which the young men visiting the dormitories do not have. While I have not heard about or witnessed any violence against unmarried women, I have personally witnessed husbands beating their wives. Such cases are comparatively rare. If the woman's parents or brothers are alive, she will run home and seek their protection, and in cases of repeated marital violence, the village neighbours interfere. Thus, married Dongria women are seen to have creative power, but they have partially lost control over their bodies and over the sexual encounter, a control that is so characteristic of the dormitory girls.

Pregnancy (*pota ate* or "she got a belly")
Although actual sexual intercourse between boys and girls is the exception, it certainly occurs, and dormitory girls do become pregnant. This leaves the woman with several options. If the girl is promised to somebody and if both are willing to stay together, she moves to his village. The fact that somebody else may be the child's genitor does not bother Dongria too much, as they are aware that a man normally does not know who the genitor of his first child is. As mentioned above, girls are allowed to sleep in dormitories before marriage and even after the wedding until the time husband and wife, with the blessing of the villagers, are joined in their house to spend their first night together. Even afterwards, the girl may visit dormitories and sleep with other men when she attends festivals or pays a visit to her parents' house. Only once the first

---

71 In the event of divorce, the children will remain with the father or the father's brother.

child has been born are both husband and wife expected to refrain from sleeping in dormitories.

If the pregnant girl is deeply in love with a particular boy who is not her arranged husband, she can elope with him or show little resistance when he comes to capture her. This may lead to a conflict with her fiancé's village if he insists on marrying her. The following case illustrates such a conflict and shows how strongly Dongria women do resist the pressure of their social group. A young woman of Gumma named Sikoka Site was promised to a man from Sutangoni, a village belonging to the Pusika clan. She had lived in his village for some time before returning home, as they did not get along well with each other. For some years she continued to sleep in various dormitories and had numerous love affairs, allegedly even with a clan brother from her own village, which caused a scandal. Finally, she fell in love with a man from Tamkaseli, a village of the Kadraka clan, became pregnant, and following the *bali yatra*, ran away with him. She stayed in his home for some time, and her lover's family agreed to pay a fine to her former husband. One day, her new husband's mother brought her back to her natal village because they were unable to pay the total fine or – as an outsider might speculate – to force Site's parents to reduce their demands. Site was angry because she did not want to stay at her father's house but wished to live with her new husband. I was present on that day and overheard a quarrel between Site and one of the Dombo women. The latter blamed her for being reluctant to marry the man from Sutangoni, whose fellow villagers were threatening to send their god to bring harm to Site's parental village. As the Dombo woman explained to me later, the villagers of Sutangoni are feared on account of a certain deity whom they can command to bring sickness and infertility to other people. As before, Site was not willing to submit to the pressure exerted by either her parents or the village authorities and returned to her new husband from Tamkalseli, where she continued to live. A few months later her baby was born, and she was accepted as a daughter-in-law in the Kadraka's family.

When a dormitory girl becomes pregnant, a competition may break out between several men who are known to have been her lovers. In one such case, a woman from Sutangoni became pregnant, and two men from the Sikoka clan were competing to become her husband. One of them was from the village where I lived, so that I got first-hand information about the events. The father of the boy, named Sikoka Mishra, had arranged a marriage for him in his childhood, but his bride was unwilling to marry him. His family was eager to have a daughter-in-law to help working in the fields, and when one day a girl of the Wadaka clan with whom Mishra had slept in the Sutangoni dormitory was reported to be pregnant, his parents made arrangements to bring her to Gumma. The girl had been promised to a man from Salpajala, and anybody intending to capture her was aware that her first husband's[72] villagers were entitled to demand compensation. For this reason, Mishra's father one day went all the way to Sutangoni to bargain about the fine in advance. Word spread that around Rs 12,000 were demanded as a payment for the pregnant girl, and Mishra's father began collecting money from his relatives and from the anthropologist living in his village. A plan was set up to capture the girl on the following Wednesday and to give a large feast the next day, i.e., the occasion when the boy's father is expected to give a buffalo to the villagers who helped him during the enterprise. As Mishra, his father, and several fellow villagers left for Sutangoni to capture the girl, they learned that a Sikoka from the neighbouring village of Dongormati had already captured her two days before. After his return, I asked the loser of the contest whom he considered to be the father of the child, and he answered that the one who captured the girl and kept her in his village would be the father. He did not worry too much about who the actual genitor of the child might have been, although he admitted that his competitor had slept with the girl more often than he. For this reason, he explained to me, the other fellow could be the father, because a woman only gets pregnant from a man if he sleeps with her quite often.

If the girl becomes pregnant without anybody claiming her as his wife, she may be forced to put her child to death. In the village where I lived, a woman had become pregnant after sleeping in various dormitories and houses, but nobody had asked her to become his wife. According to information given by the well-informed local development officers, this happened to her twice. The first time she neglected the child until it died, and the second time she was forced to keep the baby alive, as the local policeman threatened her to put her in jail if the child died. She raised her second child and continued to live in her parents' house until a widower paid a small "betrothal fee" in the form of two buffaloes to the village in order to marry her. I do not have any statistical data about often such cases of infanticide actually do occur, but my general impression is that they are rare.

"Virgin Birth" debate

Leach's (1969) distinction between dogma and actual knowledge rests on the idea that people may in certain contexts, such as myths or rituals, articulate a collective doctrine, while in other contexts they may express a knowledge based on other premises and deviating from that doctrine. For him the question

---

[72] As mentioned before, once a girl is promised to another man, he is considered to be her "husband" (*dakera*), and she is his "wife" even if the wedding has not yet taken place.

then remains why people sometimes stress the dogma although they know about the "facts of life." His answer is that the dogma must be seen as part of philosophical speculations about the relation between the physical and the metaphysical and that such dogmatic statements are expressions of how people conceive of the relations between men and gods. I agree with Leach on this point, because the ideas concerning the activities of *jaura penu* establish a relation between her and women. *Jaura penu* is the original creator, and she inserts her creative power into women's wombs. Seen in this way, women are the goddess's descendants, who repeat the primordial act by which the goddess created the first human beings. This relationship stands in opposition to the relation between men and the male god in the biblical version of creation, in which Adam and his seed continue the male power of life-giving (Delaney 1986, 501). However, does this mean that there must necessarily be a contradiction between the "supernatural" and "natural" theories of procreation? Delaney, in her critique of Leach, states this point forcefully:

> In the Trobriands, virgins neither conceive nor give birth. The so-called supernatural birth among the Trobriand or Aboriginal women is in fact, the normal everyday, dare I say "natural", way of doing things, whereas the Virgin Birth is felt to be a unique event in world history. (Delaney 1986, 501)

In this statement, Delaney actually sets up two oppositions, one between supernatural and natural theories and one between these theories and the "unique" mythological event. Thus, the story of Virgin Birth appears to contradict folk models giving importance to male paternity, and it stands in contrast to the folk models of other people, which may similarly deny the importance of paternity but do not regard this as a unique mythological exception but as the regular course of events. Regarding the Dongria, I hold the view that all these levels are more or less congruent, as I can find a clear opposition neither between the supernatural and the natural nor between unique mythological events and the common folk model. The creation of the first human being was, of course, a rather unique event, but since the goddess continues to exercise her power through women in the birth of any new-born child, the emphasis lies on continuity rather than disruption between the world of gods and human beings. Furthermore, the idea of the goddess's supernatural intervention in no way contradicts the theory that the woman's will and penetration by the man play a significant role. The folk model is clearly logical and integrates various ideas in a systematic fashion.

This Dongria folk model stands in striking opposition to what Delaney found among rural Turkish people, a model that she understands to be part of a widespread Western conception going back to biblical doctrines. Here, the male god and his descendants, men, are the sole creators, while women's role consist in nourishing the foetus and the child. As in Hindu doctrines of creation, paternity is expressed in terms of semen because "the child comes from the seed," "the child comes from man," and "the child *originates* with the father, from his seed" (Delaney 1986, 497; emphasis original). In a conception similar to Hindu ideas about women, which are already described in the books of Manu (see Apffel-Marglin 1985, 66–67), Turkish women are considered to be like a "field" that the man encloses and into which he puts his "seed" (Delaney 1986, 498). The underlying concept of paternity is best captured in the following statement by Delaney:

> In the Turkish village, men are imagined to have creative power within them, which gives a core of identity, self-motivation or autonomy. Women lack the power to create and therefore to project themselves. (Delaney 1986, 499)

As stated above, semen does not figure prominently in Dongria myths or daily talk, and I have not heard Dongria say that a woman is like a cultivated field (*nelu* or *neta*), although women are clearly considered to be similar to the earth. It is, however, clear that among the Dongria semen does not make a man a "pater" in the sense described by Delaney, because women, not men, are imagined to have the creative power within them. Can we thus state that Dongria, in contrast to the Turkish villagers described by Delaney, do not have a concept of paternity, because for Delaney "paternity means that the male role in the production of a child is understood as *the* generative and creative one" (Delaney 1986, 501; emphasis original)? Are they more like the matrilineal Trobrianders, who ascribe a "formative role" to men but lack a "concept of paternity" (Delaney 1986, 507)? Furthermore, how can we interpret the relation between the Dongria's emphasis on "maternity" and their polytheistic system?

Dongria ideas about conception are highly complex, as pregnancy for them depends on the interplay of a series of conditions: the activity of *jaura penu*, who gives life; the will of the woman, who controls sexual intercourse; long and frequent penetration by a man, who opens the woman's belly; and marital practices such as bride capture, betrothal, etc. Dongria, like the Trobriand people and unlike Hindus, may be said to have a concept of "maternity" rather than "paternity," because they ascribe all creative powers to female goddesses and women. However, to reduce the question of "paternity" and "maternity" to the question of who is regarded to be "*the* generative and creative one" is to neglect cultural constructions of the interdependence of both male and female powers. In my interpretation, Dongria women are regarded as representatives of the earth, through whom the goddess repeats her original creation of humankind each time a woman gets pregnant. Men, on the other hand, have to penetrate the women, just as the sun god penetrated the earth. Like the sun, they must be active to help the women to be creative and in order to obtain the result of their reproductive powers.

As described in this chapter, there are two legitimate ways for a man to have access to a woman's creative force, one being arranged marriage and the other being bride-capture. In the first case, the man makes considerable gifts in exchange for the woman's "life"; in the second case, he takes her by force. Exchange and violence are also appropriate ways to obtain rights in land, which in the past could either be bought from a different clan (see p. 505) or taken by force. In chapter five I will show that exchange and violence are also the two legitimate ways to acquire the fertility of the earth, the purpose for which Dongria conduct the elaborate buffalo sacrifice. In other words, Dongria men sustain life, less in the sense of "nurturing" it, more in the sense of being active and providing an order to creation. The ideal god is a king who establishes the order of things, without which creation remains in an incomplete condition. Giving order also means solving the question of whom the creation actually belongs to, and marriage, with "betrothal fee" or by capture, and land acquisition, by purchase or by force, may be understood as two ways to tackle this problem.

This argument helps us to find an answer to the second question. Delaney sees a congruence between monotheism and the monogenetic theory of creation (Delaney 1986, 503–4; 2001, 545). In our case, I would rather assert a congruence between the interdependence of male and female powers for creation and the fact that in many Dongria rituals pairs of male and female gods are worshipped. The most important festival, the sacrifice for the earth goddess, contains long sequences worshiping her husband, *koteiwali*, who stands for the mountain gods, particularly *niamraja*, who rules over all Dongria.

In conclusion, we may state an interesting difference between biblical and Turkish notions of creation as identified by Delaney and Dongria ideas concerning procreation. In both cases, women can be described as "vessels" for creation. In the Bible and in Turkish representations recorded by Delaney the spiritual power of the god or the semen of the men is considered to be the source of creation, while in Dongria mythology this power is ascribed to the goddess. In contrast to the biblical god, the Dongria's most important male god, the sun, is not described as the primary creator but rather as someone who helps to finish and to sustain the creation of the goddess. Similarly, Dongria men are expected to be active in terms of ritual, exchange, and violent action in order to acquire and promote fertility. Violence in the form of bride capture can be considered one of the major ways for a man to get access to the creative powers of a woman.

4.4.3 Bride capture (*ahpa tana* or "let's catch and bring")

An article on bride capture by Barnes (1999) gives the impression that this form of marriage has become a phenomenon of the past. The examples cited by Barnes from Eastern Indonesia, the Caribbean, Northwest Amazonia, Northeast Arnhem, and New Guinea derive from either older ethnographies whose authors occasionally witnessed bride capture in the field or newer ethnographies that mostly contain informants' reminiscences concerning bride capture as it used to be practised in the past. For example, Barnes mentions his own ethnographic experiences in Eastern Indonesia:

> While doing research in Lamalera, Lembata, Eastern Indonesia, I was once told that in the past, if a young man had made up his mind that he wished to marry a certain young woman and was encountering resistance, he would wait at an appropriate hiding place and capture the woman. (Barnes 1999, 57)

> Bride capture appears in the published Lamaholot ethnography as something which belongs to the past. It is not available for ethnographers to witness, and it would certainly not be possible for one and the same ethnographer to witness and make a comparable study of several cases. (Barnes 1999, 59)

Similarly, the Desia Kond, who inhabit the valleys and foothills of the Niamgiri mountain range, told me that their forefathers used to capture their brides, but that they gave up this custom some decades ago. Taking into account that bride capture seems to be a vanishing custom worldwide, it is important to record that Dongria Kond have not abandoned it but on the contrary practise it to a great extent.[73] In contrast to their "brothers" from the valleys, the Desia Kond, Dongria do not feel the need to adopt the more "civilised" manners of the plains people but are rather proud of the manliness involved in this type of marriage.

As mentioned above, Dongria may resort to capture when their affines are not willing to arrange a wedding even though all their demands have been fulfilled or when they aim to reduce the amount of the "betrothal fee'. Apart from bride capture as part of on-going marriage negotiations, however, it may also serve the purpose of acquiring a wife who has been demanded by somebody else or who has become pregnant. This leads to disputes and conflicts to be solved by the elders of all villages concerned, who must agree on certain fines to be paid to the fiancé

---

[73] Similarly, in the high mountains of the Belgarh area, Kuttia Kond seem to be involved in bride capture rather frequently, as Götzelmann and Pfeffer directly observed in March 1990 (personal communication). In 1983, Pfeffer similarly observed extended and controversial negotiations in a Kuttia Kond bride's village (personal communication). Though the Kuttia appear to be more peaceful than the Dongria, Kuttia affinal rules offer many similarities.

and his family (see section 4.4.4). For this reason, bride capture should not be regarded as a cheap way of acquiring a wife, since the fines to be paid can be as high or even higher than the "betrothal fee" in a regular arranged marriage. However, if the girl has not been promised to anybody else, bride capture may indeed be a way to avoid the high costs involved in "betrothal fee" marriages. As a procedure for bringing the bride from her natal village to the boy's village, bride capture has the same legitimacy as an arranged marriage with a formal wedding procession. Many Dongria who have more than one wife acquired their spouses through negotiations and through capture. Thus, in Gumma several men had two wives (*ireli* or "co-wives"), one acquired through formal arrangements by their elders, the other a former dormitory girl captured after a love affair. The following case studies illustrate the range of actions falling into the local category of capture (*ahpa tana* or "let's catch and bring").

Bride capture may be a very imprudent affair carried out singlehandedly and without any preparations. I witnessed such an attempt when attending a marriage ceremony in Sana Dengoni. On the second day of the wedding ceremonies, when the *jani* chant their verses while sitting in the river, I saw a young man approaching a small group of girls, among them a young woman for whom his parents had paid a substantial "betrothal fee". He was eager to bring her home as his wife, and in his drunken state it must have come into his mind that this was a good opportunity to seize her. Without hesitation he grabbed the girl and pulled her along the path, but her girlfriends reacted quickly, holding on to her tightly. The bride, with the help of her girlfriends, resisted as well as she could, but her groom was very strong and managed to drag her slowly in his direction. The hue and cry of the girls did not escape the attention of others, and within a short time the village chief from Sana Dengoni turned up and intervened. The chief was enraged and expressed his anger by stamping his feet on the ground, twirling his moustache, shouting at the young man, and kicking him. To my surprise, the latter showed no resistance, although he could have easily overpowered the much weaker chief. Instead, he let the girl loose, and as soon as he lost his grip onto her, she and her girlfriends ran away. The girl was crying loudly, and as she was afraid to encounter her groom again, she left the place along with her girlfriends, returning home immediately. A year later, their marriage was solemnised in an official procession attended by all parties in an amicable atmosphere.

In the second case, which I witnessed only partially, the capture was well planned and organised and appeared to be more like a ceremony than an aggressive conquest. One day in July 2001, ten young men from Gumma left for Sana Denganali to "catch" a woman and her new-born baby. The woman, named Kadraka Drimbi, had been married to a Sikoka from Niskhal but had abandoned him to live in the house of her married sister. Being away from her husband, she slept in different dormitories and finally became pregnant, most probably by Sikoka Kangu, a member of the richest family in Gumma. When her husband heard about her pregnancy, he brought her back to his village, but when he died after some months, Kadraka Drimbi again returned to her brother-in-law's village, where she gave birth to her son. A month later, the ten men from Gumma turned up to "capture" her. Neither she nor the other villagers showed any resistance, and when I met the group of "abductors" on the way to Gumma, Kadraka Drimbi was walking calmly among them while one of the men carried her baby. On the way they had stopped in Bada Denganali to drink a few bottles of country liquor, which the "husband" had to give his fellow villagers as remuneration for their participation. When they reached the village, all proceeded to Kangu's house, where an elderly female shaman sprinkled her with water, the rest of which she poured on the roof. The woman entered the house and sat down in the back room, where new clothes were given to her before she began breastfeeding her child. The village chief turned up and made libations of liquor to the ancestors in a corner of the inner room next to the door leading to the back of the house. The *bejuni* sat down in front of the sacred wall and made offerings of liquor to the house goddess, *lahi penu–sita penu*, before everybody present shared the rest of the alcohol. In this way, the ancestors and the house goddess were informed about the arrival of the new members of the house and asked to protect them. Finally, all shared a meal of cooked rice prepared by the new daughter-in-law.

The third case exemplifies the rather casual, sportsmanlike manner in which a bride capture may be performed. One evening I was informed by a friend that some young fellow villagers were about to capture a girl from Lamba, a village located about thirty minutes walk from Gumma. The two dormitories of this village are regularly frequented by the young men of Gumma, as they can be reached fairly easily and in a short time. In this case, the abductors planned to capture a girl for a boy who, at that time, had had neither a serious love affair nor an arranged marriage. The whole enterprise appeared to me to be a spontaneous operation conceived the same evening while sitting under the *salap* tree. As darkness set in, I joined the eleven men on their way across the hills to Lamba. When we approached the village, conversations were continued in whispers, and the young men sat down behind some bushes to discuss their strategy. They came up with the following plan: two boys should go ahead and knock on the door of the dormitory. As soon as the girls opened the door, the others were to rush forward and help to pull the victim out of the dormitory and carry her back to Gumma.

While I was hiding along with others behind the bushes, two boys went ahead to put the plan into action. They knocked on the door, talked to the girls until the door was opened, and rushed inside. At that moment, the others left their hiding place and rushed towards the dormitory, but on reaching it they learned that the girl they were looking for was not present. The earlier seriousness of the enterprise was immediately gone, and people began joking and laughing. Meanwhile, the villagers had learned about the failed attempt to capture one of their girls, but nobody seemed to feel angry about it. Instead, the inhabitants of the second dormitory invited us to come and sit in their house. For a while, chatting and joking continued, until the abductors returned to Gumma in a relaxed mood.

The strategic planning of a bride capture can best be illustrated by the following case of an attempted abduction during the day. The father of Sikoka Mishra, to whom I referred above in the context of the events leading to the capture of a pregnant woman, had arranged a marriage for his son with the daughter of a fellow villager. When the girl's father died, Mishra's father bore all the expenses for his funeral in the expectation that her lineage members would agree to an early marriage. However, the girl ran away to a distant village named Railima, where she stayed in the house of her father's brother. On several occasions, Mishra's father tried in vain to persuade her family members to arrange the marriage ceremony.

One day, a man of the Huika clan residing in Gumma received a visit from the girl's sister and brother-in-law. She spread the news that her sister, Mishra's bride, was presently living in Kancharu, a small village about an hour's walk away from Gumma. Next morning, a group of men consisting of Mishra's friends, his parents, and married fellow villagers was formed to capture his bride. I was asked to join them on the condition that I would not disclose the real purpose of our trip to anybody. As is customary on such an occasion, everybody carried a stick while walking in a line through the jungle, although nobody actually feared that the group could be attacked by the bride's relatives. The time passed in a joking atmosphere, the men constantly teasing each other by alluding to the feminine appearance, childish behaviour, or alleged sexual impotence of their companions. When we met somebody on the road and were asked about the object of our journey, the men from Gumma pretended to be on the way to Parsali, where the DKDA has its offices. This appeared reasonable to some passers-by, since Dongria constantly visit the offices to buy rice and kerosene or to attend a "meeting," while others rightly suspected us to be on the way to capture a girl.

Shortly before we reached Kancharu, we left the path and sat down in the forest to discuss the strategy for the subsequent actions. After the group had mulled over the best course for some time, somebody came up with a plan. He suggested sending three people to the village, among them the girl's mother's brother. While the latter, along with another strong man, was to approach the house from the front, the third man was to guard the back in case the victim made an attempt to escape in this direction. He also suggested employing a subterfuge in order to distract the villagers from the real purpose of their visit: the mother's brother was to tell the members of the house where Mishra's bride was suspected to be living that he had come to discuss the matter of jewellery belonging to her. He should inform them that the girl's sister had come to Gumma to demand the jewellery, which had remained in his possession following the death of her father. This was expected to make perfect sense to the villagers of Kancharu, as it was largely based upon truth. Once the people of Kancharu were convinced of their visitors' good intentions, they would allow them to talk to the girl. This would be the right moment for the others to leave their hiding places and help the three men to capture the girl.

The plan was accepted, and while the three men slowly walked in the direction of Kancharu, the others searched for a good ambush place. I found myself in the company of four young men, including the groom, who were hiding in a grove that offered a good view over the village and was praised by the boys as an excellent place for an amorous meeting. After about fifteen minutes of waiting, the three delegates returned with the news that Mishra's bride was not present and that the whole enterprise was in vain. A bit disappointed but still in a good mood, the men from Gumma went home. Only a few weeks later, their endeavours were crowned with success when they managed to capture the girl while she was working in a swidden. I was not present on this occasion but met the abductors when they arrived in Gumma with their "prey."

Bride capture is like a hunt, and not coincidentally, most cases of bride capture occur in late winter and spring when Dongria, along with professional hunters from the valleys, move through the forests in search for prey. Writing about abduction among the Kond more than a hundred and fifty years ago, Campbell stated:

> Marriages are usually celebrated in the hunting time, and then in almost every village may be heard the sound of their shrill musical instruments. (Campbell 1864, 43)

That a bride capture is likened to a hunt can be deduced from the expression used for such an operation as well as from the manner in which it is carried out. One expression used to encourage somebody to join a bride capture is to ask *ahpa beta hanagi*, meaning "shall we go hunting?" If he agrees, the venture may indeed turn into an activity that in many ways resembles an animal hunt. This is well illustrated by the following case.

As mentioned above, the people of Dongormati had succeeded in capturing a pregnant woman from Sutangoni two days before the young men from Gumma were planning to bring her to their village. In retaliation for this affront, the married and unmarried men of Gumma, including the prospective groom, Sikoka Mishra, formed a band for the purpose of capturing the girl from Dongormati. I joined the party, and we left the village in the morning along a narrow path that leads through the forest and across the hills from Gumma to Dongormati. The men had gained information that the girl was working in the swidden of her new husband. A plan was made. Instead of following the path that leads directly to the village, the men took a trail up into the hills belonging to Dongormati. The trail was well selected, as it led through the forest and protected the "hunters" from being seen by the Dongria working in the swidden fields. Slowly approaching the girl's husband's hill and communicating only in whispers, the men planned how to capture the girl. Everybody agreed to approach the field hut where the girl was supposedly staying from different sides, and so the party split up into smaller groups. I remained with one group at the foot of the hill, in some bushes a few meters away from the trail. We were to catch the girl if she ran down the path back to the village. The mood was very tense, as everybody was afraid of being caught by the people from Dongormati, but nothing happened until we heard some members of our party coming down from the hill, where they had searched in vain for the girl. I later asked what might have happened if we had been caught, and one of my informants answered that we could have faced angry men from Dongormati throwing stones at us. He ruled out more serious reactions, since Dongria usually abstain from attacking bride abductors with their axes. The whole affair strongly resembled a hunt, as the group of men silently walked through the jungle, encircled the girl, and planned to cut off her escape route. In contrast to other cases of bride capture, the abductors did not approach the village but instead approached the girl on the hill slope like a beast of prey.

All these cases clearly demonstrate that bride capture has a playful character, perhaps less so for the young man who wants to obtain a wife than for the other abductors, for whom such an operation is a welcome change from their daily working routine. They enjoy the thrill of "hunting" the girl and the risk of being caught in the act. When successful, everybody is served alcohol and in most cases even given a large portion of buffalo meat. This gift of a buffalo made by the abductor to his fellow villagers is called *ahpa kodru* or "catching buffalo." A bride capture, like a formal marriage, must furthermore be a collective affair and involves reciprocity, as those who ask their fellow villagers for help offer the same service in return on a later occasion. The village as a whole obtains the wife, and when the capture leads to quarrels and demands for compensation from other villages, the abductor can rely on the assistance of his fellow villagers in settling the conflict.

4.4.4 Conflict settlement

A bride capture may be carried out by a man who intends to obtain the bride for whom he and his family members have paid a considerable "betrothal fee" or by a lover who wants to bring his beloved to his own village. While in the former case normally only two parties are involved, the bride's and groom's families, the second case may lead to a conflict between three villages if the girl was promised to somebody else. When the girl does not run back home but prefers to stay with her lover, her former fiancé may either try to recover her or enter into negotiations about an appropriate fine (*tapu*) to be paid by the abductor. If the negotiations fail because the lover does not meet the demands, violence may break out between the two parties. For example, Nayak reports the following case that occurred fifteen to twenty years prior to his research:

> A *Nundruka* family from Merkabondeli had proposed the marriage of their son with the daughter of a *Nisika* family of Nisikabondeli. Retu, a young man from Garata, along with two of his friends abducted a *Nisika* maiden. The *Nundruka* failed to obtain the brideprice [the author means the fine for settling the dispute, R.H.] from the *Pusika* in spite of several rounds of discussion in Garata village. A few months passed. It was the day of the dussehra festival in the year 1966 at Bissamcuttack. The Dongria came down to observe the festival in large groups. The Dongria in divided groups indulged in displaying their traditional dances amidst songs and hurling of clubs and axes on the main road of Bissamcuttack. In the course of dancing the *Nandruka* and the *Pusika* exchanged abuses and there was a confrontation. All of a sudden the feud erupted and it was seen that *Pusika* Madakau, elder brother of Retu, was hacked into three pieces just in front of the police station. (Nayak 1989, 76–77)

During the period of my fieldwork, I witnessed such violent disputes only in the context of *meria* sacrifices, hardly any of which take place without somebody being injured or even killed. Instances of collective violence on the occasion of major Hindu festivals celebrated in the towns seem to occur less frequently today than in the past, although Dongria still threaten each other by saying, "Wait until we meet on the day of *siva yatra*" or "I'll see you at the *ratha yatra*." One reason may be the measures taken by the police to avoid the riots that according to many informants regularly used to occur when members of several villages assembled in the towns on festive occasions and seized the opportunity to take revenge for a previous misdeed. On the occasion of *ratha yatra* in Kalyansingpur, I witnessed the police forcing the young Dongria men to hand over their axes to them. Their names were written on the axe handles, and they could reclaim them at the end of the festival. In this way the officers nowadays try to prevent fatal injuries, which were very common in Kalyansingpur according to the shop owner I talked to.

Apart from direct assault on the members of the bride-seizing party, Dongria have other ways to retaliate against the abduction of one of their wives. As mentioned above, the villagers of Sutangoni threatened to send their village god to afflict the people of Gumma with diseases because they did not force one of their girls to agree to a long-arranged marriage. In one case, when the boys of my village captured a woman demanded by a man from a neighbouring village, the conflict was fought out at a buffalo sacrifice the same year, where some of the boys received serious blows. Another way to revenge a capture is to destroy the other village's crops. For example, two DKDA development officers remembered an occasion when a man from Gumma ran away with a girl claimed by another village. When no proper settlement was reached, these villagers became so enraged that one day they went to the fields belonging to Gumma, damaged as many fruit trees as possible, and chopped down the valuable palm-wine trees. This clearly shows the equivalence between natural wealth, i.e., the crops of the field and the fruits of the trees, and the woman acquired in the process of marriage negotiations.

Those cases I personally witnessed or heard about during the time of my research were not as violent as those described by Nayak. Nevertheless, threats and counter-threats were very much part of the negotiations among the three parties. The *barika* of Gumma told me several times that nowadays Dongria "sell" (Oriya: *bikuchonti*) their women, because they would rather agree to a settlement based on fines than try to recover their brides. Indeed, in those cases that came to my notice, the men preferred to accept a fine instead of insisting on their fiancée being returned. I think there are several reasons for this. First, if the girl prefers to stay with her abductor, who is normally a lover she frequently met in the dormitory, her former fiancé will find it difficult to persuade her to live with him. Second, he himself may be in love with another girl and therefore has no real interest in recovering his former bride. Third, a fine is accepted in those cases in which no real "betrothal fee" has been paid but only a few buffaloes and a few thousand rupees to solemnise the betrothal.

The whole process of reaching an amicable settlement may take several months and involves the following steps:
1. Village A captures a woman from Village B betrothed to a man from Village C.
2. The *barika* and some Dongria men from Village C visit the woman's parents in Village B and demand double the amount they have already paid as "betrothal fee".
3. The woman's parents send a delegation including their *barika* to Village A to demand double the amount of the "betrothal fee" already paid by Village C. When both parties agree on a certain amount of money, the bride's delegation receives the money and returns home.

4. Village C sends a delegation to the woman's village to demand their share of the money paid by the woman's abductors.
5. Village C sends their *barika* to Village A to demand a fine for capturing one of their brides. When the fine is paid, both parties undergo a ceremony called "pouring out water" (*eyu wapkoli*) to restore peace between them.

In other words, two different negotiations take place, one about the repayment of the "betrothal fee", the other about the fine to be paid by the abductors to the girl's former fiancé. When "betrothal fee" and fine are dealt with separately, Dongria refer to this reimbursement as a payment made *ra bata* or "on a single way." In actual fact, the two types of compensation are sometimes combined, in which case Dongria speak of a payment *ri bata* or "on two ways."

wrepoli takang ("paying back money")

Once a girl has been captured, the bride's parents and the parents of her former groom begin the negotiations. According to my experience, the family members of the first "husband"[74] waste no time but immediately send a delegation or at least their village *barika* to their former in-laws. In this preliminary meeting, the total amount of money and all the animals that were presented as part of the "betrothal fee" contribution are enumerated. Next, the husband's representatives demand double the amount they originally gave to the bride's parents. The bride-givers do not pay this money out of their own funds but approach the abductors on one of the following days and urge their new affines to give them enough money to meet the demands of their former affines. Nowadays, these meetings are often attended by members of the local police, such as the *chaukidar* and village home guards, or by the officers of the DKDA, who serve as so-called Multiple Purpose Workers (MPW). As a *chaukidar* once explained to me, in the past Dongria used to fight in order to enforce their will during such negotiations, while nowadays they ask these officials to help them in achieving a settlement. In my experience, none of these officers assumes a completely neutral role, least of all the village workers, who may fear to be reproached if they do not argue in favour of their own people.

Unlike the marriage negotiations, which take place inside the bride's parents' house, these negotiations are always held in a public space, either on

---

[74] I here adopt the language used by Dongria and Dombo when talking about these cases. The fiancé is usually called the girl's "husband" (*dakera*), while the bride-seizing people are referred to as *ahpa loku* or "abductors."

the central village plaza near the place of the earth goddess and her husband or on the veranda of the school (or the anthropologist's house). These meetings are usually attended by at least one man from each house as well as by two *barika* representing the bride's and the abductor's party, and sometimes even by a third *barika* commissioned by the first husband's family. Women stay inside the house or on the front veranda, from where they may shout their comments to the male assembly. The whole affair has a much greater public aspect than the marriage negotiations, and almost everybody feels obliged to make a comment. The atmosphere on such occasions may vary, from a highly aggressive tone to the usual exchange of arguments in a loud but not offensive way. When negotiations do not develop according to expectations, both parties employ the tactic of walking out of the discussion, the abductors withdrawing into their houses, the visitors actually going out of the village to a place where they wait to be called back by the other party.

To illustrate how these negotiations actually proceed, I describe the following case I observed in the village of Lamba in December 2001. Some years previously, a Pusika woman from Naringtola had married a Sikoka man from Niskhal. She stayed with him for five years, but since she did not become pregnant, her husband got himself a second wife and began to neglect the first one. Consequently, she moved around and slept in several dormitories until she finally got pregnant. Another Sikoka of Lamba was deeply in love with her, and when he heard about her pregnancy, he captured her along with some friends. Following some preliminary discussions, a date was fixed to negotiate the return of the "betrothal fee" to the people from Naringtola. For this occasion, the *chaukidar* of this area was invited to preside over the meeting. On the morning of the scheduled day, the bride's father, his elder and younger brothers, and the *barika* of all three parties involved in the case arrived in Lamba, where they were expected by the village elders and the *chaukidar*. The abductor himself remained in the background, and his elder brother intervened in the discussions only towards the end. Two cots were set up near the *koteiwali*, one for the guests and one for the hosts. The negotiations began with the *chaukidar* enumerating all items that were given as "betrothal fee" by the first husband's family to the bride's people. He wrote down the following list, in which he noted the actual worth of each gift:

two buffaloes	Rs 2,000
two sheep	Rs 1,000
two canisters of alcohol	Rs 500
two *puti* of rice	Rs 400
money gift	Rs 1,500
total	Rs. 5,150

4.4 Youthful deviation: Love marriage, bride capture, and collective settlements — 393

From this list we can conclude that the first husband paid only the minimum "betrothal fee", which, apart from a small amount of money and some minor gifts such as sheep, basically consists of a feast for which the groom provides two buffaloes, rice, and alcohol.

After listing these items, the *chaukidar* calculated the total worth of all the gifts and then stated publicly that according to the rules the abductors should pay back double the amount, i.e., Rs 10,300. Next, an elder from Lamba rose to speak and stated that neither could the people of Lamba pay such a huge amount of money nor would the people of Naringtola be able to "eat" this vast sum. He therefore suggested that the opposing party should be satisfied with only Rs 1,000, which he felt able to offer them. The bride's people considered this sum ridiculously low and instead demanded a payment of Rs 15,000 from the abductors. This set the stage for a series of arguments exchanged between the parties, the *chaukidar*'s role being to effect a compromise. As a result, the elders from Lamba gradually increased their offers, from Rs 1,500 to Rs 2,000, Rs 2,500 to Rs 3,000. The other party, on the other hand, was reluctant to reduce their demands and continued to insist on their first amount for a long time.

From time to time people got up from the cots and went a short distance away to engage in private negotiations with members of the opposing parties. When the bride's people refused to accommodate themselves to the offers made by the abductors, the latter discontinued the negotiations and went to the other end of their village. After some time, the visitors approached them again with an offer of Rs 9,000. However, the villagers of Lamba regarded this amount to be beneath any serious consideration. This attitude enraged the bride's people, who now on their part broke off the talks and made an attempt to leave the village. Both parties threatened each other with filing a "case," while at the same time ostentatiously expressing their complete lack of concern about the threats made by the other side. The *chaukidar* and the *barika* moved back and forth between the negotiators. As a "final offer" (*are ana hin:ambu* or "we give nothing more"), the bride's people finally signalled their willingness to accept only Rs 5,000 only, an offer turned down by the abductors, who raised their final offer from Rs 3,000 to Rs 4,000.

Now, the angry guests actually left the village and sat down on the path half a kilometre outside from the village to discuss their next moves. Meanwhile, the *barika* of Gumma, who represented the abductors' interests, argued in favour of a unanimous settlement of the conflict and suggested to the villagers of Lamba that they give their consent to the payment of Rs 5,000. However, the abductor and his elder brother continued to resist and agreed to a maximum payment of Rs 4,500 only. The moment they had decided to send the *barika* to the people of Naringtola to convey this message, the bride's father's younger brother suddenly appeared in the village and suggested agreeing on a payment of Rs 5,000 *ri bata* or "two ways," meaning that this money would compensate for the "betrothal-fee" as well as for the fine to the bride's former husband. The people of Lamba were, of course, delighted at this news and readily accepted the offer, but before anything could be finalised the *barika* of Naringtola arrived on the scene and revoked the father's younger brother's proposal. This move, of course, aroused the resentment of the abductors, who insisted on adhering to the original suggestion, but the *barika* from Naringtola was adamant and stubbornly repeated his demand for Rs 5,000 for the "betrothal fee" only.

Again, members of both parties began talking about a "case," but at this point the *chaukidar* intervened and explained that a "case" would only cause high expenses to all parties concerned. He convincingly argued that a "case" would cost the abductors at least Rs 10,000 to Rs 15,000, while an amicable settlement of the negotiations at this point would allow them to solve the conflict with a payment of only Rs 5,000. After some more discussions among themselves, the villagers of Lamba finally agreed to a payment of Rs 5,000 *ra bata* or "single way," which meant that the fine remained to be paid by them, as it was not included in this transaction. A villager brought a winnowing fan filled with husked rice, which was placed on the ground in the centre of the village where everybody assembled. The abductor's elder brother began placing banknotes into the winnowing fan, each thousand rupees being referred to as one *mana*, a unit used for measuring rice. When the total sum had been given and counted by various people present, the *chaukidar* was asked to write a *rasi* or "bill" mentioning the names of those involved in the settlement, the amount of money paid, and the reason for the transaction. He gave this bill to the abductor's family as a proof of their fulfilment of the agreement.

Now the atmosphere changed drastically. The bride's people were invited to a meal in the house of the girl's new husband. People stressed the fact that they were now related to each other as *samdhin* or "in-laws" and that there should be no more quarrels between them. To stress this fact, members of both parties joked with each other, and the villagers of Lamba remarked that they gave the compensation money without resentment. The following days, however, showed that the overall conflict was far from being settled. When a delegation from the first husband came to the bride's village a few days later, the villagers refused to hand over the Rs 5,000 given them by the people of Lamba. They argued that their daughter had spent five years altogether in the village of Niskhal, a long time, which, given the fact that the girl worked in her husband's field, might be considered a sufficient counter-value to the "betrothal fee". Furthermore, they were angry with the family from Niskhal because they had mistreated their daughter when she did not become pregnant. For all these reasons, they refused to return the "betrothal fee" and threatened their former in-laws with a "case" when they kept insisting on a reimbursement. The people from Niskhal, on the other hand, threatened to involve the police if their demands were not fulfilled. At this point, the negotiations led into a blind alley. When I later talked to the *barika* of Gumma about the events, he explained to me that the people of Naringtola are "valley people" who are feared by the Dongria because they know how to deal with the police. He therefore expected the Dongria from Niskhal to step back from their demands, despite the obvious legitimacy of their claims.

This case illustrates some of the basic norms and strategies involved in paying back the "betrothal fee". First, the former husband demands the reimbursement of double the money and gifts given by his family to the bride's village in the past. This duplication of the original amount is considered to be a "norm" (*niam*) and in my interpretation is linked to the idea that the value of things grows. Dongria are aware that the value of money increases and that a piece of land that was bought for a few rupees a hundred years ago is now worth several thousand rupees. The same holds for "betrothal fee" payments, which were considerably lower in the past. Thus, older Dongria recall the time when they paid "betrothal fees" in the range of Rs 2,000 to Rs 4,000. For example, the present *member* of Gumma, a man of perhaps sixty, remembered having paid Rs 3,700 in addition to certain other gifts for his bride about thirty-five years previously. The standard number of gifts such as buffaloes or pigs may not have changed, but their price has certainly increased. For this reason, I think that the right to claim double the amount originally paid as "betrothal fee" may be seen as an attempt to counter-balance inflation.

Second, the bride's parents do not return this "betrothal fee" themselves but forward the request to those people who, by capturing their daughter, expect to be accepted as their new affines. The question is why the former husband does not claim the reimbursement of his "betrothal fee" directly from the abductors. Again, I can only offer an interpretation but no definite explanation for this rule. In my view, the first husband cannot claim the return of the "betrothal fee" from the abductors because the latter never received any payment from him. Only the bride's people are actually liable for returning something they actually received in the past. On the other hand, the bride's people feel only partially responsible for the conflict and therefore approach their new affines, who actively created the disturbance by abducting the girl. The latter are normally prepared to pay a substantial amount of money because they want to be on good terms with their new in-laws. Furthermore, they are perhaps more willing to reimburse the "betrothal fee" because they themselves are not expected to give another substantial "betrothal fee" to the girl's family. They are not completely exempted from making gifts to their bride-givers, but their contribution usually consists of the standard feast they have to provide to the girl's fellow villagers.

Third, once the bride's people have managed to obtain a substantial payment from the abductors, the family of the girl's former husband again approaches them in order to claim their "betrothal fee" a second time. According to one of my Dongria informants, it depends on the skill of the negotiators how much money will actually be transferred. Several situations may occur. If their daughter's former husband has strong arguments or other means to enforce his will, he may insist on getting the total amount paid by the abductors or even more than that. In this case, the bride's people have to pay the additional money out of their own funds. If the latter find themselves in a stronger position, they try to bargain about the actual amount to be handed over to their former affines. For example, they may argue that their daughter already worked for her husband's family and that this work must be calculated against the "betrothal fee" paid. Another argument is to claim that a portion of the money they received from the abductors was meant as a "betrothal fee" payment from their new in-laws. Thus, a Dombo woman experienced in these matters once told me that the bride's people often retain about Rs 2,000 of the total amount as their *mahala*. If they are skilful and have good arguments on their side, they may manage to retain a substantial part of the money they receive from the abductors.

The process leading to the repayment of "betrothal fee" thus involves three parties, each of which tries to strike the best bargain in the situation: the abductors by giving as little as possible, the first husband's family by claiming as much as possible, and the bride's people by demanding the maximum from their new affines and at the same time giving the minimum to their former in-laws.

A special situation arises when the captured girl's former husband has died recently. In this case, a gift of a buffalo called *srangu kodru* has to be provided by the abductor to the former husband's village. The word *srangu* means "ashes," and the name of the gift may therefore be translated as "buffalo given in memory of the deceased." I witnessed such a case during the time of my fieldwork in Gumma. In section 4.4.3 I mentioned the case of Sikoka Kangu, who captured a woman from Sana Denganali. She had abandoned her husband from Niskhal and slept in various dormitories until she got pregnant. Soon afterwards, her former husband died and she was formally "captured" by Sikoka Kangu, as described above. A day later, a group of women from Sana Denganali turned up along with the *barika* from Niskhal and demanded the return of double the amount paid by the former husband, altogether Rs 14,000. The people of Gumma wanted to wait for their *barika* to represent them in this case, but he was away from the village. After some time, all assembled on the central village plaza, where the

4.4 Youthful deviation: Love marriage, bride capture, and collective settlements — 397

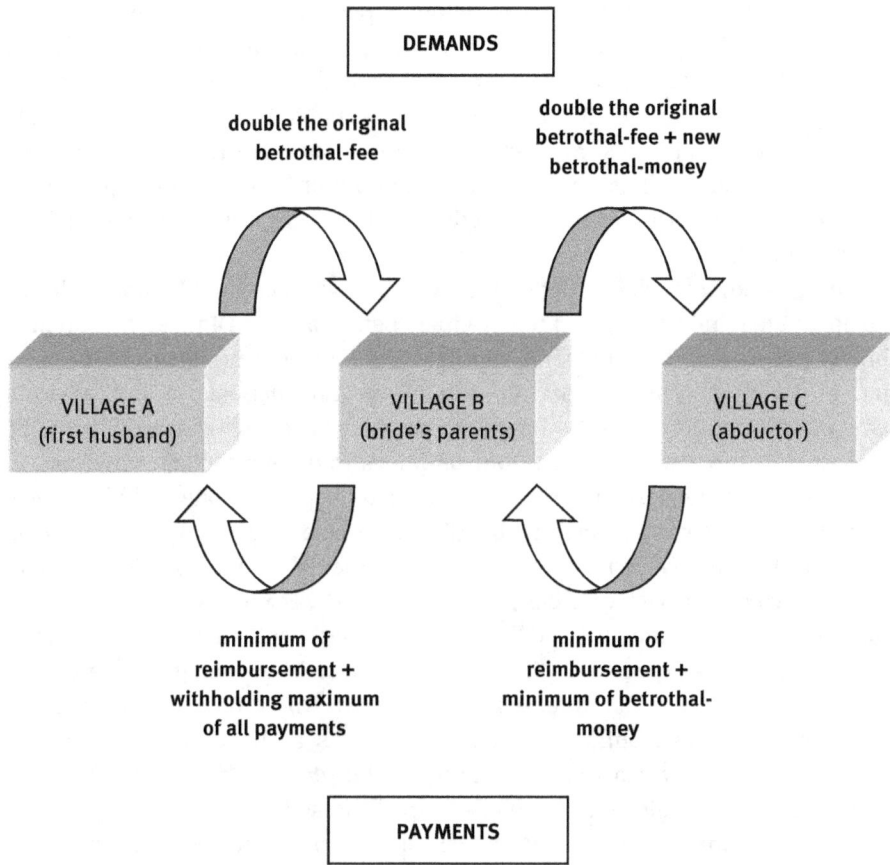

Figure 26: Model of negotiations concerning the reimbursement of a "betrothal fee"

barika of Niskhal and the women from Sana Denganali publicly announced their demands. When the abductors flatly refused to pay anything, the *barika* resorted to the usual threat of filing a "case" with the police.

The discussion then focused on the question of norms, the people of Gumma claiming that Kangu would have to pay Rs 14,000 if the girl's husband were alive, but since he had died recently, they did not have to accede to the demands from the *barika* of Niskhal. This man, on the other hand, insisted upon the legitimacy of his claims. The abductors reacted to his persistency by threatening to apply the same rule in any future case involving not only Niskhal but the whole clan territory (*padari*), including the villages of Ambadani, Sarijala, and Kucheli, if they were made to pay the total amount. This appeared to me a clever move, because the *barika* now had to decide about a matter far beyond his actual sphere of influence, making him careful not to push his case too far without consulting others. The expression used by the villagers when arguing with the *barika* of Niskhal was *badulu kina*, which can be translated as "to exchange" or "to give and take"; in this context this meant that the people of Niskhal may *take* money on this occasion but must be prepared to *give* money in the future when they capture a woman claimed by Gumma. An important aspect of this argument is the idea that the case creates a precedent with binding consequences for both sides in future.

In the end, a much smaller sum of Rs 4,000 was accepted by both sides as an adequate reimbursement of the original "betrothal fee". Of this total sum, the bride's people kept Rs 2,000 for themselves and handed over the rest to their former in-laws from Niskhal. Apart from this *wrepoli takang*, Sikoka Kangu had to pay a fine (*tapu*) of Rs 3,000 directly to the first husband's village. Finally, he was expected to present at least four buffaloes to different villages involved in the case. According to Dongria rules, he had to present one buffalo (*sringa kodru*) to the deceased former husband's village and a second buffalo (*tengeda kodru*) to his first wife's fellow villagers. In the latter case, Sikoka Kangu managed to avoid this payment, perhaps because he was not on good terms with his former affines after he and his first wife had separated. A third buffalo (*ahpa kodru*) was expected by Sikoka Kangu's own fellow villagers as a gift for helping him capture his wife. Finally, his new wife's people demanded at least one if not two buffaloes (*mahala kodru*) as a "betrothal fee". Each of these buffaloes serves a different purpose. The *ahpa kodru* is given to one's own village community, whose people helped the abductor to acquire his wife. The *mahala kodru* is given in exchange for the bride who has been captured. The *sringa kodru* is meant to appease those people whose wife has been taken and may therefore be seen a part of the fine to be paid by the abductor. Finally, the *tengeda kodru* serves to assure the abductor's other affines that he is willing to continue the marriage relation.

Table 25: Buffaloes presented as gifts by abductor

Gift	Meaning	Recipient
sringa kodru	"buffalo for ashes"	deceased former husband's village
tengeda kodru	unclear; *tenga* means "a tier, layer, tower, platform" according to Winfield (1929, 119)	first wife's parents' village
ahpa kodru	"buffalo for capture"	abductor's own village
mahala kodru	"buffalo for betrothal"	bride's village

4.4 Youthful deviation: Love marriage, bride capture, and collective settlements — 399

Taking all these gifts into account, the bride capture caused Sikoka Kangu expenses almost as high as those of a formal marriage arrangement, although he did not fulfil all his responsibilities, since he presented neither a *tengeda kodru* nor a *sringa kodru*. The following table lists all the gifts and payments made by Sikoka Kangu after abducting the woman from Sana Denganali:

Table 26: Gifts and payments by Sikoka Kangu

Gift / Payment	Recipient	Amount
tapu (fine for capture)	Niskhal (former husband's village)	Rs 3,000
wrepoli taking (reimbursement of "betrothal fee")	Sana Denganali (bride's village) + Niskhal	Rs 4,000 (Rs 2,000 handed over to Niskhal)
mahala kodru (buffalo for betrothal)	Sana Denganali	Rs 1,150 Rs 1,200
mahala kalu (alcohol for betrothal)	Sana Denganali	Rs 200
5 *mana manjing* (5 x 4 kg rice)	Sana Denganali	Rs 200
2 *mana hiko gunda* (2 x 4 kg millet flour for the feast)	Sana Denganali	Rs 40
2 *mana luna* (2 x 4 kg salt for the feast)	Sana Denganali	Rs 40
ahpa kodru (buffalo for capture)	Gumma	Rs 1,200
ahpa kalu (alcohol for capture)	Gumma	Rs 200
Total		**Rs 11,730**

Except for the *ahpa kodru*, all these buffaloes are handed over to the particular families related to the abductor, but the final recipient of the gift is always the village as a whole. As is apparent by now, anthropological usage opposing wife (or bride) givers and takers would offer quite an inadequate picture of this situation, because the exchange partners are identified by relations of descent and affinity on the analytical level of rules, while in practice their solidarity derives from joint residence. Thus, the abductor has to give the *ahpa kodru* to his village irrespective of whether he belongs to the dominant clan of this village or not. His own fellow villagers may equally be the recipients of the *sringa kodru* if the deceased husband of his new wife was a fellow villager. Thus, in Sikoka Kangu's case, his new wife's former husband belonged to the Sikoka clan and lived in a village owned by the same clan. This does not represent an exception, because I documented several cases in which a woman married either a direct brother of her deceased husband or a man belonging to the same clan, in other words a "classificatory brother." When the abductor lives in the same village as the deceased husband, the *sringa kodru* is given by the new husband to his own village in a ceremony (*eyu wapkoli* or "to pour out water") meant to smooth over relations between him and his wife's former in-laws, who are his "brothers."

The bride herself must belong to a clan different from that of the abductor, but both villages may be "owned" by the same dominant clan. In Sikoka Kangu's case, the abducted bride (Kudruka Drimbi) was neither of the dominant clan of Sana Denganali (Sikoka) nor actually a village daughter, since her native place is located in the valley beyond the Dongria homeland. However, since she lived with her married sister in Sana Denganali, the people of this village felt justified in behaving as "bride-givers." This means that a group of Sikoka clan members assumed the role of "bride-givers" against another group of Sikoka people acting as "bride-takers." Consequently, villages themselves must be regarded as "agents" vis-à-vis the abductor's family. Clan membership has an impact on the legitimacy of affinal relations between families, but it has no relevance for marriage transactions between villages, which once again underscores the importance of separating the two analytical levels.

The four types of buffaloes may thus be divided into two groups. *Ahpa kodru* and *sringa kodru* are given to those who in the context of a particular case act as bride-receiving people, while those who receive a *mahala kodru* or a *tengeda kodru* can be termed bride-giving people, as they provided ego with a spouse. Within each of these two categories, the different types of buffaloes distinguish those people who either gave or received a bride in the past from those who act as givers and takers in the present (fig. 27).

The buffalo called *sringa kodru* serves to appease the first wife-takers. If the husband is alive, no *srangu kodru* is given, but a fine (*tapu*) has to be paid and a ceremony performed, the main purpose of which is to establish peace between the families who have taken the same woman. The negotiations concerning these fines are discussed in the next section.

4.4 Youthful deviation: Love marriage, bride capture, and collective settlements — 401

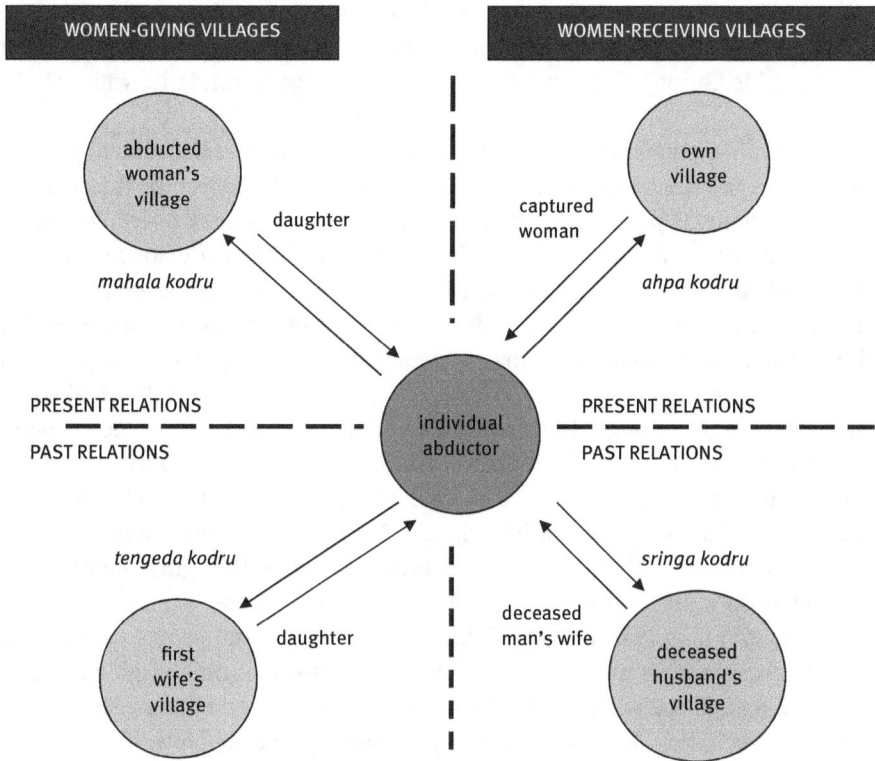

Figure 27: Abductor's gifts to four villages

tapu takang ("monetary fine")

When peace between the abductor's village and the two other parties is settled "on two ways" (*ri bata*), the negotiations (*nia kina*) about the fine (*tapu*) are conducted separately from the talks about the reimbursement of the "betrothal fee". In the cases I witnessed personally, the former husband and his family members did not attend the meeting but rather sent their *barika* as their representative and spokesman. The amount to be paid as a fine is not fixed but has to be negotiated separately for each case. This practice derives from the rule that a fine must be calculated by the concerned villages according to the amounts paid in previous cases of bride capture. For example, if Village A captured a bride claimed by Village B and paid Rs 1,000 as *tapu* ten years ago, then Village B has to pay double the amount, i.e., Rs 2,000, when abducting a girl claimed by Village A. Usually matters are not so simple, of course, since many cases of bride capture involve several villages and all these different claims must be taken into account, leaving room for negotiations that may continue over a span of several weeks. The *barika* of the demanding village is in the most difficult position, since he must represent his patrons alone in front of a whole village in solidarity with the abductor.

When an agreement has finally been reached, the former husband or his representative, the *barika*, comes to the abductor's village to collect the fine. On this day, a ceremony is performed, one that is essential to restoring peace, for example in cases of conflict with physical fights or feuds.[75] The abductor calls for the *jani* of his village to join the elders who assemble on the village plaza. Everybody sits down on the ground, since it is explicitly forbidden to sit on a cot during this ritual. The reason seems to be that everyone should be equal on this occasion when peace is to be established between former enemies. A bowl of fresh water is brought, along with the stem of a leaf belonging to a creeper plant (*siali*). This stem is twisted to form two rings, which are given to the two representatives of the conflicting parties. Then the *jani* takes the bowl containing water and a fifty-*paisa* coin in his hands, telling the two representatives sitting next to him to hook their index fingers together before he begins chanting certain verses in a fast and almost incomprehensible manner.

I was told later that he asks all the gods, ancestors, and people to assemble at this place, repeats the cause of the conflict, states that an amicable solution has been agreed on, and asks for the gods' help in preserving this peace. At the end of his recitation, he pours some of the water (*eyu wapkoli*) over the hands of both representatives. The ceremony usually ends with the *jani* or one of the two other participants grabbing the bowl and splashing the others with the rest of the water. This kind of joking symbolises the newly achieved harmony between the parties. If the bride's former husband is deceased, his representative is now given the *sringa kodru* to take home, where it is slaughtered and shared in a feast. If the former husband is alive, the *tapu* money is handed over to him. This money cannot be retained by his family, since it belongs to his village as a whole. The villagers buy buffaloes with this money and arrange one or more feasts. The development officers living in Gumma remembered occasions when, following the payment of a huge fine, the villagers consumed one buffalo every two or three days. The man whose bride was captured does not participate in these feasts, since others may say that "he has sold a vagina" (*pira prateyu*) and should not eat the profit gained from this transaction.

---

[75] A comparable ritual was documented by Macpherson in the nineteenth century (see Boal 1999, 191–92).

4.5 Conclusion: Forms of marriage, reciprocity, and social distance

Following long-term fieldwork among the Makuna, a small indigenous group inhabiting the tropical forests of the Colombian Vaupés, Kaj Arhem published an article (Arhem 1981) in which he takes up Sahlins's concepts of reciprocity and relates them to the forms of marriage he identified among the Makuna. In his famous article "On the Sociology of Primitive Exchange" Sahlins (reprint in Sahlins 1972) distinguishes reciprocity from redistribution because the former involves symmetrical transactions *between* at least two sides who are socially separated, while the latter typically occurs *within* relatively centralised social units. Since marriages in patrilineal exogamous clan societies such as the Mukuna and the Dongria Kond are often regarded as transactions *between* rather than *within* social units, affinal relations appear as ideal cases for studying forms of reciprocity.

Sahlins (1972, 191–95) himself sets up a typology of three forms of reciprocity: (i) generalised reciprocity of seemingly altruistic or generous transactions; (ii) balanced reciprocity implying an equal exchange; and (iii) negative reciprocity involving a violent appropriation of somebody's else's belongings. These types are said to correspond to the "social distance" of the parties involved. Social distance, according to Sahlins, exists in different degrees along a scale of relatedness and expresses itself in various, often interconnected forms such as spatial, genealogical, and segmentary distance. Taking up the notion of the segmented tribe made up of ever more encompassing sectors, starting from the house and expanding out to the lineage, the village, and finally the tribe, Sahlins demonstrates that generalised reciprocity characterises transaction between people who are considered to be closely related in terms of space, genealogy, and segmentation. At the other end of the scale, he finds negative reciprocity and a more or less unsocial attitude typical of transactions between distantly related people, like those belonging to different tribes. In this sphere, interactions are impersonal, are conducted with an eye toward utilitarian advantage, and often involve various degrees of violence, since negative reciprocity "is the attempt to get something for nothing" (Sahlins 1972, 195). Balanced reciprocity or equal exchange typically occurs in intermediary sectors where people neither are very closely related nor see each other as foreigners with whom one may haggle or barter.

The model presented by Sahlins rests on the idea that "tribal societies" are segmented in all spheres of life and ordered on different levels of socio-cultural integration, a concept earlier developed by Julian H. Steward. Repeating what he wrote in a general statement on the structure of "tribal society" in his book entitled *Tribesmen*, Sahlins claims that these levels of integration correspond not only to different types of reciprocity but also to forms of morality:

> The norms are characteristically relative and situational rather than absolute and universal. A given act, that is to say, is not so much in itself good or bad – it depends on who the "Alter" is. The appropriation of another man's goods *or his woman*, which is a sin ("theft," "adultery") in the bosom of one's community, may be not merely condoned but positively rewarded with the admiration of one's fellows – if it is perpetrated on an outsider. (Sahlins 1972, 199; my emphasis)

The reference to the theft of a man's wife as morally acceptable when occurring between relatively unrelated people suggests a correspondence between bride capture, intertribal relations, and negative reciprocity, which Kaj Arhem (1981) identified in the marriage relations of the Makuna. In contrast to Sahlins, Arhem does not use the segmentary descent model of the African clan to represent the social structure of these Amazonian people. Instead, he develops his own categories, partly corresponding to native categories, by distinguishing between descent-ordered residence groups and alliance-ordered local groups. The latter are usually located alongside a river or river system and form what Arhem calls a territorial group. The members of the residence group or longhouse should not intermarry, while the local groups are clusters of intermarrying neighbours. Marriages occur within and between all of these territorial units. Arhem (1981, 55) speaks of "local marriages" when they occur within the local unit, of "territorial marriages" when they are conducted between local groups of the same river territory, and of "inter-territorial marriages" when they are established between different river territories. On one end of a scale of social and territorial distance, local marriages occur between genealogically relatively closely related allies occupying the same area. On the other end, inter-territorial marriages represent links between genealogically unrelated, often hostile groups residing in separate, far-away places. Arhem places territorial marriages in an intermediate position on this scale.

Each of these marriage types goes along with a statistical preference for certain marriage practices. Arhem identifies three such forms of marriage among the Makuna. The first form identified is direct sister exchange formally arranged between two exchanging groups. Such an exchange may be part of an alliance defined as the diachronic continuity of affinal relationships. The idea of two perpetually intermarrying "classes" of people corresponds with the two-line prescriptive terminology of the Makuna and with their preference for direct or classificatory bilateral cross-cousin marriage (Arhem 1981, 50–51). It also matches Sahlins's definition of balanced reciprocity, since one bride is directly exchanged for another. The second form of marriage among the Makuna consists of bride capture, particularly of the arranged ritual type. According to Arhem (1981, 54), such a ritualised seizure of a woman corresponds to the Makuna ideological opposition between friendly kin and aggressive, even hostile affines and to their gender constructions representing men as hunters and women as prey. Bride capture is conceived of as a one-sided action, taking without giving, although in actual fact it often leads to counter-capture or to a sort of delayed marriage exchange in response to demands and threats from the bride's side (Arhem 1981, 53). It thus corresponds to what Sahlins has termed "negative reciprocity" or the violent appropriation of something that is only reciprocated in the face of countervailing pressure. A third form of marriage recognised by Arhem is gift marriage, about which he provides rather sparse information. The expression "gift marriage" seems to express the idea that the bride is given as a present without an overt demand. In this sense, it corresponds to the type of exchange called generalised reciprocity by Sahlins, since the bride's people give without openly[76] expressing expectations for reciprocity.

How do these forms of marriage correspond to the types of territorial alliances? According to Arhem, his statistical data provide evidence that local marriages normally follow the practice of gift marriages, while territorial and interterritorial marriages are established through either direct sister exchange or bride capture. Generalising from his statistical data, Arhem presents us with a model in the form of a scale of increasing social and territorial distance starting from close allies practicing gift marriages (generalised reciprocity) and moving to more distant allies linked by direct sister exchange (balanced reciprocity) and very distant or unrelated groups mutually capturing their women (negative reciprocity) (Arhem 1981, 50, fig. 3).

Can we similarly apply Sahlins's model to marriage relations and forms of marriage among the Dongria? Arranged marriage among the Dongria ideally unites two families who are strangers to each other and reside in separate, distant territories. In practice, this model often remains an ideal, as the Niamgiri Hills are just too small and the Dongria too few. All in all, not many marriages are arranged in childhood, and only a few weddings are celebrated in a grand style, as it involves expenses only a few can afford. Usually, families are not total strangers to each other and may perhaps reside only a few kilometres away. However, bride and groom are kept separate as long as possible and thereby kept "strangers" to each other until the day of their wedding. This form of marriage typically

---

76 As has been well known since Marcel Mauss's ([1925] 1990) seminal essay, every gift implies the obligation to reciprocate, but often this obligation is not made explicit, since such an open demand would have a negative impact on the status of the giver.

unites "noble" families, i.e., those who in their territories are considered descendants of the village founders and who, as proof of their status, possess the sacred objects exhibited during the *meria* festival.

Bride capture and love marriages, of which I have given several examples in this chapter, are different. In bride capture, the man usually knows the woman very well, having made her acquaintance during his visits to her dormitory. Although young men sometimes go to distant dormitories when they accompany their elder brothers on visits to their affines, they normally visit dormitories in the immediate neighbourhood of their own village, since they have to be back early in the morning. Thus, bride capture usually involves people from villages at a medium distance from each other. Exceptions are those cases in which the two parties are linked by a betrothal. Then the boy's party may go to a relatively distant place to obtain his girl. A bride capture is never just an individual affair of the couple concerned but always involves their respective groups. It is participated in by men of the whole village and evokes a collective response from the women of the bride's village and, if she has been promised to somebody else, from her fiancé's village as well. While the individual partners may be attached to each other by mutual feelings or love, the act of capture and the responses from the various groups involve different degrees of violence.

All this stands in contrast to love marriages between two young people who normally have known each other for a long time, have had sexual intercourse in the dormitory, and are perhaps even expecting the birth of a child. Since they have usually been visiting each other regularly, her dormitory may not be far away, perhaps in a neighbouring village, where everybody considers the two to be husband and wife. When the girl has not been promised to somebody else and the girl's father demands no excessive gifts, there will be relatively little collective action. She may be captured in a very formal, ceremonial way, and the boy or his parents may give a buffalo to the girl's village and perhaps another one to their own village. No major disputes and settlements follow, and no major prestations are given to the girl's side. People may say that "she has gone for nothing" (*edi chucha hace*).

These three forms of marriage can be viewed as a continuum with bride capture as a kind of intermediate form. The extremes in terms of social relations and space are arranged marriages and love marriages. The former occur between relatively "distant" parties – if not in terms of space, at least in terms of contacts between bride and groom. It takes the longest, involves many prestations and ceremonies, has a highly collective character, and devalues the intentions and emotions of the couple concerned. Love marriages, in contrast, are established by these individuals, who usually reside in each other's neighbourhood, on the basis of their emotional attachments and do not require any elaborate collective actions such as rituals, prestations, or peace settlements.

Bride capture occupies a middle position. It may involve violence if the bride and her villagers are not willing to accept the marriage; it may be based on love and affection if the capture is just a formal way of concluding the marriage preparations. Unlike in love marriages, the bride captor does not necessarily seek the girl's consent, and unlike in arranged marriages, he and his family do not provide gifts before they take the girl. Instead, they first capture her and then await the other side's demands. The more violent the capture, the more distant the relations between boy and girl, who may have met in the dormitory but are usually not considered to be husband and wife, mostly because the girl either has other lovers as well or is already engaged. For this reason, a bride capture often produces two opposed results: on the one hand, it leads to a new contract with the bride-givers; on the other hand, it sparks a conflict and perhaps even a feud with a third party who demanded the girl first. This stands in contrast to both arranged and love marriages, since the former transform relatively distant relationships into cordial ones, and the latter have no major influence on collective relations at all.

Table 27: Differences between forms of marriage

Arranged marriage	Bride capture	Love marriage
between distant villages	between close to semi-distant villages	between close villages
strangers	potential enemies	acquaintances
collective affair	personal affair turns into collective affair	personal affair
arranged by elders	collective capture (with or without the girl's agreement)	mutual love
many years of negotiations about on-going payments and prestations	may lead to conflicts and feuds; often followed by months of negotiations; payment of fines	no negotiations, few prestations
many ceremonies and prestations	few ceremonies and less valuable prestations; high fines	very few prestations, no fines
creates amicable relations	creates peace and conflict	no collective influence

The overall scheme of relations thus deviates from Sahlins's ideal model: violence is not greatest between the most distant people, but rather between neighbouring villages belonging either to another organisation (*muta*) of the same clan or to another clan. These are the people who are close and at the same time distant enough to make claims on one's land, capture one's brides, or steal one's palm wine. In my experience, most feuds and quarrels occur not between people from relatively distant villages, nor between people of the same village, but between people residing in neighbouring villages.

Do these three forms of marriage correspond to Sahlins's three types of reciprocity, as in the case of the Makuna studied by Arhem? Compared to the Makuna marriage system, affinal relationships among the Dongria differ markedly. While Makuna terminology and rules imply a two-line system of intermarrying classes similar to those described for many South Indian groups, neither Dongria terminology nor their rules stress alliance in the sense given to the word by Dumont, i.e., the diachronic repetition of affinal relationships. Unlike in the Makuna case, Dongria rules forbid symmetrical exchange of women, either in the form of bilateral cross-cousin marriage or as direct sister exchange. In practice, we have seen that Dongria marry into related local lines (see section 3.4.5) and that cases of bride capture are rationalised as attempts to restore a balance between two groups (see section 3.4.6).

Since marriage among the Dongria does not appear to be an exchange of one woman for another, we do not find a type of marriage that completely corresponds to what Sahlins calls balanced reciprocity. We may argue that an arranged marriage can be viewed as a direct reciprocal act in which a woman is exchanged for money, but I think that this interpretation does not agree with the facts. When we view the whole process of an arranged marriage, which may take many years, it becomes clear that this form of marriage shows the characteristics of balanced reciprocity or gift marriage. From the beginning, a status difference exists between the bride-givers, who possess something very valuable, their daughter, and the bride-takers, who demand this highly valuable woman. The bride is a source of status for her family because, like money spent on a feast or animals sacrificed in a grand ceremony, she can be given away. As mentioned above, status among the Dongria does not arise from keeping and displaying something valuable, but from giving it away.

The bride herself is the most important part of this gift solicited by the money presented by the bride-takers. While the groom's people make their gifts with the specific intention of receiving something in return, the bride's party makes a putatively voluntary prestation when presenting their "wedding gift" (*lahi jau*). This is the source of their high status; as mentioned in the ethnographic part of this chapter, the bride's people continue to make gifts, such as pigs and rice, whenever her daughter comes to visit them. The higher status of the bride-givers therefore continues to exist beyond the actual wedding ceremony, and I think this is best expressed in the statement by the *barika* of Gumma that the bride's mother's brother is expected to make a gift worth double the amount he received as his share of the "betrothal fee". The girl's mother's brother, of course, represents the bride-givers of the bride-givers, and the implicit expectation is that he is manifesting his superior status through lavish gifts. The highest gift of the bride's party is, of course, the bride herself. First of all, she is valued because she bears children who will belong to the group that presented her family with a considerable "betrothal fee". Furthermore, she is seen as a most valuable labourer, which is one reason why her parents always hesitate to actually give her to her husband and try to postpone the wedding day as long as possible. The higher status of the bride-givers in an arranged marriage thus derives from two facts: first, they give away their daughter; second, they give a "wedding gift" that is at least of equal if not higher value than the payments made by the other side. These monetary payments are demanded by the bride's people in order to verify the status and earnestness of the groom's people, and they are made by the bride-takers in order to solicit the much more valuable gift of a bride and her "wealth," the "wedding gift".

How does Dongria bride capture fit into Sahlins's model of three types of reciprocity? As in the case of the Makuna, it may be classified as a case of negative reciprocity in the sense that it is "an attempt to get something for nothing" and based on the knowledge that reciprocity will be "contingent upon mustering countervailing pressure or guile" (Sahlins 1972, 195). Bride capture can be seen as a violent act likened to hunting, undertaken by the men in the explicit knowledge that the "theft" will arouse the revenge of the opposing party. Therefore, either they must be convinced that they are more powerful than the bride's people and their affines, or they must be prepared to pay a substantial fine to them. In this sense, bride capture indeed appears to be the opposite of an arranged marriage, in which payments are made first in order to solicit the gift of the bride. However, when compared to the situation among the Makuna, the place of bride capture in the overall marriage system differs markedly. Bride capture among the Dongria does not occur between the most distant people in terms of social relatedness and space, but on the contrary between neighbouring villages. This puts Sahlins's segmentary model of the congruence between hostility and territorial distance into question.

As argued above, the concepts of "balanced reciprocity" and "negative reciprocity" can be applied to the forms of marriage existing in this society, but these expressions do not fully capture the nature of reciprocity involved in this case. In an arranged marriage, the bride's people indeed make a real gift to the groom's party when they send a daughter and a huge "wedding gift" to his house on the day of the wedding, but this gift has been solicited over years. Both sides in the transaction gain status, the bride-givers more in relation to the bride-takers, but the latter in relation to their own people, their "brothers" who have established less prestigious marriages. In order to capture these characteristic aspects of exchanges in arranged marriages – solicitation, unequal value, and status competition – I call this type of transaction "prestige reciprocity" rather than "balanced reciprocity". The expression "negative reciprocity" similarly does not fully correspond to what actually happens in a bride capture. As Sahlins himself states, acts of this type are clearly performed in the knowledge that it will be necessary to deal with the demands arising from the more or less violent appropriation of things belonging to somebody else. In this sense, violence or "force" is the opposite of betrothal but leads to the same results, since it creates a relationship between different parties who exchange valuables that become markers of their status. To stress the involuntary character of this type of transaction and the general aggressive atmosphere in which it occurs I prefer to call this form of exchange "violent reciprocity." Modified in this way, Sahlins's model can be used to represent the system of affinal relations among the Dongria, as shown in the following diagram:

4.5 Conclusion: Forms of marriage, reciprocity, and social distance

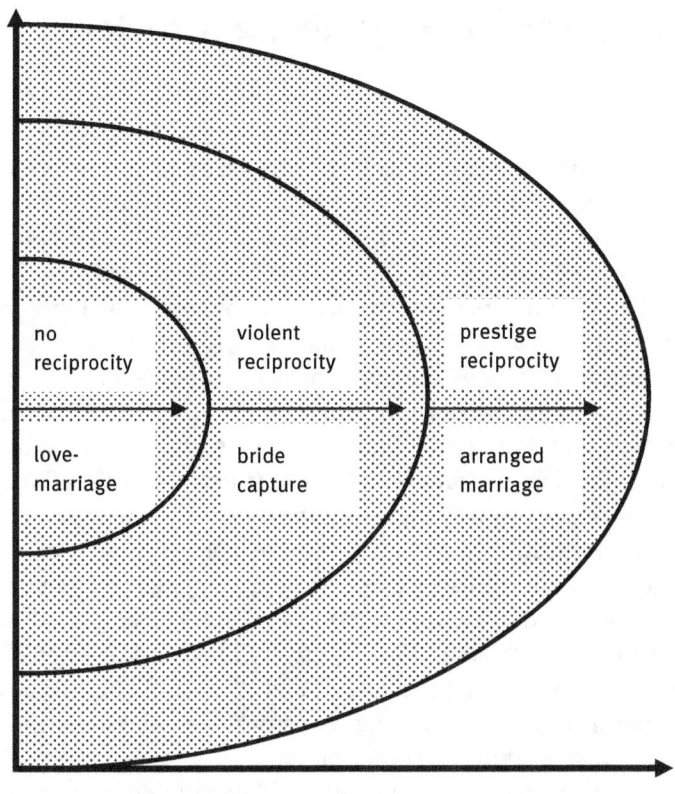

Figure 28: Types of reciprocity, forms of marriage, and degrees of distance and hostility

5 The clan sacrifice: Creating Niamgiri society

5.1 Introduction

In the previous chapters of this book, various levels of social relations between different social categories have been analysed. The second chapter addressed the role of the Dombo, who provide a number of services and link the tribal landowners, the Dongria, to the outside world through their trading activities. The third chapter focussed on the principles structuring relations within the Dongria Kond community, in particular affinity, descent, and territory. An analysis of terminology, rules, and practices revealed the importance of marriage (or affinity) as a way of establishing relations between social categories that are distinct in terms of territory and descent. The fourth chapter addressed the various ways through which marriage relations are forged and the different statuses resulting from such unions. In this chapter, I will argue that the Dongria's buffalo sacrifices provide the context for creating another, more encompassing dimension of society: these sacrifices bring society as a whole into being. During these events, all social relations distinguished in previous chapters – between communities, descent categories, territorial units, and affines – are activated and renewed in a single context. The rituals mark social boundaries and at the same time establish valued relations between these groups and categories, including the dead, ancestors, and deities worshipped on this occasion.

The following account will provide the first detailed description of the buffalo sacrifices of the Dongria Kond. I first offer an introduction to the history of Dongria human sacrifices and the interpretations offered by various authors who have studied this rite. I will then present my ethnographic data about the buffalo sacrifices that replaced the human sacrifices once these were repressed by the British. I begin by describing the sacred layout of the Dongria villages, where most of the ritual events take place, and by explaining the temporal framework of the rituals and summarizing the main costs of the sacrifice. This introduction will be followed by an overview of the preparations for the festival, which begin a whole year before the actual sacrifice with the "festival of pigeon peas," called *kanga parbu*. Other preparations include building a small house for the earth goddess, planting the stake to which the buffalo will be tied, constructing a wall near the stone that represents the earth goddess's husband, and fencing off the whole village. Another important preparation for the festival involves the purchase and of the victim, a buffalo, and its exhibition to a number of different households and villages. Before dealing with the main events, I will go on to introduce the main objects and actors of the buffalo sacrifice. I shall point out that all the objects displayed in the festival have a double function: on the one hand, they are used in the sacrifice itself, and on the other hand, they signify a particular relationship of the sacrifiers to their land. Thus, the pots, the hearth, and the iron spoon are not only used during the festival but were also, in the past, transferred from seller to buyer at the time land was sold. The axe is not only used to symbolically sacrifice the buffalo but also stands for the clearing of forest, which made the land arable. The brass pot carried around on top of a long bamboo pole at the beginning of the festival seems to represent control over the territory. The knife used to inflict the first wound on the victim is, like the brass pot, passed on from village to village within the sacrificial community. Not only the objects, but also the sacrificial specialists are ordered according to a complex system of classification that will be discussed in the ensuing part of the chapter. I will first describe how colonial officials and anthropologists understood the order of religious priests among the Kond, before I distinguish their different functions on the basis of my own ethnography. My particular focus will be the different categories of the so-called *jani*, who appear to be most closely linked to the worship of the earth goddess. This will be followed by a description of the actual performance of buffalo sacrifices I observed during my fieldwork between 2001 and 2003. After dealing briefly with some further preparations, I will focus on the three main days of the *kodru parbu*. I intend neither to give an ideal-typical description nor to deal individually with each of the eleven sacrifices I observed. Instead, I place one buffalo sacrifice, witnessed in the year 2001 in the village of Tebapada, at the centre of my description and mention additional aspects or variations observed in other performances where necessary.

In my conclusion, I interpret these events from different theoretical perspectives. I begin my analysis by pointing out certain similarities between various feasts of merit and the *kodru parbu*, in which the status of certain actors is clearly marked and negotiated. The idea that feasts of merit often involve rivalry and forms of drama that reveal the organisation and structure of the society concerned leads me to the second part of my conclusion, which analyses the relationships between various actors and the social categories they represent. The most important among these are the relationships between affines, and for this reason the third part of my conclusion attempts a comparison between sacrifice and marriage. This is followed by an inquiry into the relations between Dongria political and ritual organisation, addressing the question of whether one may have been derived from the other. The last two parts of the conclusion deal with cosmological ideas pertaining to sacrifice. I interpret some of the Kond myths available for analysis by comparing them with events in the ritual and by identifying those common themes and structures present in both myth and ritual. In the final part of the conclusion, I try to bring together the different aspects discussed by arguing that both marriage and sacrifice are linked to the same cosmological beliefs, which represent goddesses and women as the main creators and sources of fertility. Men can acquire fertility through the activities of gift exchange or violent appropriation.

5.1.1 From human sacrifices (*meria*) to buffalo sacrifices (*kodru parbu*)

When the British first entered the Kondmals on the heels of the Raja of Ghumsur, who had fled into the mountains after being unable to pay tribute, they met with fierce resistance from the people they referred to as the "Conds" (Padel 2000, 41). Following an attack by about two thousand "Conds," who killed several army officers and sepoys, Captain John Campbell – later promoted to Major-General – was summoned to take control of the situation and on arrival immediately took revenge on the attackers. This was the beginning of the so-called Ghumsur Wars: villages were raided, chiefs were executed, and many Kond were killed in battles against the colonial soldiers with their superior weapons. The main enemy of the British, apart from the Kond, who ambushed them again and again, was malaria, which resulted in many deaths among European officers (Padel 2000, 45). In August 1836, a British revenue officer named Russell sent Campbell to Madras with a written report containing the first official mention of a custom the British soldiers had learned about while fighting in the hills: human sacrifice (Padel 2000, 48–49).

The task of putting an end to this "barbarous" custom was entrusted to Campbell, and he began to tour the Ghumsur Hills, rescuing the human victims, called *meria*, wherever he could. At the same time, the directors of the East India Company ordered the severe punishment of those Dom traders who captured the victims and sold them to the Kond (Padel 2000, 65). In the following years, up until he left Odisha in 1841–42 to serve in the so-called "Opium War" against China, Campbell continued to tour different districts occupied by the Kond with the aim of rescuing the human victims and convincing the local people to give up the practice. He was succeeded by Captain Samuel Charters Macpherson, who in the following years conducted three tours through the Kond country, until he declared that he had been successful in instigating the discontinuation of the *meria* sacrifices in Ghumsur district (Padel 2000, 71). In order to extend this achievement to the whole of the area inhabited by Kond, an "Agency for the Suppression of Human Sacrifice and Female Infanticide in the Hill Tracts of Orissa" was established in December 1845, headed by Macpherson and responsible for areas administered by both the Madras and the Bengal Presidencies. Soon the new agent found himself in trouble with both the local Kond and the Raja of Boad when he demanded the surrender of *meria* victims. His order stirred up a general "spirit of resistance" (Padel 2000, 79), and fighting broke out in several places. A message was sent to the government that Macpherson's policy of coercion was responsible for a lack of peace in the hills, and in March 1847 Macpherson was relieved of his post and succeeded first by Brigadier-General Dyce and then by Captain Campbell, who became the new *"meria* Agent" (Padel 2000, 87–97). Campbell continued to tour different districts, this time as far as Rayagada, demanding the release of *meria* victims. Padel estimates that between 1836 and 1854 – the last year of Campbell's service – about two thousand *meria* victims were removed from Kond villages (Padel 2000: 106).

Up until 1859, the agency promoted the sacrifice of animals instead of human beings. As early as 1842, Macpherson began to allow the Kond to sacrifice buffaloes and monkeys "with all the ceremonies usual on occasions of human sacrifice" in an area of Ghumsur district (Macpherson 1865: 179–80). MacNeill, the last officer of the *meria* agency, which was abolished in 1861, tried to prohibit the buffalo sacrifices, because they were becoming too frequent and could be seen as a form of resistance to the British Government (Padel 2000, 105). However, his orders had no lasting effect. In 1894, the *Madras Mail* published an eyewitness report of a sacrifice with a buffalo substitute in the Ganjam Hills. The description is very lucid and stresses the fact that the people were singing almost the same songs to the buffalo as had previously been sung in the presence of the human victim (cited in Thurston [1909] 1987, 381–85). The same theme emerges from the ritual songs translated by Friend-Pereira in 1899. In these songs, the Kond remember the appearance of two "Saheebs" named Kiabon (Campbell) and Mokadella (Macpherson),[1] represented as culture heroes who brought "wisdom and reading" and helped all of the people "to become wealthy" (cited in Thurston 1987, 380). In another famous song translated by Friend-Pereira, the Kond ask the earth goddess to provide them with "large granaries" and "large store-baskets" in return for the sacrifice of the victim, a buffalo (cited in Boal 1999, 305–6).

The first detailed account of a buffalo sacrifice in the twentieth century was written by a Kond schoolteacher named Kogera Pradhan between 1910 and 1915. His notebook was discovered in 1975 and contains descriptions of twenty-six rites celebrated in the village of Mallikapori (Boal 1999, i–ii). It is probably the

---

[1] They are given various names according to different sources, most commonly Mukman Sahib (Macpherson) and Kiramal Sahib (Campbell). Niggemeyer (1964a, 211) recorded myths mentioning these two officers and provides evidence that the Kuttia Kond excuse themselves for not being able to give human blood to their goddess and blame these officers for this.

first report of the festival – called *kedu laka* or "buffalo sacrifice" – that concentrates not only on the actual killing of the victim but also on the long preparations as well as the ritual actions following the sacrifice. It is not entirely clear to me whether Barbara Boal presents us with the original text or a revised version of it. The style of the text is identical to that of her own account of the buffalo sacrifice as celebrated by the Kond of Mallikapori in the period between 1950 and 1992.[2] Both descriptions of the buffalo sacrifice are written in the form of an ideal or model account of the festival without reference to any specific performances observed by the authors. In contrast, Hermann Niggemeyer gives us a very vivid description of the buffalo sacrifices he himself observed in two different Kuttia Kond villages (Burlabaru and Batipadar)[3] in March 1956, along with two additional accounts based on information from assistants who were eyewitnesses to the festival in two other places (Bilamel and Gurlimaska) the same year (Niggemeyer 1964a, 186–208). Albert Götzelmann followed in the footsteps of Hermann Niggemeyer and conducted additional fieldwork among the Kuttia Kond. He visited the hills every year over a period of twelve years between 1984 and 1996 and collected information on marriages and various rituals, including the elaborate buffalo sacrifices.[4]

Regarding the Dongria Kond, we do not have any elaborate account of their buffalo sacrifices (*kodru parbu*), despite the fact that they continue to be celebrated to this day. All the descriptions we have were written by Indian officials and researchers, mostly from Odisha, who concentrate on an ideal course of events and present the festival in the typical "Gazetteer style". Thus, in the first depiction of the ceremony by Patnaik and Das Patnaik, the authors briefly deal with what they consider to be an eight-day festival by mentioning only the main ritual events on each of these days (Patnaik and Das Patnaik 1982,

---

[2] Barbara Boal either wrote her own report in the same style as Kogera Prodhan's, in order to make it more comparable, or she reorganised the schoolteacher's account to fit her own style of representation.

[3] Niggemeyer released a short documentary film of these two festivals. The 16 mm film is available at the Institut für den Wissenschaftlichen Film in Göttingen.

[4] From personal communication and from the few unpublished papers and documents I have, I infer that Albert Götzelmann has not only collected substantial data on this sacrifice but also written in detail about it. In particular, his translation of certain Kuttia Kond myths and recitations is very impressive, and we can only hope that this material will soon be made available to the public. In order not to anticipate Götzelmann's analysis, I have not included some of his data made available to me by Professor Pfeffer with his permission.

164–69).⁵ In the same way, Prasanna Kumar Nayak, who in his book focuses on the feuds of the Dongria Kond, provides only a sketchy, ideal-typical description of several of their festivals, including the buffalo sacrifice (*kodru parbu*) (Nayak 1989, 168–71). Again, in a publication dealing with the Dongria Kond, Jena et al. devote only four pages to the *kodru parbu*, which they describe in the same eclectic, ideal-typical manner as all the other authors (Jena et al. 2002, 213–16).

In this chapter, I will provide the first elaborate account of the buffalo sacrifice as conducted by the Dongria Kond of the Niamgiri Hills. The account will combine both generalisations from ethnographic observation and interviews, on the one hand, and descriptions of actual performances and events, on the other. The data was collected over three consecutive years in villages either located in the Niamgiri Hills (Dongria Kond) or in the valleys around the small market town of Kalyansingpur (Desia Kond). I observed various sequences of the *kodru parbu*, including the elaborate preparations, in eleven different villages during the years 2001 to 2003 (see table).

Table 28: Buffalo sacrifices (*kodru parbu*) observed by the author (year, name of village, community)

Year	Name of village	Community
2001	Railima	Dongria Kond
	Kuskedeli	Dongria Kond
	Tebapada	Dongria Kond
	Mundawali	Dongria Kond
2002	Lekhpadar	Dongria Kond
	Hundijali	Dongria Kond
	Kadalichua	Desia Kond
	Gopalpur-Dulumguda	Desia Kond
	Depaguda	Desia Kond
	Sana Bamanaguda	Desia Kond
2003	Sana Dengoni	Dongria Kond

---

5 A very similar account of the sacrifice – sometimes corresponding almost word for word to the descriptions by the previously mentioned authors – was later provided by Upali Aparajita, who claims to have observed the festival in February 1987 (Aparajita 1994, 232–36).

5.1.2 Interpretations of Kond human sacrifice (*meria*)

Previous interpretations of the sacrifice were almost exclusively concerned with the human, not the buffalo sacrifice. With the introduction of the buffalo as a substitute for the human being, European interest in the religion of the Kond ceased almost immediately. Among modern writers, only Barbara Boal (1979, 1997, 1999) analyses both human and buffalo sacrifices, as her aim is to understand Kond values, ideas, and ritual practices.[6] In this she differs both from the British colonialists, whose feelings and sense of righteousness were violated by customs such as human sacrifice and female infanticide, and from Felix Padel (2000), who reflects on the *meria* (human) sacrifice mainly in order to critically evaluate the motives of Europeans, i.e., those of the colonialists, missionaries, and anthropologists.

The earliest accounts of the *meria* sacrifice were produced by colonial officers who were convinced that the culture of the Kond represented a barbarous stage in the evolution of humankind. To them, the Kond's human sacrifices provided vivid evidence of conditions once observable in the civilised world. They were certain that the Kond could be "enlightened" – by force if necessary – and convinced to give up their primitive way of life, if only they were confronted with "rational" arguments. This attitude is clearly expressed in the following statement by Major-General John Campbell:

> I thought it better to confess that we, like them, had once sacrificed human beings; like them, had indulged in similar cruel offerings; like them, had believed that the judgement of the gods could only be averted by a bloody expiation and the slaughter of our fellow-creatures; but this was in days of gross ignorance, when we were both fools and savages, knowing nothing and living a debased and brutal life; but we emerged from this darkness, gradually obtained light, and at last gave up for ever our barbarous and unholy practices. And what has been the consequence? I inquired. All kinds of prosperity have come upon us since we abolished those sinful rites; we now possess learning and wisdom, and see clearly the great folly we all committed. I told them that they must think of this, and be certain that their real welfare did not depend, as they falsely supposed, upon the continuance of this ceremony of their religion. (Campbell 1864, 71)

While Campbell utterly despised not only the Kond religion, but probably any form of theology, Macpherson showed, to the contrary, an immense interest in

---

[6] Boal compares human and buffalo sacrifices in order to find out what changes have taken place since the intervention of the British (1979, 1997). She further analyses cycles of different buffalo sacrifices and comes to the conclusion that villages are linked through mutual cooperation in the context of three-year ritual cycles (1997, 203). Among the Dongria, such short cycles between only a limited number of villages do not exist, to the best of my knowledge.

Kond religious beliefs and practices, perhaps partly because he intended to obtain influence over the priests, as Barbara Boal (1997, 111) has suggested. In his first report from 1842 (Macpherson [1842], 1863), based on a short tour through the hills and on interviews with Kond prisoners (Padel 2000, 68), he was already attempting to gain an understanding of human sacrifice by exploring Kond mythology, religious ideas, and ceremonies. Although in this first account Macpherson still confuses many details,[7] he already links the sacrifice to ideas concerning the fertility of the earth (Macpherson 1863, 62). While Campbell regards Kond myths as "foolish legends" and "fables" (Campbell 1864, 140, 141), Macpherson clearly sees them as a key to understanding what motivates Kond to sacrifice human beings. His second report, published ten years later in the *Journal of the Royal Asiatic Society* (Macpherson 1852), singles out Kond religion as its main theme and presents the reader with an account of two conflicting sects, namely that of the earth goddess (*tari pennu*) and that of the sun god (*boora pennu* or *bela pennu*). According to the myths collected by Macpherson, the supreme male deity, *boora penu*, created for himself a consort, the earth goddess, *tari penu*, who became the main source of conflict and evil in the world.[8] Both competed for supremacy and divided their human followers into two sects, one killing female infants in the name of the sun god, the other offering human beings to the earth goddess out of fear of her power (Macpherson 1852, 225). Although Macpherson's report clearly contains many details proving his knowledge of Kond ritual practices, he probably exaggerated the "contest" between two conflicting cults, the followers of which he located in different areas. As Padel notes, this helped him to explain the British suppression of human sacrifices in the light of events described in Kond mythology:

> The majority of Konds held the Earth Goddess supreme, and propitiated her with human sacrifices to avert her anger. Macpherson claimed, in this Report, to have turned them towards the God of Light, whom he identified with the Christian God, by whose power Konds considered they had been subdued in the Ghumsur wars. (Padel 2000, 81)

In Kond mythology, Macpherson identified the following main reasons for performing human sacrifices: first, human blood helps to firm the soil and make it suitable for agriculture; and second, it satisfies the earth goddess and thus brings about general wellbeing (Macpherson 1865, 96–98).

---

[7] For example, he calls the main deity of the *meria* sacrifice Bera Pennoo and thinks the offering of a human being is made in the name of this male "earth god" (Macpherson 1863, 62).
[8] These myths contradict the myths told by Dongria Kond (see Jena et al. 2002, 133 ff), which represent the goddess as the original creator.

Drawing upon the work of Campbell, Macpherson, and other British officers, George James Frazer included the *meria* of the Kond in his book *The Golden Bough* as an example of "human sacrifices for the harvest," which he identifies among various South, Middle, and North American Indians, in West Africa and the Philippines, and among the Naga of Northeast India and the Oraon of Central India (Frazer [1922] 1968, 628–32). Frazer disagrees with the colonial officers, who in his view interpret the *meria* mainly as a sacrifice of expiation. In his opinion, the sacrifice is considered to satisfy the earth goddess, but the fact that the victim's flesh is buried in the soil indicates to him that the Kond ascribe certain powers of fertility to the victim's body: it gives colour to the turmeric and causes the rain to come and the crops to grow (Frazer 1968, 636). Taking into account the powers of fertility imagined to be inherent in the victim and considering the respect shown to the victim on the eve of the sacrifice, Frazer comes to the conclusion that the *meria* is not simply a human being but a divine one (Frazer 1968, 637). This accords with the way in which the Kond explain the origin of the sacrifice themselves in myths published by Macpherson (1865), Thurston (1987), and Elwin (1949, 40–42; 1954, 545–51). In many of these myths, either a human incarnation of the goddess or the first daughter of the earth spills blood and asks to be sacrificed in order to make the soil fertile.

From descriptions of human sacrifices (Campbell 1864; Macpherson 1865) we know that the Kond would indeed bury pieces of human flesh near their shrine of the earth goddess and in their fields, in order to enhance the fertility of the land. The burial of flesh continued in many areas where inhabitants had abandoned human sacrifice and replaced it by the sacrifice of a buffalo. Thus, Boal herself provides us with an account of a buffalo sacrifice in Mallikapori in which the young men, having killed the buffalo, rush back to their villages to bury it in their own sacred groves (Boal 1997, 399). In their interpretation of the sacrifice, Hubert and Mauss ([1899] 1968) focus on this burial of flesh. They consider the *meria* of the Kond to be one of many variants of their general scheme. These variations arise out of certain special functions ascribed to the sacrifice, i.e., "when it is performed on behalf of the sacrifier himself or of a thing in which he has a special interest" (Hubert and Mauss 1968, 61). These authors deal with the Kond's human sacrifices in the context of what they call "agrarian sacrifices," the effect of which, in their view, is twofold: first, they remove prohibitions protecting the land, thus allowing people to cultivate it, and second, they fertilise the fields (Hubert and Mauss 1968, 66). In some of these sacrifices, the remains of the victim must first be desacralised in order to allow them to be consumed by the sacrifiers and thus function effectively in the rite. In contrast, the human sacrifices of the Kond[9] represent a variant in which such desacralization appears to be unnecessary, because its main aim is "to fertilize the earth, that is, to infuse into it a divine life, or to render more active the life it may possess" (Hubert and Mauss 1968, 71).

Like Hubert and Mauss, Eliade considered the *meria* sacrifice to be part of a fertility cult and interpreted it as an expression of a "primitive theory of the seasonal regeneration of the forces of the sacred" (Eliade 1958, 345) According to this theory, the creative powers in plants are renewed by suspending time and returning to the moment when creation began. This original creation, according to Eliade, is often conceived of in terms of the violent death of a "primeval giant." In human sacrifices, the death of this creator being is re-enacted in order to return to the time when life began and fertility was at its greatest. In Eliade's words:

> *The ritual makes creation over again*; the force at work in plants is reborn by suspending time and returning to the first moment of the fullness of creation. The victim, cut into pieces, is identified with the body of the primeval being of the myth, which gave life to the grain by being itself divided ritually. (Eliade 1958, 346; emphasis original)

This does indeed neatly correspond to a myth first published by Thurston, quoted at length in the conclusion of this chapter. According to this myth, the mother of all human beings is killed and her flesh placed in holes in the earth to make it dry and fertile. After being killed, she appears to her children in a dream and instructs them to repeat the sacrifice with another human being in order to increase the fertility of their fields.

An interpretation of the Kond human sacrifices finds its staring point in Girard's scapegoat theory.[10] According to Girard, the human victim appears to be a surrogate who is put to death so that others do not turn against each other. Because of the victim's particularly violent death, the other members of the community may live together harmoniously and prosper. Padel points out that for Girard, human and animal sacrifices are not altogether different, since they are both substitutes for the sacrifier's life. The question then arises of the historical circumstances in which human sacrifices become prominent. It is this question that Padel attempts to answer in his analysis of the *meria* sacrifice. In Padel's view, human sacrifices typically occurred in contexts in which a society

---

9 As their source they mention Macpherson 1865.
10 For a more detailed discussion of the relevance of Girard's theory for understanding the *meria* festival, see Pfeffer 1997c. In this article Pfeffer analyses the Kond's human sacrifices by applying the theories of Eliade, Turner, Girard, and Maurice Bloch.

was expanding and began to develop forms of domination, such as slavery and kingship (Padel 2000, 139). To support his thesis, Padel mentions a number of cases, from the Aztec and the Ashanti to the Naga and the Indians of North America. It is not entirely clear how the Kond fit into this picture, because Padel maintains that rather than the Kond, it was the Dom traders and the Hindu kings who were dominant and expanded their influence. In this situation, the Kond sacrificed an "outsider" as a "symbolic recompense" for their increasing domination by others. Does this mean that the Kond are completely different from the numerous other societies mentioned by Padel, or is he suggesting that in all these cases human sacrifice was a "symbolic recompense"? Who sacrificed human beings, the dominators or the dominated? What also remains unclear is why only the Kond, and not any of the other major tribes of Odisha, developed the rite of human sacrifice on a large scale.

Leaving this question unanswered, Padel goes on to argue that the suppression of human sacrifices caused, in many cases, a massive increase in the incidence of violence, and he illustrates his point with a range of examples ranging from the time of the Roman empire to the Portuguese and Spanish conquest of South America (Padel 2000, 139). He identifies a similar development in areas inhabited by the Kond at the time of their invasion by British soldiers. As evidence he cites statements by Campbell and Hill to the effect that the trade in *meria* victims increased in the first years of British domination. Padel explains this development by suggesting that the British and the Kond faced a paradox: the colonialists were trying to suppress a rite they abhorred, but in actual fact achieved just the opposite, namely an increase in the number of human sacrifices, because the Kond probably believed these to be a means of acquiring the power necessary to repel the outside invasion they were facing at the time.

This part of Padel's argument appears convincing to me, because he takes the Kond point of view into account. Throughout the rest of the book, local views are almost entirely neglected, because the author is very hesitant to use historical sources to interpret Kond human sacrifice. On the one hand, he is highly critical of the data collected by the colonial officers, because it "comes to us through the double filter of what it means to the Hindus and what it meant to Christian Britons" (Padel 2000, 136). On the other hand, he appears to be sceptical about whether we can gain an understanding of Kond ideas from these texts, because they represent only "a highly selective and Hinduized version of the common, 'free' knowledge, available to all Konds, while the esoteric, priestly understanding of the ritual has never been written down" (Padel 2000, 137). All this calls for ethnographic fieldwork, which Padel did not undertake. Instead, he preferred to focus on "much surer ground interpreting British ideas and customs, because these can be tested against a multitude of written evidence" (Padel 2000, 136).

What follows will not offer an "esoteric, priestly understanding of the ritual" because in my view this does not exist independent of the "common, 'free' knowledge available to all Konds." Even if it did exist, it would have no superior value for understanding what the *meria* is all about. Understanding of this sacrifice derives partly from collecting "cosmological beliefs" and partly from interpreting the events in the context of other ritual actions and social relations between actors in the sacrificial drama. Such an approach makes it necessary to pay full attention to the details instead of focusing only on a limited number of aspects, which can then be explained as typical of "agrarian cults" or of reactions to "dominance and suppression."

5.2 The buffalo sacrifice (*kodru parbu*): An overview

5.2.1 Place: The sacred layout of a village

In the course of the *kodru parbu*, various places inside and outside the village become the focus of ritual activities. Shrines are newly constructed, ritual sites refashioned, and sacrificial poles set up. To facilitate an understanding of the ritual events during the sacrifice, I will first describe the ideal-typical layout of a Dongria Kond village and its most important sacred sites. Examples from various villages will be given to illustrate the scope of deviation from this ideal model.

Ideally a village (*nayu*) is made up of two rows (*chahada*) of houses (*ilu*) standing on a relatively flat, only slightly inclined slope near hills used for cultivation. The two rows should be of equal length, and enough space should be left between them for a village plaza referred to as the "front road" (*rechagiri*). Houses in each row are often connected by a common veranda (*pinda*) that faces out onto this front road and by a second veranda facing the "back road," known as *akagiri*. Ideally, each row is shaped like a semi-circle, so that the last houses in each row are close together and leave only small entrances to the village at both ends. These entrances lie at the eastern and western ends of the village, these being the only directions named in the Dongria language. East is referred to as *dharmu giri*, west as *surju giri*, with the word *giri* meaning "path" or "way," while *dharmu* and *surju* are two expressions for the sun. The sun is considered to be a man when rising in the east and a woman when setting in the west. Due to particular features of the topography, some villages have their entrances to the south and north, and in such cases it can be inferred from ritual actions that south is identified with east and north with

Photo 6: Village of Phakeri and the remains of the earth goddess's house

west. For example, while a shaman will normally face east when performing a ritual in a village that accords with the "ideal model," he or she will look towards the south in a village aligned on a south-north axis. The dual division of space (and time) into east (including south) and west (including north) provides a meaningful order to the layout of the village as a whole. The following description will enumerate the different sites used for worship, starting from the westernmost point of the village and progressing to the easternmost point.

A few hundred meters west of the village are the cremations grounds of both, Dongria and Dombo, often located on opposite sides of the path. A cremation ground is referred to as *mahanenga*, literally meaning "(place of) ancestors." In the same direction are the cremation ground for people who died following an accident and the trees where their dangerous souls are hog-tied with iron chains in a ceremony performed by a local shaman.[11]

Closer to the western entrance of the village stands the *yatra kudi*, a small shrine made of four wooden pillars and a canopy of leaves and branches. In

---

[11] I observed this ceremony in December 2001 after an accident that killed a young Dongria man. He fell from a *salap* tree and died instantly. The elaborate rituals that followed cannot be described here.

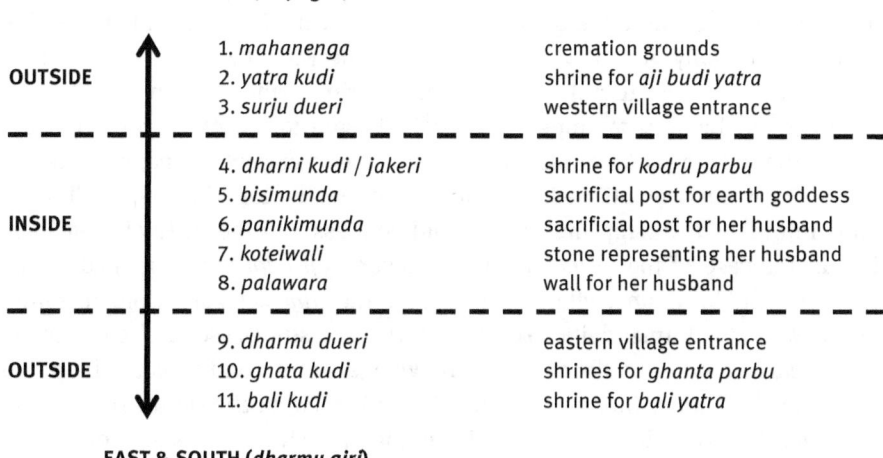

Figure 29: Sacred sites in a Dongria village

the centre of the shrine, soil is piled up in the shape of an "X," upon which an earthen pot is placed during ceremonies in order to represent different gods and goddesses, most importantly the goddess of smallpox, *aji budi*. The name *yatra kudi* derives from the site's function in the context of village festivals. A *kudi* is a small hut, and the word *yatra* refers to all festivals involving movement into and out of the village. On various occasions, deities are called into the village to the earth goddess's shrine, where they are worshipped by the village community. For this purpose, the shamans face towards the east, the direction from which the deities are expected to arrive. Following the worship, a pot representing the main deity of the festival is carried by the shaman, accompanied by some villagers and the sacrificial animal (usually a buffalo or a cow), to the *yatra kudi* in the west. The purpose of this procession is to "throw away" (*tuchpoli*) the deities and ancestors, in other words to lead them out of the village to a place where people bid them farewell with some final offerings. While the souls of the dead are said to reside on the cremation ground, the deities live in the sky (*jauragada*) and only come when called to attend a ceremony where they can eat, drink, and dance with the help of the shaman's body. As mentioned before, the *yatra kudi* serves as a watch post, keeping away evil influences that may come from the west and affect the village. Rituals for ancestors, ghosts, and the village's protecting deity are usually performed by and in the presence of women, who present to them food that has been cooked in their houses.

In Gumma, two further sacred objects are found near the *yatra kudi*, but I am uncertain whether these are typical of the majority of sites or distinctive of this particular one only. About two meters east of the *yatra kudi* a sacrificial stake was inserted in the ground and received offerings whenever the goddess of smallpox was being worshipped. This stake is said to have been set up at the time of the *ghanta parba* of Sikoka Kuli, the *saanta* or *sana bismajhi* of the village. As previously mentioned, the *ghanta parba* is performed by single households in order to worship their household goddess and the deity of their local line. In the case of the *bismajhi* status category, *aji budi* is worshipped as the deity of their local line, while members of the *jani* category worship either *kona* or *lada*, the former deity also being part of the stone assemblage representing the earth goddess in the centre of the village. The second object to be found near the *yatra kudi* of Gumma is a large flat stone (*kajawali*). On the occasion of the *aji budi* festival, the village chief is permitted to sit on it as a sign of his status. Such stones are also used for cutting the meat of sacrificial animals, in particular pigs, which meat is then cooked at the place of worship itself.

Just before a village's western entrance there are normally one or two rows of houses occupied by members of the Dombo caste. From the Dongria's perspective, the Dombo live outside, or more precisely in the backyard of, the Dongria's own settlement. The path behind the houses is taken when carrying a dead body to the cremation ground. Menstruating women and Dombo traders from the plains who are travelling through the hills usually use this back road instead of going directly through the village. The area between the Dombo houses and those of their patrons can be relatively dirty, since the latter throw their rubbish into their backyards, where they also keep pigs and cows. Yet, in contrast to the houses of the Dongria, the domiciles of the Dombo are kept scrupulously clean, with attractive wall paintings and the floors plastered with cow dung or black soil every other day. The girls' dormitories, as well as dancing grounds in those places with flat terrain, are usually found some distance from the houses of the Dombo but still near the village.

On the road leading towards the western entrance of the village, certain rituals pertaining to death are performed. When a person dies, the goddess of wealth, *sita penu-lahi penu*, is believed to desert the house and must be called back by a shaman. This ritual is called *giri takoli* or "bringing from the path," which literally means that the goddess is invoked on this western path and brought back to the house in an earthen pot carried by the shaman on her head. Several months or perhaps years after a person's death, the family members provide a large feast called *dosa* ("mistake") for relatives residing in various villages. During the night following the feast, three symbolic sacrificial stakes, as well as food cooked by the bereaved in their house, are carried to the path leading to the western entrance. A ritual specialist calls various ancestors and offers them food before asking them to leave and not bring any harm to the village.

Continuing along this path and passing the row of houses occupied by the Dombo (*Dombo sahi*), we reach the village's western "entrance," which is clearly marked out on festive occasions only. For example, before the worship of *aji budi* in the month of *caitra*, I witnessed the Dongria of Gumma setting up poles on either side of both entrances of the village, to which they tied ropes adorned with mango leaves. When, on the festive day, a Dombo visitor arrived in Gumma from a village where a man reportedly had killed himself, people shouted at him, preventing him from stepping over the imagined border of the village marked by the rope. They were afraid that the wrath of the earth goddess responsible for the casualty might spread to their own village. Shortly before the main days of the *kodru parbu*, all openings in the two rows of houses, as well as both entrances, are closed with a bamboo fence (*salabada*) clearly marking the borders of the settlement. At this time, visitors can enter and leave the village only through two small gates, one at each end of the residential area. After the festival, the fence does not remain standing for long, mostly because the villagers take it away piece by piece to fence their own gardens in the backyards of their houses.

Entering the village plaza through the western entrance, we first come across the earth goddess's shrine, called *jakeri*. Her location in the village centre marks an important difference between Dongria and Desia Kond, since the latter prefer to reside away from the sacred grove containing the *jakeri* shrine. I saw only a few Dongria villages where this was the case. In these places, people explained that their houses originally stood next to the *dharni* before they began building a new settlement in a neighbouring area that was better suited for habitation. In a case like this, the *jakeri* cannot be moved. This marks a major difference between the shrine of the earth goddess and that of her husband, whose stone can be shifted and always stands in the centre of the village.

Depending on when the last *kodru parbu* was celebrated, the earth goddess's shrine area may vary in appearance. In the event that more than fifteen or twenty years have passed since the last buffalo sacrifice, some stones covered with dust and sand and a few pillars and beams may be the only visible remains of the goddess's house, and the sacrificial stakes may be in various states of decay due to weather, ants, and termites. Nobody pays particular attention to the stones, and only on festive occasions like the community festivals (*yatra*) does their site becomes a focus of ritual attention.

When only a couple of years have passed since the last festival of the goddess, a complete building is still visible, perhaps with a tin roof provided by the government, and walls from which the clay is slowly crumbling away. Inside the house, people may sit and chat, and visitors from distant places with no relatives in the village may find shelter here at night. The house is usually built around the stones marking the place of the earth goddess, and in this sense it resembles a temple. However, nobody takes care to preserve or rebuild the house before the next *kodru parbu,* and in contrast to the sacred images in a Hindu temple, the stones receive no regular worship and can be touched by anybody and even stepped on.

In a village that has recently organised a buffalo sacrifice, we find a newly built house of the goddess with decorated walls and a roof thatched with grass or made of tin. Inside the house, the stones are neatly arranged on an earthen platform, which is usually covered with thick layers of cow dung. The stone assemblage normally consists of either three or seven stones divided into three different types. One flat stone referred to as *pata* will form the centre. In many villages, two further, similarly shaped flat stones (*patang*) are positioned next to this central one and referred to as *ade* or "friends" of the goddess. On the main *pata*, a round, moveable stone named *bayriwali*[12] is placed. It functions as a grinding stone during the pigeon-pea festival (*kanga parbu*; see section 5.3.1), when a few seeds are crushed by the *jani* on the *pata* with the *bayriwali*. Next to the main *pata*, one or three small, often conically shaped stones protrude from the ground and are known as *konang*, a name also given to the stones marking the place of the shrine of most local lines of the *jani* status category. If three such stones are present, the largest, in the centre, will be called "mother," the other two "children" (*milang*).[13]

The words *pata* and *kona* can have different meanings. According to Jena et al. (2002, 370), the word *pata* denotes both the flat stones and the horizontal beams in a house, but according to my knowledge, the latter are rather called *pati* or *pate* (pl.: *pateng*). Winfield (1929, 91) in his vocabulary of the Kui language translates *pata* or *patang* as "a slate; a board, a board or boards used as a door or as a harrow." The word *kona* may correspond to two words mentioned in this dictionary, either *kana*, translated as "a hole, aperture, orifice" (Winfield 1929, 58) or *kona*, "darkness" (Winfield 1929, 64). Given the myth that the "Dongaria Kondh emerged from a small orifice in the earth, created by an insect called *kaniledra*" (Jena et al. 2002, 135), the *pata* may be understood as the door to and the *kona* as the orifice into the earth. According to this interpretation, the stone ar-

---

12 In Israel's (1979, 395) vocabulary the word *bōyeri vali* is translated as "slab for pounding.".
13 According to Niggemeyer (1964a, 168), the Kuttia Kond refer to these three stones as *rondi riara mila*, an expression meaning "one, two together, child." Two of these stones are considered to be husband and wife or *pundri riara*. In Dongria, too, *pundri* means husband and wife, and *riara* "two together." The third stone is considered to represent a child (*mila*).

Photo 7: *Jakeri* inside the house of the earth goddess (Kanharu, 2001)

rangement marks an opening in the earth similar to the place where the first human beings were born. In the myth recorded by Jena et al., after emerging out of the earth, the Dongria immediately collected three stones to represent the goddess, before they began building their own houses:

> The *adivasis* were the ones who were resolute about finding a way to come up to the earth: after a long search they spotted a ray of light entering through a small crack. They followed it to its source and thus arrived at *sapangada-(sativada) batangada (batativala)*. The *adivasis* then divided themselves into groups which they termed *kuda*. The first of these was the Nandruka *kuda*, being those who bore lamps in their hands when they emerged from the darkness. They also carried axes, knives and other weapons which they used to clear their way through a hill called Adaberu Horu (Badaberu Horu). The path was brightly lit and it is believed that the predecessors of the various Dongaria *kudas*, as well as other people, had taken the same route out of the earth. The first task they undertook was to establish the *dharani vali* in the direction facing the sun god. For this purpose they sought two small, smooth, round stones. Together with a bigger stone, the arrangement symbolised *dharani penu*. Each *kuda* then selected an area to build their settlement. (Jena et al. 2002, 142)

Given the possible translations of *pata* and *kona* mentioned above, the stone arrangement can be interpreted as a representation of the dark hole in the earth through which the humans rose up to the place where they live today. Each stone arrangement can be seen as the local equivalent of *sapangada-batangada*, a place also mentioned in various myths collected by Niggemeyer among the Kuttia Kond. While I am not aware of any site identified with this mythological birthplace in the Niamgiri mountain range, Elwin (1954, xlvi) and Niggemeyer (1964a, 74, 140) report a spot called *saphaganna-sarchangada* near the village of Karenja (Phulbani district) where all Kond are said to have emerged from the earth.[14]

Further insights into the meaning of the stone arrangement may be gained from looking at the contrast between the flat *pata* stones and the conical *kona* stones. In the eastern part of the village there are other small conical stones named *konang*, which are worshipped by the members of a particular local line as the deities of their descent group (see p. 433). They are considered to have been set up by the local line's ancestors and can be interpreted as symbols of the continuity of the male line. One of my informants identified the *konang* stones with the knife (*suri*) that is worshipped on the occasion of the *kodru parbu*. At the time of sacrifice, the ritual specialist takes the knife and uses it to pierce the goddess's house through one of the two openings in its wall, at the place where the victim is tethered to a post. As will be described in more detail later, the sacrificial hut and the buffalo are clearly representations of the earth goddess. In a similar way, the stone pierces the earth, and the association between *kona* and a phallus emerges clearly from what the Desia Kond from the village of Kamatana told me about this stone at the site of their earth goddess. According to them, the *kona* stone rises out of the earth each time the villagers organise a *kodru parbu* and disappears again into the ground once the festival has come to an end. Like the *konang*, the knife is considered to be a male deity, and both the stones and the knife penetrate the earth. Seen in this way, the flat *pata* stones may be interpreted as the female earth goddess,[15] while the conical *konang* stones represent the male deity penetrating her.

Another meaning of the stone arrangement can be derived from a myth collected around the turn of the twentieth century by A. B. Jayaram Moodaliar and cited by Thurston (1987, 368–71). This myth will be discussed in more detail in the concluding part of this chapter (see section 5.7.5), but a few details should be mentioned at this point. According to the myth, the mother of all human beings cut her little finger, and her blood dripped onto the earth, which was at that time completely covered by water. The place where the blood fell became dry im-

---

14 In spring 2000, I visited this place in the company of Professor Pfeffer. We were told that three weeks previously, an old man and a child had been sacrificed at the spot.

15 Typically, the horizontal beams in a house are female, the vertical pillars are male. Seen in this way, the large, flat *pata* stones are like the beams of the house, while the conical stones are like the pillars. This interpretation is substantiated by Jena et al. (2002, 370), who state that *pata* describes both the beams in a house and the *dharni* stones.

mediately, so in order to make the whole earth firm and fertile, the mother asked her son to sacrifice her. She instructed him to cut off her flesh, dig holes in the earth, put the flesh into these holes, and cover them with stones (Thurston 1987, 368–9). Taking this myth into account, the stone arrangement in each Kond village can be viewed as one of the holes where the son buried the flesh of the mother of all human beings.

The stone arrangement as a whole is called *jakeri* or *dharni*, the latter expression having a wider meaning in the sense of "the earth goddess," while the former is explicitly applied to the site of the buffalo sacrifice in each village.[16] The *jakeri* of different villages are considered to be related, either as younger (*boi*) or elder (*nana*) sisters, particularly when the villages belong to the same or closely related local lines, or else as friends (*ade*). They are said to exchange meat offerings made to them by their respective villagers, for example on the occasion of the *kodru parbu*, when young men present their *jakeri* with the flesh of a buffalo obtained at the sacrifice to another *jakeri* in a different village. The villagers themselves will address the *jakeri* as their mother, distinguishing between an elder (*kayaya*) and a younger (*ichaya*) mother or between a mother (*aya*) and her children (*milang*) when referring to more than one *jakeri* on their territory. This classification according to age implies a history of migrations or geographical dispersal, in which villages occupied or purchased first are considered to be "older." Each *jakeri* has a name by which it is identified in ritual invocations.

A few meters east of the *jakeri* are the remnants of sacrificial posts set up in the course of previous *kodru parbu*. In some villages, two such posts are set up for each buffalo, a carved one painted with red or white stripes and a plain one to which the animal will actually be tied. As will be described later, the carved stakes are basically all of the same height and shape, and apart from functioning as sacrificial posts, they are themselves representations of a deity named *bisimunda*. The fence (*garada*) constructed around the sacrificial site on the eve of the festival to keep away the young men who try to kill the buffaloes before the proper time of sacrifice usually disappears within a few days after the sacrifice is over.

Further east, most often only a few meters away from the *jakeri*, another shrine area can be seen, consisting of a T-shaped wooden stake (*panikimunda*), a conical stone (*koteiwali*), and the remains of a wall (*palawara*), together with three long poles that look like lances. During the *kodru parbu*, the heads of the

---

[16] According to Jena et al. (2002, 48) the large flat stone is called *jhankiri pata* – the word is probably identical with *jakeri pata* – who is considered to be the mother, while the smaller stones or *kana* are conceived of as her children.

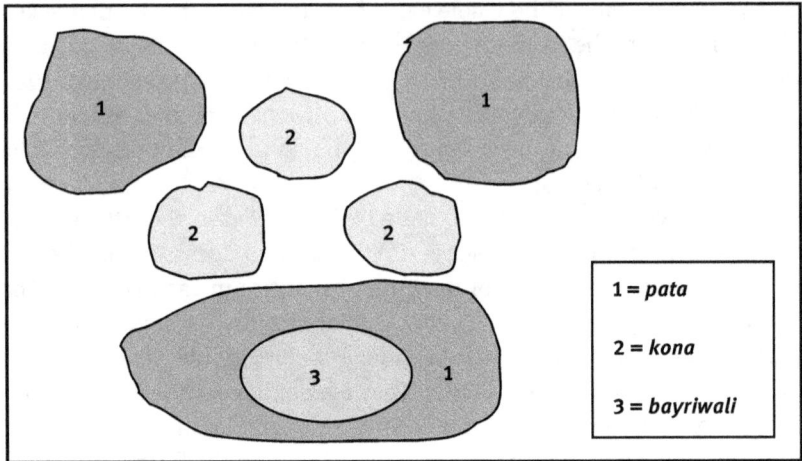

Figure 30: Diagram of the *jakeri* of Gumma

fowls offered to the *koteiwali* are placed on the horizontal plank of the *panikimunda*, while the head of the ram that is killed in his name is tied to the middle one of the three long poles, which protrude out from the wall. The stone representing the husband of the earth goddess and father of the Dongria may be of various sizes. I have seen small stones, perhaps twenty to thirty centimetres in height, as well as very large menhirs, in one case as tall as two metres. All of them have a wide base and a conical peak, thus resembling a miniature model of a hill or mountain. While most Dongria Kond villages have only a single stone on the central plaza, Desia Kond villages usually contain two such stones, one at each entrance. The wall to the east of the *koteiwali* is made of bamboo and wooden pillars and is plastered with clay and painted with simple triangles in different colours. Like the eastern wall of the *dharni kudi,* it usually has two round holes in the centre, which look like the deity's eyes.

Apart from these community shrines, large flat stones (*kaja wali*) and smaller sacrificial posts of a different shape from the *kodru parbu* stakes may be found on the village plaza. Both of these types of objects are located in front of particular houses, the owners of which claim a comparatively high status. In Gumma, there were two such stones, one in front of the house of the *jani*, who keeps the old axe from the time of human sacrifices, and one in front of the house of the *bismajhi* – sometimes also referred to as *saanta* – who preserves the brass symbol of the clan. In the morning or evening, these householders would sit on these stones in front of their houses, but I never heard of other people who sat on them being chased away. The stones appeared to be signs of the house's status without being exclusively reserved for the householders. The sacrificial poles found next to the doors of some houses are set up by the main householder for a ceremony named *ghanta parba*, in which rams are sacrificed to the house deity.

Outside the village to the east, there are only a few permanent places of worship, although many rituals take place facing in this direction. As mentioned in the context of arranged marriages in the fourth chapter, the goddess of wealth, *sita penu-lahi penu*, is brought from the path just outside the eastern end of the village after the wedding. On the second day of the wedding itself, the goddess is worshipped by three *jani* sitting in a river, east of the residential area. In the same place, the *bada* ceremony is performed during the *ghanta parba* and on other auspicious occasions. The only permanent places of worship are the shrines of the "house" deities located outside the eastern entrance of the village. The location is marked by stones, each stone being identified with one "house" in the sense that all householders worshipping the same stone claim common ancestry. The ancestor's name may not be remembered, but members of related households claim that their common "grandfather" (*tadi*) had initially placed the stone.[17] The stones can usually be found at the edge of the forest, where they are placed next to each other in a line. The number of stones varies according to the size of the village. In Gumma, people worshipped seven stones identified with three deities: the members of the local line of *kaja bismajhi* referred to their deity as *ma budi*, one local line of *icha jani* worshipped the god *lada penu*, and five local lines belonging to the categories of *kaja* and *icha jani* made their offerings to the god *kona*. According to one informant, this *kona* is the same as the knife (*churi*) worshipped during the *kodru parbu*, while others referred to their deity as *konabera*, which may be identical to the fire god.

Every house belonging to the local lines of the village founders has such a stone outside the village, with two or three houses often sharing one stone when they belong to the same descent group. People who later migrated into the village may still continue to perform worship at their local line's stone in its original village. Among the immigrants, only those families who have been well established in their new villages for two or three generations and are able to perform major rituals like the *ghanta parba* have their own stones. These stones mainly become the focus of ritual activities on two major occasions, the *ghanta parba* and the *kodru parbu*. During the former, the household builds a new shrine around its stone in the same way that the village as a whole sets up a

---

17 The ceremony of planting a stone may take place even today, and in the village of Desia Kond I once witnessed a young man who had recently migrated to the village establishing his own shrine area by placing a stone into a hole in the ground.

new house for the earth goddess prior to the buffalo sacrifice. The house for the god of the local line is called *ghata kudi*,[18] and its exact form depends on the deity represented by the stone. For example, the shrine for the god *lada penu* looks like a small house, while the shrine for *aji budi* resembles a tent with a roof extending to the ground. For a *ghanta parba*, sacrificial stakes are put into the ground, the number depending on the quantity of rams to be sacrificed, this being mainly an affair of the men of the village. Except for the female shamans, hardly any women are present at this site during the *ghanta parba*. In the context of the *kodru parbu*, no such posts are erected, although on the second day (Saturday) of the festival, many white fowls and rams are offered to the stones in a ceremony referred to as *walka puja* ("stone worship"). On this occasion, women as well as men participate in worship.

In villages where members of the local line of *pujari* are present, the shrine constructed for worshipping the god *bera* and the goddess *bali ma* is often located close to these *ghata kudi*, towards the eastern end of the village. There was no such *bali kudi* in Gumma, but I saw them in villages with a majority of *pujari* families, such as Parsali and Lekhpadar. The *bali kudi* contains not a stone but a three-step pyramid, often with *tulsi* leaves on top. In front of the shrine is a pit several meters long, used for fire walking during the *bali yatra* (Hardenberg 2014), which is celebrated annually in these villages in either *phalgun* or *caitra*. We thus have three festivals all celebrated roughly at the same time but associated with different status categories: the *bismajhi* annually worship the goddess of smallpox at the *yatra kudi* in the west; the *pujari* celebrate a festival for the god of fire and the goddess of sand at the *bali kudi* once in a year in the east; and the *jani* are mostly responsible for the worship of the earth goddess at the *dharni kudi* in the centre of the village.

What are the main structures behind this village layout? The main opposition between the east and the west has already been mentioned. Dongria consider the east to be the direction where the sun god is born and the west the place where he dies each evening. Correspondingly, rituals pertaining to life, such as bringing the harvest or a bride into the village, are performed in the east, while all ceremonies linked to death take place in the west. The places of the recently

---

18 Jena et al. (2002, 28) mention a place called *ghata kudi*, which according to them is also named "*kuda-kudi*." This place is said to be linked to a particular clan (*kuda*). On the occasion of *ghata parava* – probably the same as *ghanta parbu* – sacrificial posts are reported to be set up by members of the clan conducting the ceremony (Jena et al. 2002, 28–29). In the places where I recorded data concerning the *ghata kudi*, I often found more than one *ghata kudi* belonging to the same clan, since these places belonged to specific local lines, not entire clans.

deceased, just like the houses of the Dombo,[19] are located in this western region, while the houses of the Dongria and the shrines of the local lines founded by their ancestors stand in the east. Evil forces are expected to come from the west, and for this reason the *yatra kudi* guards this entrance to the village. Gods and benevolent ancestors arrive from the east and leave the village in the west. Finally, the gender opposition appears to correspond to the distinction of east and west, since the sun is considered to be a man when rising in the morning and a woman when setting in the evening. It fits into this structure that the "father" of the Dongria, the *koteiwali*, always stands east of their "mother," the *jakeri*.

Table 29: Binary pairs structuring the sacred village layout

east (south)	west (north)
life rituals	death rituals
arrival of deities and ancestors	departure of deities and ancestors
Dongria houses	Dombo houses
representation of local line	individual souls
male deity	female deity
male worshippers	female worshippers

Many villages I visited during my fieldwork corresponded more or less to the ideal model described above. Without variation the *yatra kudi* guards the western (or northern) entrance to the village, and in most cases the *jakeri* is indeed located on the main village plaza west (or south) of the *koteiwali*. The latter arrangement may only deviate from the ideal in places where a former village site was abandoned for various reasons. For example in Mundawali, a village belonging to the Jakesika clan, the *dharni kudi* stands a few hundred meters outside the present residential area after the villagers constructed their houses in a different place.

While the location of the *dharni* outside the settlement appears to be an exception among the Dongria Kond, it seems to be a regular pattern among the Desia Kond. In villages inhabited by the latter, the *koteiwali* often stands in the centre of the main road, although I also visited villages where two such stones could be found, one at each entrance. The *dharni*, however, is almost always located outside the settlement in a sacred grove. Similarly, the axe representing the goddess is often not kept in the *jani*'s house but instead hidden in

---

[19] In the second chapter I already pointed out the fact that Dongria jokingly call the Dombo *dhumba*, the Oriya word for dead people.

the crevice of a nearby hill or in the knothole of a tree standing in this sacred grove. The sacred grove usually lies to the west of the village and is dominated by large mango trees, but no branches should grow above the *jakeri*. Smaller stones used as a cooking hearth for the preparation of sacrificial food can usually be found next to the earth goddess's shrine. In one place the grove also contained seven stones (*konang*) representing the seven local lines of the dominant clan plus an additional larger stone for the village community (*kutumba*). In this case, *yatra kudi* and *ghata kudi* were all located in the vicinity of the *jakeri* outside the residential area.

When I discussed the location of the *dharni* in Desia Kond villages with my Dongria informants, one of them immediately related the position of the goddess on the central plaza to the strict rules observed by their own women in the context of menstruation. While Desia women at the time of their menses are allowed to move around within the village, Dongria women are confined to a room in the rear of their house for at least three to four days and should under no circumstances walk on the main road. Dongria and Desia Kond fear the earth goddess's wrath should menstrual blood fall onto the ground near her shrine, but since the former remain in the rear of their houses and towards the back of the village, the goddess' shrine can safely be kept on the village plaza. In the case of the Desia Kond, women may move around more freely as long as they do not go near the *jakeri*'s sacred grove.

5.2.2 Time: Date and intervals

The *kodru parbu* normally takes place in the months of *pausa* (December – January) and *magh* (January – February) among the Desia Kond, while Dongria Kond celebrate it a month or two later, usually in *phalgun* (February – March) or *caitra* (March – April). Among the latter group, the important rites of the sacrifice are performed on the same days as wedding rituals, i.e., from Friday to Sunday. However, the date of the festival itself is not fixed, not even by the phases of the moon, as is the case in many Hindu ceremonies. Dongria try to avoid celebrating the festival in two places at the same time unless the villages involved are located far away from each other. In some cases, Dongria ask a *dissari* or local Hindu astrologer to determine an auspicious day for the rite, but schedules are changed constantly for various reasons: the sacrificial buffalo runs away or is stolen; conflicts arise between villages, between brothers, or between affines and agnates; important people become sick; the government does not provide the tin roof for the goddess's hut of the goddess; the villagers run out of money; and/or preparations cannot be completed in time. Among the Desia

Kond, the celebration of the *kodru parbu* is not confined to the days from Friday to Saturday. I attended sacrifices in which the animals were killed on Tuesday, Wednesday, or Sunday. These differences between Dongria and Desia Kond may be related to the greater importance the latter attach to astrology for determining the time of rituals.

The typical period for conducting the *kodru parbu* falls between the reaping of the harvest and the preparing of the fields for the next agricultural year. The festival ends with a ceremony of the mango twig (*ambadadi yatra*), which signifies the end of the old year and the beginning of the new. This period is considered to be a time of happiness (*rasa wela*) during which people are to some extent released from the arduousness of agricultural work. The young people find time to play games during the day and to visit each other more often in the dormitories at night. The alcoholic *salap* sap (*mada kalu*) flows once again, and the adult men spend many hours sitting under a palm tree drinking and chatting. After the harvest people have enough to eat and may have earned a substantial amount of money from the sale of their cash crops, so that they can afford to buy new clothes, cooking utensils, and from time to time some liquor distilled by the Dombo.

The intervals between two *kodru parbu* celebrated by the same village appear to be connected to the agricultural cycle, yet the exact intervals depend on various factors and are certainly not simply determined by the practice of shifting cultivation. In contrast to festivals observed by Hindus in the plains (e.g., Hardenberg 1999, 2000), the intervals between sacrifices to the earth goddess are fixed neither by a calendar based on astrological calculations nor by any central authority such as a king or a temple committee. Upon questioning, Desia Kond residing in the valleys told me that they should celebrate the *kodru parbu* every three to five years. In contrast, Dongria Kond never mentioned any definite interval but rather stressed that any number of years may lapse before a village decides to perform the sacrifice again. According to my data, a time interval of ten or more years is not exceptional, and in some villages, such as Bada Denganali, people informed me that the last *kodru parbu* was celebrated about twenty years ago. Often villagers do not remember the exact number of years that have passed since they last gave a buffalo to the earth goddess but rather point to a child, explaining that this boy or girl was a baby at the time of the last *kodru parbu*. Some hints about a particular village's activities may also be deduced from the condition and number of sacrificial posts near the *dharni*, which stand in different stages of decay.

I found two practices or institutions that provide a certain framework for the timing of the festival yet still allow for the flexibility we observe in practice. On the one hand, the interval between two *kodru parbu* of the same village seems to depend on the practice of starting shifting cultivation in a new territory (*padari*) when deserting an old village and constructing a new one (*nayu*) in cases of epidemics, deaths, fire, or other disasters. On the other hand, the interval seems to derive from the circulation of sacred objects. Each clan organisation consists of an association of a definite number or villages, usually seven, twelve, or seventeen, which together own certain objects that must be displayed on the occasion of the *kodru parbu*. These objects are transferred from place to place each time a village of the clan association organises the festival.

The people of Gumma explained to me that the buffalo sacrifice has to be performed when the village as a whole begins cultivating a hill territory that belongs to a former settlement. After cutting down the trees, the villagers wait for three years and for a successful harvest before they make a sacrifice to the earth goddess of that territory. The logic followed seems to be the same for a household and for the village as a whole. When a family starts cutting down the trees on a hill slope (*nela*), its members wait three years before performing the great harvest ritual. This ceremony is referred to as *neta dakina* or "making a ritual for the swidden."[20] I observed this ceremony several times, recording and translating the ritual invocations, but I will not go into any details here, since this would lead us away from the main topic, the *kodru parbu*. It suffices to say that the ritual is performed after the harvest, when the crops are on the threshing ground, usually located near the watch hut in the swidden itself. This hill slope (*nela*), the threshing ground (*kada*), and the watch hut (*menda*) are considered to be representations of the goddess of wealth, *sita penu-lahi penu*.[21] The ritual involves the sacrifice of fowl to the goddess of wealth, of a ram to the god of the particular hill (*horu penu* or *dandang*), and of a small pig to the river goddess named *gungi penu*. The ceremony ends with a feast provided by the household that cultivated the swidden, to which the whole village will be invited.

The ceremony conducted by the household to its hill god corresponds on the higher segmentary level of the village and its territory (*padari*) to the sacrifice performed by the community to its local earth goddess (*jakeri*). As in the case of a single swidden, the rituals pertaining to the whole village territory involve a three-year cycle.

---

20 While the word *nela* is used for a swidden that lies fallow, the term *neta* is applied to a hill slope on which its owners have begun cultivating crops.

21 For example, in ritual invocations, the husband of *sita penu* is invoked by calling him *nela-mendakayra alo mendabamana* ("hill slope-watch hut-*kayra*, hey, watch hut-*bamana*").

Table 30: Harvest ritual (*neta dakina*) and buffalo sacrifice (*kodru parbu*)

Name of ritual	Agricultural unit	Cycle	Sponsor	Place	Main sacrifices
Neta dakina (harvest ritual)	single hill slope (*nela / neta*)	three years after first cultivation	house (*ilu*) cultivating the field	field hut (*lahi penu*)	ram to *dandang*, pig to *gungi penu*, fowls to *lahi penu*
kodru parbu (buffalo sacrifice)	whole village territory (*bondeli / padari*)	three years after first cultivation	village (*nayu*) cultivating the territory	village hut (*jakeri*)	ram to *koteiwali*, buffalo/pig to *dharni*

When Dongria begin cutting down trees in a *padari* that has lain fallow for several years, they first perform a small ceremony at the *jakeri*. In the month of *caitra*, shortly before they burn the dried wood and begin sowing, they hang a gourd filled with seeds (*hiko, kahada, kanga, joda*, etc.) above the stone representation of the goddess. This ritual is referred to as *nela nespoli* or "charging the hill fields." A year later, around the same time, the villagers perform a more elaborate ceremony, which is called *derupripka*. I personally never witnessed this ceremony, but Dongria informants described the major events to me.[22] It begins at night with incantations by three *jani* at the earth goddess's shrine. In the middle of the night, they go to the place marking the border of the village territory and sacrifice a pig to the wandering ghosts (*marha*).[23] The next morning, the shamans come and fall into a trance before the earth goddess's shrine. They dance by holding a pig hanging from a stick between them, before the animal is sacrificed in the name of the souls of the ancestors (*mahane*). Apart from a ram and some fowls given to the earth goddess and her husband, the major sacrifice is performed on behalf of the goddess protecting the village site, the *yatra kudi*. The name of the whole ceremony derives from the particular way of killing a cow that is offered to her. The sacrificers take a piece of bamboo (*deru*), split it (*pripka*), trap the cow's head between the two

---

[22] In 2002, the *derupripka* took place in Waliamba, a *padari* belonging to Gumma. It was postponed so many times that it finally took place in the rainy season, after I had left for Germany. The events were described to me by an old man from Gumma the following year when I returned to Gumma.

[23] According to other informants, a pig has to be sacrificed at each border (*handi*) of the *padari*.

halves of the bamboo, and begin turning it until the neck breaks.[24] The aim of killing the animal in this peculiar way is to prevent the spilling of blood, a practice that is just the opposite of the one that takes place during the *kodru parbu*, when everybody lays their axes into the buffalo.[25] Afterwards, the whole village assembles to share the sacrificial animals in a feast. Through this ceremony, the evil spirits are banished from the territory and driven beyond its boundaries, the ancestors residing on the village land are satisfied, and the goddess guarding the area and preventing evil forces from entering it receives the most important sacrifice.

When the harvest has been abundant for three years, the *kodru parbu* is celebrated. If the harvest has not been as successful as expected, people may wait for one or two more years and in this case have to perform a sacrifice to the goddess *yatra kudi* each year. The *kodru parbu* marks the final stage of this agricultural and ritual cycle. By giving one of the most precious gifts, in the past a human, today a buffalo, the villagers repay the goddess for providing them with fertility throughout the years of cultivation. Thus, during a trance session by the shaman, the goddess will demand a sacrifice from the villagers by asking, "I have given you rice, millet and water, what will you give to me?" (*manjing, hiko are eyu hitee, nange ana hineru?*).

Table 31: Three-year ritual sequence and agricultural cycle

Year	Name of ritual	Stage of agriculture	Purpose of ritual
one	nela nespoli	broadcast sowing of seeds in new swidden; first harvest	increasing the growth of the seeds
two	derupripka (or yatra kudi niktari)	second harvest	protecting the village territory from evil forces
three	kodru parbu	third harvest	thanksgiving to the earth goddess

---

24 In Gumma in 2001, I witnessed the ceremony for the goddess of smallpox, *aji budi*, which appears to be very similar to the *derupripka*. Three strong young men made the cow lie down on the ground before twisting the animal's head with their bare hands until its neck broke.
25 In my interpretation the practice derives from the power of a cow's blood to attract the most evil spirits, the wandering ghosts. When a person turns into a ghost through a "bad death," he or she receives a cow as an offering. If in this case the blood of the cow were to be spilled freely, the ghosts would be attracted and assemble at this site. This would cancel out the efforts to keep the ghosts out of the territory by sacrificing pigs to them at the borders of the village.

The rule mentioned above, i.e., that the *kodru parbu* is performed three years after the village begins cultivation in a new *padari*, suggests a clear link between the ritual cycle and the shifting of the place of cultivation. However, this rule seems to apply only when a community abandons a former village site and returns to it after a lapse of several years. The informants from Gumma who told me about this rule found themselves in exactly this situation. The "grandfathers" of the village elders lived in Gumma until many people fell prey to the "attacks of tigers."[26] At that time, the village is said to have been much larger than it is today, containing more than one hundred houses. When the inhabitants left Gumma, they began building new houses at two other village sites (*jakeri*), one in Kadengeyu and the other in Waliamba. About twenty years ago, first the families residing in Kadengeyu, and later those living in Waliamba, abandoned their villages and resettled in Gumma. Presently, members of the younger generation, whose fathers used to live in Waliamba, are making plans to return to this location and establish a new village. For this reason, they first began clearing the forest on the hill slopes around the *jakeri* of Waliamba. Next, they performed the ceremony of "charging the swidden" (*nela nespoli*), and a year later, they conducted the sacrifice of a cow to the *yatra kudi*. The next step should be the performance of the *kodru parbu*, which the villagers, for various reasons, have postponed several times. Once all ritual duties have been observed, many, if not all, of the villagers may abandon Gumma and build new houses in Waliamba.[27]

In this case, the buffalo sacrifice is clearly linked to tilling the land and to taking up residence in a formerly abandoned village site (*bondeli*). However, not all *kodru parbu* are timed according to the movements of all or part of the village community from one *padari* to another. I witnessed festivals (e. g., Lekhpadar, Railima) in which in one year several buffaloes were sacrificed to all the *jakeri* claimed by the village community. Dongria make the same distinction as

---

26 In Gumma, the old people still remember places where a person was killed by a tiger (*krani*) and turned into one of the most feared wandering ghosts (*krani marha*). There are now no more tigers in the woods, but in their invocations the shamans continue to beg the gods to take the tigers to faraway places. When they hear sounds in the night, Dongria often attribute this to *krani marha*.

27 People may forgo these plans due to the activities of development officers from the United Nations and the local government. In 2003, a new housing project began with the aim of providing the "poor" Dongria with new, more solid houses made of bricks and covered with tin roofs. They offered each family a – by local standards – huge amount of money to build new houses according to standards set by the United Nations and offered a free supply of tin roofs. In spring 2003, almost all Dongria in the Niamgiri Hills were busy making bricks and building walls. Upon questioning, many Dongria families appeared to be willing to remain in Gumma instead of moving to Waliamba.

442 — 5 The clan sacrifice: Creating Niamgiri society

Photo 8: A swidden in the Niamgiri Hills (near Kadrakabondeli, 2001)

the Kuttia Kond (Niggemeyer 1964a, 168)[28] between a *jakeri* that marks a possible village site – a *bondeli* – and a *jakeri* that defines a certain territory used for cultivation but not necessarily for building a settlement. This distinction between the two types of *jakeri* seems to lie behind two different practices of sacrificing buffaloes:

1) When the *jakeri* marks the place where a settlement presently stands, where a settlement used to be, or where people are planning to build a new settlement, then the buffalo sacrifice is performed at this particular stone arrangement.
2) When the *jakeri* marks only a village territory but not the site of a settlement – neither in the past, present, nor future – then the buffalo for this territory is sacrificed not at this *jakeri* but at the *jakeri* of the settlement the residents of which claim the village territory.

---

28 Niggemeyer distinguishes between a "village *dharni*" (in German, "Dorf *dharni*") and a "field *dharni*" ("Feld *dharni*"), with the latter considered to be smaller, i.e. of lower status, compared to the former.

In the case of a *kodru parbu* celebrated for a field *jakeri* (in opposition to a village *jakeri*), shifting from one *padari* to the other does not determine the timing of the sacrifice. A small *padari* may indeed be wholly abandoned and left fallow, but in a larger *padari* there are always portions of land under cultivation, while other areas are covered by thick forest. The relationship between the size of a *padari* and the number of households determines how long the members of a village cultivate a certain village territory. Each field can be cultivated for about three, or at the most four years before the quality of the soil deteriorates and the crops no longer grow properly. Most families till more than one field at a time, because certain crops grow well in the first year and others in the second or third year. In order to have a selection of all crops, it is advantageous to cultivate more than one field at one time. If the relation between land and number of households is favourable, villagers may cultivate two or more hill slopes of the same *padari*, but if the *padari* is too small, villagers will cultivate land in other territories as well.

As argued above, the long intervals between two *kodru parbu* may derive from the practice of abandoning old settlements and building new ones. They may, however, also result from the practice of transferring holy objects within a related group of villages belonging to the same clan. As will be described in more detail later, a clan territory (*muta*) as a whole owns a clan symbol (*bonda*) and sometimes a sacred knife (*suri*) that is taken from the village where the *kodru parbu* last took place to the village that organises it next. These organisers have the right to keep the object for one year or more, until the next village belonging to their *muta* sends their delegates to demand the sacred symbols to perform their own buffalo sacrifice. In my experience, only one village in every *muta* organises the festival each year. From this it is possible to infer a system of circulation in which the number of villages belonging to a *muta* determines the intervals at which each village organises the festival. However, in practice no definite sequence exists, since some villages in a *muta* perform the *kodru parbu* at short intervals and others at longer ones. This may be due to the relative differences in agricultural surplus, but the fact that a village must claim the sacred object from an agnatically related village suggests that the relative status and power of the organising local lines is of importance too. A village that organises the *kodru parbu* needs the cooperation of the villages where their "brothers" live, not only to obtain the clan symbol but also to prepare and conduct the ceremonies.

The exact sequence of *kodru parbu* among a group of villages united in a *muta* seems to be determined by several other factors. First of all, Dongria often stress the fact that the festival will only be celebrated when every household has had a successful harvest. In winter 2001, for example, the villagers of Gumma discussed whether or not they should organise the sacrifice for the next spring season, but finally decided against it. One reason was that some households had had a bad harvest that year. Another reason why a *kodru parbu* may be cancelled in the preparatory stages is that deaths or other calamities occur, such as a major fire destroying several houses of the village. I know of two cases in which one or more deaths caused the villagers to postpone their plans to celebrate the *kodru parbu*. In one case, first the daughter-in-law of the most respected *jani* of the village died in childbirth, and then his wife also died. Before these tragic incidents, the villagers were making plans to buy three buffaloes for their three village territories (*padari*), but following the two deaths, the *jani* cancelled the sacrifice for the coming year. In another case, the villagers of Sana Dengoni decided not to go ahead with the preparations for a *kodru parbu* after some of their fellow villagers died. The following year brought a good harvest and no further deaths, and the villagers performed the festival that spring.

5.2.3 Costs: Financing the sacrifice

No other religious event requires more preparations, expenditures, and investments than the buffalo sacrifice. For any of the regular village festivals (*yatra*) held throughout the year, Dongria need hardly more than an old, usually cheap buffalo, a few fowl, some liquor, and perhaps new clothes for the shaman. Within a few hours most of these festivals are over, and people can start cooking the sacrificial meat and rice, which they do not have to share with outsiders, since no guests come to attend these village celebrations. On the occasion of the *kodru parbu*, however, things are different.

First of all, the organisers have to buy one or more young, well-fed buffaloes, the exact number depending on the number of earth goddess shrines (*jakeri*) owned by the community. Such a buffalo costs a minimum of Rs 3,000 to Rs 4,000, depending on the skill of the Dombo trader. When a village owns four sites sacred to the earth goddess, the amount required for the main sacrificial animals adds up to a sum between Rs 12,000 and Rs 16,000. At least three more buffaloes of the less expensive type (Rs 1,500 to Rs 2,000) are required for other events during the *kodru parbu*. One buffalo, or alternatively one cow, has to be slaughtered in order to provide a feast for the people who assist in building the sacrificial hut for the goddess (*dharni kudi*). Another buffalo is needed for the so-called "mango-twig festival" (*ambadadi yatra*), which is celebrated a few days after the sacrifice to the earth goddess in order to bring the *kodru parbu* to an end. Finally, one buffalo has to be given to the village the male members of which are selected as *mudrenga*. They help to guard the sacrificial animal during the first two days of the festival and ensure that nobody kills the animal before the proper time for sacrifice.

The cost of these buffaloes is borne by different people. The so-called *padari kodru* or buffalo to be sacrificed to the earth goddess must be acquired by those households that, on the basis of their clan title, claim territorial rights in the land. When, for example, the *dharni* of a village belongs to the Sikoka clan, only members of the Sikoka clan residing in this village contribute money. This is considered to be a privilege and not a duty, since the purchase of the buffalo offered to the earth goddess is proof of status as a landowner, i.e., of membership in the dominant local clan. The exact application of the rule can vary. In some villages, such as the place I conducted my fieldwork, all members of the dominant clan were allowed to buy the *padari kodru,* irrespective of whether they were regarded to be members of the founding line or immigrants who came later from other villages. In other villages, the buffalo for the earth goddess will only be bought by the main *jani*, whose ancestors are said to have purchased the land. As proof of this claim this *jani* usually keeps the most sacred objects of the festival, an old knife (*suri*), an axe (*tangi*), an iron stove (*halu*), and a cooking spoon (*hetu*), in his house. In villages of Desia Kond, for example, I witnessed several *kodru parbu* for which basically all expenses were borne by the keeper of these holy objects. Sometimes more than one household claims rights in the land on the basis of their ancestry and ownership of sacred objects. These households are collectively called "chief people" (*mukhya loku*) and are distinct from those families of the village who bear the same clan title but have no connection to the place in which they are residing. I have been told that in some Dongria villages, such as Niskabondeli, only these "noble men" have the right to purchase the buffalo for the earth goddess.

When agnates and affines from different villages come to build the house for the earth goddess and the fence around the village, the feast is sponsored by those villagers who do not belong to the dominant clan and are collectively referred to as *raiti loku* (see section 3.3.4). They must buy a buffalo or a cow that is slaughtered and shared among all, along with cooked rice. The buffalo to be sacrificed during the mango-twig festival is purchased by the *barika* of the village and given as a gift to all his patrons. This festival is celebrated every spring and marks the end of the year, when contracts, in this case between the village as a whole and the *barika*, are renewed. Finally, the buffalo that is to be given to the *mudrenga* is bought from the collective village funds. The *mudrenga* will usually present a buffalo to the organisers of the *kodru parbu* in return.

Apart from buffaloes, the organisers have to buy a number of rams for sacrifice on various occasions. For the worship of the *koteiwali*, the husband of the earth goddess, the organisers set up sacrificial posts (*panikimunda*) near the stone that represents him. On the day these are set up, the god receives a white, well-fed ram whose horns are fixed to the stakes. Such a ram costs a minimum of Rs 1,000, if not more. On the first day of the festival, when the symbol representing the clan (*bonda*) is set in place on a long bamboo pole (*satara uhnari*), a ram of the same, if not higher, quality has to be sacrificed to the husband of the earth goddess. In one case (village of Railima), the organisers worshipped the *koteiwali* at four sites belonging to the village and sacrificed one ram at each place.[29] When the festival is over and the object representing the clan is taken down (*satara lipnari*) and returned to its owner, another white ram has to be killed, or alternatively at least a white fowl and a dove, adding further to the already high costs. The rams are paid for out of the common village funds, and only in one case was I informed that the ram sacrificed to the *koteiwali* was actually bought by the *mudrenga*. Apart from these collective offerings of rams, individual households may decide to sacrifice their own rams to various deities. Thus, on the second day of the festival, each household will make an offering to the god of its local line (*kana penu*) and to its house deity (*lahi penu*), and in both cases they may – depending on their financial standing – present a white, costly ram or alternatively a large white rooster.

Only a small amount of money has to be raised to buy the pigs that are offered to the earth goddess or given away to villages with which the organisers maintain relations of friendship. At least two small pigs worth Rs 100 to Rs 200 are sacrificed to the earth goddess on two consecutive nights, when the three *jani* make their incantations. In some cases these pigs were provided by the owner of the knife and axe, i.e., the village *jani*; in other cases I witnessed agnates from neighbouring villages handing over these pigs as gifts to the sponsors when they brought their knife and axe to the site of the *kodru parbu*. To the friends (*tonenga*) who come and present a buffalo as a gift to the organisers, the villagers as a whole present a pig, rice, and alcohol as a farewell present.

---

[29] Railima does not have a tradition of setting up the clan symbol. Where such a tradition exists, the festival starts with the sacrifice of a ram at the *koteiwali* on a Friday morning. In the case of Railima, one ram was given to each of their four *koteiwali* on Saturday morning, shortly before the villagers went to the stone representations of their local lines to sacrifice rams or fowls.

5.2 The buffalo sacrifice (*kodru parbu*): An overview

Table 32: Animals bought for the *kodru parbu*

Occasion	Giver	Value	Number
Buffaloes			
sacrifice to the earth goddess	village households of the local dominant clan (*padari loku*) or descendants of original land owners (*mukhya loku*)	Rs 3,000 – Rs 4,000 each	depends on the number of *jakeri* worshipped by the village
feast for constructing the house of the earth goddess	village households not belonging to the local dominant clan (*raiti loku*)	Rs 1,500 – Rs 2,000	one
sacrifice at the *ambadadi yatra* (mango-twig festival)	the village *barika*	Rs 1,500 – Rs 2,000	one
feast shared by *mudrenga* for protecting the sacrificial animals	village as a whole	Rs 1,500 – Rs 2,000	one
Rams			
setting up the sacrificial pole (*paniki munda*)	village as a whole	Rs 1,000 – Rs 1,500	one
setting up the clan symbol (*satara uhnari*)	village as a whole (alternatively *mudrenga*)	Rs 1,000 – Rs 1,500	one (or one at each *koteiwali* worshipped by the village)
taking down the clan symbol (*satara lipnari*)	village as a whole	Rs 1,000 – Rs 1,500	one (or alternatively a fowl or a dove)
worshipping the god of the local line (*kana penu*)	individual households	Rs 700 – Rs 1,000	one
worship of the house goddess	individual households	Rs 700 – Rs 1,000	one
Pigs			
sacrifice to the earth goddess on the first night (Friday)	*jani* or agnates bringing sacred knife	Rs 100 – Rs 150	one

Table 32: Animals bought for the *kodru parbu (Continued)*

Occasion	Giver	Value	Number
sacrifice to the earth goddess on the second night (Saturday)	*jani* or agnates bringing sacred knife	Rs 100 – Rs 150	one
farewell to ritual friends (*tonenga*)	village as a whole	Rs 100 – Rs 150	depends on the number of villages invited as friends

Finally, a great number of fowl, small chickens and doves, are sacrificed to various deities on different occasions. It is difficult to estimate the exact number of animals needed, so they are not included in the table above. Some are bought collectively, for example when they are offered at the shrines of the earth goddess or her husband, but an even larger number of fowl are bought and sacrificed by individual households. When the buffalo or the metal symbol of the *koteiwali* is taken from house to house, each family will offer a chicken, and on the second day of the festival, when the god of the lineage and the goddess of the house receive their share, each house must provide at least one large white rooster worth Rs 200 and one or two brown or black chickens, which are available for around Rs 100 to Rs 150 each. The animals must be purchased, but since the price of fowl rises considerably at the time of *kodru parbu*, some householders buy them well in advance.

Further expenditures are necessary to pay the ritual specialists for their services. The three *jani* who sit for two long nights in front of the stone representation of the earth goddess and recite incantations receive a monetary remuneration, the exact amount being an object of heavy bargaining.[30] For their work, the villagers have to provide them with new clothes, paddy, and the huge amounts of liquor they consume during the course of the ritual. They demand a certain share of the harvest, in particular from the fruit trees, and at the end of the *kodru parbu* they go from house to house collecting rice and money. Similarly, the village has to pay the shamans, *beju* and *bejuni*, for their services and present them with new clothes to wear when they fall into a trance and dance for the gods. A small amount of money has to be given to the blacksmith who comes to "renew" the old sacrificial weapons with his instruments the day before the actual sacrifice, but I do not have any exact information about the amount he can demand.

---

[30] For example, in Depaguda each *jani* was given Rs 500 for his services.

The great number of feasts held in the course of the whole *kodru parbu* imposes another financial burden on the sponsors. At least two feasts must be given during the preparations for the festival, one when the main pillars of the earth goddess's house have been set up and another when the roof of the house, the fence around the village, and the sacrificial site have been completed. On both occasions the women of the village cook either rice or little millet and – if the men do not slaughter a cow or a buffalo and cook the meat – they prepare a side dish consisting of boiled vegetables or lentils. During the three main days of the festival, each household will provide food to the many guests in attendance. The girls will cook rice and serve it collectively to the young men who have come to dance with them. On Friday, a feast with rice and meat will be held for all the guests on the village plaza following the sacrifice of the white ram at the shrine of the *koteiwali*. On Sunday morning, following the sacrifice of the buffaloes to the earth goddess, the young men are each given a piece of meat along with half a kilo of rice or little millet and some salt. In the evening, the sacrificial rice (*bana paga*) is cooked at the shrine of the earth goddess and distributed among the male villagers. On the following day, all are invited to a feast called *purta bhoji* or "feast for the whole world," when the majority of the buffalo meat is served along with rice or little millet. Ideally, two more feasts should take place, one on Tuesday when the legs of the buffalo are cooked and shared among the villagers, and another on Wednesday when the clan symbol is taken down and the cooked heads are eaten. Often, however, these parts have already been consumed by Monday.

In order to meet the requisite costs, the members of a village that intends to celebrate the *kodru parbu* meet several months in advance to discuss the contribution each household should make. The approximate amount depends on the number of buffaloes and rams to be sacrificed and the number of houses in the village. In small villages, like Kancharu with eleven houses, I have been told that each household had to provide Rs 2,000 to the village fund (total: Rs 22,000) while in larger villages the amount was considerably less. In Railima, which consists of about twenty-five houses and which sacrificed four buffaloes to the earth goddess and four rams to her husband, each household contributed Rs 500, i.e., a total of Rs 12,500. I assume that this amount was demanded from ordinary households, while members of the dominant clan, who are responsible for buying the costly buffaloes, paid a higher share. The *naika* of Gumma once explained to me that the wealthy families of the village are expected to contribute a larger share to the village fund than poorer households. He estimated the total costs of a *kodru parbu* to range between Rs 15,000 and Rs 20,000, with each additional village site with its own *jakeri* and *koteiwali* raising the amount by another Rs 5,000. In a village inhabited by Desia Kond I was told by an educated local politician that at total of Rs 17,000 was raised, including Rs 2,000 to meet unexpected expenses. The amount collected by the village to cover its collective expenses for the *kodru parbu* thus roughly equals the standard betrothal fee paid by the groom's family to the bride's side in an arranged marriage!

The money is collected by the *barika* of the village and handed over to a reliable village elder, often the *jani*, who is the keeper of sacred objects. The same *barika* is responsible for providing the village with sacrificial animals, which he purchases from the markets or obtains from Dongria who are indebted to him. In addition to these joint expenses, each household has to meet the costs for carrying out its own sacrifices and providing food and alcohol to its guests. More affluent families may offer a ram to the god of the local line or to the house goddess, while poorer ones must be satisfied with a fowl. For the worship of the buffaloes and sacred objects by the *jani*, each household has to offer a few smaller chickens. Taking into account all these different expenses, I estimate that a *kodru parbu* costs a normal household between Rs 1,500 and Rs 2,000, while wealthier families may have to bear expenses ranging from Rs 3,000 to Rs 5,000, or even Rs 9,000 as claimed by the *naika* of Gumma. Although this may not sound like much, it should be kept in mind that the overall income from selling cash crops is relatively low. One of my closest informants from Gumma, a relatively young man with only one son, who was too young to help him in his fields, revealed to me that in the last twelve months he had earned Rs 5,000 from selling his cash crops in the market. For him, a contribution of Rs 2,000 to the *kodru parbu* would amount to more than a third of his total income. Other villagers with larger families, better land, and more valuable cash crops, like turmeric or castor beans, certainly made a higher profit that year. For example, a Dombo from Gumma informed me that a Dongria of the same village had recently sold castor beans for Rs 3,600 and had another 140 kilograms, worth Rs 10 per kilo, in his house, raising his total income to Rs 5,000. Since this was not the only cash crop he cultivated, his total income that year must have been considerably higher than that of the younger Dongria with only one small child. On the occasion of a *kodru parbu*, both families would be expected to make a contribution to the village fund relative to the profit gained from selling their harvested produce.

5.3 Preparations

5.3.1 *kanga parbu:* The "pigeon-pea festival"

One year before the main buffalo sacrifice, most villages celebrate a "pigeon-pea festival" (*kanga parbu*) in the months of *phalgun* or *caitra*, roughly at the same time as the *kodru parbu*. It is sometimes referred to as the "little" festival for the earth goddess, as it is attended by fewer visitors, requires very little preparation, and costs the villagers only a fraction of what they invest in the main festival for the goddess. However, like the *kodru parbu*, it takes place over three days – from Friday to Sunday – and includes the worship of the old axes and other iron tools from the time of human sacrifices.

I observed the *kanga parbu* once, in the village of Dongormati, and the following description is based on data collected on this occasion. Preparations begin a few days before the main Friday of the festival, when the *jani*, together with some villagers, heads out into the hills to the sites where the different *jakeri* of the village are located. Dongormati owns five village territories (*padari*), the main one being the place where the present settlement is situated, while four others (Sakode, Askata, Bondeli, and Kataghati) are spread out over the hills of the surrounding area. Before the *kanga parbu* is performed, the villagers have to place a gourd filled with seeds (*kanga* or pigeon pea, *kahada* or little millet, and *kabang* or ricinus) at each of these four stone assemblages. As described above, the same ritual, known as *nela nespoli*, is performed when Dongria begin cultivating hill slopes near a former settlement the territory of which has lain fallow for many years. Each day, the *jani* pay a visit to one *jakeri* only. He and his helpers cut a small teak tree (*hergi mara*), carve it into a sacrificial post with a pointed top, dig a hole, and set the stake upright in the ground. The gourd containing the seeds is hung on the post, and the *jani* lights some incense. After this the delegation returns to the village, with no animal sacrifices having taken place on this occasion.

Friday: "Sending away the ancestors" (*mahane tuchpoli*) and "taking out the axe" (*tangi wecoli*)

On Friday morning, the last village territory is "charged" in this way by the *jani*. When he and his assistants return, the villagers are in the midst of preparations for the festival. As in the case of the *kodru parbu*, they are not allowed to go into the forest to collect wood during the festival, and for this reason everybody takes the opportunity to chop firewood beforehand. In front of every house, the wood is piled up in stacks, reaching several meters in height on the occasion of the *kodru parbu*. To collect the rice (*manjing*) and little millet (*kahada*) that will be cooked for the feast on Sunday, two large winnowing fans are placed on the village plaza. A female member of each household comes and pours one *ada* (two kilograms) of each type of grain into the respective fan. Additionally, every family has to provide two bowls of sacred rice (*akat manjing*), which are kept on the roof of their house and represent the goddess *sita penu-lahi penu*. This special rice is used to prepare food to be served on two ritual occasions that take place in the main *jani*'s house, first the worship of ancestors, and second, the ceremony for the axes representing the earth goddess.

From midday onwards, rituals are performed in basically all the sacred centres of the typical Dongria village described above. The stones, sacrificial posts, rotten pillars, crumbling walls, and dusty shrines suddenly become the focus of intense worship. As in the case of a wedding, collective ritual first centres upon the ghosts, the ancestors, and the protective deity of the *yatra kudi*. As on the first day of a wedding, the *jani* and his two assistants seat themselves in the *kandadae*, or room of the ancestors, the difference being that in this case the room is not in the house of the bride but in the house of the *jani*, who preserves the old iron tools from the time of human sacrifices. The three ritual specialists sit in this small, narrow room, face the eastern wall, pour paddy or husked rice into three heaps in front of them, drink alcohol, make a chicken peck at some rice from time to time, and chant incantations (*dakina*) to the ancestors. As on the day of the wedding, they "explain" the object of the festival to the ancestors and request their help. The recitations end with the sacrifice of a chicken and the cooking of *bana paga*, literally "forest rice," as is the case on all important ritual occasions. The rice is cooked in a newly made earthen pot and offered first of all to the gods and ancestors, before the *jani* or the *bejuni* gives a handful first to the family of the *jani* who owns the sacred axe (which may not be the family of the religious specialist) and then, second, to all those present.

Towards evening, the worship of the ancestors shifts from the *jani*'s house to the communal part of the village. The *bejuni* takes a large winnowing fan and sits down in the centre of the village, where she lights some incense. Facing east, she calls the ancestors, during which time women from each household come one by one with a winnowing fan containing a handful of raw rice (*manjing*) and a large leaf plate (*sipidi*), upon which cooked rice (*paga*), boiled lentils (*jau*), and pieces of dried fish (*sukhua*) have been placed. These two types of food are referred to as *lita manjing* and *lita paga*, the term *lita*, like the Oriya word *pinda*, implying that the gift serves to feed as well as to form the body of the deceased. The *bejuni* takes a small chicken, asks the ancestors for their blessings, and induces the chicken to peck at some grains of rice as a sign that the ancestors accept the offered food. Women then collect the leaf plates from each household in a basket and carry this to the *yatra kudi*, where several young and old women of the village are present, but no men. This corresponds to the paradigmatic relations among the west, cremation grounds, protective deities, and female worshippers mentioned above. The women remove the leaf plates from the basket and arrange them on the ground next to the *yatra kudi*. The *bejuni* seats herself before the shrine, this time facing west, and again spreads some raw rice on the ground and coaxes the chicken to peck at it. Subsequently a young girl comes, twists off the chicken's head, and smears the blood on the pillars of the *yatra kudi*. The *bejuni* and the *jani* never carry out the actual killing of an animal themselves, although they may symbolically sacrifice larger animals like rams or buffaloes with a wooden sword or by touching them with the old iron weapons.

Following this worship of the protective deity (*yatra kudi*), a second woman places some smaller leaf cups filled with rice on the path a few meters west of the shrine and pours a few drops of alcohol into them. This offering is made in the name of wandering spirits (*marha*), who died an unnatural death and cannot reside on the cremation ground in the same way as those deceased who died a "good" death. The latter are divided into two categories, the ancestors of all Dongria (*jati mahane*) and the ancestors belonging to the houses (*ilka mahane*) of the village that is performing the worship. For these two categories of ancestors, small leaf cups provided by each household and filled with boiled rice are placed in two separate locations between the *yatra kudi* and the "dining corner" of the wandering spirits, which is situated far to the west. For this part of the worship, each woman brings a cup of alcohol and pours some of it into the leaf cups, asking the family's ancestors for help and requesting them to protect the family from illness and death. Finally, the *bejuni* takes some rice into her hands and throws it toward the west, thereby sending the ancestors away (*mahane tuchpoli*).

In the meantime, young girls present at the site collect the dried fish contributed by each household together in one place and pour the boiled rice from the leaf plates into a large basket. They mix the rice and then distribute it between the leaf plates again, along with one piece of dried fish. This clearly expresses the village ideal of commensality, since everybody partakes in the food cooked by others, even if at the end of the ritual each woman only takes home one leaf plate of rice, which she shares with just her family members. Before leaving, the women sit down around the *yatra kudi* and consume the alcohol brought for the ancestors.

By the time they return to the village, darkness has set in, and the young men are singing and dancing with their drums on the village plaza. The *bejuni* goes to her house and begins grinding large amounts of turmeric in preparation for taking a purifying bath before the next events of the ritual. While the *bejuni* bathes behind her house, the *jani* who owns the sacred axes, as well as two or three other ritual specialists responsible for the incantations, take a bath on the village plaza. Everyone then proceeds to the *jani*'s house, where his son climbs into the attic in order to bring down the sacred iron objects, such as axes, knives, bells, cups, and chains. Carrying these objects in a winnowing fan on his head, he leaves the house and proceeds to the *jakeri,* where he places the fan near the stones. In other contexts, too, it was always young men or even small boys who carried these sacred objects, never older people.

The shamans sit down in front of the *jakeri* facing east and induce a small chicken to peck at some rice from the three *konang* and from the iron weapons. In Dongormati, this took rather a long time, since the chicken proved unwilling to eat the rice. When it finally did, it was met with loud whistles and shouts of jubilation, since this meant that the earth goddess had finally accepted the offerings. Next, the *jani*'s son once again picks up the winnowing fan and carries it to the *koteiwali*, where the shamans repeat the actions performed earlier at the earth goddess's shrine. When the *koteiwali,* through the chicken, has accepted the gift of rice made by the villagers, the young man brings the holy objects back to his house. The whole sequence of events, beginning with the taking down of the iron weapons, the showing of them to the earth goddess and her husband, and their return to the *jani*'s house, is referred to as *tangi wecoli,* meaning "the taking out of the axe."

Inside the *jani's* house, the winnowing fan containing the holy objects is placed in front of the *handani kuda,* or the wall used for worshipping the house goddess. What follows resembles both the wedding ceremony and the *kodru parbu.* As described in the fourth chapter, the cooking utensils brought into the house as part of the bride's dowry are kept near the *handani kuda,* before ideally three *jani* begin reciting incantations while standing in front of these objects. In the same way, three *jani* take up positions before the iron tools, holding rice in their right hands while others hold a new white cloth above the winnowing fan. The three specialists begin their incantations and finally throw the rice onto the cloth spread out in front of them before they sit down on a cot facing the *handani kuda.* The cloth is tied into a knot (*puda gahja*) and, according to one of my informants, is kept until the time that this family celebrates the *bada* or river ceremony. On the occasion of the latter ceremony, the rice is thrown into the flowing water in order to dispose of all evil influences affecting the household.

On this night and the one after, the three *jani* continue their incantations until sunrise. This clearly resembles the *kodru parbu,* during which the ritual specialists also chant for two nights – on Friday and Saturday – in front of the sacred objects (see below). The main difference, however, is that in the *kanga parbu,* the recitations take place inside the *jani*'s house, whereas at the time of the collective buffalo sacrifice, the goddess is invoked inside her hut built on the village plaza. While the ritual specialists chant their verses, interrupted only by sessions of drinking, during which they consume distilled *mohua* liquor provided by the community, the young men continue to dance and drum. Young visitors from neighbouring villages also come along and reside in the dormitories, where on their arrival the girls cook rice and lentils for them.

Saturday: "Planting the sacrificial stake" (*panikimunda uhpoli*) and "worshipping the god of war/hunting" (*lada penu dakoli*)

On Saturday morning, a new sacrificial post for the *koteiwali*, known as *panikimunda*, is set up. For this purpose, a few young men proceed into the woods and search for a teak tree. Without any help from a ritual specialist, they select a suitable tree, chop it down, remove the bark and branches on the spot, and return with just a two- to three-meter-long trunk. Inside the village, a man cuts the trunk into two pieces, one of which is carved and inserted into the ground, while the other is turned into a plank and placed horizontally on top, thus giving the stake its T-shaped appearance. A rope with a wooden diamond[31] is attached to each end.

The *bejuni* prepares a mixture of water, ground turmeric, and crushed castor beans and distributes it between two leaf cups. The new sacrificial post, in addition to the stones belonging to the *jakeri,* are smeared with this liquid, before a shaman – in the case of Dongormati a male shaman or *beju* – draws a circle with rice powder upon the ground, west of the place where the old *panikimunda,* set up during the last *kodru parbu,* stands. Taking a iron rod in both his hands, he whispers some verses before striking it into the earth and beginning to dig a hole. After a few minutes the *beju* hands the tool over to a young man who continues the work. Meanwhile, a cord holding mango leaves and three turmeric rhizomes is tied to the *koteiwali,* the *panikimunda,* and the last remaining pillar of the collapsed *dharni kudi.* Women bring clay and cow dung to create a new earthen platform around the stones of the *jakeri.* When the hole for the sacrificial post is deep enough, the shaman takes the new *panikimunda,* whispers some prayers

---

31 According to Jena et al. (2002, 28) these diamonds are called *golakanu* – an Oriya word – which literally means "round ear" and which they translate as "earrings.". Other Indian authors identify the objects as wooden combs: "Two wooden combs with coloured thread balls are fixed at the two extreme ends of the horizontal piece of wood fixed on the cross bars. As a male Dongria uses comb always on the tuft of hair as a mark of adornment, Kotebali as the husband of Darani Penu is also supposed to use the comb" (Patnaik and Das Patnaik 1982, 141).

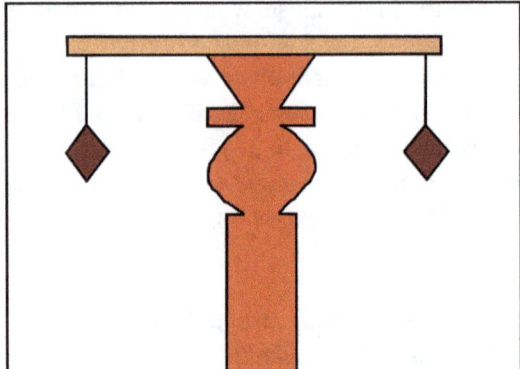

Figure 31: T-shaped sacrificial post (*panikimunda*)

while holding rice in his right hand, and finally throws the rice into the hole and quickly inserts the stake. At this point, somebody fires a gunshot, and hit by the force of the deity, the *bejuni* falls into a trance (*banga ate*), i.e., she becomes possessed by the *koteiwali*, whom the villagers identify with the god *niamraja* (see below).

First of all, the main *bejuni* steps onto the horizontal plank of the *panikimunda*, and with the help of her assistants, performs a wild dance on top of it. This may coincide with the time when other recognised shamans likewise fall into a trance. At the festival I observed in Dongormati, a total of eight *bejuni* climbed onto and danced on top of the sacrificial stake, among them a very young woman who had only recently been accepted as a shaman. During the *kodru parbu*, the *bejuni* become similarly possessed by the god *niamraja* and also dance wildly, but on this occasion a long bamboo pole with a symbol of the clan on the top is erected. This element is missing during the *kanga parbu*, which in contrast to the *kodru parbu* is not an affair of the whole clan organisation but more or less of a single village.

From the *koteiwali* the attention shifts next to the *jakeri*, where all the *bejuni* will assemble and continue their dancing. The main shaman takes some of the water mixed with turmeric and castor beans and sprinkles the coloured liquid first over the stones and then, in jest, over the men standing around her. Finally, she sits down in front of the stones, invokes the earth goddess, and utters her requests for help and protection. When this is over, the young men perform three sacrifices in quick succession. Using a knife, they first cut the throat of a small pig near the *jakeri* and let its blood drip onto the *konang* stones. Then they proceed to the *koteiwali*, where they kill a dove and a fowl, smear the blood on the *panikimunda*, and place the heads on top of it. In Dongormati, an additional sacrifice was performed for a huge sacrificial stake standing at the upper, eastern end of the village. This post was called *tadimunda,* meaning "grandfather post," and had been erected some years ago at a time when an epidemic afflicted the whole village.

When the sacrifices on the central plaza have been completed, ritual activities turn towards the shrines standing to the east of the settlement. In Dongormati, the situation differs slightly from the ideal model described above in the sense that in addition to the *ghata kudi,* each local line possesses a stone under a mango tree. On the day of *kanga parbu,* each house takes a fowl and some rice to its *ghata kudi,* and the *bejuni* induces the fowl to peck at the rice before a family member sacrifices it to the deity of the local line. In Dongormati, everybody then proceeded a little further up the hill, where eight stones – one for each local line – were protruding from the ground under a mango tree. The men carried old guns, mostly muzzle-loaders, and leaned them against the tree trunk. On the occasion of *kodru parbu* I witnessed a very similar ceremony also performed on a Saturday morning and referred to as *walka puja* or "stone worship." This ritual addresses two deities, the god of the local line – often a form of *bera* or *aji budi* – and the god *lada,* the god of hunting.[32] In Dongormati and perhaps also in other places, these two deities are worshipped in separate places, whereas in most villages I am familiar with, both categories of deities receiving their offerings at the site of the *ghata kudi,* which contains a single stone for each local line (*kona*). Although hunting no longer plays a major role in Dongria life, the god *lada,* who controls wild animals and decides upon the success of hunting, still receives many offerings on festive occasions. Among the Desia Kond, whose environment provides even fewer opportunities to hunt, the worship of *lada* is an essential feature of the *kodru parbu.* As will be described in more detail later, the young Desia boys become the "friends" (*tone*) of *lada* during the *kodru parbu* when they dance, play, and eat with the *bejuni* while she is possessed by the god of hunting.[33] On the occasion of *kanga parbu,* the ritual specialists (*jani*) will invoke *lada* in their guns by chanting verses with rice held in their right hands. At the same time, the *bejuni* sits on the ground slowly

---

[32] Macpherson describes the worship of "Loha Pennoo," who is probably the same as *lada penu.* According to Macpherson, this deity is invoked at the time of war and is considered to be the god of arms. Before a fight, a shaman becomes possessed by Loha Pennoo and distributes the weapons to the young men on behalf of the deity. Success in battle is attributed to this deity, who has command over the weapons (Macpherson 1863, 68).

[33] Among the Dongria, I only witnessed one *kodru parbu,* during which the young boys were involved in the worship of *lada penu* in the sense that it was their duty to carry the guns home after the shaman had made offerings to them.

whispering words until she falls into a trance and becomes possessed by *lada*. At that moment, the three *jani* step aside and make way for the *bejuni*, who approaches the weapons and makes rice offerings to them. Finally, the owners of the guns come forward and kill a fowl, smearing its blood on the weapon as well as on the stone protruding from the ground.

Everyone then returns to the village, where in the evening the events of the previous day are repeated: the sacred iron weapons are taken from the house of the *jani* to the *jakeri* and the *koteiwali*, receive offerings, and are returned to their owner. Throughout the night, the three *jani* sit in front of the *handani kuda* and recite their incantations until the next morning, while the young people of the village enjoy themselves with their singing, dancing, and drumming.

Sunday: "Playing with turmeric water" (*hinga eyu kayoli*)

Sunday is the last day of the *kanga parbu* and begins with a ritual that I have not observed at first hand. According to my informants, the *jani* takes some pigeon peas and crushes them on the *pata* with the help of the *bayriwali*. After that, each woman uses a grinding stone to repeat the same ritual in her own household, this ritual marking the time from which villagers are allowed to cook pigeon peas. A little later on the same morning, visitors arrive, including Dongria and Dombo from neighbouring villages, and in particular people who on the occasion of the *kodru parbu* perform the functions of *mudrenga* or watchmen of the sacrificial buffalo (see below). They often are members of a village owned by a dominant clan that stands in affinal relation to the organisers of the buffalo sacrifice. In the case I observed, the *jani* of Dongormati (Sikoka clan) had invited the Pusika from a neighbouring village named Lamba, with whom they maintain an intense and positive relationship. They basically consider themselves to be one village, in the sense that they invite each other to feasts and celebrate festivals collectively.

On their arrival, the visitors are caught hold of by the young villagers, who drag them to the *koteiwali* and force them to sit on a cot. Four strong men carry one or two visitors three times around the menhir, while others sprinkle them with turmeric water and make jesting remarks to them. When he gets up from the cot, each visitor has to pay between five and ten rupees if he does not want to get drenched with water.[34] Next, the main *jani* of the village is made to take

---

[34] The whole event resembles to some extent the famous *holi* festival celebrated by Hindus (see Marriott 1966). In the area where I conducted my research, people were familiar with the *holi* tradition but did not celebrate this festival, while in the area around Kambesi, where Dombo

a seat on the cot, gets carried around the *koteiwali*, and is splattered with the yellowish liquid and mocked by everybody present. The overall atmosphere is one of unrestrained fun and enjoyment. Completely soaked, the *jani*, together with one or two ritual specialists, sits down on a second cot, and some girls of the village come forward and place leaf plates with uncooked food in front of them, thereby humiliating the chiefs in yet another way. Next, the old women who serve as *bejuni* for the village catch hold of a few young men and drag them to the cot where the chiefs are sitting. They make them squat in front of the chiefs and then begin to accuse the young men in a joking manner of using derogatory language or telling lies on certain occasions. For their misdemeanours the young men have to pay ten rupees to the old women. The former gain their revenge by making the old female shamans sit on a bamboo mat and accusing them of spreading untrue rumours, for which they are sprinkled with water.

When this is over, things turn more serious, and people begin the *ambadadi yatra* or festival of the mango twig, which ends the same evening with a buffalo sacrifice and a feast. As is the case for the *kodru parbu*, the celebration of the *ambadadi* festival marks the end of the festive period and the beginning of the new year.

Interpretations
The *kanga parbu* described above is connected in many ways to the *kodru parbu*. The timing of both festivals is the same, since both rituals take place over three days, from Friday to Sunday, in the months of *phalgun* or *caitra*. Only during these two festivals are the old iron weapons and tools from the time of human sacrifices brought out from the *jani*'s house. It is only on this occasion that these objects are worshipped by the ritual specialists (*jani*), who recite incantations to the earth goddess for two consecutive nights. The main difference between the two festivals is that during the *kanga parbu*, the activities focus on the *jani*'s house, whereas during the *kodru parbu*, a special hut is built for the earth goddess in the centre of the village. According to some villagers, the festival is held a year before the *kodru parbu* and is thus a kind of initiatory ceremony for the more elaborate buffalo sacrifice. It can be interpreted as a promise to the earth goddess to provide her with a grand sacrifice after the next harvest. The *panikimunda* appears to be the visible sign of this promise to the earth goddess.

---

from the valleys have settled in large numbers and which is strongly affected by modern Hindu influences, I once arrived in a village on the day of *holi* and was literally bathed in various colours. Dongria also play with turmeric water on the occasion of the threshing ritual, when young boys chase girls from their village through the harvested fields.

In a short trip to the Niamgiri Hills, Barbara Boal (1997, 367–69) witnessed the setting up of the *panikimunda* in a village occupied by people of the Jakesika clan. They erected the *panikimunda* in mid-November, i.e., four to five months[35] before the actual festival. The rituals she describes resemble the ceremony I observed, with the difference that in her case the villagers carved two breasts on the horizontal beam. The diamonds attached to this plank are interpreted as the deity's earrings. In Boal's interpretation, the *panikimunda* represents the unity of the male pole with the female plank, and the act of erecting this pole is comparable to sexual intercourse (Boal 1997, 369).[36] This corresponds to my observation that the beams (*pate*) in a house are regarded as female, while posts (*munda*) are considered to be male. When building the sacrificial hut (see below), the Dongria carve breasts on the massive wooden beams that hold up the roof. Keeping in mind that the *panikimunda* is seen as a symbol of the promise to perform the *kodru parbu*, we can interpret the unity of male and female aspects as an indication that both the earth goddess and her husband, the *koteiwali*, are to be worshipped and united in the course of the next year's sacrifice.

In contrast to the *kodru parbu*, the *kanga parbu* does not involve the cooperation of the whole clan organisation. The agnates are not required to build a sacrificial hut, nor are they asked to provide the symbols of the clan, the brass pot (*bonda*) and the knife (*suri*). The affines who guard the buffaloes before the *kodru parbu* are invited to the *kanga parbu*, but only as guests and not to perform any functions. While the grand festival for the earth goddess can be seen as a gift by the whole clan to the *dharni* of their territory, the *kanga parbu* mainly focuses on the relationship between the single *jani* household, which owns the sacred weapons, and the *jakeri* of a particular village. The main object preserved by the *jani* is an axe (*tangi*), and in each Dongria village there is at least one household that is in possession of such an axe. At a *kodru parbu*, the axes of all villages belonging to the clan organisation are ideally assembled at the *jakeri* of the organisers. In case of the *kanga parbu*, only one such axe is brought to the

---

35 Boal (1997, 367) writes that the time was three months before the festival, but she is apparently not aware that Dongria, unlike the Kond she studied, do not sacrifice the buffalo in January, but in March or April. Another, more serious mistake in her description relates to the sex of the deities. According to her, the *koteiwali* represents the female and the *jakeri* the male aspect, information that contradicts the data I collected among the Dongria Kond.

36 Among the Kuttia Kond, we find a very similar practice, although the *panikimunda* appears slightly different. One year before the sacrifice, Kuttia Kond set up a forked post (vertical) with a crossbar (horizontal) near the *dharni* (see drawing in Niggemeyer 1964a, 169) as a promise to perform the buffalo sacrifice the following year (Niggemeyer 1964a, 170).

jakeri, one which, unlike in the *kodru parbu*, is relevant not to the relationship between the clan and its territory but to that between the *jani* and "his" village.

To what extent does the axe symbolise a special relationship between the *jani* and a particular village? In the past, the *jani* would buy the human victim to be sacrificed during the *kodru parbu*. According to informants, the child was reared in the *jani*'s house until the time of sacrifice. The sacrifice itself was performed with the help of knives and axes, the knife being owned by the whole clan, the axe by a member of this clan in each village. Axes are not only used for sacrificing animals but serve various functions. When Dongria begin cultivating new hill plots, axes are necessary for felling the trees. In their daily work, axes are needed for various tasks in the village and in the swidden. Dongria men will not go anywhere without their axes, which are always useful for clearing a path of creepers and bushes and for protection against wild animals. Furthermore, when fights break out, Dongria may attack and kill each other with these axes. Given these various functions, the old axe worshipped at the time of the *kanga parbu* and the *kodru parbu* can be interpreted as a symbol of the activities that legitimise claims to territory. It was with axes that the *jani*'s ancestors cleared a place in the forest, established the village, defended it from enemies, and transformed the hill slopes into cultivated fields. This territory belongs to the earth goddess, represented by the stones, to whom the *jani*'s ancestors gave a human victim who had been reared in their house, i.e., who was one of their "children," and was sacrificed with the help of axes. During the *kanga parbu*, the relationship between the *jani* and "his" *jakeri* is clearly expressed by the fact that the axe preserved in his house is carried to the stones on the village plaza and then back to his house, where it is worshipped in front of his own house shrine. By worshipping the axe in the *kanga parbu*, the *jani* makes a statement about his plans to perform the *kodru parbu* next year. This explains why, apart from a pig and some fowl, no other sacrifices are performed at the *jakeri* and the shrine of the earth goddess's husband, the *koteiwali*.

The *kanga parbu* thus entails the bestowing of a gift on the goddess in the form of animals and a portion of agricultural produce (pigeon peas), in return for a successful harvest. It also includes a promise to offer a larger sacrifice the following year if no epidemics break out and the harvest is abundant. The fact that pigeon peas are offered to the goddess in the year before the *kodru parbu* may be related to the separate cultivation of pulses and grains. In a regular swidden, Dongria do not sow all types of seeds at the same time but follow a certain rhythm. In the first year, pulses such as cow peas (*jununga, katinga*), beans (*balang*), and most important of all, pigeon peas (*kanga*) are sown, as these grow best in a field that has lain fallow for many years. Pigeon peas are always the last crop to be harvested in this first year and have a particular importance for the Dongria diet, as they are served at almost every meal. In the second year, mainly various types of millet (*kahada, hiko, arka, kuyeng*) are sown, since these also grow in hill plots less rich in minerals. The two types of crops forming the basis of Dongria daily nutrition are thus produced in successive years: pulses for preparing sauces and soups called *kachpe* (or *jau*) and grains that serve as the staple food named *lahi* (or *paga*). This two-year cultivation scheme for a particular hill plot can be seen as analogous to the consecutive celebration of the *kanga parbu* and the *kodru parbu*. Viewed in this way, the *kanga parbu* corresponds to a partial and the *kodru parbu* to a complete harvest. In other words, when the goddess has provided the people with all her gifts, including pulses and grains, she receives the highest gift – a human in the past and a buffalo in the present – in return.

When a family makes an offering to the goddess of wealth (*lahi penu*) after threshing the first millet in a hill plot, the young people invited to partake in the threshing chase each other through the harvested crops throwing turmeric water over one another. Unmarried boys and girls tease one another, although their exchanges are without sexual content, since they usually come from the same village and are therefore considered brothers and sisters. Like this harvest ritual of an individual house, the *kanga parbu* is celebrated in a very joyful atmosphere. The jesting takes place on a collective level involving different age groups as well as the immediate affines who come as guests from a neighbouring village. Joking occurs between the young men and the old women, between men of roughly the same age belonging to affinal villages, and between the people of high status and the ordinary villagers, including young girls. Role reversals known from the famous *holi* festival occur here in a less dramatic form: guests should be welcomed with respect but are drenched in water, chiefs should be served proper food but receive uncooked rice, young men should be feared for their strength and aggressiveness but are ridiculed as liars, and old women serving the village as shamans should be honoured but are humiliated for spreading rumours.

5.3.2 Purchasing the sacrificial animals

In the time of human sacrifices, the victims were known as *meria, toki,* or *kedi* (Macpherson 1865, 114). According to Macpherson (1865, 114), the word *meria* derives from Oriya and denotes the human victim. The word *toki* clearly corresponds to the local Desia word for little girl, *toki*, while *kedi* may be derived from the Kui term for sacrifice, *kedu*. Today, the buffalo sacrifice in the Kui-speaking regions is referred to as *kedu* (Boal 1997, 210). The human victims were normally provided by the clients of the Kond, according to Macpherson either "Panwa" (i.e., Pano),

"Dombango" (i.e., Dombo), or "Gahinga" (i.e., Ghasi), who reportedly purchased or kidnapped them in the plains or sold one of their own children (Macpherson 1865, 115). These clients procured the victims either on order of the Kond priests or on their own speculation (Macpherson 1863, 64). A victim was only considered to be acceptable if he or she was purchased.[37] Macpherson provides two reasons for this prerequisite. In his first report he states that a "life" not bought by the sacrifier would be an "abomination to the Deity" (Macpherson 1863, 64), while in a later account of the *kodru parbu* he explains that only a victim bought for a price was considered to be "the full property of the person who devotes him" (Macpherson 1865, 115). The average cost of a human victim was fifty to one hundred lives, one hundred lives corresponding to approximately "ten bullocks, ten buffaloes, ten sacks of corn, tens sets of brass pots, twenty sheep, ten pigs and thirty fowls" (Macpherson 1863, 50). Compared to the average gifts presented by the groom's people to the bride's parents – twenty to thirty lives (Macpherson 1863, 54) – the cost of a human victim was therefore about three times as high as the price of a bride. According to Stevenson (cited in Boal 1999, 290), the price of a human being ranged from sixty to two hundred rupees in the first part of the nineteenth century and was paid in either brass vessels, cattle, or coins. Campbell reports that a victim could cost between 60 and 130 rupees (Campbell 1864, 56–57) and that the prize was usually not paid in money but instead in livestock (cattle, pigs, goats), valuable metal items (brass vessels, ornaments), or products of the hills (saffron, wax) (Campbell 1864, 53). The victims could be of any caste[38] except the Kond themselves[39] and of either sex, although males were preferable, as they were the most costly (Stevenson cited in Boal 1999, 289). According to Campbell (1864, 52), adult victims were the most appropriate for the same reason, i.e., because they were more costly and therefore "the most acceptable to the deity." The victim was kept in the chief's house, where he or she was raised until the time of sacrifice some years later, usually before the victim reached maturity (Macpherson 1865, 116). From the beginning, the victim was considered a consecrated

---

37 Children born to a potential victim or promised to the deities in their childhood could equally be sacrificed even if they were not bought for a price (Macpherson 1865, 115).
38 The victims could be of any caste, but Macpherson (1865, 114–15) reports that Brahmins were not purchased, since they have already been devoted to the gods when receiving the sacred thread. In Mundawali, a Dongria village near Kambesi, I was told that a Brahmin woman was sacrificed many years ago, yet it might still be claimed that this is not an exception, since women do not receive the sacred thread.
39 According to Macpherson (1865, 115), the Kond sometimes sold their children when in distress, for example at a time of famine, but it is not clear from this statement whether these children could be sacrificed as well. They may well have been the "Possia Poes" Campbell (1864, 53) reports, who work for their Kond masters but "run little or no risk of being sacrificed."

being and treated well unless he or she attempted to escape (Macpherson 1865, 116).

Considering all these reports together, certain ideas concerning the victim emerge as particularly important. First, the victim had to be purchased, which means that the victim's life had to be acquired in exchange for the lives of other objects owned by the Kond. Structurally, the victim thus resembles the bride obtained in exchange for the giving of gifts. This analogy between the bride and the human victim may help us to understand why the goddess would consider a victim not purchased for a price an "abomination." Exchange and capture (or "hunting") are the two legitimate ways to acquire "life." While one shares with one's own people, one bargains, argues, and fights over the property belonging to others (see section 2.5.9). Any object bought for a price is defined as something originating outside one's own community. On the other hand, if an object was not purchased but given freely, it will be defined as something belonging to one's own community, the members of which share it. In the same way, a victim who has not been purchased would be considered to belong to one's own community. In this case, people would sacrifice their own kind, which is an act similar to incest and thus an "abomination" to the deity.

One reason given to explain the preference for a male victim is that middle-aged men were the most costly. The *kodru parbu* thus seems to be comparable to a "feast of merit" in which the organisers give away as many valuables as possible. In order to satisfy the goddess, she has to be provided with a substantial gift, and the sums mentioned by the British officers are indeed impressive. Two hundred rupees must have been a considerable amount of money in the nineteenth century, and the great number of animals and objects corresponding to one hundred "lives" confirms this assumption. The Kond of the nineteenth century can hardly be considered to have been poor peasants when they were able to perform such costly sacrifices at regular intervals.

Finally, we may conclude from these descriptions that the victims were not like ordinary human beings but from the beginning considered consecrated and deserving of special treatment. Some appear to have been kept in chains to prevent them from running away, while others were left to walk around freely and treated well. To what extent do these ideas of the past carry any importance today, when it is no longer human beings but buffaloes sacrificed to the earth goddess?

First of all, the buffaloes still have to be purchased from the Dombo, or more concretely, from the *barika* of the village that is organising the sacrifice. His right to buy and sell the victim to his patrons is fiercely defended, and a Dombo from another village trying to strike a deal by offering the organisers a cheaper buffalo will meet stern opposition. On the other hand, Dombo are of the opinion that by selling a buffalo for the *kodru parbu* they accumulate sin (*papa*). For this reason they customarily receive some additional gifts, such as one *mana* (ca. four kilograms) paddy and five or ten rupees, from their patrons when they provide a buffalo for the *kodru parbu*. The prospect of making a good profit and receiving some additional gifts appears to make the accumulation of sin bearable in the eyes of the Dombo. For example, I once experienced an attempt by the *barika* of Gumma to sell a *meria* buffalo to a neighbouring village named Lekhpadar. The village had already bought three victims but was in need of a fourth, less expensive one for the last of their village territories. The first three buffaloes had been provided by a Dombo residing in a village outside the Niamgiri Hills who was accepted as Lekhpadar's *barika*. When the *barika* from Gumma attempted to interfere with his business, this man became so angry that he attempted to slap him with his shoe. Faced with the accusation of trying to take away the other man's profit, the *barika* of Gumma justified himself by saying that selling the *meria* buffalo brings no profit (*laba*) but only sin (*papo*) and that the other Dombo should be happy that he was relieving him of a burden. It is tempting to interpret the attribution of sin to the selling of the *meria* buffalo as a relict from the time of human sacrifice, when the Dombo knowingly purchased or captured children to be killed by the Dongria. Yet the *barika* of Gumma never alluded to these times when asked why selling of the victim burdens him with sin. Instead, he mentioned two reasons why the trade with *meria* buffaloes amounts to committing a sin: first, on this occasion Dongria do not sacrifice old animals that are likely to die soon anyway, but instead young bulls and cows, and second, the buffaloes are not killed with one stroke by a single person but hacked into pieces by visitors coming from several different places (*dunia loku*, lit. "people of the whole world").

A buffalo designated to be sacrificed to the earth goddess is referred to as *padari kodru* or *meria*, an observation that does not tally with Boal's (1997, 210) statement that the meaning of the word *meria* is confined to human sacrifices. As mentioned above, the exact number of buffaloes to be offered to the earth goddess depends on different factors. Some villages own more than one territory, and in this case they may decide to perform the *kodru parbu* for all of them at one time. It seems, however, that not many villages in the Niamgiri Hills own several village territories. In addition, I have been told that regional variations exist concerning the number of buffaloes that are customarily sacrificed. The Dongria villages in the northern part of Kalyansingpur district, bordering Lanjigada district, are renowned for sacrificing three to five buffaloes at a time. In other areas, such as Muniguda district, villagers offer only one buffalo to the earth goddess each time they celebrate the festival. Such local variations may explain the practice of the people of Gumma, who claim to own three territories (Gumma, Waliamba, Kadengeyu), but unlike their direct neighbours in northern Kalyansingpur district (e.g. Lekhadar, Dongormati, Lamba), do not present buffaloes to all their *jakeri* at once. Instead, they follow the practice of their "own people," i.e. that of the Sikoka of Muniguda district, from where they reportedly have migrated, who offer only one buffalo to a particular territory each time they perform the sacrifice.

This leads me to the second point stressed in the accounts of the British officers, namely the high value of the victim. For an annual village festival, old buffaloes worth between Rs 1,000 and Rs 1,500 are sacrificed by the Dongria, yet such a victim would not be an appropriate gift to the highest goddess. Instead, she requires a young animal costing between Rs 3,000 and Rs 5,000. When asked about the preferred sex of the buffalo, Dongria usually answer that buffaloes of either sex can be sacrificed, but in my experience buffalo cows are preferred. The main reason may be that they are more valuable. On the market, a female buffalo attracts higher prices, as it can bear calves and give milk. From the Dongria's perspective, a buffalo's value is also determined by certain physical features. The *meria* buffalo must be completely dark without a single white spot, not even on its neck. The horns should be slightly curved, point away from the head, and have neither cuts nor bulges. Similarly, the ears must be well shaped and not be torn. The victim must be free of any diseases, particularly those affecting the eyes and the nose. In the event that several buffaloes are to be sacrificed, one of them tends to be larger and more costly than the others. This buffalo is presented to the main *jakeri*, while smaller and less valuable ones are given to the *jakeri* located somewhere in the forest. The hierarchy between these victims is expressed in terms of kinship. Thus, the animal dedicated to the main *jakeri* will be referred to as *aya* or "mother," while the other buffaloes are considered to be her "children" or *milang*.

In one village I was informed that the sacrificial victim must be approved of by the goddess. For this reason, the buffalo is shown to the goddess in a ceremony I myself have never observed. On such an occasion, the village shaman (*bejuni*) falls into a trance in front of the earth goddess's shrine and becomes possessed by her, and then the victim is brought to her for inspection. If the deity is not satisfied with the animal, the *bejuni* rejects it in her trance, and the village community has to buy a new one.

The human victims in the past were taken care of by the village community, in particular by the chief, in whose house the boy or girl was reared, sometimes for several years. This may be interpreted as meaning that the victim was turned into a member of the community, similar to an adopted child. The organisers of the festival might have purchased the victim, yet they sacrificed him or her only after a long time of socialization in their families. Nowadays, the buffaloes are purchased not years, but at least months before the festival. Some Dombo residing in the village are given the responsibility of herding and watching them day and night. For this they receive a sum of money from the village community. Like the human victim in the past, it may happen that during these many months the buffalo runs away or is stolen because of its high value, or simply to humiliate the organisers of the festival. One of these reasons led to the disappearance of a *meria* buffalo a few weeks before the sacrifice in a village named Kuskedeli, where I observed the preparations for the festival in the year 2001. The organisers sent out delegations of young men in search of the buffalo, getting messages from different places where the victim had allegedly been seen. After several weeks of searching in vain, the organisers decided to purchase another buffalo but could only afford a rather meagre animal with their remaining funds. This victim was then killed by Dongria from a neighbouring village a day before the proper time of sacrifice, and the whole festival ended more or less in disaster when other visitors turned up, saw the killed animal, and began to ravage the place.

5.3.3 Preparing the sacrificial site

Probably no other Kond celebrate the *kodru parbu* in the same elaborate fashion as the Dongria of the Niamgiri Hills. Weeks before the actual sacrifice, they begin preparations, transforming the whole village step by step into a sacrificial site. The settlement is fenced off, sacrificial posts are set up, a wall is built near the *koteiwali*, and a new house is constructed for the earth goddess. Of all the Kond described in anthropological literature, the Dongria appear to be the only ones who construct such a sacrificial hut. Only Niggemeyer (1964a, 189–90), in his work on the Kuttia Kond, describes the making of a conical, loosely woven bamboo fence above the representation of the goddess in the centre of the village. Niggemeyer calls it a "hut" (in German, "Hütte"), but it is more comparable to a large inverted basket,[40] placed over the stone arrangement.[41]

In the following section I will describe these preparations in detail. I begin with the construction of the goddess's sacrificial hut, *dharni kudi*, which in my interpretation is itself an image of the goddess. Her breasts are represented on

---

[40] In a comment on one of his photographs (Niggemeyer 1964a, plate 30.3), Niggemeyer calls this bamboo construction a "Bienenkorbhütte" or beehive hut.
[41] See for example Niggemeyer's photographs (Niggemeyer 1964a, plates 30 and 31) in the appendix of his book. I saw a similar bamboo construction in a Kuttia village I visited along with Professor Pfeffer in 2000.

the wooden beams, and her walls are painted in the same colours and patterns as the shawls worn by young people at the time of festivals and during wedding ceremonies. In other contexts, the goddess is seen as a mother (*aya*) or as the wife (*dakeri*) of the *koteiwali*, but in the *kodru parbu* she resembles a girl, perhaps on her wedding day, waiting for a man to take her away with him. All of the major construction work for the goddess's hut is performed by the villagers with the help of their "brothers," i.e., people from villages belonging to the same clan organisation.

Next, I will describe how the villagers set up the sacrificial post to which the buffalo is to be tethered. In my interpretation, the post has multiple meanings and functions depending on the context. The wooden stake itself appears to be a sacrificial victim, is identified with various deities, can function as a pole to which the sacrificial victim is tied, and serves as a symbol of two interrelated aspects, namely the gift the villagers owe to their earth goddess and the fulfilment of reciprocal obligations.

East of the site of the earth goddess's hut, at the site of the stone representing the *koteiwali*, the sacrificial site is prepared by building a wall bearing the same colourful decorations as the *dharni kudi*. In most cases, the construction work has to be carried out by a special category of affines called *mudrenga*. Their main duty is to protect the sacrificial animal from possible attackers who attempt to kill the animal before the proper time of sacrifice. As part of their protective functions, they construct a fence around the whole village and at the site where the buffalo will be tethered. Upon the successful completion of these tasks, the village is ready to start with the celebration.

Building the goddess's hut (*dharni kudi*)

Dongria refer to the goddess's shrine as *kudi*, a word probably derived from the Oriya term *kudia*, meaning "small hut." In contrast to a proper Dongria house, it has neither three rooms nor an attic, but simply one quadrangular room covered with a pitched roof. This simple building is also named *dharni kudi* or "hut of the earth goddess" and *padari kudi* or "hut of the clan territory." In some areas of the Niamgiri range, the hut serves as the place where men meet to discuss village affairs. Due to this function, the hut is also named *sadar kudi* or "public hut." In ritual incantations, the goddess's house is referred to in the following verses:

> *birimunda kambimunda*
> *iwaru gundi nara cuna nara*
> *tala nara wana nara rajanga*

The first verse invokes a deity who, in accordance with the typical parallelism of these incantations, has two names, *birimunda* and *kambimunda*. The word *munda* means post and denotes the wall post of a house as well as the sacrificial stake set up at a festival. This particular deity is identified with the posts upon which the sky rests. *Birimunda-kambimunda* was set up at the beginning of the world to hold up the sky and to create a space where the deities can reside. When the god *dharmu* wanted to destroy the world, he let the sky fall down onto the earth, creating a great flood (see appendix six). When building the sacrificial hut at the time of *kodru parbu*, the Dongria will first put up two very strong posts, which support a massive beam.

The second verse mentions the names of two types of people (*nara*), *gundi nara* and *cuna nara*, the word *iwaru* just meaning "you are." *Gundi* and *cuna* can be translated as red and white coloured soils that are used to decorate the walls of a house. In this context, the verse addresses the people who came to the first *kodru parbu* and brought colours in order to paint the goddess's house. These days the women search for red and white soil with which to paint the walls of the hut.

The third verse names two other types of people who are associated with "hair" (*tala*) and "appearance" (*wana*). These people are said to have been those who provided the straw – in the figurative sense the hair – to cover the roof of the first *meria* house and who by painting it with the mentioned colours lent it an attractive appearance. The word *rajanga* indicates that the first constructors of the *meria* house were not ordinary people but "kings," a term used to address important deities. Jena et al. collected a story that tells how the sun god, following the completion of the first *sadar kudi*, orders the construction of a hut made of iron and thatched with human hair:

> The first *sadar kudi* was mainly built with *sal* wood. Bamboo (*madi*) and thatching grass (*wika*) are used for the roof covering. Once the first *sadar kudi* was built, *dharam devata* began to convene meetings there. He soon sought a blacksmith who would wrought iron slabs, poles, swords and other weapons, using the iron dust available in the *sadar kudi*. Thus, an iron house was constructed. Since the material required for its thatching was long hair (*tala*), his followers went to the Kalyansingpur area, where the King Sijimadi ruled. But nobody volunteered to give his hair, and this King offered ten cartfuls of good thatching grass instead. As *dharam devata's* followers could not accept grass as a substitute, they approached two other kings, Birigamu and Mugagamu, who lived not far from Sijimadi. The women as well as men there had long hair and the two kings advised *dharam devata's* followers to take their hair after killing all the men and women. [...] Thus, *dharam devata's* followers killed the men and women, and thatched the iron *sadar kudi* with their hair. This type of *sadar kudi* was termed *talakudi-banakudi* (hair hut). (Jena et al. 2002, 148–49)

Weeks before the festival, men cut straw on the hill slopes, dry it on a high platform, and use it to cover the roof of the sacrificial hut. Women, on the other hand, are responsible for decorating the hut by painting triangles on the walls.

Taken together, these verses refer to the three main elements comprising the goddess's house: the large wooden posts (*munda*) and beams (*pate*), the painted walls (*kuda*), and the roof (*tudi*), which is covered with a particular type of mountain grass (*wikang*). Over a period of several weeks, these three key parts are built anew by the organisers, with the help of agnates from villages belonging to their own clan organisation. The construction begins with the setting up of the main posts of the house. Depending on the number of years that have passed since the celebration of the last *kodru parbu*, the posts of the former sacrificial hut may be completely rotten or – at least the larger posts – may still be firm and strong. In the latter case, they can be used again, and only the smaller posts will be carved anew. The main posts, as well as the beams, are made from a special kind of teak (*hergi mara*). A Dongria once explained to me that during the *waya wela* or "time of extraordinary perception"[42] people could speak with trees, and when searching for a teak tree with which to build the sacrificial hut, they would ask the trees whether they were willing to be cut, in other words whether they would sacrifice themselves for the goddess. This ability was lost when a son of *niamraja* tasted some of the offerings that he should have given to the trees:[43]

> A long time ago, the youngest son (*kununja*) of the sun god went to visit the Teli Sahi [street occupied by oil pressers] and the Mali Sahi [street occupied by gardeners] in order to buy flattened rice (*siudang*) and rice balls (*leyang*). He bought seven *kaudi* [one *kaudi* is equivalent to the load a man carries with a stick resting on his shoulder] of flattened rice and seven *kaudi* of rice balls. Then he went to the different trees and offered these sweets to them. At that time, the trees could speak, and they demanded these offerings from him. After presenting these gifts to the trees, some leftovers remained, and thinking that they must taste good, he ate them himself. Suddenly, he grew large ears, his mouth become longer and longer, and hair sprouted all over his body. He had turned into a dog. Thus he went to his father and asked him what he should do. The sun god sent him back to earth to live with the *adivasi*. He told his son, "From now on you will live with the *adivasi*. They cultivate

---

[42] The word *wayu* is an Oriya term meaning "insanity" or "craziness," but this translation does not correspond to what was implied by the informant, who intended to stress the increased ability of people at a time when they could converse with non-human beings.

[43] A relatively similar story was recorded by Jena et al. In their version, a young boy is sent out to smear a particular plant named *bailia* on the bark of the trees after the latter refuse to sacrifice themselves to build the *sadar kudi*. The boy cannot resist tasting the plant and turns into a dog. After that, the trees could no longer speak, and only then could the deities cut them down as wood to build the *sadar kudi* (Jena et al. 2002, 148).

the hill slopes, where they cut the trees. When they move to their fields, you must accompany them. You will see monkeys, elephants, wild boars, and bears. Your duty will be to drive away these animals. The people will beckon you by calling 'dru, dru,' and you must bark."

Nowadays, as the informant further explained to me, people no longer have the ability to understand the trees, and in order to be sure that they do not cut a tree against its will, they search for a dead tree that has completely dried up. Such a tree is referred to as *rengena,* and the posts *(munda)* and beams *(pate)* as *rengena munda-rengena pate.* With this expression Dongria shamans invoke the deity of the shrine of *aji budi,* which stands outside the village, as well as that of the *dharni kudi,* which is found inside the settlement.

The frame of the sacrificial hut consists of three quadrangular beams, held up by a minimum of six round posts, three on either side. The two posts carrying the central beam *(tudi pate)* are the largest and most carefully carved. They can be 3 to 3.5 meters tall with semi-circular notches to receive the rooftree.[44] The two beams supporting the lower edges of the roof are held up at both ends by shorter posts, about 1.5 meters high. Both ends of the beams are carved and in form resemble the *makara* figure typically found in Hindu temples. The central beam has representations of the goddess's breasts on both sides, while the lower side beams display them only on the side facing the hut's interior.

The two main posts stand at the places where the hut opens towards the village plaza. In a village located along an east-west axis, these openings face towards the north and the south. In other words, the two doors of the hut open out in the same directions as the doors of a typical Dongria house. However, the main beam held up by these two posts is aligned on a north-south axis, while the central beam of a Dongria house, just like the village as a whole, is oriented along an east-west axis. Correspondingly, the hut's roof stands at a right angle to the roofs of the two rows of Dongria houses that make up the village.

The building of the hut does not follow a strict timetable, but the first trunks of teak are carved and set up about two months before the actual sacrifice. This work is always performed by men, but nobody in particular has the right – or duty – to make these posts. Anybody with the skills and some experience does this work, which is carried out with axes *(krali)* for felling the trees, daggers *(katri)* for chopping off branches and finer work, and adzes *(barseli)* for removing the bark and cutting the wood down to the required thickness.

---

[44] In shape they are identical to the sacrificial posts I have seen in villages occupied by Kuttia Kond. I saw a similar stake in only one village (Dongormati) in the Niamgiri Hills.

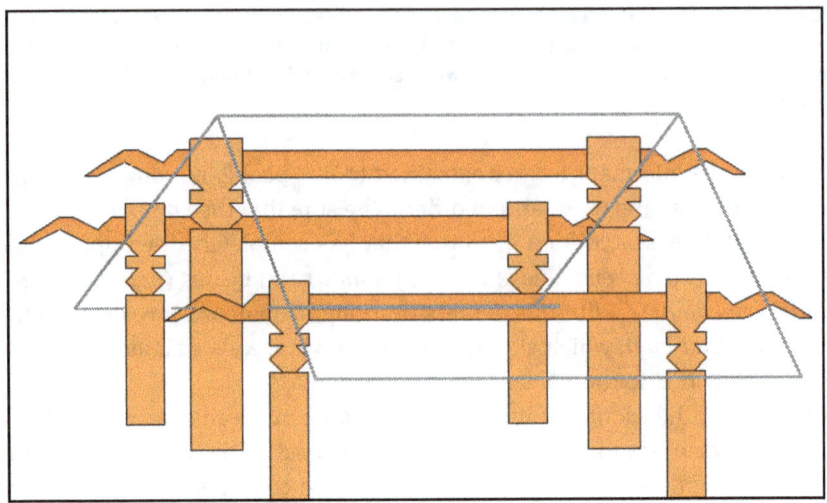

Figure 32: Basic frame of sacrificial hut

Once the basic frame is standing, further roof posts are set up with notches to hold the two lower roof beams. In addition, the required number of wall posts are put into the ground on the two sides where the openings of the hut will be. These wall posts are of roughly the same height as the roof posts but differ in shape, since they have a pointed top and look like long lances. Their main purpose is to provide stability to the walls, which are made of bamboo and plastered with clay.

On a set day about three to four weeks before the beginning of the festival, Dongria from those neighbouring villages that belong to the same clan organisation (*muta*) arrive in the morning carrying large bamboo poles (*mading mara*). Each village has a certain number of such brother villages the members of which come to build the goddess's hut. Some must rely on the cooperation of only of two or three such villages, while others have five or more villages the inhabitants of which join the organisers in their preparation. The exact number of villages willing to cooperate depends on the quality of relations existing between these agnates. If relations are strained or if the brothers live far apart, they may not be willing to come and offer their assistance. In Gumma for example, villagers told me that their relatives from Muniguda would not join them at the time of building the sacrificial hut, since their villages are at a distance of several hours walk. This is due to the fact that the ancestors of the people of Gumma migrated to their present location several generations ago.

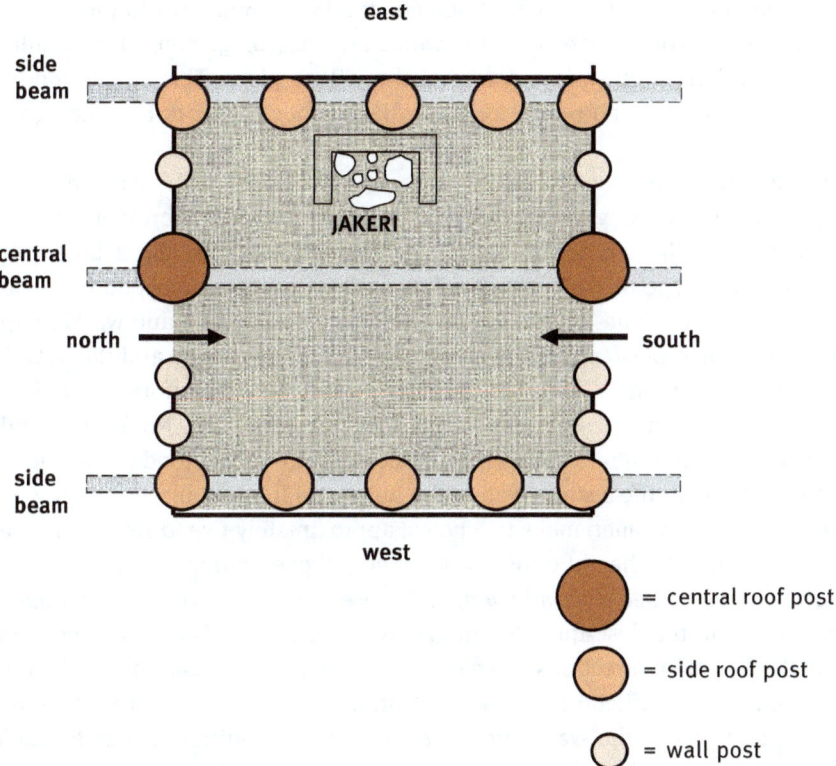

Figure 33: Layout with three types of posts

At the beginning of my fieldwork, I received seemingly contradictory information concerning the identity of the men who come to help build the sacrificial hut. While some insisted that it is their clan brothers who join in, others pointed out to me that some of the helpers belong to different affinal clans. These contradictions vanish if we take into account that cooperation is defined in terms of villages and not in terms of the clan identity of individuals. For this reason, all residents of a brother village come to offer their assistance, i.e., not only those belonging to the dominant clan of the organisers, but affines as well.

The helpers coming from brother villages begin their work by splitting the bamboo into halves and quarters of about 1.50 to 2 meters in length. These are fixed into the ground five to ten centimetres apart all along the four sides of the hut. In order to create a wattle, these stakes are next interwoven with slender strips of bamboo, with the green side facing outwards. Every twenty or thirty centimetres, the wattle is tied to the wooden posts with ropes made from the bark of a tree. Depending on the number of helpers, it takes roughly two to three hours to complete the work. Meanwhile, the women of the village cook rice or millet and some variety of pulse in a corner of the village plaza. This simple food is served to the guests, who return to their villages once the work has been completed.

The green bamboo has to dry for at least a week before the women of the village, sometimes along with their female helpers from the brother villages, begin plastering the walls with earth. For this purpose they dig a hole, take out a particular type of dark brown soil, mix it with water, and pound it with their feet until it becomes mouldable. Starting from the bottom and working upwards, the women plaster over the bamboo wattle on the inside and the outside of the hut. In addition to this, some women prepare a clay platform around the *jakeri* stones and smear cow dung on the floor inside the hut. No feast is held, but if women from brother villages have come, they are served food in the houses of their relatives. In the eastern wall of the hut – and in some places in the western wall, too – the women make two holes, approximately five to seven centimetres in diameter, at a height of about one meter above ground. The holes in the eastern wall are named *dharmu dueri*, and those in the western wall *surju dueri*. As mentioned in the description of an ideal village, the words *dharmu* and *surju* denote the two main directions, the east and the west, while *dueri* means door. In other words, the sacrificial hut has two "entrances," one in the east where the sun rises and one in the west where the sun sets. In addition, it has two side doors used by Dongria when they enter and exit the goddess's house. I once asked whether the holes symbolise the deity's eyes, but my informant denied this. A few weeks later I attended a *ghanta parba* for which a hut had been constructed above the stone representing the organiser's local line. In the eastern wall of this hut I saw the same holes as in the *dharni kudi*, and a painting of a deity was on the wall. The eyes of this deity were the two holes in the earthen wall.

About two weeks before the beginning of the festival, the sacrificial hut's roof is constructed. For this purpose, the brothers from related villages again come carrying long bamboo poles. On the same day, Dongria belonging to a particular type of affinal village turn up to build several fences. The activities they are involved in are dealt with in more detail below. The construction of the roof takes place in two phases. First, on both sides of the roof, reaching from the lower to the central beam, whole bamboo poles (*kandra*) are placed at intervals of about twenty centimetres and tied with ropes. Next, bamboo poles are cut into halves and quarters and fixed at right angles onto the *kandra*. Finally, the rest of these flexible bamboo strips are interwoven to form a coarsely meshed wattle (*kadri*).

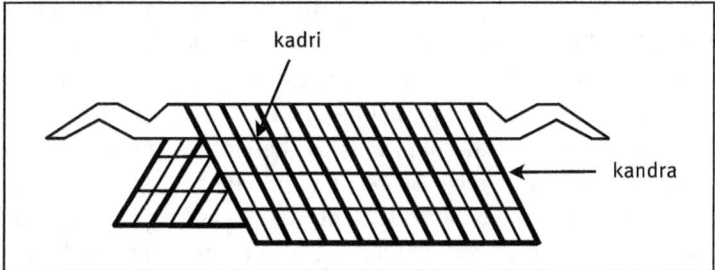

Figure 34: Frame of the roof

In the second phase, the roof is thatched with bundles of grass (*wikang*) that are placed in layers from the lower to the upper end of the roof. Nowadays, the Dongria prefer to cover the sacrificial hut with a tin roof provided by the government development agency (DKDA). In some villages the Dongria claim that they have no thatching grass on their hill slopes and would have to buy it from other villages for Rs 500 or more, whereas the government supplies the tin for free. I further suspect that compared to a thatched house, most Dongria consider the tin roof a sign of high status.

The final task, which is often carried out on the first day of the festival (Friday), consists in painting the sacrificial hut's walls. This work is the duty of the unmarried girls of the village, who go out into the hills in search of two types of soil, called *cuna wirga* (white coloured soil) and *kambit wirga* (red coloured soil). When mixed with water, they constitute an excellent, durable paint. In addition to red and white soil, soot obtained from holding a pot over a fire is used to make a black paint.[45] To carry out the painting, the girls use either their hands, in particular for painting larger surfaces, or small wooden sticks that they chew at one end to produce a brush. First, all the walls are smeared with a white colour. Next, the girls draw lines in black with a brush. Above and below each line, they draw triangles, mostly with the apex pointing upwards, but sometimes also the other way round. Then the triangles are filled in with either black or red, following no strict pattern but often using the same colour for a whole row of triangles. In between these lines of triangles, the girls also paint other patterns, in particular diagonal lines crossing each other in a zigzag style and resembling the bamboo fences around the village.

---

45 In the Dongria language, all colours are classified by three words. 1) *rinji tadi* can be translated as "light colours" including white, grey, and yellow; 2) *kambi tadi* means literally "ripe colour" and covers the whole range from orange to deep red; and 3) *kadi tadi*, finally, can be interpreted as "dark colours," such as green, blue, dark brown, and black.

When the sacrificial hut is ready, the building has become a representation of the earth goddess. The Dongria themselves recognise this, for example when saying that the thatched grass is like her hair, or when pointing to the carvings on the beams and explaining that these depict her breasts. The walls may be interpreted as forming her skin, and the paintings as the clothes she wears. The shawls (*ganda*) worn by girls and boys on festive occasions, in particular on the day of their wedding, are of exactly the same design as the paintings on the wall, i.e., rows of triangles in red, white, and black. In other words, the earth goddess is adorned in the same way as the many young Dongria women who come to attend her festival, or as a bride at the time of her wedding. The latter interpretation is corroborated by the fact that young girls decorate the bride on the day of the wedding just as girls paint the house of the goddess on the first day of the *kodru parbu* festival.

The two openings in the eastern and western walls define the way in which the sun god enters and exits the goddess's house, or figuratively speaking "her body." The hut resembles the village as a whole, as the latter also has two entrances, one facing the direction of the sunrise, the other facing the direction of the sunset. The central beam of the goddess's house divides the space absolutely into east and west. In particular, it divides the hut into two parts, an eastern part where the *jakeri* stones are located, and a western part with the doors through which the human beings enter. In other words, the sun moves into the village and the goddess's hut from the east, whereas the Dongria, being inside the village, step into the house from the west. The inside-outside opposition to the village is further expressed by the fact that the holes of the hut face in exactly the same direction as the two entrances of the village, while the doors used by the Dongria to enter the deity's dwelling face in the same direction as the doors of their own houses. Since the villagers consider the earth goddess their mother, they enter her residence in the same way as they do their own houses. In accordance with the layout of the houses, the earth goddess's hut divides the village space absolutely into a front side (*recha giri*), or inner part of the village, and a back side (*aka giri*), or space outside the village.

The openings of the sacrificial hut clearly define two opposite sets of relationships. The small holes mark the path of the sun god – we may call it the divine entrance and exit – which is associated with a number of different movements: from east to west, from morning to evening, from outside to inside. East and west further correspond to the opposition between man and woman, and if we take into consideration the relationship between *koteiwali* and *jakeri*, also between husband and wife. Similarly, I was informed by the Dongria that sun and earth are like husband and wife, and in this sense the *koteiwali* is simply a local representation of the all-pervading sun god. If we follow this understanding of the relationship between the male and female deities, east and west can be said to stand in an affinal relationship. This is confirmed by other characteristics of the spatial layout and by ritual proceedings that will be described later.

The doors of the sacrificial hut used by the villagers lie on an axis perpendicular to the divine entrance/exit and may be termed "human doors." While the east-west axis is primarily linked to movement into and out of the village, the perpendicular axis has contrary connotations. Like the earth goddess itself, it seems to be associated with locality, i.e., with belonging to a certain place. Her hut is the focal point of the village and represents its unity. When Dongria step out of their front doors, they come out onto the village plaza, the space collectively shared by all householders. The earth goddess is considered the mother, and the villagers her children. In this sense, the hut's doors connect the members of a family. This is particularly true for the male population, who consider the village territory as their own property and perform all major rituals. The village plaza is usually a domain of male activities. Married women, in contrast, have come from outside the village, and their activities should be restricted to the place behind the houses, away from the goddess. Similarly, unmarried girls, who will leave the village when they get married, reside in the dormitories behind the houses, where they also dance and sing with their visitors. In relation to the goddess, the male residents of the village are like consanguines.

The opposition between gods and humans is linked to an inversion in terms of gender. In the divine sphere, the earth goddess always remains in one place, while the sun god is born in the east and dies in the west. In the world of human beings, men may move around, but like the goddess, they ideally remain in the same village throughout their lives. In contrast, women, like the sun god, are born in one place and die in another.

Planting the buffalo post (*kodru munda uhpoli*)
A week before the sacrifice, usually on Sunday at the time "the cock crows" (*kayu knepa*), a sacrificial post is set up in front of the eastern wall of the *dharni kudi*. The exact time is determined by a specialist referred to as *dissari* or *joga jani*, who can be a Kond, a Dombo, or a member of a Hindu caste. The word *joga* means "auspicious, right time" and is linked to this man's ability to select a good time at which to perform a sacrifice. He usually knows how to read the local astrological almanac (*panji*) and is familiar with certain rituals linked to astrological constellations. Hardly any Dongria possesses these abilities, and in most cases I witnessed, the specialist came from the valleys. In the context of the *kodru parbu* they assist in the selection of the right tree for the manufac-

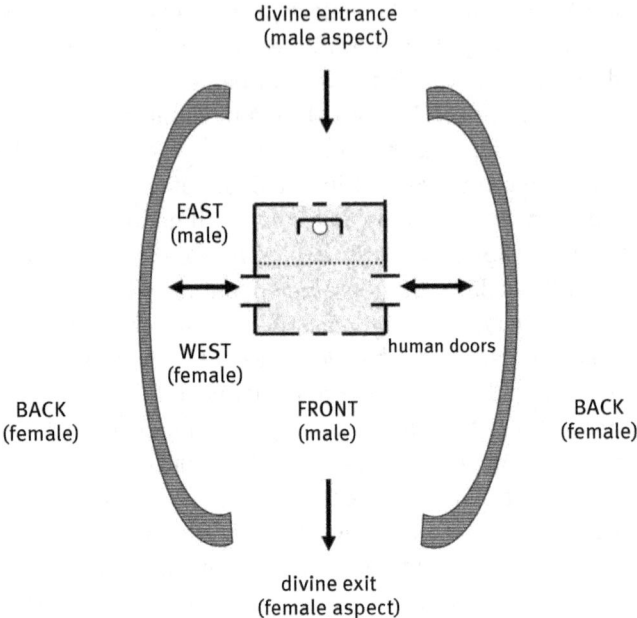

Figure 35: Spatial oppositions in the village

ture of the stake, determine the proper time for planting it, place the post into the hole, and decide upon the correct moment for sacrificing the victim.

Among the Kuttia Kond, Niggemeyer personally observed the selection of the tree used for making the *dharni munda* or "stake of the earth goddess." The timing differs from that of the Dongria, since the whole task begins on Friday, the first day of the festival, and not a week before the main events as in the Niamgiri Hills. Niggemeyer (1964a, 192–94) elaborately describes the selection of the tree for a festival that took place in a Gondo-Pano village the land of which was claimed by the Kuttia. On the Friday before the sacrifice, the male members of the village as a group, with their drums, went into the forest and searched for a specific type of tree: it had to have a straight trunk, be standing in an open place, not fall onto another tree when felled, not be overgrown with creepers, and have no dead branches or birds' nests and no holes inhabited by animals beneath its roots. The men played their instruments during the search and only ceased drumming when they had spotted a suitable tree. The *majhi* threw a handful of rice against the trunk, explained to the tree their intention to fell it in order to make a sacrificial post, and begged it not to punish them by causing diseases. He then punched his fist three times against the tree, each time pressing his ear against the trunk and listening for the goddess's cries, which would cause the men to abstain from felling the tree. When no sounds could be heard, two young men started to fell the tree, while the others resumed playing the drums. On the spot, the villagers selected a suitable part of the trunk, four *hata* (from elbow to fingertips) in length, cut it, and removed the bark. By turns and more running than walking, pairs of strong young men carried the log back to the village, where it was placed on a heap of leaves, having circumambulated the *dharni* and the old sacrificial posts twice.[46] Immediately after this, men began carving the post, dividing it in four parts of equal length, of which the upper part was used to make the "horns," the lower part was inserted into the earth, and the two middle parts constituted the actual post.[47]

On the night from Saturday to Sunday, the ritual specialist moved to the site of the old posts, sprinkled rice on them, and made a circle of rice at the place where the new post was to be erected. Before others began digging the hole, he uttered the following verse: "No stones, no roots may come, the door [of the earth] may open, termites should not destroy the post" (Niggemeyer 1964a, 193; my translation). When the hole had the appropriate depth, the ritual specialist fell into a trance and joined two other men in circumambulating the site with the post. The moment the post was inserted into the hole, the *majhi* jumped onto it, shouting, "I have given a good place to *sargi munda-margi munda*. I stand on the post, I like the post. I give you plenty of grain, I will not make you sick" (Niggemeyer 1964a, 193; my translation). Then the post was properly fixed in the ground and washed with turmeric water before offerings of rice were made to a fowl while calling the names of different hill gods of the surrounding area.

In another village, Niggemeyer observed how the *majhi* examined the tree trunk after it had been brought out from the forest to the place of the *dharni*. He first spoke to the stake and beat it in the same way as is later done with the sacrificial victim. Then he rubbed his hands against the wood and smelled his palms in order to determine whether a corpse had been burned or buried under the tree, which would have meant it was unsuitable for making the sacrificial post. At four o'clock in the morning, the post was first carried around the village, then placed near the hole, washed, and smeared with turmeric. A fowl and a pig were offered to the stake, the pig by smashing it against the post. Later, the buffalo was tethered to the stake with a strong rope. In a third village, before inserting the post into the ground, the Kuttia sacrificed a pig and let its

---

46 In this village, a total of thirteen old posts from previous sacrifices were standing, an indicator of the high frequency of buffalo sacrifices in this area. In Dongria villages, it is rare to see more than one or two old posts.

47 Several photographs in the appendix of Niggemeyer's book give a good impression of what the stakes look like.

blood drip into the hole. In a fourth village, the tree trunk was placed under a tree at the entrance of the village after it had been brought from the forest. The young men then sat on the stake, beat it like they beat the buffalo, and said, "Oh *sargi munda-margi munda*, we brought you here to make a sacrificial post. Our ancestors did the same at the behest of Nirantali-Kapantali, Ururengan-Penarengan, so do we" (Niggemeyer 1964a, 205; my translation).

These descriptions reveal the multiple identities and functions of the sacrificial stake. First, the tree itself must possess certain qualities, and from the way the Kuttia beg the tree not to cause any diseases, it can be inferred that they consider the tree to have divine powers. If it does not cry, the tree can be felled, and we may interpret this in two ways. Either the life-soul has left the tree, or the absence of any response signals a kind of agreement from the deity for the tree to be felled or "sacrificed. Second, like the tree, the stake itself appears to be a kind of sacrificial victim when it is brought into the village. This may be inferred from the fact that before entering the village the young men beat the stake in the same way that they beat the buffalo. Inside the village, the tree trunk is treated like prey brought from the forest. Thus, in order to trim the stake, the Kuttia place it on a heap of leaves, as they would do with an animal when cutting it into pieces. Third, the posts appear to be a representation or image of the earth goddess and other deities such as the mountain gods. When the stake is inserted into the hole – the door to the earth – the *majhi* becomes possessed by the earth goddess and promises a good harvest and health to the people. After that, the post receives offerings, such as fowls, pigs, and later the buffalo. Finally, the stake has the very practical function of a pole to which the buffalo is tethered before the sacrifice.

Concerning the Dongria, Jena et al. (2002, 254–55) provide a relatively similar list of qualities that the tree selected for making the sacrificial post must have: "the tree must be straight and sturdy; it should not lean on another tree; there should be no bushes or dry trees around it; the tree must be fresh and green in colour; the tree must not be overgrown by orchids; none of the branches of the tree are withered or hollow or cut off or broken; there should neither be an axe mark on it, nor should it be girdled" (Jena et al. 2002, 254). If a tree has been selected, the *jani* will strike it with an axe and put his ear on the trunk to find out whether the tree cries or whether he can hear a person moving up and down. If this is the case or if a nearby animal shrieks loudly, the villagers will not fell this tree but continue their search. Once a proper tree has been found, the *jani* offers rice and optionally a pigeon to the hill god before the men begin felling it. The trunk is divided into three parts,[48] which are carried to the village and placed near the bank of a small stream close to the settlement, where they are trimmed into sacrificial stakes. On Sunday morning, the *jani, dissari,* and *bejuni,* accompanied by the villagers, who beat drums, proceed to the stream where the stake is kept. From there they carry it to the place of worship, where a hole is dug. The *dissari* listens to find out whether or not he can hear a man moving up and down in the hole. If this is the case, it is considered an auspicious sign for setting up the post. Before the stake is actually put into the hole, the gods receive a rice offering, and a lamp is lit inside a winnowing fan. The moment the post enters the hole, gunshots are fired. Then the ritual specialist offers a fowl to the stake and bathes it with *mohua* liquor before himself drinking the remaining alcohol.

From this description, the contrast between the tree without life and the hole with life clearly emerges. Movements inside the body are interpreted as signs of the life-soul (*jiu* or *jella*).[49] Thus, the heartbeat and the pulse in the solar plexus, in the wrists, and near the throat are considered to be movements of the life-soul, which leaves the body at the time of death. Among the Dongria, Jena et al. (2002, 263) recorded the idea that in "human beings, *jella* is believed to be present at the site known as *sibdaki,* the place at which the ribs of the lower thorax meet the upper abdomen. *Jiu* is in constant motion between the *sibdaki* and the feet, and this is believed to be the process which maintains the vitality of the human body." Like human beings, trees possess a life-soul, and the procedure of beating the tree and listening for movements and cries described above may be interpreted as an attempt to verify the presence or absence of this life-soul. As previously mentioned in the context of cutting the wood in order to build the *meria* shrine, the Dongria explained to me that the trees must be dead. Since human beings can no longer talk to the trees in order to convince them to sacrifice themselves, they have to find other ways to make certain they are not committing sacrilege when felling the tree.

While the presence of sounds in the tree is interpreted as a bad sign, the same sounds are considered auspicious when coming out of the hole where the post will be planted. According to Niggemeyer's description, the hole is the door to the earth, and we may therefore interpret the movements heard by the *dissari* as signs of the deity's presence. Once the post has been inserted into the hole, the ritual specialist standing on the stake becomes possessed by

---

48 This number seems to apply only to the particular case observed by the authors. The exact number always depends on the number of buffaloes to be sacrificed by the villagers.
49 While Jena et al. clearly distinguish between stagnant *jela* and agile *jiu*, my own data does not support such a radical distinction.

this deity. In other words, the deity, in this case primarily the earth goddess, moves from the ground into the post and then into the body of the *majhi*. In other words, from being a vessel without life, the tree trunk has been turned into an object where deities reside and can be worshipped.

Photo 9: Sacrificial stake placed near stream (Railima, 2001)

The data I collected during my fieldwork confirm these interpretations. According to my informants, the tree selected for making the sacrificial stake must be a teak tree (*hergi mara*) with a straight trunk and be standing in an open space. Neither birds nor ants should be living in the tree, which must also be free of creepers and bulges (*madang*), interpreted as signs of disease. On either Friday or Saturday a week before the beginning of the festival, the *dis-*

sari and some villagers search for the proper tree in an easterly direction. A Desia Kond *dissari* once explained to me that *bhagwan* ("god") himself shows him the right tree for the stake. I never personally witnessed the selection of a tree, but I was informed that the *dissari* make a small rice offering to the tree before the young men begin felling it. Then the log is trimmed and the stake carried to a stream near the village, where it is kept until Sunday morning when the *dissari* comes, in the company of villagers, to carry the post into the village.

I observed the installation of the stake in the village of Railima, where the *dissari* planted four different stakes in four village sites (*padari*) in one night. The activities began around two o'clock in the morning, when the ritual specialist, together with some male villagers with drums and a Dombo, made their way to a small stream east of the village. There, leaning against a mango tree, stood the already carved sacrificial stake. Like all *meria* posts I saw in the Niamgiri Hills, it had a straight base followed by a flange and a pointed top. The lower portion is inserted into the ground and is one *hata* (from elbow to fingertips) in length, as is the pointed top. The flange is the length of one *chakondi* (locally also *cakedi*) which corresponds to the distance between the thumb and the tip of the middle finger. The pointed top distinguishes this style of post from the other type found in this area, which has a flat top. In contrast to the Kuttia, the Dongria do not make stakes with an upper portion that resembles a buffalo horn. I have not come across major variations in the shape of the buffalo stake; only the exact height seems to differ from place to place. Sacrificial posts set up on other occasions, in particular at the time of the *ghanta parba* and the *bali yatra*, differ markedly from the stake erected before the *kodru parbu* (see figure 36).

In order to worship the stake at the stream, the *dissari* – a Dombo from a nearby Desia village – had brought an earthen pot, a thread, tobacco powder, turmeric rhizomes, ground turmeric, and a special type of grass (*durba ghasa*). A thread holding turmeric and mango leaves was tied around the pot, which had been filled with water from the nearby stream to which turmeric powder was added. With this water, the *dissari* bathed the stake from top to bottom before he smeared the tobacco powder on it. Then he tied a second thread with five mango leaves around the middle section of the sacrificial post. When these preparations were finished, he sat down in front of the stake, pressed his right hand against it, and silently whispered a prayer. Next, he made three heaps of rice in front of the post and coaxed a small fowl to peck at the rice from these heaps and from the upper part of the stake. He then lifted the stake up onto his head, with the top pointing forward, and carried it back to the village while the others beat their drums or whistled loudly.

When they arrived in the village, the *dissari* first went to the *jakeri*, where he stood for a few seconds facing east and balancing the stake on his head without

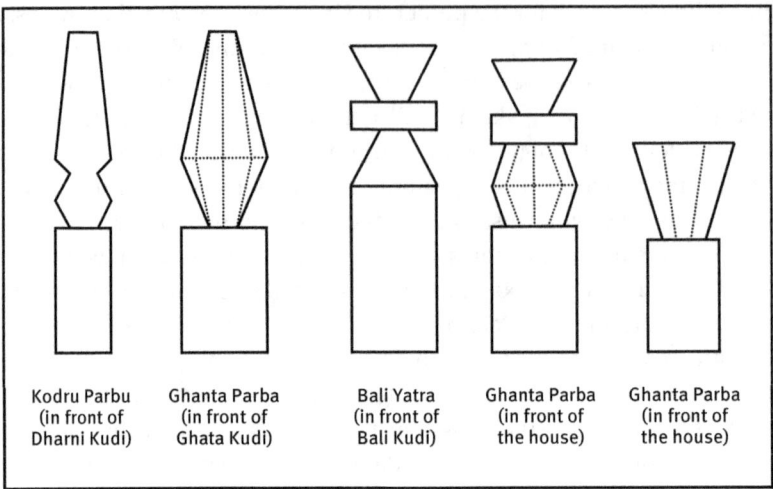

Figure 36: Different types of sacrificial stakes (examples)

touching it with his hands.[50] Then he placed the stake next to a forty-to-fifty-centimetre-deep hole east of the *dharni,* which had been dug by a Dongria the same night. The *dissari* took a twenty-five-*paisa* coin and some *durba* grass into his right hand while the young men beat wildly on their drums or whistled through their fingers. After some time, he began to tremble, threw the money and the grass into the hole, and with a single, quick motion inserted the stake into the hole. At that moment, somebody fired a gunshot, while others rushed up and filled in the hole with earth until the post was firmly fixed in the ground. Then the *dissari* seated himself in front of the stake and, as in the woods near the stream, made three heaps of rice. After a small white chicken had pecked at rice from each heap, he cut off the animal's head, took the bleeding body, and rubbed it from the top to the bottom of the stake. Finally, he took an earthen pot filled with turmeric water, poured it over the stake, and put the vessel upside down over the top of the post.

The same procedure was repeated with three other poles that were set up in places where the villagers intended to sacrifice a buffalo to their earth goddess. In the morning, at around five o'clock, when the first villagers were waking up, the *bejuni* of the village, together with some old women, approached the *dharni* accompanied by young men who were playing their drums. From each house a

---

50 In this village, the *jakeri* was not inside the *dharni kudi* but in front of its eastern wall under the open sky.

woman emerged carrying a winnowing fan with some husked rice. The main *jani* of Railima, i.e., the descendant of the village founders, came to the *jakeri*, and the *bejuni* poured some rice into his right hand and made a chicken peck at some grains. The same happens when a householder performs a ritual at his own shrine and welcomes his house deity by offering her rice from his hand. If the chicken pecks at the rice, the deity appears to be satisfied with the offering. In this case, the *jani*, being the "owner" of the village as a whole, offered rice from his hand, and when it was accepted, it was a clear indication that the village deity was satisfied with the sacrificial post set up for her. The *bejuni* rubbed the rice in her winnowing fan and began to dance. One after the other, the women from each household poured their rice into the collective winnowing fan used by the *bejuni*. They danced alternately, i.e., each in turn allowed the deity to use her body to move to the rhythm of the drums and rubbed the rice in circular movements with her right hand. Finally, when the dancing stopped, the *jani* took a small pig, cut its throat, and placed the head on top of the *jakeri* stones.

As previously mentioned, about a week later the buffalo is tethered to this stake. In some villages, however, I observed the setting up of another simple post with no carvings and no elaborate ritual. In these villages, the second post served as the actual stake to which the buffalo was tied before the sacrifice, whereas the well-trimmed post had no practical function whatsoever. From this we can infer that the sacrificial post is first of all set up as a representation of the deity. The stake is sometimes referred to as *bisimunda*. The stake receives offerings in the same way as a deity, and since the actual killing of the buffalo takes place directly at this site, the post is the first to come into contact with the victim's blood. However, apart from being an image of a deity, the post can be seen as a sign, a *cinha* as Dongria call it, of the sacrificial offering itself and of the number of village territories claimed by the people. In contrast to the stone *dharni*, it is made of transient wood. After the sacrifice, it remains a symbol of the villagers' religious devotion and of the grand festival they organised in the name of the earth goddess. However, since the wooden post slowly disintegrates over the years, it gradually becomes a reminder of their debts to the *jakeri*, who provides them with fertility and requires an offering of blood in return.

Constructing the wall (*koteiwali palawara*)
In contrast to the earth goddess, her husband (*koteiwali*) remains in an open space, perhaps a clear indication that in contrast to his consort, he is not confined to a certain location during the festivities. This deity is carried up and down the village plaza in the form of a brass pot attached to a long bamboo

pole. His dwelling place is marked by the *panikimunda* and a single wall referred to as *palawara*.⁵¹ In between these two objects stands the menhir that permanently represents the husband. I received contradictory information concerning the setting up of the sacrificial pole and the construction of the wall. While in some villages people informed me that the organisers themselves are responsible for preparing the sacrificial site of the *koteiwali*, others insisted that erecting the wall is basically the task of a certain category of affines named *mudrenga* (see photo 10).

In those cases in which it was the affines who were responsible for constructing the *palawara*, they supplied the necessary wood and bamboo, carried out the work, and provided the banana trees for decoration as well as the ram to be sacrificed on the Friday, the first day of the *kodru parbu*. The work follows the same pattern as the construction of the sacrificial hut: first posts are set up, then a wattle is made out of bamboo, and then the women plaster this with clay before finally painting it with colours. A *palawara* always has three poles shaped like lances, not dissimilar to those used in the *meria* hut, as wall posts. The middle stake is higher than the ones at either side. To this approximately two-meter-tall stake, the head and later the horns of the ram are tied following the sacrifice on the Friday morning. The exact construction may differ, since in some places simple posts without carvings are put into the ground to hold the wattle made of bamboo strips, whereas in others a ready-made wattle is simply tied with ropes to the three pointed poles. When the bamboo is dry, women belonging to the village of *mudrenga* come and plaster the wall with clay and make an earthen platform around the sacrificial site. On Friday, when village girls paint the *dharni kudi*, other girls of the affinal village draw the same colourful lines and triangles on the *palawara*. Like the eastern wall of the goddess's hut, her husband's wall has two holes at a height of about one meter above the ground.

Fencing the village (*sala bada*) and the sacrificial site (*garada*)
A task unequivocally ascribed to the organisers' "affines" is the construction of two fences, one around the village and another at the place where the buffalo is to be tethered. I place the word "affines" in quotation marks because these people in fact belong to a highly ambiguous category: they are from marriageable

---

51 According to two Indian authors this wall is "erected to protect the deity from the sight of women during their period of pollution" (Patnaik and Das Patnaik 1982, 141). I find this explanation highly unlikely, as no Dongria woman enters the village plaza during her menstruation.

Photo 10: *Koteiwali*

clans but act like brothers during the sacrifice.[52] They are referred to as *mudrenga* (sing.: *mudria*), a word probably derived from the Oriya term *mudra*, meaning "coin," "seal," or in its verbal form (*mudriba*) "to close." This designation may be derived from two practices associated with these affines. First, on the day when the deity's wall is built, or alternatively on the first day of the festival, one of the organisers, normally a *jani*, ties a thread with a piece of turmeric

---

[52] In the beginning I was often confused when they were introduced to me as *bhai* although they clearly belonged to different clans. I now think that the organisers put them into the category of brothers because they help them with the preparations and because they protect the buffalo.

Figure 37: Wall for the husband of the earth goddess (*koteiwali palawara*)

and three mango leaves around the right wrist of those men who have been selected as *mudrenga*.[53] In addition to this wristlet, the *mudrenga* are given long bamboo sticks as a symbol of their authorisation to defend the sacrificial animals against attackers. This "seals" the contract between them and the organisers. From the beginning through to the end of the three days of celebrations, they guard the victims with these bamboo sticks and beat anybody who dares to attack them with axes.

Second, these people are responsible for constructing fences out of bamboo poles that are split into halves and then loosely woven together. One kind of fence is used to close off both entrances to the village and any breaches in the two rows of houses and is referred to as *sala bada*. The expression seems to derive from Oriya, *bada* meaning "fence" while *sala* denotes a "house," and in this context probably alludes to the village as a whole. To allow people to

---

53 My wife and I were given the same thread on the day of our "wedding" before we jointly entered my hut in the village.

enter and leave the village, a small gate is built into the fence at each end of the village. The second fence is much smaller and encloses only the space between the eastern wall of the sacrificial hut and the post to which the victim is tied. It is referred to as *garada* or *kodru bada*, the first term clearly being of Oriya origin and meaning "lockup" or "prison," while the second expression represents a mixture of Dongria (*kodru* = buffalo) and Oriya (*bada* = fence). The term *mudra* appears to be linked to this function of "closing" a place where gods and humans assemble to participate in a sacrifice. This can be deduced from the invocations made by shamans when performing the ritual. In combination with the term *gati* ("knot") the word *mudra* occurs frequently in these recitations, for example in the following verses, which are repeated again and again at various moments during a several-hour-long trance session:

gada gati gude mudra aisi
("knot of town, seal of village, to be")

ida gati aiba ida mudra aiba
("this knot to be, this seal to be")

ida aba gati ai mudra ai wamu aya
("this, father, knot to be, seal to be, come mother")

These verses refer in highly metaphorical language to the assembly of worshippers and deities on ritual occasions. With these words, the shamans inform the deities that they have prepared the site for them by purifying the ground, hanging up a rope for them to climb down, and constructing a small shrine with an earthen pot for them to reside in. Everybody is assembled, and the deities are now asked to come to the sacrificial site in order to partake in the offerings. In this sense, the duty of the *mudrenga* consists in protecting both the victims and the site, so that the deities can safely come and receive their sacrifice.

The making of the fence usually occurs on the same day as the construction of the roof of the goddess's house. For this reason, both agnates (from brother villages) and affines (from *mudrenga* villages) assemble on this day. In one village named Tebapada, I witnessed an interesting division of labour between these two categories of people. While the agnates normally make the hut and the affines the fences, in this case the whole village was divided into two sections, east and west. The agnates, including the organisers, were members of five villages owned by the Kadraka clan and were responsible for constructing the goddess's house and the fence closing off the western entrance. The affines

Photo 11: Fence at entrance to village (*kodru parbu* in Railima, 2001)

came from five villages[54] claimed by the Sikoka clan and built the god's wall, the pen for the buffalo, and the eastern fence.

On the day of roof and fence construction, a feast called *kudi bhoji* takes place. A buffalo or a cow is provided by the *raiti* of the village, i.e., the people who do not belong to the dominant clan or organisers but reside in their village and cultivate their land. The animal is slaughtered without any ceremonies, and the meat is cooked on the village plaza while the women prepare rice or millet. In the village mentioned above, where affines worked in the east and agnates in the west, everybody received one plate with dark brown little millet (*kahada*) and a layer of white rice on top. This can be interpreted in terms of the *kodru parbu*, where at the *koteiwali* a white ram is sacrificed to the deity worshipped on a long bamboo pole higher up, and a black buffalo is sacrificed to the earth goddess on the ground.

---

54 In discussions, the organisers later told me that there are nine brother villages altogether, linked to seven Sikoka villages. I had the impression that only people living in neighbouring villages actually came and offered their help.

Table 33: Oppositions on the day of *kudi bhoji*

East	West
God	Goddess
Above	Below
Affines	Agnates
White	Black

Among the Desia Kond, neither of these fences are constructed at the time of *kodru parbu*. Instead, four-to-five-meter-long teak logs are set up around the village at a distance of about ten meters to hold up a rope with mango leaves. This kind of symbolic "fencing" is practised by Dongria Kond on certain festive occasions, but never during the *kodru parbu*. Furthermore, the buffalo victim is not shut up in a pen; instead, its head is caught between the slats of a simple wooden fence in order to constrain its movement. This fence (*madada*) consists of two or three posts holding up two beams, the upper of which may be lifted. Once the buffalo's head is resting between these beams, the upper beam is pushed down and fixed so that the buffalo, due to the size of his horns, can move neither forward nor backward. Among the Dongria, I witnessed the use of such a device only during the *bali yatra* but not during the worship of the earth goddess.

In the past, both entrances to a Kond village in the southern districts[55] were closed "by a strong wooden barrier gate" (Macpherson 1863, 58). More than one hundred years later, Niggemeyer reports that all larger Kuttia Kond villages located in remote areas are protected by a fence made either of bamboo or strong wooden posts bending outwards slightly. For Niggemeyer (1964a, 27), the fence serves the function of keeping away wild animals and hindering domesticated animals from escaping from the settlement.[56] According to my own interpretation, the fence constructed during the *kodru parbu* marks the border of the settlement and thereby defines the spatial as well as social unity of the village. The term *sala* indicates that the village has been turned into one "house," a place for the sacrifice to the earth goddess. In the past, the permanent fence probably served the very practical function of protecting the village, not only from wild

---

55 In the northern districts, villages were not planned in the same systematic way (Macpherson 1863, 59). After his visit to Kond villages in the northern Sambalpur district, Professor Pfeffer informed me that these villages were also not of the typical two-row structure but rather consisted of small hamlets that formed a village on the conceptual rather than empirical level (personal communication).
56 In Dongria villages, the few cows owned by the villagers are kept in stables, and the goats in the front room of their houses. Desia Kond, on the other hand, often own large numbers of cows and buffaloes, and these are tethered in the evening to small posts set up on the village plaza.

animals but also from attacks in the event of feuds with other Kond.[57] During the *kodru parbu*, it helps the organisers to keep out young men who threaten to kill the buffalo before the proper time and to hinder the victim from escaping from the village when it manages to break free in the turmoil of sacrifice. The small pen for the buffalo serves the same purpose, and often the organisers tie two or three further layers of bamboo wattle to the fence in order to increase its stability.

The absence of such protective devices among the Desia Kond reflects differences in the celebration of the *kodru parbu*. While in a Dongria village young men from many different villages assemble to kill the victim with their axes, the Desia Kond are proud of the fact that in their villages only one person, referred to as *banaja* ("sister's son"), cuts off the buffalo's head in a "civilised" manner. Since they normally do not fear attacks from young men eager to kill the victim at any possible opportunity, the Desia Kond can keep the buffalo in an open space instead of putting the victim into a pen. However, like the Dongria, they appoint a few men as *mudrenga,* whose main function consists in taking the buffalo to different villages and showing him to their relatives (see below). If the *kodru parbu* is attended by the Dongria Kond, as happens to be the case in Desia Kond villages located in the foothills of the Niamgiri, these people will additionally have the function of preventing their "wild" neighbours from attacking the buffalo. For this purpose, they carry long bamboo poles and do not hesitate to use them against the Dongria.

Who are the *mudrenga,* and how durable are bonds between them and the organisers? The *mudrenga* are usually the married men of either a single village or a number of villages belonging to a clan different from that of the organisers. In this sense, they can be termed "affines," since they are potentially marriageable and in actual fact are often linked to the organisers as either bride-givers or bride-takers. On the other hand, the organisers also call them "brothers," because like their agnates, they assist them with the preparations for the festival. When more than one village supplies men to build the fences and to protect the buffalo, these belong to the same clan organisation. For example, at the *kodru parbu* I witnessed in the village of Tebapada (Kadraka clan), the *mudrenga* came from five villages dominated by the Sikoka clan and were all joined in one *muta.* Furthermore, a hierarchy often exists among these villages depending

---

[57] Among some of the Naga tribes of Northeast India, for example, who like the Kond were renowned for their clan feuds, villages were similarly protected by stone walls, fences, and heavy wooden doors (e.g. Mills 1937, 47–48), which quickly fell into disuse in the British-administered territories.

on who is selected to perform the major tasks.[58] Ideally, such a *mudrenga* relationship with one or more villages lasts for many generations and continues on a reciprocal basis: people from village A will serve as *mudrenga* for village B, and in return village B sends their men to help village A at the time of the buffalo sacrifice. In practice, the relationship appears to be highly unstable, basically because the position of the *mudrenga* is inherently ambiguous. On the one hand, the *mudrenga* are protectors and help the organisers like their own brothers. On the other hand, they belong to an affinal clan and as such are allowed to kill the buffalo. The responses to my question of whether or not *mudrenga* are allowed to kill the victim reflect this ambiguity. Some Dongria clearly stated that a *mudria* has no right to participate in sacrificing the animal, while others were more hesitant and mentioned certain exceptions. For example, *mudrenga* are said to be entitled to kill the buffalo once the proper time has come. Others pointed out to me that only the elder, married men from the *mudria* village protect the victim, whereas young men have permission to attack the animal. Nayak (1989, 170) reports that a man belonging to the category of *mudrenga* symbolically hits the buffalo with an axe three times before others kill the animal.

Given the ambivalent nature of the relationship, it is hardly surprising that conflicts with *mudrenga* arise frequently. For example, the people of Lamba, a village belonging to the Pusika clan, had been the *mudrenga* of Gumma. During the last *kodru parbu* they had attacked the buffalo already on the first day of the festival due to a conflict over money, which led to the break up of the relationship. As a substitute, the people of Gumma were planning to assign the responsibilities of *mudrenga* to their *raitimane*, i.e., affines residing in their own village. Meanwhile, another Sikoka village named Lekhpadar, the residents of which had long been engaged in a land dispute with Gumma, established close contacts with the Pusika of Lamba. Finally, when they began their preparations for the sacrifice to the earth goddess, they requested the villagers of Lamba to act as their *mudrenga*. This, however, aroused the anger of the Pusika of Gundawayu, who had traditionally performed this function for Lekhpadar. This clearly demonstrates how unstable alliances between affines are and how they can be rearranged each time Dongria perform the *kodru parbu*. In one case, the Dongria distrusted their own affines so much that they asked people of a different caste to protect their sacrificial site. This happened in Railima, where the Huika organ-

---

58 For instance, among the five Sikoka villages serving the Kadraka of Tebapada, villagers belonging to Patalamba were referred to as *icha* ("junior") *mudrenga*, while the residents of Phakeri were addressed as *kaja* ("senior") *mudrenga*. The reason given was that the people from Patalamba had only been chosen as helpers in recent years, while the *mudrenga* relationship with the villagers of Phakeri had long been in existence.

ised the festival in 2001. They had long-standing relations of mutual help with the Dongria of Musidi, a village divided into two hamlets – Talamusidi and Uparamusudi – and belonging to the Pdiska, but when men from this village came on the second day of the festival to be sprinkled with water by the shamans, a Dongria from Railima began to quarrel with them, and they left the village, refusing to cooperate. Being without helpers to protect the buffalo, the people from Railima approached the residents of a neighbouring village populated by Desia Kond, Sondhi, Gauda, Paika, and Dara. They offered their assistance and performed their task so well that this festival became one of the few occasions I witnessed where all the proper rituals could be concluded before the young men were allowed to kill the victim.

5.3.4 Showing round (*trehnari*) and feeding (*tisnari*) the buffalo

In the fourth chapter (section 4.3.6), I described how the bride and groom visit their relatives and friends in neighbouring villages before the wedding ceremony. The bride, and in a less elaborate way also the groom, first goes to his or her mother's brother's house and then to all those places where relatives reside. Accompanied by friends (*ade / tone*), they are served food (*tone paga*) by the housewife, who smears oil in their hair and turmeric on their face. When the wedding ceremony begins, the bride remains in her village, where she pays a visit to every house in order to receive food and be anointed.

The sacrificial victim is treated in a very similar way in the weeks leading up to the actual sacrifice. Whenever the organisers find time, they tether the buffalo to a long rope, take their drums, and drive (*trehinari, keda kinari*) the animal with their sticks to certain villages. Only those villages the residents of which offered their help in preparing the *kodru parbu* are selected. These are first of all those villages where the *mudrenga* or protectors of the victim live. The buffalo is also driven to the villages belonging to the same clan organisation the inhabitants of which helped to construct the hut of the earth goddess. Finally, a few villages in the neighbourhood with which the organisers entertain amicable relations may be visited as part of the tour. However, when relations are strained due to unsettled disputes and conflicts, the organisers will avoid these villages.

For example, during my time in Gumma, the residents of a neighbouring village named Lekhpadar organised the *kodru parbu*. On the day they drove the buffalo to their *mudrenga* in a village named Lamba, the chief of Gumma, along with the eldest men of the village, made their way to this place. They asked the delegation from Lekhpadar to take the four sacrificial animals to Gumma for them to be fed. Immediately a dispute broke out among the organisers, as some were in favour of this suggestion while others were vehemently against it, mainly because of a land dispute concerning a place named Waliamba. The hills of Waliamba are presently cultivated by the Sikoka of Gumma, but the Sikoka of Lekhpadar and Dongormati, who belong to another clan organisation, claim ownership of the hills. The people from Gumma explained to me that the claims were related to the story of a boy from Dongormati (see p. 223) who was allegedly adopted by the local line of *naika* in Gumma. The members of this local line are today recognised as the main landowners of Waliamba. I was told that following the last *kodru parbu* in Waliamba, the people of Dongormati and Lekhpadar stole one leg of the victim and carried it to their *dharni* in order to claim the territory as their own. Since then, relations had been strained, and for this reason the request to take the sacrificial animals to Gumma did not meet with uniform approval and perhaps even aroused suspicion among the villagers of Lekhpadar. The chief of Gumma suggested that the Sikoka of all three places (Gumma, Dongormati, and Lekhpadar) should unite and become "one village" (*ra nayu*), and plans were made to bring about a reconciliation on both sides. A meeting was scheduled for the next day, when the leader from Gumma was expected to go to the border of Lekhpadar to receive a piece of cloth and be anointed with oil by the leader of Lekhpadar. In return, it was planned that the villagers of Lekhpadar would bring the buffaloes to Gumma, where they would be presented with oil and cloth on reaching the border. This plan aroused opposition in both villages and was therefore not carried out.

There can be two reasons why a village like Lekhpadar may not be willing to take their sacrificial victims to certain villages. First, the organisers relinquish control over the proceedings as soon as they reach the borders of another village. Concretely, this means that they cease playing their own drums and hand the buffalo over to the residents of the host village. The latter will lead the buffalo to their village plaza, where they play their own drums, and sing and dance. It is easy to imagine that the organisers are not prepared to allow members of a hostile village to exercise such control over their valuable sacrificial animal. Second, gifts of food that are typically only exchanged between close relatives and friends are presented to the organisers on this occasion. Thus, the buffalo is first driven to the houses where the chiefs of the village, such as the *jani* or *bismajhi*, reside. There the housewife presents the victim with cooked rice and lentils on a brass plate, which she places in front of the animal. This is referred to as "feeding the buffalo" (*kodru tisnari*). Such brass plates are only used on festive occasions, such as during the visit of a bride prior to her wedding, or when a man establishes a new friendship relation (*tone paga*). She pours water mixed with pieces of turmeric on the buffalo's head from a gourd and smears castor oil on its face and neck. If the victim is not willing to eat, the husband and

Photo 12: Feeding and anointing the buffaloes

wife try to coax the buffalo into eating by talking to it and offering it food out of their hands. Once the buffalo has accepted the boiled rice, it is driven to the next house and in this way visits all the houses in a village. The Dombo's settlement is included in this tour, but in contrast to the Dongria, the Dombo offer only husked, uncooked rice, placed on a winnowing fan, to the victim. This clearly illustrates the principle that the buffalo belongs to the Dongria community: the victim is one of them, it shares their cooked food, and it takes only uncooked food from their clients. The commensality between the buffalo and the Dongria reaches its high point when, following the feeding of the *meria*, each housewife brings her plateful of leftovers to the village plaza. There, a man pours the cooked food onto a large winnowing fan or into a large pot and mixes it with his hands before again distributing it between various plates. These are given to the organisers, who eat their share while sitting on the veranda of their hosts.

In some houses, white cloths are tied around the horns of the buffalo as a gift to the deity. The villagers of Lamba, for example, bound several cloths to the horns of the largest of the four buffaloes to be sacrificed in Lekhpadar, saying that this particular victim was the "mother," meaning the earth goddess of the main settlement, while the smaller buffalos were regarded as her "children," or representations of the less important earth deities located in the forest. In other words, the buffaloes are not only victims to be sacrificed to the goddess but also representations of the earth goddess. Offerings to the deity can be made through the medium of the buffalo, who like an important guest will be anointed with oil and turmeric and given food to eat and clothes to wear.

Both the bride and the groom visit their respective agnates and affines in different villages before their wedding, with the house of the mother's brother being the most important. Soon after fixing the day for the wedding, the bride and groom go to their respective mother's brother's houses and receive offerings from them. In the same way, the buffalo has to be taken to the village of *mudrenga* before the festivities begin. While the buffalo will be treated kindly by the organisers and their brothers, I saw the victim treated in a teasing, even rude manner in villages occupied by *mudrenga*. In 2001, for example, I accompanied the villagers of Kuskedeli with their buffalo to their *mudrenga* in Buduni, whose chief was introduced to me as the *samdin* (CSpF) of the *jani* from Kuskedeli, who was organising the festival. The victim was a very thin, sick-looking buffalo that had been purchased after the first buffalo had run away or been stolen, as reported above. When the buffalo was standing in front of the *samdin* house and refused to eat the offerings, the chief from Buduni and his wife began to scold, even ridicule it in a way I never witnessed in any other village.

As mentioned above, the *mudrenga* have an ambivalent relationship with the organisers, being at the same time protectors and – at least potentially – sacrificers. On certain occasions, this ambiguity is expressed in more or less hostile forms of jesting. For example, on the first day of the *kodru parbu*, the *mudrenga* will drive the buffalo from house to house in the organisers' village. In Tebapada, I witnessed how the *mudrenga* from Phakeri used the opportunity to beat their bamboo sticks on the roof of each house in order to demand gifts from the householders. In contrast to this kind of jesting, the "real" affines, i.e. those who come to sacrifice the buffalo, behave like enemies: they destroy the fence and perhaps even the organisers' houses[59] and kill the buffalo in the most brutal fashion.

---

59 For instance, in Kuskedeli, some young men hacked the victim into pieces a whole day before the scheduled time. Later, men from other villages turned up to join the festivities, but when they saw that the buffalo had already been killed, their disappointment turned against the organisers, and they began to demolish the *jani*'s house by hitting their axes and sticks against his roof.

If my interpretation is correct, the relationship between cross-cousins, who address each other as *mama* (MB) or *banaja* (ZS) (see section 3.2.2), resembles the relationship between the organisers and the *mudrenga*, who support them in the way that would be expected from cross-cousins. Both types of relationships share a common ambiguity. Cross-cousins cannot intermarry (or exchange sisters), although their relationship was originally established through marriage (see pp. 210–11). In the same way, certain people are selected because they are affines or potential sacrificers, but as soon as they have become *mudrenga*, they may no longer act as sacrificers. In Tebapada, the Dongria explicitly stated an analogy between their *mudrenga* and their cross-relatives. They had purchased two buffaloes, and when I asked them what they were for, they informed me that they would be given to their *mamu gan* (Oriya for MB's village), meaning their *mudrenga*.

Table 34: Types of relations

Organisers to Brothers	Organisers to *mudrenga*	Organisers to Sacrificers
same clan	different clans	different clans
agnates	cross-cousins (addressed as *banaja*, ZS, and *mama*, MB)	potential affines
brotherly help	help, jesting, ambiguity (protective functions but potentially hostile)	rivalry

Like the bride (or the groom) who goes to visit her relatives as soon as the day of her wedding has been fixed, the organisers of the *kodru parbu* drive the buffalo to the villages of their friends and relatives as soon as a particular date for the sacrifice has been selected. They send young men further out to more distant villages to invite their relatives to the festival. For a whole month[60] before the beginning of the ceremonies, young men will use every opportunity to take out their drums, in particular the conical, large *tamaka* – called *niseni* by Desia Kond – and circumambulate the *dharni* counter-clockwise. In the hills, the deep sound of the heavy drums can be heard over long distances. Some men will put on anklets, which consist of small bells that tinkle melodically while dancing. When brothers or affines come to join the organisers in their work, they form groups of young men who drum, sing, and dance in a particular fashion around the goddess's hut. In this kind of dance, one man with a flat drum

---

60 According to Nayak (1989, 169), the villagers begin dancing round the *dharni* a whole year before the start of the festival. This does not coincide with my own observations.

(*dhapu*) faces the others while singing one or two verses, then he turns around, and everyone moves a few steps forward together while continuing their song and beating their axes with small sticks. They then stop and the drummer turns around again to face the others and sings his lines of song before everybody continues with the circumambulation of the shrine.[61] Within days, the news of the upcoming festival will have spread throughout the hills.

5.4 Sacrificial objects

The brass figures displayed by the Kond at certain festivals have gained a certain amount of prominence in recent decades due to their popularity in circles dealing with tribal art (see Hacker 2000a, 2000b). Only a few scholars concerned with these objects have actually conducted research among the Kond, and Cornelia Mallebrein appears to be the only specialist in the field who combines Indological knowledge with extensive fieldwork. She organised an exhibition of various objects of tribal art at the Rautenstrauch-Joest-Museum in Cologne in 1993–94 and edited an extensive catalogue with articles and photographs (Mallebrein 1993; see also Mallebrein 2001). Mallebrein distinguishes five categories of brass images[62] manufactured by metalworkers (Ghasi) and owned by the Kond, in particular the so-called Malliah Kond, whom she studied in Phulbani district. The categories are comprised of (1) images belonging to the realm of ancestors; (2) figures of plants, animals, and spirits, along with objects linked to sacrifices to the earth goddess; (3) objects related to a magical being named Jebangrodu; (4) images of cattle and ploughing peasants worshipped before harvest; and (5) gifts presented at the time of marriage rituals as part of the bride's dowry (Mallebrein 1993, 471).

To illustrate the second category, which is of particular interest in the context of the *kodru parbu*, Mallebrein provides us with a number of photos of various brass objects, two of which represent human figures at the time of sacrifice, while the rest are images of different animals. Of the two human figures, one

---

[61] Nayak (1989, 169) appears to describe the same type of dance when he writes, "Each group is constituted by a leader who composes the songs for singing on the spot and is called *nokeyu* and a number of followers termed as *pendesi*." The native terms mentioned by Nayak are not titles but verbal phrases. *Nokeyu* literally means "he who goes in front," while *pendesi* can be translated as "they who are at the back."

[62] In German, the author refers to these objects as "Kondh Bronzen," but an analysis of them has clearly shown that the alloy used to make these figures is not bronze but brass (Riederer 1993, 509).

is a tall figure with breasts, perhaps the earth goddess herself, holding a long sword and standing behind a stake to which a human victim, apparently a child, is tied. The second figure represents a Kond participating in the sacrifice. In his right hand he holds a long sacrificial axe resting on his shoulder, and in his left hand he has a knife. According to Mallebrein, both instruments serve a specific function in the sacrifice: the axe is swung into the victim's neck, while the knife is used to cut meat off of the bones (Mallebrein 1993, 481). Curiously, the man's penis is exposed, a gesture that normally signifies aggressiveness and would be interpreted by opponents as a deliberate insult. Among the animal figures, two images representing peacocks differ from the others in that they may have been attached to a stick. According to Mallebrein, their exact use is not yet known; however, she does mention Taylor's report from the nineteenth century, according to which the peacock was worshipped as the earth goddess in Goomsur district, and she also states that her Kond informants spoke of such figures being kept near the *dharni* in the past.[63] The other brass images are of various animals, like peacocks, hornbills, lizards, fish, tortoises, snakes, tigers, elephants, and monkeys.

Mallebrein distinguishes six different groups of Kond and states that the existence of brass figures has only been reported in conjunction with two of them, the Malliah and the Desia Kond. Drawing on information supplied to her by Albert Gözelmann and Dagmar Stachowski, she comes to the conclusion that neither the Kuttia Kond nor the Dongria Kond worship any brass figures. In my own fieldwork, I witnessed the worship of brass items in several Dongria Kond villages, although animal figures are relatively rare, and only a few houses own as many items as the *jani* in Lekhpadar and Padangpadari. When the inhabitants of Lekhpadar, a village located in the northernmost part of Kalyansingpur district bordering Kalahandi, performed the buffalo sacrifice in 2002, four winnowing fans, two holding iron objects and another two holding brass objects, were placed near the *dharni*. The main items were an arrow (iron), a bow (iron), an axe (iron), a knife (iron), chains (iron), a bell (brass), a bowl (brass), an umbrella (brass), an elephant figure (brass), and a fish figure (brass). To explain the origin

---

63 Macpherson mentions the use of images made of wood and clay, not of brass, at the time of the human sacrifice in Goomsur: "In some parts of Goomsur where this practise prevails, small rude images of beasts and birds, in clay and wood, are made in great numbers for this festival, and stuck on poles, – a practice, the origin or meaning of which is not at all clear" (Macpherson 1852, 247).

of these sacred objects, one *jani* from a Desia Kond village told me the following myth:[64]

> In the beginning, there were four demons (*rakhyasura*) who ate everything, the mountains, the fields, everything. For this reason the gods sent to the earth four elephants that killed the demons and swallowed them. After that, new mountains came into being, and the fields started to grow. At that time, the human beings came from heaven down to the earth, and their numbers increased. When they were many, they went back to heaven to fight a war against the gods. In this war they obtained the weapons and brought them to earth. These weapons belong to the *raja*.

Among the Desia Kond, brass figures of animals, in particular peacocks and elephants with riders, are more common than among the Dongria Kond. However, a clear distinction between Desia Kond and Dongria Kond on the grounds of their use of brass figures is clearly not possible. Given the fact that members of both Kond categories participate in *kodru parbu* organised by members of the other category and taking into account the fact that many Desia Kond reportedly migrated from the valleys into the Niamgiri Hills, an exchange of ideas and material culture appears quite likely.

All of the metal objects worshipped by the Kond are usually preserved in the houses of certain families of high status who only take them out at the time of the *kodru parbu* and a few other festivals. Niggemeyer does not mention the worship of any brass figures among the Kuttia Kond but reports the existence of certain iron objects, such as knives, axes, chains, rings, and lamps, collectively known as *mala dupa*. These instruments are considered to have been given to the Kond by the creator goddess *nirantali-kapantali*, who brought them from a dark house inside the earth. At that time the *mala dupa* were crying, and for this reason the ancestors of the Kuttia Kond performed a sacrifice to them. In the same way, the Kond nowadays conduct sacrifices when the weapons cry (Niggemeyer 1964a, 200). The Kond ask them to bring the small amount of flesh the Kond can give to "their parents" (Niggemeyer 1964a, 200), which probably means to the earth goddess and her husband. In his descriptions of the buffalo sacrifice he witnessed among the Kuttia Kond, Niggemeyer mentions that following the killing of the buffalo, a blacksmith requested his share of the meat. The man justified his claims by saying:

---

[64] The connection between these iron objects, in particular the bow and arrow, and hunting or fighting will be discussed in more detail when dealing with the first and second day of the main festival (see below).

> When you [i.e. the Kond] were not yet born, the blacksmith was already there. He made the iron pillars to support the sky. At that time you were still sacrificing human beings. At that time the blacksmith gave to you the axe for hacking, the knife for cutting, the spoon for cooking. Nirantali-Kapantali lifted the sky with the iron pillars. At that time you gave the blacksmith the intestines of the animals, and since then the intestines of the buffalo have always been his share. Now I only brought you this knife. (Niggemeyer 1964a, 204; my translation)

Among the Dongria Kond, the greatest ritual attention at the time of the *kodru parbu* is given to specific old iron objects. They are preserved by high-status families in their houses, or sometimes also outside the villages in caves and trees, and reportedly stem from the time when the Kond practised human sacrifice. Among the iron objects, axes (*tangi*), knifes (*suri*), trivets (*halu*), and spoons (*hetu*) receive worship as representations of divine beings and at the same time are used during the *kodru parbu* – at least symbolically – as instruments for sacrificing the victim, cutting its meat, and preparing the feast. As in the past, the blacksmith arrives in the village on the eve of the festival bringing a few iron instruments, such as a hammer (*mutla*), a knife (*katri*), and a spoon (*hetu*). In one village I was told that the blacksmith, together with the *jani*, touches the buffalo's head with his instruments, and elsewhere that he renews the weapons by briefly holding them in the fire and symbolically hammering them afterwards. A blacksmith living in a Desia Kond village explained to me that his duty is to lift his instruments as a sign that the right time for killing the victim has come. Among the brass items, two objects have the greatest importance in the context of the *kodru parbu*, the pots that are taken out of a house or a cave before the sacrifice and an umbrella-like figure set on top of a long bamboo pole.

Brass images of certain animals, such as elephants and fishes, are worshipped by the Dongria as divine objects, but in contrast to other items, they neither play any major role in the ritual proceedings nor are clearly linked to any specific rights or claims to status. In my view, land ownership and socio-ritual status derive most clearly from the objects discussed in this chapter, i.e., the cooking utensils (*daka, halu, hetu*) for preparing the sacred food (*bana paga*), the instruments (*tangi, suri*) for symbolically sacrificing the victim, and the umbrella (*satara bonda*) representing the divine ruler presiding over the sacrifice.

5.4.1 Sale of village territory: Transfer of pots (*daka*), hearth (*halu*), and spoon (*hetu*)

When I first saw the *kodru parbu*, I noticed some old earthen pots and a few new ones in the goddess's house but did not pay much attention to them. These are such common objects in every Dongria household that I did not expect them to have any specific ritual significance. My opinion changed, however, when I attended a buffalo sacrifice in Mundawali, where on the first day of the festival a delegation of men walked into the nearby hills to a cave where they kept three brass pots (*kasa daka*). The name of the cave was Bamanadeo, literally meaning "Brahmin deity," and was apparently related to the sacrifice of a Brahmin girl a long time ago.[65] Every time one of the seven villages belonging to the Jakesika *muta* celebrates the *kodru parbu*, the organisers go to the cave, make a small sacrifice to Bamanadeo, and then take the three brass pots to the earth goddess's hut. Patnaik and Das Patnaik (1982, 167) report that people of the *pujari* category preserve such old brass pots for use the night before the sacrifice, when three girls take these pots and fetch water from a nearby stream to give the victim a purificatory bath.

In other places, I came across the use of earthen pots (*wirga daka*) that are preserved until the time of the next *kodru parbu*, when they are exchanged for new ones. In most places, they are kept in the house of a male villager who is considered to be a descendant of the original village founders. One or more of these pots are stored in the attic of his house, and inside are placed two metal objects, a kind of iron trivet called *halu* or "hearth" and a long iron "spoon" referred to as *hetu*. These cooking utensils are taken to the earth goddess's hut when the *kodru parbu* begins, and their function becomes apparent when, following the actual killing of the buffalo, a special kind of food named *bana paga* ("forest food") is cooked in the earth goddess's shrine.

The tradition of preparing *bana paga*[66] does not belong exclusively to the *kodru parbu* but is part of every elaborate sacrifice. The cooking and sharing of this kind of food mark the final stage of the ritual proceedings, which usually consist of four phases: first, the deities are called to the place of worship; second, the worshippers communicate with the deities either through the *daka jani*, who chant (*dakina*) certain ritual invocations, or through the *bejuni* and

---

65 The *jani* of Muniguda is said to preserve three strips of dried human flesh in his house. I personally never saw these strips, but everybody assured me that they are taken out of the house on the eve of the festival and kept near the *dharni*.
66 Among the Desia this sacred food is called *onda*, a Kuwi word that should not be confused with the Oriya term *onda*, meaning "egg."

504 —— 5 The clan sacrifice: Creating Niamgiri society

Photo 13: Pots placed near the earth goddess (at night in Mundawali, 2001)

her helper (*gurumeni*), who talk with the deities (*male wenbina*) and make a rice offering to them; third, young men kill the animals, offer blood to the gods, and place the victim's head in front of the deities; and finally, at the sacrificial site, rice is cooked in a new earthen pot placed either on an iron hearth or on three stones. The rice, together with some meat, usually the liver, is laid out on a large leaf plate by either the *daka jani* or the *bejuni*, who then offers it to the deity while repeating the worshippers' intentions in their performance of the ceremony. Finally, the food is shared by all present, the organisers of the sacrifice receiving their share first.

In the *kodru parbu*, the *bana paga* is prepared next to the earth goddess by the male members of certain households, referred to as *bana jani*. The old pots from previous sacrifices are placed next to the new pots, in which rice and the meat of the sacrificial animal will be cooked separately. Depending on the traditions of the particular clan performing the *kodru parbu*, this cooking is done either on the iron hearth or – when such an object is not available – on three conical stones standing near the *dharni*. The iron hearths are said to be of divine origin in the same way as the brass pots kept in the cave of *bamanadeo* are. The deities fashioned these iron hearths along with the iron spoons and brass pots and distributed them to the Kond, who settled in different villages.

The relationship between these cooking utensils, the *kodru parbu*, and claims on landownership only became clear to me when I heard about a dispute between Gumma and their former *mudrenga* from Lamba. As mentioned before, the Sikoka, who nowadays reside in Gumma, originally came from the valleys and only later moved into the mountains. At the time of their migration, they left behind the brass pots originally given to them "by the gods." While most of their relatives established villages in Muniguda district in the Niamgiri Hills, their own ancestors migrated further west into what is now Kalyansingpur district, where they bought the village land from the Timaka. Presently, a few members of the Timaka clan reside in a street in the town of Kalyansingpur, but the Timaka do not own any villages in the Niamgiri Hills. They are said to have moved further west, and Niggemeyer mentions their presence in the Kuttia Kond country (Phulbani district), where their settlements can be found in the extreme south-eastern part of the area. The Pusika of Lamba, a neighbouring village, were present as witnesses (*sakhi*) when the Timaka sold the village to the Sikoka.

A few years ago, this land purchase became the cause of a conflict between the Sikoka and the Pusika when the latter demanded money for their earlier role as witnesses of the land transaction. When explaining the reason for this conflict to me, the people of Gumma mentioned the words *halu hetu* ("hearth and spoon") several times, but at first I could not make any sense of this. Only after witnessing the use of these objects in the *kodru parbu* did I realise that the sale of land and the performance of the *kodru parbu* are linked. When I inquired a second time, people explained to me that the Timaka gave neither a hearth nor a spoon to the Sikoka at the time they sold the village. These items have to be handed over to the new owners as signs of their right to perform the *kodru parbu* to the earth goddess. Since the Sikoka from Gumma had not been given a hearth and a spoon, they possessed no definitive proof of their rightful acquisition of the territory. At the time they began preparing for the *kodru parbu*, the Pusika of Lamba approached them and claimed that they could prove these rights, since their forefathers had been witnesses of the land transaction. In return for this favour, they demanded a payment of Rs 2,000 from the people of Gumma. It seems that the Sikoka first paid the money but later reclaimed it and thereby aroused the anger of the Pusika, who had traditionally acted as their *mudrenga*. When the *kodru parbu* in Gumma began, the Pusika took the first possible opportunity to humiliate the Sikoka by attacking the sacrificial animal, which suffered several blows from an axe but did not die. Policemen were called to the spot in order to protect the buffalo and to keep away the Pusika, who were excluded from the celebrations. Since that time, relations between both villages have been strained, and their former cooperation and reciprocity at the time of festivals and weddings has been discontinued.

This case clearly illustrates the connection between landownership and the *kodru parbu*. In order to prepare the sacrificial food that is offered to the earth goddess to satisfy her demands, it is necessary to use the cooking utensils made by the gods. Without these objects, the sacrifice cannot be properly completed, and the *kodru parbu* will not bring about the desired results. My informants compared the purchase of a village with that of a house: when a person buys a house from somebody else, he purchases it including the hearth, the pots, and the spoons. In the same way, when the members of a local line acquire a village as their property, they have to be given *halu hetu*, "hearth and spoon," in order to prepare food for the goddess.

5.4.2 Clearing the village land: The axe (*tangi*) of the first settlers

Another object of great ritual importance at the time of the *kodru parbu* is an iron axe called *tangi*. The word is derived from Oriya, in which it means "ceremonial axe" as opposed to *tangia* or "working axe." The corresponding words in the Dongria language are *simeni* for the former and *krali* for the latter. Nowadays, only a few Dongria own such ceremonial axes, the blades of which are not straight but shaped like the wings of a bird.[67] They are said to be very expensive and presently only available at important markets such as the one at Lanjigarh, as they are no longer produced by local blacksmiths. The axe worshipped during the buffalo sacrifice may be called *tangi*, but most specimens I saw at first hand on such occasions resembled the simple working axe used daily by the Dongria for felling trees or cutting wood. Every village owns one *tangi*, which is usually preserved in the house of a *jani*, where it is kept near the central roof beam (*tudi pathei*). In Gumma, for example, a member of the local line of *icha jani* (small *jani*) kept the *tangi* in a bundle of cloth tied to the central beam. His ancestors were considered to be village founders in the sense that they had bought the land from the Timaka. In other places, the owners of the axe were regarded as

---

[67] Good paintings of the different kinds of axes can be found in Niggemeyer's (1964a, 105, 167) book. He distinguishes the "working axe" (Kuttia *kurari*), from the "bear-axe" (Kuttia *kakar tangi*) used as a weapon in war and from the "ceremonial axe" (Kuttia *tangi*).

Photo 14: Jani carrying the sacrificial axe (*tangi*) (Mundawali, 2001)

descendants of the village founders who had established the *dharni* stones in the village. These keepers of the axe were sometimes introduced to me as *gauntia*, a word designating a village headman in Oriya villages.

Every village owns only one such axe, usually the same person who keeps the sacred cooking utensils. It is taken out at the time of the *kodru parbu* and placed on a winnowing fan near the *dharni*. In many places, not just one village's axe, but all the axes preserved in villages belonging to the same *muta* are taken out at the time of the *kodru parbu* and collectively worshipped in the village of the organisers. In such a case, each *jani* who owns an axe brings it down from his attic and first places it in front of the wall (*handani kuda*) where all of his house rituals take place. A *beju* or *bejuni* invokes the deity of the axe and offers her rice, alcohol, and a chicken. Next, the axe is carried to the local *dharni*, where further offerings are made before the *jani* takes the axe from house to house, allowing each family to make offerings to the deity. Finally, he carries it in a winnowing fan balanced on his head to the village organising the *kodru parbu* that year. When the *jani* reaches the village border with his axe, the organisers ask him to sit on a cot and then carry their guest, now holding the axe in his hand, to the *dharni kudi*. All the axes are collected in a winnowing fan placed in front of the stone arrangement. Like the earth goddess, the *tangi* is considered to be a female deity and addressed as "our mother" (*ma aya*). Among the Desia Kond, I witnessed how shortly before the actual killing of the buffalo, the ritual specialist (*jani*, *bejuni*, or *dissari*) takes the axe and symbolically swings it at the animal's neck three times. Only then is a strong man allowed to come and actually put the victim to death by chopping off its head with a proper axe.

In settlements inhabited by Desia Kond, as well as in villages of Dongria Kond located in the foothills of the Niamgiri mountain range, the sacred axe is often not kept inside the house of the *jani* but instead outside the residential area. On the first or second day of the festival the eldest member of the founding lineage, together with the ritual specialist, brings the axe out of its hiding place and takes it back to the village where the inhabitants, including the different groups of clients, can worship it. The axe – in some places also more than one axe – may have been hidden either in a small cave in the rocks called Prahiwali (*prahi* = "old axe," *wali* = "stone, rock") or in the hollow of a tree standing next to the *jakeri* in the sacred grove outside the village.

In the first case, the *dissari*, together with some male villagers carrying drums, goes into the forest to the place where the axe is hidden. I observed this ceremony in three villages (Railima, Uparali, and Kadalichua), and each time the axe was kept in a small crevice between some rocks overgrown with bushes and creepers. The ritual specialist first removes the earth and leaves before putting his arm into the hole and bringing out a bundle of cloth containing the old axe in a dramatic gesture. As the *tangi* is considered to be a deity, it first receives an offering. The *dissari* pours some rice onto the bundle, and when a chicken pecks at least a few grains, this is interpreted as a sign that the deity has accepted the offering and is willing to be worshipped. If the chicken refuses to eat, all those present will talk to the deity, promising further offerings and asking forgiveness for possible mistakes or for their long neglect of their sacrificial duties. The chicken is killed on the spot, drops of its blood are sprinkled on the sacred object, and the animal's head is placed before it. Then the *dissari* removes the cloth and fixes the old axe head onto a new wooden handle. While the young men drum, everyone leaves the forest, and on reaching the path leading to the village, the *dissari* and the descendant of the village founder, the *jani*, take their seats upon a cot. If the *jani* has a son, he gives the sacred object to him, and all are carried into the village together. In a Desia Kond village I witnessed the two axes brought out of the cave being shown after their arrival in the village first to the Kond's clients, in this case the Dombo *barika* and the Lohar (blacksmith). The *barika*'s wife poured turmeric water over the axes and placed a mark on the ritual specialist's forehead before tying white cloths around the two sacred objects. Next, the axes were taken to the house of the local blacksmith, who offered a gold ring to them. Then everybody proceeded to the *jani*'s house, where a sacrificial post had been set up near his door. After some further offerings, the axes, together with the two buffaloes to be sacrificed at this village's two *jakeri*, were taken from house to house in order to allow each family to worship them.

When the axe is kept in a tree, preferably a mango tree, it is usually kept hidden in a knothole, as I witnessed myself in two different villages (Sana Bamanaguda and Dulumguda). From his house, where a special post has been set up to worship the axe, the *jani* is carried on a cot by the villagers to the sacred grove outside the shrine. They stop under the tree containing the axe, the *jani* climbs off the cot, and a *dissari* coaxes a chicken to peck at some rice on the *jani*'s feet. Then the *jani* climbs up the tree until he reaches the knothole where the axe has been kept since the last *kodru parbu* was celebrated. He brings out the sacred object, wrapped in a piece of cloth, and takes it to the *jakeri*. While he sits in front of the earth goddess holding the bundle with both his hands, the ritual specialist bends over him and suddenly becomes possessed by the deity. In trance, he moves to the different stakes set up for the sacrifice and embraces them before placing a sacred mark (*tika*), consisting of rice and turmeric, on the *jani*'s forehead. The latter, along with his younger brother or son, again takes his seat on a cot and is carried back to the village, where some women await them to wash their feet. In front of his own house, the *jani* unwraps the bundle, fixes the old axe head onto a new handle, and carries it to the western entrance of the village, where the Dombo *barika* is waiting together with his wife. The Dombo woman washes the *jani*'s feet, smears the axe with turmeric, and a chicken given by her husband pecks at rice on the *jani*'s feet and is then sacrificed in the name of the deity. Only then does the *jani* return to his house, where he ties the axe to the sacrificial post set up at his door. Later, the axe, together with the buffalo, is taken to every house in the village to allow each family to worship them with offerings of oil, turmeric water, rice, and chickens.

These events reflect the intimate connection between the sacrifice's patron (*jani*), the sacrificial instrument (axe), the sacrificial victim (buffalo), and the sacrifice's recipient (earth goddess). The Kond's clients recognise the central role of the *jani* in relation to the earth goddess by worshipping the axe. The axe can be said to symbolise the patrons' two main functions: they chop down the forest with the help of axes, thus turning the forest into cultivable land, and they kill the sacrificial victim with the help of this instrument in order to give its blood to the earth goddess and thereby ensure the fertility of the soil. Furthermore, there is one axe for each *dharni*, and therefore the axe clearly represents the earth goddess and the rights of its owner, the *jani*, over the village. The unity of the whole clan organisation, the *muta*, is established when all axes, in the figurative sense all local *dharni*, are assembled in one place to take part in the sacrifice. After the festival, all of the axes are returned to their owners and thus basically remain in one place, just like the earth goddess herself. All of this stands in contrast to the other two divine objects worshipped in the course of events, the "umbrella" and the knife. These objects are often identified not with single villages but with the whole clan organisation, and instead of remaining in one place, ideally they circulate within the *muta*.

5.4.3 Clan land and rulership: The umbrella (*satara bonda*) of the king

On the first day of the *kodru parbu* the most important event is the setting up of one or two long bamboo poles to which a finial is attached. Both objects are together referred to as *satara bonda* or simply *satara penu*. Whereas the axe (*tangi*) symbolises the earth goddess or "mother" and is kept inside the hut, the *satara penu* is a male deity and displayed in public on the village plaza. The word *satara* is probably derived from the Oriya term *chatra*, meaning "umbrella," an etymology supported by the fact that the Dongria attach a small shade made of bamboo strips or metal to the upper part of the post, just beneath the finial. The expression *satara penu* can thus be translated as "umbrella deity." The second term, *bonda*, is mentioned by Israel in his book on the Kuvi language of southern Odisha. His vocabulary list provides two translations of this word (Israel 1979, 395). First, *bonda* can mean "heart" and occurs in combination with *jela*, a word the Dongria use when talking about the "life" or "soul" of a person or object. Second, Israel gives "bud (flowers)" as a possible translation of the word.

Some days before the festival begins, a son of the local *jani* takes a bath, dresses himself in new clothes, and without having eaten anything, proceeds into the forest to collect one or two long, straight bamboo poles (*mading mara*), depending on the number of *bonda* to be worshipped in his particular village. He cuts the bamboo with a knife and carries the pole back to the village, where it is first placed in a stream for some time in order to straighten it.[68] On the first day of the festival (Friday), the pole is taken to the main village plaza and cut down to the appropriate length, usually twelve *hata*. If two poles are set up, they are of unequal length, one being twelve *hata* and the other thirteen.

---

[68] A more dramatic account of the collection of the bamboo pole is provided by two Indian authors: "Before four days of the celebration of the festival, the *Pujari* along with four persons proceeds to the forest being unnoticed by anybody to cut a bamboo pole of about 14 feet in height to prepare *Meria* Umbrella, called, *Chhatri*. This he cuts being completely nude, as it is reported. If the bamboo is cut in this manner the spirit who resides in the bamboo clamps may not do any harm to him. To make the bamboo pole strong, it is soaked for two days after which it is used as a stand for the umbrella" (Patnaik and Das Patnaik 1982, 165).

Photo 15: *Bonda* (Tebapada, 2001)

The segments of the bamboo pole are next painted alternately in red and white or red and black. If the organisers do not possess a small iron shade, a person experienced in making baskets will weave thin bamboo strips into an umbrella, which is fixed onto the upper part of the bamboo pole.

On the very top of the post, the organisers finally attach the finial, known as the *bonda*. The *bonda* is made usually of brass or iron and rarely of wood. Should the latter be the case, however, it is carved anew[69] each time the *kodru parbu* is celebrated. On the first day of the *kodru parbu*, the keeper of the *bonda* takes a bath before he cleans the holy object with a mixture of water and millet flour (*hiko gunda*) and decorates it with small chains to which small nacreous dia-

---

69 Professor Pfeffer and I saw a wooden *bonda* in Depaguda, a village near Kalyansingpur inhabited by the Desia Kond. The renewal of wooden objects representing divine beings is a widespread phenomenon in Odisha and carries particular importance in the famous Jagannatha cult. For an analysis of the renewal of the wooden deities of the Jagannatha temple see Tripathi 1978 and Hardenberg 1999.

Photo 16: *Satara bonda* with white cloths (Tebapada, 2001)

mond-shaped pendants are attached. Along with the *bonda*, an iron-tipped arrow, peacock feathers, and white cloths are tied to the upper part of the bamboo post. Not all villages own such an arrow,[70] but if one is available, it is kept together with the *bonda*. Like the peacock feathers, it is considered to be an object of kings. In some villages, the arrow stands for *lada penu*, the deity of war and hunting, and is not attached to the pole but driven into the ground near the *koteiwali* with the arrowhead pointing upwards.

Some Dongria expressed the view that the *bonda* was originally fashioned by the gods out of a metal unknown to human beings, at the time of the creation of the world. Others were of the opinion that their *bonda* was made from an amalgamation of gold and silver. It usually consists of a handle or shaft, into

---

[70] This arrow is used on various ritual occasions. Niggemeyer (1964a, 183–84) elaborately describes how the Kuttia Kond shaman removes diseases from the *dharni* with the help of an arrow.

which the top of the bamboo pole will be inserted, and a body that may look like an umbrella, have the form of a single upside-down bowl with a flat or pointed top, or resemble a cone comprised of different layers. Of all the different *bonda* I saw during my fieldwork, no two looked alike.

Like the axe, the *bonda* is preserved in the attic of a house, either in a casket or inside a closed earthen pot. A few days before the festival begins, the organisers send a delegation to the house where the *bonda* is kept. Unlike in the case of the axe, not every village owns a *bonda*; instead, all villages belonging to the same clan organisation ideally share one *bonda*. This *bonda* circulates within the *muta* in the sense that each village may retain the *bonda* until the next village begins the celebration of the *kodru parbu*. Then it has to part with the *bonda* and hand it over to the people who are organising the buffalo sacrifice next. Since villages belonging to the same clan organisation do not normally conduct the *kodru parbu* in the same year, each village can retain the *bonda* for at least one year. The same applies to the knife (*suri*, see below), which, like the *bonda*, circulates among the *muta* in the course of the *kodru parbu*. The connection between these two ritual objects and the clan is so strong that people define a *muta* by saying that it consists of those villages sharing the same "knife and umbrella" (*suri bonda*).

Apart from the *bonda* that moves from village to village, another type of "umbrella" exists that is kept permanently by one household only. This latter type of *bonda* is used in two different ways. In some cases, it is lent by its owner to the organisers of the *kodru parbu*, who have to return it at the end of the festivities. In other cases, the owner may only consent to the *bonda* being set up in his own village and perhaps one or two closely related villages. In the Jakesika *muta*, for example, seven villages of the same clan share two *bonda* of this kind, one of which belongs permanently to a family residing in the village of Kurli. Whenever one of the seven villages celebrates the *kodru parbu*, the people of Kurli bring them their *bonda* on a long bamboo pole, and as soon as the festivities are over, take it back to their village. In Gumma, on the other hand, one household possesses a *bonda* that is set up in the three places owned by the local lines of this settlement (i.e. Gumma, Waliamba, Kadengeyu). The same holds for another *bonda* owned by the Sikoka, which is used at the time of the *kodru parbu* only in two neighbouring villages, Goilunga and Penewali. In contrast to other *bonda*, this particular "umbrella" cannot be attached to a bamboo pole but has to be placed on the ground next to the *dharni*, as otherwise people are believed to die.

The situation is complicated by the fact that not all *muta* show such strong unity as is expressed in the sharing of the same set of sacred objects. The *muta* of the Huika clan, for example, owns a knife that travels from village to village with each *kodru parbu* but has no *bonda* and therefore does not set up bamboo poles in the course of the buffalo sacrifice. Other *muta* appear to be so segregated that only small units consisting of three to four villages exchange *suri* and *bonda*. The Sikoka of Kalyansingpur district, for instance, formed a *muta* of seventeen villages in the "times of the king" (*raja wela*) that later split up into smaller units comprising only a few villages. The people of Lekhpadar belong to this *muta*, and when they conducted the *kodru parbu* in 2002, they invited only Sikoka from two other neighbouring villages, Dongormati and Patangpadari, to their festival.[71] These three villages jointly own two *bonda*, one of which is passed around while the other remains permanently in Patangpadari. In the past, more villages, including those inhabited by the Desia Kond in the valleys, were part of this exchange circle, but later the Desia Kond began to celebrate the *kodru parbu* independently. For this purpose, the Desia Kond made new *bonda* or bought them in the market. The people of Lekhpadar claim to be the owners of the old and original *bonda*, which was presented by the king.

When two *bonda* are jointly owned by all villages united in a *muta*, these two objects are considered to be of unequal value. The *bonda* that is handed over from one residential unit to the next is regarded as the senior or "big umbrella" (*kaja bonda*) and is attached to the longer bamboo pole, while the second one is known as the junior or "small umbrella." In accordance with the hierarchy of the objects, differences in status exist between the people who preserve them. The wandering *bonda* is kept in the house of a person who is of senior status in comparison to the owner of the small *bonda*. In Gumma, for example, the *kaja jani* or "senior *jani*" has the right to retain an axe and knife in his house following the completion of the sacrifice. He carries the title *mutadhar* or "owner of the *muta*" and is of higher status than the *icha bismajhi* or "junior *bismajhi*" who possesses the second *bonda*, which does not get passed on to other villages. His status is also considered to be superior to that of the *icha jani* or "junior *jani*" who owns the axe (*tangi*) and claims to be a descendant of the village founders. The status difference between the two *bonda* is further expressed by way of their association with certain mountain gods. In Gumma, the senior *bonda* is identified with Nebaharu, the highest mountain of the area and the abode of the god *niamraja*. Most villages belonging to the same *muta* as Gumma are located in the immediate vicinity of this mountain. The junior *bonda*, on the other hand, is regarded as a representation of Anuharu, a smaller but nonetheless impressive mountain situated between Gumma and Waliamba. This seems to indicate that

---

[71] A third village named Puyubhata has been abandoned, and its former inhabitants now reside in Patangpadari.

the junior *bonda* is associated with the village territory (*padari*), whereas the senior *bonda*, which is passed on from place to place, symbolises the clan territory (*muta*).

Table 35: Hierarchy of "umbrellas" (*satara bonda*)

senior *bonda*	junior *bonda*
mobile	static
senior status group	junior status group
central hill deity (high)	local hill deity (low)
clan territory (*muta*)	village territory (*padari*)

Among the Desia Kond, I heard that the *bonda* was originally owned by the king of Jeypore. When the Kond and the king of Jeypore were in the midst of a dispute, the latter became so angry that he threw the *bonda* at them. They picked it up and, fearing his wrath, left the area and migrated north towards their present location near Kalyansingpur. The Dongria similarly draw a connection between the *bonda* and a king, saying that the latter once gave them the *bonda*, but they neither refer to a particular king nor make clear whether they are speaking of a human ruler or of their divine kings, the mountains. In recitations, great gods, in particular mountain deities, are addressed as *raja* (pl.: *rajang*), and in many mythological stories the high hills are given the title *raja*. In the context of the *kodru parbu*, the *bonda* is often identified with *niamraja*, the king of the Dongria, whose residence is the highest mountain of the area, or with other important mountain deities.

In my interpretation, the *satara bonda* functions as a kind of passage between the world of humans down on earth and the sky above where the gods reside. Depending on the deity, different objects may serve this purpose. In house rituals, for example, the Dongria tie a thread from the upper part of the *handani kuda* (the sacred wall) to the ground to allow the house goddess, *sita penu–lahi penu*, to come down to the place of worship. When summoning the same deity to the river, an iron-tipped arrow is stuck into the ground and a thread attached to facilitate the passage from the sky to the site where offerings are made. It is possible that a sacrificial pole serves the same purpose, since it provides a vertical connection between the ground, where the victim to be offered to the deity is tethered, and the realm above the ground, in an extended sense the sky. During the *kodru parbu*, as well as during the *bali yatra*, the Dongria and the Desia Kond use bamboo or teak poles several meters long and known as *satara* or "umbrella," which represent different deities. As mentioned above, the *bonda* on top of the pole represents a mountain god who is intimately connected with the area of the *muta* organising the festival. All of these mountain gods are, however, only junior relatives of the highest mountain, the *niamraja*, who is invoked on this occasion.[72] The mountain gods, in particular, are associated with high altitude and are said to live high up on the upper part of the mountain. When on the first day of the *kodru parbu* the *bejuni* climbs up the *satara bonda*, she symbolically goes to the abode of the mountain god. She leaves the ground, enters the deity's realm, and brings him down in her body.

5.4.4 Clan land and sacrifice: The knife (*suri*) that "eats" the victim

The second object circulating within a *muta* is a knife identified with a male deity called *suri penu* (knife god).[73] According to my Dongria informants, these weapons were fashioned by the gods and then distributed to human beings. The Sikoka of Gumma claim that they once owned three such knives, made of iron, silver, and gold respectively. The gold one was reportedly stolen, the silver one was lost during a *kodru parbu*, and now only the iron one remains. It moves from village to village in the course of the buffalo sacrifices celebrated by the *muta*. In the past, every Dongria man used to carry such a knife, which he kept inside his long loincloth (*drilli*), whereas nowadays these weapons have gone out of fashion. The knife worshipped at the time of the *kodru parbu* has a long, straight blade and is kept in a sheath. It is preserved in a black, hardly recognisable bundle of bamboo strips and cloth and covered with several layers of residue from the castor oil that is poured on the holy object on each ceremonial occasion. Like all the other metal objects, it is kept in the attic, in this case of the house owned by the man who also retains the *bonda* following the sacrifice.

---

[72] This corresponds to the information provided by Jena et al. (2002, 191): "The entire territory inhabited by the Dongaria Kondh is thought to be the kingdom belonging to Niyamraja. [...] Niyamraja is also believed to be the chief of the gods of small hillocks.".
[73] The word *suri* derives from the Oriya *churi* or "knife." In villages of the Desia Kond I have been told that both the axe and the knife are of female gender and together represent the earth goddess, identified with the Hindu goddess Durga. Both objects are taken out of their hiding place, be it a cave or a tree, because they want to "eat a child" (*toki khaibe*). In the past, the Desia Kond used the *tangi* to hack the human victim's neck, while the knife was used to pierce the victim's heart.

A few days before the festival begins, the organisers send a young man to their relatives who celebrated the last *kodru parbu* and retained the "umbrella" and the knife. The young man should ideally be a son of the householder who will later keep these holy objects in his attic, but in any case he must be mature but unmarried, i.e., belonging to the category of male youths (*dawe*). After receiving the sacred symbols, he ties them into a new piece of cloth, which he then binds around his waist. Concealing the objects in this way, he returns to the village, accompanied by his friends, on Thursday evening. The axe (female) and the knife (male) are tied together and placed on a winnowing fan near the *dharni* when the three main *jani* start their incantations during the night from Friday to Saturday. On Saturday the blacksmith arrives in the village with the tools he produces, such as a hammer, knife, and spoon, in the same way as he did in the past. These instruments are placed next to the *dharni* along with the old weapons preserved by the Kond. On the following night, when the time for the sacrifice has come, one of the ritual specialists takes the knife and looks through one of the holes in the wall of the goddess's house through which he can see the sacrificial victim tethered to the post.[74] He thrusts the knife through the other hole, thereby symbolically sacrificing the victim.[75] In the Dongria language this is called *suri penu tine* or "the knife god eats." This is the sign that the young men can rush to the fence and kill the buffalo. I personally never witnessed the moment when the specialist thrusts the knife through the hole, as normally the visitors hack the victim into pieces before the organisers have time to complete all the necessary rituals.

In summary, whereas the *tangi* is linked to claims of rights to a particular village territory, the *bonda* and *suri* represent the higher level of organisation, the *muta*, among the Dongria Kond. The senior *bonda* and the knife stand for the unity of the *muta* and circulate among those families in the *muta* who are recognised as having the most senior status. Before discussing the relevance of these objects for our understanding of Dongria ritual and political organisation (see conclusions), I will next discuss the different categories of ritual specialists who use these objects in their own particular forms of worship.

---

[74] According to a very well informed MPW (multiple purpose worker) of the local development agency, the *dissari* holding the knife looks for a certain star rising in the east. As soon as he can see the star through the hole, he performs the act of symbolic sacrifice by thrusting the knife through the hole.

[75] Among the Desia Kond, who do not build a sacrificial hut, the ritual specialist instead takes the sacrificial weapon and symbolically strikes the victim's neck with it three times.

5.5 Sacrificial specialists

The *kodru parbu* is celebrated by everyone, but in many ways it is an affair of the *jani*, who are the ones who own the important sacred objects and conduct many of the rituals. It is therefore necessary to take a closer look at the various categories of ritual specialists and the place of the *jani* in the sacrificial organisation.

5.5.1 Historical and modern accounts

The first detailed accounts of Kond ritual specialists were written by Macpherson, initially in his report on the Kond in Ganjam and Cuttack (Macpherson 1863) and later in his famous article on the religion of the Kond, first published in 1852 in the *Journal of the Royal Asiatic Society*.[76] In his first account, Macpherson (1863, 74) draws a distinction between the Kond priests who conduct the worship of the "Earth God" and the Hindu priests who serve the local gods and the goddess Kali. For these two types of priests, the Oriya titles "Jauni" and "Dehri"[77] are said to be used "occasionally."[78] In his later paper, the author distinguishes within the category of Kond priesthood between a "great" *jani* – perhaps a direct translation of the title *kaja jani* used by Kond today – who renounces the world and the householder priest who officiates at minor ceremonies (Macpherson 1852, 236–37).[79] The former has no property, avoids women and does not marry, resides in a filthy hut, walks around semi-naked, appears unclean, as he does not bath in water, and is, most of the time, intoxicated. This figure, described in terms reminiscent of Hindu ascetics such as the Aghori, performs the rites for the "great deities," in particular the human sacrifice to the earth goddess and the worship of the god of war, and has the right to receive a

---

[76] A later reprint of this account appeared in the book edited by Macpherson's brother (1865) after his death.
[77] The *dehri* appears to be similar to the *dihera* in Schulze's (1912, 4) account, where he is called an astrologer. Nowadays, these astrologers are often referred to as *dissari*, another word clearly related to the title *dehra*.
[78] This expression indicates that Macpherson thought these titles were becoming substitutes for what he considered to be the original titles, such as "Koottagottaroo," "Sorumba," and "Jackora," which were used in different regions (1863, 74). In my view, Macpherson confused two types of priests, the *jani* and the shaman, the latter indeed having different titles depending on the region.
[79] The Hindu "ministers" mentioned in the first account appear again in his second report, when Macpherson (1852, 236) states that only Kond priests can worship the god of war, while all other gods "accept divided service from their ministers."

share of the sacrificial animal, such as the feet or the head. Members of the other class of priests are excluded from performing the most important sacrifices but may conduct many other rituals, and in this sense "the two classes pass insensibly into one another" (Macpherson 1852, 236). In contrast to the great *jani*, the "householder" priests live like any ordinary man but eat separately from others and do not participate in wars and fighting. For their services, the community provides them with a few offerings, like vessels and a share of the harvest, but they receive no land, nor do the villagers cultivate the fields on their behalf.

Table 36: *jani* and *dehri* according to Macpherson

	Kond priesthood		Hindu priesthood
Title	*jauni* or *janni*		*dehri*
Status	great *jani*	small *jani*	Hindu ministers
Way of life	ascetic	householder	
Deities	earth goddess/ god of war	other important deities	local, lesser deities and Kali

According to Macpherson, a major part of a priest's work consists in divination combined with a period spent in a trance-like state, in the event that a person has been afflicted with a disease by a certain deity. In his earlier account, Macpherson (1863, 75) ascribes this type of ritual to the Koottagottaroo, while in his second report he only makes reference to "a priest," without mentioning any local title. Perhaps by the time of writing his second account Macpherson had begun to sense a difference between the *jani* and another type of Kond priest acting as a medicine man and shaman. Among the Kuttia Kond, the priest concerned with sickness and accidents is known as the *kutaka* (Niggemeyer 1964a, 158), a name clearly resembling the title Koottagottaroo mentioned by Macpherson. For divination, the Kond priest makes heaps of rice, dedicates them to different deities, and places some grains of rice on a sickle hung from a silk thread (Macpherson 1863, 75; 1852, 238). When the sickle quivers, this is taken as an indication that the patient is afflicted by the deity from whose rice heap the grains were taken. Calling out the god's name, the priest counts the number of grains in the heap, an odd number indicating that the deity is displeased.[80] In this case the "priest becomes full of the god, shakes his head wildly with dishevelled hair and pours a torrent of incoherent words" (Macpherson 1852, 238). The priests are said to have gained this ability in a prolonged state of confusion, sometimes lasting

---

[80] Among the Dongria, this kind of divination is called *kadi kama* or *panji kama*.

one to fourteen days, when their "third or moveable soul" is summoned by the deities, who instruct them in their duties (Macpherson 1852, 236). This knowledge can pass from father to son, but anyone can be selected by the gods to serve as a priest. Macpherson emphasises that a *jani* may exercise considerable power as an individual but does not unite with others and stands in a difficult relationship to the chief (*abbaya*) (Macpherson 1852, 238).

Modern ethnographers similarly report different categories of ritual specialists among the Kond. Niggemeyer (1964a, 158–64) stresses the difference between the "Janni," the hereditary "priest" of the village, whose particular duty lies in the worship of the earth goddess (*banga pinnu*), and the *kutaka*, a kind of medicine man and magician[81] who acquires his abilities in a dream in which he "marries" a goddess who henceforth assists him in his trance sessions. Usually one *kutaka* works for several villages, but sometimes two or three *kutaka* are found in a single village. Among the Kuttia Kond, most *kutaka* are men, but Niggemeyer also collected some information concerning female shamans, whose overall significance, however, appears limited (Niggemeyer 1964a, 163). According to Niggemeyer, the two categories of ritual specialists, *jani* and *kutaka*, are clearly separated but not in terms of their responsibilities for different deities. In his view, their work involves them in different social contexts: the *jani*'s rituals are concerned with the life of the community, while the *kutaka* is involved in the affairs of individuals who have been affected by diseases or supernatural forces (Niggemeyer 1964a, 163–64).[82] The same deities may be worshipped by both types of mediators, for example in the course of agricultural rites performed by the *jani* or in the context of healing sessions conducted by the *kutaka* (Niggemeyer 1964a, 164).

Table 37: Distinction between *janni* and *kutaka* according to Niggemeyer

	"Janni"	"Kutaka"
Level	community (village)	individual
Nomination	hereditary	vocational
Rituals	yearly rituals and festivals	healing rituals, trance and possession
Gender	men	mostly men, a few women

---

81 In Oriya, this man is called *gunnia*, a title carried by magical specialists throughout Odisha (see Otten 2006).
82 Niggemeyer does not mention Durkheim at this point, but his conclusion is clearly reminiscent of Durkheim's ([1912] 1984) famous distinction between priest and magician, between church and individual.

Macpherson's "filthy" "world renouncer" appears again in a relatively recent description of "specialists of knowledge" among the Dongria Kond (Jena et al. 2002, 105–28), although not as a *jani,* as in Macpherson's account, but as a *peju* or shaman.[83] The authors of this study distinguish six different categories in addition to the drummer, who will not be considered in this context. Among these six, the male shaman or *peju* demonstrates his vocation through various characteristics, primarily his unkemptness: "He is a man who rarely brushes his teeth and does not bathe daily, has a dishevelled appearance and is dirty in the eyes of the community. Similarly, he lives in a filthy house and wears dirty clothes" (Jena et al. 2002, 113).

Table 38: Ritual specialists among the Dongria Kond according to Jena et al.

Title	Status	Nomination	Gender	Function
jani	Teacher	hereditary	male	village priest, religious head
pujari	Assistant			village priest, cook
dissari	Teacher	self-chosen, skill	male	astrologer, medicine man
sisa	Assistant			
beju	Teacher	vocational, unkemptness	male	village shaman, medicine man, worship, sacrifices, invoking of ancestors and spirits
bahuki	Assistant			
pejuni	Teacher	vocational	female	village shaman, worship, sacrifices
gurumeni	Assistant			

The *peju* has a higher status than the female shaman or *pejuni,* since the latter are "not able to invoke and appease ancestral spirits," but both male and female shamans acquire their offices by receiving instruction from gods and goddesses. Both have students, known as *bahuki* in the case of a *peju* and *gurumeni* in the case of a *pejuni.* The *bahuki* will have received a divine calling but must learn the ritual techniques by attending the ceremonies conducted by his superior, the *peju.* The same holds true for the *gurumeni,* who will become a *pejuni* after having learnt the art of falling into a trance and dancing. These shamans are distinguished from the *dissari* and his assistant, the *sisa.* Like the *peju,* the *dissari* performs the functions of a medicine man, with the difference that he is not selected on the basis of certain signs alluding to his vocation but due to his skills and

---

[83] In some areas of the Niamgiri Hills Dongria pronounce this title *peju* (or *pejuni*), in others *beju* (or *bejuni*).

desire to become a ritual specialist. Both *peju* and *dissari* acquire their medical knowledge in dreams in which they are instructed by the deity *lada penu*, who is their ritual friend. The woman who marries a *dissari* must first be wed to a mango tree,[84] the abode of *lada* (Jena et al. 2002, 117). Another difference from the *peju* is that the *dissari* possesses astrological knowledge and can determine the correct time for performing rituals. The *jani* does not appear in this enumeration of specialists,[85] but his priestly functions are mentioned in the description of Dongria festivals (Jena et al. 2002, 198, 201, 204) and in the context of Dongria "political organisation," where the *jani* is characterised as the hereditary "head or priest of a village." The *jani* is assisted in his religious duties by the *pujari*, whose post is also hereditary.

The data I collected during my own fieldwork among the Dongria contradicts the information provided by Jena et al. on several points. My general impression is that we should abstain from searching for watertight categories, especially since some individuals have more than one ritual specialisation. Our understanding of the situation will instead be enhanced by analysing the ideas linked to these various titles and functions.

5.5.2 Forms of ritual specialisation among Dongria

In Macpherson's account of the Kond "priesthood," women are not mentioned as ritual specialists, and according to Niggemeyer, they play only a minor role among the Kuttia Kond. Among the Dongria Kond, the situation appears to be reversed, as almost all rituals are performed by women called *bejuni*.[86] From the time of their birth, these women are said to have a sign called *linga* on their foreheads, one that can only be seen by the initiated, i.e., other shamans. A shaman's child has a good chance of also bearing such a mark, but it is not necessarily passed down from parent to child.[87] Through this *linga*, deities can

---

84 The name of the ritual is *amba marata biha,* which means not "marriage to a mango tree" (Jena et al. 2002, 117) but "marriage in (or at) a mango tree." For the locative case in the Kuwi language, marked by the suffix *–ta* in the singular, see Israel 1979, 71–73.
85 The chapters of this book were obviously written by different authors who made little effort to compare their findings.
86 It is possible that this title derives from the royal title *baidya,* denoting a man with particular medical knowledge. During my fieldwork in Puri I came across the title *baidya* in the context of the Jagannatha cult as well as in the rituals of the Gajapati palace (Hardenberg 1999, 2000).
87 Elwin (1955, 133) states the same about the Soara shamans: "The office of shaman is not hereditary, but in practice it often runs in families."

enter the head of the *bejuni* and speak to her in dreams and later in trance sessions.[88] Every *bejuni* has her own personal deity particularly associated with her house. However, to become a full-fledged shaman, she has to undergo a marriage ceremony near a stream at a mango tree. Das Patnaik (1972) provides us with a detailed account of the four ritual stages that, over several years, turn a young *bejuni* into a chief shaman (*pat bejuni*). I personally witnessed only the last of the four stages, the so-called *ghanta parbu*, in which a sacrificial stake was erected near to a platform outside the village, alongside two water pitchers. As soon as the post had been set up, two *bejuni* fell into trance. They began dancing around the stake and asked the organiser of the festival to join them.[89] Holding a sari above their heads, the three moved around the stake near the platform before one *bejuni* placed her foot onto the foot of the festival's patron. I watched this ceremony together with the chief from Gumma, who commented on the event by saying in Oriya *bibaha heigola*, meaning "the marriage is complete." At the time, his explanation made no sense to me, but I now believe that through the *bejuni*, the organiser of the festival was wed to the deity.

In the same way, I interpret the "marriage" at the mango tree as a wedding between the deity and the *bejuni*'s spouse and not between her and the god. As in the case of the *dissari* described by Jena et al., the wedding at the mango tree involves the active participation of the spouse, in this case the husband of the prospective *bejuni*.[90] Das Patnaik (1972, 12) first states that a *bejuni* has a special relationship to female deities and a male shaman, a *beju*, to male deities. He goes on to describe the ceremony as a "spiritual marriage" between the shaman and her particular god, whom he calls the "ancestor spirit" (Das Patnaik 1972, 13).[91] From this description one gets the impression that the deities establish

---

[88] Otten (2006) provides a detailed account including a few case studies of such divine experiences by the *gurumai*, a female shaman among the Desia people of Koraput.

[89] I do not know whether any kinship relationship existed between the organiser and the *bejuni*.

[90] This appears to be a major difference from the initiation of the Sora shaman, who marries a "tutelary" spirit from the underworld. No human spouse has to attend the "wedding," which takes place inside the house in front of a painting showing the tutelary spirit's house. In this ceremony, the tutelary spirit is believed to take his "bride" down into the underworld (Elwin 1955, 156–58).

[91] According to Otten, the *gurumai* in Koraput are also considered to be married to a deity: "In order to confirm publicly that somebody is a Gurumai, a marriage (*biba*) will be established with the god who first entered her body. This ritual is called 'holding the winnowing fan' (*kula daraiba*). Every Gurumai, whether a woman or a man, is conceptualised as a 'bride' of the gods [...]. This conception of the Gurumai as female in relation to the gods confirms the hypothesis that humans in general are regarded as female in relation to the gods" (Otten 2006, 90; my transla-

marriage relations with human beings of the same gender. However, from the detailed description of the ceremony (Das Patnaik 1972, 13–14), another interpretation emerges. Das Patnaik reports that the "bride *bejuni*," together with her husband and an "assistant *bejuni*,"[92] goes to a mango tree near the stream and then invokes her particular god. She becomes possessed by her personal deity, represented by a water pitcher decorated with a garland, and begins to dance. At this moment, the husband gives her a sari and joins her in dancing. Various offerings are made to the deities, and the assistant *bejuni* places her right hand on both the bride *bejuni* and her husband. Then the *bejuni*, dressed like a bride, circumambulates the mango tree several times before the god finally leaves her body. A few days later they assemble at a marriage altar, and both the *bejuni* and her husband go around the mango tree seven times. After that, the *bejuni* places her right foot on her husband's left foot, while another *bejuni* kills a fowl. This is exactly the same ritual that takes place in the wedding ceremony before the bride enters her husband's house (see p. 337). On the third day, the water pitcher kept under the tree is removed and its water poured over the bride *bejuni* and her husband (Das Patnaik 1972, 14).

From these events we can infer that the *bejuni*'s husband[93] and not the *bejuni* herself is wedded to the female deity represented by the *bejuni* in the ceremony.[94] The deity as a bride marries a human being, i.e., the *bejuni*'s husband, through a mediator, the *bejuni*. In the case of the *dissari* described above, the male deity named *lada penu* marries a human being, i.e., the *dissari*'s bride, through a mediator, the *dissari*.

According to Jena et al., *beju* and *dissari* basically undergo the same ritual initiation; in other words, the *beju*'s wife, like the *dissari*'s, is wedded to her husband's "spiritual partner". During my fieldwork I met only one married *beju*, a

---

tion). Otten could not witness a complete *kula daraiba* (actually meaning "to make (someone) hold a winnowing fan") ritual, as these are quite rare, so it is not clear whether the *gurumai*'s human husband or wife must be present or not. She mentions that following this ritual, the *gurumai* cannot marry a man in the formal way (*boi bandiba*); she may, however, have been married in this way before becoming a shaman.

92 Otten (2006, 93) states that the new *gurumai* must find an older *gurumai* to teach her and help her to carry out the ritual, since otherwise she will find it difficult to be accepted by the community.

93 Otten (2006, 310–33) gives an excellent description and analysis of the so-called *bato biba* among the Rona, in which a child is married to a sacrificial post, her husband, before being "desacralised," i.e., returned to the community. Like the *gurumai* after she undergoes the *kula daraiba* ritual, such a child cannot marry again in the formal way (Otten 2006, 330).

94 This stands in contrast to what Elwin (1955, 130–41) reports for the Sora, among whom the shaman marries a "tutelary" spirit living in the underworld.

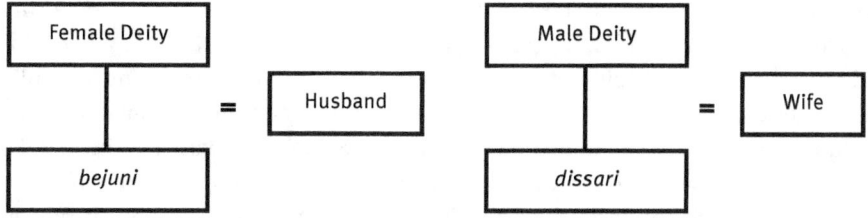

Figure 38: Marriage relation between gods and humans

man from the village of Lamba who served as a *jani*, could become possessed like a *beju*, and was summoned to ascertain the proper time for rituals in the same way as a *dissari*. A *dissari* can therefore be defined as a male, married person, possessing a particular knowledge of time, ritual techniques, and medicinal plants. These specialists appear to have a special relationship to the god of war and hunting, *lada penu*, who imparts his knowledge to them (Jena et al. 2002, 114).

All other *beju* I came across were unmarried, dressed in female clothes, spoke in high-pitched voices, and adopted behaviours considered to be typically female in this society.[95] Such unmarried shamans may despite their male physiology be addressed as *bejuni* or "sister", sleep in girls' dormitories, or reside in their own houses.[96] Often they entertain either casual or permanent homosexual relations with Kond men or with men from other communities, in particular Dombo and Ghasi. Compared to the *bejuni*, a male shaman has a higher status.[97] This becomes obvious at particular festivals when male shamans take the lead and conduct all important ceremonies.[98]

This raises the question of why such a wedding has to be performed at all. During my stay in Gumma, the eldest son of the chief *bejuni* married a young woman, a marriage that had been arranged in their childhood. The woman had shown early signs of her vocation as a *bejuni*, and everyone expected her to become a shaman in the near future. During the time of my fieldwork, how-

---

[95] For example, they do not get involved in fights, sit and chat with women behind their houses, and are very keen to take care of and to play with children.
[96] I never asked whether these *beju* undergo the same initiation ceremony as the *bejuni*. This would help us to understand the exact relation between the shaman and the deity. Does somebody play the husband of the *beju* or is he (she) indeed married herself to the deity?
[97] This may be because the *bejuni* menstruate, but I never directly inquired into this matter.
[98] Elwin (1955, 164–66) reports such "eunuchs" among the Sora who have a particularly high status among the shamans.

ever, she could not participate in public rituals, because the "marriage" at the mango tree had not yet been performed due to financial constraints. When I inquired why such a wedding at the mango tree had to take place prior to public acknowledgment of her status as a *bejuni*, I was told by a Dombo woman that the wedding is necessary to unite the woman's personal god with her husband's house. In other words, the human marriage must be accompanied by a divine marriage in which the in-married wife's god is joined to her husband's household. Until the *bejuni*'s "immigrant" personal deity has contracted such a marriage with her husband, the *bejuni* will not perform any rituals in her spouse's village. The question remains of whether it is the husband or his house deities who are married to the personal deity that his wife brought into the village. In the wedding ceremony at the mango tree described above, the husband also joins in the dance, and Das Patnaik (1972, 14) says that the "the *penu* [god] gets into both of them." This suggests that both the *bejuni* and her husband become possessed by gods. This, however, contradicts my findings that only people having the *linga* on their foreheads can fall into a trance. The question remains open until future fieldwork can provide additional data on this aspect of Dongria cosmology.

Neither *beju* nor *bejuni* are shamans in the sense Niggemeyer defines the concept in his analysis of the role of the *kutaka* among the Kuttia Kond. Like the *kutaka*, *beju* and *bejuni* are summoned to perform healing rituals when individuals suffer from diseases, but unlike the *kutaka*, they are not exempted from officiating at collective village festivals. On the contrary, almost all annual village festivals are conducted solely by *beju* or *bejuni* who summon the gods to the place of worship, fall into a trance, mediate between humans and gods in dialogues, allow gods to use their body for dancing, make offerings to them, and finally send them out of the village. What differentiates *beju* and *bejuni* from all other specialists is their relationship to a "spiritual partner" who enables them to fall into a trance (*banga ate*). No other specialist has this ability, not even the *gurumeni*, as Jena et al. claim. The *gurumeni* will never speak with the voice of the gods nor allow them to take possession of their bodies. A *gurumeni* has no *linga*; she is just an experienced, usually older woman who knows the complicated metaphors with which to speak to the deities[99] on behalf of the community. A *beju* or *bejuni* may perform the functions of a *gurumeni*, for example when assisting a more experienced shaman, but not the other way

---

[99] In the course of a ceremony, some of the observers, either men or women, may join the *gurumeni* in her work. Almost everyone knows some of these incantations and can use his or her knowledge to convey certain wishes to a particular deity.

around. Due to their ability to communicate with deities, *beju* and *bejuni* are the only ones who perform a certain type of ritual called *male wenbina* (in Desia Oriya *puciba*). They sit in front of a winnowing fan containing a handful of rice and rub it with their right hands while invoking the gods. By calling the names of different deities they can identify the one responsible for an illness or accident.

During festivals, *beju* or *bejuni* call the deities to the earth goddess's shrine in order to present offerings from the village community to them. A woman from each household approaches the shaman and hands over a winnowing fan filled with *akat manjing*. This kind of rice is preserved in each house in a gourd or small basket kept in the attic, above the sacred wall. It represents *lahi penu*, the deity of the house and the goddess of wealth, and portions of it are offered each time a festival takes place in the village. By offering this rice, each woman symbolically brings the wealth of her household as a gift to the deity. One woman after another hands over her winnowing fan to the main *bejuni* or *beju*. He or she rubs the rice with circular movements of his or her right hand while uttering verses expressing the demands of both humans and the deity. In my interpretation, this rubbing derives its meaning from the idea that the gods are asked to assemble in one place, the winnowing fan, where they receive their share of the rice offering. By rubbing the rice the shaman spreads the grains and thereby distributes the gift among all the deities called to come to the site of worship.

Jena et al. claim that one major difference between a *beju* and a *bejuni* is that only the former can worship the ancestors. This statement does not comport with my own observations; in fact, on the contrary, it is in most cases women who are concerned with making offerings to the deceased, to the exclusion of men. Jena et al. may derive their conclusion from the separation of the *jani* and the *beju/bejuni* in the context of house rituals. Inside the house, the male *jani* sits in a small room known as a *kandadae*, where he is assisted by at least one or two other men in invoking the ancestors, while behind him, in front of the wall named *handani kuda*, the *beju/bejuni* worships the deities. However, in my view, this division of labour is not based on the opposition between ancestors and gods, as can be inferred from the fact that during death ceremonies *beju/bejuni* get possessed by these ancestors inside the house. It rather derives from the distinction between the *jani*, who never falls into a trance, and the *beju/bejuni* who has acquired this ability. The *jani* recites certain verses while offering rice and alcohol to the ancestors as well as to the gods. This kind of incantation is referred to as *dakina*, a term Dongria also mention when asked to translate the Oriya term *puja* ("ritual offering"). The word *dakina* is applied to any offering involving ritual speech, including the trance sessions of the *bejuni*, but in a restricted sense it denotes a special type of recitation performed ideally by three *jani*.

In contrast to Niggemeyer and Jena et al., I am not aware of any hereditary specialisation among the *jani*. These authors seem to confuse three different meanings of the term: *jani* as a member of a particular status category, as owner of the sacred objects, and as ritual specialist. As mentioned above, each Dongria belongs to a certain status group, such as *jani*, *pujari*, *bismajhi*, and *mondal*, each of which is divided into senior and junior segments. Among the families belonging to the *jani* status group in a village, one will keep the sacred objects used at the time of the *kodru parbu*. In daily speech, the eldest man in this family will be referred to as the *jani* of the village, meaning that he keeps the sacred objects with which his ancestors performed the human sacrifices to the earth goddess. Membership in such a status group, in addition to the right to keep the old sacrificial objects, is inherited in the father's line. The knowledge needed to chant the proper verses to the gods at the time of worship is not, however, necessarily passed on from father to son. As Macpherson states, the *jani* are selected by the gods themselves, who train them. Additionally, they learn by participating in the ceremonies, when the main *jani* sitting in the centre utters verses that will then be repeated by the two younger, less experienced *jani* at his right and left side.

Macpherson gives an impressive description of the unkempt ascetic, whom Jena et al. seem to identify with the unmarried *beju* among the Dongria today. Both indeed differ from other specialists in that they are not married, and given that Macpherson does not clearly distinguish between *jani* and shaman, it is possible that he confuses the two in his description. Certain doubts remain, however, particularly because he explicitly states the high status of the "world renouncer", the "great *jani*," and mentions neither cross-dressing nor any other female characteristics of this group of specialists. The three *beju* I became familiar with during the time of my fieldwork[100] showed no particular lack of cleanliness, rather the opposite, as they were generally more concerned about their appearance than their fellow villagers. None of them lived in filthy huts, although at least one of them was given shelter in a rather small house at the rear of the village. I am not aware of an unmarried *beju* cultivating his own fields or having his own household in the same way as a householder, and in this sense a *beju* may indeed become an outsider like the ascetic described by Macpherson. However, in my experience, they join their family members in their agricultural work on the hill slopes, and their direct relatives as well as the com-

---

100 These are the *beju* from Parsali, Sana Denganali, and Mayawali.

munity at large take care of them. For these reasons I suspect that not the *beju*, but some of the *jani* who chant the verses to the earth goddess at the time of the *kodru parbu* are similar to the filthy "world renouncer" in Macpherson's account. This idea struck me when I attended the *kodru parbu* in Kuskedeli and two rather odd-looking *jani* turned up. Both appeared quite unkempt, had dishevelled hair, and wore unusual, dirty clothes[101] that they put on before entering the village. These ritual specialists receive the greatest respect of all and perform a highly specialised function that only a few people are familiar with (see below).

This leads me to a final point, namely the distinction between *jani* and *pujari*. To the best of my knowledge, the *pujari* does not have any particular office or function, although both Nayak (1989, 134) and Jena et al. (2002, 51) state that his duty consists of cooking sacrificial food and assisting the *jani*.[102] As in the case of the *jani*, we have to distinguish between status category and office. Thus, in certain villages, such as Tebapada, Parsali, and Lekhpadar, we come across families collectively known as *pujari*. Among them, one person, very often a *beju*, acts as the officiating priest at the festival most clearly identified with this status category, the *bali yatra*. Just as everyone is of the opinion that the *kodru parbu* is the festival of the *jani*, the *bali yatra*, with its worship of the god *bera*, is immediately linked to the *pujari*. As I have argued elsewhere (Hardenberg 2014), the cult of *bera* originated outside the Dongria Kond area and stands in clear opposition to the cult of the earth goddess intimately linked with the *jani* and Kond ritual traditions.

Table 39: Ritual specialists among the Dongria Kond according to Hardenberg

	Gender	Marital Status	Functions	Cult/Deity
jani	male	married	chanting (*dakina*), other functions (see below)	earth goddess (*dharni penu*)
pujari	male	married	cooking (*wajina*)	fire god (*bera penu*)
dissari	male	married; *dissari*'s wife married to male deity	chanting (*dakina*), applying medicine (*osa hina*), determining time (*joga*)	god of war/hunting (*lada penu*)

---

[101] For example, one of them wore a kind of army coat that was much too warm for the hot summer weather.
[102] In this sense the *pujari* resembles the *randari* among the Gadaba (see Berger 2015, 483).

beju	"female"	unmarried	healing (*male wenbina*), chanting (*dakina*), dancing (*endina*)	god of war/ hunting (*lada penu*)
bejuni	female	married; *bejuni*'s husband married to female deity	healing (*male wenbina*), chanting (*dakina*), dancing (*endina*)	personal deities
gurumeni	female	married	chanting (*dakina*), assisting *bejuni*	none

In the description above I presented a simplified picture of the functions of the *jani*. A closer look at the various categories of *jani* involved in the *kodru parbu* attests the intimate link between this kind of ritual specialist and the earth goddess.

5.5.3 Worshippers of the earth goddess: *janinga*

In earlier accounts of the buffalo sacrifice, no distinctions are drawn between the various categories of *jani* involved in performing the festival. In the context of my fieldwork, I collected information about six different types of *jani*. Arranged according to the sequence of their functions in the festival, these are:
1. *jani* (of the village; keeper of sacred objects)
2. *joga jani* (determines auspicious time)
3. *daka jani* (invokes the goddess)
4. *surjani* (thrusts a knife through the hole in the goddess's house)
5. *gripa jani* (offers victim's head and blood to the goddess)
6. *bana jani* (cooks food in the *dharni kudi*)

As mentioned above, families belonging to the status category of the *jani punja* preserve the sacred objects worshipped at the time of the *kodru parbu* in their houses, in particular the axe (*tangi*) and knife (*suri*). A young, unmarried man from the *jani* family of the organisers goes and fetches the knife from the place where it has been kept since the last *kodru parbu*. The same boy also climbs up to the attic of the house to bring down the axe, which is tied to the central beam of the roof. The axe is first placed in front of the *handani kuda*, where the shaman makes offerings of rice and sacrifices a fowl. Afterwards, the three *jani* who are specialised in ritual incantations come and chant their verses to the sacred object. When the axe is not kept inside the house but outside the village in a cave or in the knothole of a tree, the *jani*'s son is responsible for carrying it to the village after it has been taken out of its hiding place by one of the ritual specialists (*beju, bejuni,* or *dissari*).

Whenever the objects are shifted from one place to another, either between the house and the *dharni kudi* or between villages, only the *jani*, or more specifically one of his sons, carries the axe belonging to his family. The knife, in contrast, changes hands from the *jani* of the village that organised the last *kodru parbu* to the *jani* of the village that is to perform the sacrifice next. On one of the three days of the festival, the *jani*'s eldest son goes from house to house, holding the axe and knife in his hands or carrying them on his head. Just like the buffalo or the *satara bonda* when it is being taken from house to house, the young man stops in front of each door, where a woman pours turmeric water over his feet or head and pours a cup of uncooked rice into the winnowing fan held by the man who accompanies the *jani* on his tour.

The second type of *jani* has already been mentioned in the description of the rituals during which the earth goddess's sacrificial post is set up. His title, *joga jani*, derives from his knowledge of auspicious moments (*joga*) for performing certain ceremonies. Unlike the first type of *jani*, he often does not belong to the same village or clan as the organisers and may even be an outsider from a Desia Kond community or a Hindu caste. He is also addressed as *dissari* due to his knowledge of astrological calculations. His work includes finding the sacred trees for making the sacrificial post and determining the appropriate time to plant the stake and kill the sacrificial victim.

The highest status among all *jani* is held by the *daka jani*, the title being derived from his particular function, *dakina*, "to chant." For a complete ritual, three *daka jani* are necessary, one senior leader and two junior assistants. In some cases, the trio is made up of a father and his two sons, but this is not necessarily always the case. The assistants may be relatives or gifted students who have decided to learn their master's skills. Together, the three men are addressed by the villagers as *gurka*, an honorific title deriving from the Oriya word *guru* ("teacher," "spiritual adviser"), to which the plural suffix *-ka* is attached. In their appearance and behaviour they differ from other men. They do not mingle with others, remain in the *dharni kudi* most of the time, do not join the joyous dances of the other men, wear strange clothes, eat hardly anything, and seem to live on tobacco and alcohol provided by the organisers. Their main duty is to make the deities understand why the community is performing the sacrifice and what they expect from the deities in return. For this reason, they chant for many hours words only the initiated are able to understand.[103]

---

103 I was not allowed to record these incantations at the time of the *kodru parbu*, but I was

Photo 17: *Daka jani* and *bahuki* carried into the village on a cot

Their work ideally starts at night, when the *joga jani*, together with the villagers, brings the sacrificial post and plants it in the ground. From sunset until the time the stake is inserted into the ground early the next morning, the three *daka jani* sit in front of the *dharni* and chant their invocations. Ideally, every night of the following week, they continue their work. In practice, however, they generally stop after this first night and turn up in the village again on Friday morning a week later, when the main festival begins. The villagers await them with a cot at the border of the village and carry them in upon their arrival as a sign of their respect for the *dharni*. For the following two nights, from Friday to Saturday and from Saturday to Sunday, they recite their verses at the stones representing the earth goddess. All three sit on a cot facing east towards the *dharni*, with the leader in the middle. He usually speaks two or three words

---

permitted to record the utterances at the time of the *ambadadi yatra*. The reason given was that invocations during the buffalo sacrifice manifest a "great work" (*kaja kama*) not to be known to outsiders. Even if permission to record these chants were given, the recordings would probably be difficult to transcribe due to the fact that sometimes the three *jani* utter their verses at the same time. This makes the invocations almost unintelligible, particularly in advanced stages of the ritual when the three *jani* become intoxicated and can no longer pronounce the words properly. Whenever I asked other people to translate for me what the *daka jani* were saying, they had to admit that they themselves only understood bits and pieces.

that will immediately be repeated by his assistants before the next series of words is uttered. They keep up a certain rhythm while uttering the words and striking small bells against their knees with their right hands. Every ten minutes or so the three *jani* interrupt their work, drink some alcohol, and chat with those sitting around them. They will be remunerated for their work with rice from each household and about Rs 500, a rather small amount of money given that they work continuously for at least two to three nights.

My information about the fourth type of *jani* is rather limited, as these days this individual does not seem to play any major role in sacrifices. The title *surjaninga* is carried by only a few families, and members of this local line are not present in every village. I was given two explanations for this name. According to some, the people who keep the knife (*suri*) that circulates in the *muta* are called *surjaninga*. Others explained to me that the name is related to the functions of these *jani* at the time of the buffalo sacrifice. When the right time has come, the higher *daka jani* hands the knife to the *surjani*, who looks through one hole in the wall of the goddess's hut and thrusts the knife through the other. In practice, it seems that this function is mostly performed by the *dissari* (or *joga jani*).

The fifth type of *jani* carries the title *gripa jani*. I received different information regarding his particular duties during the *kodru parbu*. In some villages I was told that his task involves carrying the head of the buffalo from the place of the sacrifice to the *dharni*. According to my observations, the *gripa jani* performs this task in some villages, while in others the right to carry away the buffalo's head is not restricted to him. As Patnaik and Das Patnaik (1982, 168) state, the "*Meria* head is brought back in the procession by an outsider (*Padria*) other than the *Mutha* clan-members. It is tabooed for the *Mutha* clan members to touch the *Meria* head." Not every village has a *gripa jani*, but if this tradition is followed, as among the Sikoka, one particular family may possess the hereditary right to perform this work. A Dombo woman from Gumma informed me that the work of the *gripa jani* consists in cleaning the *dharni kudi* after the sacrifice with a broom and a winnowing fan. He takes the dirt to the border of the village, throws it away, and then whistles loudly through his still dirty fingers.

In Winfield's (1929, 47) dictionary, the word *gripa* is translated as "to cremate, burn the dead." It is possible that the human victim in the past was cremated after being sacrificed to the earth goddess and that the function of the *gripa jani* was to remove the corpse from the *dharni kudi* to a place outside the village for cremation. The idea that his function is linked to cleaning the *kudi* and that he is considered to be unclean may be an indication of his former role as a death priest. I personally never witnessed the *gripa jani* cleaning the *dharni kudi,* but it may be a tradition in the area where my informant, the Dombo woman, originally came from (Muniguda district).

In Lekhpadar, another Sikoka village in the Niamgiri Hills, the *gripa jani* was at the same time the main *daka jani.* I witnessed a fierce quarrel between him and the organisers of the *kodru parbu.* On the second day, Saturday, he began to demand certain gifts from the villagers of Lekhpadar, saying that he had the right to a share of the fruit cultivated in the village's orchards. When the people of Lekhpadar told him that they had already sold all the fruit and "eaten the profit," he became very angry and shouted at them. A dispute broke out until some Dongria began to intervene, saying that that "neither the buffalo nor the *gripa jani* should cry during the *kodru parbu*" and that "nothing will grow in the twelve *padari* when the *gripa jani* is not satisfied." The dispute could not be settled by the next day, when, on the morning following the sacrifice, the *gripa jani* sat on a cot in front of the sacrificial stakes and refused to perform his work. At that point, it was explained to me that the *gripa jani* has to take some blood from the sacrificial site in a cup or in his hands and carry it inside the *dharni kudi.* There he offers the blood to the stones representing the earth goddess before whistling loudly through his bloody fingers. After long discussions, the organisers finally tied a white *dhoti* around the *gripa jani* and promised to fulfil some of his demands. Only then did he get up, put some of the bloody earth into a cup (*tale*) with both his hands, and take it as an offering to the *dharni.* After that, others took the heads of the four buffaloes sacrificed that morning into the hut. Later the same day, the *jani* and his sons went from house to house to receive offerings, most probably for their services as *daka jani.* His sons carried a winnowing fan with a measuring pitcher (*mana*). Each woman gave one pitcher of rice and a ten-rupee note and poured some oil over the three *jani.*

The final type of *jani* is responsible for preparing food at the end of the *kodru parbu.* After the killing of the buffaloes in the morning, this man cooks rice inside the *dharni kudi* in the evening. In order to do so, he uses a new pot and the spoon preserved from the time of the human sacrifice. This rice is referred to as *bana paga* or "forest food." It is first served to the earth goddess, accompanied by meat, before the descendants of the village founders, together with the main priests, sit down and consume their share. Then other villagers belonging to the clan of the organisers are allowed to partake in the feast.

5.6 Performing the sacrifice

When I first came to the Niamgiri Hills in 2001, I visited a Dongria village where the people were busy preparing for the buffalo sacrifice. I inquired about the events that would take place, and instead of giving me an elaborate answer, a young man recited three verses that capture the essence of the ritual activities:

> *sukrawar satar line*
> *saniwar desa runda ane*
> *adiwar dine kodru mada ane*

These lines contain a mixture of Dongria and Desia terms – an indication that they may be part of a local song – that I only slowly began to understand in the course of my fieldwork. The verses mention the three main days of the festival, *sukruwar* or Friday, *saniwar* or Saturday, and *adiwar* or Sunday. When I asked the young man what *satar line* meant, he translated it for me using the Oriya expression *debata tiar*. The word *debata* means "deity," while *tiar* denotes the act of standing, so that the first line can be translated as "on Friday the deity will stand." The first day of the festival is thus associated with the setting up of the *bonda* described above, which is fixed to a long bamboo pole.

When I asked about the meaning of the second verse, the young man told me that on Saturday people will assemble to share a feast (*bhoji heba*). Only when I became more familiar with the local language and the ritual events did I began to have doubts about the accuracy of this translation. On Saturday no collective feast takes place, and instead each family prepares food in their house and invite relatives and friends to share rice and sacrificial meat with them. I now think that the verse refers to another event that takes place on Saturday, namely the arrival of guests from all over the hills. The word *desa* literally means "country" but in the figurative sense also denotes the people who "assemble" (*runda ane*) in the village as representatives of their territory. In other words, Saturday is identified as the day when not only relatives but visitors from all directions come together in the village that is celebrating the *kodru parbu*.[104]

Finally, on Sunday the buffalo (*kodru*) will be killed. The expression used is *mada ane*, the first word clearly derived from the Oriya verb *mariba*, "to beat" or "to kill." In everyday speech, *mada ane* also means "a fight will take place," and when I first experienced a *kodru parbu*, I began to understand the similarities between a fight and a sacrifice. On Sunday morning, young Dongria rush to

---

104 This interpretation corresponds to Nayak's (1989, 169) findings: "the assemblage of the non-kin on the eve of the sacrifice is called *desa-rundam*."

the sacrificial site and strike the victim with their axes until it dies. In the course of these events, one or more young men usually get hurt, sometimes intentionally, as in a "fight" (*mada*).

These three verses capture some of the regular elements of a festival that may feature many different local variations. Every *muta* or clan-based sacrificial organisation follows its own peculiar traditions, even within the rather small area of the Niamgiri Hills. The scope for variation increases when we leave the hills and move into the valleys of the Desia Kond, where we come across quite different traditions. In my own fieldwork, I observed the festival in Dongria and Desia Kond villages, but for purposes of this study, I restrict myself to describing the festival among the former and refer to the Desia Kond only in order to indicate certain major differences. In my description, I focus on one particular *kodru parbu* I observed in the village of Tebapada in the year 2001. There are two main reasons for this: first, I was able to collect enough data to provide a relatively complete picture of this particular sacrifice, and second, this festival was not too complex, as it involved only one village territory, and its relative simplicity enables us to grasp some of the basic sequences of the event. Given that a single ethnographer can never document everything at one time, simply for the reason that sometimes several rituals take place simultaneously but in different locations, or because he or she will be informed too late or not at all about an important event, the field notes I gathered concerning the *kodru parbu* in Tebapada do not offer a complete picture of the whole festival. In order to provide a more comprehensive account, therefore, I refer the reader at important points to festivals I observed in other villages.

5.6.1 Preparations

In 2001, the inhabitants of a small village named Tebapada (no. 62 on the map in section 3.4.4.2) celebrated the *kodru parbu*. The village belongs to the Sunakhondi Grama Panchayat of Rayagada district and is located in the south-western foothills of the Niamgiri mountain range. It consists of eleven Dongria houses standing in two rows aligned on the east-west axis, as well as three Dombo houses built in the western corner of the settlement. The majority of households belong to the Kadraka clan, whose members claim ownership of the village territory (*padari*). The Kadraka of the Niamgiri Hills differ from other clans with regard to their status categories, since they do not have any local lines of *bismajhi*. Instead, all Kadraka are assigned to one of four status categories: *jani*, *pujari*, *saanta*, and *kirchani*. These are ordered hierarchically in terms of seniority, the *jani* having a higher status than the *pujari*, and the *saanta* being senior to the *kirch-*

ani. The latter pair correspond to the status categories of *mondal* and *bismajhi* in other clans. On the level of local lines, each category is again divided into senior and junior subdivisions, although the words used to mark this distinction differ slightly from those used by other Dongria.[105]

The Kadraka as a whole are very widespread in Dongria and Desia country and are identified with the *bagha* or "tiger" clan. Among them, the *pujari* category dominates, and accordingly most people in Tebapada and some of the adjacent villages belong to this category, whose members are locally referred to as *pudria* (pl.: *pudrenga*). Tebapada belongs to one *muta* consisting of a total of twelve villages, most of them located in the Niamgiri Hills, while others can be found in the foothills and valleys. They are 1. Panchkodi; 2. Katigucha; 3. Kadrakabondeli; 4. Damanapanga; 5. Tebapada; 6. Padarmali; 7. Tamkaseli; 8. Taripayu; 9. Giriguda; 10. Badaduari; 11. Puibata; and 12. Kodrukheri. These twelve villages jointly own one sacrificial knife that is passed on from place to place with the celebration of each *kodru parbu*. In what follows I give a detailed account of the events I observed in 2001 during the preparation for and the actual performance of the sacrifice in Tebapada. Where necessary, the description is complemented by data collected in other villages.

When I first visited Tebapada in early March 2001, villagers were making plans to build the sacrificial site but had not yet begun to construct the *dharni kudi*. The wooden remains of the hut that had been set up for the goddess during the last *kodru parbu* at least ten years ago were still standing in the eastern part of the village. Most of the posts and beams were gone, but the two central pillars were still strong enough to be used again. Nobody was able to tell me exactly when the festival would start, but plans were made to perform the sacrifice in the following month, known as *caitra* (March-April) in Oriya. In order to give me a demonstration of how they would celebrate the festival, the young men took out their large conical drums (*niseni* or *dhapu*), put on anklets with small bells (*muyang*), and began drumming and dancing counter-clockwise around the earth goddess's old post.

When I arrived in the village again on March 21, things had changed considerably. A week before, on March 14, the male villagers, together with their "clan brothers" (see below), had set up the wooden frame of the hut and built the walls out of bamboo wattle. The organisers had served a simple meal of rice and boiled pulses to everybody after the work had been completed. On the following day, the women of the village had begun to plaster the walls with mud

---

[105] For example, for the junior subdivision Kadraka use the word *una*, which has the same meaning as *icha* ("small," "junior") but is more typically used by Desia Kond.

and clay, make a new earthen platform for the *jakeri*, and smear the floor with cow dung. To make the hut more attractive, they had built a small platform with bricks around the inner walls of the hut. The work had been carried out over five days, ending on March 20. On the next day, when I visited the place again, young men from different villages arrived in Tebapada carrying long bamboo poles for the roof of the goddess' hut. Not all of these helpers were of the Kadraka clan, but they all came from one of the four Kadraka villages that joined the organisers as "clan brothers" in their work. All four villages are located not more than half an hour's walk from Tebapada in different directions, and together they form a cooperative unit of villages jointly celebrating the *kodru parbu*: Tebapada, Kadrakabondeli, Padarmali, Panchkodi, and Tamkaseli.[106] Their main duty is to build the goddess's hut, and in recognition of their cooperation the organisers hold a feast on the day they finish the roof. For this purpose the men killed a buffalo (Rs 1,500) in a non-ceremonial way, while the women cooked rice and pulses. As is the case at all these feasts, the male villagers met in public to consume the food, while the women and small children ate their share later inside their houses. The feast was not only attended by people from the "clan brother" villages. Around midday, a few men from Patalamba had arrived carrying bamboo for the roof. When I inquired why these people belonging to the Sikoka clan had joined in the work, people informed me that these young men were *mudrenga* or "protectors," who offer their help like "brothers." The "protectors" remained in the minority, since their main day of work was yet to come. The Dombo of the village participated in the feast, although they had not joined the others in building the sacrificial hut. They had, however, bought the sacrificial animals and were now taking care of them. In their part of the village, the Dombo *sahi*, the *meria* was roaming around freely. The victim was a relatively unimpressive, young buffalo that the villagers had purchased for Rs 2,500.

On the day of my visit (March 21), the people of Tebapada were making more concrete plans concerning the timing of the festival, and most people agreed to celebrate the three main days around the full moon on April 8. However, on March 28, I met a few Kadraka men who informed me that the festival had been postponed for a week due to a ceremony in their brother village of Kadrakabondeli. A year previously, a fire had devastated almost the entire village, and the villagers had interpreted this event as an expression of the wrath of their vil-

---

106 This ritual unit overlaps with the modern revenue unit known as *mauza*. Three of the brother villages (Kadrakabondeli, Padarmal, and Panchkodi) fall into the same *mauza* as Tebapada, but unlike the sacrificial unit, the *mauza* also contains a village named Railima belonging to a different clan (Huika).

lage gods, in particular the earth goddess. Before celebrating the sacrifice to the earth goddess in Tebapada, they decided to make an offering to the local *dharni* of Kadrakabondeli in order to satisfy her first.

On April 4, the villagers of Tebapada arrived in the village of Parsali with two buffaloes. At that time I was living in a house associated with the project settlement of the Dongria Kond Development Agency, which is located a few hundred meters from Parsali. The young men carried sticks with which to drive the two buffaloes, led by ropes, through the mountains and show them to their relatives. One of the buffaloes was the *meria* I had already seen in the Dombo *sahi*; the other had only recently been purchased and was destined to be sacrificed at the end of the festival in a ceremony called *ambadadi yatra*. Starting at the house of the main *jani*, the buffaloes were led from door to door to be given rice, bathed with turmeric water, and anointed with castor seed oil. The visitors had come to this particular village with their buffaloes because the people of Parsali were intending to help them as "protectors." On that day, they visited a total of four villages, two of which belonged to their "clan brothers" (Padarmali and Tamkaseli) and two to their "protectors" (Parsali and Tuta). This was only the first of several such tours, during which the men play their drums and can be heard far and wide throughout the mountains.

On Sunday, April 8, the "brothers" from Kadrakabondeli sacrificed several animals to their village deities because of the fire that had destroyed most of their houses. On the same day, the young men from Tebapada went into the woods and returned with two pieces of teak. Out of these they fashioned the *panikimunda*, which was set up near the *koteiwali* in the early hours of the morning. As an offering to the deity, the villagers sacrificed a white ram, hung its head on the post, and held a feast with its meat.[107]

Early in the morning of April 10, a *dissari* from Phakeri (clan: Ataka) went out into the hills to search for a teak tree to use for the construction of the sacrificial stake (*joga munda* or *kodru munda*). He was accompanied by two men, one from the local dominant clan (Kadraka) and one from the Sikoka clan. The latter's family originally came from Phakeri, the main "protector" village of Tebapada. Both were selected on the strength of their skill in carving the stake. They returned in the morning carrying one log of teak wood (three and two-thirds *hata*), which they placed near the goddess's hut before giving it its proper form and painting red stripes on it.

---

107 I was unable to observe these rituals in Kadrakabondeli and Tebapada (although I did observe them in other places), because I decided to attend the *kodru parbu* celebrated on the same weekend in another village, named Railima.

On the next day (April 11), at the time the cock crowed, the *dissari* planted the stake in a hole in the ground east of the hut. After that, during the morning, the *bejuni* of the village welcomed the deity by dancing in front of the stake and presenting the deity with the rice offerings from each household. In the late morning of the same day, more and more groups of young men, some drumming and dancing, poured into the village. A few of them came from "clan brother" villages, but the majority belonged to one of five villages where the "protectors" of the Kadraka reside: Phakeri, Patalamba, Bangapadi, Tuta, and Parsali. Five "clan brother" villages were thus joined with five "protector" villages in an organisation of mutual help. This unit of five villages, the exact composition of which is subject to change, can be seen as the subdivision of the larger *muta* that actually organises and performs the *kodru parbu*. The other villages belonging to the *muta* of either "clan brothers" or "protectors" come as guests but do not necessarily play the same central role in the preparations and actual conduct of the festival. Among the five villages of "protectors," a still smaller subdivision consisting of two villages was expected to fulfil all major duties in the festival. These were the villages of Phakeri and Patalamba, of unequal size, since the former is one of the largest villages in the area with more than sixty houses, while the latter has hardly more than ten houses. However, size was not mentioned as a reason for why Phakeri was considered to be the "great protector" (*kaja mudrenga*) and Patalamba the "small protector" (*icha mudrenga*). This hierarchy was said to be based on "seniority" in the sense that the relationship between Tebapada and Phakeri was already in existence "at the time of grandfathers" (*tadi wela*), while the mutual cooperation between Tebapada and Patalamba was of relatively recent origin. Moreover, close affinal links existed between the former two villages and their respective clans. Among the nine Kadraka households of Tebapada, six men were married to Sikoka women, and four of these women came from Phakeri. The two families not belonging to the dominant local clan were both from the Sikoka clan, and their fathers had probably remained in Tebapada after having married Kadraka women. In a reflection of these close affinal ties, the people from Tebapada referred to the "protectors" of the Sikoka clan as *mama* ("MB/FZH") and to their villages as *mama nayu* ("MB/FZH village"). Furthermore, the young men addressed each other as brothers (*tada-buda*), and when I asked why, I was told that their relationship was one of *mehna tai* ("PosSbC"), literally "cross-brothers."

On this Wednesday, at least forty to fifty "protectors" arrived in the village carrying dozens of long bamboo poles. They split each pole into four long pieces and immediately began building fences around the village (*sala bada*) and the sacrificial stake (*garada*). Others were busy building the wall (*palawara*) behind the *koteiwali* when men from "clan brother" villages arrived and joined the "protectors" in their work. After some time, I asked a few Dongria who were sitting with me near the *dharni kudi* and observing the different activities whether my impression that "protectors" and "clan brothers" were working in different parts of the village was correct. They confirmed that the *mudrenga* do indeed carry out most of the work east of the *jakeri*, whereas the organisers and their brothers build the fence in the western part of the settlement. In this village, unlike in some others, the Dombo's houses were included within the fence.

While the work was still going on, one of the organisers brought a cow[108] to the village plaza and killed it with a single stroke, using the sharp side of his axe. Two Dombo men turned up and skinned the animal there on the spot.[109] Once the hide was removed, the Dongria began to cut the animal into pieces and remove the flesh from the bones. The head and the bones were set aside for the people of Tebapada, while the flesh was cooked in large aluminium pots inside the village. At the same time, the women of the village began to boil rice and millet in another corner of the village. Around midday, the men had completed their work and began drumming and dancing through the village. After some time, the *kajaru*, literally the "senior people" of both organisers and "protectors," called a meeting in the *dharni kudi*. While they themselves sat down on cots around the *jakeri*, other men piled into the hut in order to listen to the discussion between the elders. During this meeting the date for the festival was finally fixed and the major tasks distributed among the people present, including the nomination of those men who would protect the buffalo during the night before the sacrifice.

When the meeting was over, the people from Tebapada invited their "protectors" for a drink, an event for which they had bought a whole jerkin of country liquor from the Dombo. In good spirits, those *mudrenga* selected to guard the victim took hold of the two buffaloes and drove them to the house of Kadraka Muni,

---

108 It is quite unusual to offer beef on such an occasion. In most other villages, buffaloes were killed for the feast attended by the "protectors." One explanation may be that these Kadraka live in close vicinity to the Desia Kond, and some of their "clan brothers," for example the people of Tamkaseli, who reside in the valleys rather than in the hills, follow marriage practices typical for the Desia rather than the Dongria Kond. Thus, a young man from Tamkaseli once explained to me that they marry their cross-cousins (*mehna tangi*), and unlike the Dongria, who present buffaloes for the wedding feast, they slaughter cows in order to entertain their wedding guests. If this is correct, the killing of a buffalo for the feast for the "protectors" stresses the affinal character of the relationship between the Kadraka and the Sikoka.

109 This work is often performed by Dombo, not because of any considerations of impurity, but rather because they typically deal in these hides. After cutting the hide off in one piece, they carefully remove all remaining flesh and then dry it on the ground in front of their houses. They later sell the dried hide in the city to members of a Muslim caste locally known as Pathan.

a blind man in his forties who was considered the village chief. He, like most other Kadraka families in Tebapada, belongs to the *pujari* status category. The *mudrenga* hit the roof of the house with their bamboo sticks and demanded offerings for the buffaloes. The village chief's wife offered the victims rice to eat and anointed them with turmeric and oil before handing over some rice and ten rupees to two Sikoka men who were following the others and carrying a winnowing fan. In this way, the "protectors" went from door to door, beating their sticks on the eaves of the houses in jest. At the end of this tour, they counted the money and went straight to the Dombo *sahi* to purchase more country liquor.

At that point, one of the Dombo arrived with three more buffaloes that he had taken to the woods for grazing. Five buffaloes were now assembled on the village plaza, all of them destined to be killed in connection with the *kodru parbu*, but by different people and on different occasions. One buffalo was to be sacrificed on Sunday morning to the earth goddess, and another one at the end of the festival near a mango tree. A third one had been presented as a gift to the people of Tebapada by the "protectors" and was to be slaughtered for a feast for the organisers, after the completion of the festival. The last two buffaloes were purchased as counter-gifts to the "protectors," the "senior" ones from Phakeri and the "junior" ones from Patalamba, and would be handed over to them after they had performed their duties.

When the Sikoka returned from the Dombo *sahi*, they were called to sit down near the *dharni kudi*. The organisers had tied the two victims to the earth goddess's sacrificial stake, and a woman from each household had come and placed a plate with boiled rice and pulses in front of them. When the animals had stopped eating the offerings, the organisers took the food to a few of their "protectors" and asked them to consume it. A little later, all *mudrenga* were invited to attend the main feast, which consisted of cooked beef, boiled rice, and millet served on large leaf plates. After the feast, all the visitors left the village, and the people of Tebapada could eat their share of the food. The next day, the men were busy collecting wood, cutting it into pieces, and piling it up in stacks in front of their houses. The reason behind this is that once the festival has begun, the villagers are no longer allowed to go into the woods to collect firewood.

5.6.2 *sukruwar satara line* ("on Friday the umbrella will stand")

The major event on this first day of the sacrifice is the setting up of the *satara bonda* in front of the stone representing the male principle, the husband of the earth goddess. For this occasion a number of visitors come to the village, the most important among them being the brothers, who bring their sacred objects, the protectors, who help to decorate the sacrificial site, and the friends, i.e., a delegation from those villages with which the organisers have a particular relationship that may have been in existence for many generations. All of them are in a way "brothers" of the organisers, since they cannot kill the sacrificial buffalo in this particular village. On the other hand, their relationships to the organisers also differ. The clan brothers and the organisers exist in a hierarchical relationship, as they are either "older" or "younger," or consider themselves to be of higher or lower status depending on the particular status objects owned and displayed by them on the occasion of the festival. The protectors are not from the same or another brother clan, but instead from a clan into which the organisers may potentially marry. In this sense they are affines, but on this occasion can be viewed more as cross-cousins. Like cross-cousins, who help each other on different occasions, the *mudrenga* protect the organisers' buffalo. Furthermore, in the same way that people belonging to the cross category may not marry each other (see p. 211), the *mudrenga* may not kill the buffalo. People from Tebapada, for example, referred to the "protectors" of the Sikoka clan as *mama* ("MB/FZH") and to their villages as *mama nayu* ("MB/FZH village"). In addition, the young men addressed each other as brothers (*tada-buda*), and when I asked why, I was told that they stand in a relationship of *mehna tayi* ("PosGC"), literally meaning "cross-brothers". Finally, the friends, like the protectors, should not kill the animal, but in contrast to the *mudrenga* they are also excluded as marriage partners. Unlike the clan brothers, they are neither superior nor inferior; rather, their relationship with the organisers should be characterised by equality, love, and affection.

Arrival of brothers (*tada-buda*), protectors (*mudrenga*), and friends (*tonenga*)
On Friday, April 14, the first of the three main days of the festival, the *jani* from the "clan brother" villages arrived in Tebapada early in the morning, together with their wives, bringing gifts such as money, bottles of alcohol, rice or millet, and fowls and pigs. These were handed over to the chief of Tebapada, who stored everything in his house. I was informed on this and on other occasions that most of these gifts are used on the two subsequent nights by the three *daka jani*, when they interrupt their incantations in the *dharni kudi* at around midnight to make an offering of rice, alcohol, a fowl, and a pig to the earth goddess. Unlike in other places, the clan brothers brought neither a *bonda* nor their axes to be worshipped along with the sacred objects preserved by the people of Tebapada.

In other villages such as Lekhpadar (Sikoka clan), which celebrated the *kodru parbu* in 2002, the axe and the *bonda* were brought to the organisers of the sacrifice on Friday morning. In Lekhpadar, for example, the men, women, and children of the neighbouring village of Patangpadari arrived in a procession, accompanying their three *jani*, and with the young men dressed in new loincloths and carrying their village's sacred objects. After a circumambulation of the *dharni kudi*, these young men placed everything next to the *koteiwali*: a one-meter-long iron-tipped arrow, one winnowing fan holding iron objects (axe, knife, and arrow), and another one holding brass objects (the figure of an elephant on wheels, bells, and a *bonda*). A little later, a delegation from the second "clan brother" village, Dongormati, arrived, and their *jani* handed over the following items: a large iron-trimmed bow,[110] a winnowing fan holding iron weapons (axe, knife, chains), and another one holding brass objects (fish figurine, bells, and a *bonda*). While the two *bonda* were set up on two long bamboo poles and worshipped, all the other objects remained near the *koteiwali* until the afternoon, when everything except for the two *bonda* and the bow and arrow was carried inside the *dharni kudi* and placed next to the earth goddess.

Another difference between the *kodru parbu* in Tebapada and in Lekhpadar was that in the latter village, the male villagers, together with a *beju* and a drummer, went into the forest in procession before the beginning of the ceremony at the *koteiwali*. They returned after about an hour with a bundle of roots and herbs collectively known as *osa* or "medicine." This was then placed on top of the sacred weapons, and the *bejuni* made some chickens peck at rice from it. After the ritual, the bundle was taken into the house of the *jani*, who was recognised as a herbal medicine specialist (*cheru mula loku*).

In Tebapada, the *bonda* had been preserved in the house of the blind Kadraka Muni, who asked his son to bring it down from the attic on Friday morning. It appears that the five "clan brother" villages mentioned above share this *bonda*, but after the festival is over, it is not kept by the organisers but returned to its owner in Tebapada. Since the total *muta* consists of twelve villages altogether, it is possible that the other villages jointly worship another *bonda*, but I have no clear information about this. Following brief worship of the *bonda* at Kadraka Muni's house shrine, it was taken to a nearby river to be washed. Meanwhile, Kadraka Muni's son had gone into the woods with some of his friends and came back after some time carrying a long bamboo pole, which the group straightened by holding it over a fire. A man experienced in basketry then made a small umbrella out of bamboo strips and placed it over the long bamboo pole, just below its top end. The small umbrella was then covered with a white

---

[110] Both the iron bow and the iron arrow were said to belong to the god *bhagwan*, who used them in a war a long time ago.

piece of cloth, before the village chief, Kadraka Muni, attached the iron umbrella, the *bonda*, to the top of the pole. Others helped him to decorate the holy object with long, colourful threads.

Meanwhile, several young women had begun to paint the walls of the *dharni kudi*, as well as the goddess's husband's wall, with patterns of triangles. In other villages, the women were joined by girls from the "protector" villages, but in Tebapada hardly anyone from the five Sikoka villages, not even the men, was present on Friday morning. I attended several other *kodru parbu* where the *mudrenga* actively participated in decorating the village, not only by helping to paint the walls but also by supplying banana trees and items for the worship of the *koteiwali*.[111] For example, in Mundawali, a Jakesika village that celebrated the *kodru parbu* in 2001, two banana trees were tied to the doors of each house in the village, as well as to the entrances of the goddess's hut of the goddess and to her husband's wall. In Lekhpadar, many of these banana trees were presented as gifts by the people of Lamba, their "protectors," who turned up on this first day in a very ceremonial fashion. When Lekhpadar performed the *kodru parbu* in 2002, the men and women of Lamba left their village early on Friday morning, bringing with them leaves to make plates, rice collected from each household, a fowl for the *koteiwali* ceremony, an earthen pot to prepare the sacrificial rice, three banana trees full of fruit, and a goat. On the way to Lekhpadar, some of the men were drumming, while others whistled loudly through their fingers. When they reached the entrance to the *meria* village, they stopped and waited for the organisers to welcome them. Before they were asked to enter the village, they were received in a highly respectful manner. A large winnowing fan was placed in front of them, into which one woman from each household of Lekhpadar placed a small basketful of rice. Next, a woman from the organisers' side took a gourd filled with water and symbolically washed the feet of the chief "protectors" from Lamba. She handed them the winnowing fan filled with rice, and the visitors took a few grains each and pressed them against their foreheads as a *tilak* or auspicious sign. Only then did everyone enter the village. The men from Lamba tied the three banana trees to the *palawara* while their sisters and daughters joined the local women in painting it. Later, more banana trees were brought, and as in Mundawali, all the houses of the village, including that of the goddess, were decorated.

---

111 The "protectors" provide the items required for the worship of the male deity (*koteiwali*), whereas the clan brothers, as mentioned above, bring the offerings for the female deity (*dharni*) on this Friday morning.

546 —— 5 The clan sacrifice: Creating Niamgiri society

Photo 18: *Palawara* with banana trees (Kuskedeli, 2001)

Some of these banana trees are provided by the ritual friends (*tonenga*) of the organisers. When I observed the *kodru parbu* in Tebapada, I was not yet aware of the existence of this category of people, and only later, when I moved to Gumma, was I told that each village has at least one or two villages of a particular clan with which they maintain a collective relationship as mutual friends.[112] These relationships were established in the past, usually by the village chiefs, who presented a certain headdress made of brass and known as *teyang ganawa* to each other. From that point onwards, people from these villages

---

112 For an analysis of the concept of friendship in tribal Middle India see Hardenberg (2003) and Skoda (2005).

could no longer intermarry but were considered friends who have to present one another with gifts at the time of the *kodru parbu*. In the village of Sana Dengoni I once observed the welcoming ceremony of these friends on the morning of the first day of the *kodru parbu*. Sana Dengoni belongs to the Sikoka clan and had a longstanding friendship with two villages of the Nandruka clan, Sagdi and Duherigadi. On Friday morning, a delegation of young men from both villages arrived carrying gifts, such as banana trees, baskets of rice, and a pig. They were received by the organisers at the entrance to the village and asked to take a seat on a cot. Then several strong men lifted the cot and carried their friends around the *kudi* as a sign of respect. Next, the young visitors were invited into the houses of their friends to drink alcohol and eat rice. It is usual for the friends to remain in the village throughout the festival, at least until Monday, when the main feast takes place. After this they may leave, but before they go the organisers present them with gifts, such as pigs and rice, as a token of their friendship. They should not quarrel with these friends but instead maintain amicable relations throughout the festival. The friends, for their part, should under no circumstances be involved in the sacrifice – they may not intermarry with the organisers and should not kill their victim.

Worshipping the *satara bonda*

In Tebapada, once the *bonda* had been fixed onto the pole, a band of musicians was formed, consisting of three to four Dongria drummers and a man from the Dombo community playing an oboe (*mohuri*). The sound of this instrument can be heard at many rituals, not only in the Niamgiri Hills but everywhere in tribal Middle India. Three *bejuni*, two old and one young, approached the *koteiwali*, throwing rice at the conical stone representing the earth goddess's husband. Standing in front of the *palawara*, they began to invoke the gods by chanting verses with increasing speed. When they shrugged with their shoulders, this was a clear indication that they had fallen into a trance (*banga ate*). From the *koteiwali*, the three *bejuni* approached the men behind them, who were still busy decorating the *bonda,* dancing. Reciting their verses, they took turns touching the bamboo pole lying across the men's knees and repeatedly bowed their heads before the holy objects. When the men had finished all the decorations, the *bejuni* returned to the *koteiwali,* and at that point a few young men erected the long bamboo pole, first by lifting it onto the horizontal plank of the *panikimunda* and then by tying it in an upright position to the central pillar of the *palawara*. Everyone shouted or whistled through his fingers while the drummers played their instruments in a fast rhythm. In the middle of this crowd, right in front of the *satara bonda*, the three *bejuni* began to dance in the fashion of the divine "kings" (*rajanga*): keeping their left hands on their waists, they rhythmically raised their right fists and made a step forward; then after a few such steps, they turned round and repeated the same dance into the opposite direction. This performance continued for two to three minutes until the music stopped and the shamans again faced the *satara* bamboo. Standing next to each other, the *bejuni* talked to the deity in trembling, high-pitched voices and using a metaphorical language consisting of parallelism. They were assisted by at least one *gurumeni* who used the same language to express the villagers' demands. Then the shamans turned around and again danced to the rhythm of the music.

On this particular occasion, two young Dombo and their perhaps twelve-year-old sister joined in the dance. The two men were tall and had long hair, which they had let down when preparing to fall into a trance. Unlike the *bejuni*, they did not recite any verses, nor did they come close to the sacred objects. Instead, they stood with closed eyes a little behind the three dancing *bejuni*, slowly swaying their heads and inhaling deeply from time to time. After some time their bodies began to shake according to the rhythm of the drums, until they danced in a manner quite different from that of the Dongria shamans. Tossing their bodies to and fro and shaking their heads wildly up and down, they danced uncontrollably. Unlike the *bejuni*, they did not follow certain dance steps and did not bend their bodies, but instead kept their upper bodies upright while dancing. When the music stopped, they remained where they were and did not advance forward to face and pray to the deity like the *bejuni*. Instead, they stood in the place where they had been dancing with closed eyes and inhaled the fumes of burning incense offered to them by some Dongria men.[113] However, even if the Dombo did not participate in the verbal communication with the gods, they nevertheless were actively involved in the offerings in the sense that they gave their bodies to the gods for dancing.

The climax of the dance then approached. A new piece of cloth was tied around the head of each *bejuni* like a turban, a clear indication that they were about to become possessed by *niamraja*, the king of gods. First, the youngest *bejuni*, dressed in a new white *sari* and wearing several of the typical heavy metal necklaces, walked towards the *satara bonda* with her right fist raised in the air and jumped up onto the *panikimunda,* from where she climbed the bamboo pole. Two to three meters above the ground she stopped climbing, and holding the pole tightly with both hands, began to shake her body wildly to and fro until

---

[113] Towards the end of the trance, people blew into the possessed Dombo's ears. In contrast, the *bejuni* needed no assistance when changing from one state of consciousness to another.

she became exhausted. She then climbed down and shortly before reaching the ground loosened her grip on the bamboo pole, lost consciousness, and fell into a crowd of women who caught her. Then, one after the other, the other two *bejuni* mounted the bamboo pole. As mentioned above, I interpret this as an act of bringing the mountain deity, represented by the *satara bonda,* down to earth. The *bejuni* go halfway to the realm of the gods, represented by the "umbrella," become possessed, and accompany the deity back down to the site of worship.

Once the deity had "arrived," a woman from each household came to the *palawara* carrying a winnowing fan with ritual rice (*akat manjing*). The main *bejuni* took each winnowing fan and rubbed the rice with her right hand in the typical circular motion while expressing the demands of both gods and humans in her recitations. Knowing the particular wishes of certain households, the *gurumeni* repeatedly intervened to express certain concrete demands. The women from the three Dombo households approached the *bejuni* in a similar way and handed her a winnowing fan holding rice as a gift to the gods, in particular to the *satara bonda*.

After this collective welcoming ritual,[114] some young men untied the bamboo pole and carried it in an upright position to each house of the village, beginning with the house of the chief, Kadraka Muni. In front of his house the *satara bonda* was lowered into a horizontal position in order to allow the villagers to bind white cloths around the pole below the "umbrella." This can be compared to the tying of cloths around the horns of the buffalo, with the difference that all houses wishing to make such a gift to the *satara bonda* bind it on this occasion, while in the case of the buffalo a family binds the cloth when the victim is standing in front of their door.[115] In the same way as a few day previously with the two buffaloes, each family was now given the opportunity to please the male deity with offerings. At each house, the bamboo pole was placed on a wooden pedestal in order to allow the deity "to sit down," after which the woman of the house washed the god's "feet" by pouring water from a gourd over the lower part of the bamboo pole. Next, each woman handed over a small chicken to the *bejuni,* who coaxed it to peck at some rice from the pedestal. She then handed it to somebody else, who cut off the animal's head and rubbed the neck against the pole in order to offer food, i.e., blood, to the deity. In this way, each household treated the *satara bonda* like an honoured guest before the bamboo pole was taken back to the

---

114 A certain similarity may be identified between these offerings and the welcoming ceremony of the "protectors" described above. In both cases, the whole community receives the "visitors" by presenting them with uncooked rice.

115 The simple reason for this difference may be that it would be difficult for the bearers to lower and raise the long bamboo pole again and again in front of each house.

site of the *koteiwali*, where it was carried round the *palawara* once more and then once again tied to the stake.

Now the time had come for the collective sacrifice. Holding a dark fowl and a white dove in her hands, the main *bejuni* poured some rice onto the *panikimunda* and made the birds peck at some of the grains. Then she asked the people with high status in the village to come to the *koteiwali* and placed some rice into the palms of their right hands. When the fowl and the dove had pecked at a few rice grains, the *bejuni* tore out some of their feathers and stuck them into the hair knots of all the *gurumeni* and *bejuni*, including herself. A participant, not the *bejuni*,[116] killed the birds, smeared their blood on the *satara bonda* and the *koteiwali*, and placed the heads on top of the *panikimunda*. Then the moment for the main offering approached. In the house nearest to the *koteiwali*, the organisers had kept a white male ram that was now carried by a man to the sacrificial site, where about ten other young men were ready and waiting to kill it. As soon as the man reached the open space near the *palawara*, these young men tore the victim away from him and began to hack it to pieces with their axes. Once the ram had been sacrificed in this way, the Dongria whistled loudly through their fingers and exclaimed in joy.

The head was then cut off and tied to the *satara bonda* by the chief's son. The rest of the day was spent holding a feast to which everybody, including the Dombo, was invited. I am not certain who had sponsored the ram in Tebapada, whether it was the organisers or their "protectors." In some villages, the ram was provided by the *mudrenga*, in others by the organisers themselves. The right to kill the victim also does not seem to be clearly defined. In this case, too many people were involved in hacking the animal to pieces, so it was difficult to judge who actually killed the animal. When I asked the participants, I received different answers. Some stated that only the organisers could kill the ram, while others insisted that it was the right of the protectors.[117] In practice, I have witnessed *kodru parbu* in which men from both the former and the latter categories have slaughtered the animal, and on each occasion their right to do so was disputed. For example, in Sana Dengoni, a Sikoka village where I attended the sacrifice for the *satara bonda* in 2003, a man considered to be a "clan brother" joined in the collective slaughter of the ram and immediately wiped the blood off of his axe, hoping that nobody had seen him. It was his bad luck that several people had

---

116 Elwin's (1955, 132) statement that "no shaman should ever kill an animal with his own hands" also holds for the Dongria *bejuni*.

117 The right to sacrifice the ram may depend on the gift-giver. Possibly, when the "protectors" have bought the victim, the organisers may kill it, and when the latter have provided the ram, their "protectors" are allowed to put it to death.

observed his participation and later verbally abused him with harsh words. On another occasion, namely the *kodru parbu* in Kuskedeli (2001), a man from the Huika clan joined in killing the ram at the sacrificial site of the Jakesika clan. He belonged to their "protectors," who according to some informants were allowed to sacrifice the victim. However, he also tried to hide his deed, and when I asked him directly whether he had killed the animal, he denied it.

Invoking the earth goddess
In the evening, after finishing the feast, everybody's attention shifted from the male deity (*satara bonda*) to the goddess (*dharni*) and her iron weapons. I was unable to witness these events in the evening personally but was informed about them by the villagers later. First, the axe was brought out from the house of Kadraka Kuli, the younger brother of the blind man who owned the *bonda*, and carried in a winnowing fan to the *dharni*. In analogy to the opposition between the *dharni* and *koteiwali*, the *tangi* and *bonda* were considered to be "mother" and "father." As previously mentioned, the axe may be kept inside a house or outside the village in a cave or hollow tree. In the section dealing with the symbolism of the axe I have already given a description of how in some villages, the owner of the axe, together with the buffaloes, goes from house to house. In Tebapada, too, each family welcomed the axe in the same way they had earlier received the *satara bonda* at their door. The sequence of events on this first day thus followed a pattern that characterises all Dongria rituals involving *dharni* and *koteiwali*: the male deity is summoned and welcomed first, before everybody's attention shifts towards the *dharni* and her worship.[118]

Around the time the axe is taken from the house of the *jani* (in this case a *pujari*) to the *dharni kudi*, the *daka jani* arrive in the village. In Kuskedeli in 2001, I was able to observe how several men competed for the honour of performing the ritual for the earth goddess. In the afternoon, a man from Lamba whom everybody referred to respectfully as *jani* had arrived in Kuskedeli. Later in my fieldwork I got to know this man very well, but at the time it was just his appearance that struck me: he was an unusually tall man of about forty-five, he had a face full of scars, probably due to infection with smallpox in the past, and his skin was completely yellow, as he had smeared it with turmeric paste. He already appeared quite drunk but seemed determined to conduct the ritual. Together with the *dissari*, a man from a Desia Kond village named Depa-

---

118 Jena et al. (2002, 193) write, "on most ritual occasions, worship begins at the *katei penu* and then the invocation of other gods follows."

guda (near Kalyansingpur), he took a seat on a cot in front of the *dharni*, where four *kula* had been placed containing the axes and knives from different villages tied into bundles. He first mixed raw rice and turmeric powder in a bowl with water. Then he drew a rectangle with white powder and made three heaps of rice within it. In front of this he placed three leaf cups and filled them with alcohol. This is a standard procedure in any *dakina* ceremony, whether conducted inside a house (*kandadae*) or the *dharni kudi*. A third, younger man joined them, and all three men took a handful of rice washed in water in their right hands. After uttering a few sentences in a hasty manner, the ritual specialists threw the rice onto the rectangle and then began reciting their incantations.

About an hour later, I heard loud voices from the *dharni kudi*, where the *jani* from Lamba was having a dispute with the organisers of the *kodru parbu*. They had just informed him that another *jani* had been invited to perform the worship of the earth goddess and that this man had just arrived with his assistant. In fury, the *jani* from Lamba left the village and did not return. A little later, two men turned up, who waited a few hundred meters away from the settlement to be welcomed. Meanwhile, they changed their clothes, the chief *jani* putting on a kind of army coat with a hood to which a peacock feather was attached, while his assistant put on an old, worn-out, and much too large suit. They had come from a place called Nandapur in Rayagada district and were now received by the villagers of Kuskedeli, who carried them on a cot first around the *koteiwali* and then to the *dharni kudi*. They took their seats in front of the *dharni* stones and at once began reciting the incantations in the same way as the *jani* who had angrily left. Their work was watched by the *dissari* and some of the villagers, in particular by the local chief, a young Jakesika who held most of the responsibility for organising the festival.

At midnight, after many hours of recitation and several bottles of country liquor, the *daka jani* interrupted their work, and a piglet was brought inside the *dharni kudi* by the village headman. As on all such occasions, the animal was still very young,[119] perhaps only a few weeks old, with brown stripes on its back, a variety locally called *jada paji* or "bush pig." The *dissari* fed it rice and made a chicken peck at some grains from its neck. This is done to make sure that the deity accepts the offering. After several failed attempts, the ritual specialists were finally successful, and somebody else was asked to cut off the chicken's and the piglet's heads. These were placed on top of the iron weapons

---

119 The selection of a piglet may be explained by the fact that the young still drink their mother's milk and are therefore not polluted in the same way as adult pigs that consume human faeces (Georg Pfeffer, personal communication).

as offerings to the earth goddess. Meanwhile, some men took the piglet's body outside the *dharni kudi,* where they burnt its skin, abraded the remains with a sharp knife, cut it into pieces, and began to cook it. Inside the hut, the rice is boiled and later, together with the pork, is first offered to the deity before everybody present in the hut joins in consuming the food.

5.6.3 *saniwar desa rundam ane* ("on Saturday non-relatives will assemble")

On Saturday, three main events take place: first, the whole village goes out through the eastern exit to the stones representing the local lines and/or to a tree considered to be the abode of *lada*; second, everybody returns to their houses, where each family independently worships *sita penu-lahi penu* (*laksmi*) at their own sacred wall; third, towards the evening young boys and girls from all over the "country" (*desa*), i.e., the Niamgiri mountain range, flock to the *meria* village and transform it into a place of merriment.

Sacrifice at the abode of the god of hunting (*lada penu*)

In Tebapada, the day began with a short sacrifice marking the beginning of the season in which people are allowed to collect the mango fruits available in great abundance in this area. Inside the *dharni kudi,* the *dissari* took three green mangos and, asking the gods to provide them with plenty of fruit, cut them into halves with the point of an iron-tipped arrow. In other places, such as Railima, where the Huika clan performed the *kodru parbu* in 2001, this mango ritual took place outside the village at each house's sacrificial site. Niggemeyer provides us with a detailed account of the more elaborate mango ritual among the Kuttia Kond, for whom it marks the beginning of a seven-day-long hunt (Niggemeyer 1964a, 123–6).[120]

Among the Dongria, the cutting of mango fruits is similarly linked to the worship of weapons and of *lada penu*, the god of hunting.[121] He is represented

---

[120] As among the Dongria, the sacrifice of mangos by the Kuttia Kond marks the beginning of the time for the collection of these fruits and is linked to the worship of weapons for a successful hunt. The cutting of the fruits with iron-tipped arrows takes place at two shrines, first by a *jani* at the *dharni* stones and second by two married men outside the village at the hut of *deo pinnu* (Niggemeyer 1964a, 124).

[121] Neither Nayak (1989) nor Jena et al. (2002) mention this ceremony in their short descriptions of the *kodru parbu*.

by different stones worshipped separately by each local line near or under a tree outside the village. In some villages, the stone marking the place of the *ghata kudi* (the shrine for the *ghanta parbu*) is identical to the stone where *lada penu* is invoked; in others the two stones are separate but usually located in the same forest area to the east of the settlement. The ceremony on Saturday morning is often referred to as *walka puja*[122] or "stone ritual." In Tebapada, after the mango ritual in the *dharni kudi*, eight out of eleven houses sent at least one young man, sometimes even a young boy, with a winnowing fan and guns to a tree outside the village. On the winnowing fan they carried bamboo imitations of weapons, such as a bow and arrow, an axe, a knife, a gun, and a bow net for catching fish. They were accompanied by women carrying large white fowls, which were to be sacrificed at the end of the ritual by three *bejuni* and the *dissari*, the latter having mainly a supervisory function in the ensuing rituals. When they arrived at the tree northeast of the village, they placed the winnowing fans in front of four small stones set into the ground under the branches of the tree. The heavy, old guns were leant against the tree trunk and decorated with vermilion and flowers. The three *bejuni* began to prepare the ritual site in front of each stone by drawing a rectangle with a cross inside it on the ground. An arrow or a stick was stuck into the ground, and a small lamp was placed on top of it. The winnowing fan with the bamboo weapons was placed inside the rectangle, and three rice heaps were made in front of it.

The worship began at the village chief's stone but was then continued simultaneously at several stones, always following the same pattern. First, the *bejuni* sitting in front of the winnowing fan began to call the deities, uttering the verses in a loud, high-pitched voice, at first slowly and then faster and faster until she fell into a trance. She then invoked the deity represented by the stone, took a fowl brought by the woman of the respective house, and made it peck at some grains from the three rice heaps. Then she arose and, holding the bamboo weapons in her hands, began to dance. This particular dance was performed in the name of *lada penu*, the god of war and hunting, and was accompanied by whistles, warlike howls, and the sound of drums played by the men.

Following the dance, the *bejuni* sat down again and with the help of the *gurumeni* began to communicate with the deity. In order for the members of a household to make an offering at the stone of their local line, the family mem-

---

[122] *Walka* is the plural form (*-ka* suffix) of *wali* or "stone" in the Dongria language. According to Macpherson (1852, 255), the "Valka" ceremony is conducted a year after the completion of the *meria*, with the sacrifice of a hog to the earth goddess.

Photo 19: Winnowing fan with "weapons" of *lada penu* (Tebapada, 2001)

bers were asked to come and sit down behind her. Expressing her demands in the typical metaphorical way, she placed some of the ritual rice from the winnowing fan in the hands of each family member and made the fowl peck at some grains out of their palms. In this ritual, particular emphasis was placed on the relationship between the male members of the household, in particular the boys and young unmarried men, who were each given a white thread and a white turban. The white thread was worn like a Hindu *paita* ("sacred thread") from the right shoulder down to the left side of the body. The young men repeatedly made offerings of rice to *lada penu*, and at the end of the ceremony the *bejuni* poured alcohol over the stone and then over their heads.

During other *kodru parbu*, particularly those celebrated in Desia Kond villages, the rituals involving young men were celebrated with additional performative elements. For example, in Dulumguda (2002), a village of the Hikoka clan located in the plains near Kalyansingpur, the *dissari*, together with an old *bejuni*, performed a series of different dances accompanied by men playing drums, who changed the rhythm each time a different deity was summoned. They began with the dance for *lada penu*, during which they held wooden weapons in their hands, whistled, and shouted loudly, and continued with dances for *koteiwali, bamana deo, kakudima, rakshya,* and finally again for *lada*, but this time with the participation of small boys. Wearing new loincloths, three boys were given white turbans to wrap around their heads before the *bejuni* handed them small wooden weapons, a basket containing sweets, and a long, lit cigar (*kundeli*). The *dissari* led the dance around the *jakeri*, followed by the three boys and the old *bejuni*, all holding hands. After they had circumambulated the earth goddess several times, the *dissari* and *bejuni* danced again with each individual boy, each time in a particular fashion. Holding hands, the boy and the *dissari* (or *bejuni*) crouched on the ground and bowed to one another. Then they stood up and with small dancing steps danced around the axis of their own bodies. Finally, the boys were asked to take a bow and an arrow with a kind of funnel in place of an arrowhead and to fire popped rice into the air. After this, the three young dancers were replaced by another group of young boys with whom the *dissari* and *bejuni* repeated the ritual performance. The villagers explained to me that with this dance, the young boys become the ritual friends (*tone*) of *lada penu*, who controls the wild beasts in the forest.

In Tebapada, the dance did not involve the young men in the same way, although they still played a central role in the ritual. They carried the weapons to the site of *lada penu* and back to their houses, made offerings of rice, and then put on a thread as a sign of their initiation. At the end of the dance, the *bejuni* went over to the guns leaning against the tree and made the fowls peck at some rice from them. After that, the fowls, doves, and a single white ram were sacrificed at the stones, and some of the blood was poured over the rice, the stones, the bamboo weapons, and the guns. Finally, to mark the end of the ceremony, a young man took a gun and fired a shot into the forest, the abode of *lada penu*.

Lada penu has various names and appearances. In some cases he seems to be identified with the wild beasts, in particular the tigers, whom he controls. He is worshipped at every major festival, either outside the village under a tree or inside the village at the stones representing the earth goddess. In the latter case, he is "thrown out" of the village at the end of the festival in a specific fashion: the *bejuni*, possessed by *lada*, first dance over to the western exit of the village, where they throw some rice over the village border, before repeating the same action at the eastern border. In this way, the potentially dangerous *lada* is made to reside outside the village, where he protects its entrances from the wild beasts residing in the adjacent forest.

Nowadays, hunting no longer plays a major role in the life of the Dongria, who use their guns mainly for driving animals, especially monkeys, away from their fields. Shooting large game is illegal, and since their numbers have de-

Photo 20: Dongria shooting a gun during the worship of *lada penu* (Tebapada, 2001)

clined in recent decades, hunting has become a very difficult and often fruitless affair.[123] In Gumma, only a few young men had the ability to build the complex traps used for catching birds or small game.[124] During the time of my stay I witnessed several collective hunting expeditions, but all of them were led by men from the valleys equipped with superior guns and lights and included the Dongria merely as guides. From the items worshipped – guns, bow and arrow, knives, baskets, and bow nets – the ceremony clearly seems to be concerned with hunting rather than with war. This is substantiated by statements made by the Dongria themselves, who explained to me that *lada penu* is worshipped particularly for a successful hunt and for protection from wild animals, such as tigers.

---

123 Niggemeyer (1964a, 128), writing in the early 1960s, even then mentions the decline of hunting among the Kuttia Kond. He distinguishes between individual and collective hunting, the latter commencing on the day of the mango ritual.
124 Some of these traps resembled those shown in Niggemeyer's (1964a, 131) diagrams.

Since neither hunting nor defence against tigers plays any major role in the life of the Dongria today, we might wonder why *lada penu* continues to be worshipped on almost every ritual occasion. In my view, four reasons may explain this. First, wild animals, in particular leopards, monkeys, wild boars, and elephants, continue to threaten people and their livestock, and *lada penu* promises protection from them if worshipped properly. Second, people who have died an unnatural death, especially those killed by tigers in the past, are said to roam around and haunt the villagers, causing suffering and even death.[125] *Lada penu* can provide protection from these evil ghosts if he receives the right offerings. Third, one reason for worshipping *lada penu* in the context of the *kodru parbu* is to establish a friendship between *lada penu* and young boys in their childhood and adolescence. Even if hunting is no longer practiced in a major way, friendship with the god of hunting and knowledge of the use of weapons are fierce qualities Dongria men should possess, especially on the eve of a festival when young men, including friends and enemies, arrive in the village. Finally, the word *beta* ("hunting") has a wide meaning and refers to several contexts in which Dongria acquire "life" or "wealth" by force. Thus, it is used not only in the context of hunting game but also when collecting fruit. According to a Dongria myth (see section 5.7.5), hunters once went into the forest in search of game and returned with the goddess of wealth, *sita penu-lahi penu*. As described in the previous chapter, when men go to girls' dormitories or capture a bride they also compare this to hunting. On this Saturday of the *kodru parbu*, the Dongria first worship *lada penu* outside the village and then *sita penu-lahi penu* inside their houses. They are thus like the hunters in the myth, who "capture" the goddess in the wilderness, take her home, and worship her. As argued in the conclusion of this study (see section 6.2), hunting is a male mode of acquiring female values, "life" and "wealth," i.e., representations of the goddess.

Macpherson mentions two gods worshipped by Kond in the nineteenth century, *klambo penu* for hunting and *loha penu* for making or preventing war. Like the Dongria, who nowadays bring their guns to a tree outside the village, in Macpherson's time the Kond brought their weapons to a rivulet to be worshipped by the priest in order to ensure a successful hunt (Macpherson 1852, 261). The name *lada penu* seems to be closely related to the second god mentioned by Macpherson, *loha penu*, literally the "god of iron." In my view, the name *lada* etymologically derives from *loha*, an interpretation that is corroborated by other details.

---

[125] When sitting with Dongria men under the *salap* tree, I often heard stories about these wandering ghosts, for example, "yesterday night, when I slept in my field hut, I heard a ghost moving around and howling," and then people would begin reporting similar experiences or discussing those places where people had died an unnatural death and turned into ghosts.

For example, the iron-tipped arrow worshipped at the time of the *kodru parbu* is seen as a representation of *lada penu*. In Macpherson's (1852, 263) account, the iron-tipped arrow stands for *loha penu*. In the ceremony described above, such an arrow was used to cut the mango fruits, and a bamboo imitation of the arrow was set up at each stone. The ritual specialists and boys danced with bow and arrow imitations, weapons that according to Macpherson (1852, 261, 264) were used by Kond for hunting as well as for fighting.

If we take into account that these weapons had already been worshipped on the previous day at the *koteiwali* and at the earth goddess's shrine, we may draw the following conclusion: they signify the three interrelated realms of war, hunting, and sacrifice. In the *koteiwali* ceremony they are the royal arms of the *satara bonda*; in the *dharni kudi* they symbolise the sacrificial instruments; and in the ceremony performed at the tree they represent the weapons of the hunter.

Table 40: Worship of weapons and the three main deities

Deity	*lada penu*	*koteiwali penu*	*dharni penu*
Function	Hunting	War/Rule	Sacrifice

Inviting the house goddess

When the worship of the weapons was finished, everyone returned to their houses, with the young boys carrying the heavy guns on their shoulders or the winnowing fans with the bamboo weapons on their heads. The main *bejuni* first went to the house of the chief, Kadraka Muni, and sat down in front of the *handani kuda*. She drew a rectangle with a cross inside it in front of the wall and placed three heaps of rice within it. Then she asked the woman of the house to bring her a bottle of liquor and poured some drops onto each heap before herself drinking some alcohol. Then she left and went from house to house in order to prepare the site of worship in front of each *handani kuda* in the village.[126] Meanwhile, a son of the blind chief had gone to fetch some bark from a mango tree, and on his return to the house, his mother took the bark, crushed it, and threw it into a pot with some water. Holding this pot in her hands, she sprinkled first the *handani kuda* and then all the walls of the inner room of

---

[126] This is a very typical procedure at major festivals. Either the *bejuni* or the *dissari* first prepares the sacrificial site before he or she, making a second round of the village, actually performs the ritual at every house.

the house with this liquid. This purification is always performed before every major ceremony to which the goddess of the house, *sita penu-lahi penu*, is invited.

As the chief's wife was herself a *bejuni*, she immediately commenced the ritual by standing in front of the wall, holding some rice in her right hand, and silently reciting some verses to invoke the deity. She was later joined by two other *bejuni* and a *gurumeni*, and together the three women sat down in front of the *handani kuda*, where they became possessed by various deities. The ceremony always follows the same pattern: the *bejuni* calls the name of the deity and then becomes possessed by the god the moment she shrugs her shoulders. Then the deity, through the *bejuni*, asks for offerings in a metaphorical way. The *bejuni*, together with the *gurumeni*, answers in the same way on behalf of those family members who are ready to give rice and sacrificial animals. As proof, the *bejuni* holds a white or black fowl or a dove – depending on the deity – and makes it peck at some rice from the three heaps within the rectangle on the ground. Further offerings may be demanded by the deity, or the ritual specialists may ask the deity to help them or to cure someone who is sick or injured and thus promise further sacrifices to this end.

Towards the end of the ceremony, the goddess of the house arrived, and at that point all the family members assembled in the room. Holding a dark[127] fowl, the main *bejuni* turned around and first put some rice into the blind chief's right hand and made the victim peck at some of the grains before she repeated the same process with the other family members. In this way, the people of the house can personally make an offering to their goddess. A small black ram was brought into the house, and the main *bejuni* fed it with ritual rice. At the end of the ceremony, when all the deities had been sent away, the fowl and the ram were killed, the former inside the house, the latter in front of the door.

Arrival of the young people (*dawe / dasi*)
Around midday, the worship of *sita penu-lahi penu* had been finished in all the houses, and the women began to cook the rice and meat, which was then offered first of all at each house shrine and then distributed among the family members and guests. Most of these guests had already arrived on the previous day and were mainly close kin living in different villages, such as sons who had moved to their wives' villages or daughters who were returning to their natal vil-

---

[127] In many cases, dark sacrificial animals are sacrificed to female deities and white ones to male deities.

Photo 21: Dongria with drums during *kodru parbu* (Mundawali, 2001)

lage to take part in this major festival. In the afternoon, the young men of the village took out their drums and danced around the *dharni kudi*. Others formed dancing parties without drums, walking up and down the village plaza in a warlike manner.

They held either axes, which they played like instruments by hitting small sticks rhythmically against the blade, or long wooden lances (*kallu munda*), which they pounded on the ground with each step. Many young men were already quite drunk, as the Dombo had appeared with large canisters of alcohol, which they were selling for ten rupees a bottle (*kanch*). Apart from small quarrels, the overall atmosphere was infused with joy and merriment. Everywhere one could hear the typical *meria* song being sung, which consists of one line sung by a single man and a second line sung by the other men in the dancing party. The first line is repeated in an alternating manner and consists of only three words: *saruldi sapuri sana*, meaning "drinking gourd, pineapple, smells sweet," while the second line may vary and addresses various deities. The following few verses illustrate this type of song, which can continue for hours:

saruldi sapuri sana, aba ree pondawali (father, *pondawali* [name of a mountain god])
saruldi sapuri sana, aba ree arguwali (father, *arguwali* [name of a mountain god])
saruldi sapuri sana, aya naa rengena munda (mother, *rengena munda* [name of post at the shrine of *yatra kudi*])
saruldi sapuri sana, aya naa rengena pate (mother, *rengena pate* [name of beam at the shrine of *yatra kudi*])
saruldi sapuri sana, aya naa gada jageni (mother, watching the town)
saruldi sapuri sana, aya naa gode jageni (mother, watching the village)
saruldi sapuri sana, keouti mane mane li (fishermen are there, are there)
saruldi sapuri sana, kumbara mane mane ya (potters are there, are there)
etc.

In the afternoon, a group of policemen from Kalyansingpur arrived in the village. Nowadays, Dongria have to inform the police when they celebrate the *kodru parbu*, because in the past many people have been killed during this event. The organisers have to pay the policemen a heavy bribe, usually consisting of money in addition to a goat and rice for a feast. Their main duty is to stay awake during the night and intervene should a conflict erupt, although in actual fact they normally just sit around and wait, being aware that with their *lathi* (sticks), they are hardly in a position to do anything if a fight breaks out between young men carrying axes and knifes. For this reason, bloody conflicts have perhaps lessened in frequency but can never be completely prevented (see below).

Around sunset, the first groups of girls, each accompanied by an elderly woman, arrived in the village. While some groups had already come the day before, most people, especially those from relatively distant villages with whom no permanent relations exist, appeared only on this second day of this festival. I observed the same in other villages, and this corresponds with the saying that "on Saturday the non-relatives assemble" (*sukruwar desa rundam ane*). The girls had either already donned their colourful festival clothes or, if they had relatives in the village, carried their clothing on their heads and got dressed as soon as they reached the village. In contrast to a wedding party, they did not dance or sing, but rather appeared quite controlled and even afraid. Always in groups, they mostly remained at the back of the houses or stood behind the fence at those places where there was a gap in the rows of houses and tried to get a glimpse of the dancing men.

Their behaviour stood in sharp contrast to the merry behaviour of the young dancing men,[128] many of whom did not turn up until much later. Not on this occasion but on others I accompanied groups of young men on either the Friday or

---

[128] According to Aparajita (1994, 236), these people are collectively referred to as *padria*, a word I personally never heard in this context.

Saturday evening on their way to the *meria* village. They usually begin dancing around the *dharni* in their own village in the afternoon. Before leaving, they first drink *salap* sap, then dance through the village, and finally go in groups to the *meria* village. While walking through the forest and across the mountains, they sing the *meria* song continuously, and whenever they get an opportunity to buy alcohol in a Dombo settlement, they spend their money on getting drunk. When they arrive in the *meria* village, they have to pass through the gates to enter the plaza where the other men are dancing and singing. If the organisers are suspicious, they might not allow any men carrying an axe to pass through the gate, particularly if the buffalo has already been tethered to the sacrificial post. In Railima, for example, no man with an axe was allowed to even approach the village plaza, and consequently the atmosphere around the *dharni* was not very merry. A few men danced around the earth goddess with their drums and wooden lances, but most of the boys and girls amused themselves behind the houses.

In other places, the problem was solved by locking up the buffalo inside a deserted house or cow pen. In Tebapada, for example, a house in one of the two rows had been empty for some time but still had strong walls and doors. These were given additional protection with double fences and watched from the front and back by the *mudrenga*, as well as by policemen who guarded its front door. For this reason, everyone was allowed to enter the village, which soon became crowded with boys and girls. Many young women dared to come out onto the village plaza, where they stood in front of the houses or sat on the verandas, where they could watch the boys passing by. Behind and in front of the houses, the young people teased each other, the boys touching the girls' breasts or trying to take away their shawls. In Tepabada, at least one house was turned into a kind of dormitory where couples covered by big shawls lay on the ground. As space was lacking for so many young people, many walked into the woods and slept with their partners under the trees. The strict rules of avoidance seem to lose their validity on festive occasions like these. For example, after I moved to Gumma I learnt that one man from this village had slept with his yBWeZ when he attended the *kodru parbu* in Tebapada. In normal circumstances, he should have avoided her, but since he had slept with her during the *kodru parbu*, nobody seemed to think that he had committed a grave mistake, although some villagers teased him because of this "affair." The general sexual freedom at the time of the festival is also mentioned in Macpherson's report from the nineteenth century:

> Upon occasions of human sacrifice, however, the women mingle freely and without shame, with the other sex, in the more saturnalian license by which that rite is accompanied. (Macpherson 1863, 56)

The free mingling of boys and girls among the Dongria marks a major difference between them and the more "Hinduised" Desia Kond of the valleys. Their youths similarly engage in joyful merrymaking – this Saturday is referred to as *raha dina*[129] or "day of happiness" – but without any direct sexual contact. Instead they play a game called "making a biscuit dance" (*biskut etina*). The Desia Kond girls sit on the verandas in front of their houses, wearing colourful saris, bangles, and jewellery in the style of the plains people. The Desia Kond boys, dressed in shirts and pants, form groups of three or more and move from veranda to veranda. When standing in front of the girls, they start singing songs, often the latest and most popular Hindi songs, while holding each other's hands, swaying their bodies to and fro, and kicking one leg rhythmically up and down. When the dance stops, one after another they take a few steps toward the veranda and stretch out one hand, holding a biscuit bought from one of the many petty traders who come on this day to sell their cheap goods. One of the girls gets up and goes up to the end of the veranda to take the biscuit from him. When she does, he either withdraws his hand or tries to touch or grab her in a joking manner, perhaps saying something about her good looks. The girl laughs and makes a second attempt to try to get the biscuit, perhaps making some comments on the boy's lack of ability to dance or sing. This kind of play continues for hours and does not lead to any direct sexual contact, as is the case among the Dongria.

Back to Tebapada: while the young people enjoyed themselves, the *daka jani* inside the sacrificial hut continued their incantations. At around midnight, a pig provided by the organisers was sacrificed at the *dharni* in the same way as the night before. This marked the beginning of the third day of the *kodru parbu*, when the victim was due to be killed.

5.6.4 *adiwar kodru mada ane* ("on Sunday the buffalo will be killed")

It is extremely difficult for an ethnographer to observe the final sacrificial rites inside the *dharni kudi* due to the immense crowds of people standing inside and dancing outside the sacrificial hut. Things are far easier in Desia Kond villages, where all rituals take place outside the village in a sacred grove and where nobody attempts to kill the buffalo before the proper time of sacrifice. To illustrate these differences, I will first give an example of how the sacrifice

---

129 As mentioned above, *-s-* and *-h-* are interchangeable. While Dongria Kond say *rasa*, Desia Kond pronounce the same word *raha* ("joy," "happiness").

was performed in Dulumguda, a small village of Desia Kond near Kalyansingpur, before I present my observations from Tebapada and other Dongria villages.

Killing the buffalo in a Desia Kond village
In Dulumguda, at around two o'clock Sunday morning, the *dissari*, together with a *bejuni*, brought the old axe and the iron-tipped arrow from the house of the *jani* to the *jakeri*, located in a grove about one hundred meters outside the village. They tied the axe to a small stake set up next to the main sacrificial post and drove the arrow into the ground near the stones representing the earth goddess. There were no *daka jani* to chant the incantations to the *jakeri*, but as in a Dongria village, the *dissari* killed first a fowl and then a pig at the stones. The village chief (*member*) made a symbolic axe of bamboo and a mango leaf to represent the blade of a "new" axe and placed it next to the "old" axe. Then the ritual specialists fell into a trance and, accompanied by the varying rhythms of the drummers, began to perform their dances for the various gods and goddesses: *koteiwali, kakudima, sapa rakhya, jagannatha-puri, wedakadang, lanjigadia-maringdola, janabhaira, phulabhaira, jamimadia, rayagada-majhigada, nilamani, durgadureni-taratoreni, basanta ma, kalapurusa,* and *sidiraja*. Meanwhile, some men prepared the sacrificial rice (*onda*)[130] on three stones near the *jakeri*, while others cooked the meat in a separate place. When the dance was over, three portions of rice were placed in front of the *jakeri* as "the gods' share" (*penka bata*), and behind that seven portions of rice and meat were set out on leaf plates. Seven men of high status (*kaja loku*), who were considered to be the "original people" (*mulia loku*), i.e., descendants of the village founders, sat down in front of these plates and began to eat their shares. Only when they had finished did the other people present join in the feast. Women arrived with winnowing fans and rice and handed these to the *bejuni*, who sat near the *jakeri* and began to rub the rice each household had presented to the earth goddess.

Meanwhile, the first light could be seen on the horizon, and the area around the sacred grove became crowded as more and more villagers arrived. Four strong "protectors" (*mudrenga*) pulled the buffalo towards the "fence" (*madada*) by ropes tied to his legs and pushed his head between the two horizontal beams. The *dissari* approached him, announcing loudly that this buffalo would be sacrificed in the name of the *jakeri* and sprinkling him with rice and water. As in other sacrifices I witnessed among the Desia Kond, the buffalo's head faced

---

[130] This corresponds to the *bana paga* among the Dongria Kond.

west, towards the people.¹³¹ The *dissari* walked up to the fence a second time, this time carrying the "old" and the "new" axe in his hands, and symbolically struck the victim's neck with them. At this moment, somebody fired a gunshot, a clear indication that this was considered to be the main sacrifice. Next, a strong man took one of the rare ceremonial axes (*simini*) to cut off the buffalo's head, a very bloody affair as the axe was not sharp and the sacrificer quite unskilled.¹³² As soon as blood began flowing from the wound, the *jani*, i.e., the owner of the axe and original village founder, collected some of it in his right hand and carried it as an offering to the *jakeri*, where he poured it over the stones. A few minutes later, he picked up the buffalo's head and placed it on a winnowing fan in front of the *jakeri*. On top of the head he laid down the two axes, along with an old iron knife.

Next, a mock theft was performed in a joking manner. Somebody had cut off one of the buffalo's front legs, and a young man grabbed this, threw it over his shoulder, and raced towards the village, followed by the "protectors," who chased the "thief," hitting him with their bamboo sticks. When the thief reached the village, he went straight to the *jani*'s house and discarded the leg on the roof. With this the chase ceased. I witnessed the same mock theft in two other Desia Kond villages but never in a Dongria Kond village. However, I have been told that from time to time a real theft of the victim's leg occurs among the Dongria, when an opposing party claims rights to land for which the *kodru parbu* is performed.¹³³ For example, about fifteen years ago when the people of Gumma celebrated the festival in Waliamba, the Sikoka of Dongormati and Lekhpadar came and took away one of the victim's legs. They carried it to the *dharni* of their village and circumambulated the goddess several times with it, thereby claiming ownership rights to Waliamba's territory.

As the Desia Kond do not build a sacrificial hut, they take the victim's head, along with the sacred weapons, back to the village. In Dulumguda, everything was carried to the main *jani*'s house and placed in front of it at a particular stake (in the case of the axes) or inside the house at his shrine (in the case of

---

131 The victim's relation to the worshippers was thus the same as that of the gods when they are called by the ritual specialists.
132 In this village and others, I got the impression that in comparison to the Dongria, the Desia Kond are much less experienced in handling axes, especially on sacrificial occasions.
133 Another way to establish rights over a territory involves bringing a buffalo to the site and attempting to get it sacrificed at the *dharni*. One case in which the Kadraka unsuccessfully brought a buffalo to a *kodru parbu* organised by the Wadaka and another in which the Wadaka made the same attempt in a place claimed by the Nundruka have been documented by Nayak (1989, 86–87, 90–91).

the buffalo's head and the knife). The two main ritual specialists then went from door to door demanding rice and money as gifts for their services. They were also given the heads of all the animals sacrificed during the past three days. The distribution of the meat occurred a short while later on the same day, in a way which was typical for the Desia Kond and distinct from the *malkamba* practice of the Dongria Kond (see below). Each Dulumguda household had purchased two new earthen pots, cooked rice in them, and brought them to the sacrificial site. These *tandi padari*, literally "village-territory pots," were then distributed along with a few pieces of cooked buffalo meat from the victim's hind leg. Each village has the right to be given one such pot, and the representative of the village must eat the food there on the spot. If someone breaks the earthen pot, he has to pay a fine or *tapu*, a word also used in the settlement of cases of bride capture (see pp. 401–2).

Killing the buffalo in Dongria Kond villages
In a Dongria village, the sacrifice occurs in a more dramatic atmosphere, with more violence, disorder, and ecstasy. The whole sacrifice is organised differently among the Dongria Kond. Not one person, but all the young men present, who come from various villages and neither belong to the clan of the organisers nor have been selected as "protectors," are expected to kill the buffalo. While the organisers may wish to decide when the right time for the sacrifice has come and therefore enclose the buffalo in a pen and protect it throughout the night, the young men are just waiting for an opportunity to strike the first blow against the victim. If somebody manages to break through the fence and hit or perhaps even kill the buffalo, he is considered a "hero" (*bira*), but must anticipate severe sanctions from the organisers and their *mudrenga*. However, during the course of the night, the young visitors become increasingly uninhibited due to excessive drinking. In sharp contrast to the Desia Kond, who mostly abstain from alcohol or drink it only in small quantities, the Dongria consider a felicitous festival to be one during which they get completely drunk.

Ideally, the sacrifice should take place early in the morning. As far as the exact timing is concerned, I heard two different versions. According to some Dongria, the right time to kill the buffalo has come when the first light of the sun god (*dharmu penu*) becomes visible on the horizon. An alternative explanation was provided to me by an employee of the DKDA, who had served in the Niamgiri Hills for almost twenty years. According to this man, the ritual specialists wait for a certain star to rise in the east before giving permission for the victim to be killed. Before the actual sacrifice, the *dissari* must bathe the buffalo. This was first[134] reported by Patnaik and Das Patnaik:

> In the dead night three young girls (who have just attained maturity and have not been captured) are sent to bring three brass-wares (*Meria* accessories) from the *Pujari's* house. After coming back, three of them go straight to the stream to bring three pitcherful of water without looking back. It is believed, they may be bewitched by the spirits who are supposed to be inside the pitchers, if they look back. The *Pujari* too, accompanies them brandishing a bunch of feathers to ward off evil-spirits. With water they reach the *Meria* animal (A big buffalo who is called *Meria*) and bathe it with that water. This *Meria* animal is tied to a big wooden post and is considered to be purified after the bath. Then, they come to the *Lamba* to ask for "*Podo Kandi*" (Iron-chain and plate). Forelegs of the buffalo are tied with the chain which is indicative of the fact that the *Meria* would be sacrificed within a short time. (Patnaik and Das Patnaik 1982, 167)

Only in one case was I informed of such a bath, and I have no concrete information about whether the girls played the same prominent role as described by these authors. I never saw Dongria putting chains on the victim's legs. Patnaik and Das Patnaik's account is important, however, as it suggests an analogy between bride and buffalo: just like the bride on the eve of her wedding, the buffalo is bathed by the young women of the village.

Following the bath and shortly before the sacrifice, the *dissari* offers cooked rice to the victim. Then he has to take a fowl and make it peck at rice either from the *dharni* or from the victim's head, as is done at every major sacrifice in order to ascertain whether or not the deity accepts the offering. Next he takes the knife, or both the axe and knife, and thrusts them through one of the holes in the wall of the *dharni kudi* while observing the buffalo through the other. Alternatively, I have been told that he may symbolically touch the buffalo with the knife. In order to do this, however, he would have to enter the sacrificial pen, which carries the risk that the young men might use the opportunity to attack the victim. When the *dissari* has no time to complete the rites before the visitors kill the buffalo, he at least touches the dead animal with the knife. In the following description I present the events as I observed them in Tebapada in the year 2001. As before, I also include data I collected in other villages to complement this account.

In Tebapada, the organisers kept the buffalo inside a house protected on both sides by policemen and *mudrenga* until about 5:20 in the morning, when the right time had come for it to be sacrificed to the *dharni*. Up until this

---

134 Patnaik and Das Patnaik wrote their account of the *kodru parbu* in 1982. Twelve years later, Aparajita (1994) provides an account that sometimes resembles the text written by these two authors word for word, in particular when describing the buffalo's bath.

Photo 22: Buffaloes tethered to a post two days before the sacrifice (Tebapada, 2001)

point, the three *daka jani* had continued to chant their verses inside the *dharni kudi*, seated before the axe. They prepared themselves for the final rites, when the buffalo was to be taken by the *mudrenga* from the house to the stake in front of the goddess's hut. Just as all had expected, the buffalo never reached the sacrificial site. As soon as it appeared on the village plaza, it was attacked by the crowd, who had been waiting for their chance to kill the animal. As soon as the buffalo had received wounds from a few axe blows, it suddenly panicked and with all its might managed to struggle free from the men holding it with ropes. Immediately everyone joined in the murderous frenzy and attempted to kill the victim, which, scared to death, was running through the village searching for an exit. All possible escape routes had, however, been blocked by the fence. It took less than a minute before somebody was able to administer the buffalo a deadly blow to the neck, and the victim collapsed on the village plaza. Everyone else immediately ran towards the buffalo to strike it at least once, so that they might exult in a victorious pose with a blood-stained axe.

Following this event, things began to calm down a little. The *mudrenga* cut off the head and then carried it to the *dharni* inside the sacrificial hut. With amazing precision, one of them slit open the body above the liver[135] and removed a part of the organ, which was then placed on top of the buffalo's head. Unlike in other villages, there was no *gripa jani* to take blood from the dead animal over to the *jakeri*, and I have no information about who fulfilled this function in Tebapada. Subsequently the two hind legs were removed, carried around the *dharni kudi*, and then deposited on the roofs of two different houses. One leg was placed on the roof of the main organiser, the blind Kadraka Muni, and the other on the roof of a Sikoka who represented the *mudrenga* in Tebapada. The legs are presented as indications of the high status of these two leaders but do not become their property in the sense that the meat may no longer be consumed by anyone else. On the contrary, the legs were taken down from the roofs the next day, cut into pieces, and cooked together with the rest of the buffalo meat in preparation for the main feast on Monday. Finally, the buffalo's carcass was carried by the *mudrenga* to the pen and placed by the sacrificial stake.

Except on one occasion, the victim at the festivals I observed was always killed before the final rites had been completed. The exception occurred in the village of Railima, where people from different Hindu castes (e.g., Paika, Sondi) of a neighbouring village were assigned the duty of protecting the buffalo. They took their job very seriously and were in complete control of the situation, particularly because all of them remained sober throughout the night. After midnight, while the *daka jani* were continuing their incantations, the *dissari* bathed the buffalo. I personally did not observe how the water was fetched and whether girls were involved in this, as claimed by Patnaik and Das Patnaik (1982, 167).

Around four o'clock in the morning, the *bejuni* of the village fell into a trance, in which state they first danced in front of the *dharni* before proceeding towards the *koteiwali*, accompanied the whole time by the drummers. They summoned a number of different gods and danced with their insignia, i.e., an umbrella, ceremonial axe, or lance. Then the *dissari*, a Dombo with matted hair who resembled an ascetic, took a plate of cooked rice – most probably the sacrificial food (*bana paga*) cooked in the *dharni kudi* – and held it in front of the buffalo through a small hole in the fence. Everyone watched eagerly to see whether the buffalo, as a representative of the deity, would accept the food. After the buffalo had partaken of this offering, the *dissari* went to the *dharni*, where he placed three heaps of uncooked rice in front of the stones. After a

---

135 It is possible to speculate that one of the main functions of the knife worshipped at the time of the *kodru parbu* was to remove the liver of the human victim, but I have no proof of this.

small chicken had pecked at the rice, the *dissari* left. I was unable to see whether he thrust the weapons through the hole in the wall as he was expected to, because suddenly I heard a *mudria* shouting, *"bipada!"* ("danger"), and the other "protectors" took their bamboo sticks and hit them against the fence, thereby symbolically destroying it. At that moment, the young men, who had been waiting for some time in the eastern part of the village and had only just been kept at bay by the strong Hindu men, attacked the buffalo, holding up their axes and shouting loudly as if assailing an enemy in an ambush. When the first men had pulled down the fence, the panicked buffalo somehow managed to free itself and ran towards one end of the village. It managed to escape through the western gate, which had not been properly fastened, and ran down the hills towards the next village.[136] The entire village chased the victim, and it took the young men almost half an hour before they finally managed to kill the buffalo.

In all other villages where I witnessed the *kodru parbu*, the ritual specialists did not have enough time to ensure the deity's acceptance of the offering. In Kuskedeli, for example, the victim had already been put to death by Saturday afternoon. On this day, the buffalo had been tethered to the stake and was protected by a thick fence, but the *mudrenga* had not yet arrived, and the policemen were in a nearby village attending a feast sponsored by the organisers. At that time, a small group of dancers from Nishkal arrived in the village with a few inebriated people among them and proceeded towards the *dharni kudi*. While circumambulating it, one man suddenly climbed over the fence and hit the buffalo with his axe. A few men were able to stop him from killing the victim, and several women rushed towards the pen holding long bamboo sticks to protect the wounded, moaning animal. The dance continued for some minutes, and the situation appeared to be under control when suddenly two or three boys pulled down the fence and immediately killed the buffalo. As the organisers in this small village were in the minority, they could do nothing but inform the policemen and their protectors. The attackers were too drunk and too happy to run away, and when after ten minutes the first policemen and "protectors" arrived, they were beaten up and carried to a school in the next village. There they were locked in a room with solid doors, mainly to protect them from the angry crowd, as I was assured by one of the police officers. When the young guests, many of them from Gumma, turned up later and saw that the victim had already been killed, they nevertheless remained and danced throughout the night but were so angry that they com-

---

136 Railima is located in the foothills of the Niamgiri mountain range. From there the flat, wet-rice land of the Desia people can be reached within minutes.

pletely destroyed the fence and a portion of the *jani*'s house and took away all of the meat except for the head, which was placed in front of the *dharni*.

In Mundawali the same year, the policemen escorted the buffalo safely to the *dharni*, which is not located inside the village but a few hundred meters away from the settlement in the dense forest. The site was protected by two fences, an inner one around the stake and a second one enclosing the goddess's shrine. The policemen, together with several *mudrenga*, remained inside the fence, and nobody was allowed to come anywhere near the victim. At around three o'clock, however, the buffalo's protectors were taken by surprise when an attack was carried out by some Dongria, who emerged from the forest, broke down the fence, and killed the animal with their axes. In the darkness, several people got hurt, and three suffered such severe injuries that they had to be hospitalised. In Sana Dengoni too, several people were injured when the buffalo was killed in an attack in the middle of the night. In the *kodru parbu* celebrated in Khojuriguda in 2002, a man died after being hit with an axe. When he attempted to walk to Kalyansingpur the next morning, he had already lost so much blood that he expired on the way. At the same festival, another man died in a fight, according to information given to me by a Dombo woman.

People sometimes receive these injuries accidentally during the turmoil at the sacrificial site, for example when an axe misses the buffalo and instead hits a fellow Dongria, or when somebody swings his axe wide and hurts a person standing behind him. However, people assured me that injuries are also deliberately inflicted by enemies who take advantage of the darkness and the crowd. It is not unusual for a Dongria to threaten a rival by saying, "wait until I see you at the buffalo sacrifice in ..." Nayak, for example, reports a case in which one Dongria killed another during a *kodru parbu* in order to avenge a bride capture. A Sikoka from Jangjodi had abducted a girl demanded by the Pusika from Upparagumma. When, at the festival, the elder brother of the man for whom the girl had been intended met the father's younger brother of the abductor,[137] the former took revenge:

> In 1981 the buffalo sacrifice ceremony was being observed in Jangjodi, a Kadraka village. There was a huge gathering of Dongria clans. On the eve of the sacrifice invited clansmen from other villages were busy dancing around the community house (*kudi*) in divided groups. All of them were drunk. Amidst these rejoicings a confrontation between Pusika

---

[137] Neither of these two individuals were directly involved in the case of bride capture, i.e., they were not the first husband and the abductor, but close relatives. This clearly demonstrates that not only the individual, but everyone belonging to the same category – family, local line, perhaps even village – was held responsible.

Tinu of Upparguma and Sikoka Butu of Jangjodi, ensued. Tinu gave a severe axe blow to Butu and fled away. Butu was dead. (Nayak 1989, 65)

Nayak reports that following the incident, after the buffalo had been sacrificed, the villagers immediately sat down to a meeting in order to resolve the conflict. In every *kodru parbu*, immediately after the killing of the animal, such a conciliatory meeting called *bereni kina* ("to have discussions") takes place. In Tebapada, for example, the elders took their seats on cots placed near the *koteiwali*[138] in order to settle conflicts existing between the organisers and their *mudrenga*. For this reason, the chiefs and elders of the Sikoka and the Kadraka attended the meeting. Since I had only just begun to learn the Dongria language, I could not understand exactly what was discussed between the two parties. However, I was informed that those involved were attempting to settle conflicts arising from bride capture and theft. After the mentioned sacrifice in Mundawali, the meeting's main topic was the untimely sacrifice of the buffalo, and the organisers from the Jakesika clan accused the people from a Kadraka village named Batigumma of being the main culprits. In Railima I saw how certain individuals were summoned to the assembly of elders in order to defend themselves against accusations of misbehaviour. In Gumma, everyone was waiting for the next *kodru parbu* to take place in order to get an opportunity to discuss the question of land rights. Thus, when the people of Gumma and Lekhpadar could not find a solution to their conflict about the territory of Waliamba, the main *dissari* informed me that the issue would be raised during the *bereni kina* at the next buffalo sacrifice.

Let us return to the events in Tebapada. While the elders settled their disputes, the young people of the village were busy saying goodbye to their lovers and friends. Everywhere boys – sometimes also a few girls – could be seen carrying sticks or axes to which they had tied the shawls snatched from their lovers the night before. Since early morning, the girls had been busy cooking rice and pulses, and each approached her favourite boy to invite him to come and eat on her veranda. Several times I saw young men who refused to come, but the girls did not give up and tried to push and pull them in the direction of their houses. Others carried winnowing fans with leaf plates full of food to small groups of young men and forced them by all means possible to accept the food. Other girls chased the boys who had taken away their shawls, while the latter did ev-

---

[138] As mentioned before, the *koteiwali* can be seen as a local representation of the male divine principle, in particular of the mountain god (*niamraja*), who, according to myth, has the duty to establish order.

erything they could to keep hold of them as signs of their amorous conquests. Apart from these individual attempts to invite a particular lover to share food on their verandas, the young girls as a whole had also cooked rice for all their guests. They carried two huge baskets full of white rice to the village plaza and distributed it among the young men present.

When everybody had finished eating, the guests prepared to leave the village. Before their departure, they demanded a share of the buffalo meat, an aspect that is discussed in the next section. The young men set off for home, but just before they walked out of the village they raised their axes, whistled, and displayed the meat fixed to the blades as a token of their victory. With this, the festival came to an end. On this day and those following, the villagers divided and cooked the meat, took down the *bonda* (Wednesday), and performed the *ambadadi yatra* (Thursday), but none of these events involved as many people from outside the village as the actual sacrifice of the buffalo. The *kodru parbu* is considered successful when hundreds of young people from all over the Niamgiri mountain range have come to kill the victim and to take home a portion of its meat.

5.6.5 Distribution of the meat

For a better understanding of the division and distribution of the victim's meat it is helpful to distinguish between the allocation of particular portions to a person or group category and the actual consumption of the meat. The right to receive a certain part of the buffalo often does not mean that others are excluded from consuming this meat. Dongria Kond attach great importance to commensality and consider it a sign of good hospitality when everybody attending a feast, independent of his or her status, receives an equal share.

I begin with the first aspect, the allocation of portions of meat to people from different social or ritual categories. These are:
1. *jani kapada unga:* "head," given to the *daka* (or *gripa*) *jani*
2. *duta janga:* "legs," given to the "old man" (*duta*), i.e., the chiefs
3. *panda unga* or *malkamba:* "skin meat," given to the young men who killed the buffalo
4. *wahi unga* (or *piptanga paga*): "entrails," including the stomach, given to the *mudrenga*

The first and most important part of the buffalo to be distributed is the head. It is cut off immediately and should be brought straight to the *dharni* as an offering, either by the *gripa jani* or by the *mudrenga*, but never by the organisers themselves. As for all other sacrifices, the head officially belongs to the ritual specialist who performed the sacrifice, in this case the *daka* or *gripa jani*. In actual fact, the head is later shared by everybody during the main feast.

As mentioned in the previous section, one or two legs of the buffalo are cut off and placed on the roofs of certain people of high status. These legs are called *duta janga*, *duta* meaning "old man" and *janga* referring to the whole leg, from the shoulder to the hoof. The expression may be related to the fact that these portions of meat are given to the chiefs of those villages that organised the *kodru parbu,* including the *mudrenga*. These chiefs are the *kajaru* or "senior people," those who are the most knowledgeable, own the sacred objects, and are direct descendants of the people who founded their village. Putting the leg on their roof can be interpreted as a public recognition of their status. The legs do not remain in their possession but are later removed from the roof and cooked together with the other meat.

Photo 23: Leg of sacrificial victim placed on the roof of the *jani*'s house (Tebapada, 2001)

On Sunday morning, when the young visitors are preparing to leave, having eaten rice and pulses cooked by the girls, the *mudrenga* distribute small portions of buffalo meat to them. For this purpose, a few "protectors" assemble in the sacrificial pen, while the visitors have to wait outside. The organisers are not involved in this distribution, as they are not supposed to even touch the dead victim. The *mudrenga* cut slices of hide (*panda unga*) and meat from one side of the buffalo and give one piece, along with half a kilogram of rice, salt, and chillies, to each of the young visitors.[139] The latter bind the rice, salt and chillies into a shawl and hang the hide and meat over the top edge of their axes. With this, they walk out of the village, posing like victors lifting their axes high up in the air. When they return home, they go to the *dharni* and either place the meat in the earth goddess's hut or, if the latter is too dilapidated, hand it over to the villagers, saying *malkamba taca mai, tingana* ("I have brought *malkamba*, let's come and eat"). When more than one person has brought meat from the *kodru parbu*, several people will assemble around a fire, cook the meat, and share it in a feast. The expression *malkamba* is mentioned neither in Winfield's dictionary nor in Israel's. In my interpretation it derives from the combination of two words: *mal* or "mountain," as in Kondmal ("Kond mountains"), and *kambi-*, a verb meaning "to ripen." I have been told that in the past each Dongria took the human victim's flesh back to his mountain and buried it as a gift to the earth. Macpherson provides us with an elaborate account of how, in the early nineteenth century, the Kond divided the human flesh and buried it in the ground:

> When the victim is cut into pieces, the persons who have been deputed by each village to bring its share of the flesh instantly return home. There the village priest and everyone else who has stayed at home fast rigidly until their arrival. The bearer of the flesh carries it rolled up in leaves of the googlut tree, and when he approaches the villages, lays it out on a cushion formed of a handful of grass, and then deposits it in the place of public meeting, to give assurance to all of its arrival. The fasting heads of families then go with their priest to receive the flesh. He takes and divides it into two portions, and subdivides one of these into as many shares as there are heads of families present. He then says to the earth goddess – "O Tari Pennu! our village offered such a person as a sacrifice, and divided the flesh among all the people in honour of the gods. Now, such a village has offered such a one, and has sent us flesh for you. Be not displeased with the quantity, we could only give them as much. If you will give us wealth, we will repeat the rite." The Janni then seats himself on the ground, scrapes a hole in it, and taking one of the two portions into which he divided the flesh, places it in the hole, but with his back turned, and without looking. Then each man adds a little earth to bury it and the Janni pours water on the spot from a hill gourd. Each head of a house rolls his shred of flesh in leaves, and all raise a shout of ex-

---

139 Such a provision for the road is called *pranga* in the Dongria language.

ultation at the work done. [...] Finally, each man goes and buries his particle of flesh in his favourite field, placing it in the earth behind his back without looking. (Macpherson 1865, 129)

This practice of burying the flesh has ceased, but this did not happen immediately or in all places at once. In a report from 1894, published by the Madras Mail and quoted by Boal (1999, 301–3), the author describes how at that time everyone struggled to get a piece of flesh from the buffalo, and the man who was successful "rushed away as fast as he could to his fields to bury it there, according to ancient custom, before the sun had set" (quoted in Boal 1999, 303). Similarly, in an account written in the Kondmals in the early twentieth century by an Oriya named Kogera Pradhan (quoted in Boal 1999, 307–13), we are told that the buffalo's flesh is buried in the earth, not however on the hills slopes, but in the *meria* grove (quoted in Boal 1999, 311). In her own description of the festival, which summarises her experiences between 1950 and 1992, Boal also mentions the burial of buffalo meat. According to her observations, the main priest "rapidly slashes flesh from the still breathing animal to give to the flesh-takers from other villages. Each one drops it into a brass pot, stops it up with leaves and rushes away, running and leaping, while the people of the village pelt them with clods of earth and stones, as if in a fierce quarrel. These young men escape, and leap and dance all the way to their own villages, their drummers with them, to enable the priest to bury the flesh before sundown" (Boal 1999, 324).

From this description we can infer that the buffalo's flesh increases the fertility of either the individual fields where it is buried or the whole village territory where it is placed into the ground near the *dharni*. The rule that the flesh must be placed in the ground before sunset probably derives from the idea that the male sun god activates the female powers of the earth. The buffalo's flesh, carried home by young men like a bride captured in a neighbouring village, brings fertility to the fields just like the bride after her marriage brings wealth and children to the local line of her husband.

Shortly after distributing the *malkamba*, the "protectors" cut open the body of the buffalo, take out the intestines and stomach, and first place everything on the sacrificial pole to which the buffalo had been tied. Later the same day they carry it all to the river, wash the entrails in the water, cut the meat into small slices, and boil everything. All of the *mudrenga* assemble at this place, and the *wahi unga* ("intestine meat") is distributed among them, although everyone present, even if they do not belong to the "protectors," also receives a share. In my interpretation, the consumption of the intestines sets the *mudrenga* in opposition to the other affines who took away the *malkamba*. Both are affines, but in contrast to the latter, the former may not kill the buffalo or take *malkamba* or "fertility" away from the organisers. They resemble more the mother's brother's people, with whom one has been joined in marriage in a previous generation and who are now like brothers. They have been "swallowed," i.e., transformed by marriage from affinal outsiders into quasi-consanguineal insiders or "brothers." They eat meat from inside the body of the victim, while the young men consume the meat associated with the hide, i.e., the outer part of the body.

Table 41: Differences between the two types of affines

AFFINES	
protectors (*mudrenga*)	sacrificers (*padria*)
married men	unmarried men
middle-aged	young
"mother's brothers"	potential husbands
inside meat (intestines)	outside meat (hide)

Following the sacrifice on Sunday morning, the organisers are busy cooking for the next few days. Ideally, the following feasts should take place:
1. Sunday
   daytime: *mudrenga bhoji: mudrenga* eat their *wahi unga*
   evening: *bana paga:* rice and meat cooked in the *dharni kudi* and consumed by the organisers
2. Monday *purta bhoji* (feast for the whole world) or *mulu bhoji* (main feast)
3. Tuesday *duta janga bhoji:* eating the "legs for the old men"
4. Wednesday *hadi bhoji* (finishing feast) or *kapada bhoji* (head feast)

In practice, I never witnessed a *kodru parbu* at which this sequence of feasts was observed, for the simple reason that the meat quickly starts to spoil due to the heat and the flies. In all the places where I observed the festival, everything had been consumed by Monday, when the "whole world" is invited to share the food. This expression does not mean that many people participate in the feast. Instead, most of the food is eaten by the organisers, including the clan brothers and their *mudrenga*. Those who actually killed the animal, i.e., the young people of "the country" (*desa*), do not reappear again. In other words, the buffalo is mainly consumed by those people who were not allowed to sacrifice it!

5.7 Conclusions

5.7.1 *kodru parbu* and feasts of merit

Taking into account the huge amount of money spent on sacrificial animals and the rice, millet, pulses, meat, and alcohol required to put on feasts for a substantial number of guests, it is tempting to compare the *kodru parbu* with the expensive feasts of merit that used to be – and in some places still are – performed by people living in the extreme northeast and northwest of the Indian subcontinent. We have a number of fairly good descriptions of feasts of merit as celebrated by the various Naga tribes (Hutton 1921a, 230–33; 1921b, 227–29; Mills 1922, 136–44; 1926, 257–62, 370–96; 1937, 181–95; Parry 1932, 372–78), by the Apa Tani of Arunachal Pradesh (Fürer-Haimendorf 1962, 138–43; 1980, 150–56) and the Mru of the Chittagong Hills (Brauns and Löffler 1990, 226–40). Similar types of feasts have been described among the Kafirs of Nuristan (Jones 1974, 166–85). Such elaborate forms of wealth distribution are also found in societies in other regions of the world (Birket-Smith 1967), most notably among the various Indian tribes of the northwest coast of America and Canada (e. g., Boas 1966; Rosman and Rubel 1971) and in various New Guinea societies whose members organise large pig festivals (e. g., Rubel and Rosman 1978).

Despite the immense variation in terms of social structure and culture of the ethnic communities referred to above, we may define a kind of "polythetic class" (Wittgenstein) named "feast of merit," which contains certain features often found in combination in many but not necessarily all of these societies. What are these typical features?

1. Wealth (e. g., crops, animals, money, valuable objects) is distributed on ceremonial occasions, often involving animal sacrifices (e. g., of chicken, pigs, sheep, cows, mithun).
2. By way of this distribution, givers – and sometimes also receivers – acquire privileges such as the right to wear certain ornaments, possess a particular object, decorate their houses in a special fashion, inherit honourable titles, or take a seat in the assembly of elders that decides village affairs (e. g. Kafirs). In some cases, the feast publicly confirms rights and privileges passed on according to fixed rules of inheritance (e. g., Ang chiefs of Naga); in others the feast merely provides a chance to raise one's own status (e. g., Kafirs, Kwakiutl).
3. The guests and hosts in these feasts often stand in an affinal relationship, as people who either have intermarried in the past or can potentially intermarry in the future (e. g., *potlatch* among Kwakiutl, *te* and *moka* among Enga and Melpa).

4. Feasts held between opposite – often affinal – groups characteristically involve reciprocity, often of an asymmetrical character. The asymmetry itself can become an important status marker, as honour and rank is derived from giving more than one has received (e.g., *potlatch* among Kwakiutl, *moka* among Melpa).
5. These feasts are often ordered in a sequence of increasing expense, numbers of guests attending, and merits acquired. In order to earn the right to perform a feast to which a particularly high status is attached, one has to first hold smaller feasts.
6. These societies are more or less ranked, perhaps even oscillating between "aristocratic" and more "democratic" forms of social and political organisation (Leach 1954), and link "influence" or "charisma" to a person's qualities as a warrior as well as to his or her readiness to distribute wealth to the community.
7. Initiation ceremonies (*rites de passage*), such as name-giving, entry into dormitories, marriages, succession to eminent positions, and funerals (e.g., Northwest Coast Indians, Kafirs), and communal cults, such as ancestor worship, fertility rites, and sacrifices (e.g., Enga, Naga, Dongria), are typical occasions for distributing wealth and gaining honour.
8. These feasts of merit often involve a certain degree of rivalry and contestation, whether in the form of excessive gift-giving among the Kwakiutl (Boas 1966) or the Apa Tani (Fürer-Haimendorf 1962), feuding and raiding among the Kafir (Jones 1974), or head-hunting and brutal forms of sacrifice among the Rengma Naga (Mills 1937).
9. Although certain individuals are often considered to be the "organisers" of the feast of merit, in many cases whole groups sponsor the event and claim the status and privileges acquired through it.
10. Important feasts of merit tend to be large gatherings, not only because the status of whole groups is at stake, but also because claims to a change of status through the distribution of wealth only become effective when witnessed by many people.

Among the Dongria, certain rituals occurring at the time of *rites de passage* are similar to give-away feasts among the different Naga groups and the Kafirs. Thus, each householder has to perform a series of rituals called *giri takoli* (see section 4.3.8) following his marriage, the death of his parents, and the worship of his house deities. The greatest feast given by an individual Dongria household is the so-called *ghanta parba*, for which shrines must be built, several shamans and drummers engaged, and a large number of chickens and goats sacrificed. The whole village community and kin from all over the area are invited to come and attend the distribution of meat and join in the feasting. As an external sign of the performance of the *ghanta parba*, the householder sets up a sacrificial post in front of his house and builds a shrine, as well as setting up another post at the stone representing his local line in the eastern part of the village.

In contrast to some of the other groups referred to above, the Dongria do not have an elaborate ranking system expressed in ornaments, clothing, tattoos, or house decoration. However, status differences do exist and find their expression in titles, in stones and sacrificial poles, and in certain duties expected from a person in relation to the village as a whole. Status differences are not linked to any fixed positions of power. However, a person who distributes his wealth in feasts, assists his kin and fellow villagers in performing their rituals, takes part in decision-making in village assemblies, and represents the community among outsiders is a man of influence, a *kaja loku* or "senior person." Dongria themselves express this concept by saying "without me, no work can start; without me, nothing can be done".

In the *kodru parbu*, it is not so much the status of individual householders but that of the dominant clan and the village as a whole that seems to be at stake. The descendants of the village founders are expected to pool their resources and cooperate in order to perform the sacrifice to the earth goddess. They depend on the help of other villagers, the cooperation of their "brothers" from the same clan, and the inhabitants of neighbouring villages, who come to protect the victims. A successful sacrifice thus becomes a display of the social relationships maintained by the sponsoring village. As proof of their willingness to perform their obligations towards the deities and their kin and affines, the sacrificial posts and the earth goddess's house remain at the centre of the settlement, where the number of posts and the condition of the house are visible to all. These objects mark the wealth and the status of a village as a whole, but in particular that of the people whose ancestors first conquered or bought this territory.

The *kodru parbu*, like many of the feasts of merit referred to above, involves both a contrast between hosts and guests, the latter being either real or potential affines of the former, and a rivalry or contest, most clearly expressed in the actual killing of the victim itself. The whole setup of the festival leads to a contest between the sponsors and the young affinal men, the former trying to complete all the necessary rituals, the latter keen to kill the victim as soon as possible. The rivalry may become more than symbolic when claims over the village territory are at stake. In this case, the buffalo itself becomes an object of contestation between the sponsors and those who claim rights over the territory of a particular village. The whole performance shows elements of a battle between the young men, who carry lances and axes and whirl them around in a warlike fashion. In their interpretation of potlatch rivalry among Northwest Coast Indians,

Rubel and Rosman go back to the writings of Marcel Mauss to show that marriage, like any other form of exchange, has a double effect:

> Mauss's work on the gift illustrates the way in which series of exchanges of goods, services, and women serve to integrate groups, while at the same time maintaining separateness and even hostility between them. (Rosman and Rubel 1971, 3)

This is a perfect description of the social relations in any *kodru parbu,* in which affines confront each other in a joint operation that unites and at the same time separates them. As in feasts of merit celebrated by the various Northwest Coast Indians, succession and the status of important families of the clan appear to be regulated by the *kodru parbu*. As described in the ethnographic section of this chapter, it is not usually the old people who carry the brass pots, knives, or axes they preserve in their houses, but one of their sons. I never inquired which of his sons a householder of high status selects to act on his behalf, but the public role of the young boy or man who carries the sacred objects may be interpreted as a confirmation of his succession to his father's status. I am not aware of disputes about the right to carry these holy objects. The axes and the right to preserve the brass pot and the knife are passed on from a father to his sons, and it seems plausible that the *kodru parbu* offers an occasion to make this decision publicly known.

Among the different families involved in preparing and performing the sacrifice, the high status of the village founders is further marked by placing a leg on the roof of their house. We may say that this act serves as public acknowledgement that a certain house in the village has the most important relationship to the earth goddess, upon whom everybody depends. Among the Naga, too, the organisers of the highest grade in the series of feasts of merit will sacrifice a mithun that is divided among those present, the oldest person getting a leg and the sponsor himself (like the *jani* among the Desia Kond) receiving the victim's skull.[140]

It should again be pointed out that these status distinctions are neither highly systematised nor linked to any positions of power among the Dongria. There is neither a chain of command, as in an army or centralised kingdom, nor a clear

---

[140] The cultures of the different Naga groups show an amazing degree of resemblance to Dongria culture. Certainly, there are as many differences between the different Naga groups as there are between the various Kond communities, yet the cultural "tapestry" builds upon similar elements, such as shifting cultivation, small-scale hunting and fishing, clan-based villages, village councils, dormitories, animal sacrifices, status distinctions, etc. I was particularly struck by the similarities between the Dongria Kond and the Rengma Naga, as described by Mills (1937).

political ranking order exhibited in seating arrangements or distribution sequences, as among the Kwakiutl. There are differences in terms of wealth and political influence, but in the long term these do not result in any permanent positions of power. Therefore, relatively prosperous people are expected to hold larger feasts and spend more then their poorer fellow villagers, who always approach them in times of need.[141] The elders, who have gained some influence and respect through accumulating wealth, organising large feasts, and representing the village in conflicts, are often challenged by younger and stronger men, who may physically attack them if they feel oppressed. Claims for status are thus not necessarily claims for political power; rather, they are attempts to secure and maintain the community's respect. Status does not derive from dominance, but from wealth spent at major rituals in order to improve relations with the gods, ancestors, and spirits and from seniority. The *kodru parbu,* as a kind of feast of merit, allows both the distribution of wealth and the demonstration of seniority, and even if it does not express a highly sophisticated ranking, it does reveal and create a complex social structure.

5.7.2 Creating society: Sacrifice and social structure

In their analysis of the potlatch among the Indians of the northwest coast of North America, Rosman and Rubel come to the conclusion that the "potlatch is thus a drama in which are played out the essential elements of Kwakiutl culture and society, while revealing the components of the social structure" (Rosman and Rubel 1971, 157). The same can be said with regard to the *kodru parbu* and the Dongria social structure. First of all, the festival is intimately related to the clan organisation of the Dongria Kond. This can be deduced from the rule that nobody from the clan organising the sacrifice may kill the victim. The unity of the clan is thus defined in relation to the sacrifice to the earth goddess.

Second, the first division below that of the clan level, the *muta*, is intimately linked to the performance of the festival. A *muta* is first of all a sacrificial community of people of the same clan who jointly own certain objects necessary for the performance of the sacrifice. Each *muta* identifies itself with a certain territory and clan, but the *muta* itself does not correspond to any discrete area. Rather, it is a unit of cooperation and mutual help, since ideally all people belonging

---

[141] As a relatively wealthy person, I was constantly approached by the Dongria of the village where I stayed with requests to help them pay for rituals and sacrifices.

to the same *muta* should assist one another in preparing the sacrificial site and performing the rituals. It is uncertain whether the *muta* as a sacrificial community has ever been identical with the *muta* as an administrative unit in the royal organisation for collecting revenue from the tribals. Certain titles used by Dongria, like *saanta, bismajhi,* or *naika,* may suggest this, but additional historical sources would be needed to address this question fully. From my data it can only be concluded that a *muta* is defined by collective action in the context of the sacrifice and not by any central agency from outside.

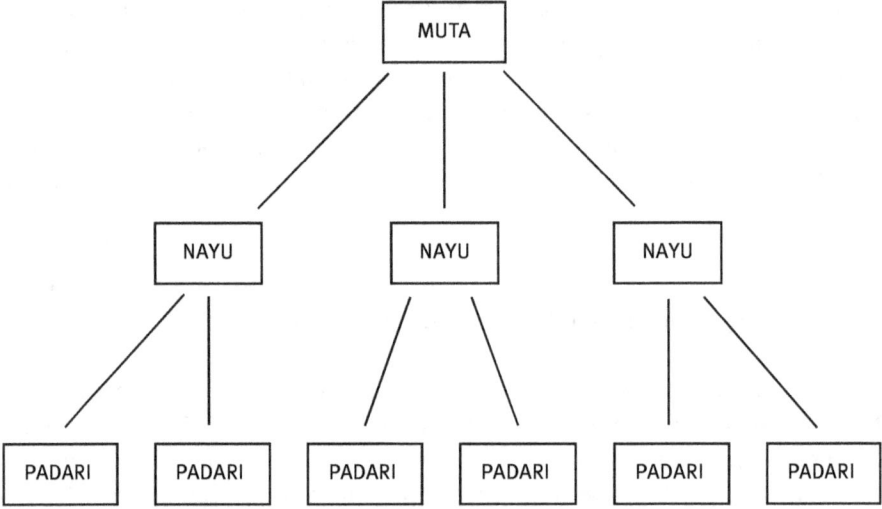

Figure 39: Territorial organisation

On the next level down in the social order we find the villages, which are relevant for the *kodru parbu* in a double sense. First, the festival is performed by the residents of the village settlement (*nayu*), who cooperate independently of their actual clan affiliation. This means that even residents belonging to clans other than those of the dominant clan provide assistance with preparing the sacrificial site or arranging the feasts. Second, each *nayu* has at least one, if not more village territories (*padari*) marked by stone arrangements representing the local earth goddess. The *kodru parbu* is performed for one or all of the *padari* of each settlement, and the dominant clan claiming rights in this *padari* is responsible for the purchase of the sacrificial victim. The village territory thus belongs to a particular *nayu* that is part of a certain *muta*. The *padari* is owned by the descendants of the village founders (or those who bought the land from another clan), who are the ones who have the right to buy the victim to be sacrificed

5.7 Conclusions — 585

to this local earth goddess. The village territory, the earth goddess, and the local dominant clan are closely interconnected, and by performing the *kodru parbu*, the members of the dominant clan demonstrate their rights over the territory and at the same time satisfy the demands of the earth goddess, who is able to make their land fertile. On the village level, people are differentiated according to their affiliation with distinct local lines (*punja*) and houses (*ijo*). The word *punja* is used in a double sense, since it refers to a certain status category as well as to a particular descent group. The titles of at least one (i.e., *jani*) but perhaps of all four status categories (*jani, pujari, bismajhi, mondal*),[142] each divided into the two further sub-sections of senior (*kaja*) and junior (*icha*), are derived from functions exercised by certain specialists during the *kodru parbu*.

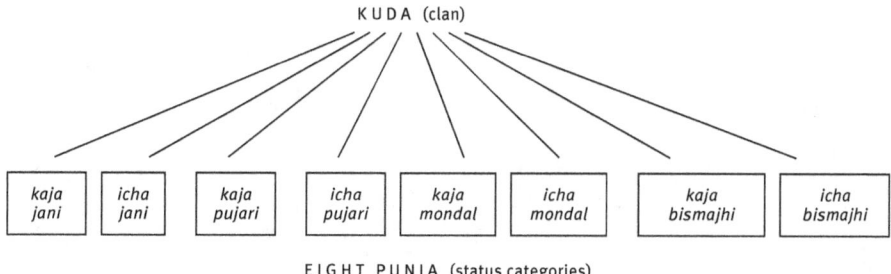

Figure 40: Descent and status categories

The *punja*, in the sense of a local descent group, plays a major role on the second day of the *kodru parbu* when the god of war and hunting, *lada penu*, is worshipped at the stones outside the village. These stones are identified with particular local descent groups, just as the stones of the local earth goddess are identified with the village as a whole.

The lowest level of the social organisation, the house, acts as a unit in different phases of the festival, most notably when the victim is driven from house to house and washed with water, anointed with oil, and fed with rice by the woman of each house. Certain houses have a prominent status due to their possession of the sacred objects, which either circulate within the *muta* or remain within the village even after the completion of the sacrifice. The seniority and status of certain houses is further expressed through the custom of placing portions of the

---

142 Instead of *bismajhi* and *mondal*, sometimes also *naika* and *saanta*. Nayak (1989, 134) cites a saying according to which the *bismajhi* brings the rice, the *jani* calls the gods, the *pujari* cooks, and the *mondal* supervises everything.

sacrificial animal on their roofs. Often, several houses together belong to one descent group named after one of the eight status categories. If there is more than one descent group of the same status category in a village, they are distinguished in two ways: first, by indicating who is to be the heir of whom, since only people of the same descent group can inherit from one another; and second, by associating a certain descent group with a particular place of origin from which its members have supposedly migrated.

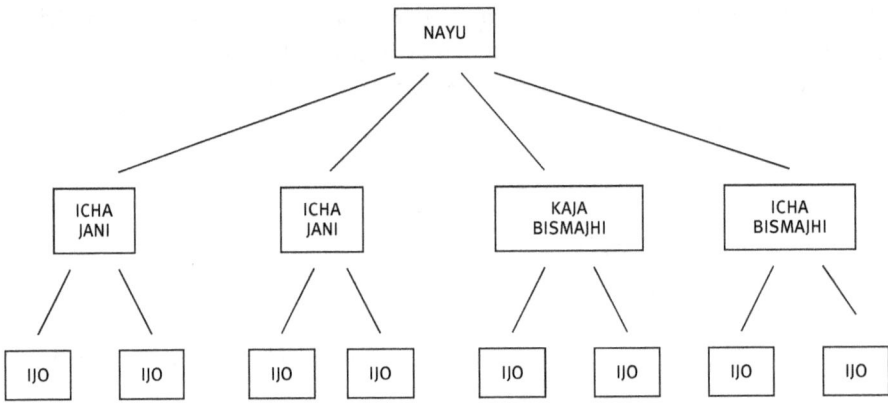

Figure 41: Descent groups and houses (hypothetical example)

This social organisation is based on the combination of descent, territory, and residence and is summarised in the table below.

Table 42: Social and territorial organisation in relation to the *kodru parbu*

Dongria	English	Definition	Example	Territory	Affiliation	Change
kuda	clan	united by a common name, the rule of clan exogamy, and a prohibition on killing the sacrificial victim they offer	Sikoka people	myths ascribe certain territories to particular clans; a clan often dominates numerically in a certain area	patrilineal descent	no change

5.7 Conclusions — 587

muta	localised sacrificial community	united by a common clan and by the exchange of objects (e.g., knife and brass pot) used in the sacrifice	twelve Sikoka villages	aggregation of villages of a certain area, no clearly bounded territory	affiliation with *muta* of one's descent group	change possible (villages join another *muta* of the same clan)
nayu	settlement	settlement occupied by members of a dominant clan who purchase the *meria* victim and by people of other clans	Gumma	boundaries only marked in ritual contexts	affiliation with the *nayu* of one's descent group; also membership through residence	change possible and frequent (e.g., migration, uxorilocal residence)
padari	village territory	named territory of a settlement containing a stone arrangement of the earth goddess for whom the victim is sacrificed	Waliamba *padari* belonging to Gumma	clearly marked boundaries	affiliation with *padari* of one's descent group	change possible (a village territory can be sold)
Punja (1)	status category	all Dongria belong to one of the eight status categories; titles imply religious or secular functions as well as seniority	*mondal* (or *saanta*), *bismajhi* (or *naika/kirsani*), *jani*, *pujari*; all these categories have a senior and a junior sub-division	people of the same status category are spread over the whole area	patrilineal descent	no change possible
Punja (2)	descent group	a number of houses recognising common de-	descent group of the senior *jani* of Gumma	members of the same descent group tend	patrilineal descent and place of origin (to dis-	change possible (migration has the effect that

		scent and worshipping the same stone (kona); named according to status category		to live together	tinguish two descent groups of the same status category, a place of origin may be recalled)	old descent links are forgotten and new ones established)
ijo	house	householder with his wife, children, and other relatives	house of Sikoka Muni	building	patrilineal descent and/or residence	change possible

The buffalo sacrifice creates and maintains certain relations not only between villages of the same clan, but also between villages of different clans. The rule that forbids someone to kill the victim sacrificed to his own earth goddess creates an opposition between clans, in this case between the clan of sacrifiers or sponsors and the clans of sacrificers. The latter are affines, but not all affines act as sacrificers. Rather, two categories of affines, the *mudrenga* and the *tonenga*, should not kill the victim. This can be compared to rules prohibiting marriage. Clan exogamy establishes an opposition between agnatic and affinal clans. However, certain additional rules prohibit the direct repetition of intermarriage among the Dongria, and thus in effect define some people within the affinal category as non-marriageable. The same holds for the buffalo sacrifice. On the one hand, all sponsors are opposed to members of affinal clans by the rule that states that clan members of the sponsors may not kill the buffalo. On the other hand, among the affines, some will join the sponsors rather than act as sacrificers, because they are also prohibited from killing the victim. Thus the organisers of the buffalo sacrifice are joined in their preparations by villagers from an affinal clan called *mudrenga*. The latter are the protectors of the sacrificial victim and are not supposed to be involved in the killing.

In addition to the *mudrenga*, the *tonenga,* or ceremonial friends, come to attend the festival as guests. The *tonenga*, although belonging to an affinal clan category, are not strictly speaking affines, because one is not supposed to intermarry with ceremonial friends. As in the case of the *mudrenga*, these friendship relations do not link individuals but whole communities, such as five Sikoka villages with five Wadaka villages. Unlike the *mudrenga*, the *tonenga* do not have to perform any functions; they are simply very honoured guests who bring gifts, such as a buffalo, rice, and alcohol, and who receive gifts from the hosts at the time of their departure. Both *mudrenga* and *tonenga*, however, may not

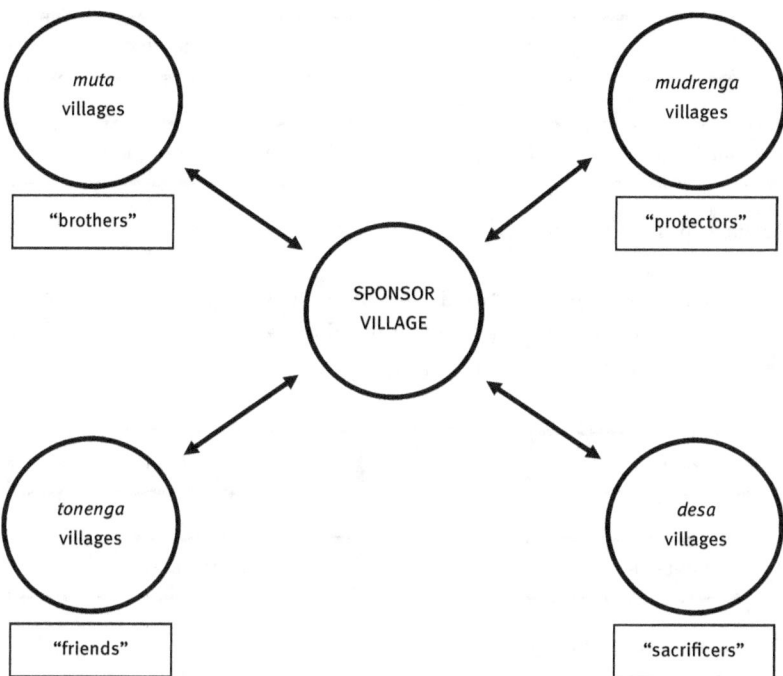

Figure 42: Villages interconnected by the *kodru parbu*

kill the buffalo, and this rule distinguishes them from the other type of affines, the young men, who are not only allowed but expected to put the buffalo to death. According to Aparajita (1994, 236), these young affines are collectively referred to as *padria*, a word I have not encountered in my fieldwork. Dongria call the assembly of these young people in their village *desa rundam ane*, meaning the "people from near and far have assembled." The word *desa* implies that these are people from various places who are neither agnates nor bound to the sponsors as protectors or ceremonial friends.

On the collective level, the *kodru parbu* thus brings together members of four types of villages (see figure 42): 1. *muta loku* or "brothers"; 2. the *mudrenga* or "protectors"; 3. the *tonenga* or "friends"; and 4. the *desa loku* or sacrificers. The distinctions between these different types are made on the basis of the following structural principles: territory, affinity, and rivalry.

First, all *muta* villages stand in opposition to all other villages in that they constitute a people who have a common clan land and cooperate in performing the sacrifice to the land, in opposition to all other people who worship the earth goddess of another clan territory:

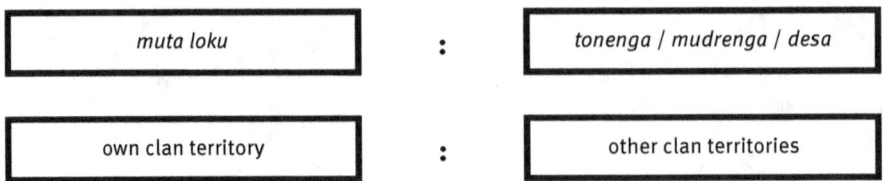

Figure 43: Relations based on territory

Second, the *muta* villages are joined with the *tonenga* because they may not marry each other, whereas they may marry into other categories of people if this is not ruled out on grounds of clan exogamy:

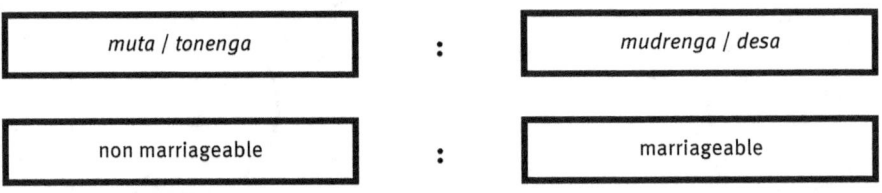

Figure 44: Relations based on affinity

Finally, *muta*, *tonenga*, and *mudrenga* villages unite in opposition to the young visitors from all other villages, as only the latter are expected to kill the victim. Furthermore, whereas members of the former three types of villages unite on the basis of mutual help and friendship, the latter are real or symbolic rivals:

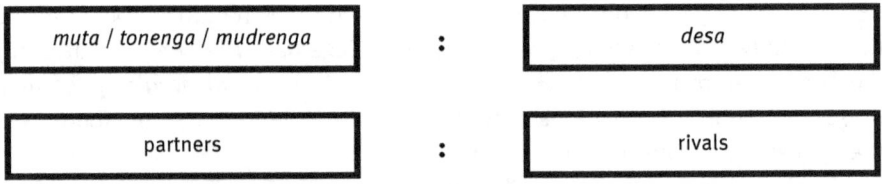

Figure 45: Relations based on rivalry

The *kodru parbu* creates Dongria Kond society by establishing differently valued relations between various social units that depend upon one another for their wellbeing and fertility. This creative aspect of the sacrifice is expressed in a myth collected by Macpherson more than one hundred and fifty years ago:

> They [the first Kond] procured and offered a sacrifice, and, says the legend, "now society with its relation of father and mother, and wife and child, and the ties between ruler and subject arose;" and the knowledge of all that relates to agriculture was imparted to men. (Macpherson 1865, 97)

The following sections of this conclusion addresses the questions of the extent to which the *kodru parbu* can be compared to marriage (5.7.3. Sacrifice and marriage), whether or not it expresses "ties between ruler and subject" (5.7.4. Ritual and political organisation), what the myths tell us about the link between the sacrifice and "the knowledge of all that relates to agriculture" (5.7.5. Myth and ritual), and the way in which the ritual performance is thought to promote the fertility of the earth (5.7.6. Fertility and wellbeing).

5.7.3 Sacrifice and marriage

If we compare Dongria Kond ideas and practices of marriage to the *kodru parbu* as described above, certain important similarities come to the fore that help us to understand specific aspects of the buffalo sacrifice.[143] First of all, the wedding ceremony follows a very similar syntax. Both the elaborate wedding ceremony and the main days of the sacrifice take place on three consecutive days, from Friday to Sunday. In both cases, the guests arrive on Friday, stay through Saturday, and leave on Sunday. The highlight of both ceremonies, the union of bride and groom and the actual killing of the buffalo, takes place on Sunday morning. On this day, the bride is taken to her new village and united with the household of her parents-in-law. In the context of the sacrifice, the young men who have killed the victim in the morning take home portions of buffalo meat, which they would once have buried in the ground but now consume along with their fellow villagers.

Second, the place of both occasions in the yearly ritual cycle is very similar. Weddings are performed just before the rainy season at the hottest time of the year, in April or May, while buffalo sacrifices are celebrated only slightly earlier, in March or April. At that time, the harvest, which begins in November-December, has come to an end with the harvest of the pigeon peas, which are brought home from the fields as late as January or February. From February onwards, Dongria fell trees in their new swiddens and let the trees and the bushy undergrowth dry up in the heat of the sun. From March onwards, people are relatively free from work, and if the harvest was good, they are able to hold large feasts

---

143 For a similar comparison between marriage and the *gotr*, the memorial festival for the dead among the Gadaba, see Pfeffer 1991, 2001, 2002b and Berger 2015, 304–32.

and buy the animals required for the completion of the wedding ceremony as well as for the *kodru parbu*. Shortly after the wedding and *kodru parbu* season, the rains set in, and people begin to sow seeds and plants in their fields at the start of the new agricultural year. Around the same time, the newlywed bride and groom, who have ideally avoided one another prior to their marriage, are invited by their friends to enter into sexual relations with each other. In this sense, the period following the completion of both rituals is characterised by activities aimed at reproduction, of the swidden in the case of the *kodru parbu* and of the people in the case of a wedding.

Third, on both occasions the rituals show certain similarities that suggest that the buffalo is treated like a bride or groom in the context of an arranged wedding. Before a marriage ceremony, a bride visits the houses of all her neighbours in her natal village and, with her friends, pays a visit to the house of her mother's brother and to all her relatives and friends living in other villages. At each of these houses, she is – mostly symbolically – bathed in turmeric water, anointed with oil, and offered cooked food to eat. Again, on the day before she leaves her natal village, i.e., on Saturday, she enters each and every house of her village, accompanied by her friends, who sing songs about her departure. She and one or two of her closest friends weep bitterly, hiding their faces in a shawl. The groom, together with his friends, is treated in a similar fashion when he goes to pay a visit to the houses in his village and a few other villages before the wedding, but these visits are not very formal, nor do people attach the same importance to them as in the case of a bride.

Not unlike bride and groom in the context of a wedding, the buffalo to be sacrificed to the earth goddess, together with at least one more buffalo to be slaughtered later during the *ambadadi yatra*, is taken to all the houses in the organising village and to several villages related to them as either "protectors" (i.e., the *mudrenga*) or "agnates" (i.e., brother villages of the same clan). On the day before the sacrifice, i.e., on Saturday, the sacrificial victim – in the case of more than one village territory, all the victims – are driven from house to house and bathed with turmeric water, anointed with oil, and offered cooked rice to eat.

These rituals suggest a certain identity between the buffalo and the main actors in a wedding ceremony. Yet, if the sacrifice appears to be similar to a marriage, this raises the questions of who marries whom and with whom the victim is identified, the bride or the groom. I think the answer to the latter question is that the sacrificial victim is similar to a bride in a wedding, because like her it is presented as a gift, and because as in a marriage, relations between the parties during the sacrifice involve rivalry and even aggression. Seen in this way, the main similarity between marriage and sacrifice is that both rituals involve actions of giving and receiving forms of "life," such as the bride, the betrothal fee, the harvest,[144] and the sacrificial victim, which create lasting alliances between potential rivals.

If my interpretation is correct, the *kodru parbu* involves two relations, an exchange relation with the goddess and a relation characterised by rivalry (or force) with the affinal villages. With regard to the goddess, the villagers provide a gift to the *dharni*, whereas they themselves take the goddess in form of the harvest provided by the earth.[145] The connection between the harvest and the sacrifice is most clearly expressed in the following Dongria saying:

> *echak loku katkiteru* (as many people sacrificed)
> *echak lahi kambitenga* (so much rice has ripened)
> *echak loku ateru* (as many people took [meat])
> *echak lahi kambitenga* (so much rice has ripened)

I have not recorded any explicit statements identifying the buffalo with the goddess's consort or husband, as is the case in Hindu festivals, where the analogy plays a central role in the worship of village deities, especially worship of forms of Durga (Kinsley 1986, 205). In the context of the *kodru parbu*, I also never encountered the idea that the buffalo represents a demon.[146] Rather, the buffalo of the *kodru parbu* is given a double identity: it represents the "mother" or earth goddess and at the same time is a sacrificial victim offered to the god-

---

144 Jena et al. (2002, 266–6 7) provide convincing evidence that trees, plants, etc. are considered to have "life" (*jela*). I myself heard, for example, Dongria talking about the "life" (*jela*) of the palm-wine tree, which is said to be located inside the tree's trunk.
145 *Sita penu-lahi penu* is the goddess of rice and of wealth in general, just like *laksmi* in the Hindu pantheon. She is considered to be the earth goddess's daughter, and her "father" is *dharmu*, the sun god. At the time of threshing, her representation, the grain heap on the threshing floor, receives elaborate worship before the Dongria take the goddess, i.e., the harvest, home and store it in the attic of their houses. Peter Berger (2015, 469–72) elaborately describes how, among the Gadaba, the rice is considered to be a bride taken home after harvest.
146 Jena et al. (2002, 146–48) collected a Dongria myth concerning the killing of a demon, but this deed is performed by a divine king (Biridanga) with bow and arrow and not by the goddess, who only helps him in putting the demon to sleep. There is, however, one connection between this demon and the *kodru parbu*, since parts of his body are said to have turned into the objects representing the *koteiwali* (the demon's horns), the *dharniwali* (the demon's head), and the roof of the goddess's house (the demon's hair) (Jena et al. 2002, 148). The rest of the demon's body is said to have turned into plants, trees, creepers, and grasses. This myth suggests that the demon, like the one conquered by the Hindu goddess, is conceived of as a buffalo. Among the Dongria, the demon is referred to as *rakesi*, a word perhaps derived from the term *rakhyasura*. Similar to the coastal people, the Dongria celebrate the demon's festival, known as *dola ghata yatra*, around October, i.e., in the Hindu month of *dasara*.

dess. Dongria emphasise that the goddess wants the buffalo in return for providing a good harvest and that the main gift to her is the "life" (*jela*), i. e., the blood (*neteri*), of the victim. The village community buys the buffalo (or in former times the human victim), thereby making it a part of their own property or "life," and then gives it away to the earth goddess as a counter-gift. It may be considered equivalent to the betrothal fee, yet with the important difference that the harvest is taken home before the sacrifice, whereas in the context of marriage it is the other way around. By giving the victim's blood, the organisers feed the goddess, just as the goddess nourishes them when she gives a good harvest. The gift of blood also prevents the goddess, who is feared for her deadly wrath, from killing someone from the village community. In this sense, the buffalo can also be seen as a substitute for the organisers themselves.

The second relationship exists between the sponsors of the festival and the young affinal men who come to kill the *meria*. As a Dongria once explained to me, the organisers cannot sacrifice the buffalo on their own, in the same ways that they may not engage in sexual relations with their own sisters. Instead, they give away the buffalo to the young men, who as affines may sacrifice the victim in the same way that they may marry (and have sex with) the organisers' sisters. They can sacrifice the buffalo and take pieces of it home just as they can bring a bride from a foreign village to their own home. By hanging the flesh in the goddess's house before consuming it, the villagers make a gift to their own *dharni* and can thus partake in the merit the festival's organisers gained through sponsoring the sacrifice. In this way, the effects of a single *kodru parbu* are multiplied.

These two types of relations, with gods and with young male affines, are established in a festival that displays elements of two forms of marriage, both arranged marriage and bride capture. On the one hand, the buffalo is treated like a bride in an arranged marriage, since like her it is led from house to house to be bathed, anointed, and fed. As previously mentioned, the *kodru parbu* occurs on the same days and at roughly the same time as elaborate weddings, and the shrines of the *dharni* and *koteiwali* are decorated with the same motifs as the shawls worn by bride and groom on the day of their marriage. The guests and young people of the village behave in very similar ways on the occasions of both weddings and buffalo sacrifices. They dance throughout the night, consume a lot of alcohol, and are open to sexual encounters with various partners in the dormitories or in the woods.

On the other hand, the way in which the young men try to kill the buffalo is reminiscent of a bride capture. Like a girl in a dormitory, the buffalo remains inside a pen, and the young men use every opportunity to catch the buffalo, i. e., to kill it. The rivalry between hosts and guests comes to the fore when the latter try to humiliate the sponsors by killing the victim before the proper time of sacrifice.¹⁴⁷ When successful, they attempt to take a piece of flesh, which they put on their axes before leaving the village making gestures of victory. In the same way, young men who have successfully managed to capture a bride express their pride with gestures of triumph. The idea that the buffalo is like the earth goddess was clearly stated by my informants. As mentioned above, Dongria who claim to have rights in the land of the village may even steal a leg of the buffalo; in other words, they "capture" a part of the earth goddess and take it to their own place. In accordance with Hubert and Mauss, we may indeed view the buffalo as a link between the sacrifiers (i.e., the sponsors) and the gods (i.e., the earth goddess) that participates in the nature of both.¹⁴⁸ Using this as a starting point, it is possible to see how an important part of the community is acquired by forcibly taking home portions of the buffalo meat, and this also holds true in the case of bride capture. In a sense, both acts may be characterised as the "stealing of fertility," since the young affines take something, i.e., the bride and the flesh, without giving any "life" back. Reciprocity exists in such relations only in the sense that those whose sisters have been captured and whose buffalo was killed will one day steal a sister and kill a buffalo of the opposite side. In the context of bride capture, I have called this type of reciprocity "violent reciprocity" (see section 4.5).

Table 43: Forms of marriage and sacrifice compared

"ARRANGED MARRIAGE"	earth goddess ←	— harvest — → buffalo blood	sponsor village
"BRIDE CAPTURE"	sponsor village	flesh of buffalo	affinal villages →

---

147 Forms of humiliation of the victim itself have been reported for the Kuttia Kond by Hermann Niggemeyer, who attended several buffalo sacrifices and reports about one of them: "Not only the priest and the Kutaka tease and ridicule the sacrificial animals from sunrise until the time of sacrifice, but also all the guests, who arrived from the neighbourhood in the course of the afternoon to attend the festival. [...] The guests from neighbouring villages sang satirical songs while beating the buffalo, pulling its genitals, and joggling its head by the horns" (Niggemeyer 1964a, 201; my translation).

148 In a Kond myth about the origin of human sacrifice cited by Elwin (1954, 550–51), the priests talk to the victim as if they were addressing the goddess herself. They ask the victim whether they will have a good harvest, and when he promises this, the Kond kill him. This myth thus establishes a clear identity between the victim and the receiver of the sacrifice, the goddess herself.

5.7.4 Ritual and political organisation

In the third part of this chapter I gave an overview of the different sacred objects worshipped by the Dongria in the course of the *kodru parbu*. It became evident that these objects are on the one hand related to the performance of the sacrifice and on the other hand serve to express land rights and the order of the local territorial organisation. Thus, the *tangi* or axe used for symbolically killing the victim is linked to claims of rights over a particular village territory, while the *bonda* (brass umbrella) and *suri* (knife) among the Dongria Kond represent the higher level of territorial organisation, the *muta*. The senior *bonda* and the *suri* stand for the unity of the *muta* and circulate between those families in the *muta* who are recognised to have the most senior status. Both objects are said to have been given to the Kond by the former kings. The *bonda*, in particular, is worshipped as a representation of the king, not so much of the human but the divine ruler, *niamraja*. In the past, the *muta* was first of all a political organisation used by the kings to administer the Kond villages and to collect revenue from them (Behura and Sahu 1970–71). This raises the question of whether ritual and political organisation are perhaps the same. Does the system formed by the ownership and circulation of divine objects used in the *kodru parbu* correspond to the system of administration in the Niamgiri Hills?

According to Nayak (1989, 180), the kings authorised "*mutha* heads" named *mondal* to administer "a cluster of twenty villages or hamlets" by furnishing them with a red sari tied to form headgear and a black coat. The *mondal* of the Dongria were distinguished from the *muta* heads of the Desia Kond, who were called *patra* and received white headgear and a khaki coat from the king as insignia of their authority (Nayak 1989, 180). The *mondal* "were given special power of arbitration in communal matters and had the power to pardon deviant Dongria Kondhs marrying outside their community" (Nayak 1989, 181). Desia Kond informed me that the *mondal* were selected by the "king" (*raja*) of Kalyansingpur, who resided in a small thatched hut in this little town. The "king" of Kalyansingpur was probably an official (*dewan*) authorised by the *thatraja* who resided in Bissamcuttack, a larger town located in the valley southeast of the Niamgiri Hills. According to these Desia Kond, one *mondal* from the Sikoka clan residing in the village of Patalamba was authorised by the *raja* to control the territory of what is now Kalyansingpur block. The *mondal* in turn chose certain families as *bismajhi* to help him as assistants, as he himself could not cover all villages. The Dongria of the Kalyansingpur block still respect two families as *mondal* over "fifty villages," i.e., approximately half of the total number of villages in the Niamgiri Hills. One is known as *kaja mondal* (in the village of Patalamba) or "senior *mondal*," since his ancestors were the first to bear this title, and the other is called *icha mondal* (in the village of Lekhpadar) or "junior *mondal*." As reported above (section 3.4.1), the *mondal* still serves this function, in particular in cases of clan incest, when either he or the *bismajhi* inquires into the case, performs the necessary rituals, and imposes the customary fines. From this diverse information I draw the conclusion that *mondal* and *bismajhi* did not perform their functions for only one clan, but were responsible for a whole territory under the leadership of a particular "*raja*." They were not "*mutha* heads" (Nayak 1989, 180) in the sense that they served a limited number of villages of the same clan joined in one organisation. They were certainly distinct from the Dongria who on the village level owned or kept the divine objects worshipped at the time of the buffalo sacrifice.

This leads to the question of whether rights to these sacred objects were perhaps linked to duties of tax and revenue collection in the former royal organisation. In many villages, those families who keep "the old things" (Oriya: *puruna jinisa*) were introduced to me in Oriya as *mula ghara*, literally "root houses," the word *mula* implying their ancient ancestry and their connection with the village's origin. Some of these families carried titles like *saanta*, *naika*, or *gauntia*. The name *saanta* seems to be a corrupt version of the royally granted title *samanta*, given by the king to his advisers. In coastal Odisha, for example, the highest Brahmins, who reside in villages given to them as tax-free grants by the Gajapati kings, carry the title *samanta* (Hardenberg 1999, 127–28). *Naika* is similarly a title given by the kings to certain chiefs on the village level. According to information I collected among the Desia Kond, *saanta* and *naika* were authorised by the king to collect taxes and revenue from the residents of their villages. In the Desia Kond villages, these families sometimes did not belong to the Kond community but were from different castes, usually of a higher status, such as Gouda and Paika. Every village had one *saanta* or *naika* who was responsible for looking after the collection of the proper amount of tax and revenue assigned to his particular village.

The third title, *gauntia*, was often used as a synonym for *saanta*. Uwe Skoda (2005) studied the *gauntia* system in northern Odisha, where he carried out ethnographic fieldwork among people of the Aghria caste. In the village where he worked, one family belonging to the Aghria caste owned most of the land, and they were paid respect by being referred to on many occasions as *gauntia* or "village king" by the villagers. According to their family history, their forefathers had cleared the forest, for which they were acknowledged by the superior king as headmen. By clearing the forest, they gained certain land rights written down in a deed called *khunt kata gaunti* (Skoda 2005, 183). In this expression, the word *khunt* refers to "the stumps of trees, which had to be cut (*kata* = to cut) in order to establish a village as a realm of a Gauntia" (Skoda 2005, 183).

To attract new settlers, the kings offered initial tax and revenue reductions, but in the long run the *gauntia* were not exempted from paying fixed dues to their overlord (Skoda 2005, 185).

It is tempting to draw parallels between this traditional *gauntia* system and the worship of an axe among the Dongria. Like the Oriya settlers, the Kond certainly acted as pioneers in transforming wild forest into arable land. As axes are used by Kond for felling trees in their swiddens, these objects can be seen as a symbol of the Kond's role in changing wilderness into cultivable land. I have not personally seen any written deeds owned by these headmen, although I heard about Dongria who had formerly possessed certificates issued by the king as proof of their rights over a certain village. In Gumma for example, the *bismajhi* who possesses the junior *bonda* reportedly once had a *pata* for the village, but it was burned during a fire affecting the whole village. However, his family has no connection with the *jani* who owns the *tangi*, and there is no clear connection between the possession of this divine object and any responsibilities for tax and revenue collection.

If *mondal* and *bismajhi* served in the royal organisation at a level higher than the clan organisation, and if the functions of the *saanta*, *naika*, and *gauntia* were restricted to the lower level of the village, who were the representatives of the *muta*, and what were their functions? Is the *muta* a political organisation at all? From my data no clear pattern can be derived concerning the relation between a certain title and the right to preserve the objects that circulate in the *muta*, i.e., the *bonda* and the *suri*. People themselves stated that both objects are always kept in the house of the *jani*, or if there is no *jani*, in the house of a *pujari*, but in actual fact they were preserved by families belonging to other status groups, like *bismajhi* and *saanta*, as well. The variations may arise from the distinction between the "wandering" *bonda* and the "stagnant" *bonda*. In Gumma for example, the "wandering" *bonda* was preserved along with the knife by the senior *jani*, while the "stagnant" *bonda* – but no knife – was kept by the junior *bismajhi*. From this it can be generalised that the more important objects symbolizing the higher level of the *muta* are passed around among the *jani*, while the other type of *bonda*, like the axe, represents the village level, but I do not have enough data to confirm this generalisation. The titles of *jani* and *pujari* are clearly linked to rituals and not to landownership, administration, and tax collection, as is the case with the other titles mentioned above. According to the Desia Kond, the king united a certain number of villages into a unit that, unlike the Dongria Kond, they refer to not as *muta* but as *moksa*. He gave these villages the sacred objects with which to perform the sacrifice and ordered them to exchange these at the time of worship. For this reason all of the villages joined in a unit must bring their divine instruments, *tangi*, *bonda*, and *suri*, to the village organising the *kodru parbu*, and those failing to do so are obliged to pay a fine (*tapu*).

In other words, the *muta* (or *moksa*) was formed on an agnatic basis in order to unite several villages for the performance of the sacrifice to the earth goddess. This organisation may itself be older than the royal division into *muta*, to which the kings provided a definite set of divine objects to be kept by selected high-status families. The *muta* as a sacrificial organisation is linked to other forms of royal administration controlled by certain families who rendered different services: the *mondal* and *bismajhi* looked after adherence to social norms within the kingdom or a part of it, the *jani* and *pujari* performed the sacrifices that guarantee the wellbeing and fertility of the clan territory, and the *saanta* (*gauntia*) and the *naika* collected taxes and revenue, or in other words, gave a share of the fertility enhanced by the sacrifice to the king. In this sense, the ritual and political organisation overlapped, but in my view one was not derived from the other, as they were implemented on different levels of the social and territorial organisation. Nayak's (1989, 179) representation of the political hierarchy as a one-dimensional chain of command does not recognise these different levels and their distinct functions.

Table 44: Levels of royal organisation among the Kond

	Kingdom / local District	Clan territory (*muta*)	Village
Kond titles	*mondal* and *bismajhi*	*jani* and *pujari*	*saanta* and *naika*
Functions	social norms	sacrifice	tax collection
Royal emblems	headgear and coat	axe, knife, umbrella, stove, pots	royal deed

5.7.5 Myth and ritual

In colonial times, several myths were collected that explain the origin of human sacrifice and provide us with detailed accounts of how the sacrifice was conducted. Thurston, for example, quotes a myth, collected by A. B. Jayaram Moodaliar, that describes how the mother of all human beings asked to be sacrificed because her blood has the power to make the ground firm and fertile. The second part of this myth contains a detailed description of how, at the mother's demand, a child obtained from a poor man was sacrificed:

Once upon a time the ground was all wet, and there were only two females on the earth, named Karaboodi and Tharthaboodi, each of whom was blessed with a single male child. The names of the children were Kasarodi and Singarodi. All these individuals sprang from the interior of the earth, together with two small plants called nagakoocha and badokoocha, on which they depended for subsistence. One day, when Karaboodi was cutting these plants for cooking, she accidentally cut the little finger of her left hand, and the blood dropped on the ground. Instantly the wet soft earth on which it fell became dry and hard. The woman then cooked the food and gave it to her son, who asked why it tasted so much sweeter than usual. She replied that she might have a dream that night and if so, would let him know. Next morning the woman told him that if he would act on advice, he would prosper in this world, that he was not to think of her as his mother, and was to cut away the flesh of her back, dig several holes in the ground, bury the flesh, and cover the holes with stones. This her son did and the rest of her body was cremated. The wet soil dried up and became hard, and all kinds of animals and trees came into existence. A partridge scratched the ground with its feet and ragi (millet), maize, dhal (lentils), and rice sprung from it [...] Then Karaboodi appeared in a dream, and told Kasarodi and Singarodi that, if they offered another human victim, their lands would be very fertile, and their cattle would flourish. In the absence of a suitable being, they sacrificed a monkey. Then Karaboodi appeared once more, and said that she was not pleased with the substitution of the monkey, and that a human being must be sacrificed. [...] The two men, with their eight children, sought for a victim for twelve years. At the end of that time, they found a poor man, who had a son four years old, and found him, his wife and child good food, clothing, and shelter for a year. They then asked permission to sacrifice the son in return for their kindness, and the father gave his assent. The boy was fettered and handcuffed to prevent his running away, and was taken good care of. Liquor was prepared from grains, and a bamboo, with a flag hoisted on it, planted in the ground. Next day, a pig was sacrificed near this post, and a feast was held. It was proclaimed that the boy would be tied to a post on the following day, and sacrificed on the third day. On the night previous to the sacrifice, the Janni (priest) took a reed and poked it into the ground in several places. When it entered to a depth of about eight inches, it was believed that the god and goddess Tadapanoo and Dasapanoo were there. Round this spot, seven pieces of wood were arranged lengthways and crossways, and an egg was placed in the centre of the structure. The Khonds arrived from the various villages, and indulged in drink. The boy was teased, and told that he had been sold to them, that his sorrow would affect his parents only, and that he was sacrificed for the prosperity of the people. He was conducted to the spot where the god and goddess had been found, tied with ropes, and held fast by the Khonds. He was made to lie on his stomach on the wooden structure, and held there. Pieces of flesh were removed from his back, arms and legs, and portions thereof buried at the Khond's place of worship. Portions were also set up near a well of drinking water, and placed around villages. The remainder of the sacrificed corpse was cremated on a pyre set alight with fire produced by the friction of two pieces of wood. On the following day, a buffalo was sacrificed, and a feast partaken of. Next day, the bamboo post was removed outside the village, and a fowl and eggs were offered to the deity. (Thurston [1909] 1987, 368–71)

This first human sacrifice is presented as a repetition of the first sacrifice of the mother of all human beings, who had asked her son to kill her, bury her flesh,

and cover the place with stones. From this we may deduce that the stone arrangement known as the *jakeri* symbolically represents the place where flesh obtained from this first sacrifice is buried. The myth explains that the mother of all human beings herself demands a repetition of this original self-sacrifice, and the description of how her children organised the human sacrifice shows a number of parallels to today's buffalo sacrifice.

The human victim in the myth, like the buffalo in a Dongria village today, is prevented from running away but at the same time treated with hospitality. To mark the beginning of the festival, a bamboo pole is set up, just as today Dongria erect a tall post with a brass pot attached to it. According to the myth, the main festival lasts for three days, which is also true for the buffalo sacrifice. As in any Dongria village today, a pig was sacrificed the night before the actual killing of the victim. Just before this deed was accomplished, the *jani* according to the myth took a "reed" and poked it into the earth. The place where the reed could pierce the soil marked the place where "the god and goddess Tadapanoo and Dasapanoo" were present. This clearly corresponds to an important element in the Dongria's buffalo sacrifice. Just before the actual killing of the buffalo, the *jani* takes a knife and thrusts it through a hole in the wall of the earth goddess's house. As argued above, the house itself represents the earth goddess, and the Dongria *jani*, like the priest in the myth, thus pierces the "earth." The act itself may be seen as a symbolic penetration of the earth, and this interpretation is supported by the myth, which claims that a god and goddess are present at the place where the "reed" can enter the soil. In the buffalo sacrifices celebrated today, it may equally be argued that the act of piercing the wall marks the sexual union of the earth goddess and her husband – perhaps represented by the buffalo tethered to the sacrificial post – which results in the fertilization of the earth.

However, the piercing of the soil or the wall may have an additional meaning that derives from the first part of the myth, stating how the mother of all human beings accidentally cut her little finger. Her blood drips on the earth and dries up the ground that was covered by water. Among the Dongria, the *jani* pierces the wall of the earth goddess, whom they consider to be their mother, and inflicts a small wound in the hide of the buffalo. This is the sign for the male Dongria, "the children of the earth," to come and kill the victim. In other words, as in the myth, the "mother" is hurt and then her representative, the buffalo, has to die in the same way as the "mother," who according to the myth was killed by her own "son."

Curiously, neither Jena et al. nor I were able to collect a similar detailed myth among the Dongria that specifically explains the origin of the *kodru parbu*. However, a closer analysis of the Dongria myths we compiled reveals that the three

days of the sacrifice are clearly related to three major cosmological events described in the myths:
1. The birth of the sun god
2. The hunting expedition and the appearance of *laksmi*
3. The beginning of cultivation

These three major events can be seen to correspond to the main themes and ritual activities of the three days of the festival:
1. The worship of the *satara bonda*
2. The worship of *lada penu* and *sita penu-lahi penu*
3. The worship of *dharni penu*

A large share of the myths collected by Jena et al. deals with the creation of the sun god, who is needed to bring light to the people and to rule them. After he was born, he appeared in the sky, and all the other gods became envious and decided to humiliate him. They challenged him to a bet, and when he lost, they laughed at him:

> The sun god returned with a pale face to his mother and told her the sad tale. *Jamarani* then decided to hide him from the eyes of the gods and goddesses by putting him into a small box. As a result, darkness descended upon the world. (Jena et al. 2002, 144)

The other deities became desperate, for they could not create any light without the sun god. For this reason they went to his mother, and after they had apologised for their conduct and "pledged to assign the sun god the highest position and status among the deities" (Jena et al. 2002, 144), she released him from the box.

As described in the ethnographic part of this chapter, the *satara bonda* is preserved by a high-status member of the village in a box or pot in his house. In this sense, the object may be compared to the sun god hiding from the other deities. Furthermore, when the *satara bonda* is taken out on the first Friday, at the hottest time of year, in the same way as the sun god, it is given the highest position by being set atop a tall bamboo pole. No other object worshipped in the ritual has a higher position than the *satara bonda,* and like the sun that moves through the village, the *satara bonda* is carried by his worshippers up and down the village plaza. When conflicts arise, the villagers meet on Sunday morning at the place where the *satara bonda*, the people's king, is kept to rule over the world and to guarantee order. The first day of the *kodru parbu* may therefore be seen as linked to the transformation from darkness to light, from lack of rule to government.

The first two events on the second day, the worship of the god of hunting and the sacrifice to the goddess of the house, seem to be related to a mythical story collected independently by both myself (see section 2.4.2) and Jena et al. (2002, 150–52). According to this story, the sun god *dharmu penu* once fell ill because he was longing for the meat of a jungle animal. He sent out his men to hunt, and after careful ritual preparations they left for the forest. They searched in vain for a long time but finally succeeded in killing a mouse deer (*gensi musa*) and a jungle fowl (*gumeti*). Since they were hungry and thirsty, they prepared rice and fetched water from a nearby stream, but when drinking it they discovered, to their surprise, that the stream contained liquor instead of water. They drank so much that they became intoxicated and forgot the purpose of their hunting expedition. The wife of *dharmu penu* brought the hunters back to their senses and, disappointed, they went home. On the way back to the village they sat down to smoke tobacco. When they inserted a dry stick of wood into a hole in the ground in order to light a fire, the goddess of wealth, *laksmi*, emerged from it. The hunters carried her back to their houses, and there they admitted to *dharmu penu* that they had not brought any prey but the goddess instead.

On the Saturday morning of the *kodru parbu*, the villagers move into the forest, in the same way as the hunters in the myth do, to a tree considered to be the abode of *lada penu*, the god of hunting. Just as in the myth, the *bejuni* gives the young men assembled at the place of *lada penu* alcohol to drink and, at least in the dances performed by the Desia Kond, long cigars to smoke. After worshipping the guns and varies deities, they return to the village without any prey but instead invoke the goddess of wealth in their houses. The goddess *sita penu-lahi penu*, as previously mentioned, represents wealth in the sense of an abundant crop and is intimately linked to the home and to food; her name *lahi penu* means "goddess of cooked rice." When the hunters in the myth do not bring back prey but instead the goddess, who emerges from the fire, they in fact achieve a transformation from hunter-gatherers to agriculturalists, from people of the forest to villagers residing in houses where they cook food. This interpretation is supported by the second part of the myth collected by Jena et al.:

> It was during the hunt that the men saw hills and forests for the first time. They were curious about whether these hills belonged to somebody. When *dharam devata* informed them that they were his possessions, they sought his consent to cultivate it. He, however, explained that they would first need *dharani penu's* approval. To this end, they approached a *pejuni* who advised that a ritual was necessary in which rice grains and a new winnowing fan were sacrificed. Once the material was procured, she performed a *malebena*, fell into a trance and became possessed by *dharani penu* who then agreed to them cultivating the hilly areas. (Jena et al. 2002, 152)

The hunting expedition is thus clearly linked to the discovery of hill cultivation, for which the people require the approval of the earth goddess.[149] The myth does not mention the sacrifice of a human being or a buffalo but continues in the following way: "When they asked for *dharma devatas's* permission to sow the seeds, he suggested that *dharani penu* be appeased. Thus, a *jani* was requested to conduct a ritual after which the seeds were sown" (Jena et al. 2002, 153). This ritual of the *jani* may be the same as the *kodru parbu,* since the latter occurs in the hottest season of the year, just before the coming of the rains and the sowing of the seeds. My hypothesis of a strong correlation between the beginning of cultivation mentioned in the myth and the timing of the *kodru parbu* is further supported by the fact that the festival ends with the *ambadadi yatra,* celebrated a few days after buffalo has been killed. A major aspect of this *yatra* consists in appeasing *bima penu,* the god of wind and storm, who has the potential to destroy the crops. According to the myth, the hunters, having cleared the slopes, turned to *dharam devata* and asked him when the slashes should be burned. The latter advised "not to light fire without the permission of *bima penu,* who, if irked, would become wrathful" (Jena et al. 2002, 152).

To summarise, comparing myths to the events of the *kodru parbu* reveals a common theme and very similar transformations. The setting up of the *satara bonda,* the king of the mountains, represented by an object placed high above the people on a bamboo pole, corresponds to the birth of the sun god, i.e., the king who brings order and light to the people. In his presence, the earth goddess and her house become established, in the same way as the objects representing the goddess, the axes, arrive on Friday, and in the same way as the final decorations for the *dharni kudi* are completed on this day. According to the myth, the sun god falls ill and sends out hunters to bring him an animal from the jungle, but instead they return with the goddess of wealth and of food. In the same way, the villagers make their way to a hunting site and on their return invoke the goddess *sita penu-lahi penu* in every house. This marks the transformation from hunter-gatherer into agriculturalist. In order to cultivate the hills that the hunters saw on their expedition, according to the myth, they are advised to seek the earth goddess's permission before they sow their seeds. This corresponds to the fact that the *kodru parbu* occurs before the time when the Dongria commence sowing their seeds on the hill slopes. The sacrifice on the third day, which is performed in the name of the earth goddess, may thus be

---

149 In a myth collected by Macpherson in the nineteenth century, the sequence of events is reversed. According to this myth, the Kond first perform the sacrifice and learn the techniques of agriculture before they begin hunting (see Macpherson 1865, 97).

viewed as an act to appease the deity of the territory that the villagers intend to cultivate.

5.7.6 Fertility: Exchange and violent appropriation

A *kodru parbu* will only be celebrated when everyone in a village has had a good harvest and when enough wealth has been accumulated to hold a large feast. The Dongria explicitly told me that a sacrifice is demanded by the goddess herself, who requests a sacrifice in return for the help she has given to them. On the other hand, we have many indications that the sacrifice not only serves as a counter-gift for the harvest received by the sponsors before the festival, but also helps to encourage fertility in the future.

The concept of making the soft soil firm so that cultivation becomes possible appears in some form multiple times in the reports of different colonial officers. These ideas are linked to mythical stories that state that sacrifices should be performed with the explicit purpose of increasing the fertility of the soil. In these myths, the knowledge of agriculture is only revealed after conducting the sacrifice. Macpherson, for example, cites the following myth:

> The earth was in a state of soft barren mud, utterly unfit for the use of man. Umbally Bylee, the name of the feminine form which Tari always assumed when she communicated with men, appeared cutting vegetables with a hook. She cut her finger, and as the blood drops fell upon earth, it became dry and firm. Umbally Bylee said, "behold the good change! cut up my body to complete it." The Khonds declined to do so, apparently believing that Umbally Bylee was one of themselves, and resolving that they would not sacrifice one another, lest their race would become extinct, but would obtain victims by purchase from other peoples. They procured and offered a sacrifice [...] and the knowledge of all that relates to agriculture was imparted to men. (Macpherson 1865, 96–97)[150]

Verrier Elwin (1954, 534–51) collected several Kond myths, mostly in Ganjam district, that address the question of how the custom of sacrificing humans came into being. All of them give a similar answer: the earth goddess demands a sacrifice, and only when people satisfy her requests is she prepared to provide them with a good harvest in return. In several of these myths the goddess or her consort sheds blood to demonstrate the effects of the sacrifice. The brass image of a large figure with breasts and a sword, which was part of the exhibition of tribal art organised by Mallebrein (1993, 480, figs. 507 and 508), can be interpreted as a visual representation of these ideas. In my view, the figure stands for the earth

---

150 The same myth is repeated in slightly different words a few pages later in the same source.

goddess, who is about to sacrifice the human being tied to a post in front of her. In Desia Kond villages, the shaman, possessed by the goddess, still approaches the buffalo victim with the old iron weapons along with a new bamboo "axe" and symbolically strikes the victim with it.

Eliade deals with these myths in the context of his interpretation of agricultural rites and fertility cults. According to him, horticulturists in tropical regions relate the knowledge of edible plants and their cultivation to a sacrifice in which a divine being is usually sacrificed or offers itself as a sacrifice (Eliade 1958, 346). The parallels with the myths told by Kond are obvious, in particular because in these myths too, the goddess takes human form and uses her own blood to make the soil firm and cultivation possible.

Boal (1997, 332) rightly states that the sacrifice was and is performed not only to increase the harvest but to achieve wellbeing, a concept expressed by her informants using the Kui expression *negi ava*. This probably corresponds to the Dongria expression *nehi ane* or "it will be good," "it will be right." The idea of general wellbeing achieved by the human sacrifice is clearly expressed in the famous dialogue between the Kond priest and the victim quoted by Macpherson at length, in which the *jani* speaks the following words on behalf of the goddess:

> cut the victim in pieces: let each man place a shred of the flesh in his fields, in his grain store, and in his yard and then kill the buffalo for food, and give a feast, with drinking and dancing to all. Then see how many children will be born to you, how much game will be yours, what crops, how few shall die. All things will become right. (Macpherson 1865, 123)

While Dongria nowadays only hang the flesh obtained in a *kodru parbu* village near their local *dharni*, the Kond studied by Barbara Boal continue to bury portions of buffalo meat in their local fields (Boal 1997, 231, 399). In the past, the sacrifice was accompanied by instantaneous shouts of triumph from the young men and a battle first between the women of the sponsors and the flesh-takers and second among the flesh-takers themselves upon reaching their own village and burying the meat in the soil. As mentioned in my description of the festival, Dongria men still exhibit gestures of triumph when leaving the sponsor's village, although no mock battle takes place between them and the women of the village as reported by Boal (1997, 399). Yet, her interpretation of the flesh's symbolic meaning may equally be applied to the Dongria Kond:

> The potency of the victim's flesh at this point seems not only to have been connected with fertility and virility but perhaps with success and strength in warfare too. (Boal 1997, 231)

In my interpretation of Dongria myths and local ideas of conception (see pp. 381–82), I came to the conclusion that neither male deities nor men are considered to be creators. Instead, any form of creation is linked to the goddess *jaura penu,* who made the first human being inside the earth and who transfers souls into women, who thereby become pregnant. The role of male deities consists mainly of bringing knowledge to the people and governing their affairs, and for this reason they are considered kings. In the human world, men are similarly not seen to be creators, yet they must sustain and acquire what has been created by female deities and women through their activities. In relation to women's creative powers, men fulfil these expectations through marriage – either arranged or by bride capture – and through penetration. In relation to the earth, they acquire and sustain this creation through their field labour and sacrifice. In Dongria, the word for shifting cultivation or agricultural work in general is *katina,* a verb having at its primary meaning "hoeing" or "pronging," i.e., opening the earth with a tool.[151] This identification of agricultural work with the act of hoeing may be comparable to the emphasis on penetration in cultural representations of men's role in procreation. The sacrifice may then be compared to marriage in the sense that it establishes rights in what has been created by women on the one hand and by the earth goddess on the other. In an arranged marriage, the bride-takers give "life" in the form of "betrothal fee" in order to obtain the future right to the children born to the woman; in a *kodru parbu,* the organisers give a victim's life to the earth goddess, and this act demonstrates their right to own the land and the harvest. In a bride capture, a group of men forcibly takes a bride, and this violence itself establishes their right to the children born to this woman; in a *kodru parbu,* the young men demonstrate their virility and aggressiveness by killing the sacrifice and triumphantly taking home the flesh that symbolises the fertility of the earth.

The specific form of male appropriation determines the relations between those involved. The organisers of a sacrifice and the bride-takers in an arranged marriage obtain the "life" and "wealth" represented by the harvest or the bride by giving other forms of wealth, a buffalo or money, to the earth goddess or the bride-givers. In contrast, force or violence are the means by which young men conquer fertility when they steal flesh in a sacrifice or capture the bride. The relation between these relations is clearly hierarchical, as Dongria attach superior value to exchange relations between gods and humans, between bride-givers

---

151 According to the myth referred to in the previous section, the hunters obtain the goddess of wealth by putting a stick into the ground. The act of rubbing the stick releases the creative female power. Also see the myth collected by me and quoted in section 2.4.2, according to which all gods and human beings came out of a hole where the hunters inserted a stick to make fire.

and bride-takers. These relations are established and expressed in the buffalo sacrifice and in an arranged marriage. On both these occasions, the opposite, relations based on force (or power), appear in more or less "ceremonial forms", such as the triumphant gestures exhibited by the flesh-takers at the time of their departure (see p. 595) and the mock battles between bride-givers and bride-takers on the third day of a wedding (see p. 338). These events hint at other occasions when force becomes real, for example when stealing the buffalo or a part of its flesh or capturing a bride. In my final analysis, the contexts discussed in this and the previous chapters are governed by a common structure: long-term, prestige reciprocity (see section 4.5) involving exchange relations between gods and humans is valued more highly than short-term, "violent reciprocity" (see section 4.5) involving relations of force between conquerors and conquered.

Table 45: Sacrifice and marriage and the hierarchy of relations

Creator	*jaura penu* and *dharni*	*jaura penu* and women
Creation	crops (*lahi penu*)	children
Male Contribution	*katina* ("hoeing"; agricultural work)	*kanbina* ("penetration"; sexual act)
Male Appropriation 1) exchange 2) violence	1) organising sacrifice 2) stealing flesh	1) arranging marriage 2) bride capture
Relations 1) prestige reciprocity 2) violent reciprocity	1) exchange relation between earth goddess and sponsors 2) relation of force between conquered sponsors and conquering flesh-takers	1) exchange relation between bride givers and bride takers 2) relation of force between conquered bride people and conquering bride capturers

6 Conclusion: A system of ideas and values

> Societies should be studied as wholes, and a comparative analysis of several societies requires that their elements be understood in terms of the particular place they occupy in each of them. Each society is ordered by the values it assigns to all social facts (its morphology, its representations and actions); this order constitutes its system of ideas and values.
> (Barraud and Platenkamp 1990, 104)

6.1 Introduction

In the central chapters of this book I have analysed relations between the Dongria and the Dombo (chapter 2), addressed social categories and marriage rules and practices (chapter 3), discussed different forms of marriage (chapter 4), and described and interpreted the rituals culminating in the grand buffalo sacrifice (*kodru parbu*) to the earth goddess (chapter 5). A number of different concepts pertaining to society, space, and cosmology have been introduced and analysed within concrete contexts such as marriage arrangements, bride capture, and collective sacrifices. In order to provide a differentiated picture of these concepts and the way they relate to each other in concrete contexts, the previous chapters provided lengthy descriptions of kinship relations between people I encountered in the field, of concrete cases of bride capture, and of rituals I observed during my time in the Niamgiri Hills. The scope of this work and the overall focus on marriage and sacrifice made it necessary to omit other contexts I studied, such as death rituals (*dosa kama*), annual festivals (*yatra*) celebrated by each village, and techniques of shifting cultivation (*nelu kama*). However, although this work provides only a partial representation of the complex social and cultural order I encountered in the Niamgiri Hills, I believe it is nonetheless possible to deduce an important configuration of "value-ideas" (Dumont 1986) from the contexts studied in this work. This does not exclude the possibility that an analysis of those contexts I did not cover may reveal further or even different values.

6.2 Female values: "life" (*jiu / jela*) and "wealth" (*lahi*)

The preceding chapters dealt with different contexts that according to "modern ideology" (see Dumont 1986) belong to three separate "domains": *economy* (trade relations between Dongria and Dombo in chapter 2), *kinship* (marriage rules and practices and forms of marriage in chapters 3 and 4), and *religion* (rituals and sacrifices in chapter 5). From a Dongria perspective these contexts do not form separate "domains" but are seen as closely related in terms of their values. The main value that is at stake in all of these contexts is fertility, or "life" (*jiu / jela*) as it is referred to by the Dongria. This "life" is essentially a female property, as is argued in the fourth chapter, where I discuss Dongria ideas concerning the role of women in creation. According to Dongria myths, all "life" comes from the goddess *jaura penu,* who created the first human beings inside the earth and continues to "impregnate" women by transferring "life" into their wombs. This "life" is contained in human beings, animals, plants, land, hills, etc.

The two words *jiu* and *jela* can both be translated as "life."[1] The word *jiu* is similar to the Sanskrit word *jiva* ("soul") and is translated by Winfield (1929, 54) as "life, spirit, soul." Israel's dictionary of the Kuwi language contains the word *jivu*. As a noun, *jivu* means "spirit, life principle, life," while in its verbal use it can be translated as "to love" (Israel 1979, 363). Somebody who lacks *jivu* is "without food" or "hopeless" (Israel 1979, 363). The word *jela* appears to be identical with the term *jeda* (with retroflex *d*) found in Winfield's dictionary. Winfield (1929, 52) translates *jeda* as "love, affection, desire, delight, pleasure, sexual passion; compassion, pity; the mind, spirit, life, soul, heart, feelings, seat of emotions and affections."

In the Dongria language, the word *jela* has a similarly extensive range of meaning. When the Dongria divide a sacrificial animal, they place the "heart," *jela*, in a separate place and make an offering of liver (*tala*) and blood (*neteri*), both containing the victim's "life" or *jela*, to the deity. In plants, *jela* is considered to reside in the stem or trunk, for example in the pith of the *salap* tree, which Dongria eat once the tree no longer produces sap (*mada kalu*). Mountains similarly contain *jela*, which is conceived of as a deity (*penu*) residing inside the mountain, its "house" (*ijo*). When a person becomes sick, a spirit or deity is considered to eat (*tinja mane*) the person's *jela*, contained in his or her blood, and when the person finally dies (male: *hateyu* / female: *hate*), his or her *jela* is said to leave (*jela hace*) the body through the head and become like wind (*widi*) that moves up into the sky (*jaura gada* or "place of *jaura*"). From there, the goddess *jaura penu* sends *jela* back to earth (*nara gada* or "place of human beings"), where it enters the "belly" (*pota*) of a woman through her "vagina" (*pira*).

The word *jiu* is less frequently used in the Dongria language, and when asked, Dongria express the opinion that *jiu* is essentially the same as *jela*. In the context of marriage, Dongria call the rice that is given along with the

---

[1] I do not agree with Jena et al. (2002, 263, 266), who distinguish more or less strictly between *jela* (mortal, stagnant, concealing) and *jiu* (immortal, active, expressive).

bride to the groom's family *jiu manjing* or "rice of life." In other contexts, the word is used to express "respect" and "affection," as in the expression *jiu kina*, "to honour." *Jela* and *jiu* are both in circulation, *jela* between gods and humans, *jiu* more specifically between affines. These concepts of "life" stand in contrast to the social aspect of a person who died a "good death", the *mahane*, on the one hand, and the perilous aspect of a person who died a "bad death", the *marha*, on the other.[2] Like *jela* and *jiu*, *mahane* and *marha* are in constant movement, although not between earth and sky, but rather between different realms on earth. Thus, the *mahane* go back and forth between the cremation ground (*mahanenga*) and the houses (*ijo*) of their family members. The *marha*, in contrast, wander through the wild forests (*kamoni*) and from time to time attack human beings near their settlements (*nayu*) or on a foot path (*giri*).

According to Macpherson, the Kond used to calculate in "lives" at a time when money was not yet known to them (Macpherson [1842] 1863, 50).[3] Crops contain "life" and are given by the earth goddess (*dharni*) to the Dongria. The highest form of "life" is rice, a representation of *sita penu-lahi penu*, the earth goddess's daughter. Dongria either buy rice from the government or acquire it by bartering with traders from the valleys, because wet-rice cultivation can only be practised in a very few areas in the Niamgiri Hills. Instead of rice, little millet (*kahada*), which is grown in the swidden, is the most important grain and is worshipped by the Dongria as a form of *sita penu-lahi penu*. The goddess is represented by the watch hut (*menda*) that serves as a granary in the swidden and by gourds (*kaktedia*) filled with grains and tied to the central beam in the attic of the house. She is present on the threshing floor where Dongria, during the winnowing of the little millet, spread the grains out in the shape of a half-moon (*jani*) before piling them up into a heap (*kupa*). In ritual invocations, the half-moon is considered to be the goddess *lahi penu*,[4] who sleeps on her

---

2 For the Gond, Fürer-Haimendorf reports a distinction between *jiv* or *jiva* ("life" or "living being"), which returns to god after death before it is again reincarnated in the form of a child, preferably a deceased person's grandchild, and *sanal* ("departed," "dead"), which contains the deceased person's personality and is worshipped in memorial feasts and ancestor cults. Such a *sanal* may turn into a *bhut* or "ghost" in cases of bad death (Fürer-Haimendorf 1953, 38, 41).
3 Unfortunately, Macpherson does not mention the Kui word he translates as "life."
4 According to Chris Gregory (personal communication), in central India rice, not millet, is usually considered to be a representation of the goddess *laksmi*. Among the Dongria, the heap of little millet (*kahada* or *hiko*) on the threshing floor is worshipped as *lahi penu* (or *laksmi*), while other types of millet are not.

side on the threshing floor before arising, i.e., turning into a heap of grain.[5] From the threshing floor she is carried home, where she is asked to fill the house and the attic with her presence.[6] God and goddess are requested to "talk," i.e., to have sex (*ma goti babu berenise*, "mother and father after talking"), so that many plants will grow (*pili gati gaja gati*, "many sprouts, many plants").

Unlike other forms of "wealth" such as bananas, oranges, castor beans, turmeric, and a variety of peas and beans, *sita penu-lahi penu* herself, i.e., the variety of grains used for cooking "rice" or *lahi*,[7] is not sold by the Dongria. Although grains and other crops are called *lahi*, meaning both "harvest" and "food," the difference seems to be that only rice (or little millet) can represent the goddess of wealth. Crops are either bartered (*patela kina*) in village markets (*banaji hata*) for rice, in particular for paddy from the plains, or sold (*prana*) in market towns (*raji hata*) for money. Money obtained in this way is used for buying other "valuables" such as paddy, cows, or sacrificial animals. To the Dongria, such market transactions appear profitable because they obtain a higher form of "wealth," the goddess represented by rice and money, by giving away something less valuable to them. The traders, on the other hand, similarly consider these transactions to be profitable, because they obtain crops that are in high demand among the plains people from the "simple-minded" Dongria for a relatively cheap price. Outsiders, such as the local development officers, are of the opinion that Dongria are cheated by these traders, but they fail to see that from the perspective of the Dongria these transactions are also considered to be highly profitable.

Wealth is closely associated with the goddess *sita penu-lahi penu*, who is considered to reside in the houses of wealthy people, such as the Komti traders or Brahmins in the towns. In ritual invocations, the Dongria request the goddess

---

5 *Aya keri ranjoli mui gae kupa ranjoli mui gae?* meaning "Mother, can I be thrown onto my side, can I be thrown into a heap?" In my interpretation, the goddess asks this question of the people who worship her. The question expresses the idea that the harvest will not necessarily be abundant every year. The people can never be certain whether the goddess will "lie" on their threshing floor and "arise" to become a heap of rice.

6 *Alo aya osum ilu osum kandra*, meaning "hey, mother, a full house, a full attic." *Kandra* refers to a particular part of the roof (see p. 475), but in this context it can be translated as "attic" or even "house," as it is being used in ritual language that operates with parallelism. The Dongria take the harvest from the threshing floor into their houses, where they store it in large baskets in their attics.

7 *Lahi* refers to the staple food consisting of boiled rice or millet. The Dongria cultivate more millet than rice. The different types of millet are *hiko* or *kahada* (little millet; Oriya *kosala*), *dare* (finger millet; Oriya *mandia*), *arka* (pearl millet; Oriya *bajra*), and *kuyeng* (sorghum; Oriya *gontia*).

6.2 Female values: "life" (*jiu* / *jela*) and "wealth" (*lahi*)

to leave the houses of these wealthy people and to come to their own settlements by saying *kumti gera wamu de bamana gera aya wamu de* ("come [to us] from the house of the Komti, mother, come [to us] from the house of the Brahmin"). They request her to increase every year (*andu hari wamu ya barca hari wamu ya*, "every year more, every year more you come, mother"), which concretely means that they ask for more wealth in the form of rice, money, animals, and children. Money is called *takang* (from Oriya *tonka*) or *lebung* and is not conceived of only as a medium of exchange but also as a representation of the goddess herself. To the Dongria, the origin of all "wealth" is the crops (*lahi*) cultivated in the swidden, which are then transformed in the market into other valuables such as money, grain, or animals. These again enter into other exchange transactions, most importantly those with bride-givers and the goddess, the former giving "life" in the form of a bride who cooks, nurtures, and bears children, the latter giving "life" by impregnating women and the earth. The bride with her wedding-gift (*lahi jau*) and her "rice-life" (*jiu manjing*) and the goddess during the *giri takoli* ritual are brought into the house and represent its wealth. When the goddess leaves the house, she has to be brought back just like a wife when she runs away. The opposites of "life" and "wealth," death and poverty, are linked to the goddess's departure. For example, when a family member dies, the goddess is believed to leave the house and must be brought back from the path into the house by a local shaman.[8]

The goddess in Dongria mythology and ritual has a number of names and functions, but in relation to the creation of life, three goddesses appear to be particularly important: *jaura penu*, who gives and takes "life"; *dharni penu*, the earth and mother of all beings, who receives "life" from *jaura penu*; and *lahi penu*, her daughter, who takes the form of "wealth" in the sense of crops. By analogy, human beings are considered to be born with the help of *jaura penu*, who puts life into the wombs of women, thereby giving them "wealth" or children. Crops (*lahi penu*) produced as part of agricultural production feed the children, who, when grown, will work in the fields and help *lahi penu* to increase.

Jaura penu gives "life" to human beings when they are born and takes "life" when they die; *dharni penu* gives her child, *lahi penu*, in the form of harvest, and demands a "child" – once a human victim, now a buffalo – in return.

---

[8] Chris Gregory pointed out to me that in the Hindu context this absence of the goddess of wealth, *laksmi*, is represented by the goddess *alaksmi*. I never heard the name of this goddess among the Dongria.

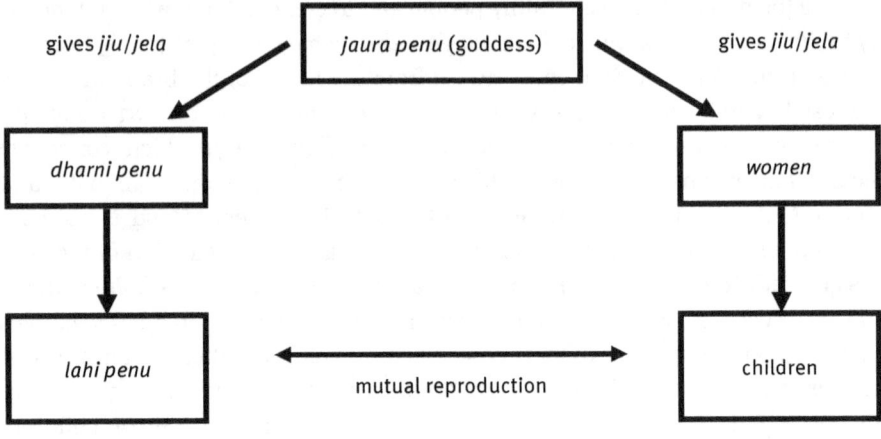

Figure 45: Female creation

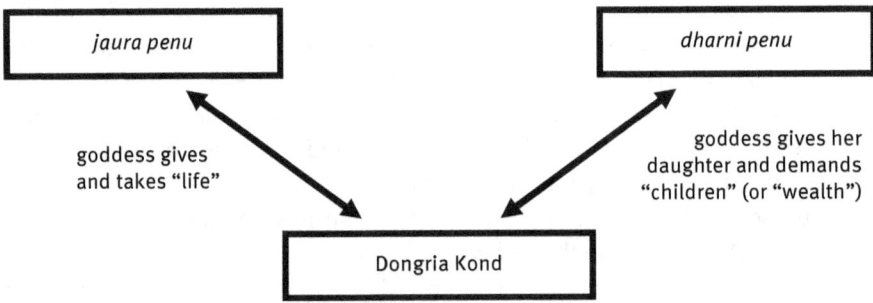

Figure 46: Relations between goddesses and human beings

6.3 Male ways of obtaining "life" and "wealth"

"Life" and "wealth" originate in female goddesses, and women and the earth are the intermediaries through which they come into being: whereas children are born (*janani ane*), plants – like the first mythical beings[9] – grow (*pdina*) from seeds. In the different contexts discussed in this book, i.e., trade, marriage, and sacrifice, I have identified three ways in which men obtain and transfer "life" and "wealth": first, by violent appropriation, which in local terms is referred to as "hunting" (*beta*); second, by negotiation and bargaining in the context

---

9 According to the creation myth, *jaura penu* created a banyan tree that bore many seeds, and one of them became the origin of *sita penu* (see Jena et al. 2002, 136).

of reciprocal exchange ("give and take" or *hinga tana*); and third, by freely sharing and distributing forms of "life" and "wealth." The first two transactions stress "social duality," while the third, sharing and distribution, emphasises "social unity" (Sahlins 1972, 188).

6.3.1 Violent appropriation: Hunting (*beta*)

"Life" and "wealth" may be obtained from another party through violence or conquest, which in the Dongria language is compared to "hunting" (*beta*). The god *lada penu* governs both hunting and war making and is worshipped prior to both hunting and war expeditions. In Dongria myths, hunters bring the goddess *lahi penu*, like a captured bride,[10] from the forest into the village. When hunting, Dongria men go into the forest, a realm ruled by the god *niamraja* and inhabited by deities and the undead (*marha*), to obtain "life" in the form of wild animals. Similarly, when making war, Dongria used to invade the territory of their enemies, kill them, and if possible drive them away from the territory. In these battles, men hacked their enemies to pieces in the same way that they nowadays sacrifice the buffalo to the earth goddess.[11] As reported, Dongria sometimes steal the sacrificial buffalo or a part of the victim in order to obtain its "life" and claim the land for which the buffalo has been sacrificed. Bride capture and visits to female dormitories is also likened to "hunting," the first being called *ahpa beta hana* ("to go, catch, and hunt"), the second *da:aska beta* ("hunting unmarried girls"). In these cases, Dongria men acquire "life" in the form of animals, land, or women through an act of violence and without giving anything in return. The "conquered" people may react by turning against the conquerors in order to reacquire the "life" they lost, and for this reason we may call this type of interaction "negative reciprocity" (Sahlins 1972, 195) or "violent reciprocity" (see section 4.5).

---

10 I thank Chris Gregory for making me aware of this similarity between bride capture and the role of hunters in the myths.
11 For a description of such a battle, see Macpherson 1863, 57–58.

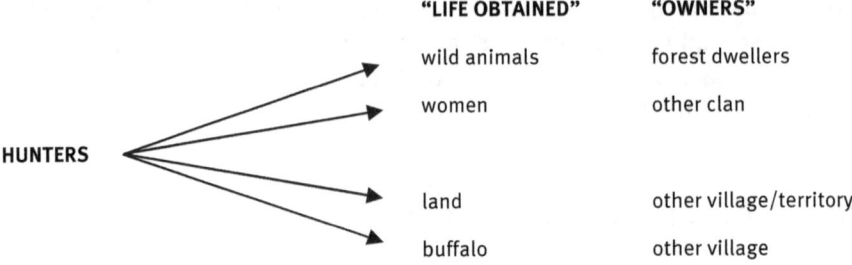

Figure 47: Obtaining "life" through "hunting"

6.3.2 Negotiation and bargaining: Reciprocal exchange (*hinga tana* or "to go, give, and bring")

The second way of obtaining "life" is through reciprocal exchange (*hinga tana* or "to go, give, and bring"), which may take various forms, characterised by negotiation (*bereni kina, nia kina* or "to have discussions") or bargaining (*wenga* or "to go and demand"). This type of exchange occurs in contexts that Western societies, but not the Dongria, typically view as belonging to two separate realms, the "sacred" and the "secular." Thus, the "buying" (*kalina*) and "selling" (*prana*) of land or items from the market, the bartering (*patela kina*) of crops, the arranging of a marriage (*hedi tana*), and the sacrifice of a buffalo (*kodru katina*) are not essentially different. In all of these contexts, the parties involved give one form of "life" and expect the return of the same value, "life," in another form. However, the cycles in which these objects circulate through processes of exchange are valued differently. For example, when a Dongria sells his crops to a Dombo or when he barters his harvest produce, he gives a form of *lahi penu* and obtains money, a buffalo, brass plates, or items for personal consumption. These transactions are part of a "short cycle of exchange" (Bloch and Parry 1989), which is linked to individual reproduction and competition.

Money and other valuables obtained through barter or market transactions with people from outside one's own community often flow into a "long-term cycle of exchange" (Bloch and Parry 1989), for example into an arranged marriage or a sacrifice to the gods, which are collective efforts to uphold and regenerate the social or cosmic order (see section 2.5.1). In an arranged marriage, both parties often continue their negotiations for years until finally, after the payment of a large "betrothal fee" (*mahala takang*) in the form of money obtained in the short cycle of exchange, the bride, along with the "life of rice" (*jiu manjing*) and her "wedding gift" (*lahi jau* or "cooked rice and vegetables/pulses"), is given to the groom's party. The bride thus brings "fertility" to the groom's family and guarantees the latter's reproduction through agricultural work, cooking, feeding, and bearing children. In a buffalo sacrifice, the main parties involved in the transaction are the gods, in particular the earth goddess and her husband, and the sponsors of the sacrifice, who have cultivated an area belonging to these deities. In return for the harvest, the villagers give "life" in the form of a victim, and this transaction involves demands and counter-demands for further gifts, fertility, and wellbeing (*nehi ane* or "it will be good").

Table 46: Obtaining "life" through reciprocal exchange

context	mode of transaction	"life" given	"life" received	cycle of exchange
1) market	buying and selling (*kalina prena*)	crops, objects, buffaloes, cows, money	crops, objects, buffaloes, cows, money	short
2) arranged marriage	giving and taking (*hinga tana*)	money, buffaloes, food	bride, objects, food, etc.	long
3) buffalo sacrifice	listening, demanding (*wena, wenbina*)	buffalo, food	crops, wellbeing	long

6.3.3 Sharing (*bat kina*)

The modes of interaction discussed above stress "social duality" in the sense that violent appropriation and exchange always occur between two parties. They can even be seen as modes for defining the boundary between social units in a constant process of "fission and fusion" (Evans-Pritchard 1940). In contrast, the sharing of "life" and "wealth" obtained through either "hunting" or "exchange" often occurs in contexts emphasising "social unity." Distribution is called *bat kina*, literally "to make shares," and involves a mode of behaviour different from both the violence involved in "hunting" and the haggling and bargaining typical of market transactions and rituals. When forms of "life" or "wealth" are shared, everybody present, irrespective of social status and community, will receive a portion. The amount of "life" and "wealth" distributed must be exactly the same for each person, and nobody dares to demand more or refuse a share. Taking part in sharing does not leave the receiver indebted to the person who distributed his "life" and "wealth" except insofar as he is expected to share his own "life" and "wealth" in the same way when the time comes. It is, however, not possible to demand a gift, for example money, in return for a share given as part of a distribution. Sharing is basically a male affair: men distribute meat, cooked food, or alcohol during feasts.

Typical occasions for distributing "life" and "wealth" are hunting expeditions, palm-wine drinking, harvesting, and feasts. When a man or a group of men returns from a successful hunt, they are expected to share the meat. They have to give equal shares of the animal's "life" at least to their neighbours, if not to the whole village, including all visitors present at the time of distribution. Similarly, whoever joins a drinking party assembling under a palm-wine tree must receive an equal share of the sap. The *salap* tree is considered to be a mother (*aya*) who gives milk (*dudu*) to her children (*milang*), the Dongria. Going into the forest to tap a *salap* tree (*mada mara*) is called *kalu beta* or "hunting alcohol," i.e., another way in which men appropriate the female "life" value. Like the owner of the *salap* tree, the owners of the village share their land with those who have no claims to the territory. When the Dongria start cultivating a hill slope that has lain fallow for many years, the men of the village first hold a meeting during which portions of land are allocated to all of the families residing in a village, irrespective of their clan membership.

The most important contexts for sharing are food distributions, in particular when the members of a village receive a buffalo, a pig, or portions of meat as part of affinal transactions. For example, if a family receives one or more buffaloes as *mahala* or "betrothal fee" for a daughter, the head of the family is expected to share the meat in a feast for all those resident in his village and certain relatives living elsewhere. When a man has been given a pig by his in-laws during a visit to his wife's village, he is expected to hand over the pig to his fellow villagers, who kill it, cook the meat, and distribute it to all the men who have assembled on the village plaza. Finally, the wealth obtained in a market transaction may similarly be shared with others, for example when a man sells his cash crops, such as bananas or pineapples, and immediately invites all those present to have a drink bought with the money he has earned.

Sharing can thus be seen as a way of distributing female values such as "life" and "wealth," obtained by individuals through violent appropriation or exchange, to the whole community. It demonstrates that the accumulation of "life" and "wealth" by individuals is not highly valued among Dongria, while the creation of social unity through sharing is. However, bringing prosperity to the larger community through sharing depends on individuals or smaller groups obtaining "life" and "wealth" through market transactions, marriage, and ritual. This appears to be a typical feature of sharing and distribution: the recipients of the shares always belong to a larger segment of society than those who obtained the "life." Just as short cycles of exchange are linked to long cycles of exchange for collective reproduction, "life" and "wealth" obtained by smaller social segments are distributed to larger social segments in order to promote collective fertility. The grand buffalo sacrifice (*kodru parbu*) appears to be the occasion upon which sharing occurs on the most "global" level: "life" obtained by the largest descent-based cooperative unit, the *muta*, is distributed to the whole of society.

6.4 Male values: Senior (*kaja*) and junior (*icha*)

Relations created through the circulation of female "life" and "wealth" do not establish permanent hierarchies between the social segments either opposed or united in these transactions. A group of men who have captured a woman will not be considered to have higher status than that of the people whose daughter they abducted. Similarly, in a monetary transaction, buyers and sellers do not stand in a hierarchical relationship. An arranged marriage begins with a slight status difference between the higher bride-givers and the lower bride-takers. However, this does not turn into a permanent status difference. Following the wedding, exchanges become more symmetrical, and the prohibition of repeating marriages with a member of a mother's brother's house prevents a perpetuation of status asymmetries from generation to generation. Permanent status in Dongria society is not achieved through transactions of "life" but is determined by birth. The birth order provides the overall scheme for the evaluation of status on all levels of society: the firstborn represents the higher value, *kaja*, which may be translated as "senior", "older," or "bigger"; the secondborn stands for the lower value, *icha*, meaning "junior," "younger," or "smaller".

Compared to all other communities in their region, the Kond consider themselves "senior" since they were the first to come out of the hole in the earth at the beginning of creation. Among the Kond, the Dongria see themselves as "senior" in relation to their brothers, the Desia Kond living in the valleys. This hierarchy exists only within a phratry or "brotherhood" (*tai bai kuda*) formed by clans from the hills (Dongria Kond) and the valleys (Desia Kond) and not between bride-exchanging clans. For example, all Kond clans that do not belong to the same phratry can intermarry and are not ordered according to status. This corresponds to my analysis that the transfer of female "life" and "wealth" does not establish a permanent hierarchical order. In the case of marriageable clans, we may even argue that the exchange of daughters suppresses status considerations based on birth order. For example, among the Dongria, the members of one clan (Wengesika or Nandruka) are considered to be descendants of the first people who reached the surface of the earth. However, the other clans are not put into a definite sequence of their appearance, and the myths stress their territorial distribution rather than their birth order.

Within each clan, the Dongria derive their status from the status category (*punja*) to which they belong by birth. This applies to both men and women, but in practice, only men seem to attach importance to the status distinctions inherited through the patriline. Status categories are paired and ordered according to status order: *jani* are senior to *pujari*, *mondal* are senior to *bismajhi*, *saanta* are senior to *naika*. The opposition between *kaja* and *icha* further segments each of these categories into two differently valued parts, such as the senior *jani* and the junior *jani* or the senior *bismajhi* and the junior *bismajhi*. At the house level, these categories are used to distinguish local lines formed on the basis of patrilineal descent, similarly known as *punja*. For example, in three different villages there may be twenty houses belonging to the same status category of junior *jani* but to different local descent groups. The members of each descent group or local line claim descent from a common ancestor and worship the same deity, represented by a stone in the eastern part of the village (see section 5.2.1). Within a village, the descendants of the village founders (*padari loku*), who claim ownership of the territory, are considered to be senior (*kaja*) because they were the first to arrive. They are addressed as *mama* or "mother's brother" by their dependents (*raitimane*), who do not belong to the village's dominant clan of the village and are known as *banaja* or "sister's sons." The status of a single house thus depends on whether or not it belongs to the dominant clan. For example, a house may be of a high status category, such as senior *jani*, but if it is not a member of the village's dominant clan, it cannot claim an elevated position in the local community. Therefore, a house's status always depends on the relation of its clan to a particular territory. Those houses of the dominant clan of a particular village who own the objects used and exhibited at the time of the buffalo sacrifice (*kodru parbu*) claim the highest status. These are the families who preserve the items that were once used at the time of human sacrifice: the axe, brass pots, knife, and "umbrella." This intimate connection between status, expressed in terms of seniority, and the sacrifice to the earth goddess of a particular territory helps us to understand the hierarchical relationship between male and female values in Dongria society.

6.5 The whole

In a number of contexts described in this work, male and female values stand in opposition to each other. For example, in a context in which female values are exchanged, such as when arranging a marriage, Dongria pay attention to the rule of clan exogamy, while the male values of the status categories of bride and groom play no role. As explained above, "life" and "wealth" are exchanged through intermarriage between clans that do not stand in a hierarchical relation to each other. The status categories, on the other hand, do express such hierarchical relations and are therefore neglected in the context of marriage, in which exchange, and not a timeless status distinction, creates a relationship between two parties. On the other hand, when people make status claims, they do not allude to forms of obtaining or exchanging female values, but employ the concept of ownership derived from their position in the system of status and descent categories. For example, a house will only be considered senior if its members descend from the original village founders and thus "own" the village (*ma nayu* or "our settlement") and the territory (*ma padari* or "our village land"). Similarly, among several houses of the *jani* category in a village, the one who preserves the axe (*tangi*) originally used at the time of human sacrifices will be considered senior (*kaja*).

The question is, then, whether these male and female values are simply opposed or actually form a system. Dumont ([1966] 1998, 1986) identifies a special configuration of values in his analysis of holistic or non-modern societies that he calls "hierarchy." Hierarchy defines a special relation between the whole and its elements. The elements are the concrete value-ideas that organise experience in a specific context. Comparing different contexts, it becomes evident that certain contexts can be grouped together because they are organised in relation to the same set of value-ideas. This opposes one set of contexts to another that is ordered according to a different set of value-ideas. For Dumont, these two sets of valued contexts are not equal, because their respective relationships to the whole differ. He illustrates this with the distinction between the right and the left hand, which are not simply opposed but also have a different relation to the whole, the body (Dumont 1985, 250). The body may be represented by one of its elements, for example the right hand, which in most societies stands for the superior value of the social whole. To express this hierarchical relationship between the differently valued sets of contexts in relation to the whole, Dumont introduced the concept of "level" (*niveau*).

My analysis above stresses the opposition between two types of contexts, those valued in relation to ideas concerning "life" and "wealth" and those organised according to the distinction of "senior" and "junior" segments. The question here is whether these types of context stand in a hierarchical relationship in which they are assigned to different levels. Does one set of value-ideas represent the social whole? Which are more highly valued, the continuous transactions of female values or the relatively unchanging male status distinctions? In my analysis, any answer to this question must take into account how the Dongria Kond, and the various other Kond communities in general, distinguish themselves from others, i.e., from the many tribal and caste communities inhabiting the Eastern

Ghats. A central marker of Kond identity is their specific relation to their territory established at the time of the grand sacrifice to the earth goddess. Kond consider themselves children of the earth, their mother, and they differ from many other communities in the territorial nature of their clans. The earth goddess represents the whole and is the womb from which the Kond sprang and the cultivators' source of wealth and fertility. In a primordial self-sacrifice, the goddess made the earth firm, and according to a Kond myth, her son distributed her body across the territory by burying her flesh in different holes and covering it with stones. Today, a Kond village can be identified by the stones that represent the earth goddess. Each Kond village thus contains a part of the whole, the mother.

In the sacrifice *to* the earth goddess, which is also a sacrifice *of* the goddess (see section 5.7.5), this primordial act is repeated by single units acting as parts of the whole, i.e., individual villages. However, the relation of each village to the whole is established by distributing portions of the victim's body, previously the human and presently the buffalo, to as many villages as possible. The Kond thereby repeat the original burial of their mother's body. In my analysis, the earth goddess represents both the whole and its parts and stands for the female value-ideas of "life" and "fertility." Contexts pertaining to these value-ideas do, therefore, belong to a higher level or *niveau* than those organised by the male value of seniority.

The buffalo sacrifice serves as an example of this particular configuration of ideas. As described in detail in the fifth chapter, this festival requires the cooperation of "brothers," i.e. villages that are "owners" of the same clan territory and of the objects used at the time of sacrifice. As brothers and as owners of the sacred objects, they are distinguished according to relative seniority. However, they cannot act as sacrificers, because they are not allowed to kill the victim. For this reason, they depend on men from other clans in the same way that they depend on members of these clans to obtain wives. The relationship between the organisers and the people from other clans is not expressed in terms of the male values of status but of the female values of "life" and "wealth." With respect to the whole of Kond society represented by the earth goddess, the functions of these affines are of the highest value: by sacrificing the victim in one place and distributing its meat across the country inhabited by the Kond, they establish a relationship between the parts, i.e., individual clans and their territory, and the whole, i.e., all Kond descending from one mother, the earth.

7 Glossary

aji budi
(also *ma budi*)
goddess of smallpox; considered to be an "old woman" (*budi*) who sows her "seeds," the disease, in different "fields", the bodies of children; worshipped at a shrine (*yatra kudi*) outside the western entrance to the village; also considered to be a *thakurani* or ruler goddess of the village

akagiri
space behind each row of houses in a Kond village; back side of the village; place where women meet during the day; location of the dormitories and dancing grounds; area where Dombo build their houses

bahuki
person who assists the *jani* during his recitations; usually two *bahuki* join a main *jani* during his recitations

barika
a village official from the Dombo community; belongs to the village council and represents the villagers in their dealings with the outside world; often acts as a middleman in marriage negotiations and conflicts; provides the village with sacrificial animals; has a right to receive cooked food for his services

beju
male village shaman; has a higher status than the female village shaman (*bejuni*) and is called to perform the more important rituals (*kaja kama*), for example at the time of death or during clan festivals; some *beju* dress in female clothing, remain unmarried, and adopt female behaviour

bejuni
female village shaman; said to have a sign (*linga*) on her forehead through which the deities enter her body in dreams and trance sessions; uses ritual language when performing rituals; can speak with the voices of gods after falling into trance (*banga ate*); identifies the causes of sickness, worships house deities (*ijo kama*), and performs village festivals (*yatra*)

beta
"hunt"; derived from the Oriya word *bentha* (hunt); the word is used for a number of different activities, such as hunting animals, collecting fruit, tapping *salap* sap, visiting female dormitories, and capturing women

bismajhi	member of the *bismajhi* status category or, in the past, a village official who performed functions in the royal revenue system and was called to issue rulings in cases of marriage outside the community
bonda	brass pot or "umbrella" fixed on top of a long bamboo pole at the time of the buffalo sacrifice; usually preserved in a box or earthen pot in the attic of the house of a senior member of the village; some *bonda* circulate within a sacrificial community (*muta*) consisting of villages of the same clan, while others always remain in the same village; represents the mountain gods, in particular *niamraja*, who resides on the highest mountain in this area (Niamgiri or Nebahoru)
Desia Kond	Kond who inhabit the valleys in Rayagada district; more numerous than the Dongria Kond, who inhabit the steep Niamgiri mountains; have been strongly influenced by Indian mainstream culture but show many similarities to the Dongria Kond in terms of social organisation
dharmu penu	sun god; highest male deity; according to some the husband of *dharni*, the earth goddess, and father of *sita penu-lahi penu* (*laksmi*); selected *niamraja* to rule over the Dongria Kond
dharni kudi	small hut in the centre of the village; constructed at the time of the buffalo sacrifice above or near the stones representing the earth goddess (*dharni*); during the buffalo sacrifice, the ritual specialists perform their incantations addressed to the goddess in this hut in front of a winnowing fan containing the metal objects from the time of human sacrifice
DKDA	Dongria Kond Development Agency
Dombo	community whose members reside in the mountains as well as in the valleys; classified as a "scheduled caste" by the government and often represented as "untouchables" in the literature; traditionally Dombo worked as weavers who produced simple white cloth; nowadays they work as traders, farmers, and alcohol distillers; Dombo are the clients of the Kond, the main land

	owners in this area; in other areas the Dombo are called Pan or Pano
garada	fence or cow pen constructed around the major sacrificial post at the time of the buffalo sacrifice
ghanta parbu	festival organised by one household; the householder sponsors several sacrifices of goats and chickens to various deities, in particular his house deities; the rituals are performed by the village shamans inside the house as well as outside the village where a shrine is built at the stone (*kona*) of the householder's local line
gota	literally "guests"; in the restricted sense "affines"
handani kuda	wall inside the central room of the Dongria house; at this wall, the shaman (*beju* or *bejuni*) performs the worship of various deities, in particular of the house goddess, *sita penu-lahi penu*
hedi	means "bride" as well as "marriage"; the elaborate type of wedding is called *hedi tana* or "to bring the bride"; the word is probably derived from a demonstrative pronoun for a woman who is far away (*hedi* or *sedi*)
icha	Dongria word meaning "small," "young," or "junior"; used to denote the lower status of a person or a social category
ijo (or *ilu*)	Dongria word for "house"; in the restricted sense the word *ijo* refers only to the central room with a cooking hearth and the sacred wall; in the wider sense it denotes the whole building including the two verandas, one in front and one in back
jakeri	stones representing the local earth goddess and "mother" of the Kond; among the Dongria Kond mostly found in the centre of the village, west of the *koteiwali*; among the Desia Kond often located in a sacred grove outside the village; a *jakeri* usually consists of three types of stones: *kona* or conical stones, *pata* or rough, flat stones, and *bayriwali* or round grinding stones

jani	either a member of the *jani* status category (*jani punja*) or a ritual specialist; among the ritual specialists, the *daka jani* is the most important as he knows how to recite (*dakina*) the incantations addressed to the gods; a *jani* specialist often belongs to the *jani* status category, which on the village level is mostly represented by one or more descent groups (local lines), but he may also be a member of another status category
jela (or *jiu*)	"life," "soul principle," "heart"; exists in every living being; returns to the goddess *jaura penu* after death; the goddess sends it back to earth at the time a new being is born; also present in animals, trees, plants, mountains, etc.; in large amounts such as grain heaps or money *jela* represents "wealth," a form of the goddess *sita penu-lahi penu* (identical with *laksmi*)
kaja	Dongria word meaning "big," "old," or "senior"; used to denote the higher status of a person or a social category
kandadae	small room in a corner of the central room of a Dongria house; usually empty and only used during rituals for worshipping gods and ancestors; among the Desia Kond, this room is used to store grain
karjame	son-in-law who serves one or more years in the village and the fields of his father-in-law; this service reduces the amount of money to be paid as "betrothal fee" for the bride
kodru parbu	buffalo sacrifice; celebrated by each village at intervals of approximately ten to twenty years; one or more buffaloes are sacrificed to the earth goddess; Dongria Kond celebrate the festival mostly between March and April, while Desia Kond perform it a month or two earlier; the festivals usually lasts for three days, from Friday to Sunday
koteiwali	menhir representing the husband of the earth goddess and "father" of the Kond; among the Dongria Kond the menhir usually stands in the centre of the village, east of the *jakeri*; among the Desia Kond, a village may have two *koteiwali*, one at the western end of the village and one at the eastern end

kuda	refers to the named, exogamous clan as well as to the exogamous phratry (*tayi bai*) consisting of two or more clans; often translated as *jati* in Oriya, although the word *jati* commonly denotes the endogamous caste and not the exogamous clan
kutumba	literally "family" but also used for the village community as a whole (otherwise referred to as *bara bhai* or twelve brothers)
mahala	betrothal; refers to the long process of establishing a marriage relation between two parties; the word also denotes the money and gifts given by the bride-takers to the bride-givers; a woman acquired in this way is referred to as *mahala dakeri*
mahane	ancestor; social aspect of a person who died a "good death" and was cremated on the cremation ground (*mahanenga*) of the village; resides on the cremation ground but also regularly visits houses and expects to be given alcohol and food on ritual occasions; protects the members of the village, but can also cause illness and sickness, in particular in close family members; will after some time be reincarnated in a new-born child
marha	undead; social aspect of a person who died a "bad death," e.g., fell from a tree, was bitten by a poisonous snake, drowned in a river, was killed in a fight, or committed suicide; cremated in a separate place and considered to roam around in the dense forests; feared because believed to attack the living
member	title of an elected representative of a village ward; also used by people who represent other government agencies such as development organisations on the village level
meria	the buffalo sacrificed to the earth goddess; in the past the word denoted the human victims as well as the practice of human sacrifice
mondal	member of the *mondal* status category or, in the past, a representative of the king who was responsible for issuing rulings in cases of incest; reportedly also played a role in the royal revenue system

mudrenga	plural of *mudria*; people who perform various functions during the buffalo sacrifice; usually selected from a neighbouring village that belongs to a clan different from the clan of organisers; they build a fence around the village and the place of sacrifice and protect the victim until the proper time of sacrifice; as a symbol of their duties they carry bamboo sticks
muta	in the literature, usually described as a territorial unit consisting of a certain number of villages belonging to several clans and administered in the past by a leader (*patro* or *mondal*) appointed by the king; in the Niamgiri Hills, a community consisting of villages belonging to the same clan and sharing certain sacred objects, such as *suri* and *bonda*, which are worshipped at the time of the buffalo sacrifice
naika	member of the *naika* status category or, in the past, a village official who annually collected taxes and revenue
nayu	Dongria word for "village"; refers to the settlement, which often consists of two rows (*chahada*) of houses built along the east-west axis
niamraja	culture hero and most important mountain god of the Dongria Kond; resides on (or in) the Niamgiri (also called Nebahoru), the highest mountain in the area, from which the region derives its name; considered a king who brought culture to the people and provided them with everything they need for life; he rules over the forest and its inhabitants, the wild animals
padari	village territory; the word *padari* has two meanings: in the limited sense, it means a certain territory marked by a *jakeri* (stones of the earth goddess); in the extended sense, *padari* refers to the whole unit consisting of a settlement and all *padari* claimed by the residents of this settlement
praja	"subjects" of the king; Dongria consider themselves "subjects" of the king; at the same time they call their clients, the Dombo, their *praja* or "subjects"

pujari	member of the *pujari* status category or ritual specialist; as a ritual specialist the *pujari* performs the worship of the god of fire (*bera penu*) during a festival called *bali yatra*
punja	a status category (like *jani* or *pujari*) or a descent group (here referred to as "local line") consisting of a number of related houses; a *punja* is opposed to other *punja* as either "senior" (*kaja*) or "junior" (*icha*)
raja	"king"; denotes human kings such as the king of Jeypore as well as the gods
rechagiri	the space between the two rows of houses in a Kond village; village plaza or front road; in Dongria villages, location of the *jakeri* and the *koteiwali*; where men of the village assemble in the morning and evening
saanta	member of the *saanta* status category or, in the past, village official who performed functions to those of the *bismajhi*; title derived from the royally granted title *samanta*
sala bada	fence constructed around the whole village at the time of the buffalo sacrifice
salap	palm tree that produces an alcoholic sap; "a mature tree is characterised by profuse inflorescence, which is where toddy is tapped from. Sap begins to be produced about 13 to 15 years after the tree germinates" (Jena et al. 2002, 252)
satara	long bamboo pole worshipped at the time of the buffalo sacrifice; on top of the bamboo pole a brass object and a bamboo shade are fixed; the word *satara* probably derives from the Oriya word *chatara*, meaning "umbrella"
sita penu-lahi penu	name of the goddess of the house and the goddess of wealth; considered identical with *laksmi* and regarded as the daughter of the earth goddess (*dharni*); represented by rice or money

suri	ceremonial knife worshipped at the time of the buffalo sacrifice; circulates within a sacrificial community (*muta*) consisting of villages of the same clan
tangi	ceremonial axe worshipped at the time of the buffalo sacrifice or during the pigeon pea festival (*kanga parbu*); usually preserved in the attic of the house of a member of the *jani* status category
tapu	fine, especially the fine paid by a bride captor to the husband of the captured woman
tayi bai	"brother and sister"; defines the category of people with whom a person cannot marry; the expression *tayi bai kuda* refers to the phratry consisting of clans whose members claim agnatic links
tonenga	plural form of *tone* or "ritual friend"; ritual friendship can exist between two individuals but also between whole villages belonging to different clans; at the time of the buffalo sacrifice new individual friendship relationships are created and the collective friends of the organising village attend the festivities and are treated as honoured guests; *tonenga* cannot kill the buffalo; female friends are referred to as *ade*

Appendix 1: Family tree of icha jani segment (Gumma)

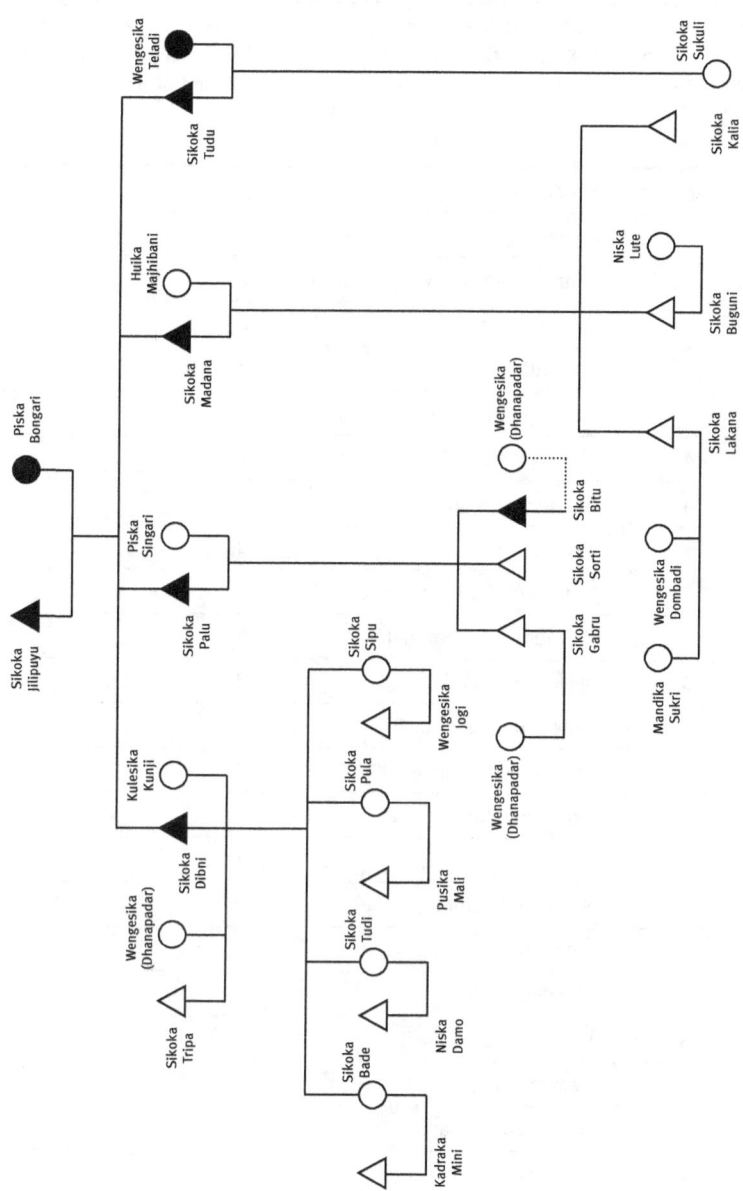

Appendix 2: Marriage relations between Gumma and other villages

Village reference number from map 3 and table 1 in Nayak (1989, 32, 221–26)	Circle in section 3.4.4.2	Name of village (spelling in Nayak 1989 in brackets)	Number of marriages with Sikokagumma (bride-givers and bride-takers)
** [unknown]	/	Kendugaradi	1
6	3	Khambesi	3
8	4	Kadrakagumma ["Kadragumma"]	2
11	4	Pusikagumma ["Bhatigumma"]	2
12	4	Jangjodi	3
13	4	Radang ["Radango"]	1
16	4	Khajuri ["Karjodi"]	1
18	4	Gandeli ["Gondeli"]	1
19	4	Sagdi	3
20	4	Lahanikuti ["Lahunikbunti"]	1
22	3	Niskabondeli ["Bondeli"]	3
23	3	Jalkirdang ["Kirdang"]	2
43	4	Penewali ["Penubali"]	1
46	3	Gundawayu ["Gunjapai"]	2
47	3	Salpajala ["Salapjhola"]	1
48	3	Garta	1
49	3	Sutangoni ["Sutanguni"]	2
51	2	Kata ["Kota"]	3
52	4	Merkabondeli	2
57	3	Dongoni ["Denguni"]	1
60	2	Damanapanga	5
62	3	Tebapoda ["Tevapada"]	1
66	2	Kurusmui ["Kuruchumuni"]	1
68	2	Chatikona ["Batikona"]	6

Continued

Village reference number from map 3 and table 1 in Nayak (1989, 32, 221–26)	Circle in section 3.4.4.2	Name of village (spelling in Nayak 1989 in brackets)	Number of marriages with Sikokagumma (bride-givers and bride-takers)
69	2	Dhanpadar	4
70	1	Kumbuli ["Kumbeli"]	4
80	4	Musudi ["Nusudi"]	5
81	4	Railima	2
84	2	Phakeri ["Fakeri"]	2
85	1	Bada Denganali ["Badas Dengnali"]	2
86	1	Sana Denganali ["Sana Dengneli"]	4
87	1	Mayawali ["Manyabali"]	3
** [near 87 "Manyabali"]	1	Kuskedeli	1
95	1	Sikokagumma	8 (intra-village)
96	1	Lamba	4
97	2	Dongormati ["Dongamati"]	1
98	2	Lekhpadar ["akhapadar" (*sic*)]	1
** [near 101 "Patangadar"]	2	Nacheniguda	2
102	2	Sarlenja ["Sorulengi"]	2
104	2	Buduni ["Batabuduni"]	4
105	2	Nirgundi	1
115	3	Phuldumberi ["Phuldumer"]	1
** [near 115 "Phuldumer"]	3	Berenipinda	1
** [near 115 "Phuldumer"]	3	Kemdipadar	2
Total:		44 villages	103 marriages

Appendix 3: Numbers and names of villages

(derived from Nayak 1989: 221–26; spelling of names has been changed)

1. Kurli; 2. Mundawali; 3. Hutesi; 4. Tuaguda; 5. Hundijali; 6. Kambesi I; 7. Karjodi; 8. Kadrakagumma; 9. Kurweli; 10. Uppargumma; 11. Batigumma (also Pusikagumma); 12. Jangjodi; 13. Radang; 14. Patalamba I; 15. Arisakani; 16. Khajuri; 17. Gortali; 18. Gondili; 19. Sagdi; 20. Lahunikunti; 21. Ranibanda; 22. Bondili; 23. Kirdang; 24. Hingabadi; 25. Kucherla; 26. Tenda; 27. Bada Duargadi; 28. Sana Duargadi; 29. Kodigumma; 30. Kinjamodi; 31. Khambesi II; 32. Ankurawali; 33. Jarpa; 34. Kesarpadi; 35. Serkapadi; 36. Batudi; 37. Dohali; 38. Jenniguda; 39. Kuncheli; 40. Monda; 41. Saragipai; 42. Gulgula; 43. Penewali; 44. Odapanga; 45. Suandipai; 46. Gundawayu; 47. Salpajhola; 48. Garta; 49. Sutangoni; 50. Panchkodi I; 51. Kota; 52. Merkabondeli; 53. Goilonga; 54. Sokota; 55. Srambi; 56. Kalierpeta; 57. Bada Dengoni; 58. Sana Dengoni; 59. Ambadoni; 60. Damanapanga; 61. Parameni; 62. Tebapoda; 63. Kadrakabondeli; 64. Panchkodi II; 65. Tuta; 66. Kurusmui; 67. Kanharu; 68. Chatikona (Hatikona); 69. Dhanpadar; 70. Kumbeli; 71. Bemberi; 73–76. [omitted]; 77. Waleri; 78. Parsali; 79. [omitted]; 80. Musudi; 81. Railima; 82. Bangapadi; 83. Sarijhola; 84. Phakeri; 85. Bada Denganali; 86. Sana Denganali; 87. Mayawali; 88–90. [omitted]; 91. Patalamba II; 92. Chipcha; 93. [omitted]; 94. Waliamba; 95. Sikokagumma; 96. Lamba; 97. Dongarmati; 98. Lekhpadar; 99. Niskhal; 100. Chamarpadar; 101. Patangpadar; 102. Sarlenja; 103. Tentulipadar; 104. Bada Buduni; 105. Nirgundi; 106. Kolti; 107. Baripadar; 108. Tadingapai; 109. [omitted]; 110. Tamkasili; 111. [omitted]; 112. Kuskedeli; 113. Ladang; 114. Kasbondeli; 115. Phuldumberi

Appendix 4: Plan of a Dongria house

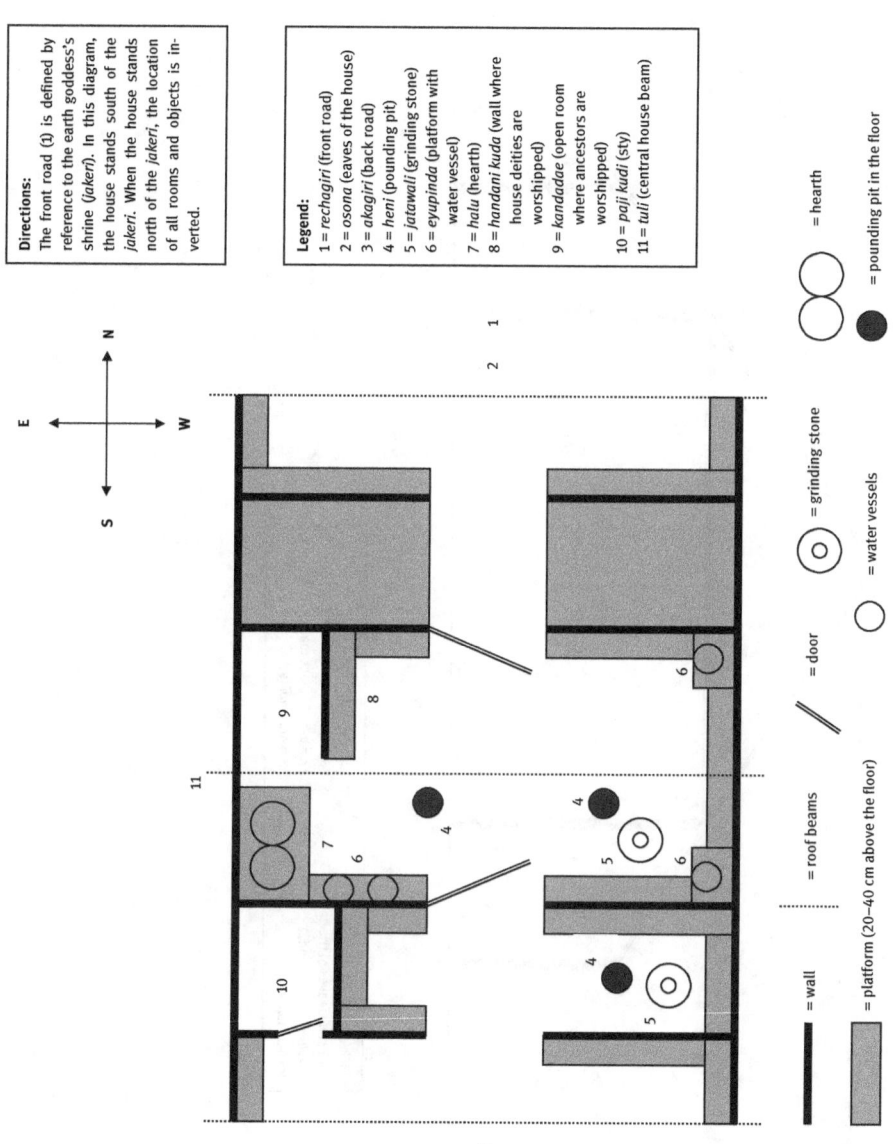

Appendix 5: Plan of a Dongria house (profile)

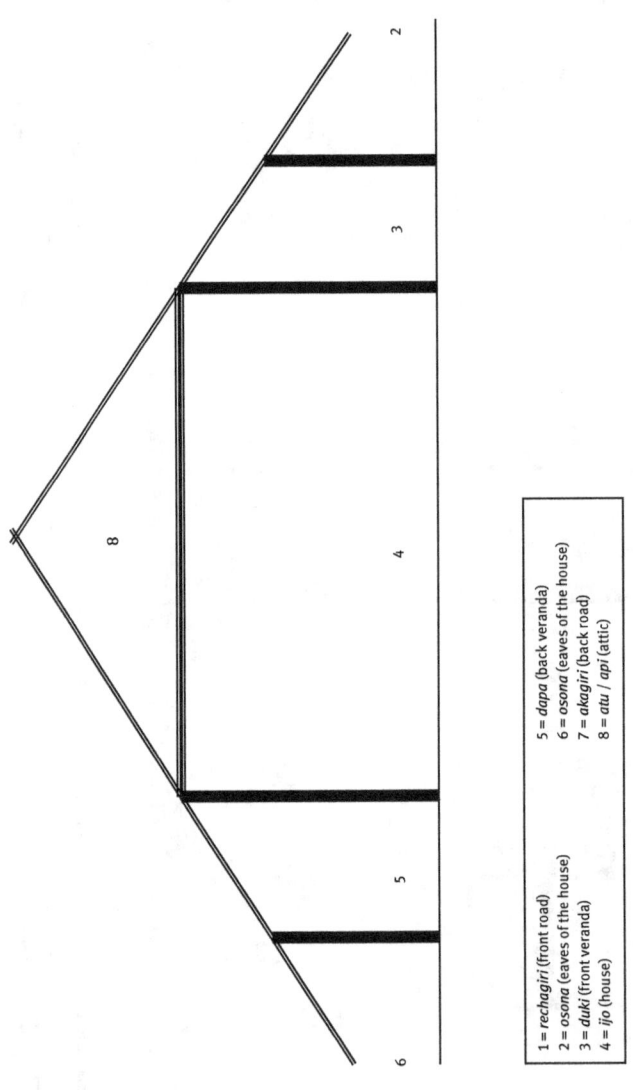

1 = *rechagiri* (front road)
2 = *osona* (eaves of the house)
3 = *duki* (front veranda)
4 = *ijo* (house)
5 = *dapa* (back veranda)
6 = *osona* (eaves of the house)
7 = *akagiri* (back road)
8 = *atu* / *api* (attic)

Appendix 6: Myths about Duke and Dumbe

Myth of Duku and Dumbe (Sikoka Lakana, 2002)

Long ago there was neither sky nor earth. The gods lived above; below them was only mud. During this time existed besides the gods two Kond, a brother called Duku and a sister named Dumbe. They said to the gods, "We want to live on earth; give us a *dharni* [shrine of the earth goddess], a village, and land where we can live and work." Thereupon the gods sent out two crows. They flew around and viewed everything. When they returned, they informed the gods that there was nothing below, no soil and no plants. Hence the gods started to search for a worm. When they found the worm, they killed it. Because the worm had eaten the soil and produced the water, the earth now started to dry up. Then the gods sowed seeds and plants, and trees began to grow. Duku and Dumbe, who belonged to the Wengesika clan, could now live on earth, but because they were brother and sister they could not marry each other. Thereupon *aji budi* disfigured the face of the sister [by smallpox], and because he could not recognise her any longer the brother married his sister. From them we all descend. When we became many, *niamraja* started to divide us and assigned different territories and names to us: Sikoka, Jakesika, Kadraka, and so on. Those who were experts in cooking became Brahmin, those who produced alcohol became Sundi, those who swept the street became Dombo, and the one who called everybody to a meeting in the morning became the *barika*. But in the beginning all were Kond.

Myth of Duke and Dumbe (Wadaka Dombu, 2002)

The first Dongria were Wengesika. At that time a king (*raja*) named Danta reigned, killed many people, and caused many wars. There were only a few Dongria villages at that time, and they were located far apart from each other. The Dongria all wore loincloths (*drilli*) and did not cut their hair but tied it in a knot, and all wore nose rings. Dharmu became very angry and decided to let the sky fall onto the earth. At that time, Duke and Dumbe went to a mountain stream (*jharana*) to hunt an antelope (*kutra*) with bow and arrow. These antelopes go to the mountain streams to drink water. When an antelope approached the stream, Duku lifted his bow to kill it, but the antelope told him that she was pregnant and that it would be a great sin to kill her. He did not kill the antelope, and because of that she disclosed to him that Bhagwan [a god; another name of Dharmu] intended to let the sky fall onto the earth. She instructed Duke and Dumbe to chop down a *leka mara* [tree, *Bombax malabricum*] and make a boat the size of a house with seven rooms. They acted according to her advice, and Dharmu made the sky fall onto the earth. Thereupon the whole earth was covered with water, and all human beings (*nara*), plants (*gacha*), and animals (*posu*) died. In the sky the gods also began to die, because there were no more human beings to provide them with food such as incense (*juna*). For this reason, Dharmu sent away his son, Gajahade Buratura, to find out whether any human beings were still alive. He went off and searched everywhere before he returned to Dharmu to tell him that nothing was alive anymore, neither humans, nor trees, nor animals, nor mountains. The whole earth was featureless and covered with water. Thereupon Dharmu made a bird, Martochteli, and gave it an iron beak and a golden headdress. He sent the bird away, and when it returned, the bird said to Dharmu that some human beings were still alive, because he had seen a piece of wood floating on the water. Thereupon Dharmu lifted the sky, and the sun dried up the earth, and everything began to grow again. Since Duke and Dumbe were brother and sister, Dharmu sent them in different directions. After walking around for a long time, Dharmu gave Duke a *raja tilak* [sign of a king] and Dumbe a *rani tilak* [sign of a queen]. For this reason, they could not recognise one another and became husband and wife.

Myth of brother and sister (Cham Kamala [Dombo woman], 2002)

In the beginning, there was water everywhere. In the water, a boat with a brother and a sister was floating. They had stored the necessary food in the boat: rice, dal, and so on. One day, the god Bera began to swell, because he had eaten too much incense. He rubbed his legs with his hands, and with the skin from one leg he made one crow, and with the skin from the other leg another crow. He sent the crows off to find out whether human beings were living on the water. The crows searched everywhere but did not see anybody. They reported this to the god Bera, who sent them away a second time. Then one of the crows saw smoke, and when she informed Bera about this, he thought, "Oh, human beings must be there." Then he untied a goat and a bear and sent them both away. The goat's excrement of the goat turned into soil and stones; the bear's excrement of the bear turned into mountains. Thereupon plants began to grow on earth. Then Bera summoned the brother and sister to come to his home, and he asked them, "Do you have a husband? Do you have a wife?" They answered him, "No, I have no husband." "No, I have no wife." Then Bera instructed them, "You go in that direction and will find a wife. You will go in the other direction and will find a husband." They both walked away in different directions and roamed around until they were tired. After some time, they met each other, and because Bera had affected their senses with *maya* (illusion), they did not recognise one another. They married and had children from whom we all descend.

References

Allen, N. 1975. "Byansi Kinship Terminology: A Study in Symmetry." *Man*, n.s., 10: 80–94.
Allen, N. 1976. "Sherpa Kinship Terminology in Diachronic Perspective." *Man*, n.s., 11: 569–87.
Allen, N. 1986. "Tetradic Theory: An Approach to Kinship." *JASO* 17 (2): 87–109.
Alter, J. S. 1997. "Seminal Truth: A Modern Science of Male Celibacy in North India." *Medical Anthropology Quarterly* 11 (3): 275–98.
Aparajita, U. 1994. *Culture and Development: Dongrias of Niyamgiri*. Tribal Studies of India Series T 167. New Delhi: Inter-India Publications.
Apffel-Marglin, F. A. 1985. *Wives of the God-King: Rituals of the Devadasis of Puri*. Oxford: Oxford University Press.
Apffel-Marglin, F. A., and P. C. Mishra. 1995. "Gender and the Unitary Self: Looking for the Subaltern in Coastal Orissa." *South Asia Research* 15 (1): 78–130.
Arhem, K. 1981. "Bride Capture, Sister Exchange and Gift Marriage among the Makuna: A Model of Marriage Exchange." *Ethnos* 46 (3–4): 47–63.
Bailey, F. G. 1957. *Caste and the Economic Frontier: A Village in Highland Orissa*. Manchester: Manchester University Press.
Bailey, F. G. 1960. *Tribe, Caste and Nation: A Study of Political Activity and Political Change in Highland Orissa*. Manchester: Manchester University Press.
Bailey, F. G. 1961. "'Tribe' and 'Caste' in India." *Contributions to Indian Sociology* 5: 7–19.
Banerjee, S. 1969. *Ethnographic Study of the Kuvi-Kandha*. Calcutta: Anthropological Survey of India.
Barnard, A., and A. Good. 1984. *Research Practices in the Study of Kinship*. London: Academic Press.
Barnes, R. H. 1999. "Marriage By Capture." *Journal of the Royal Anthropological Institute* 5 (1): 57–73.
Barnes, R. H., D. de Coppet, and R. J. Parkin. 1985. *Contexts and Levels: Anthropological Essays on Hierarchy*. Oxford: Anthropological Society.
Barnett, S. 1976. "Coconuts and Gold: Relational Identity in a South Indian Caste." *Contributions to Indian Sociology* 10 (1): 133–56.
Barraud, C. 1990a. "A Turtle Turned on the Sand in the Kei Island: Society's Shares and Values." In "Rituals and the Comparison of Societies," edited by C. Barraud and J. D. M. Platenkamp, special issue, *Bijdragen tot de taal-, land- en volkenkunde* 146 (1): 35–55.
Barraud, C. 1990b. "Wife-Givers as Ancestors and Ultimate Values in the Kei Islands." In "Rituals and the Comparison of Societies," edited by C. Barraud and J. D. M. Platenkamp, special issue, *Bijdragen tot de taal-, land- en volkenkunde* 146 (2): 193–225.
Barraud, C., D. de Coppet, A. Iteanu, and R. Jamous. 1994. *Of Relations with the Dead: Four Societies Viewed from the Angle of their Exchanges*. Oxford: Berg.
Barraud, C., and C. Friedberg. 1996. "Life-Giving Relationships in Bunaq and Kei Societies." In *For the Sake of Our Future: Sacrificing in Eastern Indonesia*, edited by S. Howell, 351–98. Leiden: CNWS Publishers.
Barraud, C., and J. D. M. Platenkamp. 1990. "Rituals and the Comparison of Societies." *Bijdragen tot de taal-, land- en volkenkunde* 146 (1): 103–23.

Bayly, S. 2000. *Caste, Society and Politics in India: From the Eighteenth Century to the Modern Age*. Cambridge: Cambridge University Press.

Behura, N. K., and B. N. Sahu. 1970–71. "Mutha: The Traditional Political Organization of the Kondh (with Specific Reference to Pusangia Mutha in the Phulbani District of Orissa). *Adibasi* 12 (1–4): 13–21.

Berger, P. 2000. "Gesellschaft, Ritual und Ideologie: Eine relationale Betrachtung der Gadaba des Koraput Distriktes, Orissa." *Mitteilungen der Berliner Gesellschaft für Anthropologie, Ethnologie und Urgeschichte* 21:15–38.

Berger, P. 2002. "The Gadaba and the 'Non-ST' Desia of Koraput, Orissa." In *Concept of Tribal Society,* edited by G. Pfeffer and D. K. Behera, 57–90. Contemporary Tribal Studies 5. New Delhi: Concept Publishing Company.

Berger, P. 2004. "Füttern, Speisen und Verschlingen: Die alimentäre Sozialordnung der Gadaba im Hochland von Orissa." Unpublished paper presented at the final conference of the Orissa Research Project in Civita Castellana (26–30 September 2004).

Berger, P. 2007. *Füttern, Speisen und Verschlingen: Ritual und Gesellschaft im Hochland von Orissa, Indien*. Berlin: LIT Verlag.

Berger, P. 2015. *Feeding, Sharing, and Devouring. Ritual and Society in Highland Odisha, India*. Boston: De Gruyter

Berreman, G. D. 1963. *Hindus of the Himalayas*. Bombay: Oxford University Press.

Berreman, G. D. 1971. "The Brahmanical View of Caste." *Contributions to Indian Sociology* 5:16–23.

Beteille, A. 1980. "On the Concept of Tribe." *International Social Science Journal* 32 (3): 825–28.

Beteille, A. 1991. *Society and Politics in India: Essays in a Comparative Perspective*. London: Athlone Press.

Bird-David, N. 1990. "The Giving Environment: Another Perspective on the Economic System of Gatherer-Hunters." *Current Anthropology* 31 (2): 189–96.

Birket-Smith, K. 1967. "Studies in Circumpacific Culture Relations: Potlatch and Feasts of Merit." *Det Kongelige Danske Videnskabernes Selskab historisk-filosofiske meddelelser* 42 (3): 3–98.

Bloch, M., and J. Parry, eds. 1982. *Death and the Regeneration of Life*. Cambridge: Cambridge University Press.

Bloch, M., and J. Parry, eds. 1989. "Introduction: Money and the Morality of Exchange." In *Money and the Morality of Exchange,* edited by M. Bloch and J. Parry, 1–32. Cambridge: Cambridge University Press.

Boal, B. 1979. "Kond Ritual Practices and Prayers: Conservation and Change." *Journal of Indian Folkloristics* 2 (3–4): 89–110.

Boal, B. 1997. *Human Sacrifice and Religious Change: The Kondhs*. New Delhi: Inter-India Publications.

Boal, B. 1999. *Man, the Gods and the Search for Cosmic Wellbeing*. Bhubaneswar: NISWAAS.

Boas, F. 1914. *Kultur und Rasse*. Leipzig: Veit & Co.

Boas, F. 1966. *Kwakiutl Ethnography*. Edited by H. Codere. Chicago: University of Chicago Press.

Bourdieu, P. 1977. *Outline of a Theory of Practice*. Cambridge: Cambridge University Press.

Burghart, R. 1978. "Hierarchical Models of the Hindu Social System." *Man,* n.s., 13: 519–36.

Brauns, C.-D., and L. G. Löffler. 1990. *Mru: Hill People on the Border of Bangladesh.* Basel: Birkhäuser Verlag.

Campbell, J. 1864. *A Personal Narrative of Thirteen Years Service amongst the Wild Tribes of Khondistan for the Suppression of Human Sacrifice.* London: Hurst and Blackett Publishers.

Casajus, D. 1985. "Why Do the Tuareg Veil Their Faces?" In *Contexts and Levels: Anthropological Essays on Hierarchy,* edited by R. H. Barnes, D. de Coppet, and R. J. Parkin, 68–77. Oxford: Anthropological Society.

Charsley, S. 1996. "'Untouchable': What Is in a Name?" *Journal of the Royal Anthropological Institute,* n.s., 2:1–23.

Clifford, J. 1986. "Introduction: Partial Truths." In *Writing Culture: The Poetics and Politics of Ethnography,* edited by J. Clifford and G. E. Marcus, 1–26. Berkeley: University of California Press.

Clifford, J., and G. E. Marcus, eds. 1986. *Writing Culture: The Poetics and Politics of Ethnography.* Berkeley: University of California Press.

Comaroff, J. L. 1980. "Introduction." In *The Meaning of Marriage Payments,* edited by J. L. Comaroff, 1–48. London: Academic Press.

Coppet, D. de. 1981. "The Life-Giving Death." In *Mortality and Immortality: The Anthropology and Archaeology of Death,* edited by S. Humphrey and H. King, 175–204. New York: Academic Press.

Coppet, D. de. 1985. "… Land owns People." In *Contexts and Levels: Anthropological Essays on Hierarchy,* edited by R. H. Barnes, D. de Coppet, and R. J. Parkin, 78–90. Oxford: Anthropological Society.

Coppet, D. de. 1992. "Introduction." In *Understanding Rituals,* edited by D. de Coppet, 1–10. London: Routledge & Kegan Paul.

Coppet, D. de. 1995. "'Are' Are Society: A Melanesian Socio-Cosmic Point of View: How Are Bigmen the Servants of Society and Cosmos?" In *Cosmos and Society in Oceania,* edited by D. de Coppet and A. Iteanu, 235–74. Oxford: Berg.

Coppet, D. de, and A. Iteanu, eds. 1995. *Cosmos and Society in Oceania.* Oxford: Berg.

Das, V. 1977. *Structure and Cognition: Aspects of Hindu Caste and Ritual.* Delhi: Oxford University Press.

Das Patnaik, P. S. 1972. "Bejunis; Their Initiation into Shamanhood." *Adibasi* 14:11–20.

Das Patnaik, P. S. 1984. "Ownership Pattern, Land Survey and Settlement and Its Impact on the Dongaria Kondhs of Orissa." *Adibasi* 23 (4): 23–32.

Das Patnaik, P. S. 1988. "Concepts of Debt among the Dongria Kondhs." *Adibasi* 28 (2): 11–15.

David, K. 1973. "Until Marriage Do Us Part: A Cultural Account of Jaffna Tamil Categories for Kinsman." *Man,* n.s., 8 (4): 521–35.

Delaney, C. 1986. "The Meaning of Paternity and the Virgin Birth Debate." *Man,* n.s., 21: 494–513.

Delaney, C. 2001. "Cutting the Ties That Bind: The Sacrifice of Abraham and Patriarchal Kinship." In *Relative Values: Reconfiguring Kinship Studies,* edited by S. Franklin and S. McKinnon, 445–67. Durham, N.C.: Duke University Press.

Dirks, N. B. 1987. *The Hollow Crown: Ethnohistory of an Indian Kingdom.* Cambridge: Cambridge University Press.

Douglas, M. 1966. *Purity and Danger: An Analysis of Concepts of Pollution and Taboo.* London: Routledge & Kegan Paul.
Dumont, L. (1957) 1986. *A South Indian Subcaste: Social Organization and Religion of the Pramalai Kallar.* Delhi: Oxford University Press.
Dumont, L. 1961. "Marriage in India: The Present State of the Question." *Contributions to Indian Sociology* 5: 75–96.
Dumont, L. 1962a. "Correspondence: 'Tribe' and 'Caste' in India." *Contributions to Indian Sociology* 6: 120–23.
Dumont, L. 1962b. "Le vocabulaire de parenté dans l'Inde du Nord." *L'Homme* 2 (2): 5–48.
Dumont, L. 1964. "Marriage in India: The Present State of the Question: Postscript to Part One." *Contributions to Indian Sociology* 7: 77–98.
Dumont, L. 1966. "Marriage in India: The Present State of the Question (III): North India in Relation to South India." *Contributions to Indian Sociology* 9: 90–114.
Dumont, L. (1966) 1998. *Homo Hierarchicus: The Caste System and its Implications.* Complete revised English edition. Delhi: Oxford University Press.
Dumont, L. 1971. *Introduction a deux théories d'anthropologie sociale.* Paris: Mouton. Translated by R. Parkin as "An Introduction to Two Theories of Social Anthropology: Descent Groups and Marriage Alliances" (manuscript available at the Free University of Berlin, Germany).
Dumont, L. 1975. "Terminology and Prestations Revisited." *Contributions to Indian Sociology* 9 (2): 197–216.
Dumont, L. 1983. *Affinity as a Value: Marriage Alliance in South India, with Comparative Essays on Australia.* Chicago: University of Chicago Press.
Dumont, L. 1986. *Essays on Individualism: Modern Ideology in Anthropological Perspective.* Chicago: University of Chicago Press.
Dumont, L., and D. Pocock. 1957. "For a Sociology of India." *Contributions to Indian Sociology* 1:7–22.
Durkheim, E. (1912) 1984. *Die elementaren Formen des religiösen Lebens.* Frankfurt am Main: Suhrkamp.
Eliade, M. 1958. *Patterns in Comparative Religion.* London: Sheed & Ward.
Elwin, V. (1947) 1991. *The Muria and Their Ghotul.* Bombay: Oxford University Press.
Elwin, V. 1950. *The Bondo Highlanders.* London: Oxford University Press.
Elwin, V. 1951. *The Tribal Art of Middle India: A Personal Record.* London: Oxford University Press.
Elwin, V. 1954. *Tribal Myths of Orissa.* Bombay: Oxford University Press.
Elwin, V. 1955. *Religion of an Indian Tribe.* London: Oxford University Press.
Evans-Pritchard, E. E. 1940. *The Nuer.* New York: Oxford University Press.
Evans-Pritchard, E. E. 1962. *Essays in Social Anthropology.* London: Faber and Faber.
Frazer, J. G. (1922) 1968. *Der Goldene Zweig: Eine Studie über Magie und Religion.* Cologne: Kiepenheuer & Witsch.
Fried, M. 1968. "On the Concepts of 'Tribe' and 'Tribal Society'." In *Essays on the Problem of Tribe,* edited by J. Helm, 3–20. Seattle: University of Washington Press.
Friend-Pereira, J. E. F. 1902. "Marriage Customs of the Khonds." *Journal of the Asiatic Society of Bengal* 71 (3): 18–28.
Fruzetti, L., A. Östör, and S. Barnett. 1976. "The Cultural Construction of the Person in Bengal and Tamil Nadu." *Contributions to Indian Sociology* 10 (1): 157–82.

Fuller, C. J. 1989. "Misconceiving the Grain Heap: A Critique of the Concept of the Indian *jajmani* System." In *Money and the Morality of Exchange,* edited by M. Bloch and J. Parry, 33–63. Cambridge: Cambridge University Press.

Fuller, C. J. 1992. *The Camphor Flame: Popular Hinduism and Society in India.* Princeton: Princeton University Press.

Fürer-Haimendorf, Chr. V. 1938. "The Morung System of the Konyak Nagas, Assam." *Journal of the Royal Anthropological Institute of Great Britain and Ireland* 68: 349–78.

Fürer-Haimendorf, Chr. V. 1948. *The Raj Gonds of Adilal.* London: Macmillan.

Fürer-Haimendorf, Chr. V. 1950. "Youth-Dormitories and Community Houses in India." *Anthropos* 45: 119–44.

Fürer-Haimendorf, Chr. V. 1953. "The After-Life in Indian Tribal Belief." *Journal of the Royal Anthropological Institute of Great Britain and Ireland* 83 (1–2): 37–49.

Fürer-Haimendorf, Chr. V. 1979. *The Gonds of Andhra Pradesh: Tradition and Change in an Indian Tribe.* New Delhi: Vikas Publishing House.

Fürer-Haimendorf, Chr. V. 1980. *A Himalayan Tribe: From Cattle to Cash.* New Delhi: Vikas Publ. House.

Galey, J.-C., ed. 1984. *Différences, valeurs, hiérachie: Textes offerts à Louis Dumont.* Paris: Éditions de l'École des Hautes Études en Sciences Sociales.

Galey, J.-C., ed. 1989. "Reconsidering Kingship in India: An Ethnological Perspective." *History and Anthropology* 4: 123–87.

Gell, A. 1982. "The Market Wheel: Symbolic Aspects of an Indian Tribal Market." *Man,* n.s., 17:470–91.

Gell, S. M. S. 1992. *The Ghotul in Muria Society.* Chur: Harwood Academic Publishers.

Gellner, E. 1977. "Patrons and Clients." In *Patrons and Clients in Mediterranean Societies,* edited by E. Gellner and J. Waterbury, 1–6. London: Duckworth.

Gellner, E., and J. Waterbury, eds. 1977. *Patrons and Clients in Mediterranean Societies.* London: Duckworth.

Godelier, M. 1977. "The Concept of 'Tribe': A Crisis Involving Merely a Concept or the Empirical Foundations of Anthropology Itself?" In *Perspectives in Marxist Anthropology,* edited by M. Godelier, 70–96. Cambridge: Cambridge University Press.

Gofman, A. 1998. "A Vague but Suggestive Concept: The 'Total Social Fact'." In *Marcel Mauss: A Centenary Tribute,* edited by W. James and N. J. Allen, 63–70. New York: Berghahn Books.

Good, A. 1980. "Elder Sister's Daughter Marriage in South Asia." *Journal of Anthropological Research* 36: 474–500.

Good, A. 1981. "Prescription, Preference and Practise: Marriage Patterns among the Kondaiyankottai Maravar of South India." *Man,* n.s., 16:108–29.

Goodenough, W. H. 1956. "Componential Analysis and the Study of Meaning." *Language* 32: 195–216.

Goody, J. 1973. "Bridewealth and Dowry in Africa and Eurasia." In *Bridewealth and Dowry,* edited by J. Goody and S. Tambiah, 1–58. Cambridge: Cambridge University Press.

Gough, K. 1956. "Brahmin Kinship in a Tamil Village." *American Anthropologist* 58: 826–53.

Guzy, L. 2000. "'On the Road with the Babas': Some Insights into Local Features of Mahima Dharma." *Journal of Social Sciences* 4 (4): 323–30.

Guzy, L. 2001. "Voices of Gods: Ecstatic Alekhs and Local Configurations of Mahima Dharma." *Adivasi* 40–41:61–70.

Guzy, L. 2002. *Baba-s und Alekh-s – Askese und Ekstase einer Religion im Werden: Vergleichende Untersuchungen der asketischen Tradition Mahima Dharma in Orissa/östliches Indien.* Berlin: Weissensee Verlag.
Hacker, K. F. 2000a. "Displaying a Tribal Imaginary: Known and Unknown India." *Museum Anthropology* 23 (3): 5–25.
Hacker, K. F. 2000b. "Travelling Objects: Brass Images, Artisans, and Audiences." *Anthropology and Aesthetics* 37: 147–66.
Hardenberg, R. 1999. *Die Wiedergeburt der Götter: Ritual und Gesellschaft in Orissa.* Hamburg: Dr. Kovac.
Hardenberg, R. 2000. *Ideologie eines Hindu-Königtums: Struktur und Bedeutung der Rituale des ‚Königs von Puri' (Orissa/Indien).* Berlin: Das Arabische Buch.
Hardenberg, R. 2003. "Friendship and Violence among the Dongria Kond (Orissa/India)." *Baessler Archiv* 51: 45–57.
Hardenberg, R. 2014. "Bali Yatra of the Kond: A Ritual Performance and its socio-historical context." In: *Dialogues with Gods: Possession in Middle Indian Rituals*, edited by T. Otten and U. Skoda, 135–74. Berlin: Weissensee Verlag.
Howell, S., ed. 1990. Special issue, *Ethnos* 55 (3–4): 137–259.
Hugh-Jones, C. 1979. *From the Milk River: Spatial and Temporal Processes in Northwest Amazonia.* Cambridge: Cambridge University Press.
Hutton, J. H. 1921a. *The Angami Nagas: With Some Notes on Neighbouring Tribes.* London: Macmillan & Co.
Hutton, J. H. 1921b. *The Sema Nagas.* London: Macmillan & Co.
Iteanu, A. 1990a. "The Concept of the Person and the Ritual System: An Orokaiva View." *Man* 25: 35–53.
Iteanu, A. 1990b. "Sacred and Profane Revisited: Durkheim and Dumont Considered in the Orokaiva Context." *Ethnos* 55 (3–4): 169–83.
Iteanu, A. 2004. "Partial Discontinuity: The Mark of Ritual." *Social Analysis* 48 (2): 98–115.
Israel, M. 1979. *A Grammar of the Kuvi Language.* Trivandrum: Dravidian Linguistics Association.
Jackson, E. 1984. "Vaupés Marriage Practices." In *Marriage Practices in Lowland South America*, edited by K. M. Kensinger, 156–79. Urbana: University of Illinois Press.
Jacobs, J. 1990. *The Nagas: Society, Culture and the Colonial Encounter.* London: Thames and Hudson.
Jamous, R. 1992. "The Brother-Married-Sister Relationship and Marriage Ceremonies as Sacrificial Rites: A Case Study from Northern India." In *Understanding Rituals*, edited by D. de Coppet, 52–73. London: Routledge & Kegan Paul.
Jena et al. (Jena, M. K., P. Pathi, J. Dash, K. Patnaik, and K. Seeland). 2002. *Forest Tribes of Orissa: Lifestyle and Social Conditions of Selected Orissan Tribes.* Vol. 1, *The Dongaria Kondh.* Man and Forest Series 2. New Delhi: D. K. Printworld.
Jones, S. 1974. *Men of Influence in Nuristan: A Study of Social Control and Dispute Settlement in Waigal Valley, Afghanistan.* London: Seminar Press.
Kanungo, A. K. 2004. "Problems in Educating Tribal Children: The Dongria Kondh Experience." Accessed 20 October 2004. www.anthroglobe.ca/docs/Dongria.pdf.
Karve, I. (1953) 1965. *Kinship Organization in India.* 2nd rev. ed. Bombay: Asia Publishing House.

Kirchhoff, P. 1932. "Verwandtschaftsbezeichnungen und Verwandtenheirat." *Zeitschrift für Ethnologie* 64: 41–72.
Kolenda, P. 1981a. "Aspects of the Religion of the Untouchable Sweepers of Khalapur." In *Caste, Cult and Hierarchy: Essays on the Culture of India*, 161–68. Meerut: Folklore Institute.
Kolenda, P. 1981b. "Religious Anxiety and Hindu Fate." In *Caste, Cult and Hierarchy: Essays on the Culture of India*, 169–84. Meerut: Folklore Institute.
Kroeber, A. L. 1909. "Classificatory Systems of Relationship." *Journal of the Royal Anthropological Institute* 39: 77–84.
Kuper, A. 1988. *The Invention of Primitive Society: Transformations of an Illusion*. London: Routledge.
Kuper, A. 1999. *Culture: The Anthropologists' Account*. Cambridge, Mass.: Harvard University Press.
Leach, E. R. 1951. "The Structural Implications of Matrilateral Cross-Cousin Marriage." *Journal of the Royal Anthropological Institute* 81:54–104.
Leach, E. R. 1954. *Political Systems of Highland Burma*. London: Athlone Press.
Leach, E. R. 1955. "Polyandry, Inheritance and the Definition of Marriage." *Man* 55: 105–13.
Leach, E. R. 1960–61. "The Frontiers of Burma." *Comparative Studies in Society and History* 3: 49–68.
Leach, E. R. 1969. "Virgin Birth." In *Genesis as Myth and other Essays*, 85–112. London: Jonathan Cape.
Lévi-Strauss, C. 1965. "The Future of Kinship Studies." *Proceedings of the Royal Anthropological Institute of Great Britain and Ireland*, 13–22.
Lévi-Strauss, C. 1969. *The Elementary Structures of Kinship*. 2nd ed. London: Eyre and Spottiswoode.
Lounsbury, F. G. 1956. "A Semantic Analysis of Pawnee Kinship Usage." *Language* 32: 158–94.
Lowie, R. H. 1928. "A Note on Relationship Terminologies." *American Anthropologist* 30:263–68.
Macpherson, S. C. (1842) 1863. *Lieut. Macpherson's Report upon the Khonds of the Districts of Ganjam and Cuttack*. Madras: Graves, Cookson & Co.
Macpherson, S. C. 1852. "An Account of the Religion of the Khonds in Orissa." *Journal of the Royal Asiatic Society of Great Britain and Ireland* 13: 216–74.
Macpherson, S. C. 1865. *Memorials of Service in India: From the Correspondence of the Late Major Samuel Charteris Macpherson, C.B., Political Agent at Gwalior during the Mutiny, Formerly Employed in the Suppression of Human Sacrifice in Orissa, Edited by His Brother*. London: John Murray.
Majumdar, D. N. 1960. *Himalayan Polyandry*. London: Asia Publishing House.
Malinowski, B. 1929. *The Sexual Life of the Savages: In North Western Melanesia*. London: Routledge & Kegan Paul.
Mallebrein, C. 1993. "Bronzen der Kondh und anderer Stammesgruppen aus Orissa." In *Die anderen Götter: Volks- und Stammesbronzen aus Indien*, edited by G. Völger, 465–507. Ethnologica 17. Cologne: Gesellschaft für Völkerkunde (Verein zur Förderung des Rautenstrauch-Joest-Museums der Stadt Köln).
Mallebrein, C. 1993. 2001. "Tribal Art: Continuity and Change." In O*rissa Revisited*, edited by P. Pal, 142–61. Mumbai: Marg Publications.

Marriott, McKim. 1966. "The Feast of Love." In *Krishna: Myths, Rites, and Attitudes*, edited by M. Singer, 202–31. Chicago: Chicago University Press.
Marriott, McKim. 1968. "Caste Ranking and Food Transactions: A Matrix Analysis." In *Structure and Change in Indian Society*, in M. Singer and B. S. Cohn, 133–71. Chicago: Aldine Publishing Company.
Marriott, McKim. 1976. "Hindu Transactions: Diversity without Dualism." In *Transaction and Meaning: Directions in the Anthropology of Exchange and Symbolic Behavior*, edited by B. Kapferer, 109–42. Philadelphia: Institute for the Study of Human Issues.
Marriott, McKim. 1977. "Towards an Ethnosociology of South Asian Caste Systems." In *The New Wind: Changing Identities in South Asia*, edited by K. David, 227–38. Chicago: Chicago University Press.
Marriott, McKim. 1990. "Constructing an Indian Ethnosociology." In *India through Hindu Categories*, edited by McKim Marriott, 1–39. New Delhi: Sage Publications.
Marriott, McKim, and R. Inden. 1974. "Caste Systems." *New Encyclopaedia Britannica* 15 (3): 982–91.
Mauss, M. (1925) 1990. *The Gift: The Form and Reason for Exchange in Archaic Societies*. London: Routledge.
McDougal, C. W. 1963a. "The Social Structure of the Hill Juang." PhD diss., University of New Mexico.
McDougal, C. W. 1963b. "The Social Structure of the Hill Juang: A Précis." *Man in India* 43: 183–91.
McDougal, C. W. 1964. "Juang Categories and Joking Relationships." *South Western Journal of Anthropology* 20: 319–45.
[McLennan, J. F.]. 1863. "Hill Tribes in India." *North British Review* 38: 392–422.
[McLennan, J. F.]. (1865) 1970. *Primitive Marriage: An Inquiry into the Origin of the Form of Capture in Marriage Ceremonies*. Chicago: Cambridge University Press.
McKinley, R. 1971. "A Critique of the Reflectionist Theory of Kinship Terminology: The Crow/Omaha Case." *Man* 6 (2): 228–47.
Mencher, J. 1974. "The Caste System Upside Down, or the Not-So-Mysterious East." *Current Anthropology* 15:469–93.
Mills, J. P. 1922. *The Lhota Nagas*. London: Macmillan & Co.
Mills, J. P. 1922. 1926. *The Ao Nagas*. London: Macmillan & Co.
Mills, J. P. 1922. 1937. *The Rengma Nagas*. London: Macmillan & Co.
Moerman, M. 1968. "Being Lue: Uses and Abuses of Ethnic Identification." In *Essays on the Problem of Tribe*, edited by J. Helm, 153–69. Seattle: University of Washington Press.
Moffatt, M. 1979. *An Untouchable Community in South India: Structure and Consensus*. Princeton: Princeton University Press.
Morgan, L. H. 1870. *Systems of Consanguinity and Affinity of the Human Family*. Smithsonian Contributions to Knowledge 218. Washington, D.C.: Smithsonian Institution.
Murdock, G. P. 1949. *Social Structure*. New York: Macmillan.
Nayak, P. K. 1989. *Blood, Women and Territory: An Analysis of Clan Feuds of the Dongria Kondhs*. Delhi: Reliance Publishing House.
Needham, R. 1966. "Terminology and Alliance: I – Garo, Manggarai." *Sociologicus* 16 (2): 141–57.
Needham, R. 1967. "Terminology and Alliance: II – Mapuche; Conclusions." *Sociologicus* 17 (1): 39–54.

Needham, R. 1971. "Introduction." In *Rethinking Kinship and Marriage*, edited by R. Needham, xiii–cxvii. London: Tavistock.
Needham, R. 1973a. "Prescription." *Oceania* 42: 166–81.
Needham, R., ed. 1973b. *Right and Left: Essays on Dual Symbolic Classification*. Chicago: University of Chicago Press.
Needham, R. 1974. "Remarks on the Analysis of Kinship and Marriage." In *Remarks on the Analysis of Kinship and Marriage*, edited by R. Needham, 38–71. London: Tavistock.
Niggemeyer, H. 1964a. *Kuttia Kond: Dschungel-Bauern in Orissa*. Frankfurt am Main: Klaus Renner Verlag.
Niggemeyer, H. 1964b. "Kuttia Kond und Pano: Zur Stellung der verachteten Klassen in Indien." In *Festschrift für Ad. E. Jensen (Teil 2)*, edited by E. Haberland, M. Schusters, and H. Straube, 407–12. Munich: Renner.
O'Flaherty, W. D. 1973. *Siva: The Erotic Ascetic*. Oxford: Oxford University Press.
O'Flaherty, W. D. 1976. *The Origins of Evil in Hindu Mythology*. Berkeley: University of California Press.
Otten, T. 2000a. "In a Remote Area: Categories of the Person and Illness among the Desia of Koraput, Orissa." *Journal of Social Sciences* 4 (4): 347–56.
Otten, T. 2000a. 2000b. "Krankheitskonzepte und Heilungsexperten bei den Desya, Orissa: Erste Einblicke." *Mitteilungen der Berliner Gesellschaft für Anthropologie, Ethnologie und Urgeschichte* 21:129–38.
Otten, T. 2000a. 2006. *Heilung durch Rituale: Vom Umgang mit Krankheit bei den Rona im Hochland Orissas, Indien*. Berlin: LIT Verlag.
Padel, F. 2000. *The Sacrifice of a Human Being: British Rule and the Konds of Orissa*. New Delhi: Oxford University Press.
Panda, S. 1969–70. "Demography of a Kond Village." *Adibasi* 11: 27–35.
Parkin, R. 1985. "Munda Kinship Terminologies." *Man* 20 (4): 705–21.
Parkin, R. 1985. 1992a. "Dispersed Alliance, Terminological Change and Evidence." *JASO* 23 (1): 253–62.
Parkin, R. 1985. 1992b. *The Munda of Central India: An Account of their Social Organisation*. Delhi: Oxford University Press.
Parry, J. 1985. "Death and Digestion: The Symbolism of Food and Eating in North Indian Mortuary Rites." *Man*, n.s., 20: 612–30.
Parry, N. E. 1932. *The Lakhers*. London: Macmillan & Co.
Patnaik, N., and P. S. Das Patnaik. 1982. *The Kondh of Orissa: Their Socio-Cultural Life and Development*. Bhubaneswar: Tribal and Harijan Research-cum-Training Institute.
Peters, E. L. 1977. "Patronage in Cyrenaica." In *Patrons and Clients in Mediterranean Societies*, edited by E. Gellner and J. Waterbury, 275–90. London: Duckworth.
Pfeffer, G. 1976. "Puris Sasana-Dörfer: Basis einer regionalen Elite." Habilitation thesis, Heidelberg University.
Pfeffer, G. 1976. 1982. *Status and Affinity in Middle India*. Beiträge zur Südasienforschung 76. Wiesbaden: Franz Steiner Verlag.
Pfeffer, G. 1976. 1983. "Generation and Marriage in Middle India: The Evolutionary Potential of 'Restricted Exchange'." *Contributions to Indian Sociology* 17 (1): 87–121.
Pfeffer, G. 1976. 1985 "Verwandtschaftssysteme der südasiatischen Regionen im Vergleich." In *Regionale Traditionen in Südasien*, edited by H. Kulke and D. Rothermund, 171–90. Wiesbaden: Franz Steiner Verlag.

Pfeffer, G. 1976. 1991. "Der intra-agnatische 'Seelentausch' der Gadaba beim großen Lineageritual." In *Beiträge zur Ethnologie Mittel- und Süd-Indiens*, edited by M. S. Laubscher, 59–92. Munich: Anacon.

Pfeffer, G. 1976. 1993. "Comment: Dispersed Alliance, Terminological Change and Evidence." *JASO* 24 (1): 49–54.

Pfeffer, G. 1976. 1997a. "Die Haardebatte: Gender, Glatzen und Gewalt der Bondo." *Zeitschrift für Ethnologie* 122: 183–208.

Pfeffer, G. 1976. 1997b. "The Scheduled Tribes of Middle India as a Unit: Problems of Internal and External Comparison." In *Contemporary Society: Tribal Studies*, vol. 1, *Structure and Process*, edited by G. Pfeffer and D. K. Behera, 3–27. New Delhi: Concept Publishers.

Pfeffer, G. 1976. 1997c. "Vier Ansätze einer Ritualtheorie." *Mitteilungen der Berliner Gesellschaft für Anthropologie, Ethnologie und Urgeschichte* 18: 39–45.

Pfeffer, G. 1976. 1999. "Gadaba and the Bondo Kinship Vocabularies *versus* Marriage, Descent and Production." In *Contemporary Society: Tribal Studies*, vol. 4, *Social Realities*, edited by D. K. Behera and G. Pfeffer, 17–46. New Delhi: Concept Publishers.

Pfeffer, G. 1976. 2000. "Tribal Ideas." In "Asian World Views: Context and Structure," edited by R. Hardenberg, special issue, *Journal of Social Sciences* 4 (4): 331–46.

Pfeffer, G. 1976. 2001. "A Ritual of Revival among the Gadaba of Koraput." In *Jagannatha Revisited: Studying Society, Religion and the State in Orissa*, edited by H. Kulke and B. Schnepel, 123–48. Delhi: Manohar.

Pfeffer, G. 1976. 2002a. "The Structure of Middle Indian Tribal Society Compared." In *Concept of Tribal Society*, edited by G. Pfeffer and D. K. Behera, 208–29. Contemporary Tribal Studies 5. New Delhi: Concept Publishers.

Pfeffer, G. 1976. 2002b. "Zeit ohne Staat." In *Vom Herrscher zur Dynastie: Zum Wesen kontinuierlicher Zeitrechnung in Antike und Gegenwart*, edited by H. Falk, 255–68. Bremen: Hempen Verlag.

Pfeffer, G. 1976. 2004a. "Order in Tribal Middle Indian 'Kinship'." *Anthropos* 99: 381–409.

Pfeffer, G. 1976. 2004b. "Tribal Society of Highland Orissa, Highland Burma, and Elsewhere." In *Text and Context in the History, Literature and Religion of Orissa*, edited by A. Malinar, J. Beltz, and H. Frese, 427–56. New Delhi: Manohar.

Pfeffer, G., and D. K. Behera. 2002. "Introduction." In *Concept of Tribal Society*, edited by G. Pfeffer and D. K. Behera, 9–28. Contemporary Tribal Studies 5. New Delhi: Concept Publishers.

Platenkamp, J. D. M. 1988. *Tobelo: Ideas and Values of a North Moluccan Society*. Leiden: Repro Psychologie.

Platenkamp, J. D. M. 1990. "'The Severance of the Origin': A Ritual of the Tobelo of North Halmahera." In "Rituals and the Comparison of Societies," edited by C. Barraud and J. D. M. Platenkamp, special issue, *Bijdragen tot de taal-, land- en volkenkunde* 146 (2): 74–92.

Platenkamp, J. D. M. 1992. "Transforming Tobelo Ritual." In *Understanding Rituals*, edited by D. de Coppet, 74–96. London: Routledge & Kegan Paul.

Platenkamp, J. D. M. 2001. "Temporality and Male-Female Distinctions in the Tobelo Vocabulary of Relationships." In *Sexe relatif ou sexe absolu? De la distinction de sexe dans les sociétés*, edited by C. Alès and C. Barraud, 241–62. Paris: Éditions de la Maison des sciences de l'homme.

Pocock, D. F. 1962. "Notes on *jajmani* Relationships." *Contributions to Indian Sociology* 6: 78–95.
Pratt, M. L. 1986. "Fieldwork in Common Places." In *Writing Culture: The Poetics and Politics of Ethnography*, edited by J. Clifford and G. E. Marcus, 27–50. Berkeley: University of California Press.
Rabinow, P. 1986. "Representations Are Social Facts: Modernity and Post-Modernity in Anthropology." In *Writing Culture: The Poetics and Politics of Ethnography*, edited by J. Clifford and G. E. Marcus, 234–61. Berkeley: University of California Press.
Radcliffe-Brown, A. R. 1952. *Structure and Function in Primitive Society*. London: Cohen and West.
Raheja, G. G. 1988. *The Poison in the Gift: Ritual, Prestation, and the Dominant Caste in a North Indian Village*. Chicago: University of Chicago Press.
Randeria, S. 1992. "The Politics of Representation and Exchange among the Untouchable Castes in Western India (Gujarat)." PhD diss., Free University of Berlin.
Ray, G. 1950. "Characteristic Features of Kondh Kinship Terminology." *The Eastern Anthropologist* 3: 151–7.
Riderer, J. 1993. "Die Metallanalyse der Volksbronzen." In *Die anderen Götter: Volks- und Stammesbronzen aus Indien*, edited by G. Völger, 509–14. Ethnologica 17. Cologne: Gesellschaft für Völkerkunde (Verein zur Förderung des Rautenstrauch-Joest-Museums der Stadt Köln).
Rivers, W. H. R. (1914) 1968. *Kinship and Social Organisation*. With commentaries by Raymond Firth and David M. Schneider. London: Athlone Press.
Rivière, P. 1970. "Editor's Introduction." In J. F. McLennan, *Primitive Marriage: An Inquiry into the Origin of the Form of Capture in Marriage Ceremonies*, vii–xlvii. Chicago: Cambridge University Press.
Rosman, A., and P. G. Rubel. 1971. *Feasting with Mine Enemy: Rank and Exchange among Northwest Coast Societies*. New York: Columbia University Press.
Roy, S. C. 1915. *The Oraons of Chota Nagpur: Their History, Economic Life, and Social Organization*. Ranchi: Man in India Office.
Roy, S. C. 1935. *The Hill Bhuiyas of Orissa: With Comparative Notes on the Plains Bhuiyas*. Ranchi: Man in India Office.
Roy, S. C. 1937. *The Kharias*. 2 vols. Ranchi: Man in India Office.
Rubel, P. G., and A. Rosman. 1978. *Your Own Pigs You May Not Eat: A Comparative Study of New Guinea Societies*. Chicago: University of Chicago.
Sahlins, M. 1968. *Tribesmen*. Englewood Cliffs: Prentice Hall.
Sahlins, M. 1972. *Stone Age Economics*. London: Tavistock Publications.
Sax, W. S. 1991. *Mountain Goddess: Gender and Politics in a Central Himalayan Pilgrimage*. New York: Oxford University Press.
Sax, W. S. 2002. *Dancing the Self: Personhood and Performance in the pandav lila of Garhwal*. New York: Oxford University Press.
Scheffler, H. W., and F. G. Lounsbury. 1971. *A Study in Kinship Semantics: The Siriono Kinship System*. Englewood Cliffs: Prentice Hall.
Schneider, D. M. 1968. *American Kinship: A Cultural Account*. Englewood Cliffs: Prentice Hall.
Schneider, D. M. 1972. "What Is Kinship All About?" In *Kinship Studies in the Morgan Centennial Year*, edited by P. Reining, 32–63. Washington: Anthropological Society of Washington.

Schnepel, B. 1993. "Die Schutzgöttinnen: Tribale Gottheiten in Südorissa (Indien) und ihre Patronage durch hinduistische Kleinkönige." *Anthropos* 88: 337–50.
Schnepel, B. 2002. *The Jungle Kings: Ethnohistorical Aspects of Politics and Ritual in Orissa.* Studies in Orissan Society, Culture and History 2. Delhi: Manohar.
Schulze, F. V. P. 1912. *The Religion of the Kuvi-Konds, Their Customs and Folklore.* Madras: Graves, Cookson & Co.
Scott, J. 1977. "Patronage as Exploitation." In *Patrons and Clients in Mediterranean Societies,* edited by E. Gellner and J. Waterbury, 21–40. London: Duckworth.
Senapati, N., and N. K. Sahu, eds. 1966. *Orissa District Gazetteers: Koraput.* Cuttack: Orissa Government Press.
Silverman, S. 1977. "Patronage as Myth." In *Patrons and Clients in Mediterranean Societies,* edited by E. Gellner and J. Waterbury, 7–20. London: Duckworth.
Sinha, S. 1980. "Tribes and Indian Civilisation: A Perspective." *Man in India* 60 (1–2): 1–15.
Sinha, S. 1981. "Tribes and Indian Civilization: Transformation Processes in Modern India." *Man in India* 61 (2): 105–142.
Skoda, U. 2000. "The Kinship System of the Aghria." *Journal of Social Sciences* 4 (4): 227–93.
Skoda, U. 2001. "Transfer of Children and Inter-Group Relations in a Mixed Tribal and Caste Society." *Adibasi* 40–41: 51–60.
Skoda, U. 2005. *The Aghria: A Peasant Caste on a Tribal Frontier.* New Delhi: Manohar.
Southall, A. W. 1970. "The Illusion of Tribe." *Journal of Asian and African Studies* 5 (1–2): 28–50.
Stachowski, D. Unpublished a. (without title; chapters deal with the house, the village, the relevance of pigs, and various death rituals of the Dongria; written in German). Manuscript, 23 pages.
Stachowski, D. Unpublished b. "Haus- und Dorfanlage der Dangria-Kond in Orissa (Indien)." Paper presented at the biannual ethnological conference of the Deutsche Gesellschaft für Völkerkunde in Cologne, October 1987. Manuscript, 8 pages.
Strümpell, C. 2001. "Industrialisation in a 'Tribal Zone': The Desia of Koraput and a Hydro-Electric Power Plant." *Adibasi* 40–41: 71–81.
Strümpell, C. 2006. *'Wir arbeiten zusammen, wir essen zusammen.' Konvivium und soziale Peripherie in einer indischen Werkssiedlung.* LIT-Verlag: Münster.
Strümpell, C. 2008. "Chatamput: An Industrial 'Camp' in the Tribal Zone." In *Periphery and Centre: Groups, Categories and Values,* edited by G. Pfeffer, 319–40. Delhi: Manohar.
Tambiah, S. J. 1973a. "Dowry and Bridewealth, and the Property Rights of Women in South Asia." In *Bridewealth and Dowry,* edited by J. Goody and S. Tambiah, 59–169. Cambridge: Cambridge University Press.
Tambiah, S. J. 1973b. "From Varna to Caste through Mixed Unions." In *The Character of Kinship,* edited by J. Goody, 191–229. Cambridge: Cambridge University Press.
Tambiah, S. J. 1989. "Bridewealth and Dowry Revisited." *Current Anthropology* 30 (4): 413–35.
Taylor, R. 1989. "Chinese Hierarchy in Comparative Perspective." *Journal of Asian Studies* 48 (3): 490–511.
Tcherkézoff, S. 1985. "Black and White Dual Classification: Hierarchy and Ritual Logic in Nyamwezi Ideology." In *Contexts and Levels: Anthropological Essays on Hierarchy,* edited by R. H. Barnes, D. de Coppet, and R. J. Parkin, 54–67. Oxford: Anthropological Society.

Thurston, E. (1909) 1987. *Castes and Tribes of Southern India*. Vol. III, K. New Delhi: Asian Educational Services.
Trautmann, T. 1987. *Lewis Henry Morgan and the Invention of Kinship*. Berkeley: University of California Press.
Trautmann, T. (1981) 1995. *Dravidian Kinship*. New Delhi: Vistaar Publications.
Tripathi, G. C. 1978. "Navakalevara: The Unique Ceremony of the 'Birth' and the 'Death' of the 'Lord of the World'." In *The Cult of Jagannatha and the Regional Tradition of Orissa*, edited by A. Eschmann, H. Kulke, and G. C. Tripathi, 223–64. New Delhi: R. Jain Manohar Publications.
Tyler, S. A. 1986. "Post-Modern Ethnography: From Document of the Occult to Occult Document." In *Writing Culture: The Poetics and Politics of Ethnography*, edited by J. Clifford and G. E. Marcus, 122–40. Berkeley: University of California Press.
Vatuk, S. 1969. "A Structural Analysis of the Hindi Kinship Terminology." *Contributions to Indian Sociology* 3: 94–115.
Vatuk, S. 1975. "Gift and Affines in North India." *Contributions to Indian Sociology* 9 (2): 155–96.
Vitebsky, P. 1993. *Dialogues with the Dead: The Discussion of Mortality among the Sora of Eastern India*. New Delhi: Cambridge University Press.
Watts, N. A. 1970. *The Half-Clad Tribals of Eastern India*. Bombay: Orient Longmans.
Winfield, W. W. 1928. *A Grammar of the Kui Language*. Calcutta: Baptist Mission Press.
Winfield, W. W. 1929. *A Vocabulary of the Kui Language*. Calcutta: Baptist Mission Press.
Wiser, W. H. 1936. *The Hindu jajmani System*. Lucknow: Lucknow Publishing House.
Woodburn, J. 1982. "Egalitarian Societies." *Man*, n.s., 17: 431–51.

Index

abduction *see* bride capture
abductors
- "betrothal fee" reimbursement by, 395–396
- gifts by, 398–399, 400–401
- negotiations with bride-givers, 391–392, 393–394

address terms
- bride-takers, 190
- ego's generation, 184–185, 186, 187
- parents' generation, 177, 178
- *sadu*, 242
- "skewing," 188–189

adivasi, rituals, 60
affinal clans
- marriages, 226–228
- in villages, 231

affinal villages, 233–234, 235
affines (*gota*)
- and agnates, 194
- buffalo sacrifice, mutual work at, 489, 490
- vs. buffalo sacrifice organisers, 594
- local vs. non-local, 208
- marriage restrictions, 193
- meaning of, 203
- *samdin gota*, 203
- Tebapada, links of, 540
- types, 578
- in village community and collectivity, 230
- *see also mudrenga*; *tonenga*

affinity, 39, 140–141, 590
age-and-status categories, 345–346, 350, 352
- *see also* children; young people; middle-aged people; old people

Agency for the Suppression of Human Sacrifice and Female Infanticide, 414–415

aggressive behaviour
- of drunk men, 19–20, 33–36, 304–305
- of *mudrenga*, 497
- *see also* violence

Aghria (caste), 597
agnates
- and affines, 194
- buffalo sacrifice, mutual work at, 489

agriculture
- buffalo sacrifice in cycle of, 440–441
- *buti kam*, 98
- by Dombo, 97, 102
- hill cultivation, 101–102, 603–604
- and marriage rules, 251
- *see also* crops; fields; harvest; livestock; produce; swidden

aji budi (goddess), 318
akat manjing (rice), 527
alcohol
- drinking at *hedi tana*, 324–325
- drunk *jani*, 327–328
- drunk men, incidents with, 19–20, 33–36, 304–305
- production, 107–108
- selling, 108, 109
- sharing, 109
- *see also salap* sap

"alliance theory," 143–144
ancestors
- food offerings to, 318–319, 452
- relations to, 46
- soul in infants, 349
- summoning of, 131
- worshipping of, 452, 453

animal markets, 110
animal sacrifices
- at *bada* ritual, 329
- chickens, 318
- colour and type, 336 n.46
- cows, 439–440
- at *derupripka*, 439–440
- dove, 550
- for earth goddess, 552–553
- fowl, 550
- at "pigeon-pea festival," 456–457
- piglet, 552–553
- pigs, 329
- promotion of, 415
- rams, 445–446, 550–551
- rituals at, 503, 504
- for *satara bonda*, 550–551

– *see also* buffalo sacrifice
animals
– brass objects, 500
– for buffalo sacrifice, 447–448
– trading in, 109–110
– *see also* livestock; *specific animals*
anthropology, 11–12
– *see also* ethnographic research
Apffel-Marglin, Frédérique, 72
arbitrators, *barika* as, 117
Arhem, Kaj, 404–405
arranged marriage
– about, 257, 405–406, 407
– beginning of, 272
– vs. bride capture, 43, 44
– bride capture as part of, 273, 386–387
– buffalo sacrifice, comparison to, 594
– conflicts, 278, 290, 378–379
– dissolved, 211–212
– gifts, 44–45
– *giri takoli* ritual, 282, 326, 340, 342
– in Gumma, 276
– *ijo henga hana*, 280–281, 311–314
– "life" obtained in, 616
– "meal of friendship," 314–315
– of Muria Gond, 355
– prestations overview, 283–285
– process, 277–282
– reciprocity, 408–409, 410
– resistance against, 344–345
– *samudi sehena*, 279, 288–292
– sex, first, 343–344
– *tone paga tinja hana*, 281
– transactions, 284, 286
– uncertain outcome, 278–279
– "wedding gift," 284–285, 332–333, 334, 408–409
– *wenda kodang* visit, 282, 343
– words for, 283–284
– younger siblings, limits for, 212–213
– *see also* "betrothal fee"; *hedi tana*; *karjame*
art, tribal, 499–500
assistants, of author, 24, 26, 28, 29–30
avoidance rules, 84–85, 295
axes
– functions, 460–461

– killing of buffalo victim with, 566
– *tangi*, 506–510, 530–531, 551–552

babies *see* infants
"bad" death, 78, 611
bada (ritual), 325–328, 329
Bada Denganali (village), 223
bahuki, photo, 532
Bailey, Frederick G., 60–61, 64
bali kudi (shrine), 434
bali yatra (festival), 373
Bamanadeo (cave), 503
bamboo fences
– *garada*, 489
– *madada*, 491
– *see also sala bada*
bamboo poles
– for buffalo sacrifice, 49
– for *satara bonda*, 510, 511, 548–549
bana jani, 534
bana paga ("forest food"), 504–505, 534
banana trees, 545, 546
bananas, trading in, 105
Banerjee, Sukumar, 114 n.41
barika
– about, 113
– Banerjee on, 114 n.41
– on "betrothal fee," 308
– functions, 113–114, 116–117, 119–121
– influence, 120
– loyalty, 117–118
– Madhu Cham, 33–34
– obligations, 113
– photo, 114
Barnes, Robert Harrison
– on bride capture, 269–270, 383
– on McLennan, 268–269
– on types of marriage, 44
bat kina see sharing
beef, eating, 77
behaviour
– ego's generation, 186, 187–188
– in girls' dormitories, 361
– grandparents' generation, 174–175
– of lovers, 362–363
– parents' generation, 178–181
– spouse's siblings' spouses, 187

– *see also* aggressive behaviour; peaceful behaviour; sexual behaviour
beju (male shaman)
– about, 525, 528–529
– at buffalo sacrifice, 131–132
– *dissari*, comparison to, 521–522
– initiation, 524, 525
– *jani*, comparison to, 527–528
– in trance (photo), 129
– trance session by, 342
bejuni (female shaman)
– about, 522–523
– at bride's procession, 336
– chicken sacrifice by, 318
– dancing at *satara bonda*, 547–548
– Dombo, 129–131
– food offerings by, 322
– husband of, 524
– invocations by, 320, 321
– *jani*, comparison to, 527–528
– marriage at mango tree, 523
– photo, 129
– at "pigeon-pea festival," 456, 457–458
– potential, 525–526
– *satara bonda*, climbing of bamboo pole of, 548–549
– at "stone ritual," 554, 555
– trance sessions by, 36–37, 321
– worshipping of *sita penu-lahi penu*, 559–560
bereni kina (conciliatory meeting), 573
Berger, Peter
– author's support by, 22–23, 27
– on relations on Koraput plateau, 62–63
– study on Gadaba, 7–8
beta see hunting
"betrothal fee" (*mahala takang*)
– amount of, 292, 333
– *barika* on, 308
– conflicts, 304–306, 307–311
– of Jreda Kond, 302
– livestock and objects as, 302
– money as, 299–301, 303
– negotiations, 298–299, 301, 303–304, 305, 309, 310–311
– overview, 280
– past, 395

– payment of, 303, 308
– by poor families, 297
– reimbursement of, 392–398
– by rich families, 297–298
– shares of, 299–301
– vs. "wedding gift," 284–285, 334
"big men," 287–288
big-men festival (*ghanta parba*), 131, 340, 580–581
biological father, 198
Bird-David, Nurit, 96, 126
birimunda-kambimunda (deity), 469
birth, as impurity, 135–136
"biscuit dance" (game), 564
bismajhi (administrator), 596–597
Bissamcuttack (town), 389
– *see also* king of Bissamcuttack
blacksmith, 501–502
Bloch, Maurice, 95
blood, from buffalo victim, 534
Boal, Barbara, 73–74, 250, 328–329, 418, 460, 577, 606
bodily fluids, 371
body ornaments, 362, 363–365, 366–367
bonda
– about, 512–513
– at buffalo sacrifice, 511, 512, 513, 544–545
– at clan territories, 513–514
– at houses, 513
– photo, 511
– status, 514
– types, 598
– *see also satara bonda*
Bondo, 356
Bourdieu, Pierre, 251–252
boys
– arranged marriage, beginning of, 272
– "biscuit dance" (game), 564
– body ornaments, 364, 367
– of bride-takers at bride's procession, 334–335
– clothes, 366
– dancing and singing, 323–324, 556
– in *ghotul*, 353–354, 355
– hair style, 366
– herding by, 112
– as human victim, 600

- joking with old men, 325
- killing of buffalo victim, 571
- popularity, 362
- sexual freedom at buffalo sacrifice, 563
- sexual relations with girls, 216–217, 234, 236, 331, 354
- visits to girls' dormitories, 358–359, 360, 369

brass objects, 499–501, 502
brass vessels (*dokanga*), as "wedding gift," 332, 333
bride capture
- about, 257, 383–384, 406, 407
- vs. arranged marriage, 43, 44
- arranged marriage, as part of, 273, 386–387
- *barika* as mediator, 117
- Barnes on, 269–270, 383
- buffalo sacrifice, comparison to, 594–595
- Campbell on, 308
- ceremonial vs. real, 269–270
- as collective affair, 388
- conflict settlement, 390–391
- conflicts, 389–390
- consent by girl, 273–274
- examples, 243–244
- failed attempts, 384, 385–386, 387
- fines, 401–402
- forceful, 306–308, 384
- as hunting, 387–388
- of Kuttia Kond, 383 n.73
- of Makuna, 404–405
- McLennan on, 43, 260, 262, 270
- negotiations on, 391–398, 401–402
- peace after, 402
- planned, 384–385
- of pregnant girl, 378–379
- reciprocity, 409, 410
- as resistance against arranged marriage, 344–345
- retaliation against, 390, 572–573
- by Sikoka Dikca, 306–308, 309
- studies, 257–258
- violence, 306–307, 384, 389, 572–573
- words for, 272–273
bride-demanding people, 288, 289–290
bride-givers
- delegation of, 311–314
- demands, 273
- Desia clans, 218–219
- feast by, 291–292
- gifts by, 408–409
- gifts for, 290–291, 292
- negotiations with abductors, 391–392, 393–394
- negotiations with first husband's family, 391, 394–395, 396
- role change, 311
- status difference to bride-takers, 408–409
- villages of, 226–228
bride's father's sisters, share of "betrothal fee" for, 299
bride's parents' house, rituals at, 319–322
bride's procession, 282, 314, 334–338
bride-takers
- address terms, 190
- boys of, at bride's procession, 334–335
- delegations of, 298, 303, 304–306
- Dongria and Desia clans, 218–219
- police support for, 310
- status difference to bride-givers, 408–409
- villages of, 226–228
brides
- avoidance rules for, 295
- at *bada* ritual, 328
- buffalo victim, comparison to, 592–593
- captured, demanding release of, 307–308
- captured, recovering of, 309
- evil forces, removing of, 328–329
- exchange of, 248–249
- farewell of, 331
- groom's house, bride's arrival at, 385
- groom's parents' house, arrival at, 337–338
- groom's people heading to village of, 323
- groom's village, crossing border of, 335
- groom's village, entering, 337
- "meal of friendship," 314–315
- preparation of, 330
- purification of, 328
- Sikoka Bambu, 333
- Sikoka Kurmi, 334
- turmeric water on, 307
- visits in neighbouring villages, 494, 592

- word for, 272
- at *yatra kudi*, 336–337
British colonialists *see* Campbell; Macpherson
brooms, trading in, 106
brother and sister, myth of, 638–639
brother clans, 208–209
"brother-and-sister clans" (*tayi bai kuda*)
- about, 191–192, 205
- of Kond, 203–204, 205
brothers
- marriage with brother's daughter, 239
- marriage with father's sister, 239
- *see also* mother's brother
brother's daughter, marriage with brother, 239
Buduni (village), 497
buffalo sacrifice (*kodru parbu*)
- about, 46–47
- in agricultural cycle, 440–441
- animals for, 447–448
- arranged marriage, comparison to, 594
- author's first witnessing, 24–25, 26
- *bana paga*, 504–505, 534
- beginning of, 415
- "biscuit dance" (game), 564
- *bonda*, 511, 512, 513, 544–545
- boys dancing at, 556
- bride capture, comparison to, 594–595
- buffaloes for, 116, 444–445, 542
- cancelled, 443–444
- clan territories, role of, 583–584
- conciliatory meeting, 573
- conflict of Sikoka vs. Pusika, 505–506
- costs, 449–450
- of Desia Kond, 436–437, 491, 492, 564
- drums (photo), 561
- in Dulumguda, 555–556, 565–567
- end, 574
- feasts, 449
- gods and deities, 47–48
- and harvest, 593, 605
- vs. harvest ritual, 438–439
- houses (social units), role of, 585–586
- human sacrifices, comparison to, 601
- intervals between, 437–438, 443
- iron objects, 502

- *jakeri* outside of settlements, 229
- *jani*, types of, 530–534
- knife at, 517
- in Kuskedeli, 551–553, 571–572
- of Kuttia Kond, 416, 595 n.147
- in Lekhpadar, 543–544, 545
- main events, 49–50
- in Mallikapori, 415–416
- mango ritual, 553
- marriage, comparison to, 50, 591–593, 594–595, 607–608
- in Mundawali, 503, 561, 572
- mutual work at, 489, 490
- myths, comparison to, 601, 602–605
- objects, 50, 413
- organisers vs. affines, 594
- and ownership of land, 506
- "pigeon-pea festival," comparison to, 459, 460–461
- in Railima, 26, 570–571
- relations of organisers of, 498, 543
- reports on, 415–417
- as research topic, 21
- rituals, 49
- as rivalry, 581
- sacred objects, 530–531, 544
- in Sana Dengoni, 547
- settlements, role of, 584
- sexual freedom, 563
- shamans, 131–132
- shrines, 48
- singing at, 415, 561–562
- *sita penu-lahi penu*, worshipping of, 559–560
- status role in, 581, 582
- *tangi*, 507, 530–531
- in Tebapada, 537–538, 540–543, 544–545, 547–550, 551, 553, 554–555, 556, 557, 559–560, 561–562, 563, 568–570, 573–574, 575
- timing, 436–437, 538–539, 591
- variations, 536
- verses on, 535–536
- villages, types of, 589–590
- young people, arrival of, 560, 561, 562–563

658 — Index

– *see also* bamboo fences; buffalo victims; earth goddess's house; *koteiwali*; *mudrenga*; sacrificial post; *satara bonda*
buffalo victims (*padari kodru*)
– blood from, 534
– bride, comparison to, 592–593
– buying, 445
– of Desia Kond, 492
– disappearance, 467
– "feeding the buffalo," 495–496
– *garada*, 489
– inspection, 466
– killing, 49, 492, 493, 565–566, 567–568, 569, 571, 572, 588
– legs, 566, 570, 575
– meat, burial of, 577, 606
– meat, consumption of, 578
– meat, distribution of, 567, 570, 574–576
– meat, fertility of, 577
– number of, 465–466
– photos, 496, 569
– physical features, 466
– purification of, 568
– representation of, 593–594
– as representation of earth goddess, 497
– right to kill, 493
– rules of killing, 588
– sacrificial post for, 468
– selling, 464–465
– value, 466
– visits in neighbouring villages, 494–497, 539, 592
buffaloes
– for buffalo sacrifice, 116, 444–445, 542
– buying, 110, 445, 447
– costs, 444, 447
– exchange, 339
– as gifts, 290–291, 309, 398–399, 400–401
– head, 339, 574–575
– killing at *hedi tana*, 339
– meat of, 49–50, 179 n.34, 291–292, 313–314
– offerings to, 542
– selling, 110–111, 116
burial
– of buffalo meat, 577, 606

– of human flesh, 420, 576–577
Burma, 134–135
buti kam (labor help), 98
buying
– buffaloes, 110, 445, 447
– fieldwork equipment, 22–23
– fowl, 448
– human victims, 463, 464
– pigs, 446, 447–448
– rams, 446, 447

camera usage, 25–26
Campbell, John
– on bride capture, 308
– on female infanticide, 42
– on human sacrifices, 418
– on human victims, 463
– human victims, rescuing of, 414, 415
– on Kond exogamy, 262
– on Kond marriage, 265–266
– on Pano, 52
– rivalry with Macpherson, 258–259
capture *see* bride capture
"cases," on "betrothal fee", 301
cassette recorder usage, 36–37, 531 n.103
"caste society"
– Bailey on, 60–61
– broader view on, 132–133
– comparison on different levels, 57–58
– Dumont on, 61
– Pfeffer on, 61–62
– "tribal societies," differences to, 37–38
– "tribal societies," interrelationship with, 58
caste systems
– of Desia Kond, 4
– *see also jajmani* system
castes (*jati*)
– about, 65–66
– Aghria, 597
– and clans, 81
– Dom, 52 n.1
– Dongria-Dombo rules, similarity to, 136–137
– hierarchy, 66
– and kinship, 152
– Komti, 103–104

– marriage with lower, 93
– in myth of origin of humankind, 76
– relation between, 10
– "substance-codes," 67
– *see also* impurity; purity; "untouchables"
cattle
– usage of, 111–112
– *see also* buffaloes; cows
cave, Bamanadeo, 503
Central Indian kinship, 160
ceremonial bride capture, vs. real, 269–270
ceremonies *see* rituals
chaukidar (police representative), 118–119
chicken sacrifices, 318
"chief people," 445
chiefs *see* village chiefs
children
– about, 346–347
– clan affiliation, 197–198
– old people, comparison to, 351
– sleeping location, 347, 358
– *see also* boys; girls; infants
children's generation (–1), terminology, 173, 188
children's spouses' parents, 182, 183, 187–188
Chota Nagpur complex, 162
claims
– to land, 566
– to ownership of village, 223
"clan brothers," in Tebapada, 540–541, 543
clan exogamy, 245, 246, 263
clan incest, 216–217
clan territories (*muta*)
– about, 96–97, 220, 223–224, 245, 587
– *bonda* at, 513–514
– buffalo sacrifice, role in, 583–584
– as clan element, 194
– of dominant clans, 206–207
– of Niamgiri Hills, 224–225
– sacred object, 443
– Sikoka *muta*, 220–223
– of Tebapada, 537
clan titles, 199–202
clans (*kuda*)
– about, 586
– and castes, 81

– categories, 201–202
– children's affiliation, 197–198
– concept of, 196–199
– dependent, 196
– of Desia Kond, 4, 207, 210
– Dongria and Dombo, analogy of, 79–81
– elements of, 194
– hierarchy, 82
– Jakesika, 220
– Kadraka, 536–537
– Kausilya, 80
– Kruska, 192
– local categories, 207–208
– locality and marriageability, 210
– opposition between, 588
– Pfeffer on, 196–197
– in Pfeffer's "complexes," 161–162
– phratries of Dongria and Desia, 205–206
– as phratry element, 193
– primary value, 246
– Pusika, 312, 505–506
– status, 619
– Timaka, 505
– titles, 199–202
– in villages, 228
– women's affiliation, 198–199
– *see also* affinal clans; brother clans; dominant clans
Clifford, James, 12–14, 15
climbing, of bamboo pole of *satara bonda*, 548–549
"close marriages," 42, 250, 252–253, 254
closed spaces, 87–89
clothes, 364, 365, 366
coastal Odisha, menstruating women, 72
cock, myth on, 115–116
collective help *see* buti kam
colonial officers *see* Campbell; Macpherson
colours, 475
combat *see* violence
compensation payment *see* "betrothal fee"; fines
conception, 371, 375, 381–382
conciliatory meeting (*bereni kina*), 573
conflicts
– arranged marriage, 278, 290, 378–379
– author's involvement in, 119

– on "betrothal fee," 304–306, 307–311
– of boys when looking for sexual partner, 331
– bride capture, 389–390
– claims to land, 566
– conciliatory meeting, 573
– on divorce, 264–265
– drunk *jani*, 327–328
– in families, 350
– Ghumsur Wars, 414
– of *jani*, 552
– with *jani*, 534
– with *mudrenga*, 493
– of neighbouring villages, 407–408
– police in, 119
– settlement of, 119, 390–391
– Sikoka vs. Pusika, 505–506
– at visits of buffalo victims, 494–495
– *see also* aggressive behaviour; bride capture; violence
construction
– of earth goddess's house, 471, 472, 473–475, 537–538
– of house of author, 28, 29
– of *palawara*, 486
– of roofs, 28, 29
– of *sala bada*, 427, 489, 490, 540–541
consumption, forms of, 8
contexts, 10–11, 621
contracts, renewing, 113 n.40
cooking, by bride's younger sister, 338
cooking utensils *see* hearths; pots; spoons
cosmological events, 601–602
costs
– of animals for buffalo sacrifice, 447–448
– of buffalo sacrifice, 449–450
– of buffaloes, 444, 447
– of human victims, 463
cousins *see* cross-cousins
cows
– killing, 541
– sacrifice, 439–440
creation
– concept of, 376
– goddesses, 613
– males' role, 607
– myth, 374–375

– providing order to, 382
– source of, 381, 382
– Virgin Birth story, 380
– women's power, 376–377
cremation grounds, 424
crops
– destruction of, 390
– important, 461–462
"cross-cousin marriage," 153–154
cross-cousins
– address terms, 184–185
– marriage restrictions, 211
"crossness," concept of, 153, 154
cross-parents
– behaviour towards, 179–180
– *see also* father's sisters; mother's brother
cycles of exchange, vs. sharing, 126–127

daaska beta (dormitory visit), 360
daka (pots), 503, 504
daka jani, 531–533
dancing
– of *bejuni* at *satara bonda*, 547–548
– of boys at buffalo sacrifice, 556
– at earth goddess's house, 498–499
– of girls behind houses, 358
– at *hedi tana*, 323–324
darkness
– in houses, 374
– vs. light, 373
Das Patnaik, Pravangshu Sekhar, 117, 523–524, 568
daughter-in-law, chosen by father, 261–262
daughters *see* brother's daughter
dead and deceased *see* ancestors
death
– "bad," 78, 611
– buffalo sacrifice, postponing of, 444
– "good," 611
– as impurity, 136
– informing about, 119–120
– rituals, 426–427
– unnatural, 120
– *see also* cremation grounds
deities *see* gods and deities
Delaney, Carol, 380–381
delegations

Index — 661

– of bride-demanding people, 288, 289–290
– of bride-givers, 311–314
– of bride-takers, 298, 303, 304–306
demands
– of bride-givers, 273
– release of bride, 307–308
demographics *see* population
demon, myth of, 593 n.146
dependent clans, and dominant clans, 196
derupripka (ritual), 439–440
desa ("sacrificers"), 589
descendants, 248
– *see also* children; grandchildren's generation
descent, as marriage factor, 244–245, 246
descent categories, as marriage factor, 247
descent groups (*punja*)
– about, 587–588
– house for god of, 434
– and houses (social units), 586
– land, 285, 286–287
– marriage, 236–240, 241–242
– marriage rules, 247
– as phratry element, 193
– of Sikoka, 222
– and status categories, 585
descent lines, absence of, 197
"descent theory," 143–144
Desia Kond
– about, 4
– brass objects, 501
– buffalo sacrifice, 436–437, 491, 492, 564
– caste system, 4
– clans, 4, 207, 210
– Dongria, difference to, 251, 253
– Dongria clans, marriages with, 210, 217–219
– *jakeri*, 435–436
– peaceful behaviour, 253
– Pfeffer on, 62
– phratries of clans of, 205–206
dharmu penu see sun god
dharni see jakeri
dharni kudi see earth goddess's house
dharni penu see earth goddess
dipawali (festival), 74–75, 78–79
disputes *see* conflicts

dissari (ritual specialist)
– *beju*, comparison to, 521–522
– initiation, 524, 525
– killing buffalo victim, ritual before, 568, 570–571
– *tangi*, rituals with, 508
distances
– social, 403, 411
– between villages, 232–234
– *see also* remoteness
"distant marriages," 41–42, 166, 232, 250, 254
distrust, in *mudrenga*, 493–494
divine objects *see* sacred objects
divorce, conflicts on, 264–265
DKDA *see* Dongria Kond Development Agency
dogma, vs. knowledge, 379–380
dokanga see brass vessels
Dom (caste), 52 n.1
Dombo
– about, 1, 52
– academic discrimination, 52–53
– agriculture, 97, 102
– author's approach of topic, 53
– *barika* and wife (photo), 114
– *bejuni*, 129–131
– buffalo victims, selling of, 464–465
– clans, 79–81
– dancing at buffalo sacrifice, 548
– Dongria, difference to, 58
– Dongria, friends among, 83–84
– Dongria, interdependence with, 65, 94–95, 138–139
– Dongria, marriage with, 80
– Dongria, relations to, 37–38, 39, 53–54, 70–71, 127
– Dongria, trading with, 106–107
– Dongria-Dombo rules and castes, similarity of, 136–137
– as ghosts, 78, 137–138
– houses, 426
– in *jajmani* system, 53
– land for, 97
– land taken away by, 101
– meat as gift by, 74–75
– number of people, 63–64
– power of, 123–124

- rice cultivation, 101
- ritual function, 38–39
- as shamans, 132
- spatial separation, 87–89
- status, 73, 77–78, 79, 94
- *see also* Pano

dominance, sexual, 368–369

dominant clans
- about, 191
- and dependent clans, 196
- land of, 97
- *muta* organisation, 206–207
- status, 581
- in villages, 231
- *see also* Sikoka

Dongormati (village)
- bride capture in, 387–388
- marriages, 219
- "pigeon-pea festival," 451–459
- unity with Gumma and Lamba, 304

Dongria Kond
- about, 1, 4, 5–6, 17–18
- community, 39
- isolation of, 59
- name, 1–2, 3
- number of people, 1 n.2, 63–64
- publications on, 51

Dongria Kond Development Agency (DKDA), 18–19, 20, 30–31

Dongria language
- arranged marriage, 283–284
- bride, 272
- bride capture, 272–273
- buffaloes as gift, 291
- *gati*, 489
- *kuang*, 3
- love, 363
- *mudra*, 489
- *pata* and *kona*, 428
- sex, 274
- wives, 274
- women, 271

dormitories
- about, 353
- of Bondo, 356
- of Juang, 353
- of Muria Gond, 353–355

- of Oraon, 355–356
- types, 356–357
- *see also* girls' dormitories

dosa (feast), 426–427

dove sacrifice, 550

Dravidian kinship terminology, 150–152, 153

drinking
- alcohol at *hedi tana*, 324–325
- *salap* sap, 31, 125–126

drums
- at buffalo sacrifice (photo), 561
- at earth goddess's house, 498
- at festivals, 131

drunk men, incidents with, 19–20, 33–36, 304–305

Duke and Dumbe, myths on, 637–639

Dulumguda (village), 555–556, 565–567

Dumont, Louis
- concepts of, 6, 7, 8–12
- on contexts, 10–11, 621
- on "cross-cousin marriage," 153–154
- Dravidian kinship terminology by, 150–152
- on hierarchy, 9–10, 155–156, 621
- on holism, 11
- influence of, 6
- on *jajmani* system, 68
- kinship comparison, 150
- on marriage rules, 146–147
- on purity vs. impurity, 66
- on relationship terminologies, 144–145
- on South and North Indian kinship, 157–158
- on tribes and "caste society," 61
- on universalism, 11
- on values, 8–10
- on whole, 10–11, 621

ears, ornaments, 364

earth, impurity of the, 71 n.6

earth goddess (*dharni penu*)
- animal sacrifices for, 552–553
- food offerings to, 552–553
- myths, 419
- representation of, 47, 476, 497
- ritual for, 551–553
- and women, 73–74

earth goddess's house (*dharni kudi*)

– about, 21, 48, 428, 467–468
– appearance, 427
– assistance from neighbouring villages, 472, 473
– blood from buffalo victim taken into, 534
– construction, 471, 472, 473–475, 537–538
– dancing and singing at, 498–499
– division, 476
– first, story of, 469
– frame, 471, 472
– *jakeri* inside, 428, 429
– layout with posts (ill.), 473
– main elements, 470
– meeting in, 541
– north-south axis, 471
– opposite sets of relationships, 476–477
– remains (photo), 424
– as representation of earth goddess, 476
– roof, 474–475
– verses on, 468–469
– walls and holes, 474
earth goddess's shrine *see jakeri*
east-facing rituals, 433
east-west axis, 423, 424, 434–435, 476–477
eating
– beef, 77
– *see also* food
"eating" analogy, 368
ego's generation (0), terminology, 172–173, 181–188
Eliade, Mircea, 421
Elwin, Verrier, 353–354, 356, 370, 371, 605
entrances, to villages, 427, 490
environment, view of, 126
E.R.A.S.M.E. (research team), 6–7
ethnic groups, classification of, 302
ethnographic research
– buffalo sacrifice as topic of, 21
– by Pfeffer, 7, 161
– proposal by author, 22
– *see also* fieldwork
ethnographic studies
– on bride capture, 257
– on Central Indian kinship, 160
– on Dongria Kond, 18 n.10
– on Gadaba, 7–8

– of rituals, 12
– on "tribal societies," 6–7
ethnographic writing, 12–16
etymology, of clan titles, 200–201
evil forces
– driven away at *yatra kudi*, 337
– removing from bride, 328–329
– *see also* demon; ghosts
evolution, human, 258
exchange
– of brides, 248–249
– of buffaloes, 339
– of sisters for marriage, 238, 404
– *see also* cycles of exchange; reciprocal exchange
exogamy
– Kond, 262
– linguistic, 269
– origin of, 263
– *see also* clan exogamy; village exogamy
expenses *see* costs
experimental ethnography, 14–15

families
– conflicts in, 350
– costs of buffalo sacrifice, 449–450
– poor, 297
– rich, 297–298
– status, 285
family tree, of *icha jani* segment (Gumma), 631
farewell, of bride, 331
fatherhood, 379
fathers
– biological, 198
– daughter-in-law, choosing of, 261–262
father's sisters
– marriage with brother, 239
– *see also* bride's father's sisters
feasts
– after bride capture, 402
– by bride-givers, 291–292
– at buffalo sacrifice, 449
– *dosa*, 426–427
– earth goddess's house, after construction of, 538
– *ijo henga hana*, 280–281, 311–314

– *kudi bhoji*, 490–491
– of merit, 579–580
– sharing at, 124–125
"feeding the buffalo" (*kodru tisnari*), 495–496
fees *see* "betrothal fee"
female infanticide
– Campbell on, 42
– of Kond, 258, 263–264
– as limited phenomenon, 268
– Macpherson on, 264–265, 266, 267
– main reasons, 267
– McLennan on, 263–264
female sphere, vs. male sphere, 373, 374
female values, 51
females *see* girls; women
fences *see* bamboo fences
fertility, 420, 577
– *see also* "life"
festivals
– ancestors, summoning of, 131
– *bali yatra*, 373
– buffaloes for, 110–111
– *dipawali*, 74–75, 78–79
– food sharing at, 92
– *karjame* at, 296
– musicians at, 131
– potlatch, 581–582
– for smallpox goddess, 129–130
– *see also* big-men festival; buffalo sacrifice; "pigeon-pea festival"
fields
– cultivation of, 443
– rice fields on lease, 101
fieldwork
– on Dongria Kond, 18 n.10
– ethnographic writing, 12–16
– by Pfeffer, 7, 161
fieldwork (of author)
– assistants, 24, 26, 28, 29–30
– Berger's support, 22–23, 27
– camera usage, 25–26
– cassette recorder usage, 36–37, 531 n.103
– concerns, 22
– conflict, involvement in, 119
– data analysis, 252
– drunk men, incidents with, 19–20, 33–36

– equipment, 22–23
– ethnographic writing, 15–16
– friendship relation, 83
– Gumma, first visit to, 27–28
– Gumma, plan to stay in, 26–27
– Gumma, stay in, 28, 29–30, 31–35, 36–37
– house of author, 28, 29
– information, collecting, 31, 32, 33
– marriage of author, 33
– *member* of Gumma, relation to, 30
– Parsali (project settlement), 20, 23
– safety, 17
– suitable place, searching for, 16–17, 18–19, 21, 23–24
fights *see* violence
financial burden, wives as, 261, 262
fines (*tapu*), 35, 390, 401–402
first husband's family, negotiations with bride-givers, 391, 394–395, 396
"flatlanders" *see* Desia Kond
flesh *see* human flesh
fluids, bodily, 371
food
– *bana paga*, 504–505, 534
– at *kudi bhoji*, 490
– "meal of friendship," 314–315
– sharing, 89–92, 618
– *see also* cooking; meat; produce
food offerings
– to ancestors, 318–319, 452
– to earth goddess, 552–553
– to gods, 321, 322, 342, 527
"forest food" *see bana paga*
fowl
– buying, 448
– sacrifice, 550
Frazer, George James, 420
"friends" *see tonenga*
friendship relations, 82–87
fruit
– bananas, 105
– *mohula*, 107–108
– pineapple, 106
fruit trees
– ownership, 123
– *see also* banana trees; mango tree

Fürer-Haimendorf, Christoph von, 371, 611 n.2

Gadaba
- relations of, 62–63
- study, 7–8

games, "biscuit dance," 564
garada (fence), 489
gati (term), 489
gauntia (title), 597
Gell, Alfred, 103
Gell, Simeran, 354–355, 371
Gellner, Ernest, 69
generational levels *see* children's generation; ego's generation; grandchildren's generation; grandparents' generation; parents' generation
ghanta parba see big-men festival
ghata kudi (house for god of local line), 434
ghosts
- Dombo as, 78, 137–138
- wandering, 440 n.25
- worshipping of, 78–79

ghotul (dormitories), 353–355
Ghumsur Wars, 414
gifts
- by abductor, 398–399, 400–401
- in arranged marriages, 44–45
- for bride-givers, 290–291, 292
- by bride-givers, 408–409
- buffalo sacrifice as counter-gift for harvest, 605
- buffaloes, 290–291, 309, 398–399, 400–401
- meat, 74–75
- pig, 343
- reciprocity, 126
- villages as, 223
- watches, 85
- *see also* "wedding gift"

Girard, René 421
giri takoli (ritual), 282, 326, 340–342, 426
girls
- arranged marriage, beginning of, 272
- "biscuit dance" (game), 564
- body ornaments, 364–365, 366
- bride capture, consent to, 273–274
- buffalo sacrifice, arrival at, 562
- clothes, 364, 365
- dancing and singing, 323–324, 358
- dormitories, control of, 369
- in *ghotul*, 353–354, 355
- hair style, 365
- initiation, 355
- Kadraka Drimbi, 384–385, 400
- painting of walls of earth goddess's house, 475
- popularity, 362
- pregnant, 370, 377, 378–379
- rice distributed by, 573–574
- sexual freedom at buffalo sacrifice, 563
- sexual intercourse, control of, 368–369
- sexual partners, change of, 370
- sexual relations with boys, 216–217, 234, 236, 331, 354
- Sikoka Site, 378
- unclaimed, 379
- visits to dormitories of, 359, 360
- *see also* brides

girls' dormitories
- about, 357
- behaviour in, 361
- of Bondo, 356
- control of, 369
- leaders, 361
- male influence, lack of, 348
- number of, 357–358
- sexual behaviour in, 362
- sexual relations in, 377
- sleeping in, 361
- visits by boys, 358–359, 360, 369
- visits by girls, 359, 360

goats, 112
gods and deities
- *aji budi*, 318
- *birimunda-kambimunda*, 469
- at buffalo sacrifice, 47–48
- called into village, 425
- creation of life, 613
- creative functions of female, 375
- of descent groups, 434
- food offerings to, 321, 322, 342, 527
- "house" deities, 433–434

- *lada penu*, 457–458, 553–555, 556, 557–558
- *loha penu*, 558–559
- marriage relations with, 523–524, 525, 526
- mountain deities, 515, 516
- origin of main, 372 n.67
- relations to, 46, 614
- in sacrificial post, 481–482
- smallpox goddess, 129–130
- see also earth goddess; *sita penu-lahi penu*; sun god

Good, Anthony, 154–155
"good" death, 611
gota see affines
gota halboli (dormitory visit), 360
Götzelmann, Albert, 416
government, land settlement by, 99–100
grandchildren's generation (–2 and lower), terminology, 173, 188–189
grandparents' generation (+2), terminology, 174–175
great *jani*, 518–519
gripa jani, 533–534
grooms
- visits in neighbouring villages, 315
- see also Sikoka Dikca

groom's house, bride arrival at, 385
groom's parents' house
- bride's arrival at, 337–338
- rituals at, 319–322, 338

groom's people
- heading to bride's village, 323
- see also bride-takers

groom's village
- bride crossing border of, 335
- bride entering, 337

guests
- bride-takers' treatment as, 303
- see also affines

Gumma (village)
- abandoning and resettling, 441
- author's first visit to, 27–28
- author's plan to stay in, 26–27
- author's stay in, 28, 29–30, 31–35, 36–37
- bride capture, negotiations after, 396, 397–398
- family tree of *icha jani* segment, 631
- history, 220–221
- *jakeri* (ill.), 432
- map, 32
- marriage relations with other villages, 632–633
- marriages, 225–228, 276–277
- *member*, 27, 30
- *sadu* relationships in Sikoka clan, 244
- Sikoka descent groups, 222
- unity with Dongormati and Lamba, 304

gun, shooting of (photo), 557
gurumai (ritual specialist), 523 n.91

hair, ornaments, 364
hair style, 365, 366
halu (hearth), 505
harmful forces see evil forces
harvest
- and buffalo sacrifice, 593, 605
- rice, 100–101
- work-sharing, 99

harvest ritual (*neta dakina*), 438–439
hata (weekly markets), 102–103
head, of buffaloes, 339, 574–575
hearths (*halu*), 505
hedi tana (marriage festival)
- about, 315
- *bada* ritual, 325–328, 329
- bride, preparation of, 330
- bride's procession, 282, 314, 334–338
- buffalo exchange, 339
- dancing and singing of boys and girls, 323–324
- food offerings to ancestors, 318–319
- groom's and bride's parents' houses, rituals at, 319–322, 338
- overview, 281–282, 316–317
- sexual relations, 331
- *yatra kudi*, ritual at, 317

herding, 112
hetu (spoon), 505
hiding
- love affair, 274
- *tangi*, 508, 509

hierarchy
- in castes, 66
- in clans, 82
- concept of, 9–10
- Dumont on, 9–10, 155–156, 621
- of relations, 607–608
- of *satara bonda*, 514–515
- seniority, 75, 619, 620
- in societies, 136–137
- *see also* castes
highlanders *see* Dongria Kond
hill cultivation, 101–102, 603–604
hills *see* Niamgiri Hills
Hindi terminology
- vs. Tamil terminology, 156–157
- Vatuk on, 159–160
holes, in earth goddess's house, 474
holism, 11
holy ... *see* sacred ...
"house" deities, shrines of, 433–434
house for god of local line *see ghata kudi*
house goddess *see sita penu-lahi penu*
houses (buildings)
- area behind, 73, 358, 426
- of author, 28, 29
- *bonda* at, 513
- bride arrival at groom's, 385
- darkness in, 374
- division of, 319 n.38
- of Dombo, 426
- plan (ill.), 635–636
- rituals at groom's and bride's parents', 319–322, 338
- *see also* bride's parents' house; earth goddess's house; groom's house; groom's parents' house; roofs
houses (social units, *ijo*)
- about, 588
- buffalo sacrifice, role in, 585–586
- "chief people," 445
- and descent groups, 586
- marriage rules, 247
- share of "betrothal fee" for, 300
- status, 620
Hubert, Henri, 420
human evolution, 258
human flesh, burial of, 420, 576–577

human sacrifices (*meria*)
- Agency for the Suppression of, 414–415
- buffalo sacrifice, comparison to, 601
- Campbell on, 418
- of Kond, 258, 422
- Macpherson on, 605
- myths, 421, 599–601, 605
- Padel on, 421–422
- reasons for, 419–421
- scapegoat theory, 421
- violence due to suppression of, 422
human victims
- buying, 463, 464
- Campbell on, 463
- flesh of, 420, 576–577
- Macpherson on, 462–463, 606
- in myth, 600–601
- rescuing of, 414–415
humankind, origin of, 75–76, 372, 429–430
humiliations
- of bride-demanding people, 289–290
- of *karjame*, 294–295
hunting (*beta*)
- bride capture as, 387–388
- decline, 556–557
- "life" obtained by, 615–616
- in myth, 603
- significance, 558
- *see also lada penu*
husbands
- avoidance of friend of, 84–85
- of *bejuni*, 524
- visits to wife's village, 343
- *see also* first husband's family

icha jani segment, family tree of (Gumma), 631
identity
- of Kond, 621–622
- language as, 167
ijo see houses (social units)
ijo henga hana (arranged marriage phase), 280–281, 311–314
impersonal fieldwork account, 13–14
impurity
- about, 71
- birth as, 135–136

– death as, 136
– Dumont on, 66
– of the earth, 71 n.6
– Moffatt on, 67, 69
– vs. purity, 38
– *see also* purity
incantations *see* invocations
incest
– Boal on, 250
– clan, 216–217
– myth, 249
– in myth of origin of humankind, 76
indigenous societies *see* "tribal societies"
infanticide *see* female infanticide
infants, ancestor's soul in, 349
initiation
– of *beju*, 524, 525
– of *dissari*, 524, 525
– of girls, 355
injuries, at killing of buffalo victims, 572
"in-law service," 293–295, 296–297
in-laws (*samdin ijo*)
– behaviour towards, 180–181
– marriage restrictions, 212–213
– *see also* daughter-in-law; *karjame*
intestines (*wahi unga*), of buffalo victim, 577
invocations
– by *bejuni*, 320, 321
– by *jani*, 319–320, 454–455
– recording of, 531 n.103
– to *sita penu-lahi penu*, 122
iron, god of (*loha penu*), 558–559
iron objects, 501, 502
isolation, of Dongria, 59
Itéanu, André, 256

jajmani system, 53, 68
jakeri (sacred stones)
– about, 47, 229
– arrangement, 429–430
– of Desia Kond, 435–436
– of different villages, 431
– in earth goddess's house, 428, 429
– of Gumma (ill.), 432
– location, 427
– "pigeon-pea festival," 451, 456
– pots at (photo), 504

– sacrificial posts at, 431
– settlements, outside of, 229
– types, 428, 441, 442
– *see also kona* stone; *pata* stones
Jakesika (clan), 220
Jangjodi (village), 572–573
jani (ritual specialists)
– appearance, 529
– at *bada* ritual, 326–328
– *beju/bejuni*, comparison to, 527–528
– conflict with, 534
– conflicts between, 552
– great, 518–519
– *icha jani* segment, family tree of (Gumma), 631
– invocations by, 319–320, 454–455
– leg of buffalo victim on roof of (photo), 575
– Niggemeyer on, 520
– peace ritual after bride capture, 402
– photo, 507
– at "pigeon-pea festival," 452, 454, 458–459
– *pujari*, comparison to, 529
– sacred objects, right of keeping, 528
– with *tangi* (photo), 507
– *tangi*, rituals with, 509
– types, 530–534
jati see castes
jela ("life"), 610
Jena, Mihir K.
– myths collected by, 340–341, 429, 469, 593 n.146, 602, 603
– on ritual specialists, 521
– on tree selection for sacrificial post, 480
jiu ("life"), 610–611
jiu manjing (rice), 329–330
joga jani, 531
joking
– boys and old men, 325
– siblings' spouses and spouse's siblings, 186
– young people, 338–339
Jreda Kond, 202, 302, 332
Juang
– dormitories, 353
– marriage rules, 168

– terminology, 164–165, 169
junior *bonda*, 514–515

Kadraka (clan), 536–537
Kadraka Drimbi (girl), 384–385, 400
Kadrakabondeli (village), 442, 538–539
kaja wali (stones), 432–433
Kalyansingpur (town), 389
Kamala Cham (woman), 33
Kambesi (village)
– "betrothal fee" conflict with, 304–306
– marriages, 218, 219
Kancharu (village), 386–387
kanga parbu see "pigeon-pea festival"
karjame (serving son-in-law)
– about, 279 n.23
– avoidance rules for, 295
– humiliations of, 294–295
– "in-law service," 293–295, 296–297
– overview, 279–280
– returning home, 295–296
– status, 296–297
Kata (village), 312–314
Kausilya (clan), 80
– *see also* Sikoka
killing
– of buffalo victims, 49, 492, 493, 565–566, 567–568, 569, 571, 572, 588
– of buffaloes at *hedi tana*, 339
– of cow, 541
– of rival after bride capture, 572–573
– *see also* female infanticide; human sacrifice
king of Bissamcuttack, 133–134, 135
"kings," Dongria as, 74–75
kinship
– and castes, 152
– Central Indian, 160
– Dumont's comparison, 150
– Morgan on, 142
– North Indian, 157–158, 159
– relations, 250–251
– South Indian, 157–158
– units, 254
– various authors on, 152–153
– *see also* affines; Dravidian kinship terminology

kinship systems, 149, 169
kinship terminologies *see* relationship terminologies
knife (*suri*), 516–517
knowledge, vs. dogma, 379–380
kodru bada see garada
kodru parbu see buffalo sacrifice
kodru tisnari see "feeding the buffalo"
Komti (caste), 103–104
kona, meaning of, 428
kona stone, 430
konang stones, 430
Kond
– "brother-and-sister clans," 203–204, 205
– coexistence with clients, 64
– exogamy, 262
– features, 2–3
– female infanticide, 258, 263–264
– as first humans, 75–76
– human sacrifices, 258, 422
– identity, 621–622
– language, 3
– marriage, 170, 261–262, 265–266, 267–268
– Pano, relations to, 64–65
– phratries, 203–204
– religion, 418–419
– residence, 3–4
– ritual specialists, 519–520
– subcategories, 2
– terminology, 170
– *see also* Desia Kond; Dongria Kond; Jreda Kond; Kui Kond; Kuttia Kond
Kond complex, 161–162
Koraput complex, 161
Koraput plateau, 62–63
koteiwali (megalith)
– about, 47–48, 431, 432
– photo, 487
– rams sacrifice, 445–446, 550–551
– ritual of bride's procession at, 337
– sacrificial post for, 455–456
– *see also palawara*
Kroeber, Alfred L., 143
Kruska (clan), 192
kuang, 3
kuda

– meaning of, 82
– *see also* clans; phratries
kudi bhoji (feast), 490–491
Kui Kond, 328–329
Kui language, 3
kula daraiba (ritual), 523 n.91
kuli kam (wage labor), 98–99
Kuper, Adam, 56
Kuskedeli (village)
– buffalo sacrifice, 551–553, 571–572
– buffalo victim, 467
– *palawara* with banana trees (photo), 546
kutaka (ritual specialists), 520
Kuttia Kond
– bride capture, 383 n.73
– buffalo sacrifice, 416, 595 n.147
– iron objects, 501
– mango ritual, 553
– Pano as "intermediaries" for, 64–65
Kuwi language, 3

labor help (*buti kam*), 98
lada penu (god of hunting), 457–458, 553–555, 556, 557–558
lahi jau see "wedding gift"
lahi penu see sita penu-lahi penu
Lamba (village)
– bride capture in, 385–386
– bride capture, negotiations on, 392–395
– marriages, 219
– unity with Gumma and Dongormati, 304
land
– claims to, 566
– of descent groups, 285, 286–287
– division of, 125
– for Dombo, 97
– Dombo, taken away by, 101
– of dominant clans, 97
– ownership, 97, 285, 286–287, 506
– quality of, 287
– transactions, 221–222
– transfer as compensation for theft, 223
– *see also* territories
land settlement, by government, 99–100
languages
– as identity, 167
– of Kond, 3

– Munda, 166–167
– sister (term) in various, 299 n.30
– *see also* Dongria language
Leach, Edmund, 134–135, 379–380
leasing, rice fields, 101
legs, of buffalo victims, 566, 570, 575
Lekhpadar (village)
– brass objects, 500
– buffalo sacrifice, 543–544, 545
– buffalo victims, 495
– conflict with *jani*, 534
levirate, 187
Lévi-Strauss, Claude, 146
life, goddesses of creation of, 613
"life" (fertility)
– about, 610
– as measure, 121–122
– ways of obtaining, 614–619
– *see also jela; jiu*
life-soul, 481
light
– vs. darkness, 373
– *see also* torches
"lineal terminologies," 152
linguistic exogamy, 269
little millet, cultivation of, 202
livestock
– as "betrothal fee," 302
– *see also specific animals*
local affines, vs. non-local, 208
local lines *see* descent groups
locality, and marriageability, 210
loha penu (god of iron), 558–559
love, terms for, 363
love affair, 274
love marriage, 406–407
lovers, behaviour, 362–363
loyalty, of *barika*, 117–118
Luithle, Andrea, 33

Macpherson, Samuel Charters
– Agency for the Suppression of Human Sacrifice, 414–415
– on clan exogamy, 263
– on female infanticide, 264–265, 266, 267
– on human sacrifices, 605
– on human victims, 462–463, 606

Index — 671

- on human victim's flesh, 576–577
- on Kond marriage, 261–262, 265, 266
- Kond religion, interest in, 418–419
- on "life," 121
- myths collected by, 419
- *Primitive Marriage*, reference to, 260
- on ritual specialists, 518–520, 528
- rivalry with Campbell, 258–259
- on sect of sun god, 42–43

madada (fence), 491
Madhu Cham (*barika*), 33–34
mahala takang see "betrothal fee"
majang (dormitories), 353
Majhiguda (village), 103
Makuna (indigenous group), 404–405
male influence, on girls' dormitories, 348
male role, in creation, 607
male sphere, vs. female sphere, 373, 374
male values, 51
Malinowski, Bronislaw, 374 n.69
malkamba (meat), 576
Mallebrein, Cornelia, 499–500
Mallikapori (village), 415–416
mama ijo see mother's brother
mango ritual, 553
mango tree, marriage at, 523
maps
- of Gumma, 32
- of Odisha, 5
- of villages, 233, 235

Marcus, George E., 12–14, 15
markets, 102, 103
- *see also* animal markets; weekly markets

marriage
- of affinal clans, 226–228
- of author, 33
- brother's daughter with brother, 239
- buffalo sacrifice, comparison to, 50, 591–593, 594–595, 607–608
- choices, 216
- "close," 42, 250, 252–253, 254
- "cross-cousin," 153–154
- descent categories, 247
- descent factor, 244–245, 246
- of descent groups, 236–240, 241–242
- discussions on, 285
- "distant," 41–42, 166, 250, 254

- with distant villages, 232
- Dongria-Desia clans, 210, 217–219
- Dongria-Dombo, 80
- family status, 285
- father's sister with brother, 239
- in Gumma, 225–228, 276–277
- Iteanu on, 256
- of Kond, 170, 261–262, 265–266, 267–268
- levirate, 187
- with lower caste, 93
- of Makuna, 404–405
- at mango tree, 523
- "other people's wife," 274–275
- polygamous, 276–277, 293
- prescriptive vs. preferred, 147
- *Primitive Marriage*, 259–260
- publications on, 140
- repetition of, 40, 188–189, 190, 248, 290
- residence factor, 246, 247
- *sadu* relationships, 242–243, 244
- *samdin* relationships, 243
- of siblings, 176, 190, 241–242
- of Sikoka, 225–228
- sister exchange, 238, 404
- sororate, 187
- statistical data, 41
- status, 44–45
- tendencies, 215, 249
- territory factor, 244–245, 246, 247, 252
- timing, 591
- types of, 44–45, 256, 275–277, 404–405, 406–407, 411, 595
- *see also* arranged marriage; bride capture; love marriage

marriage alliances, 231–232, 254
marriage capture *see* bride capture
marriage festival *see hedi tana*
marriage prohibitions
- degrees of, 209–213
- generational depth, 213–214
- repetition of marriage, 40, 188–189, 190, 248, 290
- for siblings, 212–213

marriage relations
- with deities, 523–524, 525, 526
- five generations, 214

– of Gumma and other villages, 632–633
– and social categories, 209
marriage restrictions
– for affines, 193
– for brother clans, 208–209
– for cross-cousins, 211
– forbidden women, 92–93
– in-laws rule, 212–213
– mother's brother rule, 210–211
marriage rules
– and agriculture, 251
– contradictions, 141
– for descent groups, 247
– Dumont on, 146–147
– Good on, 154–155
– for houses (social units), 247
– of Juang, 168
– Lévi-Strauss on, 146
– main points, 189, 191
– readjusting, 40
– of Sarjupari Brahmins, 158
– siblings, 190
– types, 41
– *see also* exogamy
marriage transactions, 284, 286
marriageability
– and locality, 210
– of relatives, 189–190
married couples *see* husband; wives
married women *see* wives
Marriott, McKim, 66–67
Mauss, Marcel, 420
McDougal, Charles, 160, 168–169, 353
McLennan, John F.
– Barnes on, 268–269
– on bride capture, 43, 260, 262, 270
– on female infanticide, 263–264
– on Kond marriage, 265
– *Primitive Marriage*, 259–260
– Rivière on, 268
– study on bride capture, 257
"meal of friendship" (*tone paga*), 314–315
meals *see* food
meat
– of buffaloes, 49–50, 179 n.34, 291–292, 313–314
– burial of buffalo victims', 577, 606

– consumption of buffalo victims', 578
– distribution of buffalo victims', 567, 570, 574–576
– fertility of buffalo victims', 577
– as gift by Dombo, 74–75
– *malkamba*, 576
– of pig, 343
mediators
– *barika* as, 117, 119
– *chaukidar* as, 118–119
meetings
– conciliatory, 573
– in earth goddess's house, 541
– on incident with drunk men, 34–35
megalith *see* koteiwali
member (village chief), 27, 30, 287
menstruation, 72–73, 436
meria see human sacrifices
merit, feasts of, 579–580
messengers, *barika* as, 119–120
middle-aged people
– religious positions, 348
– young people, comparison to, 351–352
migration, of Sikoka, 505
millet *see* little millet
modern societies, 9
Moffatt, Michael, 67–68, 69
mohula fruit, 107–108
mondal (administrator), 92–93, 596–597
money
– as "betrothal fee," 299–301, 303
– collecting, 111
– value of, 395
moneylenders (Sahukar), 104 n.33
moon, myth on, 367–368
morality, 403–404
Morgan, Lewis Henry
– on kinship, 142
– relationship terminologies by, 147–148
mother of all human beings, 430–431, 600
"mothers," share of "betrothal fee" for, 299
mother's brother (*mama ijo*)
– behaviour towards, 179–180
– bride, removing evil forces from, 328–329
– marriage restrictions, 210–211
– negotiations on "betrothal fee" by, 305
– Radcliffe-Brown on, 150

– share of "betrothal fee" for, 300
– "wedding gift" by, 333, 334
mountain deities, 515, 516
MPW *see* Multiple Purpose Workers
mudra (term), 489
mudrenga ("protectors")
– about, 48–49, 486, 487, 488, 492–493
– aggressive behaviour, 497
– conflicts with, 493
– of Desia Kond, 492
– distrust in, 493–494
– right to kill buffalo victim, 493
– in Tebapada, 538, 540–541, 542, 543
– villages, relations with, 493, 543
– villages of, 497
Multiple Purpose Workers (MPW), 20
Munda language, 166–167
Munda-speaking tribes, 356
Mundawali (village)
– buffalo sacrifice, 503, 561, 572
– drunk men, incident with, 35–36
– *jani* (photo), 507
murder, 572–573
Muria Gond
– dormitories, 353–355
– pregnancy, 370, 371
musical instruments *see* drums
musicians, at festivals, 131
muta see clan territories
mutual help *see buti kam*
myths
– brother and sister, 638–639
– buffalo sacrifice, comparison to, 601, 602–605
– clan titles, explanation of, 199–200
– cosmological events, 601–602
– creation, 374–375
– demon, 593 n.146
– divided people, 81–82
– Dombo and Komti, 104
– Dombo status, 77
– Duke and Dumbe, 637–639
– earth goddess, 419
– food sharing, 89–90
– hill cultivation, 603
– human sacrifices, 421, 599–601, 605
– incest, 249

– Jena, collected by, 340–341, 429, 469, 593 n.146, 602, 603
– Macpherson, collected by, 419
– mother of all human beings, 430–431, 600
– origin of humankind, 75–76, 372, 429–430
– spatial separation, 88
– sun and moon, 367–368
– sun god, 76, 115–116, 419, 602–603
– various, 501

Naga, 582
naika (title), 597
names
– of brother clans, 209
– Dongria Kond, 1–2, 3
– prohibition of using, 84, 86
– of villages, 634
Nayak, Prasanna K., 18, 120, 134, 335, 339 n.47, 572–573, 596
Nayaka, 126
nayu see settlements
Needham, Rodney, 145–146
negotiations
– on "betrothal fee," 298–299, 301, 303–304, 305, 309, 310–311
– on bride capture, 391–398, 401–402
– in public space, 391–392
neta dakina (harvest ritual), 438–439
Niamgiri Hills
– about, 1 n.1, 63
– beauty of, 17
– clan territories, 224–225
– photo, 2
– population, 1 n.2, 63–64
– remoteness, 133
Niggemeyer, Hermann
– on blacksmith, 501–502
– on buffalo sacrifice, 595 n.147
– on Kond and Pano, 64
– on mango ritual, 553
– on ritual specialists, 520
– on rituals for sacrificial post, 479–480
– on tree for sacrificial post, 478
non-industrial societies, 95–96
non-local affines, vs. local, 208

"non-modern" societies, 8–9
north *see* south-north axis
North Indian kinship, 157–158, 159
northern Odisha, 597

objects
– as "betrothal fee," 302
– for buffalo sacrifice, 50, 413
– *see also* brass objects; iron objects; sacred objects
obligations, of *barika*, 113
occupations
– of Dombo, 94
– impure, 69
Odisha (state)
– map, 5
– population of highlands, 17
– *see also* coastal Odisha; Niamgiri Hills; northern Odisha
offerings
– to buffaloes, 542
– to *lada penu*, 554, 555
– *see also* food offerings
"old feet" (*wenda kodang*), 282, 343
old people, 325, 348–349, 350–351
Oraon, dormitories, 355–356
Orissa *see* Odisha
ornaments *see* body ornaments
"other," selling to, 122
"other people's wife," 274–275
Otten, Tina, 523 n.91
"outsiders," of village community, 73–74
ownership
– of land, 97, 285, 286–287, 506
– of trees, 123
– of village, 223

padari see village territories; villages
padari kodru see buffalo victims
Padel, Felix, 419, 421–423
painting, of walls of earth goddess's house, 475
palawara (wall)
– about, 48
– with banana trees (photo), 546
– construction, 486
– illustration, 488

palm wine *see salap* sap
palm-wine trees, 109, 123
Pangenga ("flatlanders") *see* Desia Kond
panikimunda (sacrificial post), 455–456, 459–460
Pano, 52, 64–65
– *see also* Dombo
parents
– behaviour towards, 179
– segregated from children during night, 358
– *see also* cross-parents; fathers; "mothers"; spouses' parents
parents' generation (+1), terminology, 172, 175–181
parents' houses *see* bride's parents' house; groom's parents' house
Parkin, Robert, 165 n.22, 166–168, 169
Parry, Jonathan, 95
Parsali (project settlement), 20, 23
Parsali (village), 539
pata, meaning of, 428
pata stones, 428
pateleyu see spouses' parents
paternity, concept of, 381
Patnaik, Nityananda, 568
patronage, 69
patron-client relationships, 69–71
payment
– by abductor, 399
– of "betrothal fee," 303, 308
– of fine of incident with drunk men, 35
– to ritual specialists, 448
peace ritual, after bride capture, 402
peaceful behaviour, of Desia Kond, 253
pedigree *see* family tree
personal narratives, 14
Pfeffer, Georg
– author accompanied by, 16–17, 19–20, 21–22, 35–36
– on clans, 196–197
– "complexes" distinguished by, 161–162
– on Dongria-Dombo relations, 127
– drunk men, incidents with, 19–20, 35–36
– on Kond and Pano, 64–65
– on Kond marriage, 170
– relationship terminologies, analysis of, 162–164, 165

– research and fieldwork, 7, 160–161
– on "tribal society," 54–55
– on tribes and "caste society," 61–62
Phakeri (village)
– author's first visit to, 23–24
– *mudrenga* for Tebapada, 540
– remains of earth goddess's house (photo), 424
photographs, 25–26
phratries (*kuda*)
– of Dongria and Desia clans, 205–206
– elements of, 192–193
– of Kond, 203–204
– relations, 192
Phulbani (area), 64
pig sacrifices, 329
pigeon peas, 461–462
"pigeon-pea festival" (*kanga parbu*)
– about, 451
– buffalo sacrifice, comparison to, 459, 460–461
– joyful atmosphere, 459, 462
– rituals, 452–459, 460
– visitors at, 458
piglet sacrifice, 552–553
pigs
– buying, 446, 447–448
– as gift, 343
– sacrifices, 329
pineapple cultivation, 106
place of residence *see* residence
plants *see* produce; trees
poles *see* bamboo poles
police
– at buffalo sacrifice, 562
– *chaukidar*, 118–119
– in conflicts, 119
– help from, 34
– at negotiations on bride capture, 391
– problems with, 110
– support for bride-takers, 310
political organisation, 596–597, 598–599
pollution *see* impurity
polygamous marriage, 276–277, 293
poor families, 297
popularity, of boys and girls, 362
population

– of highlands of Odisha, 17
– of Niamgiri Hills, 1 n.2, 63–64
posts, of earth goddess's house (ill.), 473
potlatch, 581–582
pots (*daka*), 503, 504
power
– of Dombo, 123–124
– girls' sexual dominance, 368–369
– women's creative, 376–377
preferred marriage, 147
pregnancy, 370, 371–372, 374 n.69, 377, 378–379
– *see also* conception
prescriptive marriage, 147
prestations
– arranged marriage, 283–285
– ceremonial, 157
– *see also* "betrothal fee"
priests *see* ritual specialists
Primitive Marriage, 259–260
"primitive society," 56
privileges, 579
procession, bride's, 282, 314, 334–338
produce
– trading in, 105, 106
– *see also* brooms; fruit; little millet; pigeon peas; rice; turmeric
profit, 107, 108, 612
prohibitions
– food sharing, 89–92
– friendship relations, 84, 86
– spatial separation, 87–89
– *see also* marriage prohibitions
"protectors" *see mudrenga*
puberty, 347
public space, negotiations in, 391–392
pujari (ritual specialist), 529
punda buti (work group), 98
punja see descent groups; status categories
purchase *see* buying
purification
– of bride, 328
– of buffalo victims, 568
– after death, 136
– by turmeric water, 131
purity, 38, 66

– *see also* impurity
Pusika (clan), 312, 505–506

Rabinow, Paul, 13
Radcliffe-Brown, Alfred R., 144–145, 150
Railima (village)
– buffalo sacrifice, 26, 570–571
– *mudrenga*, distrust in, 493–494
– sacrificial post, 482, 483, 484–485
– *sala bada* at entrance to (photo), 490
raiti ("tenants"), 208
rams
– buying, 447
– sacrifice, 445–446, 550–551
Randeria, Shalini, 68
ranking *see* hierarchy
Rayagada (town), 22–23
reciprocal exchange, "life" obtained by, 616–617
reciprocity
– authors's types of, 410–411
– of gifts, 126
– Sahlins' types of, 403, 408–410
recitations, of verses, 319–320
recording
– of invocations, 531 n.103
– of trance session by *bejuni*, 36–37
reference terms
– categories, 178
– children's generation, 188
– cross/parallel distinction, 190
– ego's generation, 181–184
– grandchildren's generation, 188
– grandparents' generation, 174
– parents' generation, 175–177
– relations, 183, 184
reincarnation, 349
relations
– affinity-based, 590
– of age-and-status categories, 350
– of castes, 10
– Dongria and Dombo, 37–38, 39, 53–54, 70–71, 127
– in earth goddess's house, 476–477
– to "friends," 546–547
– friendship, 82–87
– to goddesses, 614
– to gods and ancestors, 46
– hierarchy of, 607–608
– in *jajmani* system, 68
– kinship, 250–251
– Kond and Pano, 64–65
– on Koraput plateau, 62–63
– *member* of Gumma and author, 30
– *mudrenga* and villages, 493, 543
– of organisers of buffalo sacrifice, 498, 543
– patron-client, 69–71
– phratry, 192
– reference terms, 183, 184
– rivalry-based, 590
– territory-based, 590
– *see also* marriage relations; sexual relations
relationship terminologies
– categories, 171, 178
– children's generation, 173, 188
– for descendants, 248
– "descent theory" vs. "alliance theory," 143–144
– Dravidian kinship, 150–152, 153
– Dumont on, 144–145
– ego's generation, 172–173, 181–188
– eight-line system, 165–166
– four-line system, 163–165
– grandchildren's generation and lower, 173, 188–189
– grandparents' generation, 174–175
– Hindi, 156–157, 159–160
– Juang, 164–165, 169
– Kond, 170
– Kroeber on, 143
– "lineal," 152
– list of terms, 172–173
– by Morgan, 147–148
– Needham on, 145–146
– North Indian, 157–158, 159
– parents' generation, 172, 175–181
– Pfeffer's analysis of, 162–164, 165
– Radcliffe-Brown on, 144–145
– Rivers on, 142
– South Indian, 157–158
– studies on, 148
– Tamil, 156–157
– three-line system, 167–168

– usage of term, 148
– variant terms, 148–149
– *see also* address terms; reference terms
religion
– and female infanticide, 264
– of Kond, 418–419
religious positions
– of middle-aged people, 348
– *see also* ritual specialists
remoteness, of Niamgiri Hills, 133
research *see* ethnographic research
residence
– of Kond, 3–4
– as marriage factor, 246, 247
respect, to old people, 349
restrictions *see* marriage restrictions
retaliation, against bride capture, 390, 572–573
reverence *see* worshipping
rice
– *akat manjing*, 527
– *bana paga*, 534
– distributed by girls, 573–574
– *jiu manjing*, 329–330
– for "pigeon-pea festival," 452
rice cultivation, 100–101
rice fields, on lease, 101
rice harvest, 100–101
rich families, 297–298
rings, 364–365, 367
ritual friends, 83–84
ritual killing *see* animal sacrifices; human sacrifices
ritual sites *see* shrines
ritual specialists
– Jena on, 521
– knife at buffalo sacrifice, 517
– of Kond, 519–520
– list of, 529–530
– Macpherson on, 518–520, 528
– Niggemeyer on, 520
– payment to, 448
– for sacrificial post, 477, 478, 485
– selection of tree as sacrificial post, 480–481
– *see also dissari*; *gurumai*; *jani*; *kutaka*; *pujari*; shamans

ritual titles, 128
– *see also* religious positions
rituals
– of *adivasi*, 60
– at animal sacrifices, 503, 504
– *bada*, 325–328, 329
– at *bali yatra* festival, 373
– after bride capture, 402
– at bride's parents' houses, 319–322
– at bride's procession, 335–337
– at buffalo sacrifice, 49
– buffalo victim, inspection of, 466
– death, 426–427
– *derupripka*, 439–440
– at *dipawali*, 78–79
– of *dissari* before killing buffalo victim, 568, 570–571
– Dombo's function, 38–39
– Dumont's concepts applied to, 11
– for earth goddess, 551–553
– east-facing, 433
– *giri takoli*, 282, 326, 340–342, 426
– at groom's parents' houses, 319–322, 338
– harvest, 438–439
– *kula daraiba*, 523 n.91
– marriage at mango tree, 523
– and old people, 349
– at "pigeon-pea festival," 452–459, 460
– prestations, 157
– for sacrificial post, 479–480, 483, 484–485
– *satara bonda*, climbing of bamboo pole of, 548–549
– soul, 349
– "stone ritual," 554, 555
– study of, 12
– with *tangi*, 507–509
– *tangi wecoli*, 454
– three-year sequence, 440–441
– turmeric water on bride, 307
– at *yatra kudi*, 317, 453
– *see also* invocations; sacrificial rituals; worshipping
rivalry, 581–582, 590
Rivers, William H. R., 142
Rivière, Peter, 268, 269 n.17
robbery, 36

Rona (tribal group), 7
roofs
– construction, 28, 29
– of earth goddess's house, 474–475
– leg of buffalo victim on *jani's* (photo), 575
Rosman, Abraham, 581–582
Roy, Sarat Chandra, 355–356
royal organisation, 596–597, 598–599
royal rulers *see* king of Bissamcuttack
royally granted titles, 135, 597
Rubel, Paula G., 581–582
rules
– avoidance rules, 84–85, 295
– Dongria-Dombo and castes, similarity of, 136–137
– of friendship relations, 84–85, 86
– of killing of buffalo victims, 588
– for menstruating women, 72–73
– types, 41
– *see also* marriage rules; prohibitions

saanta (title), 597
sacred grove, 435–436
sacred objects
– for buffalo sacrifice, 530–531, 544
– of clan territory, 443
– representation of, 595–596
– right of keeping, 528, 598
– *tangi wecoli* (ritual), 454
– at *yatra kudi*, 426
– *see also bonda*; knife; *tangi*
sacred sites, 425
– *see also* cremation grounds; shrines
sacred stones
– *konang*, 430
– at shrines of "house" deities, 433–434
– *see also jakeri*; *koteiwali*
"sacrificers" (*desa*), 589
sacrificial animals *see* animal sacrifices
sacrificial axe *see tangi*
sacrificial community *see* clan territories
sacrificial hut *see* earth goddess's house
sacrificial post (buffalo sacrifice)
– deities in, 481–482
– function, 485
– installation, 479, 484
– photo, 482

– of Railima, 482, 483, 484–485
– ritual specialists for, 477, 478, 485
– rituals for, 479–480, 483, 484–485
– as sacrificial victim, 480
– selection of tree, 478–479, 480–481, 482–483, 539–540
sacrificial posts
– for buffalo victims, 468
– at *jakeri*, 431
– *panikimunda*, 455–456, 459–460
– types, 483, 484
sacrificial rituals
– mango ritual, 553
– *see also* animal sacrifices; human sacrifices
sacrificial stakes *see* sacrificial posts
sacrificial victims
– sacrificial post as, 480
– *see also* buffalo victims; human victims
sadar kudi see earth goddess's house
sadu relationships, 242–243, 244
safety, of author, 17
Sahlins, Marshall D.
– on morality, 403–404
– reciprocity, types of, 403, 408–410
Sahukar (moneylenders), 104 n.33
sala bada (fence)
– about, 488–489
– construction, 427, 489, 490, 540–541
– of Desia Kond for buffalo sacrifice, 491
– at entrance to Railima (photo), 490
– function, 491–492
salap sap, sharing, 31, 109, 125–126
salap trees *see* palm-wine trees
samdin gota (affines group), 203
samdin ijo see in-laws
samdin relationships, 243
samudi sehena (arranged marriage phase), 279, 288–292
Sana Denganali (village), 399
Sana Dengoni (village), 384, 547
Sapangada (place), 372 n.68
Sarjupari Brahmins, marriage rules, 158
satara bonda ("umbrella")
– about, 510
– animal sacrifices for, 550–551
– bamboo poles, 510, 511, 548–549

- dancing at, 547–548
- function, 515
- hierarchy of, 514–515
- photo, 512
- sun god, comparison to, 602
- worshipping of, 549–550
- *see also* bonda
scapegoat theory, 421
school education, 31
seasons, 591–592
sect of sun god, 42–43
Seeland, Klaus, 65
segregation
- children from parents, 358
- spatial separation, 87–89
self-reflexive fieldwork account, 14
selling
- alcohol, 108, 109
- buffalo victims, 464–465
- buffaloes, 110–111, 116
- to "other," 122
semen, 371, 381
senior *bonda*, 514–515
senior people *see* old people; village chiefs
seniority, 75, 619, 620
serving son-in-law *see karjame*
settlements (*nayu*)
- about, 245, 587
- buffalo sacrifice, role in, 584
- changes in, 230
- *jakeri* outside of, 229
- as village element, 195
- villages, difference from, 230
sex, words for, 274
sexual behaviour, in girls' dormitories, 362
sexual dominance, of girls, 368–369
sexual freedom, at buffalo sacrifice, 563
sexual intercourse
- in arranged marriage, 343–344
- "eating" analogy, 368
- frequency, 370
- girls' control of, 368–369
- in "in-law service" period, 295–296
- and time, 368
sexual partners, 331, 370
sexual relations
- in *ghotul*, 354

- in girls' dormitories, 377
- at *hedi tana*, 331
- in villages, 234, 236
- *see also* incest
shamans
- at *bali yatra* festival, 373
- at buffalo sacrifice, 131–132
- Dombo as, 132
- at "pigeon-pea festival," 454, 455–456
- ritual specialists, comparison to other, 526–527
- students, 521
- transgender, 330
- *see also* beju; bejuni
sharing (*bat kina*)
- alcohol, 109
- buffalo meat, 313–314
- concept of, 95–96
- vs. cycles of exchange, 126–127
- at feasts, 124–125
- food, 89–92, 618
- land division, 125
- "life," 617–619
- rice harvest, 100–101
- *salap* sap, 31, 109, 125–126
shooting, of gun (photo), 557
shrines
- for buffalo sacrifice, 48
- of "house" deities, 433–434
- near *jakeri*, 431, 432
- *see also* earth goddess's house; *jakeri*; *koteiwali*; *yatra kudi*
sibling clans *see* "brother-and-sister clans"
siblings
- limits by arranged marriages, 212–213
- marriage, 176, 190, 241–242
- reference terms, 181
- *see also* brothers; sisters; spouse's siblings
siblings' spouses, 181–182, 183, 184, 185–187
- *see also* spouse's siblings' spouses
Sikoka (clan)
- clan incest, 217
- descent groups, 222
- marriages, 225–228
- migration, 505

– vs. Pusika, 505–506
– *sadu* relationships, 244
– villages, 222
– *see also* Kausilya
Sikoka Bambu (bride), 333
Sikoka Dikca (groom), bride capture by, 306–308, 309
Sikoka Kangu (young man), 385, 396, 398–400
Sikoka Kuca (villager), 306, 309–310
Sikoka Kurmi (bride), 334
Sikoka Mishra (boy), 378, 379
Sikoka Mukuna (village elder), 86
Sikoka *muta*, 220–223
Sikoka Ranu (village elder), 84
Sikoka Site (girl), 378
Sikokagumma (village) *see* Gumma
sin, 465
singing
– at buffalo sacrifice, 415, 561–562
– at earth goddess's house, 498–499
– of girls behind houses, 358
– at *hedi tana*, 323–324
Sinha, Surajit, 59
sisters
– cooking by bride's younger, 338
– exchange for marriage, 238, 404
– share of "betrothal fee" for, 299–300
– terms in various languages, 299 n.30
– *see also* father's sister
sita penu-lahi penu (goddess of wealth)
– about, 87–88, 611–612
– *giri takoli* ritual, 282, 326, 340–342, 426
– invocations to, 122
– in myth on food sharing, 89
– request to come, 612–613
– worshipping of, 326–327, 559–560
"skewing," 188–189
Skoda, Uwe, 597
sleeping
– in girls' dormitories, 361
– location for children, 347, 358
smallpox goddess, festival for, 129–130
social categories, 209
social distance, 403, 411
social facts, 47
social organisation, 586–588

societies
– hierarchy in, 136–137
– modern, 9
– non-industrial, 95–96
– "non-modern," 8–9
– "primitive," 56
– *see also* "caste society"; "tribal societies"
songs *see* singing
son-in-law *see* karjame
sororate, 187
soul, 349
– *see also* violent soul
South Asian studies, 6, 7
South Indian kinship, 157–158
Southall, Aidan W., 55–56, 60
south-north axis, 471
spatial oppositions
– in village (ill.), 478
– *see also* east-west axis
spatial separation, 87–89
speaking, with trees (story), 470–471
spoon (*hetu*), 505
spouses *see* husbands; siblings' spouses; wives
spouses' parents (*pateleyu*), 176 n.31
– *see also* children's spouses' parents
spouse's siblings, 181–182, 183, 184, 185–187
spouse's siblings' spouses, 182, 184, 187
status
– of *bonda*, 514
– of bride-givers vs. bride-takers, 408–409
– in buffalo sacrifice, 581, 582
– of clans, 619
– competing for, 255
– differences, 581, 582–583, 619
– of Dombo, 73, 77–78, 79, 94
– of dominant clan, 581
– of families, 285
– of houses (social units), 620
– of *karjame*, 296–297
– of marriage, 44–45
– and transactions, 124
– and types of marriage, 275
– of village, 581
– *see also* age-and-status categories
status categories (*punja*)

– about, 128, 129, 587
– and descent groups, 585
– grouped, 192–193, 222
– of Kadraka, 536–537
– seniority, 620
– *see also* bismajhi; jani; mondal; pujari
status markers, of "big men," 288
stealing *see* theft
"stone ritual" (*walka puja*), 554, 555
stones
– *kaja wali*, 432–433
– *see also* sacred stones
structuralism, vs. substantialism, 55
students, of shamans, 521
studies *see* ethnographic studies
"substance-codes," 66–67
substantialism, vs. structuralism, 55
sun, myth on, 367–368
sun god (*dharmu penu*)
– followers of, 264
– myths, 76, 115–116, 419, 602–603
– sect of, 42–43
suri (knife), 516–517
surjaninga, 533
Sutangoni (village), 378
swidden
– harvest ritual, 438
– photo, 442

Tamil terminology, 156–157
Tamil "untouchables", 67–68, 69
tangi (axe), 506–510, 530–531, 551–552
tangi wecoli (ritual), 454
tapu (fines), 35, 390, 401–402
taxes, 117, 597
tayi bai kuda see "brother-and-sister clans"
Tebapada (village)
– about, 536–537
– affinal links of, 540
– *bonda* (photo), 511
– buffalo sacrifice, 537–538, 540–543, 544–545, 547–550, 551, 553, 554–555, 556, 557, 559–560, 561–562, 563, 568–570, 573–574, 575
– clan territory, 537
– *sala bada*, construction of, 489, 490
– *satara bonda* (photo), 512

"tenants" (*raiti*), 208
tensions *see* conflicts
terminologies *see* relationship terminologies
territorial organisation, 584, 586–588
territories
– as marriage factor, 244–245, 246, 247, 252
– relations based on, 590
– *see also* clan territories; land; village territories
theft
– of buffalo victim's legs, 566
– land transfer as compensation for, 223
– *see also* robbery
Thurston, Edgar, 599–600
Timaka (clan), 505
time, and sexual intercourse, 368
titles
– clan, 199–202
– royally granted, 135, 597
– *see also* ritual titles
tone paga see "meal of friendship"
tone paga tinja hana (arranged marriage phase), 281
tone relationships *see* friendship relations
tonenga ("friends"), 206, 546–547, 588, 589–590
torches, rechargeable, 359 n.56
towns *see* Bissamcuttack; Kalyansingpur; Rayagada
traders, 102
trading
– in animals, 109–110
– Dongria-Dombo, 106–107
– in produce, 105, 106
– profit from, 107
– *see also* buying; markets; selling
trance
– *beju* in (photo), 129
– sessions by *beju/bejuni*, 36–37, 321, 342
transactions
– in arranged marriage, 284, 286
– Dombo, dependence on, 123–124
– land, 221–222
– in non-industrial societies, 95–96
– profitable, 612
– and status, 124

transgender shamans, 330
Trautmann, Thomas
– on "crossness," 153
– on Dravidian kinship terminology, 153
– on Hindi vs. Tamil terminology, 156–157
– on Kond terminology, 170
trees
– ability to speak with (story), 470–471
– life-soul, 481
– ownership, 123
– selection of, for sacrificial post, 478–479, 480–481, 482–483, 539–540
– *tangi* hidden in, 509
– *see also* fruit trees; palm-wine trees
tribal art, 499–500
tribal groups, Rona, 7
"tribal societies"
– "caste society," differences to, 37–38
– "caste society," interrelationship with, 58
– concept of, 57
– hierarchy in, 136 n.48
– Pfeffer on, 54–55
– segmented, 403
– Sinha on, 59
– studies, 6–7
– study, types of, 57
tribes
– Bailey on, 60–61
– Dumont on, 61
– Munda-speaking, 356
– Pfeffer on, 61–62
– Southall on, 55–56, 60
– *see also* "primitive society"
Turkish villagers, 380–381
turmeric cultivation, 104–105
turmeric water
– on bride, 307
– at "pigeon-pea festival," 458–459
– as purifying substance, 131
Tyler, Stephen A., 12

"umbrella" *see satara bonda*
universalism, 11
unnatural death, 120
untouchability *see jajmani* system
"untouchables"
– categories, 68–69

– menstruating women as temporary, 72
– Randeria on, 68
– Tamil, 67–68, 69

vagina, common idea on, 368
value-ideas
– and contexts, 10–11
– female vs. male, 51
– opposite sets of, 38
– *see also* clans; friendship relations; ghosts; "kings"; "outsiders"; seniority
values, 8–10
Vatuk, Sylvia, 158, 159–160
veneration *see* worshipping
verses
– on buffalo sacrifice, 535–536
– on earth goddess's house, 468–469
– recitations by, 319–320
– of song at buffalo sacrifice, 561–562
– terms *mudra* and *gati* in, 489
victims *see* sacrificial victims
video shooting, 25
village chiefs
– legs of buffalo victim for, 575
– *see also* member
village collectivity, affines in, 230
village community
– affines in, 230
– "outsiders," 73–74
– share of "betrothal fee" for, 299
village council, 119
– *see also* village chiefs
village exogamy, 230–231
village settlements *see* settlements
village territories (*padari*), 195, 584–585, 587
villages (*padari*)
– abandoning, 229–230
– about, 228–229, 245
– affiliation of people, 585
– affinal, 233–234, 235
– assistance from neighbouring, 472, 473
– author's first visits to, 21, 23–24
– Bada Denganali, 223
– bride crossing border of groom's, 335
– bride entering groom's, 337
– bride visits in neighbouring, 494, 592

- of bride-givers/takers, 226–228
- Buduni, 497
- buffalo victims visits in neighbouring, 494–497, 539, 592
- as clan element, 194
- of clan territories of Niamgiri Hills, 224–225
- clans, 228
- conflicts after bride capture, 389–390
- conflicts between neighbouring, 407–408
- cremations grounds, 424
- deities called into, 425
- of descent groups, 222
- distances between, 232–234
- dominant and affinal clans, 231
- dominant and dependent clans, 196
- Dulumguda, 555–556, 565–567
- elements of, 195, 196
- entrances, 427, 490
- as gifts, 223
- groom visits in neighbouring, 315
- groom's people heading to bride's, 323
- husband's visits to wife's, 343
- *jakeri* of different, 431
- Jangjodi, 572–573
- Kadrakabondeli, 442, 538–539
- Kancharu, 386–387
- Kata, 312–314
- layout, 423, 424, 434–435
- Majhiguda, 103
- Mallikapori, 415–416
- map, 233, 235
- marriage alliances between, 231–232
- marriage relations with Gumma, 632–633
- marriages with distant, 232
- *member* (chief), 287
- of *mudrenga*, 497
- *mudrenga*, relations with, 493, 543
- numbers and names, 634
- ownership, 223
- Parsali, 539
- sacred sites, 425
- Sana Denganali, 399
- Sana Dengoni, 384, 547
- settlements, difference from, 230
- sexual relations in, 234, 236
- of Sikoka *muta*, 220–221, 222
- spatial oppositions in (ill.), 478
- spatial separation, 88
- status, 581
- Sutangoni, 378
- turmeric rhizomes (photo), 105
- types of, and buffalo sacrifice, 589–590
- visitors from outside world, 120
- Waliamba, 223, 441, 495
- *see also* Dongormati; Gumma; Kambesi; Kuskedeli; Lamba; Lekhpadar; Mundawali; Phakeri; Railima; Tebapada

violence
- about, 18, 253
- bride capture, 306–307, 384, 389, 572–573
- clan incest, 217
- crops, destruction of, 390
- human sacrifices, due to suppression of, 422
- "life" obtained by, 615–616

violent soul, 78

visitors
- from outside world, 120
- at "pigeon-pea festival," 458

visits
- author's first to Gumma, 27–28
- author's first to villages, 21, 23–24
- of bride in neighbouring villages, 494, 592
- of buffalo victims in neighbouring villages, 494–497, 539, 592
- to girls' dormitories, 358–359, 360, 369
- of groom in neighbouring villages, 315
- of husband to wife's village, 343
- *wenda kodang*, 282, 343

wage labor (*kuli kam*), 98–99
wahi unga see intestines
Waliamba (village), 223, 441, 495
walka puja see "stone ritual"
walls
- of earth goddess's house, 474
- *see also palawara*
wandering ghosts, 440 n.25
watches, as gifts, 85
water *see* turmeric water
wealth
- significance of, 612–613

– ways of obtaining, 614–619
wealth, goddess of see sita penu-lahi penu
weapons
– carrying, 253
– imitation of (photo), 555
– worshipping of, 559
– see also axes; gun; knife
wedding see marriage
"wedding gift" (lahi jau), 284–285, 332–333, 334, 408–409
weekly markets (hata), 102–103
wenda kodang ("old feet"), 282, 343
west see east-west axis
whole, 10–11, 621
wine see salap sap
winnowing fan, photo, 555
wives
– of author, 33, 186
– of barika (photo), 114
– as financial burden, 261, 262
– husband's friend, avoidance of, 84–85
– husband's visits to village of, 343
– vs. unmarried women, 376, 377
– words for, 274
women
– captured bride, demanding release of, 307–308
– captured bride, recovering of, 309
– clan affiliation, 198–199
– creative power, 376–377
– of DKDA, 30–31
– and earth goddess, 73–74
– forbidden, 92–93
– menstruating, 72–73, 436
– pregnant, 371–372
– unmarried vs. wives, 376, 377
– words for, 271

– see also bejuni; brides; sisters; wives
Woodburn, James, 95–96
work group (punda buti), 98
work-sharing, 99
worshipping
– of ancestors, 452, 453
– of ghosts, 78–79
– of lada penu, 457–458, 553–555, 556, 557–558
– of satara bonda, 549–550
– of sita penu-lahi penu, 326–327, 559–560
– of stones at shrines of "house" deities, 433
– of tangi, 509, 551–552
– of weapons, 559
– see also shrines
Writing Culture, 12–14

yatra kudi (shrine)
– about, 318, 424, 425
– bride at, 336–337
– rituals at, 317, 453
– sacred objects at, 426
young people
– arranged marriage, resistance against, 344–345
– buffalo sacrifice, arrival at, 560, 561, 562–563
– drinking alcohol at hedi tana, 324–325
– independence of, 347–348
– joking between, 338–339
– middle-aged people, comparison to, 351–352
– old people, comparison to, 351
– puberty, 347
– see also boys; children; girls

www.ingramcontent.com/pod-product-compliance
Lightning Source LLC
Chambersburg PA
CBHW070753300426
44111CB00014B/2391